C26.7

LIBRARY OF CONGRESS

SUBJECT
HEADINGS

Prepared by the Policy and Standards Division,
Library Services

SUPPLEMENTARY VOCABULARIES:

Free-floating Subdivisions
Genre/Form Terms for Library and Archival Materials
Children's Subject Headings

Library of Congress, Cataloging Distribution Service, Washington, D.C., 2010

ISSN 1048–9711

Library of Congress Subject Headings is
published annually.

For sale by the Library of Congress,
Cataloging Distribution Service,
Washington, D.C. 20540–4910
(202) 707–6100

Library of Congress • CDS • 101 Independence Ave., S.E. • Washington, D.C. 20540–4910

Preface

The thirty-second edition of *Library of Congress Subject Headings* contains subject headings created by catalogers and used in cataloging at the Library of Congress since 1898.

This edition contains headings established through December 2009. Responsibility for the maintenance of the data base is held by the staff of the Data Integrity Section under the direction of the editor, Ronald A. Goudreau. Elizabeth Rinn prepared headings in the database.

The Cataloging Distribution Service (CDS) produced *LCSH* from records in the MARC 21 subject authorities format. Authority and reference entries were generated from the MARC 21 records, the entries sorted, and the data formatted. The resulting data was used by a commercial printer for final processing.

Barbara B. Tillett
Chief, Policy and Standard Division

June 2010

Contents

Introduction to Free-Floating Subdivisions

This is a list of subdivisions that are authorized for free-floating use in the Library of Congress Subject Heading system. This current list was generated from data gleaned from subdivision authority records that are online in the LCSH Master Database at the Library of Congress. The Library of Congress began to create subdivision authority records to control free-floating topical, form, and chronological subdivisions in 1999. The list represents the full set of free-floating subdivisions in existence at the end of December 2009 and includes one geographic subdivision, —**Foreign countries.** New subdivisions are added and existing subdivisions are revised at weekly editorial meetings at the Library of Congress. Announcements of new and revised free-floating subdivisions are made in the Summary of Decisions accompanying the *L.C. Subject Headings Weekly Lists* that are posted to the World Wide Web at URL <http://www.loc.gov/aba/cataloging/subject/weeklylists>. New and revised subdivision authority records are distributed to subscribers in the weekly MARC Distribution Service—Subject Authorities. More information on free-floating subdivisions and their use may be found in the *Subject Headings Manual*. Questions on free-floating subdivisions may be sent to the Policy and Standards Division at policy@loc.gov.

Authorized subdivisions appear in boldface type following a long dash, e.g., —**Anatomy;**—**Civilization.** Some subdivisions consist of more than one subfield, e.g., —**Antiquities—Collection and preservation.** For those subdivisions that are authorized for further geographic subdivision, the legend *(May Subd Geog)* appears following the subdivision, e.g.,—**Commerce** *(May Subd Geog).* Indented under the subdivision in the next line are the code(s) that identify the controlling instruction sheet number(s) for the subdivision in the *Subject Headings Manual* (H 1095– H 1200).

A usage note that identifies the category of the subdivision (topical, form, or chronological) and the types of headings with which its use is authorized appears with each subdivision entry. Dual entries have been made for many form subdivisions that can also function as topical subdivisions. For some subdivisions, there is an additional note with further information or restrictions on use of the subdivision, e.g., "Further subdivide by subdivisions used under classes of persons"; "Do not subdivide geographically under names of individual persons."

Cross-references similar to those made to subject headings appear with subdivision entries in this list. USE references are made from an unauthorized or non-preferred subdivision term to an authorized or preferred subdivision, e.g., —Anniversary celebrations USE Anniversaries, etc.; —Assimilation, Cultural USE—Cultural assimilation. Under authorized subdivisions, tracings of those references appear following the code UF (Used For). UF references that represent earlier forms of a subdivision are identified by the legend *[Former subdivision].* Authorized subdivisions are linked to each other hierarchically by reciprocal BT/NT references. BT references represent broader term subdivisions while NT references represent narrower term subdivisions.

COVERAGE

The free-floating subdivision list contains 3,586 subdivisions established through December, 2009.

CONTACT

Questions and comments may be sent to:

Policy and Standards Division
Library of Congress
101 Independence Avenue, S.E.
Washington, DC 20540-4262
Phone: 202-707-4467
Email: policy@loc.gov

—**To 221 B.C.**
H 1148
Use as a chronological subdivision under headings for art forms qualified by the adjective Chinese.

—**To 794**
H 1148
Use as a chronological subdivision under headings for art forms qualified by the adjective Japanese.

—**To 935** *(Not Subd Geog)*
H 1148
Use as a chronological subdivision under headings for art forms qualified by the adjective Korean.

—**To 1500** *(Not Subd Geog)*
H 1156; H 1160
Use as a chronological subdivision under headings for drama and forms and types of musical compositions.

—**To 1600** *(Not Subd Geog)*
H 1148
Use as a chronological subdivision under headings for art forms qualified by the adjective Japanese.

—**To 1868**
H 1148
Use as a chronological subdivision under headings for art forms qualified by the adjective Japanese.

—**To 1900**
H 1148
Use as a chronological subdivision under headings for art forms qualified by the adjective Korean.

—Three kingdoms, six dynasties-Sui dynasty, 220-618
USE   —Three kingdoms-Sui dynasty, 220-618

—**Three kingdoms-Sui dynasty, 220-618**
H 1148
Use as a chronological subdivision under headings for art forms qualified by the adjective Chinese.
UF   —Three kingdoms, six dynasties-Sui dynasty, 220-618
[Former subdivision]

—Ch'in-Han dynasties, 221 B.C.-220 A.D.
USE   —Qin-Han dynasties, 221 B.C.-220 A.D.

—**Qin-Han dynasties, 221 B.C.-220 A.D.**
H 1148
Use as a chronological subdivision under headings for art forms qualified by the adjective Chinese.
UF   —Ch'in-Han dynasties, 221 B.C.-220 A.D.
[Former subdivision]

—**500-1400**
H 1160
Use as a chronological subdivision under forms and types of musical compositions.

—**Tang-Five dynasties, 618-960**
H 1148
Use as a chronological subdivision under headings for art forms qualified by the adjective Chinese.

—**Heian period, 794-1185** *(Not Subd Geog)*
H 1148
Use as a chronological subdivision under headings for art forms qualified by the adjective Japanese.

—**10th century**
H 1148
Use as a chronological subdivision under headings for art and art forms of all nations, regions, and ethnic groups, except those headings for art and art forms of China, Japan, and Korea.

—**Koryŏ period, 935-1392**
H 1148
Use as a chronological subdivision under headings for art forms qualified by the adjective Korean.

—**Song-Yuan dynasties, 960-1368**
H 1148
Use as a chronological subdivision under headings for art forms qualified by the adjective Chinese.
UF   —Sung-Yüan dynasties, 960-1368
[Former subdivision]

—Sung-Yüan dynasties, 960-1368
USE   —Song-Yuan dynasties, 960-1368

—**11th century**
H 1148
Use as a chronological subdivision under headings for art and art forms of all nations, regions, and ethnic groups, except those headings for art and art forms of China, Japan, and Korea.

—**12th century**
H 1148
Use as a chronological subdivision under headings for art and art forms of all nations, regions, and ethnic groups, except those headings for art and art forms of China, Japan, and Korea.

—**Kamakura-Momoyama periods, 1185-1600**
H 1148
Use as a chronological subdivision under headings for art forms qualified by the adjective Japanese.

—**13th century**
H 1148
Use as a chronological subdivision under headings for art and art forms of all nations, regions, and ethnic groups, except those headings for art and art forms of China, Japan, and Korea.

—**14th century**
H 1148
Use as a chronological subdivision under headings for art and art forms of all nations, regions, and ethnic groups, except those headings for art and art forms of China, Japan, and Korea.

—Ming-Ch'ing dynasties, 1368-1912
USE   —Ming-Qing dynasties, 1368-1912

—**Ming-Qing dynasties, 1368-1912**
H 1148
Use as a chronological subdivision under headings for art forms qualified by the adjective Chinese.
UF   —Ming-Ch'ing dynasties, 1368-1912
[Former subdivision]

—**Chosŏn dynasty, 1392-1910**
(Not Subd Geog)
H 1148
Use as a chronological subdivision under headings for art forms qualified by the adjective Korean.
UF   —Yi dynasty, 1392-1910
[Former subdivision]

—Yi dynasty, 1392-1910
USE   —Chosŏn dynasty, 1392-1910

—**15th century**
H 1148; H 1160
Use as a chronological subdivision under headings for art and art forms of all nations, regions, and ethnic groups, except those headings for art and art forms of China, Japan, and Korea. Also use under forms and types of musical compositions.

—**16th century**
H 1148; H 1160
Use as a chronological subdivision under headings for art and art forms of all nations, regions, and ethnic groups, except those headings for art and art forms of China, Japan, and Korea. Also use under forms and types of musical compositions.

—**Early modern, 1500-1700**
H 1154; H 1155.2; H 1156
Use as a chronological subdivision under individual languages and groups of languages, groups of literary authors, and individual literatures except drama.

—**17th century**
H 1148; H 1156; H 1160
Use as a chronological subdivision under headings for art and art forms of all nations, regions, and ethnic groups, except those headings for art and art forms of China, Japan, and Korea. Also use under forms and types of musical compositions and headings for drama.

—**Edo period, 1600-1868** *(Not Subd Geog)*
H 1148
Use as a chronological subdivision under headings for art forms qualified by the adjective Japanese.

—**18th century**
H 1148; H 1154; H 1155.2; H 1156; H 1160
Use as a chronological subdivision under headings for art and art forms of all nations, regions, and ethnic groups, except those headings for art and art forms of China, Japan, and Korea. Also use under individual languages and groups of languages, groups of literary authors, individual literatures, including drama, and forms and types of musical compositions.

—**19th century**
H 1148; H 1154; H 1155.2; H 1156; H 1160
Use as a chronological subdivision under headings for art and art forms of all nations, regions, and ethnic groups, except those headings for art and art forms of China and Korea. Also use under individual languages and groups of languages, groups of literary authors, individual literatures, including drama, and forms and types of musical compositions.

—**1868-**
H 1148
Use as a chronological subdivision under headings for art forms qualified by the adjective Japanese.

—**Meiji period, 1868-1912**
H 1148
Use as a chronological subdivision under headings for art forms qualified by the adjective Japanese.

—**20th century**
H 1148; H 1154; H 1155.2; H 1156; H 1160
Use as a chronological subdivision under headings for art and art forms of all nations, regions, and ethnic groups. Also use under individual languages and groups of languages, groups of literary authors, individual literatures, including drama, and forms and types of musical compositions.

—**Taishō period, 1912-1926** *(Not Subd Geog)*
H 1148
Use as a chronological subdivision under headings for art forms qualified by the adjective Japanese.

—**21st century**
H 1160
Use as a chronological subdivision under headings for art and art forms of all nations, regions, and ethnic groups. Also use under individual languages and groups of languages, groups of literary authors, individual literatures, including drama, and forms and types of musical compositions.

—**2-harpsichord scores**
H 1160
Use as a form subdivision under forms and types of musical compositions.

—**2-organ scores**
H 1160
Use as a form subdivision under forms and types of musical compositions.

—**2-piano scores**
H 1160
Use as a form subdivision under forms and types of musical compositions.

—**3-piano scores**
H 1160
Use as a form subdivision under forms and types of musical compositions.

—Abandonment of nests
USE —Nests—Abandonment

—**Abbreviations**
H 1095
Use as a topical subdivision under topical headings for works about abbreviations pertaining to those topics.
NT —Acronyms

——**Dictionaries**
H 1095
Use this subdivision combination as a form subdivision under topical headings for works containing alphabetical lists of abbreviations pertaining to those topics.
BT —Dictionaries

—**Abbreviations of titles**
H 1095
Use as a form subdivision under types of periodicals for works containing lists of abbreviations of titles of those periodicals.
UF —Title abbreviations
NT —Periodicals—Abbreviations of titles

—**Abdication, [date]**
H 1110
Use as a topical subdivision under names of individual persons.

—Abdication of kings and rulers
USE —Kings and rulers—Abdication

—**Ability testing** *(May Subd Geog)*
H 1095; H 1154
Use as a topical subdivision under topical headings, including languages, for tests and testing of native aptitude or acquired proficiency in a particular topic.
BT —Testing

—**Abnormalities** *(May Subd Geog)*
H 1147; H 1164; H 1180
Further subdivide by subdivisions used under diseases when used under animals and organs and regions of the body.
Use as a topical subdivision under individual animals and groups of animals, individual plants and groups of plants, and individual organs and regions of the body.
UF —Abnormities and deformities
[Former subdivision]
—Deformities
NT —Spermatozoa—Abnormalities

—Abnormities and deformities
USE —Abnormalities

—**Abrasion resistance** *(May Subd Geog)*
H 1158
Use as a topical subdivision under individual materials and types of materials.
BT —Mechanical properties

—**Abridgments**
H 1188
Use as a form subdivision under uniform titles of sacred works.

—**Abscess** *(May Subd Geog)*
H 1164
Further subdivide by subdivisions used under diseases.
Use under individual organs and regions of the body.
BT —Diseases

—**Absolute constructions**
H 1154
Use under individual languages and groups of languages.

—**Absorption and adsorption**
(May Subd Geog)
H 1149
Use as a topical subdivision under individual chemicals and groups of chemicals.

—**Abstracting and indexing**
(May Subd Geog)
H 1095; H 1100; H 1103; H 1140; H 1188
Use as a topical subdivision under names of countries, cities, etc., classes of persons, ethnic groups, and uniform titles of sacred works, and under topical headings for works on preparing abstracts or indexes of publications about the subject. Also use under types of publications for works on preparing abstracts or indexes of those types of publications.
UF —Indexing

—**Abstracts**
H 1095; H 1100; H 1103; H 1105; H 1110; H 1140
Use as a topical subdivision under names of countries, cities, etc., and under classes of persons, ethnic groups, and topical headings for works about lists of publications on the subject and provide full bibliographical information together with substantive summaries or condensations of the facts, ideas, or opinions presented in each publication listed. Use under names of individual persons and corporate bodies for works about abstracts of works by or about the person or corporate body. Also use under types of publications for works about summaries of the contents of those publications.
UF —Summaries of publications

—**Abstracts**
H 1095; H 1100; H 1103; H 1105; H 1110; H 1140
Use as a form subdivision under names of countries, cities, etc., and under classes of persons, ethnic groups, and topical headings for works that list publications on the subject and provide full bibliographical information together with substantive summaries or condensations of the facts, ideas, or opinions presented in each publication listed. Use under names of individual persons and corporate bodies for abstracts of works by or about the person or corporate body. Also use under types of publications for works that summarize the contents of those publications.

UF —Summaries of publications
NT —Digests

—**Abuse of** *(May Subd Geog)*
H 1100
Use as a topical subdivision under classes of persons.

—Abuse of drugs
USE —Drug use

—Abuse of substances
USE —Substance use

—**Accents and accentuation**
H 1154; H 1188
Use as a topical subdivision under individual languages and groups of languages and under Bible. O.T. and individual books of the Old Testament.
UF —Accentuation

—Accentuation
USE —Accents and accentuation

—**Access control** *(May Subd Geog)*
H 1095
Use as a topical subdivision under types of archives, records, computers, computer networks, and statistical and data-gathering services.
UF —Control, Access

—Access for the physically handicapped
USE —Barrier-free design

—**Accidents** *(May Subd Geog)*
H 1095; H 1153
Do not subdivide geographically under names of individual space vehicles.
Use as a topical subdivision under names of individual space vehicles and under types of industries and other topical headings.
NT —Officials and employees—Accidents

——**Investigation** *(May Subd Geog)*
H 1095
Use as a topical subdivision under topical headings.
UF —Investigation of accidents

—Accidents and injuries
USE —Wounds and injuries

—**Accounting**
H 1095; H 1105; H 1151.5; H 1153; H 1159
Use as a topical subdivision under names of individual corporate bodies and under types of corporate bodies and industries, military services, and topical headings.

——**Law and legislation** *(May Subd Geog)*
H 1153
Further subdivide by subdivisions used under legal topics.
Use as a topical subdivision under types of industries.
BT —Law and legislation

—**Accreditation** *(May Subd Geog)*
H 1095; H 1105; H 1151.5
Do not subdivide geographically under names of corporate bodies.
Use as a topical subdivision under names of individual corporate bodies, especially institutions, educational institutions, and services, and under types of institutions, educational institutions, and services.

—**Acoustic properties** *(May Subd Geog)*
H 1149; H 1158
Use as a topical subdivision under individual chemicals and groups of chemicals and individual materials and types of materials.
BT —Properties

—Acoustic properties of mufflers
USE —Motors—Mufflers—Acoustic properties

—**Acoustics**
H 1161
Use as a topical subdivision under individual musical instruments and families of instruments.

—**Acquisition**
H 1154
Use as a topical subdivision under individual languages and groups of languages.

—**Acronyms**
H 1095; H 1154
Use as a topical subdivision under individual languages other than English, groups of languages, and topical headings for works about acronyms in those languages or pertaining to those topics.
BT —Abbreviations

——**Dictionaries**
> H 1095; H 1154
> Use this subdivision combination as a form subdivision under individual languages other than English, groups of languages, and topical headings for works containing lists of acronyms in those languages or pertaining to those topics.
> BT —Dictionaries

—Action, Mechanism of
> USE —Mechanism of action

—**Acupuncture** (May Subd Geog)
> H 1164
> Use as a topical subdivision under individual organs and regions of the body.

—**Adaptation** (May Subd Geog)
> H 1147; H 1164; H 1180
> Use as a topical subdivision under individual animals and groups of animals, individual plants and groups of plants, and individual organs and regions of the body.

—**Adaptations**
> H 1110; H 1155.8; H 1156
> Use as a topical subdivision under names of individual persons for works about adaptations by others of their creative works. Also use under literary works entered under title and individual literatures for works about adaptations of those works or of those literatures.
> UF —Paraphrases, tales, etc.
> [Former subdivision]
> NT —Audio adaptations
> —Film and video adaptations

—**Adaptations**
> H 1110; H 1155.8; H 1156
> Use as a form subdivision under names of individual persons for collections of adaptations by others of their creative works. Also use under literary works entered under title and individual literatures for collections of adaptations of those works.
> UF —Paraphrases, tales, etc.
> [Former subdivision]
> NT —Audio adaptations
> —Film and video adaptations

—**Additives** (May Subd Geog)
> H 1158
> Use as a topical subdivision under individual materials and types of materials.

—**Address, Forms of**
> H 1154
> Use as a topical subdivision under individual languages and groups of languages.
> UF —Forms of address

—Address, Titles of
> USE —Titles

—Addresses, sermons, etc.
> USE —Sermons

—**Adjectivals**
> H 1154
> Use as a topical subdivision under individual languages and groups of languages.

—**Adjective**
> H 1154
> Use as a topical subdivision under individual languages and groups of languages.

—**Adjuvant treatment** (May Subd Geog)
> H 1150
> Use as a topical subdivision under individual diseases and types of diseases.
> BT —Treatment

—**Administration**
> H 1095; H 1105; H 1149; H 1149.5; H 1151; H 1151.5
> Use as a topical subdivision under names of individual libraries and institutions in the spheres of health, social services, and education, and under types of such institutions. Under names of other corporate bodies, including government agencies, galleries, museums, parks, etc., use the subdivision Management. Also use under individual drugs and groups of drugs.
> NT —Business management
> —Colonies—Administration
> —Therapeutic use—Administration

——**Law and legislation** (May Subd Geog)
> H 1151.5
> Further subdivide by subdivisions used under legal topics.
> Use as a topical subdivision under types of educational institutions.
> BT —Law and legislation

—**Administrative and political divisions**
> H 1140
> Use as a topical subdivision under names of countries, cities, etc.
> UF —Political divisions
> NT —Autonomous communities
> —Cantons
> —Departments
> —Election districts
> —Provinces
> —Regions
> —Republics
> —States
> —Union territories
> —Voivodeships

—**Admission**
> H 1151; H 1151.5
> Use as a topical subdivision under names of individual educational institutions and types of educational institutions.
> NT —Open admission

——**Law and legislation** (May Subd Geog)
> H 1151.5
> Further subdivide by subdivisions used under legal topics.
> Use as a topical subdivision under types of educational institutions.
> BT —Law and legislation

—**Adult education** (May Subd Geog)
> H 1187
> Use as a topical subdivision under individual Christian denominations.
> BT —Education

—**Adverb**
> H 1154
> Use as a topical subdivision under individual languages and groups of languages.

—**Adverbials**
> H 1154
> Use as a topical subdivision under individual languages and groups of languages.

—**Adversaries**
> H 1110
> Use as a topical subdivision under names of individual persons for works about contemporaries who opposed the person's point of view or work.
> UF —Enemies
> —Opponents
> BT —Contemporaries

—**Aerial exploration**
> H 1140
> Use as a topical subdivision under names of countries, etc., for works on exploration conducted from the air
> UF —Exploration, Aerial
> BT —Discovery and exploration

—**Aerial film and video footage**
> H 1140
> Use as a topical subdivision under names of countries, cities, etc., for works about films or videos of those places taken from the air.

—**Aerial film and video footage**
> H 1140
> Use as a form subdivision under names of countries, cities, etc., for films or videos of those places taken from the air.

—**Aerial gunners**
> H 1159
> Further subdivide by subdivisions used under classes of persons.
> Use as a topical subdivision under military services.

—**Aerial operations**
> H 1200
> Use as a topical subdivision under individual wars.

—**Aerial operations, American,** [**British, etc.**]
> H 1200
> Use as a topical subdivision under individual wars.

—**Aerial photographs**
> H 1095; H 1140
> Use as a topical subdivision under names of countries, cities, etc., and under topical headings for works about photographs taken from conventional aircraft of a place or topic.
> UF —Description and travel—Aerial
> [Former subdivision]

—**Aerial photographs**
> H 1095; H 1140
> Use as a form subdivision under names of countries, cities, etc., and under topical headings for collections of photographs taken from conventional aircraft, including collections of reproductions, of a place or topic.
> UF —Description and travel—Aerial
> [Former subdivision]
> BT —Photographs
> —Remote-sensing images

—**Aerial views**
> H 1140; H 1151
> Use as a form subdivision under names of countries, cities, etc., and individual educational institutions for maps or atlases of those places or institutions observed from the air.
> UF —Description and travel—Aerial
> [Former subdivision]
> —Description and travel—Views
> [Former subdivision]
> —Views, Aerial
> BT —Maps

—**Aerodynamics**
> H 1195
> Use as topical subdivision under individual land vehicles and types of land vehicles.
> BT —Dynamics

—**Aesthetics**
> H 1110; H 1155.2
> Use as a topical subdivision under names of individual persons and groups of literary authors for works about their philosophy of art or beauty, whether explicitly stated or inferred from their creative works.

—**Affinity labeling** (May Subd Geog)
> H 1149
> Use as a topical subdivision under individual chemicals and groups of chemicals.
> UF —Labeling, Affinity

—**Affixes**
> H 1154
> Use as a topical subdivision under individual languages and groups of languages.

—**African American officers**
> H 1159
> Further subdivide by subdivisions used under classes of persons.
> Use as a topical subdivision under military services.
> BT —African Americans
> —Officers

—**African American troops**
> H 1159
> Use as a topical subdivision under military services.
> UF —Afro-American troops
> [Former subdivision]

—**African Americans**
> H 1159; H 1200
> Further subdivide by subdivisions used under classes of persons.
> Use as a topical subdivision under military services and individual wars.
> UF —Afro-Americans
> [Former subdivision]
> NT —African American officers

—**African influences**
> H 1156
> Use as a topical subdivision under individual literatures.
> BT —Foreign influences

—Afro-American troops
> USE —African American troops

—Afro-Americans
> USE —African Americans

—Age *(May Subd Geog)*
   H 1147; H 1180
      Use as a topical subdivision under individual animals and groups of animals and individual plants and groups of plants.

—Age determination *(May Subd Geog)*
   H 1147; H 1180
      Use as a topical subdivision under individual animals and groups of animals and individual plants and groups of plants.
      UF —Determination of age

—Age differences *(May Subd Geog)*
   H 1154
      Use as a topical subdivision under individual languages and groups of languages.
      UF —Differences, Age

—Age factors *(May Subd Geog)*
   H 1150
      Use as a topical subdivision under individual diseases and types of diseases.
      NT —Metabolism—Age factors
           —Toxicology—Age factors

—Aging
   H 1147; H 1164; H 1180
      Use as a topical subdivision under individual animals and groups of animals, individual plants and groups of plants, and individual organs and regions of the body.

——Genetic aspects
   H 1180
      Use as a topical subdivision under individual plants and groups of plants.
      BT —Genetics

——Molecular aspects
   H 1164
      Use as a topical subdivision under individual organs and regions of the body.
      BT —Molecular aspects

——Prevention
   H 1147
      Use as a topical subdivision under individual animals and groups of animals.
      BT —Prevention

—Agonists
   H 1149
      Further subdivide by subdivisions used under chemicals.
      Use as a topical subdivision under individual chemicals and groups of chemicals.

—Agreement
   H 1154
      Use as a topical subdivision under individual languages and groups of languages.

—Agriculture *(May Subd Geog)*
   H 1103
      Use as a topical subdivision under ethnic groups.

—Aides
   H 1159
      Further subdivide by subdivisions used under classes of persons.
      Use as a topical subdivision under military services.

—Air conditioning *(May Subd Geog)*
   H 1095; H 1195
      Use as a topical subdivision under types of buildings, individual land vehicles and types of land vehicles, and other constructions.
      NT —Housing—Air conditioning

——Control *(May Subd Geog)*
   H 1095
      Use as a topical subdivision under types of buildings, vehicles, and other constructions.
      UF —Control of air conditioning

—Air content *(May Subd Geog)*
   H 1158
      Use as a topical subdivision under individual materials and types of materials.

——Measurement
   H 1158
      Use as a topical subdivision under individual materials and types of materials.
      BT —Measurement

————Instruments
   H 1158
      Use as a topical subdivision under individual materials and types of materials.
      BT —Instruments

—Air disc brakes
   H 1195
      Use as a topical subdivision under individual land vehicles and types of land vehicles.
      BT —Brakes

—Air police
   H 1159
      Use as a topical subdivision under air forces. Under navies, use the subdivision Shore patrol. Under other military services use the subdivision Military police.

—Air suspension *(May Subd Geog)*
   H 1195
      Use as a topical subdivision under individual land vehicles and types of land vehicles.
      BT —Pneumatic equipment
           —Springs and suspension

—Airborne troops
   H 1159
      Use as a topical subdivision under military services.

——Communication systems
   H 1159
      Use as a topical subdivision under military services.
      BT —Communication systems

—Airmen
   H 1159
      Further subdivide by subdivisions used under classes of persons.
      Use as a topical subdivision under military services.

—Alabama ₍Illinois, Texas, etc.₎ delegation
   H 1155
      Use as a topical subdivision under names of individual legislative bodies.

—Alcohol use *(May Subd Geog)*
   H 1100; H 1103; H 1110
      Do not subdivide geographically under names of individual persons.
      Use as a topical subdivision under names of individual persons, classes of persons, and ethnic groups for works on their use or abuse of alcohol.
      BT —Substance use

—Algerian authors
   H 1156
      Use as a topical subdivision under individual literatures.

—Alien officials and employees
      USE —Officials and employees, Alien
—Alignment of bodies
      USE —Bodies—Alignment
—Alignment of wheels
      USE —Wheels—Alignment

—Allegorical interpretations
   H 1188
      Use as a topical subdivision under uniform titles of sacred works.
      BT —Criticism, interpretation, etc.

—Allegory
      USE —Symbolism
—Allegory and symbolism
      USE —Symbolism

—Allergenicity *(May Subd Geog)*
   H 1149
      Use as a topical subdivision under individual chemicals and groups of chemicals.

—Allusions
   H 1110
      Use as a topical subdivision under names of individual persons for contemporary (person's life span) and early brief references to the person.

—Alluvial plain
   H 1145.5
      Use as a topical subdivision under names of individual bodies of water.

—Almanacs
   H 1200
      Use as a form subdivision under individual wars.

—Alphabet
   H 1154
      Use as a topical subdivision under individual languages and groups of languages.

——Religious aspects
   H 1154
      Use as a topical subdivision under individual languages and groups of languages.

————Buddhism, ₍Christianity, etc.₎
   H 1154
      Use as a topical subdivision under individual languages and groups of languages.

—Alternative treatment *(May Subd Geog)*
   H 1150
      Use as a topical subdivision under individual diseases and types of diseases.
      BT —Treatment
      NT —Diseases—Alternative treatment

—Altitudes
   H 1140
      Use as a topical subdiviison under names of countries, etc.
      UF —Elevations (Altitudes)

—Alumnae
      USE —Alumni and alumnae
—Alumni
      USE —Alumni and alumnae

—Alumni and alumnae *(May Subd Geog)*
   H 1151; H 1151.5
      Further subdivide by subdivisions used under classes of persons.
      Use as a topical subdivision under names of individual educational institutions and types of educational institutions.
      UF —Alumnae
           —Alumni
              ₍Former subdivision₎

—Amateurs' manuals
   H 1095
      Use as a form subdivision under technical topics for works of instruction for nonprofessionals on how to acquire a skill or perform an operation.
      BT —Handbooks, manuals, etc.

—Ambulances
   H 1159
      Use as a topical subdivision under military services.

—American influences
   H 1156
      Use as a topical subdivision under individual literatures.
      BT —Foreign influences

—Amphibious operations
   H 1200
      Use as a topical subdivision under individual wars.

—Amusements
      USE —Games
           —Recreation

—Analogy
   H 1154
      Use as a topical subdivision under individual languages and groups of languages.

—Analysis
   H 1095; H 1149; H 1158; H 1180
      Use as a topical subdivision under substances, including individual chemicals and groups of chemicals and individual materials and types of materials, and individual plants and groups of plants, for works on methods of analyzing those substances, or analyzing a sample, to determine the presence or quantity of those substances. Also use under substances not produced naturally for works presenting the results of chemical analyses of those substances. For results of chemical analyses of natural substances of unfixed composition, use the subdivision Composition.
      UF —Analysis and chemistry
              ₍Former subdivision₎
           —Analysis and examination
              ₍Former subdivision₎
           —Chemical analysis

—Analysis and chemistry
      USE —Analysis
—Analysis and examination
      USE —Analysis

—Analysis, appreciation
   H 1160
      Use as a topical subdivision under forms and types of musical compositions.
      UF —Appreciation, analysis

—Anaphora
   H 1154
      Use as a topical subdivision under individual languages and groups of languages.

—**Anatomy**
H 1147; H 1164; H 1180
Use as a topical subdivision under individual animals and groups of animals, individual plants and groups of plants, and individual organs and regions of the body.
NT —Embryos—Anatomy
—Fetuses—Anatomy
—Muscles
—Respiratory organs
—Roots—Anatomy
—Seeds—Anatomy

—Ancestry
USE —Family

—**Anecdotes**
H 1095; H 1100; H 1103; H 1105; H 1110; H 1120; H 1140; H 1188
Use as a form subdivision under names of countries, cities, etc., names of individual persons, families, and corporate bodies, uniform titles of sacred works, and under classes of persons, ethnic groups, and topical headings for collections of brief narratives of incidents about those subjects.
UF —Anecdotes, facetiae, satire, etc.
[Former subdivision]
NT —Biography—Anecdotes
—History—[period subdivision]—Biography—Anecdotes
—History—Anecdotes

—Anecdotes, facetiae, satire, etc.
USE —Anecdotes
—Humor

—**Animacy**
H 1154
Use as a topical subdivision under individual languages and groups of languages.

—Animal behavior
USE —Behavior

—**Animal models** (May Subd Geog)
H 1150
Use as a topical subdivision under individual diseases and types of diseases.
NT —Pathophysiology—Animal models

—**Ankylosis** (May Subd Geog)
H 1164
Further subdivide by subdivisions used under diseases.
Use as a topical subdivision under individual organs and regions of the body.
BT —Diseases

—**Annexation to . . .**
H 1140
Use as a topical subdivision under names of countries, etc.

—**Anniversaries, etc.**
H 1095; H 1100; H 1103; H 1105; H 1110; H 1140; H 1187; H 1200
Do not use for works merely published on the occasion of an anniversary.
Use as a topical subdivision under names of countries, cities, etc., names of individual persons and corporate bodies, individual Christian denominations, and under historic and social movements, events, classes of persons, and ethnic groups for works on anniversary celebrations or commemorations of significant events.
UF —Anniversary celebrations
—Biography—Anniversaries, etc.
—Celebrations, anniversaries, etc.
—History—Anniversaries, etc.
[Former subdivision]
—Pageants
[Former subdivision]
NT —Centennial celebrations, etc.

—Anniversary celebrations
USE —Anniversaries, etc.

—**Anodic oxidation** (May Subd Geog)
H 1158
Use as a topical subdivision under individual materials and types of materials.
BT —Oxidation

—**Anonyms and pseudonyms**
H 1110
Use as a topical subdivision under names of individual persons.
UF —Pseudonyms

—**Antagonists**
H 1149
Further subdivide by subdivisions used under chemicals.
Use as a topical subdivision under individual chemicals and groups of chemicals other than enzymes. Under individual enzymes and groups of enzymes, use the subdivision Inhibitors.

—Anthologies, Literary
USE —Literary collections

—**Anthropometry** (May Subd Geog)
H 1100; H 1103
Use as a topical subdivision under classes of persons and ethnic groups.

—Anti-aircraft artillery operations
USE —Antiaircraft artillery operations

—**Anti-theft devices**
H 1195
Use as a topical subdivision under individual land vehicles and types of land vehicles.

—**Antiaircraft artillery operations**
H 1200
Use as a topical subdivision under individual wars.
UF —Anti-aircraft artillery operations
[Former subdivision]

—**Antilock brake systems**
H 1195
Use as a topical subdivision under individual land vehicles and types of land vehicles.
BT —Brakes

—**Antiquities**
H 1103; H 1140; H 1188; H 1200
Use as a topical subdivision under names of countries, cities, etc., other than extinct cities, ethnic groups extant in modern time, uniform titles of sacred works, and individual wars.

——**Collection and preservation**
(May Subd Geog)
H 1103; H 1140
Do not use under names of extinct cities.
Use as a topical subdivision under names of countries, cities, etc., and ethnic groups extant in modern times for works on methods of collection and preservation.
BT —Collection and preservation

——**Collectors and collecting**
(May Subd Geog)
H 1103; H 1140
Do not use under names of extinct cities.
Use as a topical subdivision under names of countries, cities, etc. and ethnic groups extant in modern times for works on collectors of antiquities and history of collecting.
BT —Collectors and collecting

—**Antiquities, Byzantine**
H 1140
Use as a topical subdivision under names of countries, cities, etc., other than extinct cities.
UF —Byzantine antiquities

—**Antiquities, Celtic**
H 1140
Use as a topical subdivision under names of countries, cities, etc., other than extinct cities.
UF —Celtic antiquities

—**Antiquities, Germanic**
H 1140
Use as a topical subdivision under names of countries, cities, etc., other than extinct cities.
UF —Germanic antiquities

—**Antiquities, Phoenician**
H 1140
Use as a topical subdivision under names of countries, cities, etc., other than extinct cities.
UF —Phoenician antiquities

—**Antiquities, Roman**
H 1140
Use as a topical subdivision under names of countries, cities, etc., other than extinct cities.
UF —Roman antiquities

—**Antiquities, Slavic**
H 1140
Use as a topical subdivision under names of countries, cities, etc., other than extinct cities.
UF —Slavic antiquities

—**Antiquities, Turkish**
H 1140
Use as a topical subdivision under names of countries, cities, etc., other than extinct cities.
UF —Turkish antiquities

—Antonyms
USE —Synonyms and antonyms

—**Apheresis**
H 1154
Use as a topical subdivision under individual languages and groups of languages.

—**Apologetic works**
H 1185; H 1187
Use as a topical subdivision under individual religions and Christian denominations for works about apologetic works.

—**Apologetic works**
H 1185; H 1187
Use as a form subdivision under individual religions and Christian denominations for works that explain a religion or denomination and defend it from criticism from the outside.

——**History and criticism**
H 1185; H 1187
Use as a topical subdivision under individual religions and Christian denominations.
BT —History and criticism

—Apparatus
USE —Equipment and supplies

—Apparatus and equipment
USE —Equipment and supplies

—Apparatus and supplies
USE —Equipment and supplies

—Appointment, call, and election of bishops
USE —Bishops—Appointment, call, and election

—Appointment, call, and election of clergy
USE —Clergy—Appointment, call, and election

—Appointment, qualifications, tenure, etc.
USE —Selection and appointment

—**Appointments and retirements**
H 1159
Use as a topical subdivision under military services.
BT —Retirement
—Selection and appointment

—Appointments, promotions, salaries, etc.
USE —Officials and employees—Salaries, etc.

—**Apposition**
H 1154
Use as a topical subdivision under individual languages and groups of languages.

—**Appreciation** (May Subd Geog)
H 1110; H 1148; H 1155.8; H 1156; H 1188
Use as a topical subdivision under names of individual persons active in the fine arts, literature, music, and performing arts for works on public response and reception, praise, etc., of the person's artistic or literary works. Also use as a topical subdivision under individual art forms and headings for national and ethnic art, individual literary works entered under title, uniform titles of sacred works and individual literatures.

—Appreciation, analysis
USE —Analysis, appreciation

—**Apprentices**
H 1159
Further subdivide by subdivisions used under classes of persons.
Use as a topical subdivision under military services.

—**Appropriate technology** (May Subd Geog)
H 1153
Use as a topical subdivision under types of industries.

—**Appropriations and expenditures**
H 1105; H 1140; H 1155; H 1159
Use as a topical subdivision under names of countries, cities, etc., individual legislative bodies, and military services. Also use under names of individual government agencies and institutions for works on their financial affairs. Under names of individual nongovernmental corporate bodies, use the subdivision Finance for works on their budgets and the raising and expenditure of funds. Also use the subdivision Finance under individual government bodies for works limited to their management of nonappropriated funds.
UF —Expenditures and appropriations

—**Appropriations and expenditures**
(Continued)

——**Effect of inflation on**
H 1105; H 1140
Use as a topical subdivision under names of countries, cities, etc., and individual government agencies.
UF —Effect of inflation on appropriations and expenditures

—**Arab authors**
H 1156
Use as a topical subdivision under individual literatures.

—**Arab influences**
H 1156
Use as a topical subdivision under individual literatures.
BT —Foreign influences

—**Archaeological collections**
H 1105; H 1110; H 1120
Use as a topical subdivision under names of individual persons, families, and corporate bodies for works about their collections of archaeological items or artifacts.

—**Archaisms**
H 1154
Use as a topical subdivision under individual languages and groups of languages.

—Architectural drawings
USE —Designs and plans

—Architectural plans
USE —Designs and plans

—**Archival resources**
H 1095; H 1140
Use as a topical subdivision under names of countries, cities, etc., and under topical headings for descriptions of the types of documents and historical records about a particular place or topic available in an institution or institutions.

—**Archives**
H 1095; H 1100; H 1103; H 1105; H 1110; H 1120; H 1151.5; H 1159
Use as a topical subdivision under names of individual persons, families, and corporate bodies, and under classes of persons, ethnic groups, types of corporate bodies and educational institutions, and military services for works about documents or historical records, including notes, correspondence, minutes, photographs, legal papers, etc., pertaining to those persons or organizations.

—**Archives**
H 1095; H 1100; H 1103; H 1105; H 1110; H 1120; H 1151.5; H 1159
Use as a form subdivision under names of individual persons, families, and corporate bodies, and under classes of persons, ethnic groups, types of corporate bodies and educational institutions, and military services for collections of documents or historical records, including notes, correspondence, minutes, photographs, legal papers, etc., pertaining to those persons or organizations.

——**Microform catalogs**
H 1110
Use this subdivision combination as a form subdivision under names of individual persons, families, and corporate bodies, and under classes of persons, ethnic groups, types of corporate bodies and educational institutions, and military services.
BT —Microform catalogs

—**Area**
H 1140
Use as a topical subdivision under names of countries, cities, etc., for descriptions of the physical area of a place as well as for works on measurement of the area of a place.

—**Armed Forces** *(May Subd Geog)*
H 1140
Further subdivide by subdivisions used under military services.
Use as a topical subdivision under names of countries, etc.
NT —Colonial forces

—**Armenian authors**
H 1156
Use as a topical subdivision under individual literatures.

—**Armistices**
H 1200
Use as a topical subdivision under individual wars.

—**Armored troops**
H 1159
Use as a topical subdivision under military services.

—Arranged excerpts
USE —Excerpts, Arranged

—**Art**
H 1095; H 1110
Use as a topical subdivision under names of individual persons who lived before 1400, and under names of deities and mythological and legendary characters for works about art depicting the person, deity, or character. For works about art depicting persons who lived after 1400, use the subdivision —Portraits. Also use under headings of the type [topic]—[subdivision] for works about art depicting those topics.
NT —History of Biblical events—Art

—**Art**
H 1095; H 1110
Use as a form subdivision under names of individual persons who lived before 1400, and under names of deities and mythological and legendary characters for collections of art depicting the person, deity, or character. For collections of art depicting persons who lived after 1400, use the subdivision Portraits. Also use under headings of the type [topic]—[subdivision] for collections of art depicting those topics.
NT —History of Biblical events—Art

—**Art and the war, [revolution, etc.]**
H 1200
Complete the subdivision by repeating the generic term for the type of engagement contained in the heading.
Use as a topical subdivision under individual wars for works about art depicting the war, revolution, etc.

—**Art and the war, [revolution, etc.]**
H 1200
Complete the subdivision by repeating the generic term for the type of engagement contained in the heading.
Use as a form subdivision under individual wars for collections of art, including reproductions of art, depicting the war, revolution, etc.

—**Art collections**
H 1105; H 1110; H 1120
Use as a topical subdivision under names of individual persons and families for works about their collections of art. Also use under names of individual corporate bodies provided that the corporate body is the owner or the collector of the art and the corporate body is not itself an art gallery or museum.

—**Art patronage**
H 1105; H 1110; H 1120
Use as a topical subdivision under names of individual persons, families, and corporate bodies for works about their support and patronage of the arts.
UF —Patronage of the arts
NT —Kings and rulers—Art patronage

—**Article**
H 1154
Use as a topical subdivision under individual languages and groups of languages.

—**Artificial growing media**
H 1180
Use as a topical subdivision under individual plants and groups of plants.

—**Artificial insemination** *(May Subd Geog)*
H 1147
Use as a topical subdivision under individual animals and groups of animals.

—**Artificial spawning** *(May Subd Geog)*
H 1147
Use as a topical subdivision under individual animals and groups of animals.
UF —Spawning, Artificial
[Former subdivision]

—**Artillery**
H 1159
Use as a topical subdivision under military services.

——**Drill and tactics**
H 1159
Use as a topical subdivision under military services.
BT —Drill and tactics

—**Artillery operations**
H 1200
Use as a topical subdivision under individual wars.

—**Artillery operations, American, [British, French, etc.]**
H 1200
Use as a topical subdivision under individual wars.

—**Asian Americans**
H 1159; H 1200
Further subdivide by subdivisions used under classes of persons.
Use as a topical subdivision under military services and individual wars.

—**Asian authors** *(Not Subd Geog)*
H 1156
Use as a topical subdivision under individual literatures.

—**Asian influences**
H 1156
Use as a topical subdivision under individual literatures.
BT —Foreign influences

—**Aspect**
H 1154
Use as a topical subdivision under individual languages and groups of languages.

—**Aspiration**
H 1154
Use as a topical subdivision under individual languages and groups of languages.

—**Assassination**
H 1110
Use as a topical subdivision under names of individual persons.
BT —Death and burial
NT —Kings and rulers—Assassination

—**Assassination attempt, [date]**
H 1110
Use as a topical subdivision under names of individual persons.
UF —Attempted assassination, [date]

—**Assassination attempts** *(May Subd Geog)*
H 1100; H 1110
Do not subdivide geographically under names of individual persons.
Use as a topical subdivision under names of individual persons and classes of persons.
UF —Attempted assassination

—Assaults against
USE —Violence against

—**Assaying** *(May Subd Geog)*
H 1149
Use as a topical subdivision under individual metals and types of metals for the determination of the quantity or quality of a metal in an ore, alloy, etc.

—Assessment of life skills
USE —Life skills assessment

—Assimilation, Cultural
USE —Cultural assimilation

—Associates
USE —Friends and associates

—**Asyndeton**
H 1154
Use as a topical subdivision under individual languages and groups of languages.

—Athletics
USE —Sports

—**Atlases**
H 1095
Use as a form subdivision under scientific and technical topics for works consisting of comprehensive, often systematically arranged collections of illustrative plates, charts, etc., usually with explanatory captions.
UF —Scientific atlases
BT —Pictorial works

—Atlases, Geographic
USE —Maps

—**Atrocities** *(May Subd Geog)*
H 1200
Use as a topical subdivision under individual wars.

—Attempted assassination
   USE —Assassination attempts
—Attempted assassination, [date]
   USE —Assassination attempt, [date]
—Attempted suicide
   USE —Suicidal behavior
—Attendance at congresses
   USE —Congresses—Attendance
—**Attitudes**
   H 1100; H 1103
   Use as a topical subdivision under classes of persons and ethnic groups for works on attitudes or opinions held by members of the group. For works on public opinion about the group, use the subdivision Public opinion.
—**Attribution**
   H 1148
   Use as a topical subdivision under individual art forms and headings for national or ethnic art.
   BT —Expertising
—Attribution of authorship
   USE —Authorship
—**Audio adaptations**   (Not Subd Geog)
   H 1110; H 1156
   Use as a topical subdivision under names of individual persons and individual literatures for works about audio adaptations of the person's creative works or works from that literature.
   BT —Adaptations
—**Audio adaptations**
   H 1110; H 1156
   Use as a form subdivision under names of individual persons and individual literatures for collections of audio adaptations of that person's creative works or works from that literature.
   BT —Adaptations
—**Audio equipment**   (May Subd Geog)
   H 1195
   Use as a topical subdivision under individual land vehicles and types of land vehicles.
   BT —Equipment and supplies
—**Audio-visual aids**
   H 1095
   Use as a topical subdivision under topical headings for works on audiovisual materials not specifically designed for educational purposes.
   NT —Study and teaching—Audio-visual aids
———**Catalogs**
   H 1095
   Use this subdivision combination as a form subdivision under topical headings for catalogs of audiovisual materials pertaining to those topics.
   BT —Catalogs
—**Audiocassette catalogs**
   H 1095; H 1103; H 1105; H 1110; H 1140; H 1160
   Use as a form subdivision under names of countries, cities, etc., names of individual persons and corporate bodies, and under ethnic groups, topical headings, and forms and types of musical compositions for lists or catalogs of sound recordings on audiocassettes.
   BT —Catalogs
—**Audiotape catalogs**
   H 1095; H 1103; H 1105; H 1110; H 1140; H 1160
   Use as a form subdivision under names of countries, cities, etc., names of individual persons and corporate bodies, and under ethnic groups, topical headings, and forms and types of musical compositions for lists or catalogs of sound recordings on audiotapes.
   UF —Phonotape catalogs
      [Former subdivision]
   BT —Catalogs
—**Auditing**
   H 1095; H 1105; H 1151.5; H 1153
   Use as a topical subdivision under names of individual corporate bodies, types of corporate bodies and industries, and topical headings.
   UF —Auditing and inspection
      [Former subdivision]

——**Law and legislation**   (May Subd Geog)
   H 1151.5
   Further subdivide by subdivisions used under legal topics.
   Use as a topical subdivision under types of educational institutions.
   BT —Law and legislation
—Auditing and inspection
   USE —Auditing
—Augment
   USE —Augmentatives
—**Augmentatives**
   H 1154
   Use as a topical subdivision under individual languages and groups of languages.
   UF —Augment
      [Former subdivision]
—**Australian influences**
   H 1156
   Use as a topical subdivision under individual literatures.
   BT —Foreign influences
—**Authorship**
   H 1095; H 1110; H 1155.8; H 1188
   Use as a topical subdivision under individual works entered under title, under disciplines and under literary, motion picture, radio, television, and video forms and genres. Also use under names of individual persons for works on the attribution of authorship of works to the person.
   UF —Attribution of authorship
   NT —Historiography
      —Spurious and doubtful works
———**Collaboration**
   H 1110
   Use as a topical subdivision under names of individual persons.
   UF —Collaboration in authorship
      —Collaborative authorship
———**Date of authorship**
   H 1188
   Use as a topical subdivision under uniform titles of sacred works.
   UF —Date of authorship
———**Style manuals**
   H 1095
   Use this subdivision combination as a form subdivision under disciplines.
   UF —Style manuals for authorship
   BT —Handbooks, manuals, etc.
—Autobiography
   USE —Biography
—**Autographs**
   H 1100; H 1103; H 1110; H 1200
   Use as a topical subdivision under names of individual persons, classes of persons, and ethnic groups for works about autographs of those persons. Also use under individual wars for works about autographs of persons associated with the war.
   UF —Handwriting
      —Signatures (Writing)
—**Autographs**
   H 1100; H 1103; H 1110; H 1200
   Use as a form subdivision under names of individual persons, classes of persons, and ethnic groups for collections of autographs of those persons. Also use under individual wars for collections of autographs of persons associated with the war.
   UF —Handwriting
      —Signatures (Writing)
—Autographs, Spurious
   USE —Forgeries
—**Automatic control**
   H 1095; H 1195
   Use as a topical subdivision under individual technical processes and equipment.
   UF —Control, Automatic
—Automatic transmission devices
   USE —Transmission devices, Automatic
—**Automation**
   H 1095; H 1105; H 1153
   Use as a topical subdivision under names of individual corporate bodies, and under types of corporate bodies, industries, facilities, processes, and systems.

—**Autonomous communities**
   H 1095
   Use as a topical subdivision under headings of the type [topic]—Spain for works discussing collectively the autonomous communities of Spain in relation to the topic.
   BT —Administrative and political divisions
—**Autonomous regions**   (Not Subd Geog)
   H 1095
   Use as a topical subdivision under headings of the type [topic]—China for works discussing collectively the autonomous regions of China in relation to the topic.
—Autonomy and independence movements
   USE —History—Autonomy and independence movements
—**Autopsy**   (May Subd Geog)
   H 1147
   Use as a topical subdivision under individual animals and groups of animals.
—**Auxiliary verbs**
   H 1154
   Use as a topical subdivision under individual languages and groups of languages.
—**Aviation**
   H 1159
   Use as a topical subdivision under military services.
   NT —Tactical aviation
———**Ground support**
   H 1159
   Use as a topical subdivision under military services other than air forces.   Under air forces, use the subdivision Ground support.
   BT —Ground support
———**Job descriptions**
   H 1159
   Use this subdivision combination as a form subdivision under military services for summaries of the essential activities involved in the performance of jobs.
   Use as a topical subdivision under military services for works about summaries of the essential activities involved in the performance of jobs.
   BT —Job descriptions
—**Aviation electronics technicians**
   H 1159
   Further subdivide by subdivisions used under classes of persons.
   Use as a topical subdivision under military services.
—**Aviation mechanics**
   H 1159
   Further subdivide by subdivisions used under classes of persons.
   Use as a topical subdivision under military services.
—**Aviation supplies and stores**
   H 1159
   Use as a topical subdivision under military services.
—**Awards**   (May Subd Geog)
   H 1095; H 1105; H 1110; H 1159
   Further subdivide geographically only under topical headings.
   Use as a topical subdivision under names of individual persons, corporate bodies, and military services, and under topical headings.
   NT —Medals
—**Axles**
   H 1195
   Use as a topical subdivision under individual land vehicles and types of land vehicles.
—**Ayurvedic treatment**   (May Subd Geog)
   H 1150
   Use as a topical subdivision under individual diseases and types of diseases.
   BT —Treatment
—Bacteriology
   USE —Microbiology
—Badges
   USE —Medals, badges, decorations, etc.
—**Bahai interpretations**
   H 1188
   Use as a topical subdivision under uniform titles of sacred works.
   BT —Criticism, interpretation, etc.

—Balancing of wheels
    USE —Wheels—Balancing
—Balloons   (May Subd Geog)
    H 1200
    Use as a topical subdivision under individual
    wars.
—Bandmasters
    H 1159
    Further subdivide by subdivisions used under
    classes of persons.
    Use as a topical subdivision under military ser-
    vices.
—Bands
    H 1151
    Use as a topical subdivision under names of indi-
    vidual educational institutions, and under military
    services.
    UF —Orchestras and bands
        [Former subdivision]
—Bangladeshi authors
    H 1156
    Use as a topical subdivision under individual lit-
    eratures.
—Baptist versions
    USE —Versions, Baptist
—Bareroot seedlings
    USE —Seedlings, Bareroot
—Barracks and quarters
    H 1159
    Use as a topical subdivision under military ser-
    vices.
    UF —Quarters and barracks
——Furniture
    H 1159
    Use as a topical subdivision under military
    services.
    UF —Furniture in barracks and
        quarters
—Barrier-free design   (May Subd Geog)
    H 1095
    Use as a topical subdivision under types of build-
    ings, structures, and facilities.
    UF —Access for the physically
        handicapped
        [Former subdivision]
    NT —Buildings—Barrier-free design
—Barrier-free design of buildings
    USE —Buildings—Barrier-free design
—Base maps
    USE —Maps, Outline and base
—Baseball
    H 1151
    Use as a topical subdivision under names of in-
    dividual educational institutions.
    BT —Sports
—Basketball
    H 1151
    Use as a topical subdivision under names of in-
    dividual educational institutions.
    BT —Sports
—Basque authors
    H 1156
    Use as a topical subdivision under individual lit-
    eratures.
—Basques   (May Subd Geog)
    H 1200
    Further subdivide by subdivisions used under
    classes of persons.
    Use as a topical subdivision under individual
    wars for works on Basques in relation to the war.
—Bathymetric maps
    H 1140
    Use as a form subdivision under names of coun-
    tries, cities, etc.
    BT —Maps
—Batteries   (May Subd Geog)
    H 1195
    Use as a topical subdivision under individual
    land vehicles and types of land vehicles.
—Battlefields   (May Subd Geog)
    H 1200
    Use as a topical subdivision under individual
    wars.
—Battles, sieges, etc.
    USE —Campaigns
        —Naval operations
—Beaching
    USE —Stranding

—Bearings   (May Subd Geog)
    H 1195
    Use as a topical subdivision under individual
    land vehicles and types of land vehicles.
    NT —Motors—Bearings
—Behavior   (May Subd Geog)
    H 1147
    Use as a topical subdivision under individual an-
    imals and groups of animals.
    UF —Animal behavior
        —Habits and behavior
        [Former subdivision]
——Climatic factors   (May Subd Geog)
    H 1147
    Use as a topical subdivision under individual
    animals and groups of animals.
    BT —Climatic factors
——Endocrine aspects
    H 1147
    Use as a topical subdivision under individual
    animals and groups of animals.
    UF —Hormonal aspects of behavior
    BT —Endocrinology
——Evolution   (May Subd Geog)
    H 1147
    Use as a topical subdivision under individual
    animals and groups of animals.
    BT —Evolution
——Genetic aspects   (May Subd Geog)
    H 1147
    Use as a topical subdivision under individual
    animals and groups of animals.
    BT —Genetics
—Behavior, Ethical
    USE —Conduct of life
—Belts, Seat
    USE —Seat belts
—Benefactors
    H 1151
    Further subdivide by subdivisions used under
    classes of persons.
    Use as a topical subdivision under individual ed-
    ucational institutions.
—Benefices   (May Subd Geog)
    H 1187
    Use as a topical subdivision under individual
    Christian denominations.
—Bengali authors
    H 1156
    Use as a topical subdivision under individual lit-
    eratures.
—Biblical teaching
    H 1095
    Use as a topical subdivision under religious or
    secular topics for works on the theological and/or
    ethical teachings of the Bible, or its individual
    parts, on those topics.
    UF —Teaching of the Bible
—Bibliographic catalogs
    USE —Bibliography—Catalogs
—Bibliographical catalogs
    USE —Bibliography—Catalogs
—Bibliographies
    USE —Bibliography
—Bibliography
    H 1095; H 1105; H 1110; H 1156; H 1160
    Use as a topical subdivision under subjects for
    works about bibliography on those subjects.
—Bibliography
    H 1095; H 1105; H 1110; H 1156; H 1160
    Use as a form subdivision under subjects for
    works consisting of bibliographies about the sub-
    ject. Use under names of individual persons and
    corporate bodies for lists of works by or about the
    person or corporate body.
    UF —Bibliographies
        —Lists of books
    NT —Bibliography of bibliographies
        —Bio-bibliography
        —First editions—Bibliography
        —Imprints
        —Maps—Bibliography
        —Music—Bibliography
        —Periodicals—Bibliography
——Bibliography
    USE —Bibliography of bibliographies

——Catalogs
    H 1095
    Use as a form subdivision under subjects for
    lists of publications about the subject that pro-
    vide information about their location, availabil-
    ity, etc.
    UF —Bibliographic catalogs
        —Bibliographical catalogs
    BT —Catalogs
    NT —Periodicals—Bibliography—
        Catalogs
——Early
    H 1095
    Use as a form subdivision under subjects for
    bibliographies compiled or issued before 1800.
    UF —Bibliography—Early works to
        1800
        —Early bibliography
    BT —Early works to 1800
——Early works to 1800
    USE —Bibliography—Early
——Exhibitions
    H 1095
    Use as a form subdivision under subjects.
    BT —Exhibitions
——First editions
    USE —First editions—Bibliography
——Graded lists
    H 1160
    Use as a form subdivision under forms and
    types of musical compositions.
    UF —Graded lists
——Indexes
    USE —Indexes
——Methodology
    H 1095
    Use as a topical subdivision under subjects.
    UF —Bibliography—Theory, methods,
        etc.
        [Former subdivision]
    BT —Methodology
——Microform catalogs
    H 1095
    Use as a form subdivision under subjects for
    catalogs that list works stored in microform edi-
    tions.
    BT —Microform catalogs
——Theory, methods, etc.
    USE —Bibliography—Methodology
——Union lists
    H 1095
    Use as a form subdivision under subjects for
    catalogs of materials on those subjects held by
    two or more libraries.
    BT —Union lists
    NT —Periodicals—Bibliography—
        Union lists
—Bibliography of bibliographies
    H 1095
    Use as a form subdivision under subjects for
    works consisting of lists of bibliographies on those
    subjects.
    UF —Bibliography—Bibliography
        [Former subdivision]
    BT —Bibliography
—Bilingual method of language teaching
    USE —Study and teaching—Bilingual
        method
—Bills, Private
    USE —Private bills
—Bio-bibliography
    H 1095; H 1103; H 1140; H 1186; H 1187
    Use as a form subdivision under names of coun-
    tries, cities, etc., individual Christian denomina-
    tions, and monastic and religious orders, and un-
    der ethnic groups, literatures, and topical headings
    for works containing both biographical information
    about persons associated with the subject and bib-
    liographies of writings by and/or about them.
    BT —Bibliography
        —Biography
—Bioaccumulation   (May Subd Geog)
    H 1149
    Use as a topical subdivision under individual
    chemicals and groups of chemicals.

—**Bioavailability**   (*May Subd Geog*)
  H 1149
    Use as a topical subdivision under individual
  chemicals and groups of chemicals.
—**Biocompatibility**   (*May Subd Geog*)
  H 1158
    Use as a topical subdivision under individual
  materials and types of materials.
—Biocontrol
  USE —Biological control
—**Biodegradation**   (*May Subd Geog*)
  H 1149; H 1158
    Use as a topical subdivision under individual
  chemicals and groups of chemicals and individual
  materials and types of materials.
    BT —Deterioration
    NT —Carcasses—Biodegradation
—Biographical anecdotes
  USE —Biography—Anecdotes
—Biographical dictionaries
  USE —Biography—Dictionaries
—**Biography**
  H 1095; H 1100; H 1103; H 1105; H 1140;
  H 1147; H 1151; H 1159; H 1188; H 1200
    Use as a topical subdivision under names of
  countries, cities, etc., names of individual corporate
  bodies, uniform titles of sacred works, and under
  classes of persons, ethnic groups, individual and
  groups of animals, and historic events for works
  about collective or individual biography.
    UF —Autobiography
—**Biography**
  H 1095; H 1100; H 1103; H 1105; H 1140;
  H 1147; H 1151; H 1159; H 1188; H 1200
    Use as a form subdivision under names of coun-
  tries, cities, etc., names of individual corporate
  bodies, uniform titles of sacred works, and under
  classes of persons, ethnic groups, individual and
  groups of animals, and historic events for works of
  collective or individual biography.
    UF —Autobiography
        —Correspondence, reminiscences,
          etc.
          [Former subdivision]
        —Legends and stories
          [Former subdivision]
    NT —Bio-bibliography
        —History—[period subdivision]—
          Biography
        —Toxicology—Biography
——Ancestry
  USE —Family
——**Anecdotes**
  H 1140
    Use as a form subdivision under names of
  countries, cities, etc. for anecdotes about per-
  sons in or from those places.
    UF —Biographical anecdotes
        —Biography—Anecdotes, facetiae,
          satire, etc.
          [Former subdivision]
    BT —Anecdotes
——Anecdotes, facetiae, satire, etc.
  USE —Biography—Anecdotes
        —Biography—Humor
——Anniversaries, etc.
  USE —Anniversaries, etc.
——Birth
  USE —Birth
——**Caricatures and cartoons**
  H 1140
    Use as a form subdivision under names of
  countries, cities, etc., for caricatures and car-
  toons of persons in or from those places.
    BT —Caricatures and cartoons
——Character
  USE —Ethics
        —Psychology
——Chronology
  USE —Chronology
——Death and burial
  USE —Death and burial
——Descendants
  USE —Family

——**Dictionaries**
  H 1095; H 1100; H 1103; H 1105; H 1140
    Use as a form subdivision under names of
  countries, cities, etc., names of individual corpo-
  rate bodies, and under classes of persons, ethnic
  groups, and historic events.
    UF —Biographical dictionaries
    BT —Dictionaries
——Exile
  USE —Exile
——Family
  USE —Family
——Health
  USE —Health
——**History and criticism**
  H 1095; H 1100; H 1103; H 1105; H 1140
    Use as a topical subdivision under names of
  countries, cities, etc., names of individual corpo-
  rate bodies, and under classes of persons, ethnic
  groups, and historic events.
    BT —History and criticism
——**Humor**
  H 1140
    Use as a form subdivision under names of
  countries, cities, etc., for humor about persons
  in or from those places.
    UF —Biography—Anecdotes, facetiae,
          satire, etc.
          [Former subdivision]
    BT —Humor
——Imprisonment
  USE —Imprisonment
——Last years
  USE —Last years
——Last years and death
  USE —Death and burial
        —Last years
——Marriage
  USE —Marriage
——Old age
  USE —Last years
——**Pictorial works**
  H 1100; H 1103; H 1140
    Use as a form subdivision under names of
  countries, cities, etc., and under classes of per-
  sons and ethnic groups.
    BT —Pictorial works
——**Portraits**
  H 1105; H 1140; H 1159
    Use as a topical subdivision under names of
  countries, cities, etc., individual corporate bod-
  ies, and military services for works about por-
  traits of persons in or from those places, corpo-
  rate bodies, and military services.
    BT —Portraits
——**Portraits**
  H 1105; H 1140; H 1159
    Use as a form subdivision under names of
  countries, cities, etc., individual corporate bodies, and military services for collections of portraits of persons in or from those places, corporate bodies, or military services.
    BT —Portraits
——Psychology
  USE —Psychology
——**Sermons**
  H 1188
    Use as a form subdivision under uniform titles
  of sacred works.
    BT —Sermons
——**Sources**
  H 1100; H 1103; H 1140
    Use as a topical subdivision under names of
  countries, cites, etc., classes pf persons, and ethnic groups for works about biographical source
  materials pertaining to persons from those places
  or belonging to those groups.
    Use this subdivision combination as a form
  subdivision under names of countries, cities,
  etc., classes of persons, and ethnic groups for
  collections of biographical source materials pertaining to persons from those places or belonging to those groups.
    BT —Sources
——Youth
  USE —Childhood and youth

—**Biological control**   (*May Subd Geog*)
  H 1147; H 1180
    Use as a topical subdivision under individual an-
  imals and groups of animals, and individual plants
  and groups of plants.
    UF —Biocontrol
    BT —Control
    NT —Diseases and pests—Biological
          control
        —Parasites—Biological control
        —Postharvest diseases and injuries—
          Biological control
—**Biological warfare**   (*May Subd Geog*)
  H 1200
    Use as a topical subdivision under individual
  wars.
—**Biopsy**   (*May Subd Geog*)
  H 1164
    Use as a topical subdivision under individual or-
  gans and regions of the body.
    BT —Diagnosis
        —Surgery
    NT —Needle biopsy
—Biopsy, Needle
  USE —Needle biopsy
—**Biotechnology**   (*May Subd Geog*)
  H 1149; H 1180
    Use as a topical subdivision under individual
  chemicals and groups of chemicals and individual
  plants and groups of plants.
    NT —Genetic engineering
—**Birth**
  H 1110
    Use as a topical subdivision under names of in-
  dividual persons for works about the events of an
  individual's birth, including birthdays, the date or
  year of the person's birth, etc.
    UF —Biography—Birth
          [Former subdivision]
        —Date of birth
—Birthday books
  USE —Calendars
—**Birthplace**
  H 1110
    Use as a topical subdivision under names of in-
  dividual persons.
    UF —Place of birth
    BT —Homes and haunts
—**Bishops**
  H 1187
    Further subdivide by subdivisions used under
  classes of persons.
    Use as a topical subdivision under individual
  Christian denominations.
    BT —Clergy
——**Appointment, call, and election**
  H 1187
    Use as a topical subdivision under individual
  Christian denominations.
    UF —Appointment, call, and election
          of bishops
    BT —Selection and appointment
—**Black authors**
  H 1156
    Use as a topical subdivision under individual lit-
  eratures.
—**Black interpretations**
  H 1188
    Use as a topical subdivision under uniform titles
  of sacred works.
    BT —Criticism, interpretation, etc.
—**Blacks**   (*May Subd Geog*)
  H 1200
    Further subdivide by subdivisions used under
  classes of persons.
    Use as a topical subdivision under individual
  wars for works on aspects of the war in relation to
  blacks.
—Blank forms
  USE —Forms
—Blanks (Forms)
  USE —Forms
—Blockade
  USE —Blockades

—Blockades *(May Subd Geog)*
H 1200
Use as a topical subdivision under individual wars.
UF —Blockade
[Former subdivision]
—Blogs
H 1095; H 1100; H 1103; H 1110
Use as a topical subdivision under names of individual persons, classes of persons, ethnic groups, and topical headings for works about blogs by those persons or about those persons, groups, or topics.
UF —Weblogs
[Former subdivision]
—Blogs
H 1095; H 1100; H 1103; H 1110
Use as a form subdivision under names of individual persons, classes of persons, ethnic groups, and topical headings for blogs by those persons or about those persons, groups, or topics.
UF —Weblogs
[Former subdivision]
—Blood-vessels
H 1164
Use as a topical subdivision under individual organs and regions of the body.
—Blunt trauma *(May Subd Geog)*
H 1164
Further subdivide by subdivisions used under diseases.
Use as topical subdivision under individual organs and regions of the body.
BT —Wounds and injuries
—Boats *(May Subd Geog)*
H 1103; H 1159
Do not subdivide geographically under military services.
Use as a topical subdivision under ethnic groups and military services.
—Boatswains
H 1159
Further subdivide by subdivisions used under classes of persons.
Use as a topical subdivision under military services.
—Boatswain's mates
H 1159
Further subdivide by subdivisions used under classes of persons.
Use as a topical subdivision under military services.
—Bodies *(May Subd Geog)*
H 1195
Use as a topical subdivision under individual land vehicles and types of land vehicles.
UF —Vehicle bodies
NT —Interiors
——Alignment *(May Subd Geog)*
H 1195
Use as a topical subdivision under individual land vehicles and types of land vehicles.
UF —Alignment of bodies
——Parts *(May Subd Geog)*
H 1195
Use as a topical subdivision under individual land vehicles and types of land vehicles.
BT —Parts
—Boiler technicians
H 1159
Further subdivide by subdivisions used under classes of persons.
Use as a topical subdivision under military services.
—Bomb reconnaissance
H 1200
Use as a topical subdivision under individual wars.
—Bonding *(May Subd Geog)*
H 1100
Use as a topical subdivision under occupational groups and types of employees.
—Boning *(May Subd Geog)*
H 1147
Use as a topical subdivision under individual animals and groups of animals.
—Bonsai collections
H 1105; H 1110; H 1120
Use under names of individual persons, families, and corporate bodies for works about their collections of bonsai.

—Book reviews
H 1095; H 1100; H 1103; H 1140
Use as a form subdivision under names of countries, cities, etc., and under classes of persons, ethnic groups, and topical headings for collections of appraisals of books on those places or topics.
BT —Reviews
—Books and reading *(May Subd Geog)*
H 1100; H 1103; H 1110
Do not subdivide geographically under names of individual persons.
Use as a topical subdivision under names of individual persons, classes of persons, and ethnic groups for works about books for those persons or about their reading habits or interests.
UF —Books for
[Former subdivision]
—Reading habits
—Reading interests
—Books for
USE —Books and reading
—Borders
USE —Boundaries
—Boundaries *(May Subd Geog)*
H 1140; H 1149.5
Use as a topical subdivision under names of countries, cities, etc.
UF —Borders
—Boundary disputes
—Disputes, Boundary
—Frontier troubles
[Former subdivision]
—Frontiers (Boundaries)
—Geographic boundaries
—Political boundaries
—Territorial boundaries
NT —Colonies—Boundaries
—Boundary disputes
USE —Boundaries
—Bowing
H 1161
Use as a topical subdivision under individual musical instruments and families of instruments.
—Brakes
H 1195
Use as a topical subdivision under individual land vehicles and types of land vehicles.
NT —Air disc brakes
—Antilock brake systems
—Disc brakes
—Brazilian influences
H 1156
Use as a topical subdivision under individual literatures.
BT —Foreign influences
—Brazing *(May Subd Geog)*
H 1149
Use as a topical subdivision under individual metals and metal compounds.
—Breaking in
H 1195
Use as a topical subdivision under individual land vehicles and types of land vehicles.
—Breath control
H 1161
Use as a topical subdivision under individual musical instruments and familes of instruments.
UF —Control, Breath
—Breeding *(May Subd Geog)*
H 1147; H 1180
Use as a topical subdivision under individual animals and groups of animals and individual plants and groups of plants for works on the controlled mating and selection of those organisms by humans, usually for the purpose of improving the species or breed. For works on the physiological processes, sexual or asexual, by which organisms generate offspring of the same kind, use the subdivision Reproduction.
NT —Hybridization
—Induced spawning
—Mutation breeding
——Selection indexes
H 1147
Use as a topical subdivision under individual animals and groups of animals.
UF —Selection indexes for breeding

—Brittleness *(May Subd Geog)*
H 1149; H 1158
Use as a topical subdivision under individual chemicals and groups of chemicals and individual materials and types of materials.
BT —Properties
—Brothers of kings and rulers
USE —Kings and rulers—Brothers
—Buddhist authors
H 1156
Use as a topical subdivision under individual literatures.
—Buddhist influences
H 1156
Use as a topical subdivision under individual literatures.
—Buddhist interpretations
H 1188
Use as a topical subdivision under uniform titles of sacred works.
BT —Criticism, interpretation, etc.
—Buildings
H 1095; H 1105; H 1151
Use as a topical subdivision under names of individual corporate bodies and exhibitions for works that discuss collectively the buildings of those corporate bodies or exhibitions.
NT —Buildings, structures, etc.
——Access for the physically handicapped
USE —Buildings—Barrier-free design
——Barrier-free design
H 1151
Use as a topical subdivision under names of individual educational institutions.
UF —Barrier-free design of buildings
—Buildings—Access for the physically handicapped
[Former subdivision]
BT —Barrier-free design
——Remodeling for other use
H 1151
Use as a topical subdivision under individual educational institutions.
—Buildings, structures, etc.
H 1140
Use as a topical subdivision under names of cities and city sections.
UF —Structures, etc.
BT —Buildings
—Bumpers
H 1195
Use as a topical subdivision under individual land vehicles and types of land vehicles.
—Burial
USE —Death and burial
—Burial of kings and rulers
USE —Kings and rulers—Death and burial
—Business management
H 1151.5
Use as a topical subdivision under types of educational institutions.
BT —Administration
—Buying
USE —Purchasing
—By-laws
H 1095; H 1105
Use as a topical subdivision under names of individual corporate bodies and under types of corporate bodies for works about by-laws of those bodies.
UF —Bye laws
—Byelaws
—Bylaws
—By-laws
H 1095; H 1105
Use as a form subdivision under names of individual corporate bodies and under types of corporate bodies for collections of by-laws of those bodies.
UF —Bye-laws
—Byelaws
—Bylaws
—By-products
H 1095
Use as a topical subdivision under types of industries and processes.
NT —Pickling—By-products

—Bye laws
  USE —By-laws
—Bye-laws
  USE —By-laws
—Byelaws
  USE —By-laws
—Bylaws
  USE —By-laws
—Byzantine antiquities
  USE —Antiquities, Byzantine
—**Cadenzas**
  H 1160
    Use as a form subdivision under forms and types of musical compositions.
—**Calcification** *(May Subd Geog)*
  H 1164
    Use as a topical subdivision under individual organs and regions of the body.
—**Calendars**
  H 1095; H 1105; H 1110; H 1140
    Use as a form subdivision under names of countries, cities, etc., names of individual corporate bodies, and topical headings for works that list recurring, coming, or past events occurring in those places, associated with those organizations, or relating to those topics. Also use under names of individual persons for calendars that include information on events associated with the person or quotations from the person.
  UF —Birthday books
      [Former subdivision]
    —Calendars, etc.
      [Former subdivision]
  NT —Liturgy—Calendar
—Calendars, etc.
  USE —Calendars
—**Calibration** *(May Subd Geog)*
  H 1095
    Use as a topical subdivision under types of scientific and technical instruments and equipment.
—**Camouflage**
  H 1200
    Use as a topical subdivision under individual wars.
—**Campaigns** *(May Subd Geog)*
  H 1200
    Use as a topical subdivision under individual wars.
  UF —Battles, sieges, etc.
      [Former subdivision]
    —Campaigns and battles
      [Former subdivision]
—Campaigns and battles
  USE —Campaigns
—Camshafts of motors
  USE —Motors—Camshafts
—**Cancer** *(May Subd Geog)*
  H 1164
    Further subdivide by subdivisions used under diseases.
    Use as a topical subdivision under individual organs and regions of the body.
  BT —Diseases
  NT —Precancerous conditions
—**Cannibalism** *(May Subd Geog)*
  H 1147
    Use as a topical subdivision under individual animals and groups of animals.
  BT —Food
—**Canon**
  H 1188
    Use as a topical subdivision under uniform titles of sacred works.
—**Canonical criticism**
  H 1188
    Use as a topical subdivision under uniform titles of sacred works.
  UF —Criticism, Canonical
      [Former subdivision]
  BT —Criticism, interpretation, etc.
—**Cantons**
  H 1095
    Use as a topical subdivision under headings of the type [topic]—[country] for works discussing collectively the cantons of a country in relation to the topic.
  BT —Administrative and political divisions

—Capacity, Industrial
  USE —Industrial capacity
—Capacity of fluids
  USE —Fluid capacities
—**Capital and capitol**
  H 1140
    Do not use under names of cities.
    Use as a topical subdivision under names of countries, etc.
  UF —Capitol
—**Capital investments** *(May Subd Geog)*
  H 1153
    Use as a topical subdivision under types of industries.
  UF —Investments, Capital
—Capital, Military
  USE —Military capital
—**Capital productivity** *(May Subd Geog)*
  H 1153
    Use as a topical subdivision under types of industries.
  UF —Productivity, Capital
—**Capitalization**
  H 1154
    Use as a topical subdivision under individual languages and groups of languages.
—Capitol
  USE —Capital and capitol
—**Captivity, [dates]**
  H 1110
    Use as a topical subdivision under names of individual persons for works on periods in which the person was held captive in bondage or confinement, especially under house arrest, as a hostage, or in battle. For works on periods in which the person was imprisoned in a correctional institution or prisoner of war camp, use the subdivision Imprisonment.
—**Carbon content** *(May Subd Geog)*
  H 1158; H 1180
    Use as a topical subdivision under individual materials and types of materials and individual plants and groups of plants
—Carburetors of motors
  USE —Motors—Carburetors
—**Carcasses** *(May Subd Geog)*
  H 1147
    Use as a topical subdivision under individual animals and groups of animals.
— — **Biodegradation** *(May Subd Geog)*
    H 1147
      Use as a topical subdivision under individual animals and groups of animals.
    BT —Biodegradation
— — **Grading** *(May Subd Geog)*
    H 1147
      Use as a topical subdivision under individual animals and groups of animals.
    BT —Grading
— — **Handling** *(May Subd Geog)*
    H 1147
      Use as a topical subdivision under individual animals and groups of animals.
    BT —Handling
—**Carcinogenicity** *(May Subd Geog)*
  H 1149
    Use as a topical subdivision under individual chemicals and groups of chemicals.
—**Cardiovascular system**
  H 1147
    Use as a topical subdivision under individual animals and groups of animals.
—**Care** *(May Subd Geog)*
  H 1100
    Use as a topical subdivision under classes of persons who are generally dependent upon the care or assistance of others for works on personal care in general, or covering several levels of care.
  UF —Care and treatment
      [Former subdivision]
  NT —Home care
    —Hospice care
    —Institutional care
    —Intermediate care
    —Long-term care
    —Respite care

—**Care and hygiene** *(May Subd Geog)*
  H 1164
    Use as a topical subdivision under individual organs and regions of the body.
  UF —Hygiene
  NT —Massage
—Care and treatment
  USE —Care
—**Career in [specific field or discipline]**
  H 1110
    Use as a topical subdivision under names of individual persons for works on events in the person's occupational life or participation in a profession or vocation.
  UF —Careers
    —Professional life
—Careers
  USE —Career in [specific field or discipline]
—**Caribbean authors**
  H 1156
    Use as a topical subdivision under individual literatures.
—**Caricatures and cartoons**
  H 1095; H 1100; H 1103; H 1105; H 1110; H 1120; H 1188
    Use as a topical subdivision under names of individual persons, families, and corporate bodies, and under classes of persons, ethnic groups, individual wars, and topical headings for works about caricatures or pictorial humor about those subjects.
  UF —Cartoons, satire, etc.
      [Former subdivision]
    —Pictorial humor
    —Portraits, caricatures, etc.
      [Former subdivision]
—**Caricatures and cartoons**
  H 1095; H 1100; H 1103; H 1105; H 1110; H 1120; H 1188
    Use as a form subdivision under names of individual persons, families, and corporate bodies, and under classes of persons, ethnic groups, individual wars, and topical headings for collections of caricatures or pictorial humor about those subjects.
  UF —Cartoons, satire, etc.
      [Former subdivision]
    —Pictorial humor
    —Portraits, caricatures, etc.
      [Former subdivision]
  BT —Humor
    —Pictorial works
  NT —Biography—Caricatures and cartoons
    —Comic books, strips, etc.
—**Cartography**
  H 1200
    Use as a topical subdivision under individual wars.
—Cartoons, satire, etc.
  USE —Caricatures and cartoons
    —Humor
—**Case**
  H 1154
    Use as a topical subdivision under individual languages and groups of languages.
  NT —Ergative constructions
    —Locative constructions
—**Case grammar**
  H 1154
    Use as a topical subdivision under individual languages and groups of languages.
  BT —Grammar
—**Case studies**
  H 1095; H 1100; H 1103; H 1105
    Use as a form subdivision under names of individual corporate bodies and under classes of persons, ethnic groups, and topical headings.
  UF —Cases, clinical reports, statistics
      [Former subdivision]
    —Clinical reports
  NT —Longitudinal studies
—**Cases**
  H 1154.5
    Use as a form subdivision under individual legal topics.
— — **Digests**
    USE —Digests

SD-11

—Cases, clinical reports, statistics
  USE —Case studies
        —Statistics
—**Casualties** *(May Subd Geog)*
  H 1200
    Use as a topical subdivision under individual
    wars.
  UF —Casualties (Statistics, etc.)
        [Former subdivision]
——**Statistics**
  H 1200
    Use this subdivision combination as a form
    subdivision under individual wars.
  UF —Casualties (Statistics, etc.)
        [Former subdivision]
  BT —Statistics
—Casualties (Statistics, etc.)
  USE —Casualties
        —Casualties—Statistics
—**Catalan authors**
  H 1156
    Use as a topical subdivision under individual lit-
    eratures.
—**Catalogs**
  H 1095; H 1105; H 1110; H 1120; H 1148
    Use as a topical subdivision under types of ob-
    jects, including types of merchandise, art objects,
    products, publications, collectors' items, technical
    equipment, etc., for works about listings of those
    objects that have been produced, that are available
    or located at particular places, or that occur on
    a particular market, often systematically arranged
    with descriptive details, prices, etc., accompany-
    ing each entry. Use the topical subdivision Cata-
    logs under the heading Excavations (Archaeology)
    as well as under headings for individual archaeo-
    logical sites for works about lists of objects found.
    Use the topical subdivision Catalogs under names
    of individual corporate bodies and types of organi-
    zations for works about lists of objects, art works,
    products, etc., produced by, located in, or available
    from those organizations. Also use the topical sub-
    division Catalogs under names of individual artists,
    craftspersons, families of artists and craftspersons,
    and corporate bodies for works about lists of their
    art works or crafts which are available or located
    in particular institutions or places. Also use under
    persons or families doing business as sellers under
    their own names.
  NT —Catalogs and collections
—**Catalogs**
  H 1095; H 1105; H 1110; H 1120; H 1148
    Use as a form subdivision under types of ob-
    jects, including types of merchandise, art objects,
    products, publications, collectors' items, technical
    equipment, etc., for listings of those objects that
    have been produced, that are available or located
    at particular places, or that occur on a particular
    market, often systematically arranged with descrip-
    tive details, prices, etc., accompanying each entry.
    Use the subdivision Catalogs under the heading Ex-
    cavations (Archaeology) as well as under headings
    for individual archaeological sites for works listing
    objects found. Use the subdivision Catalogs under
    names of individual corporate bodies and types of
    organizations for works listing objects, art works,
    products, etc., produced by, located in, or avail-
    able from those organizations. Also use the subdi-
    vision Catalogs under names of individual artists,
    craftspersons, families of artists and craftspersons,
    and corporate bodies for works listing their art
    works or crafts which are available or located in
    particular institutions or places. Also use under
    persons or families doing business as sellers under
    their own names.
  NT —Audio-visual aids—Catalogs
        —Audiocassette catalogs
        —Audiotape catalogs
        —Bibliography—Catalogs
        —Catalogs and collections
        —Catalogues raisonnés
        —CD-ROM catalogs
        —Compact disc catalogs
        —Curricula—Catalogs
        —Data tape catalogs
        —Discography
        —Exhibitions
        —Film catalogs

        —Manufacturers' catalogs
        —Manuscripts—Catalogs
        —Microform catalogs
        —Thematic catalogs
        —Union lists
        —Video catalogs
—**Catalogs and collections** *(May Subd Geog)*
  H 1095; H 1147; H 1161; H 1180
    Use as a topical subdivision under types of nat-
    ural objects, individual musical instruments and
    families of instuments for works about catalogs or
    collections of those objects and instruments.
  BT —Catalogs
—**Catalogs and collections** *(May Subd Geog)*
  H 1095; H 1147; H 1161; H 1180
    Use as a form subdivision under types of natural
    objects, individual musical instruments, and fam-
    ilies of instruments for catalogs or collections of
    those objects and instruments.
  BT —Catalogs
  NT —Germplasm resources—Catalogs
        and collections
—Catalogs, Manufacturers'
  USE —Manufacturers' catalogs
—**Catalogues raisonnés**
  H 1110
    Use as a form subdivision under names of in-
    dividual persons for comprehensive listings of an
    artist's or craftperson's works in one medium or all
    media, usually chronologically or systematically
    arranged, and accompanied by descriptive or crit-
    ical notes.
  UF —Oeuvre catalogues
  BT —Catalogs
—**Catalytic converters**
  H 1195
    Use as a topical subdivision under individual
    land vehicles and types of land vehicles.
—**Cataphora**
  H 1154
    Use as a topical subdivision under individual
    languages and groups of languages.
—**Catechisms**
  H 1185; H 1187
    Use as a topical subdivision under individual
    religions and Christian denominations for works
    about catechisms of those religions or denomina-
    tions.
  UF —Catechisms and creeds
        [Former subdivision]
—**Catechisms**
  H 1185; H 1187
    Use as a form subdivision under individual reli-
    gions and Christian denominations for catechisms
    of those religions or denominations.
  UF —Catechisms and creeds
        [Former subdivision]
——**English, [French, German, etc.]**
  H 1187
    Use as a form subdivision under individual
    Christian denominations.
——**History and criticism**
  H 1187
    Use as a topical subdivision under individual
    Christian denominations.
  BT —History and criticism
—Catechisms and creeds
  USE —Catechisms
        —Creeds
—**Categorial grammar**
  H 1154
    Use as a topical subdivision under individual
    languages and groups of languages.
  BT —Grammar
—Categories, Grammatical
  USE —Grammatical categories
—**Catholic authors**
  H 1156
    Use as a topical subdivision under individual lit-
    eratures.
—Catholic versions
  USE —Versions, Catholic
—Catholic vs. Protestant versions
  USE —Versions, Catholic vs. Protestant
—**Caucuses**
  H 1155
    Use as a topical subdivision under names of in-
    dividual legislative bodies.

—**Causative**
  H 1154
    Use as a topical subdivision under individual
    languages and groups of languages.
—**Causes**
  H 1200
    Use as a topical subdivision under individual
    wars.
—**Cavalry**
  H 1159
    Use as a topical subdivision under military ser-
    vices.
——**Drill and tactics**
  H 1159
    Use as a topical subdivision under military
    services.
  BT —Drill and tactics
—**Cavalry operations**
  H 1200
    Use as a topical subdivision under individual
    wars.
—**Cavitation erosion** *(May Subd Geog)*
  H 1158
    Use as a topical subdivision under individual
    materials and types of materials.
  BT —Erosion
—**CD-ROM catalogs**
  H 1095
    Use as a form subdivision under subjects.
  BT —Catalogs
—Celebrations, anniversaries, etc.
  USE —Anniversaries, etc.
—Celtic antiquities
  USE —Antiquities, Celtic
—**Celtic authors**
  H 1156
    Use as a topical subdivision under individual lit-
    eratures.
—**Celtic influences**
  H 1156
    Use as a topical subdivision under individual lit-
    eratures.
  BT —Foreign influences
—**Censorship** *(May Subd Geog)*
  H 1095; H 1110; H 1156; H 1200
    Use as a topical subdivision under names of in-
    dividual persons and under individual literatures,
    wars, and topical headings, especially forms of
    communication.
  UF —Prohibited books
—**Censures**
  H 1110; H 1155
    Use as a topical subdivision under names of in-
    dividual persons and legislative bodies.
—**Census**
  H 1103; H 1140
    Use as a topical subdivision under names of
    countries, cities, etc., and ethnic groups for works
    about official counts of the population of the place
    or group.
  BT —Statistics
—**Census**
  H 1103; H 1140
    Use as a form subdivision under names of coun-
    tries, cities, etc., and ethnic groups for official
    counts of the population of the place or group, in-
    cluding data relating to economic and social condi-
    tions.
  BT —Statistics
——**Law and legislation**
  H 1140
    Further subdivide by subdivisions used under
    legal topics.
    Use as a topical subdivision under names of
    countries, cities, etc.
  BT —Law and legislation
—**Census, [date]**
  H 1103; H 1140
    Use as a topical subdivision under names of
    countries, cities, etc., and ethnic groups for works
    about a specific census of the place or group.
—**Census, [date]**
  H 1103; H 1140
    Use as a form subdivision under names of coun-
    tries, cities, etc., and ethnic groups for results of a
    specific census of the place or group.

—**Centennial celebrations, etc.**
  H 1095; H 1105; H 1140; H 1200
    Use as a topical subdivision under names of countries, cities, etc., and individual corporate bodies, and under historic events.
  UF —Centennials
  BT —Anniversaries, etc.
—Centennials
  USE —Centennial celebrations, etc.
—Ceremonies
  USE —Rites and ceremonies
—Ceremonies and practices
  USE —Customs and practices
—**Certification**   (*May Subd Geog*)
  H 1095; H 1100; H 1153
    Use as a topical subdivision under types of products and industries, occupational groups, and types of employees for works on official confirmation that standards have been met.
  NT —Seeds—Certification
—**Channelization**
  H 1145.5
    Use as a topical subdivision under names of individual bodies of water.
—**Channels**
  H 1145.5
    Use as a topical subdivision under individual bodies of water.
—**Chapel exercises**
  H 1151.5
    Use as a form subdivision under types of educational institutions.
  UF —Exercises, Chapel
—**Chaplains**   (*May Subd Geog*)
  H 1105; H 1159; H 1200
    Further subdivide by subdivisions used under classes of persons.
    Further subdivide geographically only under individual wars.
    Do not use under headings of the type [place]—Armed Forces; use Military chaplains—[place] instead.
    Use as a topical subdivision under names of individual corporate bodies, military services and wars.
—**Chaplain's assistants**
  H 1159
    Further subdivide by subdivisions used under classes of persons.
    Use as a topical subdivision under military services.
—**Characters**
  H 1110; H 1155.8
    Use as a topical subdivision under names of individual literary authors and literary works entered under title for works about the author's or work's characters in general.
——**Children, [Jews, Physicians, etc.]**
  H 1110
    Complete the subdivision with subdivisions for classes of persons or ethnic groups.
    Use as a topical subdivision under names of individual literary authors for works about specific groups or categories of characters of an author.
——[**name of individual character**]
  H 1110
    Complete the subdivision with subdivisions for individual named characters in uninverted forms.
    Use as a topical subdivision under names of individual literary authors for works about specific named characters of the author.
—**Charitable contributions**   (*May Subd Geog*)
  H 1095; H 1100; H 1103
    Use as a topical subdivision under classes of persons, ethnic groups, and types of organizations.
  UF —Contributions, Charitable
    —Contributions to charity
—**Charities**
  H 1103; H 1105; H 1185; H 1187
    Use as a topical subdivision under names of individual corporate bodies and under individual religions and Christian denominations for works about charities sponsored by the corporate body, religion, or denomination. Use under ethnic groups for works about charities serving or benefitting the group.

—**Charters**
  H 1105; H 1140
    Use as a topical subdivision under names of states, counties, cities, etc., of the United States, under names of indigenous jurisdictions in the United States, and under names individual corporate bodies for works about charters of those places or corporate bodies.
—**Charters**
  H 1105; H 1140
    Use as a form subdivision under names of states, counties, cities, etc., of the United States, under names of indigenous jurisdictions in the United States, and under names of individual corporate bodies for individual or collections of charters of those places or corporate bodies.
—**Charters, grants, privileges**
  H 1140
    Use as a topical subdivision under countries, etc., other than the United States, and under names of cities other than those of the United States for works about charters, grants, etc., of those places.
—**Charters, grants, privileges**
  H 1140
    Use as a form subdivision under names of countries, etc., other than the United States, and under names of cities other than those of the United States for individual or collections of charters, grants, etc., of those places.
—Charts
  USE —Charts, diagrams, etc.
—**Charts, diagrams, etc.**
  H 1095
    Use as a form subdivision under topical headings for works consisting of miscellaneous charts or diagrams illustrating those topics.
  UF —Charts
    [*Former subdivision*]
    —Charts, tables, etc.
    [*Former subdivision*]
    —Diagrams
    [*Former subdivision*]
    —Outline drawings
  BT —Pictorial works
  NT —Chord diagrams
    —Fingering—Charts, diagrams, etc.
—Charts, tables, etc.
  USE —Charts, diagrams, etc.
    —Tables
—**Chassis**
  H 1195
    Use as a topical subdivision under land vehicles and types of land vehicles.
—Chat groups, Online
  USE —Online chat groups
—Chemical analysis
  USE —Analysis
—**Chemical defenses**   (*May Subd Geog*)
  H 1147; H 1180
    Use as a topical subdivision under individual animals and groups of animals and individual plants and groups of plants.
  BT —Defenses
—**Chemical resistance**
  H 1158
    Use as a topical subdivision under individual materials and types of materials.
  UF —Resistance, Chemical
—**Chemical warfare**   (*May Subd Geog*)
  H 1200
    Use as a topical subdivision under individual wars.
  UF —Chemistry
    [*Former subdivision*]
—Chemistry
  USE —Chemical warfare
—**Chemoprevention**   (*May Subd Geog*)
  H 1150
    Use as a topical subdivision under individual diseases and types of diseases.
  BT —Chemotherapy
    —Prevention
—**Chemotaxonomy**   (*May Subd Geog*)
  H 1180
    Use as a topical subdivision under individual plants and groups of plants.
  BT —Classification

—**Chemotherapy**   (*May Subd Geog*)
  H 1150
    Use as a topical subdivision under individual diseases and types of diseases.
  BT —Treatment
  NT —Chemoprevention
    —Diseases—Chemotherapy
    —Photochemotherapy
———**Complications**   (*May Subd Geog*)
  H 1150
    Further subdivide by other subdivisions used under diseases.
    Use as a topical subdivision under individual diseases and types of diseases.
  UF —Chemotherapy—Complications and sequelae
    [*Former subdivision*]
  BT —Complications
———Complications and sequelae
  USE —Chemotherapy—Complications
—**Childhood and youth**
  H 1110
    Use as a topical subdivision under names of individual persons.
  UF —Biography—Youth
    [*Former subdivision*]
    —Early life
    —Youth
—**Children**   (*May Subd Geog*)
  H 1200
    Further subdivide by subdivisions used under classes of persons.
    Use as a topical subdivision under individual wars for works on aspects of the war in relation to children, especially the war's effects on them. For works on the participation of children in the military actions of a war, use the subdivision Participation, Juvenile.
—Children of kings and rulers
  USE —Kings and rulers—Children
—Children's dictionaries
  USE —Dictionaries, Juvenile
—Children's encyclopedias
  USE —Encyclopedias, Juvenile
—Children's humor
  USE —Juvenile humor
—Children's literature
  USE —Juvenile literature
—Children's plays
  USE —Juvenile drama
—Children's poetry
  USE —Juvenile poetry
—**Children's sermons**
  H 1188
    Use as a form subdivision under uniform titles of sacred works.
  BT —Juvenile literature
    —Sermons
—Children's software
  USE —Juvenile software
—Children's stories
  USE —Juvenile fiction
—**Children's use**   (*May Subd Geog*)
  H 1188
    Use as a topical subdivision under uniform titles of sacred works.
  UF —Use by children
—**Chinese authors**
  H 1156
    Use as a topical subdivision under individual literatures.
—**Chinese influences**
  H 1156
    Use as a topical subdivision under individual literatures.
  BT —Foreign influences
—**Chiropractic treatment**   (*May Subd Geog*)
  H 1150
    Use as a topical subdivision under individual diseases and types of diseases.
  BT —Treatment
  NT —Diseases—Chiropractic treatment
—**Choral organizations**
  H 1151
    Use as a topical subdivision under names of individual educational institutions.

—**Chord diagrams**
H 1161
Use as a form subdivision under individual musical instruments, and families of instruments.
BT —Charts, diagrams, etc.

—**Chorus scores with organ**
H 1160
Use as a form subdivision under forms and types of musical compositions.

—**Chorus scores with piano**
H 1160
Use as a form subdivision under forms and types of musical compositions.

—**Chorus scores without accompaniment**
H 1160
Use as a form subdivision under forms and types of musical compositions.

—Chrestomathies and readers
USE —Readers

—**Christian authors**
H 1156
Use as a topical subdivision under individual literatures.

—Christian church history
USE —Church history

—**Christian influences**
H 1156
Use as a topical subdivision under individual literatures.

—**Christian Science authors**
H 1156
Use as a topical subdivision under individual literatures.

—Chronological lists
USE —Chronology

—**Chronology** (Not Subd Geog)
H 1110; H 1155.2; H 1188
Use as a topical subdivision under names of individual persons and groups of literary authors for works about the chronology of events in the person's life or dates when works were produced. Also use under uniform titles of sacred works for works on the dating or order of occurrence of events mentioned in the sacred work.

—**Chronology**
H 1095; H 1110; H 1148; H 1155.2; H 1156; H 1188; H 1200
Use as a form subdivision under names of individual persons, groups of literary authors, uniform titles of sacred works, headings for art, music, and literature, and topical headings that are inherently historical for lists of dates of events pertinent to the subject in order of their occurrence.
UF —Biography—Chronology
—Chronological lists
—Lists of events
NT —History—[period subdivision]—Chronology
—History—Chronology
—Prophecies—Chronology

—**Church history**
H 1140
Use as a topical subdivision under names of countries, cities, etc.
UF —Christian church history
BT —History

——**16th century**
H 1140
Use as a topical subdivision under names of countries, cities, etc.

——**17th century**
H 1140
Use as a topical subdivision under names of countries, cities, etc.

——**18th century**
H 1140
Use as a topical subdivision under names of countries, cities, etc.

——**19th century**
H 1140
Use as a topical subdivision under names of countries, cities, etc.

——**20th century**
H 1140
Use as a topical subdivision under the names of countries, cities, etc.

——**21st century**
H 1140
Use as a topical subdivision under names of countries, cities, etc.

—**Cipher**
H 1110
Use as a topical subdivision under names of individual persons.

—**Circulation**
H 1095
Use as a topical subdivision under types of serial publications.

—**Citizen participation**
H 1095
Use as a topical subdivision under topical headings for works on the participation of citizens in carrying out an activity.
UF —Participation, Citizen

—Citizenship, Tribal
USE —Tribal citizenship

—**Civic action**
H 1159
Use as a topical subdivision under military services.

—**Civil functions**
H 1159
Use as a topical subdivision under military services.

—**Civil rights** (May Subd Geog)
H 1100; H 1103
Use as a topical subdivision under classes of persons and ethnic groups.
UF —Rights, Civil
BT —Legal status, laws, etc.

—**Civilian employees**
H 1159
Further subdivide by subdivisions used under classes of persons.
Use as a topical subdivision under military services.

—Civilian evacuation
USE —Evacuation of civilians

—**Civilian relief** (May Subd Geog)
H 1200
Use as a topical subdivision under individual wars.
UF —Hospitals, charities, etc.
 [Former subdivision]

—**Civilization**
H 1140
Use as a topical subdivision under names of countries, cities, etc.
UF —Culture (Civilization)

——**16th century**
H 1140
Use as a topical subdivision under names of countries, cities, etc.

——**17th century**
H 1140
Use as a topical subdivision under names of countries, cities, etc.

——**18th century**
H 1140
Use as a topical subdivision under names of countries, cities, etc.

——**19th century**
H 1140
Use as a topical subdivision under names of countries, cities, etc.

——**20th century**
H 1140
Use as a topical subdivision under names of countries, cities, etc.

——**21st century**
H 1140
Use as a topical subdivision under names of countries, cities, etc.

——**Foreign influences**
H 1140
Use as a topical subdivision under names of countries, cities, etc.
BT —Foreign influences

——**Philosophy**
H 1140
Use as a topical subdivision under names of countries, cities, etc.
BT —Philosophy

—**Cladistic analysis** (May Subd Geog)
H 1180
Use as a topical subdivision under individual plants and groups of plants.

—**Claims**
H 1103; H 1140; H 1200
Use as a topical subdivision under names of countries, cities, etc., ethnic groups, and individual wars.

—**Claims vs. . . . .**
H 1105; H 1110; H 1140
Complete the subdivision with the name of the jurisdiction against which the claim was brought.
Use as a topical subdivision under names of countries, cities, etc., individual persons, and corporate bodies for works on legal claims filed by the jurisdiction, person, or corporate body.

—**Classical influences**
H 1156
Use as a topical subdivision under individual literatures.
BT —Foreign influences

—**Classification**
H 1095; H 1100; H 1147; H 1154; H 1180
Use as a topical subdivision under classes of persons and topical headings for works on the theory and/or methodology of creating a systematic breakdown of a subject into its constituent categories or subtopics.
NT —Chemotaxonomy
—Cytotaxonomy
—Palynotaxonomy

—**Classification** (Not Subd Geog)
H 1095; H 1100; H 1147; H 1154; H 1180
Use as a form subdivision under classes of persons and topical headings for works that consist of a systematic breakdown of a subject into its constituent categories or subtopics.

——**Molecular aspects** (Not Subd Geog)
H 1147; H 1180
Use as a topical subdivision under individual animals and groups of animals and individual plants and groups of plants.
BT —Molecular aspects

—**Classifiers**
H 1154
Use as a topical subdivision under individual languages and groups of languages.

—**Clauses**
H 1154
Use as a topical subdivision under individual languages and groups of languages.
NT —Relative clauses
—Temporal clauses

—**Cleaning** (May Subd Geog)
H 1095
Use as a topical subdivision under topical headings.

—**Clergy**
H 1187
Further subdivide by subdivisions used under classes of persons.
Use as a topical subdivision under individual Christian denominations.
NT —Bishops

——**Appointment, call, and election**
H 1187
Use as a topical subdivision under individual Christian denominations.
UF —Appointment, call, and election of clergy
BT —Selection and appointment

——**Degradation**
H 1187
Use as a topical subdivision under individual Christian denominations.
UF —Degradation of clergy

——**Deposition**
H 1187
Use as a topical subdivision under individual Christian denominations.
UF —Deposition of clergy

——**Deprivation of the clerical garb**
 (May Subd Geog)
H 1187
Use as a topical subdivision under individual Christian denominations.
UF —Deprivation of the clerical garb

——**Installation** (May Subd Geog)
H 1187
Use as a topical subdivision under individual Christian denominations.
UF —Installation of clergy

——**Secular employment** *(May Subd Geog)*
H 1187
Use as a topical subdivision under individual Christian denominations.
UF —Secular employment of clergy
BT —Employment
—**Clerical work**
H 1159
Use as a topical subdivision under military services.
—**Climate**
H 1140
Use as a topical subdivision under names of countries, cities, etc.
——**Observations**
H 1140
Use this subdivision combination as a form subdivision under names of countries, cities, etc.
BT —Observations
—**Climatic factors** *(May Subd Geog)*
H 1147; H 1180; H 1195
Use as a topical subdivision under individual animals and groups of animals, individual plants and groups of plants and individual land vehicles and types of land vehicles for works on the relation of those topics to climate.
UF —Effect of climate changes on
—Effect of climate on
NT —Behavior—Climatic factors
—Effect of acid precipitation on
—Effect of freezes on
—Effect of global warming on
—Effect of ozone on
—Effect of storms on
—Effect of wind on
—Feeding and feeds—Climatic factors
—Geographical distribution—Climatic factors
—Metabolism—Climatic factors
—Migration—Climatic factors
—Reproduction—Climatic factors
—Seeds—Climatic factors
—Storage—Climatic factors
—Clinical reports
USE —Case studies
—**Clitics**
H 1154
Use as a topical subdivision under individual languages and groups of languages.
—**Clones** *(May Subd Geog)*
H 1180
Use as a topical subdivision under individual plants and groups of plants.
——**Selection** *(May Subd Geog)*
H 1180
Use as a topical subdivision under individual plants and groups of plants.
BT —Selection
——**Variation** *(May Subd Geog)*
H 1180
Use as a topical subdivision under individual plants and groups of plants.
BT —Variation
—**Cloning** *(May Subd Geog)*
H 1147
Use as a topical subdivision under individual animals and groups of animals.
—**Clothes**
USE —Clothing
—**Clothing** *(May Subd Geog)*
H 1100; H 1103; H 1110; H 1120
Do not subdivide geographically under names of individual persons and families.
Use as a topical subdivision under names of individual persons and families, and under classes of persons and ethnic groups.
UF —Clothes
—Costume
[Former subdivision]
—Dress
NT —Court and courtiers—Clothing
—Uniforms
—**Cloture**
H 1155
Use as a topical subdivision under names of individual legislative bodies.

—Clubs
USE —Societies and clubs
—Clubs, Officers'
USE —Officers' clubs
—Clubs, Service
USE —Service clubs
—**Clutches** *(May Subd Geog)*
H 1195
Use as a topical subdivision under individual land vehicles and types of land vehicles.
—**Cobalt content** *(May Subd Geog)*
H 1158
Use as a topical subdivision under individual materials and types of materials.
—**Code numbers**
H 1095
Use as a form subdivision under topical headings for works consisting of lists of code numbers pertaining to those topics.
UF —Numbers, Code
—**Code words**
H 1095
Use as a form subdivision under topical headings for works consisting of lists of code words pertaining to those topics.
UF —Words, Code
—**Codification**
H 1154.5
Use as a topical subdivision under individual legal topics.
—**Cognate words**
H 1154
Use as a topical subdivision under individual languages and groups of languages.
BT —Vocabulary
——**Dutch, [German, etc.]**
H 1154
Use as a topical subdivision under individual languages and groups of languages.
—Cohesion, Unit
USE —Unit cohesion
—**Coin collections**
H 1105; H 1110; H 1120
Use as a topical subdivision under names of individual persons, families, and corporate bodies for works about their coin collections.
BT —Numismatic collections
—**Cold weather conditions**
H 1095
Use as a topical subdivision under types of installations, construction activities, and technical processes for works on procedures to be followed during cold weather conditions.
—**Cold weather operation** *(May Subd Geog)*
H 1195
Use as a topical subdivision under individual land vehicles and types of land vehicles.
UF —Operation in cold weather
—**Cold working** *(May Subd Geog)*
H 1149; H 1158
Use as a topical subdivision under individual chemicals and groups of chemicals and individual materials and types of materials.
—Collaboration in authorship
USE —Authorship—Collaboration
—**Collaborationists** *(May Subd Geog)*
H 1200
Further subdivide by subdivisions used under classes of persons.
Use as a topical subdivision under individual wars.
—Collaborative authorship
USE —Authorship—Collaboration
—**Collectibles** *(May Subd Geog)*
H 1095; H 1100; H 1103; H 1105; H 1110; H 1200
Use as a topical subdivision under names of individual persons, corporate bodies, titles of works, and fictitious and legendary characters, and under classes of persons, ethnic groups, events, and topical headings for works on objects depicting or related to those subjects.
NT —History, Local—Collectibles
—Collecting of objects
USE —Collectors and collecting

—**Collection and preservation** *(May Subd Geog)*
H 1095; H 1147; H 1180
Use as a topical subdivision under types of natural objects, including plants, animals, rocks, and minerals, for works on methods of collecting and preserving those objects.
UF —Preservation and collection
NT —Antiquities—Collection and preservation
——**Licenses** *(May Subd Geog)*
H 1147
Use as a topical subdivision under individual animals and groups of animals.
BT —Licenses
—**Collective nouns**
H 1154
Use as a topical subdivision under individual languages and groups of languages.
BT —Noun
—**Collectors and collecting** *(May Subd Geog)*
H 1095; H 1195
Use as a topical subdivision under types of objects, excluding natural objects, for works on collectors, and methods of assembling and maintaining collections of those objects.
UF —Collecting of objects
NT —Antiquities—Collectors and collecting
—**Collier service**
H 1159
Use as a topical subdivision under military services.
—**Collision avoidance systems** *(May Subd Geog)*
H 1195
Use as a topical subdivision under individual land vehicles and types of land vehicles.
—**Collision damage** *(May Subd Geog)*
H 1195
Use as a topical subdivision under individual land vehicles and types of land vehicles.
UF —Damage from collisions
—**Colonial forces** *(May Subd Geog)*
H 1159
Use as a topical subdivision under military services.
BT —Armed Forces
—**Colonial influence**
H 1140
Use as a topical subdivision under names of countries, cities, etc. for works on the influence of former colonial policies and structures on the existing institutions of former colonies.
UF —Influence, Colonial
—Colonial possessions
USE —Colonies
—**Colonies** *(May Subd Geog)*
H 1095; H 1140; H 1149.5
Further subdivide headings of the type [place]—Colonies only by Africa, America, Asia and Oceania
Do not further subdivide geographically headings of the type [topic]—[place]—Colonies.
Use as a topical subdivision under names of countries, cities, etc., for works discussing collectively the colonies ruled by the country or city. Also use under headings of the type [topic]—[place] for works discussing collectively the colonies of a place in relation to those topics.
UF —Colonial possessions
BT —Territories and possessions
——**Administration** *(Not Subd Geog)*
H 1149.5
Use as a topical subdivision under names of countries, cities, etc.
BT —Administration
——**Boundaries** *(May Subd Geog)*
H 1149.5
Use as a topical subdivision under names of countries, cities, etc.
BT —Boundaries
——**Commerce** *(May Subd Geog)*
H 1149.5
Use as a topical subdivision under names of countries, cities, etc.
BT —Commerce

—**Colonies** *(Continued)*
——**Defenses**
H 1149.5
Use as a topical subdivision under names of countries, cities, etc.
BT —Defenses
——**Description and travel** *(Not Subd Geog)*
H 1149.5
Use as a topical subdivision under names of countries, cities, etc.
BT —Description and travel
——**Discovery and exploration**
H 1149.5
Use as a topical subdivision under names of countries, cities, etc.
BT —Discovery and exploration
——**Economic conditions** *(Not Subd Geog)*
H 1149.5
Use as a topical subdivision under names of countries, cities, etc.
BT —Economic conditions
——**Economic policy**
H 1149.5
Use as a topical subdivision under names of countries, cities, etc.
BT —Economic policy
——**Emigration and immigration**
(Not Subd Geog)
H 1149.5
Use as a topical subdivision under names of countries, cities, etc.
BT —Emigration and immigration
——**Geography**
H 1149.5
Use as a topical subdivision under names of countries, cities, etc.
BT —Geography
——**History** *(Not Subd Geog)*
H 1149.5
Use as a topical subdivision under names of countries, cities, etc.
BT —History
——**Officials and employees**
H 1149.5
Further subdivide by the subdivisions used under classes of persons.
Use as a topical subdivision under names of countries, cities, etc.
BT —Officials and employees
——**Population** *(Not Subd Geog)*
H 1149.5
Use as a topical subdivision under names of countries, cities, etc.
BT —Population
——**Race relations**
H 1149.5
Use as a topical subdivision under names of countries, cities, etc.
BT —Race relations
——**Religion** *(Not Subd Geog)*
H 1149.5
Use as a topical subdivision under names of countries, cities, etc.
BT —Religion
——**Religious life and customs**
H 1149.5
Use as a topical subdivision under names of countries, cities, etc.
BT —Religious life and customs
——**Rural conditions** *(Not Subd Geog)*
H 1149.5
Use as a topical subdivision under names of countries, cities, etc.
BT —Rural conditions
——**Social conditions**
H 1149.5
Use as a topical subdivision under names of countries, cities, etc.
BT —Social conditions
——**Social life and customs** *(Not Subd Geog)*
H 1149.5
Use as a topical subdivision under names of countries, cities, etc.
BT —Social life and customs
——**Social policy**
H 1149.5
Use as a topical subdivision under names of countries, cities, etc.
BT —Social policy

——**Africa** *(Not Subd Geog)*
H 1149.5
Use as a topical subdivision under names of countries, cities, etc.
——**America**
H 1149.5
Use as a topical subdivision under names of countries, cities, etc.
——**Asia** *(Not Subd Geog)*
H 1149.5
Use as a topical subdivision under names of countries, cities, etc.
——**Oceania**
H 1149.5
Use as a topical subdivision under names of countries, cities, etc.
—**Colonization** *(May Subd Geog)*
H 1100; H 1103; H 1140; H 1147; H 1180
Further subdivide geographically only under animals, plants, classes of persons, and ethnic groups to designate where the colony is being established.
Use as a topical subdivision under names of countries, cities, etc., that are being colonized, and under classes of persons and ethnic groups who are being transplanted to establish colonies in new lands. Also use under individual animals and groups of animals and individual plants and groups of plants for works about the establishment of a species in an area not currently occupied by that species.
NT —Recolonization
—**Color** *(May Subd Geog)*
H 1147; H 1180
Use as a topical subdivision under individual animals and groups of animals and individual plants and groups of plants.
——**Fading** *(May Subd Geog)*
H 1180
Use as a topical subdivision under individual plants and groups of plants.
UF —Fading of color
———**Control** *(May Subd Geog)*
H 1180
Use as a topical subdivision under individual plants and groups of plants.
UF —Control of fading of color
——**Genetic aspects**
H 1180
Use as a topical subdivision under individual plants and groups of plants.
BT —Genetics
—**Coloring**
H 1149; H 1158
Use as a topical subdivision under individual chemicals and groups of chemicals and individual materials and types of materials.
—**Combat sustainability**
H 1159
Use as a topical subdivision under military services.
UF —Sustainability of combat
—**Combustion** *(May Subd Geog)*
H 1158
Use as a topical subdivision under individual materials and types of materials.
NT —Motors—Combustion
—**Comedies**
H 1110
Do not use under names of dramatists who write principally comedies.
Use as a topical subdivision under names of individual literary authors for works of criticism about comedies by the author.
BT —Dramatic works
—**Comic books, strips, etc.**
H 1095; H 1100; H 1103; H 1105; H 1110; H 1188
Use as a form subdivision under names of individual persons and corporate bodies, uniform titles of sacred works, and under classes of persons, ethnic groups, and topical headings for fictional or nonfiction works in comic strip form.
UF —Comic strips
BT —Caricatures and cartoons
NT —History—Comic books, strips, etc.
—Comic strips
USE —Comic books, strips, etc.
—**Commando operations** *(May Subd Geog)*
H 1200
Use as a topical subdivision under individual wars.

—**Commando troops**
H 1159
Use as a topical subdivision under military services.
—**Commentaries**
H 1188
Use as a topical subdivision under uniform titles of sacred works for works about commentaries on those works.
—**Commentaries**
H 1188
Use as a form subdivision under uniform titles of sacred works for commentaries on those works.
——**History and criticism**
H 1188
Use as a topical subdivision under uniform titles of sacred works.
BT —History and criticism
—**Commerce** *(May Subd Geog)*
H 1103; H 1140; H 1149.5
For works on reciprocal trade between countries, cities, etc., assign a combination of headings: [place A]—Commerce—[place B]; [place B]—Commerce—[place A].
Use as a topical subdivision under names of countries, cities, etc., and ethnic groups for the foreign or domestic trade of the place or group.
UF —Commercial trade
—Foreign trade
—Trade
NT —Colonies—Commerce
——Treaties
USE —Commercial treaties
—**Commercial policy**
H 1140
Use as a topical subdivision under names of countries, etc.
UF —Trade policy
BT —Government policy
—Commercial trade
USE —Commerce
—**Commercial treaties**
H 1140
Use as a topical subdivision under names of countries, etc., for works about commercial treaties of those places.
UF —Commerce—Treaties
BT —Treaties
—**Commercial treaties**
H 1140
Use as a form subdivision under names of countries, etc., for collections of commercial treaties of those places.
UF —Commerce—Treaties
BT —Treaties
—**Commissariat**
H 1159
Use as a topical subdivision under military services other than navies. Under navies, use the subdivision Provisioning.
—**Committees**
H 1155
Use as a topical subdivision under names of individual legislative bodies.
UF —Legislative committees
NT —Conference committees
——**Indexes**
H 1155
Use this subdivision combination as a form subdivision under names of individual legislative bodies.
BT —Indexes
——**Rules and practice**
H 1155
Use as a topical subdivision under names of individual legislative bodies for works about rules and practice of committees of that body.
Use this subdivision combination as a form subdivision under names of individual legislative bodies for works containing the rules and practice of committees of that body.
BT —Rules and practice
——**Seniority system**
H 1155
Use as a topical subdivision under names of individual legislative bodies.
UF —Seniority system of legislative committees

—Common names
USE —Nomenclature (Popular)
—**Communication**
H 1103
Use as a topical subdivision under ethnic groups.
—**Communication systems**
H 1095; H 1105; H 1151.5; H 1153; H 1159
Use as a topical subdivision under names of individual corporate bodies and under types of industries, institutions, installations, military services, and disciplines.
NT —Airborne troops—Communication systems
——**Contracting out**   (*May Subd Geog*)
H 1151.5
Use as a topical subdivision under types of educational institutions.
UF —Contracting out of communication systems
—Communication with constituents
USE —Constituent communication
—**Communications**
H 1200
Use as a topical subdivision under individual wars.
—Communist participation
USE —Participation, Communist
—**Compact disc catalogs**
H 1095; H 1105; H 1110; H 1140
Use as a form subdivision under names of countries, cities, etc., names of individual persons and corporate bodies, and topical headings.
BT —Catalogs
—Companions
USE —Friends and associates
—**Comparative clauses**
H 1154
Use as a topical subdivision under individual languages and groups of languages.
—Comparative grammar
USE —Grammar, Comparative
—Comparative maps
USE —Maps, Comparative
—**Comparative method**
H 1095
Use as a topical subdivision under disciplines for works on methods of comparing data relevant to the discipline.
BT —Methodology
—Comparative phonology
USE —Phonology, Comparative
—**Comparative studies**
H 1095; H 1187; H 1188
Use as a form subdivision under uniform titles of sacred works, individual Christian denominations, and under religious topics.
—**Comparison**
H 1154
Use as a topical subdivision under individual languages and groups of languages.
—Compends
USE —Outlines, syllabi, etc.
—**Competitions**   (*May Subd Geog*)
H 1095
Use as a topical subdivision under topical headings.
UF —Contests
—**Complaints against**   (*May Subd Geog*)
H 1151.5
Use as a topical subdivision under types of educational institutions.
—**Complement**
H 1154
Use as a topical subdivision under individual languages and groups of languages.
—**Compliance costs**   (*May Subd Geog*)
H 1154.5
Use as a topical subdivision under individual legal topics.
BT —Costs

—**Complications**   (*May Subd Geog*)
H 1150
Further subdivide by other subdivisions used under individual diseases.
Use as a topical subdivision under individual diseases and types of diseases.
UF —Complications and sequelae
[*Former subdivision*]
NT —Chemotherapy—Complications
—Endoscopic surgery—Complications
—Hormone therapy—Complications
—Radiotherapy—Complications
—Surgery—Complications
—Treatment—Complications
—Vaccination—Complications
—Complications and sequelae
USE —Complications
—**Composition**
H 1095; H 1147; H 1180
Use as a topical subdivision under natural substances of unfixed composition, including soils, plants, animals, farm products, etc., for the results of chemical analyses of those substances. For works on the methods of analyzing substances, including individual chemicals and materials and individual plants and groups of plants, or analyzing a sample, to determine the presence or quantity of those substances, use the subdivision Analysis
NT —Mercury content
—Silica content
—**Composition and exercises**
H 1154
Use as a topical subdivision under individual languages and groups of languages.
UF —Exercises and composition
—**Compound words**
H 1154
Use as a topical subdivision under individual languages and groups of languages.
—Compressed-gas motors
USE —Motors (Compressed-gas)
—**Compression testing**   (*May Subd Geog*)
H 1158
Use as a topical subdivision under individual materials and types of materials.
BT —Testing
—**Computer-aided design**   (*May Subd Geog*)
H 1095
Use as a topical subdivision under topical headings.
—**Computer-assisted instruction**
H 1095; H 1154
Use as a topical subdivision under topical headings for works on automated methods of instruction in which a student interacts directly with instructional materials stored in a computer.
—**Computer-assisted instruction for foreign speakers**
H 1154
Use as a topical subdivision under individual languages and groups of languages.
—**Computer-assisted instruction for French, [Spanish, etc.] speakers**
H 1154
Use as a topical subdivision under individual languages and groups of languages.
—Computer control systems for motors
USE —Motors—Computer control systems
—**Computer games**
H 1095
Use as a topical subdivision under subjects for works about computer games on those subjects.
BT —Games
—**Computer games**
H 1095
Use as a form subdivision under subjects for computer games on those subjects.
BT —Software
—**Computer network resources**
H 1095
Use as a topical subdivision under subjects for works on computer network resources available for research on those subjects.
BT —Electronic information resources

—**Computer networks**   (*May Subd Geog*)
H 1095
Use as a topical subdivision under subjects.
UF —Networks, Computer
——**Security measures**   (*May Subd Geog*)
H 1095
Use as a topical subdivision under subjects.
BT —Security measures
—**Computer programs**
H 1095
Use as a topical subdivision under topical headings for works about computer programs.
—**Computer simulation**
H 1095
Use as a topical subdivision under topical headings.
BT —Simulation methods
—**Concentration camps**   (*May Subd Geog*)
H 1200
Use as a topical subdivision under individual wars.
—**Concessive clauses**
H 1154
Use as a topical subdivision under individual languages and groups of languages.
—**Concordances**
H 1095; H 1110; H 1156; H 1188
Use as a form subdivision under individual works (author-title or title entries), uniform titles of sacred works, and individual literatures and literary genres for indexes to the principal words found in those works. Also use under names of individual persons for concordances to their writings.
UF —Word indexes
BT —Indexes
NT —Liturgy—Texts—Concordances
—Rituals—Texts—Concordances
—**Concordances, English**
H 1188
Use as a form subdivision under uniform titles of sacred works.
——**Authorized, [Living Bible, Revised Standard, etc.]**
H 1188
Use as a form subdivision under uniform titles of sacred works.
—**Concordances, French, [German, etc.]**
H 1188
Use as a form subdivision under uniform titles of sacred works.
—**Condition scoring**   (*May Subd Geog*)
H 1147
Use as a topical subdivision under individual animals and groups of animals.
—**Conditionals**
H 1154
Use as a topical subdivision under individual languages and groups of languages.
—**Conduct of life**
H 1100
Use as a topical subdivision under classes of persons.
UF —Behavior, Ethical
—Deportment
—Ethical behavior
—Conductivity, Thermal
USE —Thermal conductivity
—Conference attendance
USE —Congresses—Attendance
—**Conference committees**
H 1155
Use as a topical subdivision under names of individual legislative bodies.
BT —Committees
—Conference proceedings
USE —Congresses
—Conferences
USE —Congresses
—**Confiscations and contributions**
(*May Subd Geog*)
H 1200
Use as a topical subdivision under individual wars.
UF —Finance, commerce, confiscations, etc.
[*Former subdivision*]

—**Conformation** *(May Subd Geog)*
H 1147; H 1149
Further subdivide geographically only under animals.
Use as a topical subdivision under individual animals and groups of animals and individual chemicals and groups of chemicals.

—**Confucian influences**
H 1156
Use as a topical subdivision under individual literatures.

—**Congresses**
H 1095
Use as a topical subdivision under subjects for works about conferences or congresses on those subjects.
UF —Conferences
—Congresses, conferences, etc.
[Former subdivision]
—Meetings
—Symposia
—Symposiums

—**Congresses**
H 1095
Use as a form subdivision under subjects for the proceedings or reports of proceedings of conferences or congresses on those subjects.
UF —Conference proceedings
—Congresses—Abstracts
—Congresses, conferences, etc.
[Former subdivision]
—Proceedings of conferences

——Abstracts
USE —Congresses

——**Attendance**
H 1095
Use as a topical subdivision under subjects for works about attendance at congresses on those subjects.
UF —Attendance at congresses
—Conference attendance

—Congresses, conferences, etc.
USE —Congresses

—**Conjunctions**
H 1154
Use as a topical subdivision under individual languages and groups of languages.

—**Connectives**
H 1154
Use as a topical subdivision under individual languages and groups of languages.

—**Conscientious objectors** *(May Subd Geog)*
H 1200
Further subdivide by subdivisions used under classes of persons.
Use as a topical subdivision under individual wars.

—**Conscript labor** *(May Subd Geog)*
H 1200
Use as a topical subdivision under individual wars.

—**Conservation** *(May Subd Geog)*
H 1147; H 1158; H 1180
Use as a topical subdivision under individual animals and groups of animals, individual materials and types of materials, and individual plants and groups of plants.
NT —Energy conservation
—Habitat—Conservation

——**Law and legislation** *(May Subd Geog)*
H 1147; H 1180
Further subdivide by subdivisions used under legal topics.
Use as a topical subdivision under individual animals and groups of animals and individual plants and groups of plants.
BT —Law and legislation

—**Conservation and restoration**
(May Subd Geog)
H 1095; H 1148; H 1195
Use as a topical subdivision under types of art objects, library materials, types of architecture, types of buildings, individual land vehicles and types of vehicles, etc., for works on preserving and restoring those items.
UF —Restoration and conservation

—**Consonants**
H 1154
Use as a topical subdivision under individual languages and groups of languages.

—**Constituent communication**
H 1155
Use as a topical subdivision under names of individual legislative bodies.
UF —Communication with constituents

—**Constitution**
H 1105
Use as a topical subdivision under names of individual corporate bodies for works about constitutions of those bodies.

—**Constitution**
H 1105
Use as a form subdivision under names of individual corporate bodies for individual or collections of constitutions of those bodies.

—**Construction** *(May Subd Geog)*
H 1161
Use as a topical subdivision under individual musical instruments and families of instruments.

—Construction and design
USE —Design and construction

—Construction and engineering
USE —Engineering and construction

—**Construction mechanics**
H 1159
Further subdivide by subdivisions used under classes of persons.
Use as a topical subdivision under military services.

—Consumption, Fuel
USE —Fuel consumption

—Consumption of energy
USE —Energy consumption

—Container seedlings
USE —Seedlings, Container

—Contamination of feeds
USE —Feeding and feeds—Contamination

—Contamination, Radioactive
USE —Radioactive contamination

—**Contemporaries**
H 1110
Use as a topical subdivision under names of individual persons for works about other persons flourishing during the person's life, but not necessarily in close contact with the person.
NT —Adversaries
—Friends and associates

—Contents, Tables of
USE —Tables of contents

—**Contested elections**
H 1155
Use as a topical subdivision under names of individual legislative bodies.
BT —Elections

—Contests
USE —Competitions

—**Context**
H 1154
Use as a topical subdivision under individual languages and groups of languages.

—Continuing education
USE —Education (Continuing education)

—Contracting out of communication systems
USE —Communication systems—
Contracting out

—Contracting out of services for
USE —Services for—Contracting out

—**Contraction** *(May Subd Geog)*
H 1154; H 1164
Further subdivide geographically only under organs and regions of the body.
Use as a topical subdivision under individual languages and groups of languages and individual organs and regions of the body.

—Contraction and expansion
USE —Expansion and contraction

—Contracts and specifications
USE —Specifications

—Contributions, Charitable
USE —Charitable contributions

—Contributions to charity
USE —Charitable contributions

—**Control** *(May Subd Geog)*
H 1095; H 1147; H 1180
Use as a topical subdivision under individual animals and groups of animals, individual plants and groups of plants and individual pests.
NT —Biological control
—Cultural control
—Diseases and pests—Control
—Integrated control
—Parasites—Control
—Predators of—Control

——**Environmental aspects**
(May Subd Geog)
H 1147; H 1180
Use as a topical subdivision under individual animals and groups of animals and individual plants and groups of plants.
BT —Environmental aspects

——**Law and legislation** *(May Subd Geog)*
H 1147; H 1180
Further subdivide by subdivisions used under legal topics.
Use as a topical subdivision under individual animals and groups of animals and individual plants and groups of plants.
BT —Law and legislation

—Control, Access
USE —Access control

—Control, Automatic
USE —Automatic control

—Control, Breath
USE —Breath control

—Control, Inventory
USE —Inventory control

—Control of air conditioning
USE —Air conditioning—Control

—Control of costs
USE —Cost control

—Control of fading of color
USE —Color—Fading—Control

—Control of fumes
USE —Fume control

—Control of heating and ventilation
USE —Heating and ventilation—Control

—Control of spray
USE —Spray control

—Control systems for motors
USE —Motors—Control systems

—**Controlled release** *(May Subd Geog)*
H 1149
Use as a topical subdivision under individual drugs and groups of drugs. Under individual and groups of non-drug chemicals use the subdivision Therapeutic use—Controlled release
NT —Therapeutic use—Controlled
release

—**Controversial literature** *(Not Subd Geog)*
H 1185; H 1186; H 1187; H 1188
Use as a topical subdivision under names of individual religious and monastic orders, individual religions, individual Christian denominations, and uniform titles of sacred works for works about works that argue against or express opposition to those groups or works.
UF —Doctrinal and controversial works
[Former subdivision]

—**Controversial literature**
H 1185; H 1186; H 1187; H 1188
Use as a form subdivision under names of individual religious and monastic orders, individual religions, individual Christian denominations, and uniform titles of sacred works for works that argue against or express opposition to those groups or works.
UF —Doctrinal and controversial works
[Former subdivision]

——**History and criticism**
H 1185; H 1186; H 1187; H 1188
Use as a topical subdivision under names of individual religious and monastic orders, individual religions, individual Christian denominations, and uniform titles of sacred works.
BT —History and criticism

—**Conversation and phrase books**
　H 1154
　　Use as a form subdivision under individual lan-
　　guages and groups of languages.
　　UF 　—Phrase books
　　NT 　—Dialects—Conversation and phrase
　　　　　books
——**English**
　H 1154
　　Use as a form subdivision under languages
　　other than English.
——**French, [Italian, etc.]**
　H 1154
　　Use as a form subdivision under individual
　　languages and groups of languages.
——**Polyglot**
　H 1154
　　Use as a form subdivision under individual
　　languages and groups of languages.
—**Conversation and phrase books (for
accountants)**
　H 1154
　　Use as a form subdivision under individual lan-
　　guages and groups of languages.
—**Conversation and phrase books (for air
pilots)**
　H 1154
　　Use as a form subdivision under individual lan-
　　guages and groups of languages.
—**Conversation and phrase books (for animal
specialists)**
　H 1154
　　Use as a form subdivision under languages and
　　groups of languages.
—**Conversation and phrase books (for bank
employees)**
　H 1154
　　Use as a form subdivision under individual lan-
　　guages and groups of languages.
—**Conversation and phrase books (for
businesspeople)**
　H 1154
　　Use as a form subdivision under individual lan-
　　guages and groups of languages.
—**Conversation and phrase books (for
caregivers)**
　H 1154
　　Use as a form subdivision under individual lan-
　　guages and groups of languages.
—**Conversation and phrase books (for clergy,
etc.)**
　H 1154
　　Use as a form subdivision under individual lan-
　　guages and groups of languages.
—**Conversation and phrase books (for
computer industry employees)**
　H 1154
　　Use as a form subdivision under individual lan-
　　guages and groups of languages.
—**Conversation and phrase books (for
construction industry employees)**
　H 1154
　　Use as a form subdivision under individual lan-
　　guages and groups of languages.
—**Conversation and phrase books (for
correctional personnel)**
　H 1154
　　Use as a form subdivision under individual lan-
　　guages and groups of languages.
—**Conversation and phrase books (for dental
personnel)**
　H 1154
　　Use as a form subdivision under individual lan-
　　guages and groups of languages.
—**Conversation and phrase books (for
diplomats)**
　H 1154
　　Use as a form subdivision under individual lan-
　　guages and groups of languages.
—**Conversation and phrase books (for
domestics)**
　H 1154
　　Use as a form subdivision under individual lan-
　　guages and groups of languages.
—**Conversation and phrase books (for
farmers)**
　H 1154
　　Use as a form subdivision under individual lan-
　　guages and groups of languages.

—**Conversation and phrase books (for fire
fighters)**
　H 1154
　　Use as a form subdivision under individual lan-
　　guages and groups of languages.
—**Conversation and phrase books (for first
responders)**
　H 1154
　　Use as a form subdivision under individual lan-
　　guages and groups of languages.
—**Conversation and phrase books (for fishers)**
　H 1154
　　Use as a form subdivision under individual lan-
　　guages and groups of languages.
—**Conversation and phrase books (for flight
attendants)**
　H 1154
　　Use as a form subdivision under individual lan-
　　guages and groups of languages.
—**Conversation and phrase books (for
gardeners)**
　H 1154
　　Use as a form subdivision under individual lan-
　　guages and groups of languages.
—**Conversation and phrase books (for
geologists)**
　H 1154
　　Use as a form subdivision under individual lan-
　　guages and groups of languages.
—**Conversation and phrase books (for
gourmets)**
　H 1154
　　Use as a form subdivision under individual lan-
　　guages and groups of languages.
—**Conversation and phrase books (for
homeowners)**
　H 1154
　　Use as a form subdivision under individual lan-
　　guages and groups of languages.
—Conversation and phrase books (for hotel
personnel)
　　USE 　—Conversation and phrase books (for
　　　　　restaurant and hotel personnel)
—**Conversation and phrase books (for
landscaping industry employees)**
　H 1154
　　Use as a form subdivision under individual lan-
　　guages and groups of languages.
—**Conversation and phrase books (for
lawyers)**
　H 1154
　　Use as a form subdivision under individual lan-
　　guages and groups of languages.
—**Conversation and phrase books (for library
employees)**
　H 1154
　　Use as a form subdivision under individual lan-
　　guages and groups of languages.
—**Conversation and phrase books (for
mathematicians)**
　H 1154
　　Use as a form subdivision under individual lan-
　　guages and groups of languages.
—**Conversation and phrase books (for medical
personnel)**
　H 1154
　　Use as a form subdivision under individual lan-
　　guages and groups of languages.
　　UF 　—Conversation and phrase books (for
　　　　　physical therapists)
　　　　　[Former subdivision]
—**Conversation and phrase books (for
merchants)**
　H 1154
　　Use as a form subdivision under individual lan-
　　guages and groups of languages.
—**Conversation and phrase books (for
meteorologists)**
　H 1154
　　Use as a form subdivision under individual lan-
　　guages and groups of languages.
—**Conversation and phrase books (for
museum employees)**
　H 1154
　　Use as a form subdivision under individual lan-
　　guages and groups of languages.

—**Conversation and phrase books (for
musicians, musicologists, etc.)**
　H 1154
　　Use as a form subdivision under individual lan-
　　guages and groups of languages.
—**Conversation and phrase books (for
nutritionists)**
　H 1154
　　Use as a form subdivision under individual lan-
　　guages and groups of languages.
—**Conversation and phrase books (for
personnel department employees)**
　H 1154
　　Use as a form subdivision under individual lan-
　　guages and groups of languages.
—**Conversation and phrase books (for
petroleum workers)**
　H 1154
　　Use as a form subdivision under individual lan-
　　guages and groups of languages.
—Conversation and phrase books (for physical
therapists)
　　USE 　—Conversation and phrase books (for
　　　　　medical personnel)
—**Conversation and phrase books (for police)**
　H 1154
　　Use as a form subdivision under individual lan-
　　guages and groups of languages.
—**Conversation and phrase books (for
professionals)**
　H 1154
　　Use as a form subdivision under individual lan-
　　guages and groups of languages.
—**Conversation and phrase books (for
restaurant and hotel personnel)**
　H 1154
　　Use as a form subdivision under individual lan-
　　guages and groups of languages.
　　UF 　—Conversation and phrase books (for
　　　　　hotel personnel)
—**Conversation and phrase books (for sailors)**
　H 1154
　　Use as a form subdivision under individual lan-
　　guages and groups of languages.
　　UF 　—Conversation and phrase books (for
　　　　　seamen)
　　　　　[Former subdivision]
—**Conversation and phrase books (for school
employees)**
　H 1154
　　Use as a form subdivision under individual lan-
　　guages and groups of languages.
—Conversation and phrase books (for seamen)
　　USE 　—Conversation and phrase books (for
　　　　　sailors)
—**Conversation and phrase books (for
secretaries)**
　H 1154
　　Use as a form subdivision under individual lan-
　　guages and groups of languages.
—**Conversation and phrase books (for social
workers)**
　H 1154
　　Use as a form subdivision under individual lan-
　　guages and groups of languages.
—**Conversation and phrase books (for
soldiers, etc.)**
　H 1154
　　Use as a form subdivision under individual lan-
　　guages and groups of languages.
—**Conversation and phrase books (for tourism
industry employees)**
　H 1154
　　Use as a form subdivision under individual lan-
　　guages and groups of languages.
　　UF 　—Conversation and phrase books (for
　　　　　tourist trade employees)
　　　　　[Former subdivision]
—Conversation and phrase books (for tourist
trade employees)
　　USE 　—Conversation and phrase books (for
　　　　　tourism industry employees)
—**Conversion tables**
　H 1095
　　Use as a form subdivision under topical head-
　　ings.
　　BT 　—Tables

—Cooling *(May Subd Geog)*
　　H 1095; H 1158; H 1180
　　　Use as a topical subdivision under topical headings.
　　NT　—Motors—Cooling
—Cooling systems of motors
　　USE　—Motors—Cooling systems
—Cooperation, International
　　USE　—International cooperation
—Cooperative marketing *(May Subd Geog)*
　　H 1147; H 1180
　　　Use as a topical subdivision under individual animals and groups of animals and individual plants and groups of plants.
　　BT　—Marketing
—Coordinate constructions
　　H 1154
　　　Use as a topical subdivision under individual languages and groups of languages.
—Copies (Facsimiles)
　　USE　—Facsimiles
—Copying
　　H 1148
　　　Use as a topical subdivision under individual art forms and headings for national or ethnic art.
—Coronation
　　H 1110
　　　Use as a topical subdivision under names of individual persons.
　　UF　—Crowning
—Correspondence
　　H 1100; H 1103; H 1110; H 1120
　　　Use as a topical subdivision under names of individual persons and families, classes of persons, and ethnic groups for works about correspondence to or from those persons.
　　UF　—Correspondence, reminiscences, etc.
　　　　　[Former subdivision]
　　　　—Letters
　　NT　—Records and correspondence
—Correspondence
　　H 1100; H 1103; H 1110; H 1120
　　　Use as a form subdivision under names of individual persons and families, classes of persons, and ethnic groups for individual or collections of correspondence to or from those persons.
　　UF　—Correspondence, reminiscences, etc.
　　　　　[Former subdivision]
　　　　—Letters
　　NT　—Records and correspondence
——Microform catalogs
　　H 1110
　　　Use this subdivision combination as a form subdivision under names of individual persons.
　　BT　—Microform catalogs
—Correspondence, reminiscences, etc.
　　USE　—Biography
　　　　—Correspondence
—Corrosion *(May Subd Geog)*
　　H 1095; H 1149; H 1158; H 1195
　　　Use as a topical subdivision under individual metals and metal compounds, individual materials and types of materials, and types of engineering structures, equipment, and vehicles.
　　NT　—Stress corrosion
—Corrosion fatigue *(May Subd Geog)*
　　H 1158
　　　Use as a topical subdivision under individual materials and types of materials.
　　BT　—Fatigue
—Corrupt practices *(May Subd Geog)*
　　H 1095; H 1105; H 1151.5; H 1153
　　　Do not subdivide geographically under names of individual corporate bodies.
　　　Use as a topical subdivision under names of individual corporate bodies, and under types of organizations, activities, and industries.
　　UF　—Corruption
—Corruption
　　USE　—Corrupt practices
—Cossacks *(May Subd Geog)*
　　H 1200
　　　Further subdivide by subdivisions used under classes of persons.
　　　Use as a topical subdivision under individual wars.

—Cost control
　　H 1095; H 1153; H 1159
　　　Use as a topical subdivision under types of industries, military services, and topical headings.
　　UF　—Control of costs
—Cost effectiveness
　　H 1095; H 1153
　　　Use as a topical subdivision under types of industries and topical headings.
—Cost-of-living adjustments to pensions
　　USE　—Pensions—Cost-of-living adjustments
—Cost-of-living adjustments to salaries
　　USE　—Salaries, etc.—Cost-of-living adjustments
—Cost of operation
　　H 1095; H 1195
　　　Use as a topical subdivision under topical headings.
　　UF　—Operating costs
—Costs
　　H 1095; H 1153
　　　Use as a topical subdivision under types of industries and topical headings.
　　NT　—Compliance costs
—Costume
　　USE　—Clothing
—Counseling of *(May Subd Geog)*
　　H 1100; H 1103
　　　Use as a topical subdivision under classes of persons and ethnic groups.
　　NT　—Pastoral counseling of
—Counterfeit money *(May Subd Geog)*
　　H 1200
　　　Use as a topical subdivision under individual wars.
—Counting *(May Subd Geog)*
　　H 1147; H 1180
　　　Use as a topical subdivision under individual animals and groups of animals and individual plants and groups of plants.
　　NT　—Eggs—Counting
　　　　—Nests—Counting
—Course catalogs
　　USE　—Curricula—Catalogs
—Court and courtiers
　　H 1140
　　　Use as a topical subdivision under names of countries, cities, etc.
　　UF　—Courtiers
——Clothing
　　H 1140
　　　Use as a topical subdivision under names of countries, cities, etc.
　　BT　—Clothing
——Food
　　H 1140
　　　Use as a topical subdivision under names of countries, cities, etc.
　　BT　—Food
——Language
　　H 1140
　　　Use as a topical subdivision under names of countries, cities, etc.
　　BT　—Language
—Courtiers
　　USE　—Court and courtiers
—Coverage by the press
　　USE　—Press coverage
—Cracking *(May Subd Geog)*
　　H 1158
　　　Use as a topical subdivision under individual materials and types of materials.
—Craniology *(May Subd Geog)*
　　H 1103
　　　Use as a topical subdivision under ethnic groups.
—Crankshafts of motors
　　USE　—Motors—Crankshafts
—Crash tests *(May Subd Geog)*
　　H 1195
　　　Use as a topical subdivision under individual land vehicles and types of land vehicles.
　　UF　—Crashworthiness—Testing
　　BT　—Testing
—Crashworthiness *(May Subd Geog)*
　　H 1195
　　　Use as a topical subdivision under individual land vehicles and types of land vehicles.

———Testing
　　USE　—Crash tests
—Credit guides
　　USE　—Credit ratings
—Credit ratings
　　H 1153
　　　Use as a topical subdivision under types of industries.
　　UF　—Credit guides
　　　　　[Former subdivision]
　　　　—Ratings, Credit
—Creeds
　　H 1185; H 1187
　　　Use as a topical subdivision under individual religions and Christian denominations for works about authoritative statements of belief of those religions or denominations.
　　UF　—Catechisms and creeds
　　　　　[Former subdivision]
—Creeds
　　H 1185; H 1187
　　　Use as a form subdivision under individual religions and Christian denominations for authoritative statements of belief of those religions or denominations.
　　UF　—Catechisms and creeds
　　　　　[Former subdivision]
——History and criticism
　　H 1187
　　　Use as a topical subdivision under individual Christian denominations.
　　BT　—History and criticism
—Creep *(May Subd Geog)*
　　H 1149; H 1158
　　　Use as a topical subdivision under individual chemicals and groups of chemicals and individual materials and types of materials.
—Crimes against *(May Subd Geog)*
　　H 1100; H 1103
　　　Use as a topical subdivision under classes of persons and ethnic groups.
—Criminal provisions
　　H 1154.5
　　　Use as a topical subdivision under individual legal topics.
—Criticism and history
　　USE　—History and criticism
—Criticism and interpretation
　　H 1110
　　　Use only under names of persons active in the fine arts, literature, music, and performing arts.
　　　Use as a topical subdivision under names of individual persons for works of critical analysis or interpretation of the person's artistic works or endeavors without biographical details.
　　UF　—Interpretation and criticism
　　NT　—Criticism, Textual
　　　　—Dramatic works
　　　　—Fictional works
　　　　—Motion picture plays
　　　　—Poetic works
　　　　—Prose
　　　　—Radio and television plays
——History
　　H 1110
　　　Use as a topical subdivision under names of individual persons.
　　BT　—History
———To 1500
　　H 1110
　　　Use as a topical subdivision under names of individual persons.
———16th century
　　H 1110
　　　Use as a topical subdivision under names of individual persons.
———17th century
　　H 1110
　　　Use as a topical subdivision under names of individual persons.
———18th century
　　H 1110
　　　Use as a topical subdivision under names of individual persons.
———19th century
　　H 1110
　　　Use as a topical subdivision under names of individual persons.

—— **20th century**
> H 1110
>> Use as a topical subdivision under names of individual persons.

—— **21st century**
> H 1110
>> Use as a topical subdivision under names of individual persons.

— Criticism, Canonical
> USE —Canonical criticism

— **Criticism, Form**
> H 1188
>> Use as a topical subdivision under uniform titles of sacred works.
>
> UF —Form criticism
> BT —Criticism, interpretation, etc.

— **Criticism, interpretation, etc.**
> *(May Subd Geog)*
> H 1188
>> Use as a topical subdivision under uniform titles of sacred works.
>
> NT —Allegorical interpretations
>> —Bahai interpretations
>> —Black interpretations
>> —Buddhist interpretations
>> —Canonical criticism
>> —Criticism, Form
>> —Criticism, interpretation, etc., Jewish
>> —Criticism, Narrative
>> —Criticism, Redaction
>> —Criticism, Textual
>> —Feminist criticism
>> —Gay interpretations
>> —Hindu interpretations
>> —Islamic interpretations
>> —Postcolonial criticism
>> —Reader-response criticism
>> —Social scientific criticism
>> —Socio-rhetorical criticism
>> —Structuralist criticism

—— **History**
> H 1188
>> Use as a topical subdivision under uniform titles of sacred works.
>
> BT —History

——— **Early church, ca. 30-600**
> H 1188
>> Use as a topical subdivision under uniform titles of sacred works.

——— **Middle Ages, 600-1500**
> H 1188
>> Use as a topical subdivision under uniform titles of sacred works.

——— **Modern period, 1500-**
> H 1188
>> Use as a topical subdivision under uniform titles of sacred works.

———— **16th century**
> H 1188
>> Use as a topical subdivision under uniform titles of sacred works.

———— **17th century**
> H 1188
>> Use as a topical subdivision under uniform titles of sacred works.

———— **18th century**
> H 1188
>> Use as a topical subdivision under uniform titles of sacred works.

———— **19th century**
> H 1188
>> Use as a topical subdivision under uniform titles of sacred works.

———— **20th century**
> H 1188
>> Use as a topical subdivision under uniform titles of sacred works.

———— **21st century**
> H 1188
>> Use as a topical subdivision under uniform titles of sacred works.

— **Criticism, interpretation, etc., Jewish**
> H 1188
>> Use as a topical subdivision under Bible. O.T. or individual books of the Old Testament.
>
> UF —Jewish criticism, interpretation, etc.
> BT —Criticism, interpretation, etc.

— **Criticism, Narrative**
> H 1188
>> Use as a topical subdivision under uniform titles of sacred works.
>
> UF —Narrative criticism
> BT —Criticism, interpretation, etc.

— **Criticism, Redaction**
> H 1188
>> Use as a topical subdivision under uniform titles of sacred works.
>
> UF —Redaction criticism
> BT —Criticism, interpretation, etc.

— **Criticism, Textual**
> H 1110; H 1155.6; H 1155.8; H 1156; H 1188
>> Use as a topical subdivision under names of individual persons, individual works (author-title or title entries), and individual literatures.
>
> UF —Textual criticism
> BT —Criticism and interpretation
>> —Criticism, interpretation, etc.
>> —History and criticism

— **Cross-cultural studies**
> H 1095
>> Use as a topical subdivision under topical headings for works about the methods and techniques of conducting cross-cultural studies on those topics.

— **Cross-cultural studies**
> H 1095
>> Use as a form subdivision under topical headings for works that report the results of cross-cultural studies on those topics.

— **Cross references**
> H 1188
>> Use as a form subdivision under uniform titles of sacred works.

— **Cross-sectional imaging** *(May Subd Geog)*
> H 1164
>> Use as a topical subdivision under individual organs and regions of the body.
>
> BT —Imaging
> NT —Magnetic resonance imaging
>> —Tomography
>> —Ultrasonic imaging

— Crowning
> USE —Coronation

— **Cruise,** [date]
> H 1159
>> Use as a topical subdivision under military services.

— **Cryopreservation** *(May Subd Geog)*
> H 1164
>> Use as a topical subdivision under individual organs and regions of the body.
>
> BT —Preservation
> NT —Germplasm resources—Cryopreservation

— **Cryosurgery** *(May Subd Geog)*
> H 1150; H 1164
>> Use as a topical subdivision under individual diseases and types of diseases and individual organs and regions of the body.
>
> UF —Diseases—Cryosurgery
> BT —Surgery

— **Cryotherapy** *(May Subd Geog)*
> H 1150
>> Use as a topical subdivision under individual diseases and types of diseases.
>
> BT —Treatment

— **Cryptography**
> H 1200
>> Use as a topical subdivision under individual wars.

— **Cult** *(May Subd Geog)*
> H 1095; H 1110
>> Use as a topical subdivision under individual deities, divine persons, saints, and persons worshipped for works on systems of beliefs or rituals associated with them.

— **Cultural assimilation** *(May Subd Geog)*
> H 1103
>> Use as a topical subdivision under ethnic groups.
>
> UF —Assimilation, Cultural

— **Cultural control** *(May Subd Geog)*
> H 1147; H 1180
>> Use as a topical subdivision under individual animals and groups of animals and individual plants and groups of plants.
>
> BT —Control
> NT —Diseases and pests—Cultural control

— **Cultural policy**
> H 1140
>> Use as a topical subdivision under names of countries, cities, etc.
>
> BT —Government policy

— Culture (Civilization)
> USE —Civilization

— **Cultures and culture media** *(May Subd Geog)*
> H 1164
>> Use as a topical subdivision under individual organs and regions of the body.

— **Curing** *(May Subd Geog)*
> H 1158
>> Use as a topical subdivision under individual materials and types of materials.

— Curiosa and miscellanea
> USE —Miscellanea

— Curious editions
> USE —Editions, Curious

— Currency, Military
> USE —Military currency

— **Curricula** *(May Subd Geog)*
> H 1095; H 1151; H 1151.5
>> Do not subdivide geographically under names of individual educational institutions.
>>
>> Use as a topical subdivision under names of individual educational institutions and under types of education and educational institutions for works on courses offered at those institutions or in those fields.
>
> NT —Honors courses

——— **Catalogs**
> H 1151; H 1151.5
>> Use this subdivision combination as a form subdivision under names of individual educational institutions and types of educational institutions for listings of courses offered.
>
> UF —Course catalogs
> BT —Catalogs

— **Customer services** *(May Subd Geog)*
> H 1095; H 1105; H 1153
>> Do not subdivide geographically under names of individual corporate bodies.
>>
>> Use as a topical subdivision under names of individual corporate bodies and under types of organizations and industries.

— **Customizing** *(May Subd Geog)*
> H 1161; H 1195
>> Use as a topical subdivision under individual musical instruments and families of instruments and individual land vehicles and types of land vehicles.

— Customs
> USE —Social life and customs

— **Customs and practices**
> H 1185; H 1186; H 1187
>> Use as a topical subdivision under names of individual religions and monastic orders and under individual religions and Christian denominations.
>
> UF —Ceremonies and practices
>> [Former subdivision]

— **Cuttings** *(May Subd Geog)*
> H 1180
>> Use as a topical subdivision under individual plants and groups of plants.

— Cycles, Life
> USE —Life cycles

— Cylinder blocks of motors
> USE —Motors—Cylinder blocks

— Cylinder heads of motors
> USE —Motors—Cylinder heads

— Cylinders of motors
> USE —Motors—Cylinders

—**Cysts** *(May Subd Geog)*
　H 1164
　　Further subdivide by subdivisions used under diseases.
　　Use as a topical subdivision under individual organs and regions of the body.
　　BT　—Diseases
　　NT　—Hydatids
—**Cytochemistry**
　H 1164; H 1180
　　Use as a topical subdivision under individual plants and groups of plants and individual organs and regions of the body.
　　BT　—Cytology
—**Cytodiagnosis** *(May Subd Geog)*
　H 1150
　　Use as a topical subdivision under individual diseases and types of diseases.
　　BT　—Diagnosis
—**Cytogenetics**
　H 1147; H 1180
　　Use as a topical subdivision under individual animals and groups of animals and individual plants and groups of plants.
　　BT　—Cytology
　　　　—Genetics
—**Cytology**
　H 1147; H 1164; H 1180
　　Use as a topical subdivision under individual animals and groups of animals, individual organs and regions of the body, and individual plants and groups of plants.
　　NT　—Cytochemistry
　　　　—Cytogenetics
　　　　—Cytotaxonomy
　　　　—Ultrastructure
—**Cytopathology**
　H 1150; H 1164
　　Use as a topical subdivision under individual diseases and types of diseases and organs and regions of the body.
　　UF　—Diseases—Cytopathology
—**Cytotaxonomy** *(May Subd Geog)*
　H 1180
　　Use as a topical subdivision under individual plants and groups of plants.
　　BT　—Classification
　　　　—Cytology
—**Czech influences**
　H 1156
　　Use as a topical subdivision under individual literatures.
　　BT　—Foreign influences
—**Dalit authors**
　H 1156
　　Use as a topical subdivision under individual literatures.
　　UF　—Untouchable authors
　　　　　[Former subdivision]
—Damage from collisions
　USE　—Collision damage
—Data bases
　USE　—Databases
—**Data processing**
　H 1095; H 1105
　　Use as a topical subdivision under names of individual corporate bodies and under topical headings.
—**Data tape catalogs**
　H 1095
　　Use as a form subdivision under subjects.
　　BT　—Catalogs
—**Databases**
　H 1095
　　Use as a topical subdivision under subjects for works about databases on those subjects.
　　UF　—Data bases
　　　　　[Former subdivision]
—**Databases**
　H 1095
　　Use as a form subdivision under subjects for databases on those subjects.
　　UF　—Data bases
　　　　　[Former subdivision]
—Date of authorship
　USE　—Authorship—Date of authorship
—Date of birth
　USE　—Birth

—**Dating**
　H 1095
　　Use as a topical subdivision under types of objects for the techniques of fixing the date of their origination.
　　NT　—Texts—Dating
—Dead, Registers of
　USE　—Registers of dead
—Dead, Repatriation of
　USE　—Repatriation of war dead
—**Death**
　H 1100; H 1103
　　Use as a topical subdivision under classes of persons and ethnic groups.
　　NT　—Kings and rulers—Death and burial
—**Death and burial**
　H 1110
　　Use as a topical subdivision under names of individual persons for works on the person's death, funeral, or burial, including the person's last illness.
　　UF　—Biography—Death and burial
　　　　—Biography—Last years and death
　　　　　[Former subdivision]
　　　　—Burial
　　　　—Funeral
　　　　—Funeral and memorial services
　　　　　[Former subdivision]
　　　　—Interment
　　　　—Last illness
　　NT　—Assassination
—**Death mask**
　H 1110
　　Use as a topical subdivision under names of individual persons.
　　BT　—Relics
—Debate, Freedom of
　USE　—Freedom of debate
—**Decay**
　H 1149
　　Use as a topical subdivision under individual chemicals and groups of chemicals.
—**Decentralization** *(May Subd Geog)*
　H 1151.5
　　Use as a topical subdivision under types of educational institutions.
—**Deception** *(May Subd Geog)*
　H 1200
　　Use as a topical subdivision under individual wars.
—**Decision making**
　H 1095; H 1105
　　Use as a topical subdivision under topical headings for works on the process of arriving at decisions for action, including attempts to formulate a general theory based on mathematical analysis and psychological experiment.
—**Declension**
　H 1154
　　Use as a topical subdivision under individual languages and groups of languages.
—**Decontamination** *(May Subd Geog)*
　H 1149
　　Use as a topical subdivision under individual chemicals and groups of chemicals.
—**Decoration** *(May Subd Geog)*
　H 1195
　　Use as a topical subdivision under individual land vehicles and types of land vehicles.
　　NT　—Housing—Decoration
—Decorations, Military
　USE　—Medals, badges, decorations, etc.
—**Defects** *(May Subd Geog)*
　H 1095; H 1158; H 1195
　　Use as a topical subdivision under individual materials and types of materials and types of equipment, structures, products, etc., in which defects may exist.
　　NT　—Surfaces—Defects
——**Law and legislation** *(May Subd Geog)*
　H 1195
　　Further subdivide by subdivisions used under legal topics.
　　Use as a topical subdivision under individual land vehicles and types of land vehicles.
　　BT　—Law and legislation

——**Reporting** *(May Subd Geog)*
　H 1095; H 1158; H 1195
　　Use as a topical subdivision under individual materials and types of materials and types of equipment, structures, products, etc.
　　BT　—Reporting
—**Defense measures** *(May Subd Geog)*
　H 1095; H 1153
　　Use as a topical subdivision under types of industries, utilities, installations, etc., for measures undertaken for their protection during times of conflict.
—**Defenses** *(May Subd Geog)*
　H 1140; H 1149.5
　　Do not subdivide geographically under names of countries, etc.
　　Use as a topical subdivision under names of countries, etc., individual animals and groups of animals, and individual plants and groups of plants.
　　NT　—Chemical defenses
　　　　—Colonies—Defenses
——**Economic aspects**
　H 1140
　　Use as a topical subdivision under names of countries, etc.
　　BT　—Economic aspects
——**Law and legislation**
　H 1140
　　Further subdivide by subdivisions used under legal topics.
　　Use as a topical subdivision under names of countries, etc.
　　BT　—Law and legislation
—**Definiteness**
　H 1154
　　Use as a topical subdivision under individual languages and groups of languages.
—Deformities
　USE　—Abnormalities
—Degradation of clergy
　USE　—Clergy—Degradation
—**Degrees**
　H 1151
　　Use as a topical subdivision under names of individual educational institutions.
—**Deinstitutionalization** *(May Subd Geog)*
　H 1100
　　Use as a topical subdivision under classes of persons.
—**Deixis**
　H 1154
　　Use as a topical subdivision under individual languages and groups of languages.
—**Deletion**
　H 1154
　　Use as a topical subdivision under individual languages and groups of languages.
—Demand and supply
　USE　—Supply and demand
—**Demobilization**
　H 1159
　　Use as a topical subdivision under military services.
—Demography
　USE　—Population
—**Demonstratives**
　H 1154
　　Use as a topical subdivision under individual languages and groups of languages.
—**Denaturation**
　H 1149
　　Use as a topical subdivision under individual proteins and groups of proteins.
—**Density**
　H 1149; H 1158
　　Use as a topical subdivision under individual chemicals and groups of chemicals and individual materials and types of materials.
　　BT　—Properties
—**Dental care** *(May Subd Geog)*
　H 1100; H 1103; H 1159
　　Use as a topical subdivision under classes of persons, ethnic groups, and military services.
—**Deoxidizing** *(May Subd Geog)*
　H 1158
　　Use as a topical subdivision under individual materials and types of materials.

—**Departments**
H 1095; H 1151.5
Use under headings of the type [topic]—[country] for works discussing collectively the departments of a country in relation to the topic. Also use under types of educational institutions for works on the administrative divisions of those institutions.
BT —Administrative and political divisions

—**Dependency grammar**
H 1154
Use as a topical subdivision under individual languages and groups of languages.
BT —Grammar

—**Dependency on foreign countries**
H 1140
Use as a topical subdivision under names of countries, etc.

—**Dependency on [place]**
H 1140
Use as a topical subdivision under names of countries, etc.

—Deportment
USE —Conduct of life

—Deposition of clergy
USE —Clergy—Deposition

—Deposition of kings and rulers
USE —Kings and rulers—Deposition

—Deprivation of the clerical garb
USE —Clergy—Deprivation of the clerical garb

—**Deputy speakers** *(Not Subd Geog)*
H 1155
Further subdivide by subdivisions used under classes of persons.
Use as a topical subdivision under names of individual legislative bodies.
BT —Leadership

—**Deregulation** *(May Subd Geog)*
H 1153
Use as a topical subdivision under types of industries.

—**Derivatives** *(May Subd Geog)*
H 1149
Further subdivide by subdivisions used under chemicals.
Use as a topical subdivision under individual chemicals and groups of chemicals.

—Description
USE —Description and travel

—**Description and travel**
H 1140; H 1149.5
Use as a topical subdivision under names of countries, cities, etc.
UF —Description
[Former subdivision]
—Description, geography
[Former subdivision]
NT —Colonies—Description and travel

——Aerial
USE —Aerial photographs
—Aerial views

——Gazetteers
USE —Gazetteers

——Guide-books
USE —Guidebooks

——Guidebooks
USE —Guidebooks

——Tours
USE —Tours

——Views
USE —Aerial views
—Pictorial works

—Description, geography
USE —Description and travel

—Descriptions of jobs
USE —Job descriptions

—**Desertions** *(May Subd Geog)*
H 1200
Use as a topical subdivision under individual wars.

—**Design**
H 1095; H 1149
Use as a topical subdivision under topical headings for which the subdivision —Design and construction is not appropriate. Also use under individual drugs and groups of drugs.

—**Design and construction**
H 1095; H 1195
Use as a topical subdivision under individual examinations and types of examinations. Also use under types of structures, machines, equipment, etc., for works discussing their engineering and/or construction.
UF —Construction and design
NT —Housing—Design and construction

——**Law and legislation** *(May Subd Geog)*
H 1195
Further subdivide by subdivisions used under legal topics.
Use as a topical subdivision under individual land vehicles and types of land vehicles.
BT —Law and legislation

——**Optical methods**
H 1195
Use as a topical subdivision under individual land vehicles and types of land vehicles.
UF —Optical methods of design and construction

—**Designs and plans**
H 1095
Use as a form subdivision under architectural headings, including types of buildings and rooms, and under landscape headings, including types of gardens and parks, for works containing architectural drawings.
UF —Architectural drawings
—Architectural plans
—Plans, Architectural
BT —Drawings

—**Destruction and pillage** *(May Subd Geog)*
H 1200
Use as a topical subdivision under individual wars.
UF —Pillage

—**Desulfurization** *(May Subd Geog)*
H 1158
Use as a topical subdivision under individual materials and types of materials.
UF —Desulphurization
[Former subdivision]

—Desulphurization
USE —Desulfurization

—**Detection** *(May Subd Geog)*
H 1147
Use as a topical subdivision under individual animals and groups of animals.

—**Deterioration** *(May Subd Geog)*
H 1095; H 1158
Use as a topical subdivision under individual materials and types of materials and types of substances, products, etc.
NT —Biodegradation
—Erosion

—Determination of age
USE —Age determination

—**Determiners**
H 1154
Use as a topical subdivision under individual languages and groups of languages.

—Detoxification, Metabolic
USE —Metabolic detoxification

—**Development** *(May Subd Geog)*
H 1147; H 1149; H 1180
Use as a topical subdivision under individual animals and groups of animals, individual drugs and groups of drugs, and individual plants and groups of plants.
NT —Metamorphosis

——**Endocrine aspects**
H 1147
Use as a topical subdivision under individual animals and groups of animals.
BT —Endocrinology

—**Devotional literature**
H 1188
Use as a topical subdivision under uniform titles of sacred works for works about devotional literature on those works.

—**Devotional literature**
H 1188
Use as a form subdivision under uniform titles of sacred works for devotional literature on those works.
NT —Meditations

—**Devotional use**
H 1188
Use as a topical subdivision under uniform titles of sacred works.
UF —Use in devotion

—Devotions
USE —Prayers and devotions

—**Dewatering** *(May Subd Geog)*
H 1158
Use as a topical subdivision under individual materials and types of materials.

—**Diacritics**
H 1154
Use as a topical subdivision under individual languages other than English and groups of languages.

—**Diagnosis** *(May Subd Geog)*
H 1150
Use as a topical subdivision under individual diseases and types of diseases.
NT —Biopsy
—Cytodiagnosis
—Diseases—Diagnosis
—Examination
—Immunodiagnosis
—Molecular diagnosis
—Serodiagnosis
—Wounds and injuries—Diagnosis

—**Diagnostic use** *(May Subd Geog)*
H 1149
Use as a topical subdivision under individual chemicals and groups of chemicals.
UF —Use in diagnosis

—Diagrams
USE —Charts, diagrams, etc.

—**Dialectology**
H 1154
Use as a topical subdivision under individual languages and groups of languages.

—**Dialects** *(May Subd Geog)*
H 1154
Use as a topical subdivision under individual languages and groups of languages.

——**Conversation and phrase books**
H 1154
Use this subdivision combination as a form subdivision under individual languages and groups of languages.
BT —Conversation and phrase books

——**Glossaries, vocabularies, etc.**
H 1154
Use this subdivision combination as a form subdivision under individual languages and groups of languages.
BT —Glossaries, vocabularies, etc.

——**Grammar**
H 1154
Use as a topical subdivision under individual languages and groups of languages.
BT —Grammar

——**Lexicology**
H 1154
Use as a topical subdivision under individual languages and groups of languages.
BT —Lexicology

——**Morphology**
H 1154
Use as a topical subdivision under individual languages and groups of languages.
BT —Morphology

——**Mutual intelligibility**
H 1154
Use as a topical subdivision under individual languages and groups of languages.
BT —Mutual intelligibility

——**Phonetics**
H 1154
Use as a topical subdivision under individual languages and groups of languages.
BT —Phonetics

——**Phonology**
H 1154
Use as a topical subdivision under individual languages and groups of languages.
BT —Phonology

——**Research** *(May Subd Geog)*
H 1154
Use as a topical subdivision under individual languages and groups of languages.
BT —Research

—Dialects
———Research   *(Continued)*
————Law and legislation   *(May Subd Geog)*
> H 1154
> Further subdivide by subdivisions used under legal topics.
> Use as a topical subdivision under individual languages and groups of languages.
> BT   —Law and legislation

———Syntax
> H 1154
> Use as a topical subdivision under individual languages and groups of languages.
> BT   —Syntax

———Texts
> H 1154
> Use this subdivision combination as a form subdivision under individual languages and groups of languages.
> BT   —Texts

—Diaries
> H 1100; H 1103; H 1110; H 1120; H 1159
> Use as a topical subdivision under names of individual persons and families, classes of persons, and ethnic groups for works about diaries of those persons. Also use under military services for works about diaries of persons belonging to those services.
> UF   —Journals (Diaries)

—Diaries
> H 1100; H 1103; H 1110; H 1120; H 1159
> Use as a form subdivision under names of individual persons and families, classes of persons, and ethnic groups for individual or collections of diaries of those persons. Also use under military services for diaries of persons belonging to those services.
> UF   —Journals (Diaries)

—Dictation exercises
> USE   —Exercises for dictation

—Diction
> H 1154
> Use as a topical subdivision under individual languages and groups of languages.

—Dictionaries
> H 1095; H 1105; H 1110; H 1154
> Use as a form subdivision under subjects.
> UF   —Dictionaries and encyclopedias
> *[Former subdivision]*
> —Dictionaries, indexes, etc.
> *[Former subdivision]*
> NT   —Abbreviations—Dictionaries
> —Acronyms—Dictionaries
> —Biography—Dictionaries
> —Gazetteers

———Early works to 1700
> H 1154
> Use as a form subdivision under individual languages and groups of languages.
> BT   —Early works to 1800

———French, [Italian, etc.]
> H 1095; H 1154
> Use as a form subdivision under subjects.

———Juvenile literature
> USE   —Dictionaries, Juvenile

———Polyglot
> H 1095; H 1154
> Use as a form subdivision under subjects.

—Dictionaries and encyclopedias
> USE   —Dictionaries
> —Encyclopedias

—Dictionaries, indexes, etc.
> USE   —Dictionaries
> —Indexes

—Dictionaries, Juvenile
> H 1095; H 1154
> Use as a form subdivision under subjects.
> UF   —Children's dictionaries
> —Dictionaries—Juvenile literature
> —Juvenile dictionaries
> BT   —Juvenile literature

———Hebrew, [Italian, etc.]
> H 1154
> Use as a form subdivision under individual languages and groups of languages.

—Diesel motors
> USE   —Motors (Diesel)

—Diet therapy   *(May Subd Geog)*
> H 1150
> Use as a topical subdivision under individual diseases and types of diseases.
> BT   —Treatment
> NT   —Diseases—Diet therapy

———Recipes
> H 1150
> Use this subdivision combination as a form subdivision under individual diseases and types of diseases.

—Differences, Age
> USE   —Age differences

—Differences, Sex
> USE   —Sex differences

—Differentials
> H 1195
> Use as a topical subdivision under individual land vehicles and types of land vehicles.

—Differentiation
> H 1164
> Use as a topical subdivision under individual organs and regions of the body.

—Differentiation therapy   *(May Subd Geog)*
> H 1150
> Use as a topical subdivision under individual diseases and types of diseases.
> BT   —Treatment

—Diffusion rate
> H 1149
> Use as a topical subdivision under individual chemicals and groups of chemicals.
> UF   —Rate of diffusion

—Digestive organs
> H 1147
> Use as a topical subdivision under individual animals and groups of animals.

—Digests
> H 1154.5
> Use as a form subdivision under individual legal topics.
> UF   —Cases—Digests
> BT   —Abstracts

—Digitization   *(May Subd Geog)*
> H 1095
> Use as a topical subdivision under types of library materials.

—Dilatation   *(May Subd Geog)*
> H 1164
> Use as a topical subdivision under individual organs and regions of the body.
> UF   —Enlargement
> BT   —Size

—Diminutives
> H 1154
> Use as a topical subdivision under individual languages and groups of languages.

—Dioceses   *(May Subd Geog)*
> H 1187
> Use as a topical subdivision under individual Christian denominations.

—Diphthongs
> H 1154
> Use as a topical subdivision under individual languages and groups of languages.

—Diplomatic history
> H 1200
> Use as a topical subdivision under wars established directly under the name of the war. For wars established under names of places use [country]—Foreign relations—[period].
> BT   —History

—Diplomatic service
> H 1187
> Use as a topical subdivision under individual Christian denominations.

—Dipole moments
> H 1149
> Use as a topical subdivision under individual chemicals and groups of chemicals.

—Direct object
> H 1154
> Use as a topical subdivision under individual languages and groups of languages.

—Direction and production
> USE   —Production and direction

—Directories
> H 1095; H 1100; H 1103; H 1105; H 1120; H 1140
> Use as a form subdivision under names of countries, cities, etc., individual corporate bodies, and families, and under classes of persons, ethnic groups, Christian denominations, types of organizations, and topical headings for individual directories containing names, addresses, and other identifying data.
> NT   —Telephone directories

———Telephone
> USE   —Telephone directories

—Disc brakes
> H 1195
> Use as a topical subdivision under individual land vehicles and types of land vehicles.
> BT   —Brakes

—Disciples
> H 1110
> Use as a topical subdivision under names of individual persons for works about persons who received instruction from the individual or accepted the person's doctrines or teachings and assisted in spreading or implementing them.

—Discipline
> H 1095; H 1100; H 1105; H 1185; H 1187
> Use as a topical subdivision under names of individual corporate bodies and under types of corporate bodies, classes of persons, individual religions, and Christian denominations for the enforcement of rules affecting conduct or action.

—Discography
> H 1095; H 1100; H 1103; H 1105; H 1110; H 1160
> Use as a topical subdivision under names of individual persons and corporate bodies, classes of persons, ethnic groups, forms and types of musical compositions and topical headings for works about discography of those subjects.

—Discography
> H 1095; H 1100; H 1103; H 1105; H 1110; H 1160
> Use as a form subdivision under names of individual persons and corporate bodies for lists or catalogs of sound recordings by or about those persons or corporate bodies. Also use under forms and types of musical compositions, classes of persons, ethnic groups and topics for lists or catalogs of sound recordings of those subjects.
> BT   —Catalogs
> NT   —Music—Discography
> —Songs and music—Discography

———Methodology
> H 1160
> Use as a topical subdivision under forms and types of musical compositions.
> BT   —Methodology

—Discourse analysis
> H 1154
> Use as a topical subdivision under individual languages and groups of languages.

—Discovery and exploration
> H 1140; H 1149.5
> Use as a topical subdivision under names of countries, cities, etc.
> UF   —Exploration and discovery
> —Exploring expeditions
> *[Former subdivision]*
> NT   —Aerial exploration
> —Colonies—Discovery and exploration

———French, [Spanish, etc.]
> H 1140
> Use as a topical subdivision under names of countries, cities, etc.

—Disease and pest resistance
(May Subd Geog)
> H 1180
> Use as a topical subdivision under individual plants and groups of plants.
> UF   —Pest resistance
> —Resistance to diseases and pests
> —Resistance to pests
> NT   —Insect resistance

———Genetic aspects
> H 1180
> Use as a topical subdivision under individual plants and groups of plants.
> BT   —Genetics

—**Disease-free stock** (*May Subd Geog*)
  H 1180
    Use as a topical subdivision under individual plants and groups of plants.
—**Diseases** (*May Subd Geog*)
  H 1100; H 1103; H 1147; H 1164
    Under organs and regions of the body, further subdivide by subdivisions used under diseases.
    Use as a topical subdivision under classes of persons, ethnic groups, individual animals and groups of animals, and individual organs and regions of the body.
  UF —Diseases and hygiene
        [Former subdivision]
  NT —Abscess
      —Ankylosis
      —Cancer
      —Cysts
      —Employees—Diseases
      —Hemorrhage
      —Hypertrophy
      —Infections
      —Metabolism—Disorders
      —Necrosis
      —Paralysis
      —Tumors
      —Ulcers
——**Alternative treatment** (*May Subd Geog*)
  H 1147
    Use as a topical subdivision under individual animals and groups of animals.
  BT —Alternative treatment
——**Chemotherapy** (*May Subd Geog*)
  H 1147
    Use as a topical subdivision under individual animals and groups of animals.
  BT —Chemotherapy
——**Chiropractic treatment**
    (*May Subd Geog*)
  H 1147
    Use as a topical subdivision under individual animals and groups of animals.
  BT —Chiropractic treatment
——Cryosurgery
  USE —Cryosurgery
——Cytopathology
  USE —Cytopathology
——**Diagnosis** (*May Subd Geog*)
  H 1147
    Use as a topical subdivision under individual animals and groups of animals.
  BT —Diagnosis
——**Diet therapy** (*May Subd Geog*)
  H 1147
    Use as a topical subdivision under individual animals and groups of animals.
  BT —Diet therapy
——Endoscopic surgery
  USE —Endoscopic surgery
——**Epidemiology** (*May Subd Geog*)
  H 1147
    Use as a topical subdivision under individual animals and groups of animals.
  BT —Epidemiology
——**Genetic aspects**
  H 1147
    Use as a topical subdivision under individual animals and groups of animals.
  BT —Genetic aspects
——**Homeopathic treatment**
    (*May Subd Geog*)
  H 1147
    Use as a topical subdivision under individual animals and groups of animals.
  BT —Homeopathic treatment
——Imaging
  USE —Imaging
——Interventional radiology
  USE —Interventional radiology
——Laser surgery
  USE —Laser surgery
——Magnetic resonance imaging
  USE —Magnetic resonance imaging

———**Molecular aspects**
  H 1147
    Use as a topical subdivision under individual animals and groups of animals.
  BT —Molecular aspects
———**Nursing** (*May Subd Geog*)
  H 1147
    Use as a topical subdivision under individual animals and groups of animals.
  BT —Nursing
———**Nutritional aspects** (*May Subd Geog*)
  H 1147
    Use as a topical subdivision under individual animals and groups of animals.
  BT —Nutritional aspects
———Pathophysiology
  USE —Pathophysiology
———**Prevention**
  H 1147
    Use as a topical subdivision under individual animals and groups of animals.
  BT —Prevention
———Radionuclide imaging
  USE —Radionuclide imaging
———Reoperation
  USE —Reoperation
———Spectroscopic imaging
  USE —Spectroscopic imaging
———Surgery
  USE —Surgery
———Tomography
  USE —Tomography
———**Treatment** (*May Subd Geog*)
  H 1147
    Use as a topical subdivision under individual animals and groups of animals.
  BT —Treatment
———Ultrasonic imaging
  USE —Ultrasonic imaging
———Vaccination
  USE —Vaccination
—Diseases and hygiene
  USE —Diseases
        —Health and hygiene
—**Diseases and pests** (*May Subd Geog*)
  H 1180
    Use as a topical subdivision under individual plants and groups of plants.
  UF —Pests
  NT —Roots—Diseases and pests
      —Seedlings—Diseases and pests
——**Biological control** (*May Subd Geog*)
  H 1180
    Use as a topical subdivision under individual plants and groups of plants.
  BT —Biological control
——**Control** (*May Subd Geog*)
  H 1180
    Use as a topical subdivision under individual plants and groups of plants.
  BT —Control
———**Environmental aspects**
    (*May Subd Geog*)
  H 1180
    Use as a topical subdivision under individual plants and groups of plants.
  BT —Environmental aspects
——**Cultural control** (*May Subd Geog*)
  H 1180
    Use as a topical subdivision under individual plants and groups of plants.
  BT —Cultural control
——**Identification**
  H 1180
    Use this subdivision combination as a form subdivision under individual plants and groups of plants.
  BT —Identification
——**Integrated control** (*May Subd Geog*)
  H 1180
    Use as a topical subdivision under individual plants and groups of plants.
  BT —Integrated control
——**Monitoring** (*May Subd Geog*)
  H 1180
    Use as a topical subdivision under individual plants and groups of plants.
  BT —Monitoring

———**Nutritional aspects** (*May Subd Geog*)
  H 1180
    Use as a topical subdivision under individual plants and groups of plants.
  BT —Nutritional aspects
—Disinfection of animal housing
  USE —Housing—Disinfection
—**Dislocation** (*May Subd Geog*)
  H 1164
    Further subdivide by subdivisions used under diseases.
    Use as a topical subdivision under individual organs and regions of the body.
—**Dismissal of** (*May Subd Geog*)
  H 1100
    Use as a topical subdivision under occupational groups and types of employees.
—Disparities, Regional
  USE —Regional disparities
—**Dispersal** (*May Subd Geog*)
  H 1147; H 1180
    Use as a topical subdivision under individual animals and groups of animals and individual plants and groups of plants.
  NT —Eggs—Dispersal
      —Larvae—Dispersal
      —Seeds—Dispersal
—Displaced persons
  USE —Refugees
—**Displacement**
  H 1164
    Further subdivide by subdivisions used under diseases.
    Use as a topical subdivision under individual organs and regions of the body.
—Display systems for instruments
  USE —Instruments—Display systems
—Disposal of wastes
  USE —Waste disposal
—Disputes, Boundary
  USE —Boundaries
—**Dissection** (*May Subd Geog*)
  H 1147; H 1164
    Use as a topical subdivision under individual animals and groups of animals and individual organs and regions of the body.
—**Dissertations**
  H 1151
    Use as a topical subdivision under names of individual educational institutions.
——**Style manuals**
  H 1151
    Use this subdivision combination as a form subdivision under names of individual educational institutions.
  UF —Style manuals for dissertations
  BT —Handbooks, manuals, etc.
—**Dissimilation**
  H 1154
    Use as a topical subdivision under individual languages and groups of languages.
—**Dissolution**
  H 1155; H 1158
    Use as a topical subdivision under names of individual legislative bodies and under individual materials and types of materials.
—**Distances, etc.**
  H 1140
    Use as a topical subdivision under names of countries, cities, etc.
—Distribution, Geographical
  USE —Geographical distribution
—Distribution, Seasonal
  USE —Seasonal distribution
—Distribution, Vertical
  USE —Vertical distribution
—Division, Numerical
  USE —Numerical division
—**Divorce**
  H 1110
    Use as a topical subdivision under names of individual persons.
—Doctrinal and controversial works
  USE —Controversial literature
        —Doctrines

—**Doctrines**

H 1185; H 1187

Use as a topical subdivision under individual religions and Christian denominations.

UF —Doctrinal and controversial works

[Former subdivision]

——**History**

H 1187

Use as a topical subdivision under individual Christian denominations.

BT —History

———**Modern period, 1500-**

H 1187

Use as a topical subdivision under individual Christian denominations.

—**Documentation** (May Subd Geog)

H 1095

Use as a topical subdivision under topical headings for works on the processes by which documents on those topics are made available.

—Documents, Papal

USE —Papal documents

—**Domestic animals** (May Subd Geog)

H 1103

Use as a topical subdivision under ethnic groups.

—**Doors**

H 1195

Use as a topical subdivision under individual land vehicles and types of land vehicles.

—**Dormancy** (May Subd Geog)

H 1147; H 1180

Use as a topical subdivision under individual animals and groups of animals and individual plants and groups of plants.

NT —Seeds—Dormancy

—**Dose-response relationship**

H 1149

Use as a topical subdivision under individual chemicals and groups of chemicals.

—**Dosimetric treatment** (May Subd Geog)

H 1150

Use as a topical subdivision under individual diseases and types of diseases.

BT —Treatment

—Doubtful works

USE —Spurious and doubtful works

—**Draft resisters** (May Subd Geog)

H 1200

Further subdivide by subdivisions used under classes of persons.

Use as a topical subdivision under individual wars.

—**Drama**

H 1095; H 1100; H 1103; H 1105; H 1110; H 1120; H 1140

Use as a form subdivision under names of countries, cities, etc., names of individual persons, families, and corporate bodies, and under classes of persons, ethnic groups, and topical headings for plays or musical dramatic works on those subjects.

UF —Plays

NT —Juvenile drama

—**Dramatic production**

H 1110; H 1155.8

Use as a topical subdivision under names of individual literary authors and literary works entered under the title for works on various aspects of stage presentation, e.g. acting, costume, stage setting, and scenery, etc. For works on historical aspects of dramatic production, use the subdivision Stage history.

UF —Stage presentation

—Stage setting and scenery

—**Dramatic works**

H 1110

Do not use under authors who write principally drama.

Use as a topical subdivision under names of individual literary authors for works of criticism about dramatic works by the author.

BT —Criticism and interpretation

NT —Comedies

—Tragedies

—Tragicomedies

—**Dramaturgy**

H 1110

Use as a topical subdivision under names of individual composers for works on their technique in writing operas and other dramatic works.

—**Dravidian authors**

H 1156

Use as a topical subdivision under individual literatures.

—**Drawings**

H 1095

Use as a topical subdivision under technical topics for the technique of making technical drawings on those topics, unless a separate heading for the technique has been provided.

—**Drawings**

H 1095

Use as a form subdivision under technical topics for collections of drawings, plans, etc., on those topics.

NT —Designs and plans

—Dress

USE —Clothing

—**Drill and tactics**

H 1159

Use as a topical subdivision under military services.

NT —Artillery—Drill and tactics

—Cavalry—Drill and tactics

—Infantry—Drill and tactics

—Machine gun drill and tactics

——**Handbooks, manuals, etc.**

H 1159

Use this subdivision combination as a form subdivision under military services.

UF —Drill manuals

[Former subdivision]

BT —Handbooks, manuals, etc.

—Drill manuals

USE —Drill and tactics—Handbooks, manuals, etc.

—Drought resistance

USE —Drought tolerance

—**Drought tolerance** (May Subd Geog)

H 1180

Use as a topical subdivision under individual plants and groups of plants.

UF —Drought resistance

[Former subdivision]

—Resistance to droughts

—Tolerance, Drought

—Drug abuse

USE —Drug use

—Drug effects

USE —Effect of drugs on

—**Drug testing** (May Subd Geog)

H 1100

Use as a topical subdivision under classes of persons tested.

UF —Drug use—Testing

—Testing for drug use or abuse

—**Drug use** (May Subd Geog)

H 1100; H 1103; H 1110

Further subdivide geographically only under classes of persons and ethnic groups.

Use as a topical subdivision under names of individual persons, classes of persons, and ethnic groups for works on their use or abuse of drugs.

UF —Abuse of drugs

—Drug abuse

BT —Substance use

——Testing

USE —Drug testing

—**Druze authors**

H 1156

Use as a topical subdivision under individual literatures.

—**Drying** (May Subd Geog)

H 1095; H 1158; H 1180

Use as a topical subdivision under individual materials and types of materials and types of products and objects dried, including individual plants and groups of plants.

NT —Seeds—Drying

—**Ductility**

H 1158

Use as a topical subdivision under individual materials and types of materials.

—**Dust control** (May Subd Geog)

H 1095; H 1153

Use as a topical subdivision under types of industries, industrial plants, and processes.

—Duties and powers

USE —Powers and duties

—**Dwellings** (May Subd Geog)

H 1100; H 1103

Use as a topical subdivision under classes of persons and ethnic groups for works on residential buildings for the group from the standpoint of architecture, construction, ethnology, etc. For works on social or economic aspects of the provision of housing for the group use the subdivision Housing. For works on homes of individual members of the group from an architectural or historical point of view, use the subdivision Homes and haunts.

UF —Residences

NT —Kings and rulers—Dwellings

—Dynamic testing of materials

USE —Materials—Dynamic testing

—**Dynamics**

H 1195

Use as a topical subdivision under individual land vehicles and types of land vehicles.

NT —Aerodynamics

—Early bibliography

USE —Bibliography—Early

—Early childhood education

USE —Education (Early childhood)

—Early life

USE —Childhood and youth

—Early quotations

USE —Quotations, Early

—**Early works to 1800**

H 1095; H 1100; H 1103; H 1140

Use as a form subdivision under names of countries, cities, etc., and under classes of persons, ethnic groups, and topical headings for individual works written or issued before 1800.

NT —Bibliography—Early

—Dictionaries—Early works to 1700

—Maps—Early works to 1800

—**Earthquake effects** (May Subd Geog)

H 1095

Use as a topical subdivision under types of buildings, structures, facilities, and equipment.

UF —Effect of earthquakes on

—**East Indian authors**

H 1156

Use as a topical subdivision under individual literatures.

—**Eclectic treatment** (May Subd Geog)

H 1150

Use as a topical subdivision under individual diseases and types of diseases.

BT —Treatment

—**Ecology** (May Subd Geog)

H 1147; H 1180

Use as a topical subdivision under individual animals and groups of animals and individual plants and groups of plants.

NT —Ecophysiology

—Larvae—Ecology

—Predators of—Ecology

—**Econometric models**

H 1095; H 1153

Use as a topical subdivision under topical headings for works that employ mathematical or statistical models used to test or measure economic phenomena.

—**Economic aspects** (May Subd Geog)

H 1095

Use as a topical subdivision under topical headings.

NT —Defenses—Economic aspects

—Emigration and immigration—Economic aspects

—Ethnic relations—Economic aspects

—Population—Economic aspects

—Race relations—Economic aspects

—Religion—Economic aspects

—Economic conditions
H 1100; H 1103; H 1140; H 1149.5
Use as a topical subdivision under names of countries, cities, etc., classes of persons, and ethnic groups.
UF —Economic history
—Socioeconomic status
[Former subdivision]
NT —Colonies—Economic conditions

——16th century
H 1100; H 1103; H 1140
Use as a topical subdivision under names of countries, cities, etc., classes of persons and ethnic groups.

——17th century
H 1100; H 1103; H 1140
Use as a topical subdivision under names of countries, cities, etc., classes of persons and ethnic groups.

——18th century
H 1100; H 1103; H 1140
Use as a topical subdivision under names of countries, cities, etc., classes of persons and ethnic groups.

——19th century
H 1100; H 1103; H 1140
Use as a topical subdivision under names of countries, cities, etc., classes of persons and ethnic groups.

——20th century
H 1100; H 1103; H 1140
Use as a topical subdivision under names of countries, cities, etc., classes of persons, and ethnic groups.

——21st century
H 1100; H 1103; H 1140
Use as a topical subdivision under names of countries, cities, etc., classes of persons, and ethnic groups.

——[period subdivision]

————Regional disparities
H 1140
Use as a topical subdivision under names of countries, etc.
BT —Regional disparities

——Regional disparities
H 1140
Use as a topical subdivision under names of countries, etc.
BT —Regional disparities

—Economic history
USE —Economic conditions

—Economic integration
H 1140
Use as a topical subdivision under names of regions larger than countries.

—Economic policy
H 1140; H 1149.5
Use as a topical subdivision under names of countries, cities, etc.
BT —Government policy
NT —Colonies—Economic policy

—Ecophysiology *(May Subd Geog)*
H 1147; H 1180
Use as a topical subdivision under individual animals and groups of animals and individual plants and groups of plants.
BT —Ecology
—Physiology
NT —Seedlings—Ecophysiology

—Editions, Curious
H 1188
Use as a topical subdivision under uniform titles of sacred works.
UF —Curious editions

—Education *(May Subd Geog)*
H 1100; H 1103; H 1186; H 1187
Use as a topical subdivision under names of individual religions and monastic orders, and under individual Christian denominations, classes of persons, and ethnic groups.
NT —Adult education
—Kings and rulers—Education

——Law and legislation *(May Subd Geog)*
H 1103
Further subdivide by subdivisions used under legal topics.
Use as a topical subdivision under ethnic groups.
BT —Law and legislation

—Education and the war, [revolution, etc.]
H 1200
Complete the subdivision by repeating the generic term for the type of engagement contained in the heading.
Use as a topical subdivision under individual wars.

—Education (Continuing education) *(May Subd Geog)*
H 1100; H 1103
Use as a topical subdivision under classes of persons and ethnic groups.
UF —Continuing education

—Education (Early childhood) *(May Subd Geog)*
H 1100; H 1103
Use as a topical subdivision under classes of persons and ethnic groups.
UF —Early childhood education

—Education (Elementary) *(May Subd Geog)*
H 1100; H 1103
Use as a topical subdivision under classes of persons and ethnic groups.
UF —Elementary education

—Education (Graduate) *(May Subd Geog)*
H 1100; H 1103
Use as a topical subdivision under classes of persons and ethnic groups.
UF —Graduate education

—Education (Higher) *(May Subd Geog)*
H 1100; H 1103
Use as a topical subdivision under classes of persons and ethnic groups.
UF —Higher education

—Education (Middle school) *(May Subd Geog)*
H 1100; H 1103
Use as a topical subdivision under classes of persons and ethnic groups.
UF —Middle school education

—Education (Preschool) *(May Subd Geog)*
H 1100; H 1103
Use as a topical subdivision under classes of persons and ethnic groups.
UF —Preschool education

—Education (Primary) *(May Subd Geog)*
H 1100; H 1103
Use as a topical subdivision under classes of persons and ethnic groups.
UF —Primary education

—Education (Secondary) *(May Subd Geog)*
H 1100; H 1103
Use as a topical subdivision under classes of persons and ethnic groups.
UF —Secondary education

—Educational tests
USE —Examinations

—Effect of acid deposition on *(May Subd Geog)*
H 1180
Use as a topical subdivision under individual plants and groups of plants.

—Effect of acid precipitation on *(May Subd Geog)*
H 1147; H 1180
Use as a topical subdivision under individual animals and groups of animals and individual plants and groups of plants.
BT —Climatic factors

—Effect of air pollution on *(May Subd Geog)*
H 1180
Use as a topical subdivision under individual plants and groups of plants.

——Genetic aspects
H 1180
Use as a topical subdivision under individual plants and groups of plants.
BT —Genetics

—Effect of aircraft on *(May Subd Geog)*
H 1147
Use as a topical subdivision under individual animals and groups of animals.

—Effect of altitude on *(May Subd Geog)*
H 1147
Use as a topical subdivision under individual animals and groups of animals.
NT —Reproduction—Effect of altitude on

—Effect of aluminum sulfate on *(May Subd Geog)*
H 1180
Use as a topical subdivision under individual plants and groups of plants.

—Effect of arsenic on *(May Subd Geog)*
H 1180
Use as a topical subdivision under individual plants and groups of plants.

—Effect of atmospheric carbon dioxide on *(May Subd Geog)*
H 1180
Use as a topical subdivision under individual plants and groups of plants.

—Effect of atmospheric deposition on *(May Subd Geog)*
H 1180
Use as a topical subdivision under individual plants and groups of plants.

—Effect of atmospheric nitrogen dioxide on *(May Subd Geog)*
H 1180
Use as a topical subdivision under individual plants and groups of plants.

—Effect of atmospheric ozone on *(May Subd Geog)*
H 1180
Use as a topical subdivision under individual plants and groups of plants.

—Effect of automation on *(May Subd Geog)*
H 1100
Use as a topical subdivision under occupational groups and types of employees.

—Effect of browsing on *(May Subd Geog)*
H 1180
Use as a topical subdivision under individual plants and groups of plants.
NT —Seedlings—Effect of browsing on

—Effect of cadmium on *(May Subd Geog)*
H 1180
Use as a topical subdivision under individual plants and groups of plants.

—Effect of chemicals on *(May Subd Geog)*
H 1147; H 1164
Use as a topical subdivision under individual animals and groups of animals and individual organs and regions of the body.
NT —Effect of surface active agents on

—Effect of climate changes on
USE —Climatic factors

—Effect of climate on
USE —Climatic factors

—Effect of cold on *(May Subd Geog)*
H 1147; H 1164; H 1180
Use as a topical subdivision under individual animals and groups of animals, individual organs and regions of the body and individual plants and groups of plants.
BT —Effect of temperature on

—Effect of contaminated sediments on *(May Subd Geog)*
H 1147
Use as a topical subdivision under individual animals and groups of animals.

—Effect of dams on *(May Subd Geog)*
H 1147
Use as a topical subdivision under individual animals and groups of animals.

—Effect of dichlorophenoxyacetic acid on *(May Subd Geog)*
H 1180
Use as a topical subdivision under individual plants and groups of plants.

—Effect of dredging on *(May Subd Geog)*
H 1147; H 1180
Use as a topical subdivision under individual plants and groups of plants and individual animals and groups of animals.

—Effect of drought on *(May Subd Geog)*
H 1147; H 1180
Use as a topical subdivision under individual animals and groups of animals and individual plants and groups of plants.

—**Effect of drugs on** *(May Subd Geog)*
> H 1147; H 1164
>> Use as a topical subdivision under individual animals and groups of animals and individual organs and regions of the body.
>> UF —Drug effects
>>> *[Former subdivision]*
>> NT —Receptors—Effect of drugs on
—Effect of earthquakes on
> USE —Earthquake effects
—**Effect of environment on** *(May Subd Geog)*
> H 1195
>> Use as a topical subdivision under individual land vehicles and types of land vehicles.
>> NT —Ordnance and ordnance stores—Effect of environment on
—**Effect of ethephon on** *(May Subd Geog)*
> H 1180
>> Use as a topical subdivision under individual plants and groups of plants.
—**Effect of exotic animals on**
> *(May Subd Geog)*
> H 1147
>> Use as a topical subdivision under individual animals and groups of animals.
—**Effect of explosive devices on**
> *(May Subd Geog)*
> H 1195
>> Use as a topical subdivision under individual land vehicles and types of land vehicles.
—**Effect of factory and trade waste on**
> *(May Subd Geog)*
> H 1180
>> Use as a topical subdivision under individual plants and groups of plants.
—**Effect of ferrous sulfate on**
> *(May Subd Geog)*
> H 1180
>> Use as a topical subdivision under individual plants and groups of plants.
>> UF —Effect of ferrous sulphate on
>>> *[Former subdivision]*
—Effect of ferrous sulphate on
> USE —Effect of ferrous sulfate on
—**Effect of fires on** *(May Subd Geog)*
> H 1147; H 1180
>> Use as a topical subdivision under individual animals and groups of animals and individual plants and groups of plants.
>> UF —Effect of wildfires on
——**Genetic aspects** *(May Subd Geog)*
> H 1180
>> Use as a topical subdivision under individual plants and groups of plants.
>> BT —Genetics
—**Effect of fishing on** *(May Subd Geog)*
> H 1147
>> Use as a topical subdivision under individual animals and groups of animals.
—**Effect of floods on** *(May Subd Geog)*
> H 1147; H 1180
>> Use as a topical subdivision under individual animals and groups of animals and individual plants and groups of plants.
—**Effect of fluorides on** *(May Subd Geog)*
> H 1180
>> Use as a topical subdivision under individual plants and groups of plants.
—**Effect of fluorine on** *(May Subd Geog)*
> H 1180
>> Use as a topical subdivision under individual plants and groups of plants.
—**Effect of forest management on**
> *(May Subd Geog)*
> H 1147; H 1180
>> Use as a topical subdivision under individual animals and groups of animals and individual plants and groups of plants
—**Effect of freezes on** *(May Subd Geog)*
> H 1180
>> Use as a topical subdivision under individual plants and groups of plants.
>> BT —Climatic factors
>>> —Effect of temperature on
—**Effect of gamma rays on** *(May Subd Geog)*
> H 1180
>> Use as a topical subdivision under individual plants and groups of plants.

—**Effect of gases on** *(May Subd Geog)*
> H 1180
>> Use as a topical subdivision under individual plants and groups of plants.
—**Effect of global warming on**
> *(May Subd Geog)*
> H 1147; H 1180
>> Use as a topical subdivision under individual plants and groups of plants and individual animals and groups of animals
>> BT —Climatic factors
>>> —Effect of temperature on
—**Effect of glyphosate on** *(May Subd Geog)*
> H 1180
>> Use as a topical subdivision under individual plants and groups of plants.
—**Effect of grazing on** *(May Subd Geog)*
> H 1180
>> Use as a topical subdivision under individual plants and groups of plants.
—**Effect of greenhouse gases on**
> *(May Subd Geog)*
> H 1180
>> Use as a topical subdivision under individual plants and groups of plants.
—**Effect of habitat modification on**
> *(May Subd Geog)*
> H 1147
>> Use as a topical subdivision under individual animals and groups of animals.
—**Effect of heat on** *(May Subd Geog)*
> H 1164
>> Use as a topical subdivision under individual organs and regions of the body.
—**Effect of heavy metals on** *(May Subd Geog)*
> H 1147; H 1180
>> Use as a topical subdivision under individual animals and groups of animals and individual plants and groups of plants.
—**Effect of high temperatures on**
> *(May Subd Geog)*
> H 1158
>> Use as a topical subdivision under individual materials and types of materials.
>> BT —Effect of temperature on
—**Effect of human beings on**
> *(May Subd Geog)*
> H 1147
>> Use as a topical subdivision under individual animals and groups of animals.
—**Effect of hunting on** *(May Subd Geog)*
> H 1147
>> Use as a topical subdivision under individual animals and groups of animals.
—Effect of hurricanes on
> USE —Hurricane effects
—**Effect of ice on** *(May Subd Geog)*
> H 1180
>> Use as a topical subdivision under individual plants and groups of plants.
—**Effect of implants on** *(May Subd Geog)*
> H 1164
>> Use as a topical subdivision under individual organs and regions of the body.
—**Effect of imprisonment on**
> *(May Subd Geog)*
> H 1100
>> Use as a topical subdivision under classes of persons.
—Effect of inflation on appropriations and expenditures
> USE —Appropriations and expenditures—Effect of inflation on
—Effect of inflation on pensions
> USE —Pensions—Effect of inflation on
—**Effect of insecticides on** *(May Subd Geog)*
> H 1147
>> Use as a topical subdivision under individual animals and groups of animals.
—**Effect of iron on** *(May Subd Geog)*
> H 1180
>> Use as a topical subdivision under individual plants and groups of plants.
—**Effect of lasers on** *(May Subd Geog)*
> H 1158
>> Use as a topical subdivision under individual materials and types of materials.

—**Effect of light on** *(May Subd Geog)*
> H 1147; H 1180
>> Use as a topical subdivision under individual animals and groups of animals and individual plants and groups of plants.
>> NT —Reproduction—Effect of light on
—**Effect of logging on** *(May Subd Geog)*
> H 1147
>> Use as a topical subdivision under individual animals and groups of animals.
—**Effect of low temperatures on**
> *(May Subd Geog)*
> H 1158
>> Use as a topical subdivision under individual materials and types of materials.
>> BT —Effect of temperature on
—**Effect of magnesium on** *(May Subd Geog)*
> H 1180
>> Use as a topical subdivision under individual plants and groups of plants.
—**Effect of magnetism on** *(May Subd Geog)*
> H 1147; H 1164; H 1180
>> Use as a topical subdivision under animals and groups of animals, individual organs and regions of the body, and individual plants and groups of plants.
—**Effect of manganese on** *(May Subd Geog)*
> H 1180
>> Use as a topical subdivision under individual plants and groups of plants.
—**Effect of metals on** *(May Subd Geog)*
> H 1147; H 1164
>> Use as a topical subdivision under individual animals and groups of animals and individual organs and regions of the body.
—Effect of mineral industries on
> USE —Effect of mining on
—**Effect of minerals on** *(May Subd Geog)*
> H 1180
>> Use as a topical subdivision under individual plants and groups of plants.
—**Effect of mining on** *(May Subd Geog)*
> H 1147
>> Use as a topical subdivision under individual animals and groups of animals.
>> UF —Effect of mineral industries on
—**Effect of music on** *(May Subd Geog)*
> H 1180
>> Use as a topical subdivision under individual animals and groups of animals.
—**Effect of noise on** *(May Subd Geog)*
> H 1147
>> Use as a topical subdivision under individual animals and groups of animals.
—**Effect of odors on** *(May Subd Geog)*
> H 1147
>> Use as a topical subdivision under individual animals and groups of animals.
—**Effect of off-road vehicles on**
> *(May Subd Geog)*
> H 1147; H 1180
>> Use as a topical subdivision under individual plants and groups of plants and under individual animals and groups of animals.
—**Effect of oil spills on** *(May Subd Geog)*
> H 1147
>> Use as a topical subdivision under individual animals and groups of animals.
—**Effect of oxygen on** *(May Subd Geog)*
> H 1180
>> Use as a topical subdivision under individual plants and groups of plants.
—**Effect of ozone on** *(May Subd Geog)*
> H 1180
>> Use as a topical subdivision under individual plants and groups of plants.
>> BT —Climatic factors
—**Effect of pesticides on** *(May Subd Geog)*
> H 1147; H 1180
>> Use as a topical subdivision under individual animals and groups of animals and individual plants and groups of plants.
—**Effect of poaching on** *(May Subd Geog)*
> H 1147; H 1180
>> Use as a topical subdivision under individual animals and groups of animals and individual plants and groups of plants.

—**Effect of pollution on** (*May Subd Geog*)
  H 1147; H 1180
    Use as a topical subdivision under individual an-
    imals and groups of animals and individual plants
    and groups of plants.
—**Effect of potassium on** (*May Subd Geog*)
  H 1180
    Use as a topical subdivision under individual
    plants and groups of plants.
—**Effect of predation on** (*May Subd Geog*)
  H 1147
    Use as a topical subdivision under individual an-
    imals and groups of animals.
—**Effect of radiation on** (*May Subd Geog*)
  H 1147; H 1149; H 1158; H 1164; H 1180
    Use as a topical subdivision under individual an-
    imals and groups of animals, individual chemicals
    and groups of chemicals, individual materials and
    types of materials, organs and regions of the body,
    and individual plants and groups of plants.
—**Effect of radioactive pollution on**
  (*May Subd Geog*)
  H 1147; H 1180
    Use as a topical subdivision under individual an-
    imals and groups of animals and individual plants
    and groups of plants.
—**Effect of roads on** (*May Subd Geog*)
  H 1147
    Use as a topical subdivision under individual an-
    imals and groups of animals.
—**Effect of salt on** (*May Subd Geog*)
  H 1147; H 1158; H 1180
    Use as a topical subdivision under individual an-
    imals and groups of animals, individual materials
    and types of materials, and individual plants and
    groups of plants.
—**Effect of sediments on** (*May Subd Geog*)
  H 1147
    Use as a topical subdivision under individual an-
    imals and groups of animals.
—**Effect of selenium on** (*May Subd Geog*)
  H 1147
    Use as a topical subdivision under individual an-
    imals and groups of animals.
—**Effect of soil acidity on** (*May Subd Geog*)
  H 1180
    Use as a topical subdivision under individual
    plants and groups of plants.
—**Effect of sound on** (*May Subd Geog*)
  H 1147
    Use as a topical subdivision under individual an-
    imals and groups of animals.
—**Effect of space flight on**
  H 1164
    Use as a topical subdivision under individual or-
    gans and regions of the body.
—**Effect of storms on** (*May Subd Geog*)
  H 1147
    Use as a topical subdivision under individual an-
    imals and groups of animals and individual plants
    and groups of plants.
  BT —Climatic factors
—**Effect of stray currents on**
  (*May Subd Geog*)
  H 1147
    Use as a topical subdivision under individual an-
    imals and groups of animals.
  UF —Effect of vagrant electric currents
        on
        [*Former subdivision*]
—**Effect of stress on** (*May Subd Geog*)
  H 1147; H 1164; H 1180
    Use as a topical subdivision under individual
    animals and groups of animals, individual organs
    and regions of the body, and individual plants and
    groups of plants.
—**Effect of sulfates on** (*May Subd Geog*)
  H 1180
    Use as a topical subdivision under individual
    plants and groups of plants.
—**Effect of sulfur on** (*May Subd Geog*)
  H 1180
    Use as a topical subdivision under individual
    plants and groups of plants.
  UF —Effect of sulphur on
        [*Former subdivision*]
—Effect of sulphur on
  USE —Effect of sulfur on

—**Effect of surface active agents on**
  (*May Subd Geog*)
  H 1147
    Use as a topical subdivision under individual an-
    imals and groups of animals.
  BT —Effect of chemicals on
—**Effect of technological innovations on**
  (*May Subd Geog*)
  H 1100
    Use as a topical subdivision under classes of per-
    sons.
  NT —Employees—Effect of
        technological innovations
—**Effect of temperature on** (*May Subd Geog*)
  H 1147; H 1158; H 1180
    Use as a topical subdivision under individual an-
    imals and groups of animals, individual materials
    and types of materials, and individual plants and
    groups of plants.
  UF —Effect of water temperature on
        [*Former subdivision*]
  NT —Effect of cold on
        —Effect of freezes on
        —Effect of global warming on
        —Effect of high temperatures on
        —Effect of low temperatures on
        —Expansion and contraction
        —Reproduction—Effect of
          temperature on
—**Effect of thermal pollution on**
  (*May Subd Geog*)
  H 1180
    Use as a topical subdivision under individual
    plants and groups of plants.
—**Effect of trampling on** (*May Subd Geog*)
  H 1180
    Use as a topical subdivision under individual
    plants and groups of plants.
—**Effect of trichloroethylene on**
  (*May Subd Geog*)
  H 1180
    Use as a topical subdivision under individual
    plants and groups of plants.
—**Effect of turbidity on** (*May Subd Geog*)
  H 1147; H 1180
    Use as a topical subdivision under individual an-
    imals and groups of animals and individual plants
    and groups of plants.
—**Effect of ultraviolet radiation on**
  (*May Subd Geog*)
  H 1147; H 1180
    Use as a topical subdivision under individual an-
    imals and groups of animals and individual plants
    and groups of plants.
  NT —Embryos—Effect of ultraviolet
        radiation on
        —Larvae—Effect of ultraviolet
          radiation on
—Effect of vagrant electric currents on
  USE —Effect of stray currents on
—**Effect of vibration on** (*May Subd Geog*)
  H 1164
    Use as a topical subdivision under individual or-
    gans and regions of the body.
—**Effect of volcanic eruptions on**
  (*May Subd Geog*)
  H 1147; H 1180
    Use as a topical subdivision under individual an-
    imals and groups of animals and individual plants
    and groups of plants.
—**Effect of water acidification on**
  (*May Subd Geog*)
  H 1147
    Use as a topical subdivision under individual an-
    imals and groups of animals.
—**Effect of water levels on** (*May Subd Geog*)
  H 1147; H 1180
    Use as a topical subdivision under individual an-
    imals and groups of animals and individual plants
    and groups of plants.
—**Effect of water pollution on**
  (*May Subd Geog*)
  H 1147; H 1180
    Use as a topical subdivision under individual an-
    imals and groups of animals and individual plants
    and groups of plants.

—**Effect of water quality on**
  (*May Subd Geog*)
  H 1147
    Use as a topical subdivision under individual an-
    imals and groups of animals.
—Effect of water temperature on
  USE —Effect of temperature on
—**Effect of water waves on** (*May Subd Geog*)
  H 1180
    Use as a topical subdivision under individual
    plants and groups of plants.
—Effect of wildfires on
  USE —Effect of fires on
—**Effect of wind on** (*May Subd Geog*)
  H 1180
    Use as a topical subdivision under individual
    plants and groups of plants.
  BT —Climatic factors
—**Effect of wind power plants on**
  (*May Subd Geog*)
  H 1147
    Use as a topical subdivision under individual an-
    imals and groups of animals.
—**Effectiveness** (*May Subd Geog*)
  H 1149
    Use as a topical subdivision under individual
    drugs and groups of drugs.
  NT —Therapeutic use—Effectiveness
—Efficiency of feed utilization
  USE —Feed utilization efficiency
—**Eggs** (*May Subd Geog*)
  H1147
    Use as a topical subdivision under individual an-
    imals and groups of animals.
——**Counting** (*May Subd Geog*)
  H 1147
    Use as a topical subdivision under individual
    animals and groups of animals.
  BT —Counting
——**Dispersal** (*May Subd Geog*)
  H 1147
    Use as a topical subdivision under individual
    animals and groups of animals
  BT —Dispersal
——**Geographical distribution**
  H 1147
    Use as a topical subdivision under individual
    animals and groups of animals.
  BT —Geographical distribution
——**Incubation** (*May Subd Geog*)
  H 1147
    Use as a topical subdivision under individual
    animals and groups of animals.
  UF —Incubation of eggs
—**Egyptian influences**
  H 1156
    Use as a topical subdivision under individual lit-
    eratures.
  BT —Foreign influences
—**Elastic properties** (*May Subd Geog*)
  H 1158
    Use as a topical subdivision under individual
    materials and types of materials.
  UF —Elasticity
—Elasticity
  USE —Elastic properties
—**Election districts**
  H 1155
    Use as a topical subdivision under names of in-
    dividual legislative bodies.
  BT —Administrative and political
        divisions
—**Elections**
  H 1105; H 1155
    Use as a topical subdivision under names of in-
    dividual corporate bodies and legislative bodies.
  NT —Contested elections
—**Elections, [date]**
  H 1155
    Use as a topical subdivision under names of in-
    dividual legislative bodies.
—**Elective system**
  H 1151.5
    Use as a topical subdivision under types of edu-
    cational institutions.

—**Electric equipment** (May Subd Geog)
  H 1153; H 1195
    Use as a topical subdivision under types of industries and individual land vehicles and types of land vehicles.
    BT —Equipment and supplies
—**Electric generators** (May Subd Geog)
  H 1195
    Use as a topical subdivision under individual land vehicles and types of land vehicles.
—**Electric installations**
  H 1159
    Use as a topical subdivision under military services.
—**Electric properties** (May Subd Geog)
  H 1149; H 1158; H 1164; H 1180
    Use as a topical subdivision under individual chemicals and groups of chemicals, individual materials and types of materials, individual organs and regions of the body, and individual plants and groups of plants.
    BT —Properties
—**Electric wiring**
  H 1195
    Use as a topical subdivision under individual land vehicles and types of land vehicles.
    UF —Wiring, Electric
—**Electromechanical analogies**
  H 1095
    Use as a topical subdivision under scientific and technical topics.
    BT —Simulation methods
—**Electrometallurgy**
  H 1149
    Use as a topical subdivision under individual metals and metal compounds.
    BT —Metallurgy
—**Electronic discussion groups**
  H 1095
    Use as a topical subdivision under subjects for works about electronic discussion groups on those subjects.
—**Electronic discussion groups**
  H 1095
    Use as a form subdivision under subjects for electronic discussion groups on those subjects.
—**Electronic equipment** (May Subd Geog)
  H 1153; H 1195
    Use as a topical subdivision under types of industries and individual land vehicles and types of land vehicles.
    BT —Equipment and supplies
    NT —Ignition—Electronic systems
—Electronic fuel injection systems of motors
    USE —Motors—Electronic fuel injection systems
—**Electronic information resources**
  H 1095
    Use as a topical subdivision under subjects for works about electronic information resources on those subjects.
    BT —Information resources
    NT —Computer network resources
—**Electronic installations**
  H 1159
    Use as a topical subdivision under military services.
—**Electronic intelligence** (May Subd Geog)
  H 1200
    Use as a topical subdivision under individual wars.
    BT —Military intelligence
—**Electronic publishing** (May Subd Geog)
  H 1095
    Use as a topical subdivision under types of published materials and headings for literature on particular topics.
    BT —Publishing
—**Electronic technicians**
  H 1159
    Further subdivide by subdivisions used under classes of persons.
    Use as a topical subdivision under military services.
—Elementary education
    USE —Education (Elementary)
—Elevations (Altitudes)
    USE —Altitudes

—**Elision**
  H 1154
    Use as a topical subdivision under individual languages and groups of languages.
—**Ellipsis**
  H 1154
    Use as a topical subdivision under individual languages and groups of languages.
—**Embouchure**
  H 1161
    Use as a topical subdivision under individual musical instruments and families of instruments.
—**Embrittlement**
  H 1158
    Use as a topical subdivision under individual materials and types of materials.
    NT —Hydrogen embrittlement
—Embryogenesis, Somatic
    USE —Somatic embryogenesis
—**Embryology**
  H 1147; H 1180
    Use as a topical subdivision under individual animals and groups of animals and individual plants and groups of plants.
—**Embryos** (May Subd Geog)
  H 1147; H 1180
    Use as a topical subdivision under individual animals and groups of animals and individual plants and groups of plants.
——**Anatomy**
  H 1147
    Use as a topical subdivision under individual animals and groups of animals.
    BT —Anatomy
——**Effect of ultraviolet radiation on**
  (May Subd Geog)
  H 1147
    Use as a topical subdivision under individual animals and groups of animals
    BT —Effect of ultraviolet radiation on
——**Motility**
  H1147
    Use as a topical subdivision under individual animals and groups of animals.
——**Nutrition** (May Subd Geog)
  H 1180
    Use as a topical subdivision under individual plants and groups of plants.
    BT —Nutrition
——**Physiology** (May Subd Geog)
  H 1147
    Use as a topical subdivision under individual animals and groups of animals.
    BT —Physiology
——**Transplantation** (May Subd Geog)
  H 1147
    Use as a topical subdivision under individual animals and groups of animals.
    BT —Transplantation
—**Emigration and immigration**
  H 1140; H 1149.5
    Use as a topical subdivision under names of countries, cities, etc.
    UF —Foreign population
        [Former subdivision]
      —Immigration
    NT —Colonies—Emigration and immigration
——**Economic aspects**
  H 1140
    Use as a topical subdivision under names of countries, cities, etc.
    BT —Economic aspects
——**Government policy**
  H 1140
    Use as a topical subdivision under names of countries, cities, etc.
    BT —Government policy
——**Religious aspects**
  H 1140
    Use as a topical subdivision under names of countries, cities, etc.
———**Baptists, [Catholic Church, etc.]**
  H 1140
    Use as a topical subdivision under names of countries, cities, etc.
———**Buddhism, [Christianity, etc.]**
  H 1140
    Use as a topical subdivision under names of countries, cities, etc.

——**Social aspects**
  H 1140
    Use as a topical subdivision under names of countries, cities, etc.
    BT —Social aspects
—**Emphasis**
  H 1154
    Use as a topical subdivision under individual languages and groups of languages.
—Employee participation in management
    USE —Management—Employee participation
—**Employees**
  H 1095; H 1105; H 1110; H 1151; H 1151.5; H 1153; H 1187
    Further subdivide by subdivisions used under classes of persons.
    Use as a topical subdivision under types of industries, services, establishments, etc. Also use under names of individual persons for works on persons employed by the individual, including household servants, etc. Also use under names of individual educational institutions and non governmental corporate bodies. Under names of individual international, government, and quasi-governmental agencies, use Officials and employees.
    UF —Relations with employees
      —Servants
    NT —Professional staff
——**Diseases** (May Subd Geog)
  H 1153
    Use as a topical subdivision under types of industries.
    UF —Employees—Diseases and hygiene
        [Former subdivision]
    BT —Diseases
——Diseases and hygiene
    USE —Employees—Diseases
      —Employees—Health and hygiene
——**Effect of technological innovations**
  (May Subd Geog)
  1153
    Use as a topical subdivision under types of industries.
    BT —Effect of technological innovations on
——**Health and hygiene** (May Subd Geog)
  H 1153
    Use as a topical subdivision under types of industries.
    UF —Employees—Diseases and hygiene
        [Former subdivision]
——**Job descriptions** (May Subd Geog)
  H 1153
    Use this subdivision combination as a form subdivision under types of industries for summaries of the essential activities involved in the performance of jobs.
    Use as a topical subdivision under types of industries for works about summaries of the essential activities involved in the performance of jobs.
    BT —Job descriptions
——**Legal status, laws, etc.** (May Subd Geog)
  H 1153
    Further subdivide by subdivisions used under legal topics.
    Use as a topical subdivision under types of industries.
    BT —Legal status, laws, etc.
——**Medical care** (May Subd Geog)
  H 1153
    Use as a topical subdivision under types of industries.
    BT —Medical care
——**Pensions** (May Subd Geog)
  H 1153
    Use as a topical subdivision under types of industries.
    UF —Salaries, pensions, etc.
        [Former subdivision]
    BT —Pensions

————**Law and legislation** (*May Subd Geog*)
   H 1153
    Further subdivide by subdivisions used under legal topics.
    Use as a topical subdivision under types of industries.
    BT —Law and legislation

——**Supply and demand** (*May Subd Geog*)
   H 1153
    Use as a topical subdivision under types of industries.
    BT —Supply and demand

——**Training of** (*May Subd Geog*)
   H 1153
    Use as a topical subdivision under types of industries.
    BT —Training of

—**Employment** (*May Subd Geog*)
   H 1100; H 1103
    Use as a topical subdivision under classes of persons and ethnic groups.
    UF —Working conditions
    NT —Clergy—Secular employment
       —Supplementary employment

——**Foreign countries**
   H 1100; H 1103
    Use as a topical subdivision under classes of persons and ethnic groups.

—**Enclitics**
   H 1154
    Use as a topical subdivision under individual languages and groups of languages.

—**Encyclopedias**
   H 1095
    Use as a form subdivision under subjects.
    UF —Dictionaries and encyclopedias
       [Former subdivision]

——Juvenile literature
    USE —Encyclopedias, Juvenile

—**Encyclopedias, Juvenile**
   H 1095
    Use as a form subdivision under subjects.
    UF —Children's encyclopedias
       —Encyclopedias—Juvenile literature
       —Juvenile encyclopedias
    BT —Juvenile literature

—**Endocrine aspects**
   H 1150
    Use as a topical subdivision under individual diseases and types of diseases.
    UF —Hormonal aspects
    NT —Hormone therapy
       —Metabolism—Endocrine aspects

—**Endocrinology**
   H 1147
    Use as a topical subdivision under individual animals and groups of animals.
    NT —Behavior—Endocrine aspects
       —Development—Endocrine aspects
       —Larvae—Endocrinology
       —Metamorphosis—Endocrine aspects
       —Reproduction—Endocrine aspects

—**Endoscopic surgery** (*May Subd Geog*)
   H 1150; H 1164
    Use as a topical subdivision under individual diseases and types of diseases and organs and regions of the body.
    UF —Diseases—Endoscopic surgery
    BT —Surgery

——**Complications** (*May Subd Geog*)
   H 1164
    Further subdivide by subdivisions used under diseases.
    Use as a topical subdivision under individual organs and regions of the body.
    BT —Complications

—**Endowments**
   H 1095; H 1105
    Use as a topical subdivision under names of individual corporate bodies and under types of corporate bodies and disciplines.

—**Enemies**
    USE —Adversaries

—**Energy conservation** (*May Subd Geog*)
   H 1095; H 1153
    Use as a topical subdivision under types of industries, facilities, etc.
    BT —Conservation

—**Energy consumption** (*May Subd Geog*)
   H 1095; H 1153; H 1159
    Do not further subdivide geographically under military services.
    Use as a topical subdivision under types of industries, military services, and topical headings.
    UF —Consumption of energy
    NT —Fuel consumption

—**Engineering and construction**
   H 1200
    Use as a topical subdivision under individual wars.
    UF —Construction and engineering

—**English influences**
   H 1156
    Use as a topical subdivision under individual literatures other than English.
    BT —Foreign influences

—Enlargement
    USE —Dilatation
       —Hypertrophy

—Enlistment
    USE —Recruiting, enlistment, etc.

—Enrichment of environment
    USE —Environmental enrichment

—**Entrance examinations**
   H 1151; H 1151.5
    Use as a topical subdivision under names of individual educational institutions and types of educational institutions.
    BT —Examinations

——**Law and legislation** (*May Subd Geog*)
   H 1151.5
    Further subdivide by subdivisions used under legal topics.
    Use as a topical subdivision under types of educational institutions.
    BT —Law and legislation

——**Study guides**
   H 1151.5
    Use this subdivision combination as a form subdivision under types of educational institutions.
    BT —Study guides

—**Entrance requirements**
   H 1151; H 1151.5
    Use as a topical subdivision under names of individual educational institutions and types of educational institutions.
    UF —Requirements for entrance

——**[subject]**
   H 1151
    Further subdivide by disciplines and fields of study.
    Use as a topical subdivision under names of individual educational institutions.'

—**Environmental aspects** (*May Subd Geog*)
   H 1095; H 1149; H 1150; H 1151.5; H 1153; H 1158; H 1159; H 1195; H 1200
    Use as a topical subdivision under individual military services, events, and wars, individual chemicals and groups of chemicals, individual materials and types of materials, and under types of industries, processes, machines, facilities, constructions, educational institutions, and events for environmental issues associated with their operation, creation, use, or planning and execution.
    Use as a topical subdivision under individual diseases and types of diseases for environmental aspects of their causation or development.
    NT —Control—Environmental aspects
       —Diseases and pests—Control—Environmental aspects
       —Manure—Environmental aspects
       —Parasites—Control—Environmental aspects
       —Population—Environmental aspects

—**Environmental conditions**
   H 1140
    Use as a topical subdivision under names of countries, cities, etc.

—Environmental engineering of animal housing
    USE —Housing—Environmental engineering

—**Environmental enrichment** (*May Subd Geog*)
   H 1147
    Use as a topical subdivision under individual animals and groups of animals.
    UF —Enrichment of environment

—**Environmental testing** (*May Subd Geog*)
   H 1158
    Use as a topical subdivision under individual materials and types of materials.
    BT —Testing

—**Epidemiology**
   H 1150
    Use as a topical subdivision under individual diseases and types of diseases.
    NT —Diseases—Epidemiology

—**Epithets**
   H 1154
    Use as a topical subdivision under individual languages other than English and groups of languages.

—**Eponyms**
   H 1154
    Use as a topical subdivision under individual languages and groups of languages.

—**Equipment**
   H 1159
    Use as a topical subdivision under military services.

——**Quality control**
   H 1159
    Use as a topical subdivision under military services.
    BT —Quality control

—**Equipment and supplies**
   H 1095; H 1105; H 1147; H 1153; H 1180; H 1195; H 1200
    Use as a topical subdivision under names of individual corporate bodies and under types of industries, processes, services, activities, institutions, disciplines, individual animals and groups of animals, individual plants and groups of plants, individual land vehicles and types of land vehicles, and individual wars.
    UF —Apparatus
       [Former subdivision]
       —Apparatus and equipment
       [Former subdivision]
       —Apparatus and supplies
       [Former subdivision]
       —Supplies
       [Former subdivision]
    NT —Audio equipment
       —Electric equipment
       —Electronic equipment
       —Hydraulic equipment
       —Pneumatic equipment
       —Radio equipment
       —Safety appliances

—**Ergative constructions**
   H 1154
    Use as a topical subdivision under individual languages and groups of languages.
    BT —Case
       —Syntax

—**Erosion** (*May Subd Geog*)
   H 1158
    Use as a topical subdivision under individual materials and types of materials.
    BT —Deterioration
    NT —Cavitation erosion

—Errors, inventions, etc., of history
    USE —History—Errors, inventions, etc.

—**Errors of usage**
   H 1154
    Use as a topical subdivision under individual languages and groups of languages.
    UF —Idioms, corrections, errors
       [Former subdivision]
       —Usage errors

—**Eruption, [date]**
   H 1140
    Use as a topical subdivision under names of individual volcanoes.

—Eruptions
H 1140
Use as a topical subdivision under names of individual volcanoes.

—Essence, genius, nature
H 1185
Use as a topical subdivision under individual religions.

—Estate
H 1110
Use as a topical subdivision under names of individual persons for works on the aggregate of property or liabilities of all kinds that a person leaves for disposal at his death, including discussions or cases of contested estates.

—Estimates *(May Subd Geog)*
H 1095; H 1153
Use as a topical subdivision under types of engineering, technical processes, industries, etc., for estimates of the cost of construction, installation, etc., or the carrying out of a task to completion.
UF —Estimates and cost
 [Former subdivision]

—Estimates and cost
USE —Estimates

—Etching *(May Subd Geog)*
H 1158
Use as a topical subdivision under individual materials and types of materials.

—Ethical aspects
USE —Moral and ethical aspects

—Ethical behavior
USE —Conduct of life

—Ethics
H 1110; H 1155
Use as a topical subdivision under names of individual persons for works on the individual's ethical system and values. Also use under names of individual legislative bodies.
UF —Biography—Character
 [Former subdivision]
 —Knowledge—Ethics
 —Moral ideas
 —Religion and ethics
 [Former subdivision]

—Ethics, Professional
USE —Professional ethics

—Ethnic identity
H 1103
Use as a topical subdivision under ethnic groups.
UF —Identity, Ethnic

—Ethnic relations
H 1140
Use as a topical subdivision under names of countries, cities, etc.
UF —Relations, Ethnic

——Economic aspects
H 1140
Use as a topical subdivision under names of countries, cities, etc.
BT —Economic aspects

——Political aspects
H 1140
Use as a topical subdivision under names of countries, cities, etc.
BT —Political aspects

—Ethnobiology *(May Subd Geog)*
H 1103
Use as a topical subdivision under ethnic groups.
NT —Ethnobotany
 —Ethnozoology

—Ethnobotany *(May Subd Geog)*
H 1103
Use as a topical subdivision under ethnic groups.
BT —Ethnobiology

—Ethnological collections
H 1105; H 1110; H 1120
Use as a topical subdivision under names of individual persons, corporate bodies, and families for works about their ethnological collections.

—Ethnomusicological collections
H 1105; H 1110; H 1120
Use as a topical subdivision under names of individual persons, corporate bodies, and families for works about their ethnomusicological collections.

—Ethnozoology *(May Subd Geog)*
H 1103
Use as a topical subdivision under ethnic groups.
BT —Ethnobiology

—Etiology
H 1150
Use as a topical subdivision under individual diseases and types of diseases.

—Etymology
H 1154
Use as a topical subdivision under individual languages and groups of languages.

——Names
H 1154
Use as a topical subdivision under individual languages and groups of languages.
UF —Names—Etymology

—Euphemism
H 1154
Use as a topical subdivision under individual languages and groups of languages.

—European authors
H 1156
Use as a topical subdivision under individual literatures.

—European influences
H 1156
Use as a topical subdivision under individual literatures.
BT —Foreign influences

—Evacuation of civilians *(May Subd Geog)*
H 1200
Use as a topical subdivision under individual wars.
UF —Civilian evacuation

—Evaluation
H 1095; H 1105; H 1151.5
Use as a topical subdivision under names of individual corporate bodies and under types of institutions, products, services, equipment, activities, projects, and programs for works on methods of assessing or appraising those subjects, or for works on both the methods and results of assessing them.
NT —Rating of
 —Seedlings—Evaluation

—Evidences, authority, etc.
H 1188
Use as a topical subdivision under uniform titles of sacred works.

—Evolution *(May Subd Geog)*
H 1147; H 1149; H 1164; H 1180
Use as a topical subdivision under individual animals and groups of animals, individual chemicals and groups of chemicals, individual organs and regions of the body, and individual plants and groups of plants.
NT —Behavior—Evolution

—Examination *(May Subd Geog)*
H 1164
Use as a topical subdivision under individual organs and regions of the body.
BT —Diagnosis

—Examination questions
USE —Examinations, questions, etc.

—Examinations
H 1095; H 1100; H 1105; H 1151; H 1151.5; H 1159
Use under classes of persons only if a heading for the corresponding field or activity does not exist or cannot be established.
Use as a topical subdivision under names of individual corporate bodies, educational institutions, and military services and under types of educational institutions, classes of persons, and topical headings for works about examinations given by those organizations, for those groups, or about those topics.
UF —Educational tests
 —Testing, Educational
NT —Entrance examinations
 —Graduate work—Examinations

——Law and legislation *(May Subd Geog)*
H 1151.5
Further subdivide by subdivisions used under legal topics.
Use as a topical subdivision under types of educational institutions.
BT —Law and legislation

——Study guides
H 1095
Use this subdivision combination as a form subdivision under names of individual corporate bodies, educational institutions, and military services, and under types of educational institutions, classes of persons, and topical headings for study guides for examinations given by those organizations, for those groups, or about those groups.
BT —Study guides

——[subject]
H 1151; H 1151.5
Further subdivide by disciplines and fields of study.
Use as a topical subdivision under names of individual educational institutions and types of educational institutions.

—Examinations, questions, etc.
H 1095; H 1100; H 1103; H 1188
Use as a form subdivision under classes of persons, ethnic groups, uniform titles of sacred works, and topical headings for compilations of questions and answers for examinations for those groups or about those topics.
UF —Examination questions
 —Questions, examinations, etc.

—Examples
USE —Specimens

—Excerpts
H 1095; H 1160
Further subdivide by other subdivisions for musical presentation.
Use as a form subdivision under motion picture forms and genres and under forms and types of musical compositions.
NT —Orchestral excerpts

—Excerpts, Arranged
H 1160
Further subdivide by other subdivisions for musical presentation
Use as a form subdivision under forms and types of musical compositions.
UF —Arranged excerpts

—Exclamations
H 1154
Use as a topical subdivision under individual languages and groups of languages.

—Excretion
H 1149
Use as a topical subdivision under individual chemicals and groups of chemicals.

—Executive agreements on foreign relations
USE —Foreign relations—Executive
 agreements

—Exemplars
USE —Specimens

—Exercise *(May Subd Geog)*
H 1147
Use as a topical subdivision under individual animals and groups of animals.

——Physiological aspects
H 1147
Use as a topical subdivision under individual animals and groups of animals.
BT —Physiological aspects

—Exercise therapy *(May Subd Geog)*
H 1150
Use as a topical subdivision under individual diseases and types of diseases.
BT —Physical therapy

—Exercises and composition
USE —Composition and exercises

—Exercises and studies
USE —Studies and exercises

—Exercises, Chapel
USE —Chapel exercises

—Exercises for dictation
H 1154
Use as a form subdivision under individual languages and groups of languages.
UF —Dictation exercises
BT —Problems, exercises, etc.

—Exercises, problems, etc.
USE —Problems, exercises, etc.

—Exhaust gas of diesel motors
USE —Motors (Diesel)—Exhaust gas

—Exhaust gas of motors
　USE —Motors—Exhaust gas
—Exhaust systems of motors
　USE —Motors—Exhaust systems
—Exhibit catalogs
　USE —Exhibitions
—Exhibition catalogs
　USE —Exhibitions
—**Exhibitions**
　H 1095
　　Use as a topical subdivision under subjects for
　works about exhibitions on those subjects. Also use
　under headings for types of institutions for works
　on exhibition techniques and methodology in those
　institutions.
—**Exhibitions**
　H 1095
　　Use as a form subdivision under subjects for cat-
　alogs of exhibitions on those subjects.
　　UF —Exhibit catalogs
　　　　—Exhibition catalogs
　　　　—Exhibitions—Catalogs
　　BT —Catalogs
　　NT —Bibliography—Exhibitions
——Catalogs
　USE —Exhibitions
—Exhibitions and museums
　USE —Museums
—**Exile** (*May Subd Geog*)
　H 1110
　　Use as a topical subdivision under names of in-
　dividual persons.
　　UF —Biography—Exile
　　　　[Former subdivision]
—Exile, Governments in
　USE —Governments in exile
—**Existential constructions**
　H 1154
　　Use as a topical subdivision under individual
　languages and groups of languages.
—**Expansion and contraction**
　(*May Subd Geog*)
　H 1158
　　Use as a topical subdivision under individual
　materials and types of materials.
　　UF —Contraction and expansion
　　BT —Effect of temperature on
—Expansion, Territorial
　USE —Territorial expansion
—Expenditures and appropriations
　USE —Appropriations and expenditures
—Experimental liturgy
　USE —Liturgy, Experimental
—**Experiments**
　H 1095
　　Use as a topical subdivision under scientific and
　technical topics for works on experiments and in-
　structions for carrying them out.
　　NT —Field experiments
—**Expertising** (*May Subd Geog*)
　H 1095; H 1148
　　Use as a topical subdivision under headings for
　art forms and under types of art objects, types of
　architecture, and types of buildings.
　　NT —Attribution
—**Explication**
　H 1156
　　Use as a topical subdivision under individual lit-
　eratures.
—Exploration, Aerial
　USE —Aerial exploration
—Exploration and discovery
　USE —Discovery and exploration
—Exploring expeditions
　USE —Discovery and exploration
—**Explosion,** [date]
　H 1105
　　Use as a topical subdivision under names of indi-
　vidual corporate bodies, buildings, structures, etc.
—Exposure limits, Occupational
　USE —Threshold limit values
—**Expulsion**
　H 1155
　　Use as a topical subdivision under names of in-
　dividual legislative bodies.

—**Extra-canonical parallels**
　H 1188
　　Use as a topical subdivision under uniform titles
　of sacred works.
　　UF —Parallels, Extra-canonical
—**Extrusion** (*May Subd Geog*)
　H 1158
　　Use as a topical subdivision under individual
　materials and types of materials.
—**Facilities**
　H 1155; H 1159
　　Use as a topical subdivision under names of in-
　dividual legislative bodies and military services.
——**Law and legislation**
　H 1159
　　Further subdivide by subdivisions used under
　legal topics.
　　Use as a topical subdivision under military
　services.
　　BT —Law and legislation
—Facsimile maps
　USE —Maps—Facsimiles
—**Facsimiles**
　H 1095
　　Use as a form subdivision under headings or sub-
　divisions designating types of printed or written
　materials, documents, etc.
　　UF —Copies (Facsimiles)
　　NT —Manuscripts—Facsimiles
　　　　—Maps—Facsimiles
—**Faculty**
　H 1151; H 1151.5
　　Further subdivide by subdivisions used under
　classes of persons.
　　Use as a topical subdivision under names of in-
　dividual educational institutions and types of edu-
　cational institutions.
—**Faculty housing**
　H 1151
　　Use as a topical subdivision under names of in-
　dividual educational institutions.
—Fading of color
　USE —Color—Fading
—**Fake books**
　H 1160
　　Use as a form subdivision under forms and types
　of musical compositions.
—**Family**
　H 1110
　　Use as a topical subdivision under names of in-
　dividual persons for works on the person's family
　or relations with family members as well as for ge-
　nealogical works about the person's family.
　　UF —Ancestry
　　　　—Biography—Ancestry
　　　　[Former subdivision]
　　　　—Biography—Descendants
　　　　[Former subdivision]
　　　　—Biography—Family
　　　　[Former subdivision]
　　　　—Relations with family
—Family history
　USE —Genealogy
—**Family relationships** (*May Subd Geog*)
　H 1100
　　Use as a topical subdivision under classes of per-
　sons.
—Family trees
　USE —Genealogy
—**Fatigue** (*May Subd Geog*)
　H 1149; H 1158
　　Use as a topical subdivision under individual
　chemicals and groups of chemicals and individual
　materials and types of materials.
　　NT —Corrosion fatigue
　　　　—Thermal fatigue
—Federal aid
　USE —Subsidies
—**Feed utilization efficiency**
　(*May Subd Geog*)
　H 1147
　　Use as a topical subdivision under individual an-
　imals and groups of animals.
　　UF —Efficiency of feed utilization

—**Feeding and feeds** (*May Subd Geog*)
　H 1147
　　Use as a topical subdivision under individual an-
　imals and groups of animals for works on the nutri-
　tional preparations provided for animals by humans
　as well as for works on the process of providing
　nourishment to them. For works on the nutritional
　substances that animals find on their own or pro-
　vide for themselves as well as for works on their
　food habits, use the subdivision Food.
　　UF —Feeds
———**Climatic factors** (*May Subd Geog*)
　H 1147
　　Use as a topical subdivision under individual
　animals and groups of animals.
　　BT —Climatic factors
———**Contamination** (*May Subd Geog*)
　H 1147
　　Use as a topical subdivision under individual
　animals and groups of animals.
　　UF —Contamination of feeds
———**Recipes**
　H 1147
　　Use this subdivision combination as a form
　subdivision under individual animals and groups
　of animals.
—Feeds
　USE —Feeding and feeds
—**Fees** (*May Subd Geog*)
　H 1100
　　Use as a topical subdivision under professional
　groups of persons.
—Fees for licenses
　USE —Licenses—Fees
—Fees for registration and transfer
　USE —Registration and transfer—Fees
—Fellowships
　USE —Scholarships, fellowships, etc.
—Female authors
　USE —Women authors
—Female participation
　USE —Participation, Female
—**Feminist criticism** (*May Subd Geog*)
　H 1188
　　Use as a topical subdivision under uniform titles
　of sacred works.
　　BT —Criticism, interpretation, etc.
—**Fenders**
　H 1195
　　Use as a topical subdivision under individual
　land vehicles and types of land vehicles.
—**Fertility** (*May Subd Geog*)
　H 1147
　　Use as a topical subdivision under individual an-
　imals and groups of animals.
—**Fertilization**
　H 1145.5
　　Use as a topical subdivision under names of in-
　dividual bodies of water.
—**Fertilizers** (*May Subd Geog*)
　H 1180
　　Use as a topical subdivision under individual
　plants and groups of plants.
　　UF —Fertilizers and manures
　　　　[Former subdivision]
—Fertilizers and manures
　USE —Fertilizers
—**Fetuses**
　H 1147
　　Use as a topical subdivision under individual an-
　imals and groups of animals.
——**Anatomy**
　H 1147
　　Use as a topical subdivision under individual
　animals and groups of animals.
　　BT —Anatomy
———**Physiology** (*May Subd Geog*)
　H 1147
　　Use as a topical subdivision under individual
　animals and groups of animals.
　　BT —Physiology
—**Fibrosis** (*May Subd Geog*)
　H 1164
　　Further subdivide by subdivisions used under
　diseases.
　　Use as a topical subdivision under individual or-
　gans and regions of the body.

—**Fiction**

H 1095; H 1100; H 1103; H 1105; H 1110; H 1120; H 1140

Use as a form subdivision under names of countries, cities, etc., names of individual persons, families, and corporate bodies, and under classes of persons, ethnic groups, and topical headings for collections of stories or novels on those subjects. Also use under names of individual persons and historic events for individual works of biographical or historical fiction, and under animals for individual stories about animals.

UF —Legends and stories

[Former subdivision]

—Novels

—Stories

NT —Juvenile fiction

—**Fictional works**

H 1110

Do not use under authors who write principally fiction.

Use as a topical subdivision under names of individual literary authors for works of criticism about fictional works by the author.

BT —Criticism and interpretation

—**Field experiments**

H 1180

Use as a topical subdivision under individual plants and groups of plants.

BT —Experiments

—Field guides

USE —Identification

—Field protocols

USE —Fieldwork

—**Field service**

H 1159

Use as a topical subdivision under military services.

—Field study

USE —Fieldwork

—Field work

USE —Fieldwork

—**Fieldwork**   *(May Subd Geog)*

H 1095

Use as a topical subdivision under disciplines for works on the techniques of carrying out work in the field to gain practical experience through firsthand observation and to collect data.

UF —Field protocols

—Field study

—Field work

[Former subdivision]

BT —Methodology

—**Figures of speech**

H 1154

Use as a topical subdivision under individual languages other than English and groups of languages.

—Film adaptations

USE —Film and video adaptations

—**Film and video adaptations**

(Not Subd Geog)

H 1110; H 1155.8; H 1156; H 1160

Use as a topical subdivision under names of individual persons for works about film or video adaptations of the person's creative works. Also use under individual literatures, individual literary works entered under title, and forms and types of musical compositions for works about film or video adaptations of those works.

UF —Film adaptations

[Former subdivision]

—Video adaptations

BT —Adaptations

—**Film and video adaptations**

H 1110; H 1155.8; H 1156; H 1160

Use as a form subdivision under names of individual persons for collections of film or video adaptations of their creative works. Also use under individual literatures, individual literary works entered under title, and types and forms of musical compositions for collections of film or video adaptations of those works.

UF —Film adaptations

[Former subdivision]

—Video adaptations

BT —Adaptations

—**Film catalogs**

H 1095

Use as a form subdivision under subjects for lists of films about those subjects.

BT —Catalogs

—**Films for foreign speakers**

H 1154

Use as a form subdivision under individual languages and groups of languages.

—**Films for French, [Spanish, etc.] speakers**

H 1154

Use as a form subdivision under individual languages and groups of languages.

—Films, Juvenile

USE —Juvenile films

—**Finance**

H 1095; H 1103; H 1105; H 1151; H 1151.5; H 1153; H 1159; H 1187; H 1200

This subdivision may be subdivided geographically only under wars entered under directly their own names.

Use as a topical subdivision under names of individual nongovernmental corporate bodies and under types of industries, corporate bodies, services, technical operations, etc., for works on their budgets and the raising and expenditure of funds. Use under names of individual government bodies for works limited to their management of nonappropriated funds. For works on the financial affairs of individual government agencies and institutions, use the subdivision Appropriations and expenditures.

Use as topical subdivision under ethnic groups for works on the financial affairs of the group as a whole. Also use under individual wars.

UF —Finance, commerce, confiscations, etc.

[Former subdivision]

NT —Subsidies

——**Law and legislation**   *(May Subd Geog)*

H 1103; H 1151.5; H 1153; H 1159

Further subdivide by subdivisions used under legal topics.

Do not further subdivide geographically under military services.

Use as a topical subdivision under ethnic groups, types of educational institutions, types of industries, and military services.

BT —Law and legislation

—Finance, commerce, confiscations, etc.

USE —Confiscations and contributions

—Finance

—**Finance, Personal**

H 1100; H 1103; H 1110

Use as a topical subdivision under names of individual persons, classes of persons, and ethnic groups for works about their personal financial affairs.

UF —Personal finance

—**Fingering**

H 1161

Use as a topical subdivision under individual musical instruments and families of instruments.

UF —Instruction and study—Fingering

[Former subdivision]

—Studies and exercises—Fingering

[Former subdivision]

——**Charts, diagrams, etc.**

H 1161

Use this subdivision combination as a form subdivision under individual musical instruments and families of instruments.

UF —Fingering charts

BT —Charts, diagrams, etc.

—Fingering charts

USE —Fingering—Charts, diagrams, etc.

—**Finishing**   *(May Subd Geog)*

H 1158

Use as a topical subdivision under individual materials and types of materials.

NT —Models—Finishing

——**Waste disposal**   *(May Subd Geog)*

H 1158

Use as a topical subdivision under individual materials and types of materials.

BT —Waste disposal

——**Waste minimization**   *(May Subd Geog)*

H 1158

Use as a topical subdivision under individual materials and types of materials.

BT —Waste minimization

—**Finnish influences**

H 1156

Use as a topical subdivision under individual literatures.

BT —Foreign influences

—**Fire controlmen**

H 1159

Further subdivide by subdivisions used under classes of persons.

Use as a topical subdivision under military services.

—**Fire, [date]**

H 1105

Use as a topical subdivision under names of individual corporate bodies, buildings, structures, etc.

—**Fire fighters**   *(May Subd Geog)*

H 1200

Further subdivide by subdivisions used under classes of persons.

Use as a topical subdivision under individual wars.

—Fire prevention

USE —Fires and fire prevention

—**Fire testing**   *(May Subd Geog)*

H 1158

Use as a topical subdivision under individual materials and types of materials.

BT —Testing

—**Fire use**   *(May Subd Geog)*

H 1103

Use as a topical subdivision under ethnic groups.

UF —Use of fire

—**Firearms**

H 1159

Use as a topical subdivision under military services.

——**Markings**

H 1159

Use as a topical subdivision under military services.

UF —Markings of firearms

—**Firemen**

H 1159

Further subdivide by subdivisions used under classes of persons.

Use as a topical subdivision under military services.

—**Fires and fire prevention**   *(May Subd Geog)*

H 1095; H 1153; H 1158; H 1195

Use as a topical subdivision under types of institutions, buildings, industries, materials, and vehicles.

UF —Fire prevention

BT —Prevention

—**Firing regulations**

H 1159

Use as a form subdivision under military services.

—**First editions**

H 1110; H 1156

Use as a topical subdivision under names of individual persons and individual literatures for works about first editions of their works and those literatures.

——**Bibliography**

H 1110; H 1156

Use this subdivision combination as a form subdivision under names of individual persons and individual literatures for lists of first editions of those works and those literatures.

UF —Bibliography—First editions

[Former subdivision]

BT —Bibliography

—**First performances**   *(May Subd Geog)*

H 1160

Use as a topical subdivision under forms and types of musical compositions.

BT —Performances

—**Fishing**   *(May Subd Geog)*

H 1103

Use as a topical subdivision under ethnic groups.

—**Flags**

H 1159; H 1200

Use as a topical subdivision under military services and individual wars.

—**Flammability** *(May Subd Geog)*
H 1158
Use as a topical subdivision under individual materials and types of materials.
UF —Inflammability
—**Flight** *(May Subd Geog)*
H 1147
Use as a topical subdivision under individual animals and groups of animals that can fly.
BT —Locomotion
—**Flight officers**
H 1159
Further subdivide by subdivisions used under classes of persons.
Use as a topical subdivision under military services.
—**Flight surgeons**
H 1159
Further subdivide by subdivisions used under classes of persons.
Use as a topical subdivision under military services.
BT —Surgeons
—**Flowering**
H 1180
Use as a topical subdivision under individual plants and groups of plants.
—**Flowering time**
H 1180
Use as a topical subdivision under individual plants and groups of plants.
UF —Time of flowering
—**Fluid capacities** *(May Subd Geog)*
H 1195
Use as a topical subdivision under individual land vehicles and types of land vehicles.
UF —Capacity of fluids
—**Fluid dynamics**
H 1158
Use as a topical subdivision under individual materials and types of materials.
—**Fluorescence** *(May Subd Geog)*
H 1147
Use as a topical subdivision under individual animals and groups of animals.
BT —Physiology
—**Folklore**
H 1095; H 1100; H 1103; H 1140; H 1188
Use as a topical subdivision under names of countries, cities, etc., and under classes of persons, ethnic groups, uniform titles of sacred works, and topical headings for works about those subjects as themes in folklore.
NT —Kings and rulers—Folklore
—**Folklore**
H 1095; H 1100; H 1103; H 1140; H 1188
Use as a form subdivision under names of countries, cities, etc., and under classes of persons, ethnic groups, uniform titles of sacred works, and topical headings for collections of folklore texts on those subjects.
UF —Folkloric texts
NT —Kings and rulers—Folklore
—Folkloric texts
USE —Folklore
—**Food** *(May Subd Geog)*
H 1103; H 1147
Use as a topical subdivision under ethnic groups. Also use under individual animals and groups of animals for works on substances animals find on their own or provide for themselves as well as for works on their food habits. For works on the nutritional preparations provided for animals by humans as well as for works on the process of providing nourishment to them, use the subdivision Feeding and feeds.
NT —Cannibalism
—Court and courtiers—Food
—Larvae—Food
—Food question
USE —Food supply
—**Food service** *(May Subd Geog)*
H 1095; H 1151.5; H 1155
Do not further subdivide geographically under legislative bodies.
Use as a topical subdivision under names of individual legislative bodies and under types of institutions, organized activities, etc., for works on provisions for meals and food in those enterprises.

—**Food supply** *(May Subd Geog)*
H 1200
Use as a topical subdivision under individual wars.
UF —Food question
[Former subdivision]
—**Football**
H 1151
Use as a topical subdivision under names of individual educational institutions.
BT —Sports
—**Forced repatriation**
H 1200
Use as a topical subdivision under individual wars.
UF —Repatriation, Forced
—**Forecasting**
H 1095; H 1140
Use as a topical subdivision under names of countries, cities, etc., and under topical headings.
—**Foreign authors**
H 1156
Use as a topical subdivision under individual literatures.
—Foreign auxiliaries of military police
USE —Military police—Foreign auxiliaries
—**Foreign bodies** *(May Subd Geog)*
H 1164
Further subdivide by subdivisions used under diseases.
Use as a topical subdivision under individual organs and regions of the body.
—**Foreign countries**
H 1095; H 1103; H 1154; H 1156; H 1159
Use as a geographic subdivision under ethnic groups, individual languages, individual literatures, military services, and types of publications qualified by language or nationality.
NT —Officials and employees—Foreign countries
——**History and criticism**
H 1156
Use this subdivision combination as a topical subdivision under individual literatures.
BT —History and criticism
—**Foreign economic relations**
(May Subd Geog)
H 1140
Use as a topical subdivision under names of countries, cities, etc.
BT —Foreign relations
—**Foreign elements**
H 1154
Use as a topical subdivision under individual languages and groups of languages.
——**French, [Greek, Latin, etc.]**
H 1154
Use as a topical subdivision under individual languages and groups of languages.
—**Foreign influences**
H 1095; H 1103; H 1148; H 1156
Use as a topical subdivision under ethnic groups, individual literatures, art forms, and headings for disciplines further subdivided by place for works on general outside cultural influences on those groups or topics.
UF —Influences, Foreign
NT —African influences
—American influences
—Arab influences
—Asian influences
—Australian influences
—Brazilian influences
—Celtic influences
—Chinese influences
—Civilization—Foreign influences
—Classical influences
—Czech influences
—Egyptian influences
—English influences
—European influences
—Finnish influences
—French influences
—German influences
—Greek influences
—Hebrew influences
—Hungarian influences

—Indic influences
—Iranian influences
—Irish influences
—Italian influences
—Japanese influences
—Latin American influences
—Mayan influences
—Mediterranean influences
—Mexican influences
—Mycenaean influences
—Old Norse influences
—Persian influences
—Polish influences
—Portuguese influences
—Provençal influences
—Roman influences
—Romanian influences
—Russian influences
—Sanskrit influences
—Scandinavian influences
—Scottish influences
—Slavic influences
—Slovak influences
—Soviet influences
—Spanish influences
—Turkic influences
—Ukrainian influences
—Urdu influences
—West Indian influences
—Western influences
—Yiddish influences
—Foreign language competency of officials and employees
USE —Officials and employees—Foreign countries—Foreign language competency
—Foreign language textbooks
USE —Textbooks for foreign speakers
—Foreign opinion
USE —Foreign public opinion
—**Foreign ownership**
H 1153
Use as a topical subdivision under types of industries.
BT —Ownership
—Foreign participation
USE —Participation, Foreign
—Foreign population
USE —Emigration and immigration
—**Foreign public opinion**
H 1140; H 1200
Use as a topical subdivision under names of countries, etc., and individual wars.
UF —Foreign opinion
[Former subdivision]
—**Foreign public opinion, Austrian, [British, etc.]**
H 1200
Use as a topical subdivision under names of countries, etc., and individual wars.
—**Foreign relations** *(May Subd Geog)*
H 1140; H 1187
Use as a topical subdivision under names of countries, etc., and individual Christian denominations.
UF —Relations (diplomatic)
[Former subdivision]
BT —Relations
NT —Foreign economic relations
——**Catholic Church**
H 1140
Use as a topical subdivision under names of countries, etc.

—**Foreign relations** *(Continued)*
——**Executive agreements**
> H 1140
> Use this subdivision combination as a form subdivision under names of countries, etc., for works containing texts of executive agreements on foreign relations to which the country is a party.
> Use as a topical subdivision under names of countries, etc., for works about executive agreements on foreign relations to which the country is a party.

> UF —Executive agreements on foreign relations

——**Law and legislation**
> H 1140
> Further subdivide by subdivisions used under legal topics.
> Use as a topical subdivision under names of countries, etc.

> BT —Law and legislation

——**Philosophy**
> H 1140
> Use as a topical subdivision under names of countries, etc.

> BT —Philosophy

——**Treaties**
> H 1140; H 1187
> Use this subdivision combination as a form subdivision under names of countries, etc., and individual Christian denominations for works containing texts of foreign relations treaties to which the country or denomination is a party.
> Use as a topical subdivision under names of countries, etc., and individual Christian denominations for works about foreign relations treaties to which the country or denomination is a party.

> BT —Treaties

—**Foreign relations administration**
> H 1140
> Use as a topical subdivision under names of countries, etc.

—**Foreign service** *(May Subd Geog)*
> H 1159
> Use as a topical subdivision under military services.

—Foreign trade
> USE —Commerce

—**Foreign words and phrases**
> H 1154
> Use as a topical subdivision under individual languages and groups of languages.

> NT —Gallicisms

——**Arabic, [Italian, etc.]**
> H 1154
> Use as a topical subdivision under individual languages and groups of languages.

—Forerunners
> USE —Sources

—**Forgeries** *(May Subd Geog)*
> H 1095; H 1110; H 1148
> Use as a topical subdivision under names of individual persons for works about forgeries of the person's creative works or signature. Also use under types of art objects, documents, etc.

> UF —Autographs, Spurious
> *[Former subdivision]*

—Form criticism
> USE —Criticism, Form

—**Formability**
> H 1158
> Use as a topical subdivision under individual materials and types of materials.

—Formation of words
> USE —Word formation

—**Forms**
> H 1095; H 1105; H 1154.4
> Use as a form subdivision under names of individual corporate bodies, and under topical headings for works consisting of, or containing, substantial numbers of blank forms.

> UF —Blank forms
> —Blanks (Forms)
> —Forms, blanks, etc.
> *[Former subdivision]*

—Forms, blanks, etc.
> USE —Forms

—Forms of address
> USE —Address, Forms of

—**Formulae, receipts, prescriptions**
> H 1095
> Use as a form subdivision under individual branches and systems of medicine.

> UF —Prescriptions

> NT —Medicine—Formulae, receipts, prescriptions

—Formulae, tables, etc.
> USE —Tables

—**Fracture** *(May Subd Geog)*
> H 1158
> Use as a topical subdivision under individual materials and types of materials.

—**Fractures** *(May Subd Geog)*
> H 1147; H 1164
> Further subdivide by subdivisions used under diseases.
> Use as a topical subdivision under individual animals and groups of animals and individual organs and regions of the body.

> BT —Wounds and injuries

—**Freedom of debate**
> H 1155
> Use as a topical subdivision under names of individual legislative bodies.

> UF —Debate, Freedom of

—**Freemasonry**
> H 1110
> Use as a topical subdivision under names of individual persons for works discussing the person's membership or participation in the Freemasons.

—**French influences**
> H 1156
> Use as a topical subdivision under individual literatures.

> BT —Foreign influences

—Frequency of words
> USE —Word frequency

—Frequented places
> USE —Homes and haunts

—**Freshmen**
> H 1151
> Further subdivide by subdivisions used under classes of persons.
> Use as a topical subdivision under names of individual educational institutions.

> BT —Undergraduates

—**Friends and associates**
> H 1110
> Use as a topical subdivision under names of individual persons for works on the person's close and immediate contacts, such as companions and co-workers.

> UF —Associates
> —Companions
> —Relations with friends and associates

> BT —Contemporaries

—**Front-wheel drive**
> H 1195
> Use as a topical subdivision under individual land vehicles and types of land vehicles.

—Frontier troubles
> USE —Boundaries
> —History

—Frontiers (Boundaries)
> USE —Boundaries

—**Frost damage** *(May Subd Geog)*
> H 1180
> Use as a topical subdivision under individual plants and groups of plants.

> BT —Wounds and injuries

—**Frost protection** *(May Subd Geog)*
> H 1180
> Use as a topical subdivision under individual plants and groups of plants.

> BT —Protection

—**Frost resistance** *(May Subd Geog)*
> H 1180
> Use as a topical subdivision under individual plants and groups of plants.

> UF —Resistance to frost

—**Fuel**
> H 1159
> Use as a topical subdivision under military services.

—**Fuel consumption**
> H 1195
> Use as a topical subdivision under individual land vehicles and types of land vehicles.

> UF —Consumption, Fuel

> BT —Energy consumption

——**Law and legislation** *(May Subd Geog)*
> H 1195
> Further subdivide by subdivisions used under legal topics.
> Use as a topical subdivision under individual land vehicles and types of land vehicles.

> BT —Law and legislation

—Fuel injection systems of motors
> USE —Motors—Fuel injection systems

—**Fuel supplies**
> H 1200
> Use as a topical subdivision under individual wars.

—**Fuel systems**
> H 1095; H 1195
> Use as a topical subdivision under types of equipment and vehicles.

——**Vapor lock**
> H 1195
> Use as a topical subdivision under individual land vehicles and types of land vehicles.

> UF —Vapor lock of fuel systems

—**Fume control** *(May Subd Geog)*
> H 1095; H 1153
> Use as a topical subdivision under types of industries, industrial plants, and processes.

> UF —Control of fumes

—**Fumigation** *(May Subd Geog)*
> H 1180
> Use as a topical subdivision under individual plants and groups of plants.

—**Function words**
> H 1154
> Use as a topical subdivision under individual languages and groups of languages.

—**Funds and scholarships**
> H 1151
> Use as a topical subdivision under names of individual educational institutions.

> UF —Scholarships and funds

—Funeral
> USE —Death and burial

—Funeral and memorial services
> USE —Death and burial

—**Funeral customs and rites**
> *(May Subd Geog)*
> H 1103
> Use as a topical subdivision under ethnic groups.

> UF —Mortuary customs

> BT —Rites and ceremonies

—Furloughs
> USE —Leaves and furloughs

—Furloughs of officials and employees
> USE —Officials and employees—Furloughs

—Furniture in barracks and quarters
> USE —Barracks and quarters—Furniture

—**Galician influences**
> H 1156
> Use as a topical subdivision under individual literatures.

> UF —Gallegan influences
> *[Former subdivision]*

—Gallegan influences
> USE —Galician influences

—**Gallicisms**
> H 1154
> Use as a topical subdivision under individual languages and groups of languages.

> BT —Foreign words and phrases

—**Galvanomagnetic properties**
> *(May Subd Geog)*
> H 1158
> Use as a topical subdivision under individual materials and types of materials.

—**Gambling** *(May Subd Geog)*
> H 1103
> Use as a topical subdivision under ethnic groups.

—**Games** (*May Subd Geog*)
  H 1103
    Use as a topical subdivision under ethnic groups.
  UF —Amusements
  NT —Computer games
—**Gas producers** (*May Subd Geog*)
  H 1195
    Use as a topical subdivision under individual land vehicles and types of land vehicles.
—**Gay interpretations**
  H 1188
    Use as a topical subdivision under uniform titles of sacred works.
  BT —Criticism, interpretation, etc.
—Gay participation
  USE —Participation, Gay
—**Gays** (*May Subd Geog*)
  H 1159; H 1200
    Further subdivide by subdivisions used under classes of persons.
    Further subdivide geographically only under individual wars.
    Do not use under headings of the type [Place]—Armed Forces. Use Gays in the military—[Place] instead.
    Use as a topical subdivision under individual wars for works on aspects of the war in relation to gays, especially the war's effect on them. For works on the participation of gays in the military actions of a war, use the subdivision —Participation, Gay. Also use as a topical subdivision under military services.
—**Gazetteers**
  H 1140
    Use as a form subdivision under names of countries, cities, etc.
  UF —Description and travel—Gazetteers
      [*Former subdivision*]
  BT —Dictionaries
—**Gemination**
  H 1154
    Use as a topical subdivision under individual languages and groups of languages.
—**Gender**
  H 1154
    Use as a topical subdivision under individual languages and groups of languages.
—Gender differences
  USE —Sex differences
—**Gene therapy** (*May Subd Geog*)
  H 1150
    Use as a topical subdivision under individual diseases and types of diseases.
  BT —Treatment
—Genealogies
  USE —Genealogy
—**Genealogy**
  H 1100; H 1103; H 1105; H 1140
    Use as a topical subdivision under names of countries, cities, etc., and individual corporate bodies and under classes of persons and ethnic groups for works about genealogy of persons from those places or belonging to those groups.
  UF —Family history
  NT —Kings and rulers—Genealogy
—**Genealogy**
  H 1100; H 1103; H 1105; H 1140
    Use as a form subdivision under names of countries, cities, etc., and individual corporate bodies, and under classes of persons and ethnic groups for genealogies of persons from those places or belonging to those groups.
  UF —Family trees
      —Genealogies
  NT —Kings and rulers—Genealogy
      —Pedigrees
— —**Religious aspects**
  H 1140
    Use as a topical subdivision under names of countries, cities, etc.
—**General staff officers**
  H 1159
    Further subdivide by subdivisions used under classes of persons.
    Use as a topical subdivision under military services.
  BT —Officers
—Generative grammar
  USE —Grammar, Generative

—**Generative organs**
  H 1147
    Use as a topical subdivision under individual animals and groups of animals.
—**Genetic aspects**
  H 1150
    Use as a topical subdivision under individual diseases and types of diseases.
  NT —Diseases—Genetic aspects
—**Genetic engineering** (*May Subd Geog*)
  H 1147; H 1180
    Use as a topical subdivision under individual animals and groups of animals and individual plants and groups of plants.
  BT —Biotechnology
—**Genetics**
  H 1147; H 1180
    Use as a topical subdivision under individual animals and groups of animals and individual plants and groups of plants.
  NT —Aging—Genetic aspects
      —Behavior—Genetic aspects
      —Color—Genetic aspects
      —Cytogenetics
      —Disease and pest resistance—Genetic aspects
      —Effect of air pollution on—Genetic aspects
      —Effect of fires on—Genetic aspects
      —Immunology—Genetic aspects
      —Insect resistance—Genetic aspects
      —Metabolism—Genetic aspects
      —Metamorphosis—Genetic aspects
      —Molecular genetics
      —Physiological genomics
—**Genome mapping** (*May Subd Geog*)
  H 1147; H 1180
    Use as a topical subdivision under individual animals and groups of animals and individual plants and groups of plants.
  UF —Mapping of genomes
—Genomics, Physiological
  USE —Physiological genomics
—Geographic atlases
  USE —Maps
—Geographic boundaries
  USE —Boundaries
—**Geographic information systems**
  (*May Subd Geog*)
  H 1095
    Use as a topical subdivision under subjects.
—**Geographical distribution**
  H 1147; H 1180
    Use as a topical subdivision under individual animals and groups of animals and individual plants and groups of plants.
  UF —Distribution, Geographical
  NT —Eggs—Geographical distribution
      —Home range
      —Larvae—Geographical distribution
— —**Climatic factors** (*May Subd Geog*)
  H 1147; H 1180
    Use as a topical subdivision under individual animals and groups of animals and individual plants and groups of plants.
  BT —Climatic factors
—**Geography**
  H 1140; H 1149.5; H 1188
    Use as a topical subdivision under names of countries, cities, etc., and uniform titles of sacred works.
  NT —Colonies—Geography
      —Historical geography
— —History
  USE —Historical geography
—**German Americans**
  H 1159; H 1200
    Further subdivide by subdivisions used under classes of persons.
    Use as a topical subdivision under individual military services and wars.
—**German authors**
  H 1156
    Use as a topical subdivision under individual literatures.

—**German influences**
  H 1156
    Use as a topical subdivision under individual literatures.
  BT —Foreign influences
—Germanic antiquities
  USE —Antiquities, Germanic
—**Germplasm resources** (*May Subd Geog*)
  H 1147; H 1180
    Use as a topical subdivision under individual animals and groups of animals and individual plants and groups of plants.
— — **Catalogs and collections**
  (*May Subd Geog*)
  H 1180
    Use this subdivision combination as a form subdivision under individual plants and groups of plants.
  BT —Catalogs and collections
— —**Cryopreservation** (*May Subd Geog*)
  H 1147; H 1180
    Use as a topical subdivision under individual animals and groups of animals and individual plants and groups of plants.
  BT —Cryopreservation
— —**Microbiology** (*May Subd Geog*)
  H 1147
    Use as a topical subdivision under individual animals and groups of animals.
  BT —Microbiology
—**Gerund**
  H 1154
    Use as a topical subdivision under individual languages and groups of languages.
—**Gerundive**
  H 1154
    Use as a topical subdivision under individual languages and groups of languages.
—**Gift books**
  H 1180; H 1200
    Use as a form subdivision under individual plants and groups of plants and individual wars.
  UF —Giftbooks
      [*Former subdivision*]
—Giftbooks
  USE —Gift books
—**Globalization**
  H 1154
    Use as a topical subdivision under individual languages and groups of languages.
—**Glossaries, vocabularies, etc.**
  H 1154
    Use as a form subdivision under individual languages and groups of languages.
  UF —Vocabularies, glossaries, etc.
  NT —Dialects—Glossaries, vocabularies, etc.
      —Language—Glossaries, etc.
— —**Polyglot**
  H 1154
    Use as a form subdivision under individual languages and groups of languages.
—**Gold discoveries**
  H 1140
    Use as a topical subdivision under names of countries, etc.
—**Golf**
  H 1151
    Use as a topical subdivision under names of individual educational institutions.
  BT —Sports
—**Government**
  H 1154; H 1185; H 1187
    Use as a topical subdivision under individual languages and groups of languages, and under individual religions and Christian denominations.
—Government aid
  USE —Subsidies
—Government and politics
  USE —Politics and government
—**Government jargon**
  H 1154
    Use as a topical subdivision under individual languages and groups of languages.
  BT —Jargon
—**Government ownership** (*May Subd Geog*)
  H 1153
    Use as a topical subdivision under types of industries.
  BT —Ownership

—**Government policy** (*May Subd Geog*)

H 1095; H 1100; H 1103; H 1153

Use as a topical subdivision under classes of persons, ethnic groups, and topical headings that are not inherently governmental for works describing the course of action selected by national, state, or local governments to guide decision-making and programs pertaining to the class of persons, ethnic group, or topic.

UF —Policy, Government

NT —Commercial policy

—Cultural policy

—Economic policy

—Emigration and immigration—Government policy

—Military policy

—Population policy

—Prices—Government policy

—Social policy

—**Government relations**

H 1103

Use as a topical subdivision under ethnic groups for works on relations between the group as a whole and the government of the place in which they reside.

—**Governments in exile**

H 1200

Use as a topical subdivision under individual wars.

UF —Exile, Governments in

—**Gradation**

H 1154

Use as a topical subdivision under individual languages and groups of languages.

—Graded lists

USE —Bibliography—Graded lists

—**Grading** (*May Subd Geog*)

H 1095; H 1147; H 1180

Use as a topical subdivision under individual animals and groups of animals, individual plants and groups of plants, and individual products or commodities for works on the division of commercial products into categories of uniform quality to facilitate marketing.

NT —Carcasses—Grading

—Graduate education

USE —Education (Graduate)

—**Graduate students**

H 1151

Further subdivide by subdivisions used under classes of persons.

Use as a topical subdivision under names of individual educational institutions.

BT —Students

—**Graduate work**

H 1151; H 1151.5

Use as a topical subdivision under names of individual educational institutions and types of educational institutions.

NT —Study and teaching (Graduate)

——**Examinations**

H 1151.5

Use as a topical subdivision under types of educational institutions.

BT —Examinations

—**Graduation requirements**

H 1151.5

Use as a topical subdivision under types of educational institutions.

UF —Requirements for graduation

—**Graffiti**

H 1200

Use as a topical subdivision under individual wars.

—**Grafting** (*May Subd Geog*)

H 1180

Use as a topical subdivision under individual plants and groups of plants.

—**Grammar**

H 1154

Use as a topical subdivision under individual languages and groups of languages.

NT —Case grammar

—Categorial grammar

—Dependency grammar

—Dialects—Grammar

—Grammar, Comparative

—Grammar, Generative

—Grammar, Historical

—Relational grammar

——**Terminology**

H 1154

Use this subdivision combination as a form subdivision under individual languages and groups of languages.

BT —Terminology

——**Theory, etc.**

H 1154

Use as a topical subdivision under individual languages and groups of languages.

—**Grammar, Comparative**

H 1154

Use as a topical subdivision under individual languages and groups of languages.

UF —Comparative grammar

BT —Grammar

——**French, [Latin, etc.]**

H 1154

Use as a topical subdivision under individual languages and groups of languages.

—**Grammar, Generative**

H 1154

Use as a topical subdivision under individual languages and groups of languages.

UF —Generative grammar

BT —Grammar

—**Grammar, Historical**

H 1154

Use as a topical subdivision under individual languages and groups of languages.

UF —Historical grammar

BT —Grammar

—**Grammatical categories**

H 1154

Use as a topical subdivision under individual languages and groups of languages.

UF —Categories, Grammatical

—**Grammaticalization**

H 1154

Use as a topical subdivision under individual languages and groups of languages.

—Grants, Research

USE —Research grants

—**Graphemics**

H 1154

Use as a topical subdivision under individual languages and groups of languages.

—**Graphic methods**

H 1095

Use as a topical subdivision under disciplines, types of technical processes, scientific phenomena, etc., for the technique of solving problems by means of graphs.

BT —Methodology

—Grave

USE —Tomb

—**Greek authors**

H 1156

Use as a topical subdivision under individual literatures.

—**Greek influences**

H 1156

Use as a topical subdivision under individual literatures.

BT —Foreign influences

—**Grilles**

H 1195

Use as a topical subdivision under individual land vehicles and types of land vehicles.

—**Grooming** (*May Subd Geog*)

H 1147

Use as a topical subdivision under individual animals and groups of animals for the human tending, cleaning, brushing, etc., of animals.

—**Ground support**

H 1159

Use as a topical subdivision under individual air forces. Under other military services use the subdivision Aviation—Ground support.

NT —Aviation—Ground support

—**Growing media**

H 1180

Use as a topical subdivision under individual plants and groups of plants.

—**Growth**

H 1147; H 1164; H 1180

Use as a topical subdivision under individual animals and groups of animals, individual organs and regions of the body, and individual plants and groups of plants.

——**Molecular aspects**

H 1164

Use as a topical subdivision under individual organs and regions of the body.

BT —Molecular aspects

——**Regulation**

H 1164

Use as a topical subdivision under individual organs and regions of the body.

UF —Regulation of growth

—**Guard duty**

H 1159

Use as a topical subdivision under military services.

—Guerrillas

USE —Underground movements

—Guidance, Vocational

USE —Vocational guidance

—Guide-books

USE —Guidebooks

—**Guidebooks**

H 1095; H 1105; H 1140

Use as a form subdivision under names of countries, cities, etc., individual corporate bodies and parks, etc., and under topical headings.

UF —Description and travel—Guide-books

[*Former subdivision*]

—Description and travel—Guidebooks

—Guide-books

[*Former subdivision*]

NT —Tours

—**Guided missile personnel**

H 1159

Further subdivide by subdivisions used under classes of persons.

Use as a topical subdivision under military services.

——**Training of** (*May Subd Geog*)

H 1159

Use as a topical subdivision under military services.

BT —Training of

———**Aids and devices**

H 1159

Use as a topical subdivision under military services.

—Guides, Stage

USE —Stage guides

—**Gunners**

H 1159

Further subdivide by subdivisions used under classes of persons.

Use as a topical subdivision under military services.

—**Gymnastics**

H 1151

Use as a topical subdivision under names of individual educational institutions.

BT —Sports

—**Habitat** (*May Subd Geog*)

H 1147; H 1180

Use as a topical subdivision under individual animals and groups of animals and individual plants and groups of plants.

——**Conservation** (*May Subd Geog*)

H 1147

Use as a topical subdivision under individual animals and groups of animals.

BT —Conservation

—**Habitat suitability index models**
  (*May Subd Geog*)
    H 1147
      Use as a topical subdivision under individual animals and groups of animals.
—**Habitations** (*May Subd Geog*)
    H 1147
      Use as a topical subdivision under individual animals and groups of animals for works on the natural shelters and homes that animals build for themselves, such as burrows, dens, lairs, lodges. For works on the shelters and structures that humans construct and provide for wild or domestic animals use the subdivision Housing.
    NT —Nests
—Habits and behavior
    USE —Behavior
—**Hadith**
    H 1110
      Use as a topical subdivision under names of individual imams for works on the oral tradition concerning the deeds and sayings of the imam.
—Half-life of isotopes
    USE —Isotopes—Half-life
—**Handbooks, manuals, etc.**
    H 1095; H 1100; H 1105; H 1140; H 1188
      Use under classes of persons only if a heading for the corresponding field or activity does not exist.
      Use as a form subdivision under subjects for concise reference works in which facts and information pertaining to the subject are arranged for ready reference and consultation rather than for continuous reading and study.
    UF —Manuals
        —Vade-mecums
    NT —Amateurs' manuals
        —Authorship—Style manuals
        —Dissertations—Style manuals
        —Drill and tactics—Handbooks, manuals, etc.
        —Laboratory manuals
        —Life skills guides
        —Non-commissioned officers' handbooks
        —Observers' manuals
        —Officers' handbooks
        —Petty officers' handbooks
        —Sailors' handbooks
—**Handling** (*May Subd Geog*)
    H 1147; H 1180
      Use as a topical subdivision under individual animals and groups of animals and individual plants and groups of plants.
    NT —Carcasses—Handling
        —Manure—Handling
        —Seeds—Handling
—**Handling characteristics** (*May Subd Geog*)
    H 1195
      Use as a topical subdivision under individual land vehicles and types of land vehicles.
—Handwriting
    USE —Autographs
—**Haplology**
    H 1154
      Use as a topical subdivision under individual languages and groups of languages.
—**Hardenability** (*May Subd Geog*)
    H 1158
      Use as a topical subdivision under individual materials and types of materials.
—**Hardiness** (*May Subd Geog*)
    H 1180
      Use as a topical subdivision under individual plants and groups of plants.
—**Harmonics**
    H 1161
      Use as a topical subdivision under individual musical instruments and families of instruments.
—**Harmonies** (*Not Subd Geog*)
    H 1188
      Use as a topical subdivision under uniform titles of sacred works for works about parallel texts or passages from those works.
—**Harmonies** (*Not Subd Geog*)
    H 1188
      Use as a form subdivision under uniform titles of sacred works for parallel texts or passages from those works.

——**History and criticism**
    H 1188
      Use as a topical subdivision under uniform titles of sacred works.
    BT —History and criticism
—**Harmonies, English,** [**French, German, etc.**]
    H 1188
      Use as a topical subdivision under uniform titles of sacred works for works about parallel texts or passages from those works in that language.
—**Harmonies, English,** [**French, German, etc.**]
    H 1188
      Use as a form subdivision under uniform titles of sacred works for parallel texts or passages from those works in that language.
——**History and criticism** (*Not Subd Geog*)
    H 1188
      Use as a topical subdivision under uniform titles of sacred works.
    BT —History and criticism
—**Harmony**
    H 1110
      Use as a topical subdivision under names of individual composers for works on their uses of harmony.
—**Harvesting** (*May Subd Geog*)
    H 1180
      Use as a topical subdivision under individual plants and groups of plants.
    NT —Husking
        —Seeds—Harvesting
——**Machinery** (*May Subd Geog*)
    H 1180
      Use as a topical subdivision under individual plants and groups of plants.
    BT —Machinery
—**Harvesting time** (*May Subd Geog*)
    H 1180
      Use as a topical subdivision under individual plants and groups of plants.
    UF —Time of harvesting
—Haunts
    USE —Homes and haunts
—**Headquarters**
    H 1159
      Use as a topical subdivision under military services.
—**Health** (*May Subd Geog*)
    H 1110; H 1120; H 1147; H 1180
      Do not subdivide geographically under names of individual persons and families.
      Use as a topical subdivision under names of individual persons and families for works on the person's or family members' state of health, including diseases suffered and accounts of specific diseases. Also use under individual animals and groups of animals and individual plants and groups of plants.
    UF —Biography—Health
          [*Former subdivision*]
    NT —Mental health
—**Health and hygiene** (*May Subd Geog*)
    H 1100; H 1103
      Use as a topical subdivision under classes of persons and ethnic groups.
    UF —Diseases and hygiene
          [*Former subdivision*]
        —Hygiene
—**Health aspects** (*May Subd Geog*)
    H 1095; H 1153; H 1200
      Use as a topical subdivision under topical headings.
    UF —Hygenic aspects
          [*Former subdivision*]
        —Medical and sanitary affairs
          [*Former subdivision*]
—**Health promotion services**
  (*May Subd Geog*)
    H 1151.5
      Use as a topical subdivision under types of educational institutions.
—**Health risk assessment** (*May Subd Geog*)
    H 1100
      Use as a topical subdivision under classes of persons.
    BT —Risk factors
—**Heat treatment** (*May Subd Geog*)
    H 1158
      Use as a topical subdivision under individual materials and types of materials.
    NT —Thermomechanical treatment

—**Heating** (*May Subd Geog*)
    H 1158
      Use as a topical subdivision under individual materials and types of materials.
—**Heating and ventilation** (*May Subd Geog*)
    H 1095; H 1195
      Use as a topical subdivision under types of buildings, vehicles, and other construction.
    UF —Ventilation
    NT —Housing—Heating and ventilation
——**Control** (*May Subd Geog*)
    H 1095
      Use as a topical subdivision under types of buildings, vehicles, and other construction.
    UF —Control of heating and ventilation
—**Hebrew influences**
    H 1156
      Use as a topical subdivision under individual literatures.
    BT —Foreign influences
—**Heirloom varieties** (*May Subd Geog*)
    H 1180
      Use as a topical subdivision under individual plants and groups of plants.
    BT —Varieties
—**Helium content** (*May Subd Geog*)
    H 1158
      Use as a topical subdivision under individual materials and types of materials.
—**Hemorrhage** (*May Subd Geog*)
    H 1164
      Further subdivide by subdivisions used under diseases.
      Use as a topical subdivision under individual organs and regions of the body.
    BT —Diseases
        —Wounds and injuries
—**Heraldry**
    H 1095; H 1105
      Use as a topical subdivision under names of individual corporate bodies, types of industries, and topical headings for works on the devising, granting, and use of armorial insignia pertaining to those subjects.
    NT —Kings and rulers—Heraldry
—**Herbarium**
    H 1105; H 1110; H 1120
      Use as a topical subdivision under names of individual persons and families. Also use under names of individual corporate bodies that have herbariums for which no corporate heading exists or can be established.
—**Herbicide injuries** (*May Subd Geog*)
    H 1180
      Use as a topical subdivision under individual plants and groups of plants.
    BT —Wounds and injuries
—Herd-books
    USE —Pedigrees
—**Hermeneutics**
    H 1188
      Use as a topical subdivision under uniform titles of sacred works.
    NT —Sacred books—Hermeneutics
—**Heteronyms**
    H 1154
      Use as a topical subdivision under individual languages and groups of languages.
—**Hiatus**
    H 1154
      Use as a topical subdivision under individual languages and groups of languages.
—**Hibernation** (*May Subd Geog*)
    H 1147
      Use as a topical subdivision under individual animals and groups of animals.
—Higher education
    USE —Education (Higher)
—**Hindu authors**
    H 1156
      Use as a topical subdivision under individual literatures.
—**Hindu interpretations**
    H 1188
      Use as a topical subdivision under uniform titles of sacred works.
    BT —Criticism, interpretation, etc.

—**Hispanic Americans**
> H 1159
> Further subdivide by subdivisions used under classes of persons.
> Use as a topical subdivision under military services.

—**Histochemistry**
> H 1164; H 1180
> Use as a topical subdivision under individual organs and regions of the body and individual plants and groups of plants.
> BT —Histology

—**Histology**
> H 1147; H 1164
> Use as a topical subdivision under individual animals and groups of animals and individual organs and regions of the body.
> NT —Histochemistry
>   —Histopathology

—**Histopathology**
> 1164; H 1147; H 1150
> Use as a topical subdivision under individual animals and groups of animals, individual diseases and types of diseases, and organs and regions of the body.
> BT —Histology

—**Historical geography**
> H 1140
> Use as a topical subdivision under names of countries, cities, etc.
> UF —Geography—History
> BT —Geography
>   —History

——**Maps**
> H 1140
> Use this subdivision combination as a form subdivision under names of countries, cities, etc.
> BT —Maps

—Historical grammar
> USE —Grammar, Historical

—Historical lexicology
> USE —Lexicology, Historical

—Historical phonology
> USE —Phonology, Historical

—Historical semantics
> USE —Semantics, Historical

—**Historiography**
> H 1095; H 1100; H 1103; H 1105; H 1140; H 1188; H 1200
> Use as a topical subdivision under names of countries, cities, etc., and individual corporate bodies, uniform titles of sacred works and treaties, and under classes of persons, ethnic groups, individual wars, and topical headings.
> UF —History—Authorship
>   —History—Historiography
>   *[Former subdivision]*
> BT —Authorship
> NT —History—[period subdivision]—Historiography

—**History**
> H 1095; H 1100; H 1103; H 1105; H 1140; H 1149.5; H 1154; H 1159; H 1187; H 1188
> Use as a topical subdivision under names of countries, cities, etc., and individual corporate bodies, uniform titles of sacred works, and under classes of persons, ethnic groups, and topical headings.
> UF —Frontier troubles
>   *[Former subdivision]*
> NT —Church history
>   —Colonies—History
>   —Criticism and interpretation—History
>   —Criticism, interpretation, etc.—History
>   —Diplomatic history
>   —Doctrines—History
>   —Historical geography
>   —History, Local
>   —History, Military
>   —History, Naval
>   —History of Biblical events
>   —History of contemporary events
>   —History of doctrines

——**To 1500**
> H 1095
> Use as a topical subdivision under topical headings.

——**Modern period, 1500-**
> H 1187
> Use as a topical subdivision under individual Christian denominations.

——**16th century**
> H 1095; H 1100; H 1103; H 1105; H 1140; H 1159; H 1187
> Use as a topical subdivision under names of countries, cities, etc., and individual corporate bodies, and under classes of persons, ethnic groups, military services, Christian denominations, and topical headings.

——**17th century**
> H 1095; H 1100; H 1103; H 1105; H 1140; H 1159; H 1187
> Use as a topical subdivision under names of countries, cities, etc., and individual corporate bodies, and under classes of persons, ethnic groups, military services, Christian denominations and topical headings.

——**18th century**
> H 1095; H 1100; H 1103; H 1105; H 1140; H 1159; H 1187
> Use as a topical subdivision under names of countries, cities, etc., and individual corporate bodies, and under classes of persons, ethnic groups, military services, Christian denominations, and topical headings.

——**Revolution, 1775-1783, [War of 1812, etc.]** *(Not Subd Geog)*
> H 1159
> Use as a topical subdivision under military services.

——**19th century**
> H 1095; H 1100; H 1103; H 1105; H 1140; H 1159; H 1187
> Use as a topical subdivision under names of countries, cities, etc., and corporate bodies, and under classes of persons, ethnic groups, military services, Christian denominations, and topical headings.

——**20th century**
> H 1095; H 1100; H 1103; H 1105; H 1140; H 1159; H 1187
> Use as a topical subdivision under names of countries, cities, etc., and individual corporate bodies, and under classes of persons, ethnic groups, military services, Christian denominations, and topical headings.

——**1965-**
> H 1187
> Use as a topical subdivision under individual Christian denominations.

——**21st century**
> H 1095; H 1100; H 1103; H 1105; H 1140; H 1159; H 1187
> Use as a topical subdivision under names of countries, cities, etc., and individual corporate bodies, and under classes of persons, ethnic groups, military services, Christian denominations, and topical headings.

——[period subdivision]
——**Biography**
> H 1140
> Use this subdivision combination as a form subdivision under names of countries, cities, etc.
> BT —Biography

——**Anecdotes**
> H 1140
> Use this subdivision combination as a form subdivision under names of countries, cities, etc.
> BT —Anecdotes

——**Portraits**
> H 1140
> Use this subdivision combination as a form subdivision under names of countries, cities, etc.
> BT —Portraits

——**Sources**
> H 1140
> Use as a topical subdivision under names of countries, cities, etc., for works about biographical source materials pertaining to persons from those places during a specific time period.
> Use this subdivision combination as a form subdivision under names of countries, cities, etc., for collections of biographical source materials pertaining to persons from those places during a specific time period.
> BT —Sources

——**Chronology**
> H 1140
> Use this subdivision combination as a form subdivision under names of countries, cities, etc.
> BT —Chronology

——**Historiography**
> H 1140
> Use as a topical subdivision under names of countries, cities, etc.
> BT —Historiography

——**Philosophy**
> H 1140
> Use as a topical subdivision under names of countries, cities, etc.
> BT —Philosophy

——**Sources** *(Not Subd Geog)*
> H 1140
> Use this subdivision combination as a form subdivision under names of countries, cities, etc. for collections of source materials pertaining to the history of those places during a specific time period.
> Use as a topical subdivision under names of countries, cities, etc., for works about source materials pertaining to the history of those places during a specific time period.
> BT —Sources

——**Anecdotes**
> H 1140
> Use this subdivision combination as a form subdivision under names of countries, cities, etc.
> UF —History—Anecdotes, facetiae, satire, etc.
>   *[Former subdivision]*
>   —History, Comic, satirical, etc.
>   *[Former subdivision]*
> BT —Anecdotes

——Anecdotes, facetiae, satire, etc.
> USE —History—Anecdotes
>   —History—Humor

——Anniversaries, etc.
> USE —Anniversaries, etc.

——Authorship
> USE —Historiography

——**Autonomy and independence movements** *(Not Subd Geog)*
> H 1140
> Use as a topical subdivision under names of countries, etc.
> UF —Autonomy and independence movements

——**Chronology**
> H 1095; H 1103; H 1105; H 1140; H 1159
> Use this subdivision combination as a form subdivision under names of countries, cities, etc., and individual corporate bodies, and under ethnic groups, military services, and topical headings that are not inherently historical.
> BT —Chronology

——**Comic books, strips, etc.**
> H 1140
> Use this subdivision combination as a form subdivision under names of countries, cities, etc.
> UF —History, Comic, satirical, etc.
>   *[Former subdivision]*
> BT —Comic books, strips, etc.

——**Errors, inventions, etc.**
> H 1140
> Use as a topical subdivision under names of countries, cities, etc.
> UF —Errors, inventions, etc., of history

——Historiography
> USE —Historiography

—**—Humor**
    H 1140
      Use this subdivision combination as a form subdivision under names of countries, cities, etc.
    UF —History—Anecdotes, facetiae, satire, etc.
        [Former subdivision]
        —History, Comic, satirical, etc.
        [Former subdivision]
    BT —Humor
—**—Periodization**
    H 1140
      Use as a topical subdivision under names of countries, etc.
    UF —Periodization of history
—**—Philosophy**
    H 1095; H 1140
      Use as a topical subdivision under names of countries, cities, etc., and under topical headings.
    BT —Philosophy
—**—Pictorial works**
    H 1140
      Use this subdivision combination as a form subdivision under names of countries, cities, etc.
    BT —Pictorial works
—**—Prophecies**
    H 1140
      Use as a topical subdivision under names of countries, cities, etc.
    BT —Prophecies
—**—Religious aspects** (Not Subd Geog)
    H 1140
      Use as a topical subdivision under names of countries, cities, etc.
—**——Baptists, [Catholic Church, etc.]**
    H 1140
      Use as a topical subdivision under names of countries, cities, etc.
—**——Buddhism, [Christianity, etc.]**
    (Not Subd Geog)
    H 1140
      Use as a topical subdivision under names of countries, cities, etc.
—**—Sources** (Not Subd Geog)
    H 1095; H 1100; H 1103; H 1105; H 1140
      Use this subdivision combination as a form subdivision under names of countries, cities, etc., and individual corporate bodies, and under classes of persons, ethnic groups, and topical headings not inherently historical for collections of materials of all types, such as legal documents, letters, diaries, family papers, visual and moving image materials, assembled at a later time to serve as source materials for use by students, scholars, etc., in their research on the subject.
      Use as a topical subdivision under names of countries, cities, etc., and individual corporate bodies, and under classes of persons, ethnic groups, and topical headings not inherently historical for works about materials of all types, such as legal documents, letters, diaries, family papers, visual and moving image materials, available as source materials for use by students, scholars, etc., in their research on the subject.
    BT —Sources
—**History and criticism**
    H 1095; H 1156; H 1160
      Use as a topical subdivision under literary, music, film, television program, and video recording form headings.
    UF —Criticism and history
    NT —Apologetic works—History and criticism
        —Biography—History and criticism
        —Catechisms—History and criticism
        —Commentaries—History and criticism
        —Controversial literature—History and criticism
        —Creeds—History and criticism
        —Criticism, Textual
        —Foreign countries—History and criticism
        —Harmonies—History and criticism

        —Harmonies, English, [French, German, etc.]—History and criticism
        —Hymns—History and criticism
        —Liturgy—Texts—History and criticism
        —Music—History and criticism
        —Musical settings—History and criticism
        —Paraphrases—History and criticism
        —Paraphrases, English, [French, German, etc.]—History and criticism
        —Prayers—History and criticism
        —Prayers and devotions—History and criticism
        —Rituals—Texts—History and criticism
        —Sermons—History and criticism
        —Songs and music—History and criticism
        —Translations—History and criticism
        —Translations into French, [German, etc.]—History and criticism
—**—Theory, etc.**
    H 1156
      Use as a topical subdivision under individual literatures.
—History, Comic, satirical, etc.
    USE —History—Anecdotes
        —History—Comic books, strips, etc.
        —History—Humor
—**History, Local**
    H 1140
      Use as a topical subdivision under names of countries, etc., for the collective histories of several local units. For the history of a single locality, use the subdivision —History under the name of the locality.
    UF —Local history
    BT —History
—**—Collectibles**
    H 1140
      Use as a topical subdivision under names of countries, etc.
    BT —Collectibles
—**History, Military**
    H 1140
      Use as a topical subdivision under names of countries, cities, etc.
    UF —Military history
    BT —History
—**—16th century**
    H 1140
      Use as a topical subdivision under names of countries, cities, etc.
—**—17th century**
    H 1140
      Use as a topical subdivision under names of countries, cities, etc.
—**—18th century**
    H 1140
      Use as a topical subdivision under names of countries, cities, etc.
—**—19th century**
    H 1140
      Use as a topical subdivision under names of countries, cities, etc.
—**—20th century**
    H 1140
      Use as a topical subdivision under names of countries, cities, etc.
—**—21st century**
    H 1140
      Use as a topical subdivision under names of countries, cities, etc.
—**—Religious aspects**
    H 1140
      Use as a topical subdivision under names of countries, cities, etc.
—**History, Naval**
    H 1140
      Use as a topical subdivision under names of countries, cities, etc.
    UF —Naval history
    BT —History

—**—16th century**
    H 1140
      Use this subdivision under names of countries, cities, etc.
—**—17th century**
    H 1140
      Use as a topical subdivision under names of countries, cities, etc.
—**—18th century**
    H 1140
      Use as a topical subdivision under names of countries, cities, etc.
—**—19th century**
    H 1140
      Use as a topical subdivision under names of countries, cities, etc.
—**—20th century**
    H 1140
      Use as a topical subdivision under names of countries, cities, etc.
—**—21st century**
    H 1140
      Use as a topical subdivision under names of countries, cities, etc.
—**History of Biblical events**
    H 1188
      Use as a topical subdivision under uniform titles of sacred works.
    BT —History
—**—Art** (Not Subd Geog)
    H 1188
      Use this subdivision combination as a form subdivision under uniform titles of sacred works for art depicting events in the work.
      Use as a topical subdivision under uniform titles of sacred works for works about art depicting events in the work.
    BT —Art
—**History of contemporary events**
    H 1188
      Use as a topical subdivision under uniform titles of sacred works.
    BT —History
—**History of doctrines**
    H 1095
      Use as a topical subdivision under religious topics.
    BT —History
—**—Early church, ca. 30-600**
    H 1095
      Use as a topical subdivision under religious topics.
—**—Middle Ages, 600-1500**
    H 1095
      Use as a topical subdivision under religious topics.
—**—16th century**
    H 1095
      Use as a topical subdivision under religious topics.
—**—17th century**
    H 1095
      Use as a topical subdivision under religious topics.
—**—18th century**
    H 1095
      Use as a topical subdivision under religious topics.
—**—19th century**
    H 1095
      Use as a topical subdivision under religious topics.
—**—20th century**
    H 1095
      Use as a topical subdivision under religious topics.
—**—21st century**
    H 1095
      Use as a topical subdivision under religious topics.
—**Hockey** (Not Subd Geog)
    H 1151
      Use as a topical subdivision under names of individual educational institutions.
    BT —Sports
—**Home care** (May Subd Geog)
    H 1100; H 1103
      Use as a topical subdivision under classes of persons and ethnic groups.
    BT —Care

—**Home range** (*May Subd Geog*)
> H 1147
> Use as a topical subdivision under individual animals and groups of animals.
>> BT   —Geographical distribution

—**Homeopathic treatment** (*May Subd Geog*)
> H 1150
> Use as a topical subdivision under individual diseases and types of diseases.
>> BT   —Treatment
>> NT   —Diseases—Homeopathic treatment

—Homes
>> USE   —Homes and haunts

—**Homes and haunts** (*May Subd Geog*)
> H 1100; H 1103; H 1105; H 1110; H 1120
> Use as a topical subdivision under names of individual persons, families, and performing groups, classes of persons, and ethnic groups for works on the homes of individual persons, families, or members of the group from an architectural or historical point of view. Also use for works about the favorite places of individual persons or group members or places they habitually frequent or with which they are associated. For works on residential buildings for the group from the standpoint of architecture, construction, ethnology, etc., use the subdivision Dwellings. For works on social or economic aspects of the provision of housing for the group, use the subdivision Housing.
>> UF   —Frequented places
>>   —Haunts
>>   —Homes
>>   *[Former subdivision]*
>>   —Places frequented
>>   —Residences
>> NT   —Birthplace
>>   —Palaces

—**Homiletical use**
> H 1188
> Use as a topical subdivision under uniform titles of sacred works.

—**Homing** (*May Subd Geog*)
> H 1147
> Use as a topical subdivision under individual animals and groups of animals.

—**Homonyms**
> H 1154
> Use as a topical subdivision under individual languages and groups of languages.

—**Honor system**
> H 1151
> Use as a topical subdivision under names of individual educational institutions.

—Honorary officials and employees
>> USE   —Officials and employees, Honorary

—**Honorific**
> H 1154
> Use as a topical subdivision under individual languages and groups of languages.

—**Honorific unit titles**
> H 1159
> Use as a topical subdivision under military services.

—**Honors courses** (*May Subd Geog*)
> H 1151.1
> Use as a topical subdivision under types of educational institutions.
>> BT   —Curricula

—Hormonal aspect of migration
>> USE   —Migration—Endocrine aspects

—Hormonal aspects
>> USE   —Endocrine aspects

—Hormonal aspects of behavior
>> USE   —Behavior—Endocrine aspects

—**Hormone therapy** (*May Subd Geog*)
> H 1150
> Use as a topical subdivision under individual diseases and types of diseases.
>> BT   —Endocrine aspects
>>   —Treatment

——**Complications** (*May Subd Geog*)
> H 1150
> Further subdivide by subdivisions used under diseases.
> Use as a topical subdivision under individual diseases and types of diseases.
>> BT   —Complications

—**Horns**
> H 1195
> Use as a topical subdivision under individual land vehicles and types of land vehicles.

—**Hospice care** (*May Subd Geog*)
> H 1100; H 1103
> Use as a topical subdivision under classes of persons and ethnic groups.
>> BT   —Care

—**Hospital care** (*May Subd Geog*)
> H 1100; H 1103
> Use as a topical subdivision under classes of persons and ethnic groups.
>> BT   —Institutional care
>>   —Medical care

—**Hospital ships**
> H 1159
> Use as a topical subdivision under military services.
>> BT   —Hospitals

—**Hospitals** (*May Subd Geog*)
> H 1100; H 1103; H 1150; H 1200
> Do not use under headings for persons with specific diseases. Use [disease]—Hospitals instead.
> Use as a topical subdivision under classes of persons, ethnic groups, individual diseases and types of diseases, and wars.
>> UF   —Hospitals and sanitoriums
>>   *[Former subdivision]*
>>   —Hospitals, charities, etc.
>>   *[Former subdivision]*
>>   —Medical and sanitary affairs
>>   *[Former subdivision]*
>> NT   —Hospital ships

—Hospitals and sanitoriums
>> USE   —Hospitals

—Hospitals, charities, etc.
>> USE   —Civilian relief
>>   —Hospitals
>>   —War work

—**Host plants** (*May Subd Geog*)
> H 1147
> Use as a topical subdivision under individual animals and groups of animals.

—**Hostages** (*May Subd Geog*)
> H 1200
> Further subdivide by subdivisions used under classes of persons.
> Use as a topical subdivision under individual wars.

—**Hot weather conditions** (*May Subd Geog*)
> H 1095
> Use as a topical subdivision under topical headings for works on procedures to be followed during hot weather conditions.

—**Hot working** (*May Subd Geog*)
> H 1158
> Use as a topical subdivision under individual materials and types of materials.

—**Housing** (*May Subd Geog*)
> H 1100; H 1103; H 1147
> Use as a topical subdivision under classes of persons and ethnic groups for works on social or economic aspects of the provision of housing for the group. For works on residential buildings for the group from the standpoint of architecture, construction, ethnology, etc., use the subdivision Dwellings. For works on the homes of individual members of the group from an architectural or historical point of view, use the subdivision Homes and haunts.
> Also use under individual animals and groups of animals for works on the shelters and structures that humans construct and provide for wild or domestic animals. For works on the natural shelters and homes that animals build for themselves, such as burrows, dens, lairs, lodges, use the subdivision Habitations.
>> NT   —Student housing

——**Air conditioning** (*May Subd Geog*)
> H 1147
> Use as a topical subdivision under individual animals and groups of animals.
>> BT   —Air conditioning

——Contracts and specifications
>> USE   —Housing—Specifications

——**Decoration** (*May Subd Geog*)
> H 1147
> Use as a topical subdivision under individual animals and groups of animals.
>> BT   —Decoration

——**Design and construction**
> H 1147
> Use as a topical subdivision under individual animals and groups of animals.
>> BT   —Design and construction

——**Disinfection** (*May Subd Geog*)
> H 1147
> Use as a topical subdivision under individual animals and groups of animals.
>> UF   —Disinfection of animal housing

——**Environmental engineering**
> (*May Subd Geog*)
> H 1147
> Use as a topical subdivision under individual animals and groups of animals.
>> UF   —Environmental engineering of animal housing

——**Heating and ventilation**
> (*May Subd Geog*)
> H 1147
> Use as a topical subdivision under individual animals and groups of animals.
>> UF   —Housing—Ventilation
>> BT   —Heating and ventilation

——**Insulation** (*May Subd Geog*)
> H 1147
> Use as a topical subdivision under individual animals and groups of animals.
>> UF   —Insulation of animal housing

——**Lighting** (*May Subd Geog*)
> H 1147
> Use as a topical subdivision under individual animals and groups of animals.
>> BT   —Lighting

——**Odor control** (*May Subd Geog*)
> H 1147
> Use as a topical subdivision under individual animals and groups of   animals.
>> UF   —Odor control of animal housing

——**Safety measures**
> H 1147
> Use as a topical subdivision under individual animals and groups of animals.
>> BT   —Safety measures

——**Sanitation** (*May Subd Geog*)
> H 1147
> Use as a topical subdivision under individual animals and groups of animals.
>> BT   —Sanitation

——**Specifications** (*May Subd Geog*)
> H 1147
> Use this subdivision combination as a form subdivision under individual animals and groups of animals.
>> UF   —Housing—Contracts and specifications
>>   *[Former subdivision]*
>> BT   —Specifications

——Ventilation
>> USE   —Housing—Heating and ventilation

——**Waste disposal** (*May Subd Geog*)
> H 1147
> Use as a topical subdivision under individual animals and groups of animals.
>> BT   —Waste disposal

—**Humor**
> H 1095; H 1100; H 1103; H 1105; H 1110; H 1140; H 1188
> Use as a topical subdivision under names of countries, cities, etc., and individual corporate bodies, and under uniform titles of sacred works and topical headings for works about humor on those subjects. Also use under names of individual persons for works about the person's sense of humor or use of humor.
>> UF   —Anecdotes, facetiae, satire, etc.
>>   *[Former subdivision]*
>>   —Cartoons, satire, etc.
>>   *[Former subdivision]*
>>   —Humor, satire, etc.

—**Humor**
>
> H 1095; H 1100; H 1103; H 1105; H 1110; H 1140; H 1188
>> Use as a form subdivision under names of countries, cities, etc., names of individual persons and corporate bodies, uniform titles of sacred works, and under topical headings for humorous works about those subjects.
>
> UF —Anecdotes, facetiae, satire, etc.
>> *[Former subdivision]*
>> —Cartoons, satire, etc.
>> *[Former subdivision]*
>> —Humor, satire, etc.
>> *[Former subdivision]*
>> —Jokes
>> —Satire
>
> NT —Biography—Humor
>> —Caricatures and cartoons
>> —History—Humor
>> —Juvenile humor

—Humor, satire, etc.
> USE —Humor

—**Hungarian influences**
>
> H 1156
>> Use as a topical subdivision under individual literatures.
>
> BT —Foreign influences

—**Hunting** *(May Subd Geog)*
>
> H 1103
>> Use as a topical subdivision under ethnic groups.

—**Hurricane effects** *(May Subd Geog)*
>
> H 1095
>> Use as a topical subdivision under types of buildings, structures, facilities, and equipment.
>
> UF —Effect of hurricanes on

—**Husking** *(May Subd Geog)*
>
> H 1180
>> Use as a topical subdivision under individual plants and groups of plants.
>
> BT —Harvesting

—Hussite versions
> USE —Versions, Hussite

—**Hybridization** *(May Subd Geog)*
>
> H 1147; H 1180
>> Use as a topical subdivision under individual animals and groups of animals and individual plants and groups of plants.
>
> BT —Breeding

—**Hydatids** *(May Subd Geog)*
>
> H 1164
>> Further subdivide by subdivisions used under diseases.
>> Use as a topical subdivision under individual organs and regions of the body.
>
> BT —Cysts

—**Hydraulic equipment**
>
> H 1195
>> Use as a topical subdivision under individual land vehicles and types of land vehicles.
>
> BT —Equipment and supplies

—**Hydrogen content** *(May Subd Geog)*
>
> H 1158
>> Use as a topical subdivision under individual materials and types of materials.

—**Hydrogen embrittlement**
>
> H 1158
>> Use as a topical subdivision under individual materials and types of materials.
>
> BT —Embrittlement

—Hygenic aspects
> USE —Health aspects

—Hygiene
> USE —Care and hygiene
>> —Health and hygiene

—**Hymns**
>
> H 1187
>> Use as a topical subdivision under individual Christian denominations for works about hymns of those denominations.

—**Hymns**
>
> H 1187
>> Use as a form subdivision under individual Christian denominations for hymns of those denominations.

——**History and criticism**
>
> H 1187
>> Use as a topical subdivision under individual Christian denominations.
>
> BT —History and criticism

——**Texts**
>
> H 1187
>> Use as a form subdivision under individual Christian denominations for texts of hymns of those denominations.
>
> BT —Texts

—**Hypertrophy** *(May Subd Geog)*
>
> H 1164
>> Further subdivide by subdivisions used under diseases.
>> Use as a topical subdivision under individual organs and regions of the body.
>
> UF —Enlargement
> BT —Diseases
>> —Size

—**Ice breaking operations**
>
> H 1159
>> Use as a topical subdivision under military services.

—Iconography
> USE —Pictorial works

—**Identification**
>
> H 1095; H 1100
>> Use as a topical subdivision under classes of persons and topical headings for works on the process or methods of identifying or characterizing those persons or topics.

—**Identification**
>
> H 1147; H 1180
>> Use as a form subdivision under individual animals and groups of animals, individual plants and groups of plants, and types of objects for works presenting the characteristics of a group for the purpose of determining the names of its members.
>
> UF —Field guides
>> —Identification guides
>> —Keys (Identification guides)
>
> NT —Diseases and pests—Identification
>> —Parasites—Identification
>> —Seeds—Identification

—Identification guides
> USE —Identification

—Identification, Photographic
> USE —Photographic identification

—Identity, Ethnic
> USE —Ethnic identity

—Identity, Race
> USE —Race identity

—Identity, Racial
> USE —Race identity

—**Ideophone** *(Not Subd Geog)*
>
> H 1154
>> Use as a topical subdivision under individual languages and groups of languages.

—**Idioms**
>
> H 1154
>> Use as a topical subdivision under individual languages and groups of languages.
>
> UF —Idioms, corrections, errors
>> *[Former subdivision]*

—Idioms, corrections, errors
> USE —Errors of usage
>> —Idioms
>> —Usage

—**Ignition**
>
> H 1195
>> Use as a topical subdivision under individual land vehicles and types of land vehicles.

——**Electronic systems**
>
> H 1195
>> Use as a topical subdivision under individual land vehicles and types of land vehicles.
>
> BT —Electronic equipment

—**Illustrations**
>
> H 1095; H 1110; H 1155.6; H 1155.8; H 1156; H 1188
>> Use as a topical subdivision under individual works (author-title or title entries), uniform titles of sacred works, and individual literatures, literary forms, and types of published materials for works about pictorial representation of those works. Also use under names of individual persons for works about pictorial representations of their written works.
>
> NT —Liturgy—Texts—Illustrations

—**Illustrations**
>
> H 1095; H 1110; H 1155.6; H 1155.8H 1156; H 1188
>> Use as a form subdivision under individual works (author-title or title entries), uniform titles of sacred works, and individual literatures, literary forms, and types of published materials for collections of pictorial representations of those works. Also use under names of individual persons for collections of pictorial representations of the person's written works.
>
> BT —Pictorial works
> NT —Liturgy—Texts—Illustrations
>> —Picture Bibles

—**Imaging** *(May Subd Geog)*
>
> H 1150; H 1164
>> Use as a topical subdivision under individual diseases and types of diseases and organs and regions of the body.
>
> UF —Diseases—Imaging
> NT —Cross-sectional imaging
>> —Radionuclide imaging
>> —Spectroscopic imaging

—Imitations (Parodies)
> USE —Parodies, imitations, etc.

—Immersion method of language teaching
> USE —Study and teaching—Immersion method

—Immigrant participation
> USE —Participation, Immigrant

—Immigration
> USE —Emigration and immigration

—Immunities and privileges
> USE —Privileges and immunities

—**Immunodiagnosis** *(May Subd Geog)*
>
> H 1150
>> Use as a topical subdivision under individual diseases and types of diseases.
>
> BT —Diagnosis
>> —Immunological aspects
> NT —Radioimmunoimaging

—**Immunological aspects**
>
> H 1150
>> Use as a topical subdivision under individual diseases and types of diseases.
>
> NT —Immunodiagnosis

—**Immunology**
>
> H 1147; H 1149; H 1164
>> Use as a topical subdivision under individual animals and groups of animals and under individual chemicals and groups of chemicals, and individual organs and regions of the body.
>
> NT —Transplantation—Immunological aspects
>> —Trypanotolerance

——**Genetic aspects**
>
> H 1147
>> Use as a topical subdivision under individual animals and groups of animals.
>
> BT —Genetics

—**Immunotherapy** *(May Subd Geog)*
>
> H 1150
>> Use as a topical subdivision under individual diseases and types of diseases.
>
> BT —Treatment
> NT —Radioimmunotherapy

—**Impact testing** *(May Subd Geog)*
>
> H 1158
>> Use as a topical subdivision under individual materials and types of materials.
>
> BT —Testing

—**Impeachment**
>
> H 1110
>> Use as a topical subdivision under names of individual persons.

—Imperative
H 1154
Use as a topical subdivision under individual languages and groups of languages.

—Implements   *(May Subd Geog)*
H 1103
Use as a topical subdivision under ethnic groups.
UF   —Tools

—Imprints
H 1140
Use as a form subdivision under names of countries, cities, etc. for lists of works published in those places.
BT   —Bibliography

—Imprisonment
H 1110
Use as a topical subdivision under names of individual persons on works on periods in which the person was imprisoned in a correctional institution or a prisoner of war camp. For works on periods in which the person was held captive in bondage or confinement, especially under house arrest, as a hostage, or in battle, use the subdivision Captivity, [dates].
UF   —Biography—Imprisonment
[Former subdivision]
—Imprisonment, [dates]
[Former subdivision]

—Imprisonment, [dates]
USE   —Imprisonment

—In art
H 1095; H 1105; H 1140; H 1187
Use as a topical subdivision under names of countries, cities, etc., individual corporate bodies, and Christian denominations for works about those places and organizations as themes in art. Also use under uniform titles for works about the representation of those titles as physical objects in art.

—In art
H 1095; H 1105; H 1140; H 1187
Use as a form subdivision under names of countries, cities, etc., individual corporate bodies, and Christian denominations for works consisting of reproductions of artistic works that depict that place or organization. Also use under names of uniform titles for works consisting of reproductions of artistic works that represent those titles as physical objects.
BT   —Pictorial works

—In bookplates
H 1105; H 1110; H 1140; H 1200
Use as a topical subdivision under names of individual persons, corporate bodies, countries, cities, etc., and wars for works on representation of those persons, organizations, places, and wars on bookplates.

—In fiction, drama, poetry, etc.
USE   —In literature

—In literature
H 1105; H 1110; H 1120; H 1140; H 1187; H 1188
Use as a topical subdivision under names of individual persons, families, corporate bodies, countries, cities etc., Christian denominations and uniform titles of sacred works for works on those persons, families, organizations, places, and titles as characters or themes in literary works.
UF   —In fiction, drama, poetry, etc.
[Former subdivision]

—In mass media
H 1105; H 1110; H 1120; H 1140
Use as a topical subdivision under names of individual persons, families, corporate bodies, and countries, cities, etc., for works on those persons, organizations, and places in mass media.
NT   —On television

—In motion pictures
H 1105; H 1110; H 1120; H 1140; H 1187
Use as a topical subdivision under names of individual persons, families, corporate bodies, countries, cities, etc., and Christian denominations for works about those persons, organizations or places depicted in motion pictures.

—In opera
H 1110
Use as a topical subdivision under names of individual persons.
BT   —Songs and music—History and criticism

—In popular culture
H 1140
Use as a topical subdivision under names of countries, cities, etc.

—In-service training   *(May Subd Geog)*
H 1100
Use as a topical subdivision under occupational groups and types of employees.
BT   —Training of

—In the press
USE   —Press coverage

—In-vitro propagation
USE   —Micropropagation

—Inauguration, [date]
H 1110
Use as a topical subdivision under names of individual persons.

—Inclusions   *(May Subd Geog)*
H 1158
Use as a topical subdivision under individual materials and types of materials.

—Incubation of eggs
USE   —Eggs—Incubation

—Indeclinable words
H 1154
Use as a topical subdivision under individual languages and groups of languages.

—Index maps
H 1140
Use as a form subdivision under names of countries, cities, etc.
BT   —Maps

—Indexes
H 1095; H 1100; H 1103; H 1105; H 1110
Use as a form subdivision under subjects.
UF   —Bibliography—Indexes
—Dictionaries, indexes, etc.
[Former subdivision]
NT   —Committees—Indexes
—Concordances
—Manuscripts—Indexes
—Periodicals—Indexes
—Reverse indexes

—Indexing
USE   —Abstracting and indexing

—Indian influences
H 1156
Use as a topical subdivision under individual literatures.

—Indian troops
H 1159
Use as a topical subdivision under military services.

—Indians
H 1159; H 1200
Further subdivide by subdivisions used under classes of persons.
Use as a topical subdivision under individual wars.

—Indic influences
H 1156
Use as a topical subdivision under individual literatures.
BT   —Foreign influences

—Indicative
H 1154
Use as a topical subdivision under individual languages and groups of languages.

—Indirect discourse
H 1154
Use as a topical subdivision under individual languages and groups of languages.

—Indirect object
H 1154
Use as a topical subdivision under individual languages and groups of languages.

—Induced spawning   *(May Subd Geog)*
H 1147
Use as a topical subdivision under individual animals and groups of animals.
UF   —Spawning, Induced
[Former subdivision]
BT   —Breeding

—Industrial applications   *(May Subd Geog)*
H 1095; H 1149; H 1180
Use as a topical subdivision under scientific topics, individual chemicals and groups of chemicals, and individual plants and groups of plants.

—Industrial capacity   *(May Subd Geog)*
H 1153
Use as a topical subdivision under types of industries.
UF   —Capacity, Industrial

—Industries   *(May Subd Geog)*
H 1103
Use as a topical subdivision under preliterate ethnic groups.

—Infallibility
H 1187
Use as a topical subdivision under individual Christian denominations.

—Infancy   *(May Subd Geog)*
H 1147
Use as a topical subdivision under individual animals and groups of animals.
BT   —Life cycles

—Infantry
H 1159
Use as a topical subdivision under military services.

——Drill and tactics
H 1159
Use as a topical subdivision under military services.
BT   —Drill and tactics

—Infections   *(May Subd Geog)*
H 1147; H 1164
Further subdivide by subdivisions used under diseases.
Use as a topical subdivision under individual animals and groups of animals and individual organs and regions of the body.
BT   —Diseases
NT   —Syphilis
—Tuberculosis
—Virus diseases

—Infertility   *(May Subd Geog)*
H 1147
Use as a topical subdivision under individual animals and groups of animals.

—Infinitival constructions
H 1154
Use as a topical subdivision under individual languages and groups of languages.
BT   —Syntax

—Infinitive
H 1154
Use as a topical subdivision under individual languages and groups of languages.

—Infixes
H 1154
Use as a topical subdivision under individual languages and groups of languages.

—Inflammability
USE   —Flammability

—Inflation pressure of tires
USE   —Tires—Inflation pressure

—Inflection
H 1154
Use as a topical subdivision under individual languages and groups of languages.

—Influence
H 1095; H 1105; H 1110; H 1148; H 1155.8; H 1185; H 1187; H 1188; H 1200
Use as a topical subdivision under names of individual persons and corporate bodies, uniform titles of sacred works, and literary, artistic and moving image works entered under title, and under forms and movements in the literary and visual arts, types of organizations, religions, and individual wars for works discussing their influence.
UF   —Influence and results
[Former subdivision]

——Civilization, Medieval
USE   —Influence—Medieval civilization

——Medieval civilization
H 1188
Use as a topical subdivision under uniform titles of sacred works.
UF   —Influence—Civilization, Medieval
[Former subdivision]

——Modern civilization
H 1188
Use as a topical subdivision under uniform titles of sacred works.

——**Slavic civilization**
> H 1188
>> Use as a topical subdivision under uniform titles of sacred works.

——**Western civilization**
> H 1188
>> Use as a topical subdivision under uniform titles of sacred works.

—Influence and results
> USE —Influence

—Influence, Colonial
> USE —Colonial influence

—**Influence on foreign languages**
> H 1154
>> Use as a topical subdivision under individual languages and groups of languages.

—**Influence on French, [Italian, etc.]**
> H 1154
>> Use as a topical subdivision under individual languages and groups of languages.

—Influences, Foreign
> USE —Foreign influences

—**Information resources**
> H 1095
>> Use as a topical subdivision under subjects for works about sources of information on those subjects.
>
> NT —Electronic information resources
>> —Library resources

—**Information resources management**
> *(May Subd Geog)*
> H 1095; H 1105; H 1153
>> Use as a topical subdivision under names of individual corporate bodies and under types of industries and organizations.

—**Information services**
> H 1095; H 1100; H 1103; H 1105; H 1110; H 1140; H 1153
>> Use as a topical subdivision under names of countries, cities, etc., individual persons, and corporate bodies, and under classes of persons, ethnic groups, military services, and topical headings.
>
> NT —Statistical services

——**Law and legislation** *(May Subd Geog)*
> H 1153
>> Further subdivide by subdivisions used under legal topics.
>> Use as a topical subdivision under types of industries.
>
> BT —Law and legislation

—**Information technology** *(May Subd Geog)*
> H 1095; H 1105; H 1153
>> Do not subdivide geographically under names of individual corporate bodies.
>> Use as a topical subdivision under names of individual corporate bodies, and under disciplines, types of industries, services, and organizations.

—**Inhibitors**
> H 1149
>> Further subdivide by subdivisions used under chemicals.
>> Use as a topical subdivision under individual enzymes and groups of enzymes. Under individual chemicals other than enzymes, use the subdivision Antagonists.
>
> NT —Synthesis—Inhibitors

—Injuries
> USE —Wounds and injuries

—**Innervation**
> H 1164
>> Use as a topical subdivision under individual organs and regions of the body.

—Innovations, Technological
> USE —Technological innovations

—**Inoculation** *(May Subd Geog)*
> H 1180
>> Use as a topical subdivision under individual plants and groups of plants.

—**Insect resistance** *(May Subd Geog)*
> H 1180
>> Use as a topical subdivision under individual plants and groups of plants.
>
> UF —Resistance to insects
>
> BT —Disease and pest resistance

——**Genetic aspects**
> H 1180
>> Use as a topical subdivision under individual plants and groups of plants.
>
> BT —Genetics

—**Insignia**
> H 1095; H 1105; H 1151.5; H 1159
>> Use as a topical subdivision under names of individual corporate bodies and military services and under types of corporate bodies.

—**Inspection** *(May Subd Geog)*
> H 1095; H 1147; H 1159; H 1180; H 1195
>> Do not subdivide geographically under military services.
>> Use as a topical subdivision under military services, types of merchandise, products, equipment, engineering structures, and buildings, individual animals and groups of animals, and individual plants and groups of plants.
>
> NT —Sampling

—**Inspiration**
> H 1188
>> Use as a topical subdivision under uniform titles of sacred works.

—**Installation** *(May Subd Geog)*
> H 1095
>> Use as a topical subdivision under types of equipment.

—Installation of clergy
> USE —Clergy—Installation

—**Institutional care** *(May Subd Geog)*
> H 1100; H 1103
>> Use as a topical subdivision under classes of persons and ethnic groups.
>
> BT —Care
>
> NT —Hospital care
>> —Nursing home care

—**Instruction and study** *(May Subd Geog)*
> H 1160; H 1161
>> Use as a topical subdivision under forms and types of musical compositions, individual musical instruments, and families of instruments.
>
> UF —Practicing
>> *[Former subdivision]*

——Fingering
> USE —Fingering

——**Juvenile**
> H 1160
>> Use this subdivision combination as a form subdivision under forms and types of musical compositions, individual musical instruments, and families of instruments.

——Methods
> USE —Methods

——Pedaling
> USE —Pedaling

—**Instructive editions**
> H 1160
>> Use as a form subdivision under forms and types of musical compositions.

—**Instrument panels**
> H 1195
>> Use as a topical subdivision under individual land vehicles and types of land vehicles.
>
> UF —Panels, Instrument

——**Padding**
> H 1195
>> Use as a topical subdivision under individual land vehicles and types of land vehicles.
>
> UF —Padding of instrument panels

—**Instrumental settings**
> H 1160
>> Use as a form subdivision under forms and types of musical compositions.
>
> UF —Settings, Instrumental

—**Instruments**
> H 1095; H 1195
>> Use as a topical subdivision under scientific and technical disciplines for works on instruments employed in those fields and under individual land vehicles and types of land vehicles.
>
> NT —Air content—Measurement—Instruments
>> —Laser surgery—Instruments
>> —Surgery—Instruments

——**Display systems**
> H 1195
>> Use as a topical subdivision under individual land vehicles and types of land vehicles.
>
> UF —Display systems for instruments

—Insulation of animal housing
> USE —Housing—Insulation

—**Insurance** *(May Subd Geog)*
> H 1153
>> Use as a topical subdivision under types of industries.

——**Law and legislation** *(May Subd Geog)*
> H 1153
>> Further subdivide by subdivisions used under legal topics.
>> Use as a topical subdivision under types of industries.
>
> BT —Law and legislation

—**Insurance requirements** *(May Subd Geog)*
> H 1100
>> Use as a topical subdivision under classes of persons.
>
> UF —Requirements, Insurance

—**Integrated control** *(May Subd Geog)*
> H 1147; H 1180
>> Use as a topical subdivision under individual animals and groups of animals and individual plants and groups of plants.
>
> BT —Control
>
> NT —Diseases and pests—Integrated control
>> —Postharvest diseases and injuries—Integrated control

—Integration, Vertical
> USE —Vertical integration

—**Intellectual life**
> H 1100; H 1103; H 1140
>> Use as a topical subdivision under names of countries, cities, etc., classes of persons, and ethnic groups.

——**16th century**
> H 1100; H 1103; H 1140
>> Use as a topical subdivision under names of countries, cities, etc., classes of persons, and ethnic groups.

——**17th century**
> H 1103; H 1110; H 1140
>> Use as a topical subdivision under names of countries, cities, etc., classes of persons, and ethnic groups.

——**18th century**
> H 1103; H 1110; H 1140
>> Use as a topical subdivision under names of countries, cities, etc., classes of persons, and ethnic groups.

——**19th century**
> H 1103; H 1110; H 1140
>> Use as a topical subdivision under names of countries, cities, etc., classes of persons, and ethnic groups.

——**20th century**
> H 1100; H 1103; H 1140
>> Use as a topical subdivision under names of countries, cities, etc., classes of persons, and ethnic groups.

——**21st century**
> H 1100; H 1103; H 1140
>> Use as a topical subdivision under names of countries, cities, etc., classes of persons, and ethnic groups.

—**Intelligence levels** *(May Subd Geog)*
> H 1100; H 1103
>> Use as a topical subdivision under classes of persons and ethnic groups.

—Intelligence, Military
> USE —Military intelligence

—**Intelligence specialists**
> H 1159
>> Further subdivide by subdivisions used under classes of persons.
>> Use as a topical subdivision under military services.

—**Intelligence testing** *(May Subd Geog)*
> H 1100; H 1103
>> Use as a topical subdivision under classes of persons and ethnic groups.

—Intelligibility, Mutual
> USE —Mutual intelligibility

—**Intensification**
> H 1154
>> Use as a topical subdivision under individual languages and groups of languages.

—**Interactive multimedia**
> H 1095
>> Use as a topical subdivision under subjects for works about interactive multimedia on those subjects.

—**Interactive multimedia**
H 1095
Use as a form subdivision under subjects for interactive multimedia on those subjects.

—**Interiors**   *(May Subd Geog)*
H 1195
Use as a topical subdivision under individual land vehicles and types of land vehicles.
BT   —Bodies

—**Interjections**
H 1154
Use as a topical subdivision under individual languages and groups of languages.

—**Interlinear translations**
H 1188
Use as a form subdivision under uniform titles of sacred works.
BT   —Translations

—**Interlinear translations, English, ₍French, etc.₎**
H 1188
Use as a form subdivision under uniform titles of sacred works.

—**Intermediate care**   *(May Subd Geog)*
H 1100
Use as a topical subdivision under classes of persons.
BT   —Care

—Interment
USE   —Death and burial

—**International cooperation**
H 1095
Use as a topical subdivision under topical headings.
UF   —Cooperation, International

—**International status**
H 1140
Use as a topical subdivision under names of countries, cities, etc.

—**Internet marketing**   *(May Subd Geog)*
H 1095
Use as a topical subdivision under types of commodities, products, and services.
BT   —Marketing

—**Interpretation**
H 1095
Use as a topical subdivision under individual tests and types of tests.

—**Interpretation and construction**
H 1154.5
Use as a topical subdivision under individual legal topics.

—Interpretation and criticism
USE   —Criticism and interpretation

—**Interpretation (Phrasing, dynamics, etc.)**
H 1160
Use as a topical subdivision under forms and types of musical compositions.

—**Interrogative**
H 1154
Use as a topical subdivision under individual languages and groups of languages.

—**Interventional radiology**   *(May Subd Geog)*
H 1150; H 1164
Use as a topical subdivision under individual diseases and types of diseases and organs and regions of the body.
UF   —Diseases—Interventional radiology
—Radiology, Interventional

—**Interviews**
H 1100; H 1103; H 1105; H 1110
Use as a form subdivision under names of individual persons, classes of persons, and ethnic groups for transcripts or recordings of what was said during the course of interviews with those persons. Also use under names of individual corporate bodies for interviews with persons associated with that corporate body.

—**Intonation**
H 1154; H 1161
Use as a topical subdivision under individual languages and groups of languages and individual musical instruments and families of instruments.

—**Intraoperative radiotherapy**
(May Subd Geog)
H 1150
Use as a topical subdivision under individual diseases and types of diseases.
BT   —Radiotherapy

—**Introductions**
H 1188
Use as a form subdivision under uniform titles of sacred works.
NT   —Sacred books—Introductions

—**Inventories**
H 1095; H 1153
Use as a topical subdivision under types of industries, institutions, and topical headings for works about raw materials, supplies, works in process, finished goods, etc., on hand at a particular time.

—**Inventories**   *(Not Subd Geog)*
H 1095; H 1153
Use as a form subdivision under types of industries, institutions, and topical headings for lists of raw materials, supplies, works in process, finished goods, etc., on hand at a particular time.

—**Inventory control**   *(May Subd Geog)*
H 1095; H 1105; H 1153; H 1159
Further subdivide geographically only under types of industries, organizations, and facilities.
Use as a topical subdivision under names of individual corporate bodies, military services, and types of industries, organizations, and facilities.
UF   —Control, Inventory

—Investigation of accidents
USE   —Accidents—Investigation

—Investments, Capital
USE   —Capital investments

—**Iranian influences**
H 1156
Use as a topical subdivision under individual literatures.
BT   —Foreign influences

—**Irish Americans**
H 1159
Further subdivide by subdivisions used under classes of persons.
Use as a topical subdivision under military services.

—**Irish authors**
H 1156
Use as a topical subdivision under individual literatures.

—**Irish influences**
H 1156
Use as a topical subdivision under individual literatures.
BT   —Foreign influences

—**Irrigation**   *(May Subd Geog)*
H 1180
Use as a topical subdivision under individual plants and groups of plants.

—**Islamic influences**
H 1156
Use as a topical subdivision under individual literatures.

—**Islamic interpretations**
H 1188
Use as a topical subdivision under uniform titles of sacred works.
BT   —Criticism, interpretation, etc.

—**Isotopes**   *(May Subd Geog)*
H 1149
Further subdivide by subdivisions used under chemicals.
Use as a topical subdivision under individual elements and groups of elements for works discussing collectively the isotopic forms of those elements as well as for works on individual numbered isotopes of those elements.
UF   —Radioisotopes

——**Half-life**   *(May Subd Geog)*
H 1149
Use as a topical subdivision under individual elements and groups of elements.
UF   —Half-life of isotopes

—**Italian Americans**
H 1159; H 1200
Further subdivide by subdivisions used under classes of persons.
Use as a topical subdivision under military services and individual wars.

—**Italian authors**
H 1156
Use as a topical subdivision under individual literatures.

—**Italian influences**
H 1156
Use as a topical subdivision under individual literatures.
BT   —Foreign influences

—Itineraries
USE   —Tours
—Travel

—**Jaina authors**
H 1156
Use as a topical subdivision under individual literatures.

—**Japanese Americans**
H 1200
Further subdivide by subdivisions used under classes of persons.
Use as a topical subdivision under military services and individual wars.

—**Japanese authors**
H 1156
Use as a topical subdivision under individual literatures.

—**Japanese influences**
H 1156
Use as a topical subdivision under individual literatures.
BT   —Foreign influences

—**Jargon**
H 1154
Use as a topical subdivision under individual languages and groups of languages.
NT   —Government jargon

—Jehovah's Witnesses versions
USE   —Versions, Jehovah's Witnesses

—**Jewelry**   *(May Subd Geog)*
H 1103
Use as a topical subdivision under ethnic groups.

—**Jewish authors**
H 1156
Use as a topical subdivision under individual literatures.

—**Jewish Christian authors**
H 1156
Use as a topical subdivision under individual literatures.

—Jewish criticism, interpretation, etc.
USE   —Criticism, interpretation, etc., Jewish

—Jewish participation
USE   —Participation, Jewish

—**Jews**   *(May Subd Geog)*
H 1200
Further subdivide by subdivisions used under classes of persons.
Use as a topical subdivision under individual wars for works on aspects of a war in relation to Jews, especially the war's effect on them. For works on the participation of Jews in the military actions of a war, use the subdivision Participation, Jewish.

—**Job descriptions**   *(May Subd Geog)*
H 1095; H 1100; H 1105; H 1159
Further subdivide geographically only under occupational groups.
Use as a topical subdivision under names of individual corporate bodies and under military services and occupational groups for works about summaries of the essential activities involved in the performance of jobs.
UF   —Descriptions of jobs
—Occupational descriptions
—Position descriptions
NT   —Aviation—Job descriptions
—Employees—Job descriptions

—**Job descriptions**   *(May Subd Geog)*
H 1095; H 1100; H 1105; H 1159
Further subdivide geographically only under occupational groups.
Use as a form subdivision under names of individual corporate bodies and under military services and occupational groups for summaries of the essential activities involved in the performance of jobs.
UF   —Descriptions of jobs
—Occupational descriptions
—Position descriptions
NT   —Aviation—Job descriptions
—Employees—Job descriptions

—**Job satisfaction** (*May Subd Geog*)
  H 1100
    Use as a topical subdivision under occupational groups and types of employees.
    UF —Satisfaction, Job
—**Job stress** (*May Subd Geog*)
  H 1100; H 1103
    Use as a topical subdivision under classes of persons and ethnic groups.
    UF —Stress, Job
—**Job vacancies** (*May Subd Geog*)
  H 1153
    Use as a topical subdivision under types of industries.
    UF —Vacancies, Job
—Jokes
    USE —Humor
—**Journalism, Military** (*May Subd Geog*)
  H 1200
    Use as a topical subdivision under individual wars.
    UF —Military journalism
—**Journalists**
  H 1159; H 1200
    Further subdivide by subdivisions used under classes of persons.
    Use as a topical subdivision under military services and individual wars.
—Journals (Diaries)
    USE —Diaries
—Journals (Periodicals)
    USE —Periodicals
—Journeys
    USE —Travel
—**Judging** (*May Subd Geog*)
  H 1147; H 1180
    Use as a topical subdivision under individual animals and groups of animals and individual plants and groups of plants.
—**Jungle warfare**
  H 1200
    Use as a topical subdivision under wars.
—**Juvenile**
  H 1160
    Use as a form subdivision under forms and types of musical compositions.
—Juvenile dictionaries
    USE —Dictionaries, Juvenile
—**Juvenile drama**
  H 1095; H 1100; H 1103; H 1105; H 1110; H 1140
    Use as a form subdivision under names of countries, cities, etc., names of individual persons and corporate bodies, and under classes of persons, ethnic groups, and topical headings.
    UF —Children's plays
    BT —Drama
        —Juvenile literature
—Juvenile encyclopedias
    USE —Encyclopedias, Juvenile
—**Juvenile fiction**
  H 1095; H 1100; H 1103; H 1105; H 1110; H 1140
    Use as a form subdivision under names of countries, cities, etc., names of individual persons and corporate bodies, and under classes of persons, ethnic groups, and topical headings.
    UF —Children's stories
    BT —Fiction
        —Juvenile literature
—**Juvenile films**
  H 1095
    Use as a form subdivision under subjects.
    UF —Films, Juvenile
—**Juvenile humor**
  H 1095; H 1100; H 1103; H 1105; H 1110; H 1140
    Use as a form subdivision under names of countries, cities, etc., names of individual persons and corporate bodies, and under classes of persons, ethnic groups, and topical headings.
    UF —Children's humor
    BT —Humor
        —Juvenile literature

—**Juvenile literature**
  H 1095
    Use as a form subdivision under subjects.
    UF —Children's literature
        —Literature for children
    NT —Children's sermons
        —Dictionaries, Juvenile
        —Encyclopedias, Juvenile
        —Juvenile drama
        —Juvenile fiction
        —Juvenile humor
        —Juvenile poetry
—Juvenile maps
    USE —Maps for children
—Juvenile participation
    USE —Participation, Juvenile
—**Juvenile poetry**
  H 1095; H 1100; H 1103; H 1105; H 1110; H 1140
    Use as a form subdivision under names of countries, cities, etc., names of individual persons and corporate bodies, and under classes of persons, ethnic groups, and topical headings.
    UF —Children's poetry
    BT —Juvenile literature
        —Poetry
—**Juvenile software**
  H 1095
    Use as a form subdivision under subjects.
    UF —Children's software
    BT —Software
—**Juvenile sound recordings**
  H 1095
    Use as a form subdivision under subjects.
    UF —Sound recordings for children
—Keys (Identification guides)
    USE —Identification
—**Kidnapping,** [date]
  H 1110
    Use as a topical subdivision under names of individual persons.
—**Kings and rulers**
  H 1103; H 1140
    Further subdivide by subdivisions used under classes of persons.
    Use as a topical subdivision under names of countries, cities, etc., and ethnic groups.
    UF —Rulers
——**Abdication**
  H 1140
    Use as a topical subdivision under names of countries, cities, etc.
    UF —Abdication of kings and rulers
——**Art patronage**
  H 1140
    Use as a topical subdivision under names of countries, cities, etc.
    BT —Art patronage
——**Assassination**
  H 1103; H 1140
    Use as a topical subdivision under names of countries, cities, etc. and ethnic groups
    BT —Assassination
——**Brothers**
  H 1140
    Further subdivide by subdivisions used under classes of persons.
    Use as a topical subdivision under names of countries, cities, etc.
    UF —Brothers of kings and rulers
——**Children**
  H 1103; H 1140
    Further subdivide by subdivisions used under classes of persons.
    Use as a topical subdivision under names of countries, cities, etc., and ethnic groups.
    UF —Children of kings and rulers
——**Death and burial**
  H 1103; H 1140
    Use as a topical subdivision under names of countries, cities, etc., and ethnic groups.
    UF —Burial of kings and rulers
    BT —Death

——**Deposition**
  H 1140
    Use as a topical subdivision under names of countries, cities, etc.
    UF —Deposition of kings and rulers
——**Dwellings**
  H 1140
    Use as a topical subdivision under names of countries, cities, etc.
    BT —Dwellings
——**Education**
  H 1103; H 1140
    Use as a topical subdivision under names of countries, cities, etc., and ethnic groups.
    BT —Education
——**Folklore** (*Not Subd Geog*)
  H 1103; H 1140
    Use this subdivision combination as a form subdivision under names of countries, cities, etc., and ethnic groups for collections of folklore texts about kings and rulers of those places or groups.
    Use as a topical subdivision under names of countries, cities, etc., and ethnic groups for works about folklore of kings and rulers of those places or groups.
    BT —Folklore
——**Genealogy** (*Not Subd Geog*)
  H 1103; H 1140
    Use this subdivision combination as a form subdivision under names of countries, cities, etc., and ethnic groups for genealogies of kings and rulers of those places or groups.
    Use as a topical subdivision under names of countries, cities, etc., and ethnic groups for works about genealogy of kings and rulers of those places or groups.
    BT —Genealogy
——**Heraldry**
  H 1140
    Use as a topical subdivision under names of countries, cities, etc.
    BT —Heraldry
——Journeys
    USE —Kings and rulers—Travel
——Mistresses
    USE —Kings and rulers—Paramours
——**Mythology**
  H 1103; H 1140
    Use as a topical subdivision under names of countries, cities, etc., and ethnic groups.
    BT —Mythology
——**Paramours**
  H 1140
    Further subdivide by subdivisions used under classes of persons.
    Use as a topical subdivision under names of countries, cities, etc.
    UF —Kings and rulers—Mistresses
        [*Former subdivision*]
        —Mistresses of kings and rulers
        —Paramours of kings and rulers
——**Religious aspects**
  H 1103; H 1140
    Use as a topical subdivision under names of countries, cities, etc., and ethnic groups.
——**Sisters**
  H 1140
    Further subdivide by subdivisions used under classes of persons.
    Use as a topical subdivision under names of countries, cities, etc.
    UF —Sisters of kings and rulers
——**Succession**
  H 1103; H 1140
    Use as a topical subdivision under names of countries, cities, etc., and ethnic groups.
    UF —Succession of kings and rulers
——**Tombs**
  H 1140
    Use as a topical subdivision under names of countries, cities, etc.
    BT —Tombs

—Kings and rulers *(Continued)*

——Travel *(May Subd Geog)*
H 1140
Use as a topical subdivision under names of countries, cities, etc.
UF —Kings and rulers—Journeys
[Former subdivision]
BT —Travel

—Kinship *(May Subd Geog)*
H 1103
Use as a topical subdivision under ethnic groups for works on the group's system of rules governing descent, succession, marriage, etc., and determining the relationship of individuals.

—Kirghiz authors
USE —Kyrgyz authors

—Knock of motors
USE —Motors—Knock

——Ethics
USE —Ethics

——Philosophy
USE —Philosophy

——[specific topic]
H 1110
Use as a topical subdivision under names of individual persons for works on the person's knowledge of a specific topic, whether explicitly stated or inferred from his or her life and work. Also use for discussions of the person's educational background in a specific topic. Assign an additional heading for the specific topic.

—Knowledge and learning
H 1110
Use as a topical subdivision under names of individual persons for works on the person's formal or informal learning or scholarship in general.
UF —Learning
—Scholarship

—Koranic teaching
H 1095
Use as a topical subdivision under Islamic topics.

—Korean authors
H 1156
Use as a topical subdivision under individual literatures.

—Kurdish authors
H 1156
Use as a topical subdivision under individual literatures.

—Kyrgyz authors
H 1156
Use as a topical subdivision under individual literatures.
UF —Kirghiz authors
[Former subdivision]

—Labeling *(May Subd Geog)*
H 1095
Use as a topical subdivision under types of products.
UF —Labelling

—Labeling, Affinity
USE —Affinity labeling

—Labelling
USE —Labeling

—Labiality
H 1154
Use as a topical subdivision under individual languages and groups of languages.

—Labor productivity *(May Subd Geog)*
H 1095; H 1153
Use as a topical subdivision under types of industries, occupations, and processes.
UF —Productivity, Labor

—Labor unions *(May Subd Geog)*
H 1100
Use as a topical subdivision under occupational groups and types of employees.

——Organizing *(May Subd Geog)*
H 1100
Use as a topical subdivision under occupational groups and types of employees.
UF —Organizing of labor unions

—Laboratory manuals
H 1095
Use as a form subdivision under scientific and technical topics for workbooks containing concise background information and directions for performing work, including experiments, in the laboratory.
BT —Handbooks, manuals, etc.

—Land surveys
USE —Surveys

—Land tenure *(May Subd Geog)*
H 1103
Use as a topical subdivision under ethnic groups.
UF —Tenure of land

—Landscape architecture *(May Subd Geog)*
H 1095
Use as a topical subdivision under types of buildings, institutions, and facilities.

—Language
H 1095; H 1100; H 1105; H 1110; H 1151; H 1154.5; H 1155.4; H 1155.8; H 1200
Use as a topical subdivision under names of individual persons and corporate bodies, individual works entered under title, and under classes of persons and disciplines, individual wars, and types of newspapers.
UF —Language (New words, slang, etc.)
[Former subdivision]
NT —Court and courtiers—Language

——Glossaries, etc.
H 1110; H 1155.8
Use this subdivision combination as a form subdivision under names of individual persons and individual literary works entered under title.
BT —Glossaries, vocabularies, etc.

——Style
USE —Literary style

—Language (New words, slang, etc.)
USE —Language

—Language, style
H 1188
Use as a topical subdivision under uniform titles of sacred works.
NT —Sacred books—Language, style

—Languages
H 1103; H 1140
Further subdivide by subdivisions used under languages.
Use as a topical subdivision under names of countries, cities, etc., and ethnic groups for works discussing collectively the languages spoken in those places or by those groups.

——Law and legislation
H 1140
Further subdivide by subdivisions used under legal topics.
Use as a topical subdivision under names of countries, cities, etc.
BT —Law and legislation

——Political aspects
H 1140
Use as a topical subdivision under names of countries, cities, etc.
BT —Political aspects

——Texts
H 1103; H 1140
Use this subdivision combination as a form subdivision under names of countries, cities, etc., and ethnic groups for collections of texts in languages spoken in those places or by those groups.
BT —Texts

—Larvae *(May Subd Geog)*
H 1147
Use as a topical subdivision under individual animals and groups of animals.

——Dispersal *(May Subd Geog)*
H 1147
Use as a topical subdivision under individual animals and groups of animals.
BT —Dispersal

——Ecology *(May Subd Geog)*
H 1147
Use as a topical subdivision under individual animals and groups of animals.
BT —Ecology

——Effect of ultraviolet radiation on
(May Subd Geog)
H 1147
Use as a topical subdivision under individual animals and groups of animals.
BT —Effect of ultraviolet radiation on

——Endocrinology
H 1147
Use as a topical subdivision under individual animals and groups of animals.
BT —Endocrinology

——Food *(May Subd Geog)*
H 1147
Use as a topical subdivision under individual animals and groups of animals.
BT —Food

——Geographical distribution
H 1147
Use as a topical subdivision under individual animals and groups of animals.
BT —Geographical distribution

——Microbiology *(May Subd Geog)*
H 1147
Use as a topical subdivision under individual animals and groups of animals.
BT —Microbiology

—Laser surgery *(May Subd Geog)*
H 1150; H 1164
Use as a topical subdivision under individual diseases and types of diseases and organs and regions of the body.
UF —Diseases—Laser surgery
BT —Surgery

——Instruments
H 1164
Use as a topical subdivision under individual organs and regions of the body.
BT —Instruments

—Last illness
USE —Death and burial

—Last years
H 1110
Use as a topical subdivision under names of individual persons.
UF —Biography—Last years
[Former subdivision]
—Biography—Last years and death
[Former subdivision]
—Biography—Old age
—Old age

—Lateral stability
H 1195
Use as a topical subdivision under individual land vehicles and types of land vehicles.
BT —Stability

—Latin American influences
H 1156
Use as a topical subdivision under individual literatures.
BT —Foreign influences

—Law and legislation *(May Subd Geog)*
H 1147; H 1149; H 1150; H 1151.5; H 1153; H 1158; H 1180; H 1195; H 1200
Further subdivide by subdivisions used under legal topics.
Use as a topical subdivision under individual animals and groups of animals, individual chemicals and groups of chemicals, individual diseases and types of diseases, types of educational institutions, types of industries, individual materials and types of materials, individual plants and groups of plants, individual land vehicles and types of land vehicles, and individual wars.
NT —Accounting—Law and legislation
—Administration—Law and legislation
—Admission—Law and legislation
—Auditing—Law and legislation
—Census—Law and legislation
—Conservation—Law and legislation
—Control—Law and legislation
—Defects—Law and legislation
—Defenses—Law and legislation
—Design and construction—Law and legislation
—Dialects—Research—Law and legislation
—Education—Law and legislation

—Employees—Pensions—Law and
legislation
—Entrance examinations—Law and
legislation
—Examinations—Law and legislation
—Facilities—Law and legislation
—Finance—Law and legislation
—Foreign relations—Law and
legislation
—Fuel consumption—Law and
legislation
—Information services—Law and
legislation
—Insurance—Law and legislation
—Languages—Law and legislation
—Legal status, laws, etc.
—Lighting—Law and legislation
—Maintenance and repair—Law and
legislation
—Management—Employee
participation—Law and
legislation
—Marketing—Law and legislation
—Medical care—Law and legislation
—Military construction operations—
Law and legislation
—Motors—Exhaust gas—Law and
legislation
—Navigation—Law and legislation
—Parts—Law and legislation
—Pay, allowances, etc.—Law and
legislation
—Personnel management—Law and
legislation
—Pollution control devices—Law
and legislation
—Prices—Law and legislation
—Protection—Law and legislation
—Radiography—Law and legislation
—Recruiting, enlistment, etc.—Law
and legislation
—Research—Law and legislation
—Safety regulations
—Seat belts—Law and legislation
—Statistical services—Law and
legislation
—Study and teaching—Law and
legislation
—Supplies and stores—Law and
legislation
—Taxation—Law and legislation
—Transplantation—Law and
legislation
—Transportation—Law and
legislation
—Windows and windshields—Law
and legislation

—**Lawyers**
H 1159
Further subdivide by subdivisions used under
classes of persons.
Use as a topical subdivision under military ser-
vices.

—**Lead content**   *(May Subd Geog)*
H 1149
Use as a topical subdivision under individual
chemicals and groups of chemicals.

—**Lead sheets**
H 1160
Use as a form subdivision under forms and types
of musical compositions.

—**Leadership**
H 1155
Use as a topical subdivision under names of in-
dividual legislative bodies.
NT   —Deputy speakers
—Majority leaders
—Majority whips
—Minority leaders
—Minority whips
—Presiding officers
—Speakers

—Leadership, Military
USE   —Military leadership
—Learning
USE   —Knowledge and learning
—Leave regulations of officials and employees
USE   —Officials and employees—Leave
regulations

—**Leaves and furloughs**
H 1159
Use as a topical subdivision under military ser-
vices.
UF   —Furloughs
—Left hand studies
USE   —Studies and exercises (Left hand)

—**Legal research**
H 1154.5
Use as a topical subdivision under individual legal topics for works on the use of legal research
tools, such as court reports, codes, digests, citators,
etc., in determining the status of statutory, regula-
tory, or case law on the topic.

—**Legal status, laws, etc.**   *(May Subd Geog)*
H 1100; H 1103
Further subdivide by subdivisions used under le-
gal topics.
Use as a topical subdivision under classes of per-
sons and ethnic groups.
BT   —Law and legislation
NT   —Civil rights
—Employees—Legal status, laws,
etc.
—Legendary tales
USE   —Legends

—**Legends**
H 1095; H 1110; H 1188
Use as a form subdivision under names of indi-
vidual persons, legendary characters, and uniform
titles of sacred works, and under religious topics
for collected or individual literary versions of leg-
endary tales about those persons, characters, or top-
ics.
UF   —Legendary tales
—Romances, legends, etc.
[Former subdivision]
—Tales, Legendary
NT   —Romances
—Legends and stories
USE   —Biography
—Fiction
—Legislative committees
USE   —Committees

—**Legislative history**
H 1154.5
Use as a topical subdivision under individual le-
gal topics and names of individual legislative en-
actments.
—Letters
USE   —Correspondence

—**Lexicography**
H 1154; H 1185
Use as a topical subdivision under individual
languages and groups of languages and individual
religions.

—**Lexicology**
H 1154
Use as a topical subdivision under individual
languages other than English and groups of lan-
guages.
NT   —Dialects—Lexicology
——History
USE   —Lexicology, Historical

—**Lexicology, Historical**
H 1154
Use as a topical subdivision under individual
languages other than English and groups of lan-
guages.
UF   —Historical lexicology
—Lexicology—History

—**Libraries**
H 1105; H 1200
Use as a topical subdivision under names of individual corporate bodies having library systems of
more than one library for which no corporate heading exists or can be established. Also use under
individual wars.

—Library
H 1105; H 1110; H 1120
Use as a topical subdivision under names of in-
dividual persons, families, and corporate bodies.
——**Marginal notes**   *(Not Subd Geog)*
H 1110
Use this subdivision combination as a form
subdivision under names of individual persons
for marginal notes in works belonging to the per-
son, whether written by the person or by others.
UF   —Marginal notes
——**Microform catalogs**
H 1110
Use this subdivision combination as a form
subdivision under names of individual persons.
BT   —Microform catalogs

—**Library resources**
H 1095; H 1100; H 1103; H 1105; H 1110;
H 1140
Use as a topical subdivision under names of
countries, cities, etc., names of individual persons
and corporate bodies, and under classes of persons,
ethnic groups, and topical headings for works describing the resources and special collections available on those subjects.
BT   —Information resources

—**Librettos**
H 1160
Use as a topical subdivision under forms and
types of musical compositions for works about librettos.

—**Librettos**
H 1160
Use as a form subdivision under forms and types
of musical compositions.

—**Licenses**   *(May Subd Geog)*
H 1095; H 1100; H 1153; H 1195
Use as a topical subdivision under occupational
groups and types of employees, under types of in-
dustries, facilities, and institutions, and under indi-
vidual land vehicles and types of land vehicles.
NT   —Collection and preservation—
Licenses
——**Fees**   *(May Subd Geog)*
H 1095; H 1100; H 1153; H 1195
Use as a topical subdivision under occupa-
tional groups and types of employees, under
types of industries, facilities, and institutions,
and under individual land vehicles and types of
land vehicles.
UF   —Fees for licenses

—**Life cycles**   *(May Subd Geog)*
H 1147; H 1180
Use as a topical subdivision under individual an-
imals and groups of animals and individual plants
and groups of plants.
UF   —Cycles, Life
NT   —Infancy
—Parasites—Life cycles

—**Life skills assessment**   *(May Subd Geog)*
H 1100; H 1103
Use as a topical subdivision under classes of per-
sons and ethnic groups.
UF   —Assessment of life skills

—**Life skills guides**
H 1100; H 1103
Use as a form subdivision under classes of per-
sons and ethnic groups.
BT   —Handbooks, manuals, etc.

—**Lighting**   *(May Subd Geog)*
H 1095; H 1195
Use as a topical subdivision under types of vehi-
cles, structures, buildings, rooms, installations, etc.
NT   —Housing—Lighting
——**Law and legislation**   *(May Subd Geog)*
H 1195
Further subdivide by subdivisions used under
legal topics.
Use as a topical subdivision under individual
land vehicles and types of land vehicles.
BT   —Law and legislation

—**Linear programming**
H 1095
Use as a topical subdivision under topical head-
ings.
—Liquid nitrogen motors
USE   —Motors (Liquid nitrogen)
—Lists of books
USE   —Bibliography

—Lists of events
USE —Chronology
—Lists of passengers
USE —Passenger lists
—Lists of vessels
H 1159
Use as a form subdivision under military services.
—Lists, Union
USE —Union lists
—Literary anthologies
USE —Literary collections
—Literary art
H 1110
Do not use under multi-career persons who are also recognized as literary authors.
Use as a topical subdivision under names of individual persons for works on a non-literary person's literary ability and accomplishments, including discussions of literary works by persons normally identified with another field.
UF —Writing skill
—Literary collections
H 1095; H 1100; H 1103; H 1105; H 1110; H 1120; H 1140
Use as a form subdivison under names of countries, cities, etc., individual persons and corporate bodies, and under classes of persons, ethnic groups, individual wars, and topical headings for collections including several literary forms.
UF —Anthologies, Literary
—Literary anthologies
—Literary style
H 1110
Use as a topical subdivision under names of individual literary authors for discussions of rhetoric, figures of speech, and artistic use of language in general.
UF —Language—Style
BT —Style
—Literary themes, motives
H 1160
Use as a topical subdivision under forms and types of musical compositions.
UF —Themes, motives, Literary
[Former subdivision]
—Literature and the war, [revolution, etc.]
H 1200
Complete the subdivision by repeating the generic term for the type of engagement contained in the heading.
Use as a topical subdivision under individual wars.
NT —Underground literature
—Literature for children
USE —Juvenile literature
—Literatures
H 1140
Further subdivide by subdivisions used under literatures.
Use as a topical subdivision under names of countries, cities, etc., in which one language predominates but two or more languages are spoken for works about those literatures.
—Literatures
H 1140
Further subdivide by subdivisions used under literatures.
Use as a form subdivision under names of countries, cities, etc., in which one language predominates but two or more languages are spoken for collections of literary works in several of those languages.
—Litigation
USE —Trials, litigation, etc.
—Liturgical calendars
USE —Liturgy—Calendar
—Liturgical lessons, Dutch, [English, etc.]
H 1188
Use as a form subdivision under uniform titles of sacred works.
—Liturgical objects *(May Subd Geog)*
H 1185; H 1187
Use as a topical subdivision under individual religions and Christian denominations.
—Liturgical texts
USE —Liturgy—Texts

—Liturgical use *(May Subd Geog)*
H 1188
Use as a topical subdivision under uniform titles of sacred works.
UF —Use in liturgy
—Liturgy
H 1095; H 1186; H 1187
Use as a topical subdivision under individual Jewish and Christian sects and rites; under names of individual Christian monastic and religious orders; and under individual Jewish and Christian ceremonies, rituals, holidays, etc.
——Calendar *(Not Subd Geog)*
H 1187
Use this subdivision combination as a form subdivision under individual Christian denominations.
UF —Liturgical calendars
BT —Calendars
——Texts
H 1187
Use this subdivision combination as a form subdivision under individual Jewish and Christian sects and rites; under names of individual Christian monastic and religious orders; and under individual Jewish and Christian ceremonies, rituals, holidays, etc., for liturgical texts.
Use this subdivision combination as a topical subdivision under individual Jewish and Christian sects and rites; under names of individual Christian monastic and religious orders; and under individual Jewish and Christian ceremonies, rituals, holidays, etc., for works about liturgical texts.
UF —Liturgical texts
BT —Texts
———Concordances
H 1187
Use this subdivision combination as a form subdivision under individual Christian denominations for word indexes to liturgical texts.
BT —Concordances
———History and criticism
H 1187
Use as a topical subdivision under individual Christian denominations.
BT —History and criticism
———Illustrations
H 1187
Use this subdivision combination as a form subdivision under individual Christian denominations for collections of pictorial representations from liturgical texts.
Use as a topical subdivision under individual Christian denominations for works about pictorial representations from liturgical texts.
BT —Illustrations
———Manuscripts
H 1187
Use this subdivision combination as a form subdivision under individual Christian denominations.
———Rubrics
H 1187
Use this subdivision combination as a form subdivision under individual Christian denominations.
UF —Rubrics in liturgical texts
——Theology
H 1187
Use as a topical subdivision under individual Christian denominations.
BT —Theology
—Liturgy, Experimental
H 1187
Use as a topical subdivision under individual Christian denominations.
UF —Experimental liturgy
—Local history
USE —History, Local
—Location *(May Subd Geog)*
H 1095; H 1153; H 1180
Use as a topical subdivision under types of industries, business entities, government agencies, and facilities and under individual plants and groups of plants.

—Locative constructions
H 1154
Use as a topical subdivision under individual languages and groups of languages.
BT —Case
—Syntax
—Locks
H 1195
Use as a topical subdivision under individual land vehicles and types of land vehicles.
—Locomotion *(May Subd Geog)*
H 1147
Use as a topical subdivision under individual animals and groups of animals.
NT —Flight
—Logistics *(May Subd Geog)*
H 1200
Use as a topical subdivision under individual wars.
—Long-term care *(May Subd Geog)*
H 1100
Use as a topical subdivision under classes of persons.
BT —Care
—Longevity *(May Subd Geog)*
H 1147; H 1180
Use as a topical subdivision under individual animals and groups of animals and individual plants and groups of plants.
—Longitudinal studies
H 1095; H 1100; H 1103
Use as a topical subdivision under classes persons, ethnic groups, and topical headings for works about longitudinal studies on those groups or topics.
—Longitudinal studies
H 1095; H 1100; H 1103
Use as a form subdivision under classes of persons, ethnic groups, and topical headings for works that report the results of longitudinal studies on those groups or topics.
BT —Case studies
—Losses *(May Subd Geog)*
H 1147; H 1180
Use as a topical subdivision under individual animals and groups of animals and individual plants and groups of plants.
NT —Postharvest losses
——Prevention
H 1180
Use as a topical subdivision under individual plants and groups of plants.
BT —Prevention
—Lubrication
H 1195
Use as a topical subdivision under individual land vehicles and types of land vehicles.
—Lubrication systems of motors
USE —Motors—Lubrication systems
—Lutheran authors
H 1156
Use as a topical subdivision under individual literatures.
—Luxembourg authors
H 1156
Use as a topical subdivision under individual literatures.
—Lymphatics
H 1164
Use as a topical subdivision under individual organs and regions of the body.
—Machinability
H 1158
Use as a topical subdivision under individual materials and types of materials.
—Machine gun drill and tactics
H 1159
Use as a topical subdivision under military services.
BT —Drill and tactics
—Machine translating *(May Subd Geog)*
H 1154
Use as a topical subdivision under individual languages and groups of languages.
BT —Translating

—**Machinery** *(May Subd Geog)*
    H 1180
    Use as a topical subdivision under individual
plants and groups of plants.
    NT   —Harvesting—Machinery
      —Processing—Machinery
      —Shelling—Machinery
      —Threshing—Machinery
      —Transplanting—Machinery
—**Magnetic fields**
    H 1164
    Use as a topical subdivision under individual or-
gans and regions of the body.
—**Magnetic properties** *(May Subd Geog)*
    H 1149; H 1158
    Use as a topical subdivision under individual
chemicals and groups of chemicals and individual
materials and types of materials.
    BT   —Properties
—**Magnetic resonance imaging**
    (May Subd Geog)
    H 1150; H 1164
    Use as a topical subdivision under individual dis-
eases and types of diseases and organs and regions
of the body.
    UF   —Diseases—Magnetic resonance
      imaging
    BT   —Cross-sectional imaging
—**Maintenance and repair**
    H 1095; H 1161; H 1195
    Use as a topical subdivision under types of ob-
jects, including machinery, vehicles, structures, individual musical instruments and families of instruments, etc., requiring maintenance and repair.
    UF   —Repair and maintenance
    NT   —Repairing
————**Law and legislation** *(May Subd Geog)*
    H 1195
    Further subdivide by subdivisions used under
legal topics.
    Use as a topical subdivision under individual
land vehicles and types of land vehicles.
    BT   —Law and legislation
—Majority leader
    USE   —Majority leaders
—**Majority leaders**
    H 1155
    Further subdivide by subdivisions used under
classes of persons.
    Use as a topical subdivision under names of in-
dividual legislative bodies.
    UF   —Majority leader
      [Former subdivision]
    BT   —Leadership
—Majority whip
    USE   —Majority whips
—**Majority whips**
    H 1155
    Further subdivide by subdivisions used under
classes of persons.
    Use as a topical subdivision under individual
legislative bodies.
    UF   —Majority whip
      [Former subdivision]
    BT   —Leadership
—**Male authors**
    H 1156
    Use as a topical subdivision under individual lit-
eratures.
    UF   —Men authors
—Malpractice of medical personnel
    USE   —Medical personnel—Malpractice
—Malpractice of surgeons
    USE   —Surgeons—Malpractice
—**Management**
    H 1095; H 1105; H 1153; H 1159
    Use as a topical subdivision under names of in-
dividual corporate bodies, including government
agencies, galleries, museums, parks, etc., and under types of industries, industrial plants and processes, special activities, resources, etc. Under
names of individual libraries, schools, and institutions in the spheres of health and social services,
and under types of such institutions, and types of
education and programs in the field of education
use the subdivision Administration.
    NT   —Materials management
        —Personnel management

    —Risk management
——**Employee participation**
    (May Subd Geog)
    H 1153
    Use as a topical subdivision under types of in-
dustries.
    UF   —Employee participation in
      management
————**Law and legislation** *(May Subd Geog)*
    H 1153
    Further subdivide by subdivisions used un-
der legal topics.
    Use as a topical subdivision under types of
industries.
    BT   —Law and legislation
—**Maneuvers**
    H 1159
    Use as a topical subdivision under military ser-
vices.
—**Manpower** *(May Subd Geog)*
    H 1200
    Use as a topical subdivision under individual
wars.
—Manuals
    USE   —Handbooks, manuals, etc.
—**Manufacturers' catalogs**
    H 1161
    Use as a form subdivision under individual mu-
sical instruments and families of instruments.
    UF   —Catalogs, Manufacturers'
      [Former subdivision]
    BT   —Catalogs
—**Manure** *(May Subd Geog)*
    H 1147
    Use as a topical subdivision under individual an-
imals and groups of animals.
——**Environmental aspects**
    (May Subd Geog)
    H 1147
    Use as a topical subdivision under individual
animals and groups of animals.
    BT   —Environmental aspects
——**Handling** *(May Subd Geog)*
    H 1147
    Use as a topical subdivision under individual
animals and groups of animals.
    BT   —Handling
—Manuscript maps
    USE   —Maps, Manuscript
—**Manuscripts** *(Not Subd Geog)*
    H 1095; H 1100; H 1103; H 1110; H 1120;
    H 1156; H 1188
    Use as a topical subdivision under names of in-
dividual persons and families, individual works entered under title, uniform titles of sacred works, and
under classes of persons, ethnic groups, groups of
literary authors, individual literatures, and topical
headings for works about manuscripts by those persons, of those titles or literatures, or about those
topics.
——**Bibliography**
    USE   —Manuscripts—Catalogs
——**Catalogs** *(Not Subd Geog)*
    H 1095
    Use this subdivision combination as a form
subdivision for catalogs of manuscripts.
    UF   —Manuscripts—Bibliography
    BT   —Catalogs
——**Facsimiles**
    H 1095; H 1110; H 1155.8
    Use as a form subdivision under names of
individual literary authors and composers for
facsimile editions of manuscripts of individual
works or collections of works. Also use under
literary works entered under title for facsimile
editions of manuscripts of those works.
    BT   —Facsimiles
——**Indexes** *(Not Subd Geog)*
    H 1095
    Use this subdivision combination as a form
subdivision for indexes to manuscripts.
    BT   —Indexes
——**Microform catalogs**
    H 1095
    Use this subdivision combination as a form
subdivision for catalogs of manuscripts in microform.
    BT   —Microform catalogs

——**Paragraphs** *(Not Subd Geog)*
    H 1188
    Use as a topical subdivision under uniform ti-
tles of sacred works.
    BT   —Paragraphs
—**Manuscripts (Papyri)**
    H 1188
    Use as a topical subdivision under uniform titles
of sacred works.
—**Maori authors** *(Not Subd Geog)*
    H 1156
    Use as a topical subdivision under individual lit-
eratures.
—**Map collections**
    H 1105; H 1110; H 1120
    Use as a topical subdivision under names of in-
dividual persons, families, and corporate bodies for
works on their collections of maps.
—Mapping of genomes
    USE   —Genome mapping
—**Maps**
    H 1095; H 1103; H 1105; H 1140
    Use as a topical subdivision under names of
countries, cities, etc., and individual corporate bodies, and under topical headings for works about
maps on those subjects.
—**Maps**
    H 1095; H 1103; H 1105; H 1140
    Use as a form subdivision under names of coun-
tries, cities, etc., and individual corporate bodies,
and under topical headings for individual maps or
collections of maps on those subjects.
    UF   —Atlases, Geographic
      —Geographic atlases
    NT   —Aerial views
      —Bathymetric maps
      —Historical geography—Maps
      —Index maps
      —Maps, Comparative
      —Maps for children
      —Maps for people with visual
        disabilities
      —Maps for the blind
      —Maps, Manuscript
      —Maps, Mental
      —Maps, Outline and base
      —Maps, Physical
      —Maps, Pictorial
      —Maps, Topographic
      —Maps, Tourist
      —Relief models
      —Remote-sensing maps
——**Bibliography**
    H 1095; H 1105; H 1140
    Use this subdivision combination as a form
subdivision under names of countries, cities,
etc., and individual corporate bodies, and under
topical headings.
    BT   —Bibliography
——**Early works to 1800**
    H 1095; H 1140
    Use as a form subdivision under names of
countries, cities, etc., and under topical headings
for maps of those places or topics issued before
1800.
    UF   —Maps—To 1800
      [Former subdivision]
    BT   —Early works to 1800
——**Facsimiles**
    H 1095; H 1140
    Use as a form subdivision under names of
countries, cities, etc., and under topical headings.
    UF   —Facsimile maps
    BT   —Facsimiles
——Juvenile literature
    USE   —Maps for children
——**Symbols**
    H 1095
    Use as a topical subdivision under topical
headings.
    UF   —Symbols on maps
——To 1800
    USE   —Maps—Early works to 1800

—Maps, Comparative
H 1095; H 1140
Use as a form subdivision under names of countries, cities, etc.
UF —Comparative maps
BT —Maps

—Maps for children
H 1095; H 1105; H 1140
Use as a form subdivision under names of countries, cities, etc., and individual corporate bodies, and under topical headings.
UF —Juvenile maps
—Maps—Juvenile literature
BT —Maps

—Maps for people with visual disabilities
H 1095; H 1140
Use as a form subdivision under names of countries, cities, etc.
UF —Maps for the visually handicapped
[Former subdivision]
BT —Maps

—Maps for the blind
H 1095; H 1140
Use as a form subdivision under names of countries, cities, etc.
BT —Maps

—Maps for the visually handicapped
USE —Maps for people with visual disabilities

—Maps, Manuscript
H 1095; H 1140
Use as a form subdivision under names of countries, cities, etc.
UF —Manuscript maps
BT —Maps

—Maps, Mental
H 1095; H 1140
Use as a form subdivision under names of countries, cities, etc.
UF —Mental maps
BT —Maps

—Maps, Outline and base
H 1095; H 1140
Use as a form subdivision under names of countries, cities, etc.
UF —Base maps
—Outline maps
BT —Maps

—Maps, Physical
H 1095; H 1140
Use as a form subdivision under names of countries, cities, etc.
UF —Physical maps
BT —Maps

—Maps, Pictorial
H 1140; H H 1095
Use as a form subdivision under names of countries, cities, etc.
UF —Pictorial maps
BT —Maps

—Maps, Topographic
H 1095; H 1140
Use as a form subdivision under names of countries, cities, etc.
UF —Topographic maps
BT —Maps

—Maps, Tourist
H 1095; H 1140
Use as a form subdivision under names of countries, cities, etc.
UF —Tourist maps
BT —Maps

—Maratha authors
H 1156
Use as a topical subdivision under individual literatures.

—Marginal notes
USE —Library—Marginal notes

—Marginal readings
H 1188
Use as a form subdivision under uniform titles of sacred works.
UF —Readings, Marginal

—Marginalia
USE —Scholia

—Markedness
H 1154
Use as a topical subdivision under individual languages and groups of languages.

—Marketing
H 1095; H 1147; H 1180; H 1195
Use as a topical subdivision under types of commodities, products, services, and institutions providing products or services.
NT —Cooperative marketing
—Internet marketing
—Seeds—Marketing

——Law and legislation (May Subd Geog)
H 1147
Further subdivide by subdivisions used under legal topics.
Use as a topical subdivision under individual animals and groups of animals.
BT —Law and legislation

—Marking (May Subd Geog)
H 1147
Use as a topical subdivision under animals and groups of animals.
UF —Tagging

—Markings of firearms
USE —Firearms—Markings

—Marriage
H 1110
Use as a topical subdivision under names of individual persons.
UF —Biography—Marriage
[Former subdivision]

—Marriage customs and rites
(May Subd Geog)
H 1103
Use as a topical subdivision under ethnic groups.
BT —Rites and ceremonies

—Mascots
H 1151; H 1159
Use as a topical subdivision under names of individual educational institutions and military services.

—Mass media and the war, [revolution, etc.]
H 1200
Complete the subdivision by repeating the generic term for the type of engagement contained in the heading.
Use as a topical subdivision under individual wars.

—Massage (May Subd Geog)
H 1164
Use as a topical subdivision under individual organs and regions of the body.
BT —Care and hygiene

—Masters-at-arms
H 1159
Further subdivide by subdivisions used under classes of persons.
Use as a topical subdivision under military services.

—Material culture (May Subd Geog)
H 1103
Use as a topical subdivision under ethnic groups.

—Materials (May Subd Geog)
H 1095; H 1195
Further subdivide by subdivisions used under materials.
Use as a topical subdivision under scientific and technical disciplines and under types of equipment and construction.

——Dynamic testing (May Subd Geog)
H 1195
Use as a topical subdivision under individual land vehicles and types of land vehicles.
UF —Dynamic testing of materials
BT —Testing

—Materials management (May Subd Geog)
H 1153
Use as a topical subdivision under types of industries.
BT —Management

—Mathematical models
H 1095
Use as a topical subdivision under topical headings.
BT —Simulation methods

—Mathematics
H 1095; H 1103
Use as a topical subdivision under ethnic groups for works on their systems of mathematics. Also use under topical headings for works on the mathematics employed in those fields.

—Maxims
USE —Quotations, maxims, etc.

—Maximum allowable concentrations
USE —Threshold limit values

—Mayan influences
H 1156
Use as a topical subdivision under individual literatures.
BT —Foreign influences

—Measurement
H 1095
Use as a topical subdivision under scientific and technical topics for works on the technique of making measurements.
NT —Air content—Measurement

—Mechanical properties
H 1158; H 1164; H 1180
Use as a topical subdivision under individual materials and types of materials, individual organs and regions of the body, and individual plants and groups of plants.
NT —Abrasion resistance

—Mechanism of action
H 1149
Use as a topical subdivision under individual chemicals and groups of chemicals.
UF —Action, Mechanism of

—Medals
H 1095; H 1100; H 1103; H 1105; H 1110; H 1200
Do not further subdivide geographically under names of individual persons and corporate bodies.
Use as a topical subdivision under names of individual persons and corporate bodies other than military services, and under classes of persons, ethnic groups, individual wars, and topical headings for works on commemorative or honorary medals issued or awarded in relation to the subject. Use Medals, badges, decorations, etc. under military services.
BT —Awards
—Numismatics

—Medals, badges, decorations, etc.
H 1159
Do not use under headings of the type [place]—Armed Forces; use Military decorations—[place] instead.
Use as a topical subdivision under names of individual military services.
UF —Badges
—Decorations, Military
—Military decorations

—Medical and sanitary affairs
USE —Health aspects
—Hospitals
—Medical care

—Medical care (May Subd Geog)
H 1100; H 1103; H 1159; H 1200
Use as a topical subdivision under classes of persons, ethnic groups, military services, and individual wars.
UF —Medical and sanitary affairs
[Former subdivision]
BT —Services for
NT —Employees—Medical care
—Hospital care
—Medical examinations

——Law and legislation
H 1159
Further subdivide by subdivisions used under legal topics.
Use as a topical subdivision under military services.
BT —Law and legislation

—Medical examinations (May Subd Geog)
H 1095; H 1100; H 1103; H 1159
Use as a topical subdivision under classes of persons, ethnic groups, military services, and topical headings for which medical examinations are needed, such as types of insurance.
BT —Medical care

—**Medical personnel**
H 1159
Further subdivide by subdivisions used under classes of persons.
Use as a topical subdivision under military services.
  NT —Medical technologists
    —Nurses
    —Surgeons

——**Malpractice**
H 1159
Use as a topical subdivision under military services.
  UF —Malpractice of medical personnel

—Medical statistics
USE —Statistics, Medical

—**Medical supplies**
H 1159
Use as a topical subdivision under military services.
  BT —Supplies and stores

—**Medical technologists**
H 1159
Further subdivide by subdivisions used under classes of persons.
Use as a topical subdivision under military services.
  BT —Medical personnel

—Medicinal use
USE —Therapeutic use

—**Medicine** *(May Subd Geog)*
H 1103
Use as a topical subdivision under ethnic groups.

——**Formulae, receipts, prescriptions**
H 1103
Use this subdivision combination as a topical subdivision under ethnic groups.
  BT —Formulae, receipts, prescriptions

—**Medieval influences**
H 1156
Use as a topical subdivision under individual literatures.

—**Meditations**
H 1095; H 1110; H 1188
Use as a form subdivision under names of individual persons, uniform titles of sacred works, and under religious topics for works containing collections of thoughts or reflections on the spiritual significance of the person or topic.
  BT —Devotional literature

—**Mediterranean influences**
H 1156
Use as a topical subdivision under individual literatures.
  BT —Foreign influences

—Meetings
USE —Congresses

—**Membership**
H 1095; H 1105; H 1187
Use as a topical subdivision under names of individual corporate bodies, individual Christian denominations, and types of corporate bodies for works on the conditions of belonging to those organizations.

—**Memorizing**
H 1156; H 1188
Use as a topical subdivision under individual literatures and uniform titles of sacred works.

—Men authors
USE —Male authors

—**Mennonite authors**
H 1156
Use as a topical subdivision under individual literatures.

—**Mental health** *(May Subd Geog)*
H 1100; H 1103; H 1110
Do not further subdivide geographically under names of individual persons.
Use as a topical subdivision under names of individual persons, classes of persons, and ethnic groups.
  BT —Health

—**Mental health services** *(May Subd Geog)*
H 1100; H 1103
Use as a topical subdivision under classes of persons and ethnic groups.
  UF —Psychiatric care
  BT —Services for

—Mental maps
USE —Maps, Mental

—**Mercury content** *(May Subd Geog)*
H 1147
Use as a topical subdivision under individual animals and groups of animals.
  BT —Composition

—**Mergers** *(May Subd Geog)*
H 1151.5; H 1153
Use as a topical subdivision under types of educational institutions and industries.

—**Messes**
H 1159
Use as a topical subdivision under military services.

—Metabolic detoxication
USE —Metabolic detoxification

—**Metabolic detoxification** *(May Subd Geog)*
H 1149
Use as a topical subdivision under individual chemicals and groups of chemicals.
  UF —Detoxification, Metabolic
  —Metabolic detoxication
    [Former subdivision]

—**Metabolism**
H 1147; H 1149; H 1164; H 1180
Use as a topical subdivision under individual animals and groups of animals, individual chemicals and groups of chemicals, individual organs and regions of the body, and individual plants and groups of plants.
  BT —Physiology

——**Age factors** *(May Subd Geog)*
H 1149
Use as a topical subdivision under individual chemicals and groups of chemicals.
  BT —Age factors

——**Climatic factors** *(May Subd Geog)*
H 1147
Use as a topical subdivision under individual animals and groups of animals.
  BT —Climatic factors

——**Disorders** *(May Subd Geog)*
H 1149; H 1164
Further subdivide by subdivisions used under diseases.
Use as a topical subdivision under individual chemicals and groups of chemicals and individual organs and regions of the body.
  BT —Diseases

——**Endocrine aspects**
H 1164
Use as a topical subdivision under individual organs and regions of the body.
  BT —Endocrine aspects

——**Genetic aspects**
H 1149
Use as a topical subdivision under individual chemicals and groups of chemicals.
  BT —Genetics

——**Regulation**
H 1149; H 1164
Use as a topical subdivision under individual chemicals and groups of chemicals and individual organs and regions of the body.
  UF —Regulation of metabolism

—**Metallography**
H 1158
Use as a topical subdivision under individual metals and types of metals.

—**Metallurgy**
H 1158
Use as a topical subdivision under individual metals and types of metals.
  NT —Electrometallurgy

—**Metamorphosis** *(May Subd Geog)*
H 1147
Use as a topical subdivision under individual animals and groups of animals.
  BT —Development

——**Endocrine aspects**
H 1147
Use as a topical subdivision under individual animals and groups of animals.
  UF —Metamorphosis—Hormonal aspects
  BT —Endocrinology

——**Genetic aspects**
H 1147
Use as a topical subdivision under individual animals and groups of animals.
  BT —Genetics

——Hormonal aspects
USE —Metamorphosis—Endocrine aspects

——**Molecular aspects**
H 1147
Use as a topical subdivision under individual animals and groups of animals.
  BT —Molecular aspects

—**Methodist authors**
H 1156
Use as a topical subdivision under individual literatures.

—**Methodology**
H 1095
Use as a topical subdivision under disciplines for works on both the theory and practice of procedures to be followed.
  NT —Bibliography—Methodology
  —Comparative method
  —Discography—Methodology
  —Fieldwork
  —Graphic methods
  —Statistical methods

—**Methods**
H 1161
Use as a topical subdivision under individual musical instruments and families of instruments.
  UF —Instruction and study—Methods

—**Methods**
H 1161
Use as a form subdivision under individual musical instruments and families of instruments.
  UF —Instruction and study—Methods

——**Group instruction**
H 1161
Use as a form subdivision under individual musical instruments and families of instruments.
  NT —Methods (Jazz)—Group instruction
  —Methods (Jazz-rock)—Group instruction

——**Juvenile**
H 1161
Use as a form subdivision under individual musical instruments and families of instruments.

——**Self-instruction**
H 1161
Use as a form subdivision under individual musical instruments and families of instruments.
  BT —Self-instruction
  NT —Methods (Jazz)—Self-instruction
  —Methods (Jazz-rock)—Self-instruction

—**Methods (Alternative rock)**
H 1161
Use as a form subdivision under individual musical instruments and families of instruments.

——**Group instruction**
H 1161
Use as a form subdivision under individual musical instruments and families of instruments.

——**Self-instruction**
H 1161
Use as a form subdivision under individual musical instruments and families of instruments.

—**Methods (Big band)**
H 1161
Use as a form subdivision under individual instruments and families of instruments.

——**Group instruction**
H 1161
Use as a form subdivision under individual instruments and families of instruments.

——**Self-instruction**
H 1161
Use as a form subdivision under individual instruments and families of instruments.

—**Methods (Bluegrass)**
H 1161
Use as a form subdivision under individual instruments and families of instruments.

——**Group instruction**
H 1161
Use as a form subdivision under individual instruments and families of instruments.

—Methods (Bluegrass) *(Continued)*
———Self-instruction
H 1161
Use as a form subdivision under individual instruments and families of instruments.
—Methods (Blues)
H 1161
Use as a form subdivision under individual instruments and families of instruments.
———Group instruction
H 1161
Use as a form subdivision under individual instruments and families of instruments.
———Self-instruction
H 1161
Use as a form subdivision under individual instruments and families of instruments.
—Methods (Blues-rock)
H 1161
Use as a form subdivision under individual instruments and families of instruments.
———Group instruction
H 1161
Use as a form subdivision under individual instruments and families of instruments.
———Self-instruction
H 1161
Use as a form subdivision under individual instruments and families of instruments.
—Methods (Boogie woogie)
H 1161
Use as a form subdivision under individual instruments and families of instruments.
———Group instruction
H 1161
Use as a form subdivision under individual instruments and families of instruments.
———Self-instruction
H 1161
Use as a form subdivision under individual instruments and families of instruments.
—Methods (Bop)
H 1161
Use as a form subdivision under individual instuments and families of instruments.
———Group instruction
H 1161
Use as a form subdivision under individual instruments and families of instruments.
———Self-instruction
H 1161
Use as a form subdivision under individual instruments and families of instruments.
—Methods (Celtic)
H 1161
Use as a form subdivision under individual instruments and families of instruments.
———Group instruction
H 1161
Use as a form subdivision under individual instruments and families of instruments.
———Self-instruction
H 1161
Use as a form subdivision under individual instruments and families of instruments.
—Methods (Country)
H 1161
Use as a form subdivision under individual instruments and families of instruments.
———Group instruction
H 1161
Use as a form subdivision under individual instruments and families of instruments.
———Self-instruction
H 1161
Use as a form subdivision under individual instruments and families of instruments.
—Methods (Dixieland)
H 1161
Use as a form subdivision under individual instruments and families of instruments.
———Group instruction
H 1161
Use as a form subdivision under individual instruments and families of instruments.
———Self-instruction
H 1161
Use as a form subdivision under individual instruments and families of instruments.
—Methods (Folk)
H 1161
Use as a form subdivision under individual instruments and families of instruments.

———Group instruction
H 1161
Use as a form subdivision under individual instruments and families of instruments.
———Self-instruction
H 1161
Use as a form subdivision under individual instruments and families of instruments.
—Methods (Funk)
H 1161
Use as a form subdivision under individual musical instruments and families of instruments.
———Group instruction
H 1161
Use as a form subdivision under individual musical instruments and families of instruments.
———Self-instruction
H 1161
Use as a form subdivision under individual musical instruments and families of instruments.
—Methods (Gospel)
H 1161
Use as a form subdivision under individual musical instruments and families of instruments.
———Group instruction
H 1161
Use as a form subdivision under individual musical instruments and families of instruments.
———Self-instruction
H 1161
Use as a form subdivision under individual musical instruments and families of instruments.
—Methods (Heavy metal)
H 1161
Use as a form subdivision under individual musical instruments and families of instruments.
———Group instruction
H 1161
Use as a form subdivision under individual musical instruments and families of instruments.
———Self-instruction
H 1161
Use as a form subdivision under individual musical instruments and families of instruments.
—Methods (Honky-tonk)
H 1161
Use as a form subdivision under individual musical instruments and families of instruments.
———Group instruction
H 1161
Use as a form subdivision under individual musical instruments and families of instruments.
———Self-instruction
H 1161
Use as a form subdivision under individual musical instruments and families of instruments.
—Methods (Jazz)
H 1161
Use as a form subdivision under individual musical instruments and families of instruments.
———Group instruction
H 1161
Use as a form subdivision under individual musical instruments and families of instruments.
BT —Methods—Group instruction
———Self-instruction
H 1161
Use as a form subdivision under individual musical instruments and families of instruments.
BT —Methods—Self-instruction
—Methods (Jazz-rock)
H1161
Use as a form subdivision under individual musical instruments and families of instruments.
———Group instruction
H1161
Use as a form subdivision under individual musical instruments and families of instruments.
BT —Methods—Group instruction
———Self-instruction
H 1161
Use as a form subdivision under individual musical instruments and families of instruments.
BT —Methods—Self-instruction
—Methods (Latin jazz)
H 1161
Use as a form subdivision under individual musical instruments and families of instruments.
———Group instruction
H 1161
Use as a form subdivision under individual musical instruments and families of instruments.

———Self-instruction
H 1161
Use as a form subdivision under individual musical instruments and families of instruments.
—Methods (Popular music)
H 1161
Use as a form subdivision under individual musical instruments and families of instruments.
———Group instruction
H 1161
Use as a form subdivision under individual musical instruments and families of instruments.
———Self-instruction
H 1161
Use as a form subdivision under individual musical instruments and families of instruments.
—Methods (Progressive rock)
H 1161
Use as a form subdivision under individual musical instruments and families of instruments.
———Group instruction
H 1161
Use as a form subdivision under individual musical instruments and families of instruments.
———Self-instruction
H 1161
Use as a form subdivision under individual musical instruments and families of instruments.
—Methods (Ragtime)
H 1161
Use as a form subdivision under individual musical instruments and families of instruments.
———Group instruction
H 1161
Use as a form subdivision under individual musical instruments and families of instruments.
———Self-instruction
H 1161
Use as a form subdivision under individual musical instruments and families of instruments.
—Methods (Reggae)
H 1161
Use as a form subdivision under individual musical instruments and families of instruments.
———Group instruction
H 1161
Use as a form subdivision under individual musical instruments and families of instruments.
———Self-instruction
H 1161
Use as a form subdivision under individual musical instruments and families of instruments.
—Methods (Rhythm and blues)
H 1161
Use as a form subdivision under individual musical instruments and families of instruments.
———Group instruction
H 1161
Use as a form subdivision under individual musical instruments and families of instruments.
———Self-instruction
H 1161
Use as a form subdivision under individual musical instruments and families of instruments.
—Methods (Rock)
H 1161
Use as a form subdivision under individual musical instruments and families of instruments.
———Group instruction
H 1161
Use as a form subdivision under individual musical instruments and families of instruments.
———Self-instruction
H 1161
Use as a form subdivision under individual musical instruments and families of instruments.
—Methods (Salsa)
H 1161
Use as a form subdivision under individual musical instruments and families of instruments.
———Group instruction
H 1161
Use as a form subdivision under individual musical instruments and families of instruments.
———Self-instruction
H 1161
Use as a form subdivision under individual musical instruments and families of instruments.
—Methods (Swing)
H 1161
Use as a form subdivision under individual musical instruments and families of instruments.

——**Group instruction**
　　H 1161
　　　Use as a form subdivision under individual musical instruments and families of instruments.

——**Self-instruction**
　　H 1161
　　　Use as a form subdivision under individual musical instruments and families of instruments.

—**Methods (Western swing)**
　　H 1161
　　　Use as a form subdivision under individual musical instruments and families of instruments.

——**Group instruction**
　　H 1161
　　　Use as a form subdivision under individual musical instruments and families of instruments.

——**Self-instruction**
　　H 1161
　　　Use as a form subdivision under individual musical instruments and families of instruments.

—**Methylation**
　　H 1149
　　　Use as a topical subdivision under individual chemicals and groups of chemicals.

—**Metonyms**
　　H 1154
　　　Use as a topical subdivision under individual languages and groups of languages.

—**Metrics and rhythmics**
　　H 1154
　　　Use as a topical subdivision under individual ancient languages. Under individual modern languages and groups of modern languages use the subdivisions Rhythm; Versification.

—**Mexican influences**
　　H 1156
　　　Use as a topical subdivision under individual literatures.
　　BT　—Foreign influences

—**Microbiology**　(May Subd Geog)
　　H 1147; H 1150; H 1158; H 1164; H 1180
　　　Use as a topical subdivision under individual animals and groups of animals, individual diseases and types of diseases, individual materials and types of materials, individual organs and regions of the body, and individual plants and groups of plants.
　　UF　—Bacteriology
　　　　　[Former subdivision]
　　NT　—Germplasm resources—
　　　　　Microbiology
　　　　—Larvae—Microbiology

—**Microform catalogs**
　　H 1095; H 1105
　　　Use as a form subdivision under names of individual institutions and collections for catalogs that list works stored in those institutions or collections in microform editions.
　　BT　—Catalogs
　　NT　—Archives—Microform catalogs
　　　　—Bibliography—Microform catalogs
　　　　—Correspondence—Microform catalogs
　　　　—Library—Microform catalogs
　　　　—Manuscripts—Microform catalogs

—**Micropropagation**　(May Subd Geog)
　　H 1180
　　　Use as a topical subdivision under individual plants and groups of plants.
　　UF　—In-vitro propagation
　　　　—Propagation—In-vitro
　　　　　[Former subdivision]

—**Microscopy**　(May Subd Geog)
　　H 1158; H 1164; H 1180
　　　Use as a topical subdivision under individual materials and types of materials other than metals, individual organs and regions of the body, and individual plants and groups of plants.

—**Microstructure**
　　H 1158
　　　Use as a topical subdivision under individual materials and types of materials.

—Middle school education
　　USE　—Education (Middle school)

—**Migration**　(May Subd Geog)
　　H 1147
　　　Use as a topical subdivision under individual animals and groups of animals.

—**Climatic factors**　(May Subd Geog)
　　H 1147
　　　Use as a topical subdivision under individual animals and groups of animals.
　　BT　—Climatic factors

——**Endocrine aspects**
　　H 1147
　　　Use as a topical subdivision under individual animals and groups of animals.
　　UF　—Hormonal aspect of migration

—**Migrations**
　　H 1103
　　　Use as a topical subdivision under ethnic groups.

—**Military aspects**　(May Subd Geog)
　　H 1153
　　　Use as a topical subdivision under types of industries.

—**Military capital**
　　H 1159
　　　Use as a topical subdivision under military services.
　　UF　—Capital, Military

—**Military construction operations**
　　H 1159
　　　Use as a topical subdivision under military services.

——**Law and legislation**
　　H 1159
　　　Further subdivide by subdivisions used under legal topics.
　　　Use as a topical subdivision under military services.
　　BT　—Law and legislation

—**Military currency**　(May Subd Geog)
　　H 1200
　　　Use as a topical subdivision under individual wars.
　　UF　—Currency, Military

—Military decorations
　　USE　—Medals, badges, decorations, etc.

—Military history
　　USE　—History, Military

—**Military intelligence**　(May Subd Geog)
　　H 1200
　　　Use as a topical subdivision under individual wars.
　　UF　—Intelligence, Military
　　NT　—Electronic intelligence

—Military journalism
　　USE　—Journalism, Military

—**Military leadership**
　　H 1110
　　　Use as a topical subdivision under names of individual persons.
　　UF　—Leadership, Military

—**Military life**
　　H 1159
　　　Use as a topical subdivision under military services.

—**Military police**
　　H 1159
　　　Use as a topical subdivision under military services other than air forces and navies. Under air forces, use the subdivision Air police. Under navies, use the subdivision Shore patrol.

——**Foreign auxiliaries**
　　H 1159
　　　Use as a topical subdivision under military services.
　　UF　—Foreign auxiliaries of military police

—**Military policy**
　　H 1140
　　　Use as a topical subdivision under countries, etc.
　　BT　—Government policy

——**Religious aspects**
　　H 1140
　　　Use as a topical subdivision under names of countries and regions larger than countries.

—**Military relations**　(May Subd Geog)
　　H 1140
　　　Use as a topical subdivision under names of regions, countries, cities, etc., for non-hostile military relations and/or cooperation between one region or jurisdiction and another.
　　BT　—Relations

——**Foreign countries**
　　H 1140
　　　Use as a topical subdivision under names of regions, countries, cities, etc.
　　BT　—Relations

—**Militia**
　　H 1140
　　　Further subdivide by subdivisions used under military services.
　　　Use as a topical subdivision under names of countries, etc.
　　NT　—Naval militia

—**Milling**　(May Subd Geog)
　　H 1180
　　　Use as a topical subdivision under individual plants and groups of plants.
　　BT　—Processing

—**Mimetic words**
　　H 1154
　　　Use as a topical subdivision under individual languages and groups of languages.

—**Minangkabau influences**
　　H 1156
　　　Use as a topical subdivision under individual literatures.

—Minimization of wastes
　　USE　—Waste minimization

—**Minorities**
　　H 1159
　　　Further subdivide by subdivisions used under classes of persons.
　　　Use as a topical subdivision under military services.

—**Minority authors**
　　H 1156
　　　Use as a topical subdivision under individual literatures.

—Minority leader
　　USE　—Minority leaders

—**Minority leaders**
　　H 1155
　　　Further subdivide by subdivisions used under classes of persons.
　　　Use as a topical subdivision under the names of individual legislative bodies.
　　UF　—Minority leader
　　　　　[Former subdivision]
　　BT　—Leadership

—Minority whip
　　USE　—Minority whips

—**Minority whips**
　　H 1155
　　　Further subdivide by subdivisions used under classes of persons.
　　　Use as a topical subdivision under names of individual legislative bodies.
　　UF　—Minority whip
　　　　　[Former subdivision]
　　BT　—Leadership

—**Miracles**
　　H 1110
　　　Use as a topical subdivision under names of individual persons to whom miracles are attributed.

—**Miscellanea**
　　H 1095
　　　Use as a topical subdivision under subjects for works about miscellaneous or special aspects of those subjects for which no other subdivision exists or can be established and yet, because of their unusual nature, cannot be treated as general works on those subjects.
　　UF　—Curiosa and miscellanea
　　　　　[Former subdivision]
　　　　—Miscellaneous aspects

—**Miscellanea**
　　H 1095
　　　Use as a form subdivision under subjects for compilations of unusual or miscellaneous facts about the subject without continuous text as well as for works in a question and answer format.
　　UF　—Curiosa and miscellanea
　　　　　[Former subdivision]
　　　　—Questions and answers

—Miscellaneous aspects
　　USE　—Miscellanea

—**Misfueling**　(May Subd Geog)
　　H 1195
　　　Use as a topical subdivision under individual land vehicles and types of land vehicles.

—**Missing in action** *(May Subd Geog)*
H 1200
Further subdivide by subdivisions used under classes of persons.
Use as a topical subdivision under individual wars.

—**Missions** *(May Subd Geog)*
H 1103; H 1185; H 1186; H 1187
Use as a topical subdivision under ethnic groups for works on Missions to those groups. Also use under individual religions and Christian denominations and names of individual religious and monastic orders for works on missions or missionary activities sponsored or undertaken by those religions or organizations.

—Mistresses of kings and rulers
USE —Kings and rulers—Paramours

—**Mixing** *(May Subd Geog)*
H 1158
Use as a topical subdivision under individual materials and types of materials.

—**Mnemonic devices**
H 1188
Use as a topical subdivision under uniform titles of sacred works.

—**Mobilization**
H 1159
Use as a topical subdivision under military services.

—**Modality**
H 1154
Use as a topical subdivision under individual languages and groups of languages.

—**Models** *(May Subd Geog)*
1195; H 1095; H 1164
Use as a topical subdivision under types of objects and organs and regions of the body.

——**Finishing** *(May Subd Geog)*
H 1195
Use as a topical subdivision under individual land vehicles and types of land vehicles.
BT —Finishing

——**Radio control** *(May Subd Geog)*
H 1195
Use as a topical subdivision under individual land vehicles and types of land vehicles.
UF —Radio control of models

—Modification of motors
USE —Motors—Modification

—**Moisture** *(May Subd Geog)*
H 1095; H 1158; H 1180
Use as a topical subdivision under types of farm produce, individual materials and types of materials, types of objects, technical equipment, etc., for works on their moisture content.

—**Molecular aspects**
H 1147; H 1150; H 1164; H 1180
Use as a topical subdivision under individual animals and groups of animals, individual plants and groups of plants, individual diseases and types of diseases, and individual organs or regions of the body.
NT —Aging—Molecular aspects
—Classification—Molecular aspects
—Diseases—Molecular aspects
—Growth—Molecular aspects
—Metamorphosis—Molecular aspects
—Parasites—Molecular aspects
—Phylogeny—Molecular aspects

—**Molecular diagnosis** *(May Subd Geog)*
H 1150
Use as a topical subdivision under individual diseases and types of diseases.
BT —Diagnosis

—**Molecular genetics**
H 1147; H 1180
Use as a topical subdivision under individual animals and groups of animals and individual plants and groups of plants.
BT —Genetics

—**Molecular rotation**
H 1149
Use as a topical subdivision under individual chemicals and groups of chemicals.
UF —Rotation, Molecular

—**Money** *(May Subd Geog)*
H 1103
Use as a topical subdivision under ethnic groups.

—**Mongolian authors**
H 1156
Use as a topical subdivision under individual literatures.

—**Monitoring** *(May Subd Geog)*
H 1147; H 1180
Use as a topical subdivision under individual animals and groups of animals and individual plants and groups of plants.
NT —Diseases and pests—Monitoring

—**Monosyllables**
H 1154
Use as a topical subdivision under individual languages and groups of languages.

—**Monuments** *(May Subd Geog)*
H 1100; H 1103; H 1110; H 1120; H 1200
Use as a topical subdivision under names of individual persons and families, classes of persons, ethnic groups, and individual wars.
UF —Monuments, etc.
[Former subdivision]

—Monuments, etc.
USE —Monuments

—**Mood**
H 1154
Use as a topical subdivision under individual languages and groups of languages.
NT —Subjunctive

—**Moral and ethical aspects**
(May Subd Geog)
H 1095; H 1200
Use as a topical subdivision under individual wars and non-religious or non-ethical topics.
UF —Ethical aspects
—Moral and religious aspects
[Former subdivision]
—Moral aspects
[Former subdivision]

—Moral and religious aspects
USE —Moral and ethical aspects

—Moral aspects
USE —Moral and ethical aspects

—**Moral conditions**
H 1140
Use as a topical subdivision under names of countries, cities, etc.

—Moral ideas
USE —Ethics

—**Mormon authors**
H 1156
Use as a topical subdivision under individual literatures.

—**Morphemics**
H 1154
Use as a topical subdivision under languages and groups of languages.

—**Morphogenesis** *(May Subd Geog)*
H 1147; H 1180
Use as a topical subdivision under individual animals and groups of animals and individual plants and groups of plants.
NT —Photomorphogenesis

—**Morphology**
H 1147; H 1154; H 1180
Use as a topical subdivision under individual animals and groups of animals, individual languages and groups of languages, and individual plants and groups of plants.
NT —Dialects—Morphology
—Pollen—Morphology
—Seeds—Morphology
—Spermatozoa—Morphology
—Spores—Morphology

—**Morphophonemics**
H 1154
Use as a topical subdivision under individual languages and groups of languages.

—**Morphosyntax**
H 1154
Use as a topical subdivision under individual languages and groups of languages.

—**Mortality** *(May Subd Geog)*
H 1100; H 1103; H 1147; H 1150; H 1180
Use as a topical subdivision under classes of persons, ethnic groups, individual animals and groups of animals, and individual diseases and types of diseases, and individual plants and groups of plants.
UF —Patients—Mortality

—Mortuary customs
USE —Funeral customs and rites

—**Motion picture plays**
H 1110
Do not use under authors who write principally film scripts.
Use as a topical subdivision under names of individual literary authors for works of criticism about film scripts written by the author.
UF —Moving-picture plays
[Former subdivision]
—Screenplays
BT —Criticism and interpretation

—**Motion pictures and the war, [revolution, etc.]**
H 1200
Complete the subdivision by repeating the generic term for the type of engagement contained in the heading.
Use as a topical subdivision under individual wars.

—Motives, themes
USE —Themes, motives

—**Motorcycle troops**
H 1159
Use as a topical subdivision under individual military services.

—**Motors**
H 1195
Use as a topical subdivision under individual land vehicles and types of land vehicles.

——**Bearings** *(May Subd Geog)*
H 1195
Use as a topical subdivision under individual land vehicles and types of land vehicles.
BT —Bearings

——**Camshafts**
H 1195
Use as a topical subdivision under individual land vehicles and types of land vehicles.
UF —Camshafts of motors

——**Carburetors**
H 1195
Use as a topical subdivision under individual land vehicles and types of land vehicles.
UF —Carburetors of motors

——**Combustion** *(May Subd Geog)*
H 1195
Use as a topical subdivision under individual land vehicles and types of land vehicles.
BT —Combustion

——**Computer control systems**
(May Subd Geog)
H 1195
Use as a topical subdivision under individual land vehicles and types of land vehicles.
UF —Computer control systems for motors

——**Control systems**
H 1195
Use as a topical subdivision under individual land vehicles and types of land vehicles.
UF —Control systems for motors

——**Cooling** *(May Subd Geog)*
H 1195
Use as a topical subdivision under individual land vehicles and types of land vehicles.
BT —Cooling

——**Cooling systems** *(May Subd Geog)*
H 1195
Use as a topical subdivision under individual land vehicles and types of land vehicles.
UF —Cooling systems of motors

——**Crankshafts**
H 1195
Use as a topical subdivision under individual land vehicles and types of land vehicles.
UF —Crankshafts of motors

——**Cylinder blocks**
H 1195
Use as a topical subdivision under individual land vehicles and types of land vehicles.
UF —Cylinder blocks of motors

——**Cylinder heads** *(May Subd Geog)*
H 1195
Use as a topical subdivision under individual land vehicles and types of land vehicles.
UF —Cylinder heads of motors

——**Cylinders**
H 1195
Use as a topical subdivision under individual
land vehicles and types of land vehicles.
UF —Cylinders of motors

——**Electronic fuel injection systems**
H 1195
Use as a topical subdivision under individual
land vehicles and types of land vehicles.
UF —Electronic fuel injection systems
of motors
BT —Motors—Fuel injection systems

——**Exhaust gas** *(May Subd Geog)*
H 1195
Use as a topical subdivision under individual
land vehicles and types of land vehicles.
UF —Exhaust gas of motors

————**Law and legislation** *(May Subd Geog)*
H 1195
Further subdivide by subdivisions used un-
der legal topics.
Use as a topical subdivision under individ-
ual land vehicles and types of land vehicles.
BT —Law and legislation

——**Exhaust systems**
H 1195
Use as a topical subdivision under individual
land vehicles and types of land vehicles.
UF —Exhaust systems of motors

——**Fuel injection systems**
H 1195
Use as a topical subdivision under individual
land vehicles and types of land vehicles.
UF —Fuel injection systems of motors
NT —Motors—Electronic fuel
injection systems

——**Knock** *(May Subd Geog)*
H 1195
Use as a topical subdivision under individual
land vehicles and types of land vehicles.
UF —Knock of motors

——**Lubrication systems** *(May Subd Geog)*
H 1195
Use as a topical subdivision under individual
land vehicles and types of land vehicles.
UF —Lubrication systems of motors

——**Modification** *(May Subd Geog)*
H 1195
Use as a topical subdivision under individual
land vehicles and types of land vehicles.
UF —Modification of motors

——**Mufflers**
H 1195
Use as a topical subdivision under individual
land vehicles and types of land vehicles.
UF —Mufflers of motors

————**Acoustic properties** *(May Subd Geog)*
H 1195
Use as a topical subdivision under individ-
ual land vehicles and types of land vehicles.
UF —Acoustic properties of mufflers

——**Oil filters**
H 1195
Use as a topical subdivision under individual
land vehicles and types of land vehicles.
UF —Oil filters of motors

——**Parts**
H 1195
Use as a topical subdivision under individual
land vehicles and types of land vehicles.
BT —Parts

——**Pistons and piston rings**
H 1195
Use as a topical subdivision under individual
land vehicles and types of land vehicles.
UF —Piston rings of motors
—Pistons of motors

——**Soundproofing** *(May Subd Geog)*
H 1195
Use as a topical subdivision under individual
land vehicles and types of land vehicles.
BT —Soundproofing

——**Superchargers**
H 1195
Use as a topical subdivision under individual
land vehicles and types of land vehicles.
UF —Superchargers of motors

——**Thermodynamics**
H 1195
Use as a topical subdivision under individual
land vehicles and types of land vehicles.

——**Timing belts**
H 1195
Use as a topical subdivision under individual
land vehicles and types of land vehicles.
UF —Timing belts of motors

——**Turbochargers**
H 1195
Use as a topical subdivision under individual
land vehicles and types of land vehicles.
UF —Turbochargers of motors

——**Valves** *(May Subd Geog)*
H 1195
Use as a topical subdivision under individual
land vehicles and types of land vehicles.
UF —Valves of motors

——**Vibration** *(May Subd Geog)*
H 1195
Use as a topical subdivision under individual
land vehicles and types of land vehicles.
BT —Vibration

—**Motors (Compressed-gas)**
(May Subd Geog)
H 1195
Use as a topical subdivision under individual
land vehicles and types of land vehicles.
UF —Compressed-gas motors

—**Motors (Diesel)**
H 1195
Use as a topical subdivision under individual
land vehicles and types of land vehicles.
UF —Diesel motors

——**Exhaust gas** *(May Subd Geog)*
H 1195
Use as a topical subdivision under individual
land vehicles and types of land vehicles.
UF —Exhaust gas of diesel motors

—**Motors (Liquid nitrogen)**
(May Subd Geog)
H 1195
Use as a topical subdivision under individual
land vehicles and types of land vehicles.
UF —Liquid nitrogen motors

—**Motors (Two-stroke cycle)**
H 1195
Use as a topical subdivision under individual
land vehicles and types of land vehicles.
UF —Two-stroke cycle motors

—**Mountain warfare**
H 1200
Use as a topical subdivision under individual
wars.

—**Movements**
H 1164
Use as a topical subdivision under individual or-
gans and regions of the body.
BT —Physiology

—Moving-picture plays
USE —Motion picture plays

—Mufflers of motors
USE —Motors—Mufflers

—**Mulching** *(May Subd Geog)*
H 1180
Use as a topical subdivision under individual
plants and groups of plants.

—**Multiphonics**
H 1161
Use as a topical subdivision under individual
musical instruments and families of instruments.

—**Muscles**
H 1164
Use as a topical subdivision under individual or-
gans and regions of the body.
BT —Anatomy

—**Museums** *(May Subd Geog)*
H 1095; H 1100; H 1103; H 1105; H 1110;
H 1120; H 1187; H 1200
Do not subdivide geographically under names of
individual corporate bodies.
Use as a topical subdivision under names of indi-
vidual persons, families, and corporate bodies, and
under ethnic groups, individual wars, and topical
headings for which phrase headings for the type of
museum have not been established.
UF —Exhibitions and museums
[Former subdivision]
—Museums, relics, etc.

[Former subdivision]
—Museums, relics, etc.
USE —Museums

—**Music**
H 1103
Use as a topical subdivision under ethnic groups
for works about music of the group.

—**Music**
H 1103
Use as a form subdivision under ethnic groups
for music of the group.

——**Bibliography**
H 1103
Use this subdivision combination as a form
subdivision under ethnic groups.
BT —Bibliography

——**Discography**
H 1103
Use this subdivision combination as a form
subdivision under ethnic groups.
BT —Discography

——**History and criticism**
H 1103
Use as a topical subdivision under ethnic
groups.
BT —History and criticism

—Music and songs
USE —Songs and music

—**Music and the war,** *[revolution, etc.]*
H 1200
Complete the subdivision by repeating the
generic term for the type of engagement contained
in the heading.
Use as a topical subdivision under individual
wars for works about songs or music related to the
war.

—**Musical instrument collections**
H 1105; H 1110; H 1120
Use as a topical subdivision under names of individual persons, families, and corporate bodies
for works about their collections of musical instruments.

—**Musical settings**
H 1110; H 1156
Use as a topical subdivision under names of individual persons for works on musical compositions
based on their written works or words. Also use
under individual literatures for works on musical
compositions based on texts of those literatures.

—**Musical settings**
H 1110; H 1156
Use as a form subdivision under names of individual persons for musical scores or sound recordings in which writings or words of the person have
been set to music. Also use under individual literatures for musical scores or sound recordings in
which those literary texts have been set to music.
UF —Settings, Musical

——**History and criticism**
H 1100; H 1156
Use as a topical subdivision under names of
individual persons and under individual litera-
tures.
BT —History and criticism

—**Muslim authors**
H 1156
Use as a topical subdivision under individual lit-
eratures.

—**Mutation**
H 1154
Use as a topical subdivision under individual
languages and groups of languages.

—**Mutation breeding** *(May Subd Geog)*
H 1180
Use as a topical subdivision under individual
plants and groups of plants.
BT —Breeding

—**Mutual intelligibility**
H 1154
Use as a topical subdivision under groups of lan-
guages.
UF —Intelligibility, Mutual
NT —Dialects—Mutual intelligibility

—**Mycenaean influences**
H 1156
Use as a topical subdivision under individual
languages.
BT —Foreign influences

—**Mythology** *(May Subd Geog)*
H 1095
Use as a topical subdivision under topical headings.
NT —Kings and rulers—Mythology
—**Name**
H 1095; H 1103; H 1105; H 1110; H 1140;
H 1187; H 1200
Use as a topical subdivision under names of countries, cities, etc., individual persons, deities, and corporate bodies, and under ethnic groups, Christian denominations, wars, events, etc., for works on the name's origin, history, spelling, validity, etc.
—**Names**
H 1095; H 1147; H 1151.5
Use as a topical subdivision under types of objects, events, organizations, and educational institutions for works on the rules, customs, etc., in the naming of those items. Also use under groups of animals for works on the history, origin, customs, etc., of selecting personal names for individual animals.
——Etymology
USE —Etymology—Names
—Narrative criticism
USE —Criticism, Narrative
—Narratives, Personal
USE —Personal narratives
—**Nasality**
H 1154
Use as a topical subdivision under individual languages and groups of languages.
—**National Guard**
H 1140
Further subdivide by subdivisions used under military services.
Use as a topical subdivision under names of countries, etc.
—**Natural history collections**
H 1105; H 1110; H 1120
Use as a topical subdivision under names of individual persons, families, and corporate bodies for works about their collections of natural history items or specimens.
—Naval history
USE —History, Naval
—**Naval militia**
H 1140
Further subdivide by subdivisions used under military services.
Use as a topical subdivision under names of countries, etc.
BT —Militia
—**Naval operations**
H 1200
Use as a topical subdivision under individual wars.
UF —Battles, sieges, etc.
[Former subdivision]
——**Submarine**
H 1200
Use as a topical subdivision under individual wars.
UF —Submarine operations
—**Naval operations, American, [British, etc.]**
H 1200
Use as a topical subdivision under individual wars.
—**Navigation**
H 1145.5
Use as a topical subdivision under names of individual bodies of water.
——**Law and legislation**
H 1145.5
Further subdivide by subdivisions used under legal topics.
Use as a topical subdivision under names of individual bodies of water.
BT —Law and legislation
—**Nazi persecution** *(May Subd Geog)*
H 1186
Use as a topical subdivision under names of individual religious and monastic orders.
UF —Persecution, Nazi
—**Necrology**
H 1186
Use as a form subdivision under names of individual religious and monastic orders.

—**Necrosis** *(May Subd Geog)*
H 1164
Further subdivide by subdivisions used under diseases.
Use as a topical subdivision under individual organs and regions of the body.
BT —Diseases
—**Needle biopsy** *(May Subd Geog)*
H 1164
Use as a topical subdivision under individual organs and regions of the body.
UF —Biopsy, Needle
[Former subdivision]
BT —Biopsy
—Needs assessment in prevention of diseases
USE —Prevention—Needs assessment
—**Negatives**
H 1154
Use as a topical subdivision under individual languages and groups of languages.
—**Nervous system**
H 1147
Use as a topical subdivision under individual animals and groups of animals.
NT —Sense organs
—**Nests** *(May Subd Geog)*
H 1147
Use as a topical subdivision under individual nesting animals and groups of nesting animals.
BT —Habitations
——**Abandonment** *(May Subd Geog)*
H 1147
Use as a topical subdivision under individual animals and groups of animals.
UF —Abandonment of nests
——**Counting** *(May Subd Geog)*
H 1147
Use as a topical subdivision under individual animals and groups of animals.
BT —Counting
—Networks, Computer
USE —Computer networks
—Networks, Social
USE —Social networks
—**Neutralization**
H 1154
Use as a topical subdivision under individual languages and groups of languages.
—**New words**
H 1154
Use as a topical subdivision under individual languages and groups of languages.
BT —Vocabulary
—News media coverage
USE —Press coverage
—**Newspapers**
H 1095; H 1103; H 1140
Use as a form subdivision under subjects.
BT —Periodicals
—**Nitrogen content** *(May Subd Geog)*
H 1158
Use as a topical subdivision under individual materials and types of materials.
—Nobility, Titles of
USE —Titles
—**Noise**
H 1095; H 1153
Use as a topical subdivision under types of industries and topical headings.
—Nomenclators
USE —Nomenclature
—**Nomenclature**
H 1095; H 1147; H 1180
Use as a topical subdivision under scientific and technical disciplines and types of substances, plants, and animals for works about the creation or application of systematically derived and formally sanctioned names of those topics.
UF —Scientific names
—**Nomenclature**
H 1095; H 1147; H 1180
Use as a form subdivision under scientific and technical disciplines and types of substances, plants, and animals for systematically derived lists of names or designations that have been formally adopted or sanctioned.
UF —Nomenclators
—Scientific names

—**Nomenclature (Popular)**
H 1147; H 1180
Use as a topical subdivision under individual animals and groups of animals and individual plants and groups of plants for works about common names of those organisms.
UF —Common names
—Popular nomenclature
—**Nomenclature (Popular)**
H 1147; H 1180
Use as a form subdivision under individual animals and groups of animals and individual plants and groups of plants for lists of common names of those organisms.
UF —Common names
—Popular nomenclature
———**French, [Italian, etc.]**
H 1147
Use as a form subdivision under individual animals and groups of animals.
—**Nominals**
H 1154
Use as a topical subdivision under individual languages and groups of languages.
—**Nomograms**
H 1095
Use as a form subdivision under topical headings.
—**Non-commissioned officers**
H 1159
Further subdivide by subdivisions used under classes of persons.
Use as a topical subdivision under military services.
—**Non-commissioned officers' handbooks**
H 1159
Use as a form subdivision under military services.
BT —Handbooks, manuals, etc.
—**Nondestructive testing** *(May Subd Geog)*
H 1158
Use as a topical subdivision under individual materials and types of materials.
BT —Testing
—**Northern Thai influences**
H1156
Use as a topical subdivision under individual literatures.
—**Notation**
H 1095; H 1158
Use as a topical subdivision under scientific and technical topics for works about the symbols, formulae, or signs employed in those topics.
—**Notation**
H 1095
Use as a form subdivision under scientific and technical topics for works containing the symbols, formulae, or signs employed in those topics.
—**Notebooks, sketchbooks, etc.**
H 1110
Use as a topical subdivision under names of individual persons for works about notebooks, sketchbooks, etc., of the person.
UF —Sketchbooks
—**Notebooks, sketchbooks, etc.**
H 1110
Use as a form subdivision under names of individual persons for individual or collections of notebooks, sketchbooks, etc., of the person.
UF —Sketchbooks
—**Noun**
H 1154
Use as a topical subdivision under individual languages and groups of languages.
NT —Collective nouns
—**Noun phrase**
H 1154
Use as a topical subdivision under individual languages and groups of languages.
—Novels
USE —Fiction
—**Number**
H 1154
Use as a topical subdivision under individual languages and groups of languages.
—Numbers, Code
USE —Code numbers
—Numbers, Serial
USE —Serial numbers

—**Numerals**
H 1154
Use as a topical subdivision under individual languages and groups of languages.

—**Numerical division**
H 1188
Use as a topical subdivision under uniform titles of sacred works.
UF —Division, Numerical

—**Numismatic collections**
H 1105; H 1110; H 1120
Use as a topical subdivision under names of individual persons, families, and corporate bodies for works about their numismatic collections.
NT —Coin collections

—**Numismatics**
H 1110
Use as a topical subdivision under names of individual persons for works on the representation of the person on coins, tokens, medals, paper money, etc.
NT —Medals

—**Nurses**
H 1159
Further subdivide by subdivisions used under classes of persons.
Use as a topical subdivision under military services.
BT —Medical personnel

—**Nursing** *(May Subd Geog)*
H 1150
Use as a topical subdivision under individual diseases and types of diseases.
NT —Diseases—Nursing
—Surgery—Nursing
—Transplantation—Nursing

—**Nursing home care** *(May Subd Geog)*
H 1100
Use as a topical subdivision under classes of persons.
BT —Institutional care

—**Nutrition** *(May Subd Geog)*
H 1100; H 1103; H 1147; H 1180
Use as a topical subdivision under classes of persons, ethnic groups, individual animals and groups of animals, and individual plants and groups of plants.
NT —Embryos—Nutrition

——**Requirements** *(May Subd Geog)*
H 1100; H 1147
Use as a topical subdivision under classes of persons and individual animals and groups of animals.
UF —Nutritional requirements
—Requirements, Nutritional

—**Nutritional aspects** *(May Subd Geog)*
H 1150
Use as a topical subdivision under individual diseases and types of diseases.
NT —Diseases—Nutritional aspects
—Diseases and pests—Nutritional aspects
—Surgery—Nutritional aspects

—Nutritional requirements
USE —Nutrition—Requirements

—**Obituaries**
H 1100; H 1103
Use as a form subdivision under classes of persons and ethnic groups.

—**Obscene words**
H 1154
Use as a topical subdivision under individual languages and groups of languages.
BT —Vocabulary

—**Observations**
H 1095
Use as a topical subdivision under scientific topics for works about the processing and use of data obtained by the observation of natural phenomena.

—**Observations**
H 1095
Use as a form subdivision under scientific topics for works consisting of numerical data obtained by the observation of natural phenomena.
NT —Climate—Observations

—**Observers' manuals**
H 1095
Use as a form subdivision under scientific topics for instruction books on making observations of natural phenomena.
BT —Handbooks, manuals, etc.

—**Obsolete words**
H 1154
Use as a topical subdivision under individual languages and groups of languages.
BT —Vocabulary

—Occidental influences
USE —Western influences

—**Occupant restraint systems** *(May Subd Geog)*
H 1195
Use as a topical subdivision under individual land vehicles and types of land vehicles.
UF —Restraint systems, Occupant
BT —Safety appliances
NT —Seat belts

—Occupational descriptions
USE —Job descriptions

—Occupational exposure limits
USE —Threshold limit values

—**Occupational specialties**
H 1159
Use as a topical subdivision under military services.

—**Occupations**
H 1186
Use as a topical subdivision under names of individual religious and monastic orders.

—**Occupied territories**
H 1200
Use as a topical subdivision under individual wars.

—**Odor** *(May Subd Geog)*
H 1147
Use as a topical subdivision under individual animals and groups of animals.

—Odor control of animal housing
USE —Housing—Odor control

—Oeuvre catalogues
USE —Catalogues raisonnés

—**Off-road operation** *(May Subd Geog)*
H 1195
Use as a topical subdivision under individual land vehicles and types of land vehicles.
UF —Operation off-road

—Office records
USE —Records and correspondence

—**Officer efficiency reports**
H 1159
Use as a topical subdivision under military services.

—**Officers**
H 1159
Further subdivide by subdivisions used under classes of persons.
Use as a topical subdivision under military services.
NT —African American officers
—General staff officers
—Officers on detached service

—**Officers' clubs**
H 1159
Use as a topical subdivision under military services.
UF —Clubs, Officers'

—**Officers' handbooks**
H 1159
Use as a form subdivision under military services.
BT —Handbooks, manuals, etc.

—**Officers on detached service**
H 1159
Use as a topical subdivision under military services.
BT —Officers

—**Officials and employees** *(May Subd Geog)*
H 1095; H 1105; H 1140; H 1149.5; H 1155; H 1159
Subdivide geographically only under names of countries, cities, etc.
Further subdivide by subdivisions used under classes of persons.
Use as a topical subdivision under types of government agencies. Also use under names of countries, cities, etc., and individual international, government, and quasi-governmental agencies. Under names of individual educational institutions and nongovernmental corporate bodies use Employees.
NT —Colonies—Officials and employees

——**Accidents** *(May Subd Geog)*
H 1105; H 1140
Do not subdivide geographically under names of corporate bodies.
Use as a topical subdivision under names of countries, cities, etc., and individual government agencies.
BT —Accidents

——**Furloughs**
H 1105; H 1140
Use as a topical subdivision under names of countries, cities, etc., and individual government agencies.
UF —Furloughs of officials and employees

——**Leave regulations**
H 1105; H 1140
Use as a topical subdivision under names of countries, cities, etc., and individual government agencies.
UF —Leave regulations of officials and employees

——**Payroll deductions**
H 1140
Use as a topical subdivision under names of countries, cities, etc.
UF —Payroll deductions of officials and employees

——**Pensions**
H 1155
Use as a topical subdivision under names of individual legislative bodies.
UF —Salaries, pensions, etc.
[Former subdivision]
BT —Pensions

——Salaries, allowances, etc.
USE —Officials and employees—Salaries, etc.

——**Salaries, etc.** *(May Subd Geog)*
H 1105; H 1140; H 1155
Subdivide geographically only under names of countries, cities, etc.
Use as a topical subdivision under names of countries, cities, etc., individual government agencies, and individual legislative bodies.
UF —Appointments, promotions, salaries, etc.
[Former subdivision]
—Officials and employees—Salaries, allowances, etc.
[Former subdivision]
BT —Salaries, etc.

——**Regional disparities**
H 1105; H 1140
Use as a topical subdivision under names of countries, etc., and individual government agencies.
BT —Regional disparities

——**Turnover**
H 1105; H 1140
Use as a topical subdivision under names of countries, cities, etc., and individual government agencies.
UF —Turnover of officials and employees

———**Foreign countries**
H 1140
Use as a topical subdivision under names of countries, cities, etc.
BT —Foreign countries

—Officials and employees
——Foreign countries (Continued)
———Foreign language competency
    H 1140
      Use as a topical subdivision under names of countries, cities, etc.
      UF —Foreign language competency of officials and employees

—Officials and employees, Alien
    H 1140
      Further subdivide by subdivisions used under classes of persons.
      Use as a topical subdivision under names of countries, cities, etc.
      UF —Alien officials and employees

—Officials and employees, Honorary
    H 1140
      Further subdivide by subdivisions used under classes of persons.
      Use as a topical subdivision under names of countries, cities, etc.
      UF —Honorary officials and employees

—Officials and employees, Retired
    H 1140
      Further subdivide by subdivisions used under classes of persons.
      Use as a topical subdivision under names of countries, cities, etc.
      UF —Retired officials and employees

—Oil filters of motors
    USE —Motors—Oil filters

—Old age
    USE —Last years

—Old Norse influences
    H 1156
      Use as a topical subdivision under individual literature.
      BT —Foreign influences

—On postage stamps
    H 1110; H 1140; H 1187
      Use as a topical subdivision under names of individual persons, corporate bodies, countries, cities, etc., and titles of works for works on portrayal of those entities on postage stamps.

—On television
    H 1110; H 1140
      Do not use for works about a person as a television actor, television host, news anchor, etc.
      Use as a topical subdivision under names of countries, cities, etc. Also use under names of individual persons for works that discuss television programming about the person, including dramatic or documentary shows, news programming, and advertising.
      BT —In mass media

—Online chat groups
    H 1095
      Use as a topical subdivision under subjects for works about online chat groups on those subjects.
      UF —Chat groups, Online

—Online chat groups
    H 1095
      Use as a form subdivision under subjects for online chat groups on those subjects.
      UF —Chat groups, Online

—Onomatopoeic words
    H 1154
      Use as a topical subdivision under individual languages and groups of languages.
      BT —Vocabulary

—Open admission (May Subd Geog)
    H 1151; H 1151.5
      Subdivide geographically only under types of educational institutions.
      Use as a topical subdivision under names of individual educational institutions and types of educational institutions.
      BT —Admission

—Operating costs
    USE —Cost of operation

—Operating room technicians
    H 1159
      Use as a topical subdivision under military services.

—Operation in cold weather
    USE —Cold weather operation

—Operation off-road
    USE —Off-road operation

—Operational readiness
    H 1159
      Use as a topical subdivision under military services.
      UF —Readiness, Operational

—Operations other than war
    H 1159
      Use as a topical subdivision under military services.
      NT —Stability operations

—Opinion, Public
    USE —Public opinion

—Opponents
    USE —Adversaries

—Optical instrument repairers
    H 1159
      Further subdivide by subdivisions used under classes of persons.
      Use as a topical subdivision under military services.

—Optical methods of design and construction
    USE —Design and construction—Optical methods

—Optical properties
    H 1149; H 1158
      Use as a topical subdivision under individual chemicals and groups of chemicals and individual materials and types of materials.
      BT —Properties
      NT —Surfaces—Optical properties

—Oratory
    H 1110
      Use as a topical subdivision under names of individual persons.
      UF —Public speaking

—Orbit
    H 1095
      Use as a topical subdivision under names of individual artificial satellites.

—Orchestra studies
    USE —Orchestral excerpts

—Orchestral excerpts
    H 1161
      Use as a form subdivision under musical instruments and families of instruments.
      UF —Orchestra studies
            [Former subdivision]
      BT —Excerpts

—Orchestras
    H 1151
      Use as a topical subdivision under names of individual educational institutions.
      UF —Orchestras and bands
            [Former subdivision]

—Orchestras and bands
    USE —Bands
        —Orchestras

—Order-books
    H 1159
      Use as a form subdivision under military services.

—Order of words
    USE —Word order

—Ordnance and ordnance stores
    H 1159
      Use as a topical subdivision under military services.
      BT —Supplies and stores
——Effect of environment on
    (May Subd Geog)
    H 1159
      Use as a topical subdivision under military services.
      UF —Ordnance and ordnance stores—Influence of environment
            [Former subdivision]
      BT —Effect of environment on
——Influence of environment
    USE —Ordnance and ordnance stores—Effect of environment on

——Quality control
    H 1159
      Use as a topical subdivision under military services.
      BT —Quality control

—Ordnance facilities
    H 1159
      Use as a topical subdivision under military services.

—Organ
    USE —Organs

—Organ scores
    H 1160
      Use as a form subdivision under forms and types of musical compositions.

—Organic farming (May Subd Geog)
    H 1180
      Use as a topical subdivision under individual plants and groups of plants.

—Organization
    H 1159
      Use as a topical subdivision under military services.

—Organizing of labor unions
    USE —Labor unions—Organizing

—Organs
    H 1105
      Use as a topical subdivision under names of individual corporate bodies having one or more organs, especially churches, concert halls, etc., for works discussing the organs collectively.
      UF —Organ
            [Former subdivision]

—Orientation (May Subd Geog)
    H 1147
      Use as a topical subdivision under individual animals and groups of animals.

—Origin
    H 1103; H 1147; H 1180; H 1185
      Use as a topical subdivision under ethnic groups, individual animals and groups of animals, individual plants and groups of plants, and individual religions.

—Ornaments, Radiator
    USE —Radiator ornaments

—Orthodox Eastern authors
    H 1156
      Use as a topical subdivision under individual literatures.

—Orthography and spelling
    H 1154
      Use as a topical subdivision under individual languages and groups of languages.
      UF —Spelling

—Osmotic potential (May Subd Geog)
    H 1180
      Use as a topical subdivision under individual plants and groups of plants.

—Outline drawings
    USE —Charts, diagrams, etc.

—Outline maps
    USE —Maps, Outline and base

—Outlines, syllabi, etc.
    H 1095; H 1100; H 1103; H 1110; H 1188
      Use as a form subdivision under names of individual persons, uniform titles of sacred works, and under classes of persons, ethnic groups, and topical headings for brief statements of the principal elements of a subject to be studied, usually arranged by headings and subheadings.
      UF —Compends
            [Former subdivision]
        —Study and teaching—Outlines, syllabi, etc.
            [Former subdivision]
        —Syllabi
      NT —Sermons—Outlines, syllabi, etc.

—Outside employment
    USE —Supplementary employment

—Overdosage
    USE —Overdose

—Overdose (May Subd Geog)
    H1149
      Use as a topical subdivision under individual drugs and groups of drugs.
      UF —Overdosage

—Ownership (May Subd Geog)
    H 1153
      Use as a topical subdivision under types of industries.
      NT —Foreign ownership
         —Government ownership

—**Oxidation**   (May Subd Geog)
  H 1149
    Use as a topical subdivision under individual
chemicals and groups of chemicals.
    NT —Anodic oxidation
       —Peroxidation
—**Oxygen content**   (May Subd Geog)
  H 1158
    Use as a topical subdivision under individual
materials and types of materials.
—**Packaging**   (May Subd Geog)
  H 1095; H 1180
    Use as a topical subdivision under types of prod-
ucts and merchandise for works on the techniques
of wrapping, sealing, and labeling those items for
marketing.
    NT —Seeds—Packaging
—**Packing**   (May Subd Geog)
  H 1095; H 1180
    Use as a topical subdivision under types of prod-
ucts and commodities for works on the techniques
of preparing those items for storage or shipment.
—Padding of instrument panels
    USE —Instrument panels—Padding
—Pageants
    USE —Anniversaries, etc.
—**Painting**   (May Subd Geog)
  H 1158; H 1195
    Use as a topical subdivision under individual
materials and types of materials and individual land
vehicles and types of land vehicles.
—**Painting of vessels**
  H 1159
    Use as a topical subdivision under military ser-
vices.
—**Palaces**   (May Subd Geog)
  H 1110
    Use as a topical subdivision under names of in-
dividual persons.
    BT —Homes and haunts
—**Palatalization**
  H 1154
    Use as a topical subdivision under individual
languages and groups of languages.
—**Palliative treatment**   (May Subd Geog)
  H 1150
    Use as a topical subdivision under individual dis-
eases and types of diseases.
    BT —Treatment
—**Palynotaxonomy**   (May Subd Geog)
  H 1180
    Use as a topical subdivision under individual
plants and groups of plants.
    BT —Classification
—**Pamphlets**
  H 1095; H 1200
    Use as a form subdivision under 16th, 17th and
18th century period subdivisions of European and
American history and under individual wars for
short, separately published, usually polemical es-
says or treatises regarding controversial issues of
contemporary interest, especially political or reli-
gious matters.
—Panels, Instrument
    USE —Instrument panels
—**Papal documents**
  H 1095
    Use as a form subdivision under topical head-
ings for collections of documents and other papal
pronouncements on the topic.
    UF —Documents, Papal
—**Parables**
  H 1188
    Use as a topical subdivision under uniform titles
of sacred works.
—**Parachute troops**
  H 1159
    Use as a topical subdivision under military ser-
vices.
—**Paragraphs**
  H 1154; H 1188
    Use as a topical subdivision under individual
languages and groups of languages and uniform ti-
tles of sacred works.
    NT —Manuscripts—Paragraphs
—**Parallel versions, English, [French, etc.]**
  H 1188
    Use as a form subdivision under uniform titles
of sacred works.

—**Parallelism**
  H 1154
    Use as a topical subdivision under individual
languages and groups of languages.
—Parallels, Extra-canonical
    USE —Extra-canonical parallels
—**Paralysis**   (May Subd Geog)
  H 1164
    Further subdivide by subdivisions used under
diseases.
    Use as a topical subdivision under individual or-
gans and regions of the body.
    BT —Diseases
—Paramours of kings and rulers
    USE —Kings and rulers—Paramours
—**Paraphrase**
  H 1154
    Use as a topical subdivision under individual
languages and groups of languages.
—**Paraphrases**
  H 1188
    Use as a topical subdivision under uniform ti-
tles of sacred works for works about paraphrases of
those works.
—**Paraphrases**
  H 1188
    Use as a form subdivision under uniform titles
of sacred works for paraphrases of those works.
——**History and criticism**
  H 1188
    Use as a topical subdivision under uniform ti-
tles of sacred works.
    BT —History and criticism
—**Paraphrases, English, [French, German, etc.]**
  H 1188
    Use as a form subdivision under uniform titles
of sacred works for paraphrases of those works in
those languages.
——**History and criticism**
  H 1188
    Use as a topical subdivision under uniform ti-
tles of sacred works.
    BT —History and criticism
—Paraphrases, tales, etc.
    USE —Adaptations
—**Parasites**   (May Subd Geog)
  H 1147; H 1164
    Further subdivide by subdivisions under dis-
eases.
    Use as a topical subdivision under individual an-
imals and groups of animals and individual organs
and regions of the body.
——**Biological control**   (May Subd Geog)
  H 1147
    Use as a topical subdivision under individual
animals and groups of animals.
    BT —Biological control
——**Control**   (May Subd Geog)
  H 1147
    Use as a topical subdivision under individual
animals and groups of animals.
    BT —Control
————**Environmental aspects**
   (May Subd Geog)
  H 1147
    Use as a topical subdivision under individ-
ual animals and groups of animals.
    BT —Environmental aspects
——**Identification**
  H 1147
    Use this subdivision combination as a form
subdivision under individual animals and groups
of animals.
    BT —Identification
——**Life cycles**   (May Subd Geog)
  H 1147
    Use as a topical subdivision under individual
animals and groups of animals.
    BT —Life cycles
——**Molecular aspects**
  H 1147
    Use as a topical subdivision under individual
animals and groups of animals.
    BT —Molecular aspects
—**Pardon**
  H 1110
    Use as a topical subdivision under names of in-
dividual persons for works about the person's legal
release from the penalty of an offense.

—**Parenthetical constructions**
  H 1154
    Use as a topical subdivision under individual
languages and groups of languages.
—**Parking**
  H 1151
    Use as a topical subdivision under names of in-
dividual educational institutions.
—**Parodies, imitations, etc.**
  H 1095; H 1110; H 1155.8; H 1188
    Use as a topical subdivision under names of in-
dividual persons, names of musical groups, and in-
dividual works entered under title for works about
imitations, either comic or distorted, of the person's
or musical group's creative works, or of those titles.
Also use under motion picture, television and video
forms and genres for works about parodies of them.
    UF —Imitations (Parodies)
       —Parodies, travesties, etc.
         [Former subdivision]
       —Spoofs (Parodies)
       —Travesties (Parodies)
—**Parodies, imitations, etc.**
  H 1095; H 1110; H 1155.8; H 1188
    Use as a form subdivision under names of indi-
vidual persons and individual works entered under
title for imitations, either comic or distorted, of the
person's creative works or of those titles. Also use
under topical headings for motion picture, televi-
sion, and video forms and genres for parodies of
them.
    UF —Imitations (Parodies)
       —Parodies, travesties, etc.
         [Former subdivision]
       —Spoofs (Parodies)
       —Travesties (Parodies)
—Parodies, travesties, etc.
    USE —Parodies, imitations, etc.
—**Paronyms**
  H 1154
    Use as a topical subdivision under individual
languages and groups of languages.
—**Parsee authors**
  H 1156
    Use as a topical subdivision under individual lit-
eratures.
—**Parsing**
  H 1154
    Use as a topical subdivision under individual
languages and groups of languages.
—**Participation, African American, [Indian, etc.]**
  H 1200
    Use as a topical subdivision under individual
wars for works on the participation of the ethnic
group in the military actions of the war.
    UF —Participation, Afro-American,
         [Indian, etc.]
         [Former subdivision]
—Participation, Afro-American, [Indian, etc.]
    USE —Participation, African American,
         [Indian, etc.]
—**Participation, Buddhist, [Muslim, etc.]**
  H 1200
    Use as a topical subdivision under individual
wars.
—Participation, Citizen
    USE —Citizen participation
—**Participation, Communist**
  H 1200
    Use as a topical subdivision under individual
wars for works on the participation of communists
in the military actions of the war.
    UF —Communist participation
—**Participation, Female**
  H 1200
    Use as a topical subdivision under individual
wars for works on the participation of women in
the military actions of the war. For works on aspects of the war in relation to women, including its
effect on them, use the subdivision Women.
    UF —Female participation

—**Participation, Foreign**
    H 1200
    Do not use under the headings World War, 1914-1918 or World War, 1939-1945.
    Use as a topical subdivision under individual wars.
    UF —Foreign participation
        [Former subdivision]
—**Participation, Gay**
    H 1200
    Use as a topical subdivision under individual wars for works on the participation of gays in the military actions of a war. For works on aspects of the war in relation to gays, especially the war's effects on them, use the subdivision Gays.
    UF —Gay participation
—**Participation, German, [Irish, Swiss, etc.]**
    H 1200
    Do not use under the headings World War, 1914-1918 or World War, 1939-1945.
    Use as a topical subdivision under individual wars for works on the direct participation of nationals of the country in the military actions of the war as well as for works on economics and technical assistance to the combatants from that country.
—**Participation, Immigrant**
    H 1200
    Use as a topical subdivision under individual wars for works on the participation of immigrants in the military actions of a war.
    UF —Immigrant participation
—**Participation, Jewish**
    H 1200
    Use as a topical subdivision under individual wars for works on the participation of Jews in the military actions of a war. For works on aspects of a war in relation to Jews, especially the war's effect on them, use the subdivision Jews.
    UF —Jewish participation
—**Participation, Juvenile**
    H 1200
    Use as a topical subdivision under individual wars for works on the participation of children in the military actions of a war. For works on aspects of a war in relation to children, especially the war's effect on them, use the subdivision Children.
    UF —Juvenile participation
        [Former subdivision]
—Participation, Political
    USE —Political activity
—**Participle**
    H 1154
    Use as a topical subdivision under individual languages and groups of languages.
—**Particles**
    H 1154
    Use as a topical subdivision under individual languages and groups of languages.
—**Partitives**
    H 1154
    Use as a topical subdivision under individual languages and groups of languages.
—**Parts** *(May Subd Geog)*
    H 1195
    Use as a topical subdivision under individual land vehicles and types of land vehicles.
    NT —Bodies—Parts
        —Motors—Parts
        —Transmission devices, Automatic—Parts
—**Parts**
    H 1160
    Use as a form subdivision under forms and types of musical compositions.
——**Law and legislation** *(May Subd Geog)*
    H 1195
    Further subdivide by subdivisions used under legal topics.
    Use as a topical subdivision under individual land vehicles and types of land vehicles.
    BT —Law and legislation
—Parts and scores
    USE —Scores and parts
—**Parts of speech**
    H 1154
    Use as a topical subdivision under individual languages and groups of languages.
—**Parts (solo)**
    H 1160
    Use as a form subdivision under forms and types of musical compositions.

—**Parturition** *(May Subd Geog)*
    H 1147
    Use as a topical subdivision under individual animals and groups of animals.
    BT —Reproduction
—**Party work**
    H 1105
    Use as a topical subdivision under names of individual political parties.
—**Passenger lists**
    H 1095
    Use as a form subdivision under names of individual ships.
    UF —Lists of passengers
—**Passive voice**
    H 1154
    Use as a topical subdivision under individual languages and groups of languages.
    BT —Voice
—**Pastoral counseling of** *(May Subd Geog)*
    H 1100; H 1103
    Use as a topical subdivision under classes of persons and ethnic groups.
    BT —Counseling of
—**Pastoral letters and charges**
    H 1187
    Use as a form subdivision under individual Christian denominations.
—**Patents**
    H 1095
    Use as a topical subdivision under disciplines and under types of articles and processes patented for works about patents.
—**Patents**
    H 1095
    Use as a form subdivision under disciplines and under types of articles and processes patented for collections of patents.
—**Pathogenesis**
    H 1150
    Use as a topical subdivision under individual diseases and types of diseases.
—**Pathogens** *(May Subd Geog)*
    H 1147
    Use as a topical subdivision under individual animals and groups of animals.
—**Pathophysiology**
    H 1149; H 1150; H 1164
    Use as a topical subdivision under individual chemicals and groups of chemicals, individual diseases and types of diseases, and individual organs and regions of the body.
    UF —Diseases—Pathophysiology
        —Physiopathology
    BT —Physiology
——**Animal models**
    H 1164
    Use as a topical subdivision under individual organs and regions of the body.
    BT —Animal models
—**Patients** *(May Subd Geog)*
    H 1150
    Further subdivide by subdivisions used under classes of persons.
    Use as a topical subdivision under individual diseases and types of diseases.
    NT —Surgery—Patients
        —Transplantation—Patients
——Mortality
    USE —Mortality
—Patronage of the arts
    USE —Art patronage
—**Pay, allowances, etc.**
    H 1159
    Use as a topical subdivision under military services.
    NT —Reserves—Pay, allowances, etc.
——**Law and legislation**
    H 1159
    Further subdivide by subdivisions used under legal topics.
    Use as a topical subdivision under military services.
    BT —Law and legislation
—Payroll deductions of officials and employees
    USE —Officials and employees—Payroll deductions

—**Peace**
    H 1200
    Use as a topical subdivision under individual wars.
—**Pedaling**
    H 1161
    Use as a topical subdivision under musical instruments and families of instruments.
    UF —Instruction and study—Pedaling
        [Former subdivision]
        —Studies and exercises—Pedaling
        [Former subdivision]
—**Pedigrees**
    H 1147
    Use as a form subdivision under individual animals and groups of animals.
    UF —Herd-books
        [Former subdivision]
        —Stud-books
        [Former subdivision]
        —Studbooks
    BT —Genealogy
—**Pejoration**
    H 1154
    Use as a topical subdivision under individual languages and groups of languages.
—**Penetration resistance**
    H 1158
    Use as a topical subdivision under individual materials and types of materials.
    UF —Resistance to penetration
—**Pensions** *(May Subd Geog)*
    1155; (H 1100; H 1103
    Further subdivide geographically only under classes of persons and ethnic groups.
    Use as a topical subdivision under names of individual legislative bodies and under classes of persons and ethnic groups.
    UF —Salaries, pensions, etc.
        [Former subdivision]
    NT —Employees—Pensions
        —Officials and employees—Pensions
———**Cost-of-living adjustments**
    (May Subd Geog)
    H 1100
    Use as a topical subdivision under classes of persons.
    UF —Cost-of-living adjustments to pensions
———**Effect of inflation on** *(May Subd Geog)*
    H 1100
    Use as a topical subdivision under classes of persons.
    UF —Effect of inflation on pensions
———**Unclaimed benefits** *(May Subd Geog)*
    H 1100
    Use as a topical subdivision under classes of persons.
    UF —Unclaimed pension benefits
—**Performance** *(May Subd Geog)*
    H 1161; H 1195
    Use as a topical subdivision under individual musical instruments and families of instruments, and individual land vehicles and types of land vehicles.
—**Performance records**
    H 1147
    Use as a form subdivision under individual animals and groups of animals.
    UF —Records, Performance
—**Performances** *(May Subd Geog)*
    H 1105; H 1110; H 1160
    Use as a topical subdivision under performing artists and performing groups of all types for works about their performances. Use under composers, choreographers, etc., for works about performances of their compositions or works. Also use under forms and types of musical compositions for works on performances of those compositions.
    NT —First performances
—**Periodicals**
    H 1095
    Use as a topical subdivision under subjects for works about periodicals on those subjects.
    UF —Journals (Periodicals)
        —Societies, periodicals, etc.
        [Former subdivision]
        —Yearbooks
        [Former subdivision]

—**Periodicals**
H 1095
Use as a form subdivision under subjects for periodicals on those subjects.
UF —Journals (Periodicals)
—Societies, periodicals, etc.
[Former subdivision]
—Yearbooks
[Former subdivision]
NT —Newspapers
—Students—Yearbooks

———**Abbreviations of titles**
H 1095
Use this subdivision combination as a form subdivison under subjects for works containing lists of abbreviations of titles of periodicals on those subjects.
BT —Abbreviations of titles

———**Bibliography**
H 1095
Use this subdivision combination as a form subdivision for works containing lists of periodicals on those subjects.
BT —Bibliography

————**Catalogs**
H 1095
Use this subdivision combination as a form subdivision under subjects for lists of serials or periodicals held by one organization or library, assembled as a private collection, or issued by an individual publisher.
BT —Bibliography—Catalogs

————**Union lists**
H 1095
Use this subdivision combination as a form subdivision under subjects for catalogs of serials or periodicals on those subjects held by two or more libraries.
BT —Bibliography—Union lists

———**Indexes**
H 1095
Use this subdivision combination as a form subdivision for indexes to periodicals on those subjects.
BT —Indexes

—**Periodization**
H 1156
Use as a topical subdivision under individual literatures.

—Periodization of history
USE —History—Periodization

—Periods, Transition
USE —Transition periods

—**Permeability**
H 1149; H 1158; H 1164
Use as a topical subdivision under individual chemicals and groups of chemicals, individual materials and types of materials, and individual organs and regions of the body.

—**Peroxidation**
H 1149
Use as a topical subdivision under individual chemicals and groups of chemicals.
BT —Oxidation

—Persecution, Nazi
USE —Nazi persecution

—**Persian authors**
H 1156
Use as a topical subdivision under individual literatures.

—**Persian influences**
H 1156
Use as a topical subdivision under individual literatures.
BT —Foreign influences

—**Person**
H 1154
Use as a topical subdivision under individual languages and groups of languages.

—Personal finance
USE —Finance, Personal

—**Personal narratives**
H 1095; H 1200
Use as a form subdivision under names of events and wars.
UF —Narratives, Personal

—**Personal narratives, American,** [**French, etc.**]
H 1200
Use as a form subdivision under individual wars and battles.

—**Personal narratives, Confederate**
H 1200
Use as a form subdivision under individual wars and battles.

—**Personal narratives, Jewish**
H 1200
Use as a form subdivision under individual wars and battles.

—Personality
USE —Psychology

—**Personnel management**
H 1095; H 1105; H 1153; H 1159
Use as a topical subdivision under names of individual corporate bodies and under types of industries and organizations.
BT —Management

———**Law and legislation** *(May Subd Geog)*
H 1159
Further subdivide by subdivisions used under legal topics.
Use as a topical subdivision under military services.
BT —Law and legislation

—**Personnel records**
H 1105; H 1159
Use as a topical subdivision under names of individual corporate bodies and military services.
BT —Records and correspondence
NT —Reserves—Personnel records

—Pest resistance
USE —Disease and pest resistance

—Pests
USE —Diseases and pests

—**Petty officers**
H 1159
Further subdivide by subdivisions used under classes of persons.
Use as a topical subdivision under military services.

—**Petty officers' handbooks**
H 1159
Use as a form subdivision under military services.
BT —Handbooks, manuals, etc.

—**Pharmacokinetics**
H 1149
Use as a topical subdivision under individual chemicals and groups of chemicals.

—**Phenology**
H 1180
Use as a topical subdivision under individual plants and groups of plants.

—**Philosophy**
H 1095; H 1110; H 1155.2; H 1188
Do not use under names of philosophers.
Use as a topical subdivision under names of individual persons who are not philosophers, and under groups of literary authors, uniform titles of sacred works, and topical headings.
UF —Knowledge—Philosophy
NT —Civilization—Philosophy
—Foreign relations—Philosophy
—History—[period subdivision]—Philosophy
—History—Philosophy
—Politics and government—[period subdivision]—Philosophy
—Politics and government—Philosophy

—Phoenician antiquities
USE —Antiquities, Phoenician

—**Phonemics**
H 1154
Use as a topical subdivision under names of individual languages and groups of languages.

—**Phonetic transcriptions**
H 1154
Use as a form subdivision under individual languages and groups of languages.
UF —Transcriptions, Phonetic

—**Phonetics**
H 1154
Use as a topical subdivision under individual languages and groups of languages.
NT —Dialects—Phonetics
—Tempo

—**Phonology**
H 1154
Use as a topical subdivision under individual languages and groups of languages.
NT —Dialects—Phonology

—**Phonology, Comparative**
H 1154
Use as a topical subdivision under individual languages and groups of languages.
UF —Comparative phonology

———**French,** [**German, etc.**]
H 1154
Use as a topical subdivision under individual languages and groups of languages.

—**Phonology, Historical**
H 1154
Use as a topical subdivision under individual languages and groups of languages.
UF —Historical phonology

—Phonorecords for foreign speakers
USE —Sound recordings for foreign speakers

—Phonorecords for French, [Spanish, etc.] speakers
USE —Sound recordings for French, [Spanish, etc.] speakers

—Phonotape catalogs
USE —Audiotape catalogs

—**Photochemotherapy** *(May Subd Geog)*
H 1150
Use as a topical subdivision under individual diseases and types of diseases.
BT —Chemotherapy
—Phototherapy

—**Photograph collections**
H 1105; H 1110; H 1120
Use as a topical subdivision under names of individual persons, families, and corporate bodies for works on their collections of photographs.

—**Photographers**
H 1159
Further subdivide by subdivisions used under classes of persons.
Use as a topical subdivision under military services.

—**Photographic identification**
(May Subd Geog)
H 1147
Use as a topical subdivision under individual animals and groups of animals.
UF —Identification, Photographic

—**Photographs**
H 1095
Use as a form subdivision under subjects for works consisting of actual photographs, that is, photographic prints or digital photographs, rather than reproductions of photographs.
BT —Pictorial works
NT —Aerial photographs
—Photographs from space

—**Photographs from space**
H 1095; H 1140
Use as a form subdivision under names of countries, cities, etc., and under topical headings for collections of photographs taken from outer space.
UF —Space photographs
BT —Photographs

—**Photography**
H 1200
Use as a topical subdivision under individual wars.

—**Photomorphogenesis**
H 1180
Use as a topical subdivision under individual plants and groups of plants.
BT —Morphogenesis

—**Phototherapy** *(May Subd Geog)*
H 1150
Use as a topical subdivision under individual diseases and types of diseases.
BT —Treatment
NT —Photochemotherapy

—Phrase books
USE —Conversation and phrase books
—**Phraseology**
H 1154
Use as a topical subdivision under individual languages and groups of languages.
—Phrases and terms
USE —Terms and phrases
—**Phylogeny**
H 1147; H 1164; H 1180
Use as a topical subdivision under individual animals and groups of animals, individual organs and regions of the body, and individual plants and groups of plants.
——**Molecular aspects**
H 1147; H 1180
Use as a topical subdivision under individual animals and groups of animals and individual plants and groups of plants.
BT —Molecular aspects
—Physical maps
USE —Maps, Physical
—**Physical therapy** *(May Subd Geog)*
H 1150
Use as a topical subdivision under individual diseases and types of diseases.
BT —Treatment
NT —Exercise therapy
—**Physical training** *(May Subd Geog)*
H 1159
Use as a topical subdivision under military services.
—**Physiological aspects**
H 1095
Use as a topical subdivision under types of activities and mental conditions for works on the relationship between an individual's activity, mental state, etc., and the individual's physiology.
NT —Exercise—Physiological aspects
—**Physiological effect** *(May Subd Geog)*
H 1095; H 1149; H 1158; H 1180
Use as a topical subdivision under individual chemicals and groups of chemicals, individual materials and types of materials, individual plants and groups of plants, and environmental phenomena or conditions for works on their effect on the functions of living organisms.
—**Physiological genomics**
H 1147
Use as a topical subdivision under individual animals and groups of animals.
UF —Genomics, Physiological
BT —Genetics
—**Physiological transport**
H 1149
Use as a topical subdivision under individual chemicals and groups of chemicals.
—**Physiology** *(May Subd Geog)*
H 1100; H 1103; H 1147; H 1164; H 1180
Use as a topical subdivision under classes of persons, ethnic groups, individual animals and groups of animals, individual organs and regions of the body, and individual plants and groups of plants.
NT —Ecophysiology
—Embryos—Physiology
—Fetuses—Physiology
—Fluorescence
—Metabolism
—Movements
—Pathophysiology
—Postharvest physiology
—Psychophysiology
—Reproduction
—Respiration
—Roots—Physiology
—Seeds—Physiology
—Venom resistance
—Physiopathology
USE —Pathophysiology
—**Piano scores**
H 1160
Use as a form subdivision under forms and types of musical compositions.
—**Piano scores (4 hands)**
H 1160
Use as a form subdivision under forms and types of musical compositions.

—**Pickling** *(May Subd Geog)*
H 1158
Use as a topical subdivision under individual materials and types of materials.
———**By-products**
H 1158
Use as a topical subdivision under individual materials and types of materials.
BT —By-products
———**Waste disposal** *(May Subd Geog)*
H 1158
Use as a topical subdivision under individual materials and types of materials.
BT —Waste disposal
—Pictorial humor
USE —Caricatures and cartoons
—Pictorial maps
USE —Maps, Pictorial
—**Pictorial works**
H 1095; H 1100; H 1103; H 1105; H 1110; H 1120; H 1140; H 1155.6
Use as a form subdivision under names of countries, cities, etc., individual persons, families, and corporate bodies and other named entities, such as individual parks, structures, etc., and under classes of persons, ethnic groups, individual wars, and topical headings. Also use under individual literary works entered under author for works consisting of pictures pertaining to the work as a physical object, or, in the case of dramatic works, to productions of the work.
UF —Description and travel—Views
[Former subdivision]
—Iconography
[Former subdivision]
—Pictures
NT —Atlases
—Biography—Pictorial works
—Caricatures and cartoons
—Charts, diagrams, etc.
—History—Pictorial works
—Illustrations
—In art
—Photographs
—Portraits
—**Picture Bibles**
H 1188
Use as a form subdivision under uniform titles of sacred works.
BT —Illustrations
—Pictures
USE —Pictorial works
—Pillage
USE —Destruction and pillage
—Piston rings of motors
USE —Motors—Pistons and piston rings
—Pistons of motors
USE —Motors—Pistons and piston rings
—Place of birth
USE —Birthplace
—Places frequented
USE —Homes and haunts
—**Planning**
H 1095; H 1105; H 115.1; H 1153
Use as a topical subdivision under names of individual corporate bodies and under types of activities, facilities, industries, services, undertakings, etc., for works that describe or discuss the planning process
—Plans, Architectural
USE —Designs and plans
—**Planting** *(May Subd Geog)*
H 1180
Use as a topical subdivision under individual plants and groups of plants.
—**Planting time** *(May Subd Geog)*
H 1180
Use as a topical subdivision under individual plants and groups of plants.
UF —Time of planting
—**Plastic properties**
H 1158
Use as a topical subdivision under individual materials and types of materials.

—**Platforms**
H 1105
Use as a topical subdivision under names of individual political parties for works about platforms of those parties.
—**Platforms**
H 1105
Use as a form subdivision under names of individual political parties for works containing platforms of those parties.
—Plays
USE —Drama
—Plots
USE —Stories, plots, etc.
—**Pneumatic equipment**
H 1195
Use as a topical subdivision under individual land vehicles and types of land vehicles.
BT —Equipment and supplies
NT —Air suspension
—Poems
USE —Poetry
—**Poetic works** *(Not Subd Geog)*
H 1110
Do not use under authors who write principally poetry.
Use as a topical subdivision under names of individual literary authors for works of criticism about poetic works by the author.
BT —Criticism and interpretation
—**Poetry**
H 1095; H 1100; H 1103; H 1105; H 1110; H 1120; H 1140
Use as a form subdivision under names of countries, cities, etc., names of individual persons, families, and corporate bodies, and under classes of persons, ethnic groups, and topical headings for collections of poetry and individual poems on those subjects.
UF —Poems
NT —Juvenile poetry
—Poisoning
USE —Toxicology
—Policy, Government
USE —Government policy
—**Polish authors**
H1156
Use as a topical subdivision under individual literatures.
—**Polish influences**
H 1156
Use as a topical subdivision under individual literatures.
BT —Foreign influences
—**Political activity** *(May Subd Geog)*
H 1095; H 1100; H 1105; H 1110; H 1120; H 1153; H 1155.2; H 1159; H 1187
Use as a topical subdivision under names of individual persons, families, and corporate bodies; and under classes of persons, types of industries and corporate bodies, military services, and Christian denominations for works on the political participation of those persons or organizations.
UF —Participation, Political
—Political participation
—Politics and suffrage
[Former subdivision]
—**Political and social views**
H 1110; H 1155.2
Do not use for works written by a person on political or social topics.
Use as a topical subdivision under names of individual persons and groups of literary authors for works on the person's political and/or social views in general.
UF —Social views
—**Political aspects** *(May Subd Geog)*
H 1095; H 1185
Use as a topical subdivision under individual religious sects and denominations and under topical headings for works on the political dimensions or implications of nonpolitical topics.
NT —Ethnic relations—Political aspects
—Languages—Political aspects
—Race relations—Political aspects
—Political boundaries
USE —Boundaries

—Political divisions
  USE —Administrative and political
         divisions
—Political history
  USE —Politics and government
—Political-military affairs officers
    H 1159
    Further subdivide by subdivisions used under
  classes of persons.
    Use as a topical subdivision under military ser-
  vices.
—Political participation
  USE —Political activity
—Politics
  USE —Politics and government
—Politics and government
    H 1103; H 1140
    Use as a topical subdivision under names of
  countries, cities, etc. Also use under ethnic groups
  for the internal or self-government of the groups
  and/or the political activity of the group or its individual members.
  UF —Government and politics
       —Political history
       —Politics
         [Former subdivision]
       —Politics and suffrage
         [Former subdivision]
  NT —Territories and possessions—
         Politics and government
———16th century
    H 1103; H 1140
    Use as a topical subdivision under names of
  countries, cities, etc., and ethnic groups.
———17th century
    H 1103; H 1140
    Use as a topical subdivision under names of
  countries, cities, etc., and ethnic groups.
———18th century *(Not Subd Geog)*
    H 1103; H 1140
    Use as a topical subdivision under names of
  countries, cities, etc., and ethnic groups.
———19th century
    H 1103; H 1140
    Use as a topical subdivision under names of
  countries, cities, etc., and ethnic groups.
———20th century *(Not Subd Geog)*
    H 1103; H 1140
    Use as a topical subdivision under names of
  countries, cities, etc., and ethnic groups.
———21st century
    H 1103; H 1140
    Use as a topical subdivision under names of
  countries, cities, etc., and ethnic groups.
———[period subdivision]
————Philosophy
    H 1140
    Use as a topical subdivision under names
  of countries, cities, etc.
  BT —Philosophy
———Philosophy
    H 1140
    Use as a topical subdivision under names of
  countries, cities, etc.
  BT —Philosophy
—Politics and suffrage
  USE —Political activity
       —Politics and government
       —Suffrage
—Pollen *(May Subd Geog)*
    H 1180
    Use as a topical subdivision under individual
  plants and groups of plants.
———Morphology *(Not Subd Geog)*
    H 1180
    Use as a topical subdivision under individual
  plants and groups of plants.
  BT —Morphology
—Pollen management *(May Subd Geog)*
    H 1180
    Use as a topical subdivision under individual
  plants and groups of plants.
—Pollination *(May Subd Geog)*
    H 1180
    Use as a topical subdivision under individual
  plants and groups of plants.
  BT —Reproduction

—Pollution control devices
    H 1195
    Use as a topical subdivision under individual
  land vehicles and types of land vehicles.
———Law and legislation *(May Subd Geog)*
    H 1195
    Further subdivide by subdivisions used under
  legal topics.
    Use as a topical subdivision under individual
  land vehicles and types of land vehicles.
  BT —Law and legislation
—Polysemy
    H 1154
    Use as a topical subdivision under individual
  languages and groups of languages.
—Popular nomenclature
  USE —Nomenclature (Popular)
—Popular works
    H 1095; H 1154.5
    Use as a form subdivision under scientific, tech-
  nical, and legal topics for works written for the
  layperson.
—Population
    H 1103; H 1140; H 1149.5
    Use as a topical subdivision under names of
  countries, cities, etc., and ethnic groups.
  UF —Demography
  NT —Colonies—Population
———Economic aspects
    H 1140
    Use as a topical subdivision under names of
  countries, cities, etc.
  BT —Economic aspects
———Environmental aspects
    H 1140
    Use as a topical subdivision under names of
  countries, cities, etc.
  BT —Environmental aspects
—Population policy
    H 1140
    Use as a topical subdivision under names of
  countries, cities, etc.
  BT —Government policy
—Population regeneration *(May Subd Geog)*
    H 1180
    Use as a topical subdivision under individual
  plants and groups of plants.
  UF —Regeneration, Population
—Population viability analysis
  (May Subd Geog)
    H 1147; H 1180
    Use as a topical subdivision under individual an-
  imals and groups of animals and individual plants
  and groups of plants.
—Portraits
    H 1100; H 1103; H 1110; H 1120; H 1186;
    H 1200
    Use as a topical subdivision under names of in-
  dividual persons who lived after 1400, individual
  families, classes of persons, and ethnic groups for
  works about portraits of those persons. Also use
  under names of individual religious and monastic
  orders and wars for works about portraits of persons associated with those orders or wars. For
  works about art depicting persons who lived before
  1400, use the subdivision Art.
  UF —Portraits, caricatures, etc.
         [Former subdivision]
       —Portraits, etc.
         [Former subdivision]
  NT —Biography—Portraits
       —Self-portraits
—Portraits
    H 1100; H 1103; H 1110; H 1120; H 1186;
    H 1200
    Use as a form subdivision under names of in-
  dividual persons who lived after 1400, individual
  families, classes of persons and ethnic groups for
  collections of portraits of those persons. Also use
  under names of individual religious and monastic
  orders and wars for portraits of persons associated
  with those orders and wars. For collections of art
  depicting persons who lived before 1400, use the
  subdivision Art.
  UF —Portraits, caricatures, etc.
         [Former subdivision]
       —Portraits, etc.
         [Former subdivision]
  BT —Pictorial works

  NT —Biography—Portraits
       —History—[period subdivision]—
         Biography—Portraits
       —Self-portraits
—Portraits, caricatures, etc.
  USE —Caricatures and cartoons
       —Portraits
—Portraits, etc.
  USE —Portraits
—Portuguese influences
    H 1156
    Use as a topical subdivision under individual lit-
  eratures.
  BT —Foreign influences
—Position descriptions
  USE —Job descriptions
—Positioning for radiography
  USE —Radiography—Positioning
—Positions
    H 1105
    Use as a topical subdivision under names of in-
  dividual government agencies.
—Possessions and territories
  USE —Territories and possessions
—Possessives
    H 1154
    Use as a topical subdivision under individual
  languages and groups of languages.
—Postal clerks
    H 1159
    Further subdivide by subdivisions used under
  classes of persons.
    Use as a topical subdivision under military ser-
  vices.
—Postal service
    H 1159; H 1200
    Use as a topical subdivision under military ser-
  vices and individual wars.
—Postcolonial criticism *(May Subd Geog)*
    H 1188
    Use as a topical subdivision under uniform titles
  of sacred works.
  BT —Criticism, interpretation, etc.
—Poster collections
    H 1105; H 1110; H 1120
    Use as a topical subdivision under names of in-
  dividual persons, families, and corporate bodies for
  works on their collections of posters.
—Posters *(May Subd Geog)*
    H 1095; H 1100; H 1103; H 1105; H 1110;
    H 1140
    Use as a topical subdivision under names of
  countries, cities, etc., individual persons and corporate bodies, classes of persons, ethnic groups, individual wars, and topical headings for works about
  posters on those subjects.
—Posters
    H 1095; H 1100; H 1103; H 1105; H 1110;
    H 1140
    Use as a form subdivision under names of coun-
  tries, cities, etc., individual persons and corporate bodies, classes of persons, ethnic groups, individual wars, and topical headings for individual
  posters and collections of posters about those subjects.
—Postharvest diseases and injuries
  (May Subd Geog)
    H 1180
    Use as a topical subdivision under individual
  plants and groups of plants.
  UF —Postharvest technology—Diseases
         and injuries
         [Former subdivision]
  NT —Storage—Diseases and injuries
       —Transportation—Diseases and
         injuries
———Biological control *(May Subd Geog)*
    H 1180
    Use as a topical subdivision under individual
  plants and groups of plants.
  BT —Biological control
———Integrated control *(May Subd Geog)*
    H 1180
    Use as a topical subdivision under individual
  plants and groups of plants.
  BT —Integrated control

—**Postharvest losses** (May Subd Geog)
  H 1180
    Use as a topical subdivision under individual plants and groups of plants.
  BT —Losses

——**Prevention**
  H 1180
    Use as a topical subdivision under individual plants and groups of plants.
  BT —Prevention

—**Postharvest physiology** (May Subd Geog)
  H 1180
    Use as a topical subdivision under individual plants and groups of plants.
  BT —Physiology

—**Postharvest technology** (May Subd Geog)
  H 1180
    Use as a topical subdivision under individual plants and groups of plants.
  NT —Seeds—Postharvest technology

——Diseases and injuries
  USE —Postharvest diseases and injuries

—**Postpositions**
  H 1154
    Use as a topical subdivision under individual languages and groups of languages.

—**Power supply** (May Subd Geog)
  H 1095; H 1153
    Use as a topical subdivision under types of buildings, installations, equipment, industries, etc.

—**Power trains** (May Subd Geog)
  H 1195
    Use as a topical subdivision under individual land vehicles and types of land vehicles.

—**Power utilization**
  H 1145.5
    Use as a topical subdivision under names of individual bodies of water.

—**Powers and duties**
  H 1155
    Use as a topical subdivision under names of individual legislative bodies.
  UF —Duties and powers

—**Practice** (May Subd Geog)
  H 1095
    Use as a topical subdivision under types of professions.

—Practice and rules
  USE —Rules and practice

—Practicing
  USE —Instruction and study

—Prayer-books and devotions
  USE —Prayers and devotions

—**Prayers**
  H 1151.5; H 1188
    Use as a topical subdivision under types of educational institutions for works about prayers for use in those institutions and under uniform titles of sacred works for works about prayers from those works.

—**Prayers** (Not Subd Geog)
  H 1151.5; H 1188
    Use as a form subdivision under types of educational institutions for collections of prayers for use in those institutions and under uniform titles of sacred works for collections of prayers from those works.

——**History and criticism**
  H 1188
    Use as a topical subdivision under uniform titles of sacred works.
  BT —History and criticism

—**Prayers and devotions** (Not Subd Geog)
  H 1095; H 1100; H 1103; H 1110; H 1185; H 1186; H 1187
    Use as a topical subdivision under names of individual religious and monastic orders and under individual religions, individual Christian denominations, classes of persons, and ethnic groups for works about prayers intended for their use; under names of individual saints, deities, etc., for works about devotions directed to them; and under topical headings for works about prayers and devotions on those topics.
  UF —Devotions
      —Prayer-books and devotions
      [Former subdivision]

—**Prayers and devotions**
  H 1095; H 1100; H 1103; H 1110; H 1185; H 1186; H 1187
    Use as a form subdivision under names of individual religious and monastic orders and under individual religions, individual Christian denominations, classes of persons and ethnic groups for whose use the prayers are intended; under names of individual saints, deities, etc., to whom the devotions are directed; and under topical headings for prayers and devotions on those topics.
  UF —Devotions
      —Prayer-books and devotions
      [Former subdivision]

——**History and criticism**
  H 1095; H 1100; H 1103; H 1110; H 1185; H 1186; H 1187
    Use as a topical subdivision under names of individual religious and monastic orders and under individual religions, individual Christian denominations, classes of persons, and ethnic groups; under names of individual saints, deities, etc.; and under topical headings.
  BT —History and criticism

—**Pre-existence**
  H 1110
    Use as a topical subdivision under names of individual persons for works about the person's existence in a previous state or life.

—Precancer
  USE —Precancerous conditions

—**Precancerous conditions** (May Subd Geog)
  H 1164
    Further subdivide by subdivisions used under diseases.
    Use as a topical subdivision under individual organs and regions of the body.
  UF —Precancer
  BT —Cancer

—**Precooling** (May Subd Geog)
  H 1180
    Use as a topical subdivision under individual plants and groups of plants.

—**Predators of** (May Subd Geog)
  1147
    Use as a topical subdivision under individual animals and groups of animals.

——**Control** (May Subd Geog)
  H 1147
    Use as a topical subdivision under individual animals and groups of animals.
  BT —Control

——**Ecology** (May Subd Geog)
  H 1147
    Use as a topical subdivision under individual animals and groups of animals.
  BT —Ecology

—Predators of seeds
  USE —Seeds—Predators of

—**Prefaces**
  H 1188
    Use as a form subdivision under uniform titles of sacred works.

—Prefixes
  USE —Suffixes and prefixes

—**Pregnancy** (May Subd Geog)
  H 1147
    Use as a topical subdivision under individual animals and groups of animals.
  BT —Reproduction

—**Preharvest sprouting** (May Subd Geog)
  H 1180
    Use as a topical subdivision under individual plants and groups of plants.
  UF —Sprouting, Preharvest

—**Prepositional phrases**
  H 1154
    Use as a topical subdivision under individual languages and groups of languages.

—**Prepositions**
  H 1154
    Use as a topical subdivision under individual languages and groups of languages.

—Preschool education
  USE —Education (Preschool)

—Prescriptions
  USE —Formulae, receipts, prescriptions

—**Preservation** (May Subd Geog)
  H 1095; H 1164; H 1180
    Use as a topical subdivision under individual organs and regions of the body, individual plants and groups of plants, and types of perishable products, including food, drugs, textiles, etc.
  NT —Cryopreservation
      —Radiation preservation
      —Sacred books—Preservation

—Preservation and collection
  USE —Collection and preservation

—**Presidents**
  H 1105
    Use as a topical subdivision under names of individual corporate bodies.

—Presiding officer
  USE —Presiding officers

—**Presiding officers**
  H 1155
    Further subdivide by subdivisions used under classes of persons.
    Use as a topical subdivision under names of individual legislative bodies.
  UF —Presiding officer
      [Former subdivision]
  BT —Leadership

—**Press coverage** (May Subd Geog)
  H 1095; H 1105; H 1140; H 1200
    Use as a topical subdivision under names of countries, cities, etc., individual corporate bodies, individual events, and topical headings.
  UF —Coverage by the press
      —In the press
      —News media coverage

—Pressure, Vapor
  USE —Vapor pressure

—**Prevention**
  H 1095; H 1150
    Use as a topical subdivision under individual diseases and and types of diseases, and under other situations to be avoided
  NT —Aging—Prevention
      —Chemoprevention
      —Diseases—Prevention
      —Fires and fire prevention
      —Losses—Prevention
      —Postharvest losses—Prevention
      —Vaccination

——**Needs assessment** (May Subd Geog)
  H 1150
    Use as a topical subdivision under individual diseases and types of diseases.
  UF —Needs assessment in prevention of diseases

—Preventive inoculation
  USE —Vaccination

—Price policy
  USE —Prices—Government policy

—**Prices** (May Subd Geog)
  H 1095; H 1149; H 1153; H 1158; H 1180; H 1195
    Use as a topical subdivision under types of products, objects, etc., and under industries where one general heading for the products of that industry is lacking.

——**Government policy** (May Subd Geog)
  H 1095; H 1153
    Use as a topical subdivision under types of products, objects, etc., and under industries where one general heading for the products of that industry is lacking.
  UF —Price policy
  BT —Government policy

——**Law and legislation** (May Subd Geog)
  H 1153; H 1195
    Further subdivide by subdivisions used under legal topics.
    Use as a topical subdivision under types of industries and individual land vehicles and types of land vehicles.
  BT —Law and legislation

—Primary education
  USE —Education (Primary)

—Primary sources
  USE —Sources

—Printing plants, Underground
  USE —Underground printing plants

—Prison ships
    USE —Prisons
—**Prisoners and prisons**
    H 1200
    Use as a topical subdivision under individual wars.
    UF —Prisoners, Exchange of
        [Former subdivision]
        —Prisons and prisoners
—**Prisoners and prisons, British, [German, etc.]**
    H 1200
    Qualify by nationality to refer to the country controlling the prisons and holding the prisoners of war.
    Use as a topical subdivision under individual wars.
—Prisoners, Exchange of
    USE —Prisoners and prisons
—**Prisons**
    H 1159
    Use as a topical subdivision under military services.
    UF —Prison ships
        —Prisons and prison ships
        [Former subdivision]
—Prisons and prison ships
    USE —Prisons
—Prisons and prisoners
    USE —Prisoners and prisons
—**Private bills**
    H 1155
    Use as a topical subdivision under names of individual legislative bodies for works about private bills from those bodies.
—**Private bills**
    H 1155
    Use as a form subdivision under names of individual legislative bodies for individual or collections of private bills from those bodies.
    UF —Bills, Private
—**Private collections** (May Subd Geog)
    H 1095
    Use as a topical subdivision under types of objects, including art and antiquities and excluding natural objects and musical instruments, for works on privately owned collections.
—**Privatization** (May Subd Geog)
    H 1153
    Use as a topical subdivision under types of industries.
—**Privileges and immunities**
    H 1095; H 1105; H 1151.5; H 1155
    Use as a topical subdivision under names of individual international agencies and legislative bodies and under types of organizations and educational institutions.
    UF —Immunities and privileges
—**Prizes, etc.**
    H 1200
    Use as a topical subdivision under individual wars.
—**Problems, exercises, etc.**
    H 1095
    Use as a form subdivision under topical headings for compilations of practice problems or exercises pertinent to the study of the topic.
    UF —Exercises, problems, etc.
        —Workbooks
    NT —Exercises for dictation
        —Studies and exercises
—Proceedings of conferences
    USE —Congresses
—Proceedings of trials
    USE —Trials, litigation, etc.
—**Processing** (May Subd Geog)
    H 1147; H 1180
    Use as a topical subdivision under individual animals and groups of animals and individual plants and groups of plants.
    NT —Milling
        —Seeds—Processing
— —**Machinery** (May Subd Geog)
    H 1180
    Use as a topical subdivision under individual plants and groups of plants.
    BT —Machinery

—**Procurement**
    H 1105; H 1159
    Use as a topical subdivision under names of individual government agencies and military services.
—**Production and direction** (May Subd Geog)
    H 1160; H1095
    Use as a topical subdivision under forms and types of musical compositions, under individual art forms performed on stage or screen, under motion picture forms and genres, and under types of programming for the broadcast media.
    UF —Direction and production
—**Production control** (May Subd Geog)
    H 1095; H 1153
    Use as a topical subdivision under types of industries, industrial plants, and processes.
—**Production standards** (May Subd Geog)
    H 1095; H 1153
    Use as a topical subdivision under types of industries and processes.
    BT —Standards
—**Productivity** (May Subd Geog)
    H 1147
    Use as a topical subdivision under individual animals and groups of animals.
—Productivity, Capital
    USE —Capital productivity
—Productivity, Labor
    USE —Labor productivity
—**Professional ethics** (May Subd Geog)
    H 1100
    Use as a topical subdivision under occupational groups and types of employees.
    UF —Ethics, Professional
—Professional life
    USE —Career in [specific field or discipline]
—**Professional relationships**
    (May Subd Geog)
    H 1100
    Use as a topical subdivision under classes of persons.
—**Professional staff**
    H 1151; H 1151.5
    Further subdivide by subdivisions used under classes of persons.
    Use as a topical subdivision under names of individual educational institutions and types of educational institutions.
    BT —Employees
—**Prognosis** (May Subd Geog)
    H 1150
    Use as a topical subdivision under individual diseases and types of diseases.
—**Programmed instruction**
    H 1095
    Use as a form subdivision under topical headings for programmed texts on those topics.
    UF —Programmed texts
—Programmed texts
    USE —Programmed instruction
—**Programming** (May Subd Geog)
    H 1095
    Use as a topical subdivision under individual and types of computers, microprocessors, and programmable calculators.
—Prohibited books
    USE —Censorship
—**Promotions** (May Subd Geog)
    H 1100; H 1103; H 1159
    Further subdivide geographically only under classes of persons and ethnic groups.
    Use as topical subdivision under classes of persons, ethnic groups, and military services.
    NT —Reserves—Promotions
—**Pronominals**
    H 1154
    Use as a topical subdivision under individual languages and groups of languages.
—**Pronoun**
    H 1154
    Use as a topical subdivision under individual languages and groups of languages.
—**Pronunciation**
    H 1154
    Use as a topical subdivision under individual languages and groups of languages.
    NT —Pronunciation by foreign speakers

—**Pronunciation by foreign speakers**
    H 1154
    Use as a topical subdivision under individual languages and groups of languages.
    UF —Pronunciation by foreigners
        [Former subdivision]
    BT —Pronunciation
—Pronunciation by foreigners
    USE —Pronunciation by foreign speakers
—Pronunciation of terminology
    USE —Terminology—Pronunciation
—**Propaganda**
    H 1200
    Use as a topical subdivision under individual wars.
—**Propagation** (May Subd Geog)
    H 1180
    Use as a topical subdivision under individual plants and groups of plants.
    BT —Reproduction
    NT —Vegetative propagation
— —In-vitro
    USE —Micropropagation
—**Properties**
    H 1149
    Use as a topical subdivision under individual chemicals and groups of chemicals.
    NT —Acoustic properties
        —Brittleness
        —Density
        —Electric properties
        —Magnetic properties
        —Optical properties
        —Reactivity
        —Solubility
        —Stability
        —Thermal properties
        —Transport properties
        —Viscosity
—**Prophecies**
    H 1095; H 1100; H 1103; H 1110; H 1188; H 1200
    Use as a topical subdivision under names of individual persons and deities, uniform titles of sacred works, and under classes of persons, ethnic groups, individual wars.
    NT —History—Prophecies
— —**Chronology**
    H 1188
    Use this subdivision combination as a form subdivision under uniform titles of sacred works.
    BT —Chronology
— —[subject of prophecy]
    H 1188
    Use as a topical subdivision under uniform titles of sacred works.
—**Prose** (Not Subd Geog)
    H 1110
    Do not use under authors who write principally prose.
    Use as a topical subdivision under names of individual literary authors for works of criticism about prose works or passages by the author.
    BT —Criticism and interpretation
—**Prosodic analysis**
    H 1154
    Use as a topical subdivision under individual languages and groups of languages.
—**Protection** (May Subd Geog)
    H 1095; H 1100; H 1164; H 1180; H 1195
    Use as a topical subdivision under types of equipment, structures, individual plants and groups of plants, organs and regions of the body, and under classes of persons for works on preserving these items or persons from physical damage or harm.
    NT —Frost protection
        —Seedlings—Protection
        —Snow protection and removal
— —**Law and legislation** (May Subd Geog)
    H 1180
    Further subdivide by subdivisions used under legal topics.
    Use as a topical subdivision under individual plants and groups of plants.
    BT —Law and legislation

—**Protest movements**   (*May Subd Geog*)
  H 1200
    Use as a topical subdivision under individual
  wars.
—**Protestant authors**
  H 1156
    Use as a topical subdivision under individual lit-
  eratures.
—**Provenance trials**   (*May Subd Geog*)
  H 1180
    Use as a topical subdivision under individual
  plants and groups of plants.
—**Provenances**   (*May Subd Geog*)
  H 1180
    Use as a topical subdivision under individual
  plants and groups of plants.
—**Provençal influences**
  H 1156
    Use as a topical subdivision under individual lit-
  eratures.
  BT   —Foreign influences
—**Provinces**
  H 1095
    Use as a topical subdivision under headings of
  the type [topic]—[country] for works discussing col-
  lectively the provinces of a country in relation to
  the topic.
  BT   —Administrative and political
          divisions
—**Provincialisms**   (*May Subd Geog*)
  H 1154
    Use as a topical subdivision under individual
  languages and groups of languages.
—**Provisioning**
  H 1159
    Use as a topical subdivision under navies. Under
  other military services, use the subdivision Com-
  missariat.
—**Pruning**   (*May Subd Geog*)
  H 1180
    Use as a topical subdivision under individual
  plants and groups of plants.
—Pseudonyms
  USE   —Anonyms and pseudonyms
—Psychiatric care
  USE   —Mental health services
—**Psychic aspects**   (*May Subd Geog*)
  H 1147; H 1180
    Use as a topical subdivision under individual an-
  imals and groups of animals and individual plants
  and groups of plants.
—**Psychological aspects**   (*Not Subd Geog*)
  H 1095; H 1147; H 1150; H 1200
    Use as a topical subdivision under topical head-
  ings other than religious topics for works on the
  influence of conditions, activities, objects, etc., on
  the mental condition or personality of individuals.
—**Psychological testing**   (*May Subd Geog*)
  H 1100; H 1103; H 1147
    Use as a topical subdivision under classes of per-
  sons, ethnic groups, and individual animals and
  groups of animals.
  UF   —Psychology—Testing
            [Former subdivision]
—**Psychology**
  H 1095; H 1100; H 1103; H 1110; H 1147;
  H 1185; H 1188
    Use as a topical subdivision under uniform titles
  of sacred works, religions, and religious topics for
  the psychological aspects of those works or topics.
  Use under names of individual persons for discussions or interpretations of the person's psycholog-
  ical traits, personality, character, etc. Also use un-
  der classes of persons, ethnic groups, and individ-
  ual and groups of animals for the mental processes
  or characteristics of those persons or animals.
  UF   —Biography—Character
            [Former subdivision]
          —Biography—Psychology
            [Former subdivision]
          —Personality
            [Former subdivision]
——Testing
  USE   —Psychological testing
—**Psychophysiology**   (*Not Subd Geog*)
  H 1164
    Use as a topical subdivision under individual or-
  gans and regions of the body.
  BT   —Physiology

—**Psychosomatic aspects**   (*May Subd Geog*)
  H 1150
    Use as a topical subdivision under individual dis-
  eases and types of diseases.
—**Psychotropic effects**   (*May Subd Geog*)
  H 1149
    Use as a topical subdivision under individual
  chemicals and groups of chemicals.
—**Public opinion**
  H 1095; H 1100; H 1103; H 1105; H 1110;
  H 1200
    Use under names of individual persons and cor-
  porate bodies, and under classes of persons, eth-
  nic groups, individual wars, and topical headings
  for works on public opinion about those persons or
  topics. For works on attitudes or opinions held by
  members of a group, use the subdivision Attitudes
  under classes of persons and ethnic groups.
  UF   —Opinion, Public
—**Public records**
  H 1105
    Use as a topical subdivision under names of in-
  dividual government agencies.
  BT   —Records and correspondence
—**Public relations**   (*May Subd Geog*)
  H 1095; H 1105; H 1159
    Use under names of individual corporate bodies,
  military services, and topical headings.
—**Public services**
  H 1151; H 1151.5
    Use as a topical subdivision under names of in-
  dividual educational institutions and types of edu-
  cational institutions.
—Public speaking
  USE   —Oratory
—**Public welfare**   (*May Subd Geog*)
  H 1103
    Use as a topical subdivision under ethnic groups.
—**Publication and distribution**
  (*May Subd Geog*)
  H 1188
    Use as a topical subdivision under uniform titles
  of sacred works.
  BT   —Publishing
—**Publication of proceedings**
  H 1155
    Use as a topical subdivision under names of in-
  dividual legislative bodies.
—**Publishing**   (*May Subd Geog*)
  H 1095; H 1105; H 1156; H 1187
    Use as a topical subdivision under names of in-
  dividual corporate bodies, individual Christian de-
  nominations, and types of corporate bodies, and
  under types of published materials, and headings
  for literature on particular topics.
  NT   —Electronic publishing
          —Publication and distribution
—**Pump placing**   (*May Subd Geog*)
  H 1158
    Use as a topical subdivision under individual
  materials and types of materials.
—**Punctuation**
  H 1154
    Use as a topical subdivision under individual
  languages and groups of languages.
—**Purchasing**   (*May Subd Geog*)
  H 1095; H 1147
    Use as a topical subdivision under types of
  products and services and individual animals and
  groups of animals.
  UF   —Buying
            [Former subdivision]
—**Purges**
  H 1105
    Use as a topical subdivision under names of in-
  dividual political parties.
—**Purification**   (*May Subd Geog*)
  H 1149
    Use as a topical subdivision under individual
  chemicals and groups of chemicals.
—**Puritan authors**
  H 1156
    Use as a topical subdivision under individual lit-
  eratures.
—**Quaker authors**
  H 1156
    Use as a topical subdivision under individual lit-
  eratures.

—**Qualifications**
  H 1155
    Use as a topical subdivision under names of in-
  dividual legislative bodies.
—**Quality**   (*May Subd Geog*)
  H 1147; H 1180
    Use as a topical subdivision under individual an-
  imals and groups of animals and individual plants
  and groups of plants.
  NT   —Seedlings—Quality
          —Seeds—Quality
—**Quality control**
  H 1095; H 1153; H 1158
    Use as a topical subdivision under types of in-
  dustries, industrial plants, and processes, and under
  individual materials and types of materials.
  NT   —Equipment—Quality control
          —Ordnance and ordnance stores—
            Quality control
          —Supplies and stores—Quality
            control
—**Quantifiers**
  H 1154
    Use as a topical subdivision under individual
  languages and groups of languages.
—**Quantity**
  H 1154
    Use as a topical subdivision under individual
  languages and groups of languages.
—**Quarantine**   (*May Subd Geog*)
  H 1147
    Use as a topical subdivision under individual an-
  imals and groups of animals.
—Quarters and barracks
  USE   —Barracks and quarters
—**Queens**
  H 1103
    Use as a topical subdivision under ethnic groups.
—**Quenching**   (*May Subd Geog*)
  H 1149; H 1158
    Use as a topical subdivision under individual
  chemicals and groups of chemicals and individual
  materials and types of materials.
—Questions and answers
  USE   —Miscellanea
—Questions, examinations, etc.
  USE   —Examinations, questions, etc.
—**Quotations**
  H 1100; H 1103; H 1110; H 1120; H 1188
    Use as a topical subdivision under names of in-
  dividual persons and families, classes of persons,
  and ethnic groups for works about quotations of or
  about those persons or groups. Also use under uniform titles of sacred works for works about quotations from or about those works.
  UF   —Sayings
          —Table-talk
—**Quotations**
  H 1100; H 1103; H 1110; H 1120; H 1188
    Use as a form subdivision under names of in-
  dividual persons and families, classes of persons,
  and ethnic groups for collections of quotations of
  or about those persons or groups. Also use under uniform titles of sacred works for collections
  of quotations from or about those works.
  UF   —Sayings
          —Table-talk
  NT   —Sacred books—Quotations
—**Quotations, Early**
  H 1188
    Use as a topical subdivision under uniform titles
  of sacred works for works about quotations found
  in early literature.
  UF   —Early quotations
—**Quotations, Early**
  H 1188
    Use as a form subdivision under uniform titles
  of sacred works for collections of quotations found
  in early literature.
  UF   —Early quotations
—**Quotations in rabbinical literature**
  H 1188
    Use as a topical subdivision under Bible. O.T. or
  individual parts or books of the Old Testament for
  works about quotations.

—**Quotations in rabbinical literature**
H 1188
Use as a form subdivision under Bible. O.T. or individual parts or books of the Old Testament for collections of quotations.

—**Quotations in the New Testament**
H 1188
Use as a topical subdivision under Bible. O.T. or individual books of the Old Testament for works about quotations.

—**Quotations in the New Testament**
H 1188
Use as a form subdivision under Bible. O.T. or individual parts or books of the Old Testament for collections of quotations.

—**Quotations, maxims, etc.**
H 1095; H 1140
Use as a topical subdivision under names of countries, cities, etc., and topical headings for works about quotations, maxims, etc., on those places or topics.
UF —Maxims

—**Quotations, maxims, etc.**
H 1095; H 1140
Use as a form subdivision under names of countries, cities, etc., and under topical headings for compilations of quotations, maxims, etc., about those places or topics.
UF —Maxims

—**Race identity**   *(May Subd Geog)*
H 1103
Use as a topical subdivision under ethnic groups.
UF —Identity, Race
—Identity, Racial
—Racial identity

—Race question
USE —Race relations

—**Race relations**
H 1140; H 1149.5
Use as a topical subdivision under names of countries, cities, etc.
UF —Race question
   [Former subdivision]
—Relations, Race
NT —Colonies—Race relations

———**Economic aspects**
H 1140
Use as a topical subdivision under names of countries, cities, etc.
BT —Economic aspects

———**Political aspects**
H 1140
Use as a topical subdivision under names of countries, cities, etc.
BT —Political aspects

—**Racial analysis**   *(May Subd Geog)*
H 1147
Use as a topical subdivision under individual animals and groups of animals.

—Racial identity
USE —Race identity

—**Radar**
H 1200
Use as a topical subdivision under individual wars.

—**Radiation injuries**   *(May Subd Geog)*
H 1164
Further subdivide by subdivisions used under diseases.
Use as a topical subdivision under individual organs and regions of the body.
BT —Wounds and injuries

—**Radiation preservation**   *(May Subd Geog)*
H 1180
Use as a topical subdivision under individual plants and groups of plants.
BT —Preservation

—**Radiator ornaments**
H 1195
Use as a topical subdivision under individual land vehicles and types of land vehicles.
UF —Ornaments, Radiator

—**Radiators**
H 1195
Use as a topical subdivision under individual land vehicles and types of land vehicles.

—**Radio and television plays**
H 1110
Do not use under authors who write principally radio or television plays.
Use as a topical subdivision under names of individual literary authors for works of criticism about scripts written by the author expressly for radio or television.
UF —Television plays
BT —Criticism and interpretation

—**Radio broadcasting and the war, [revolution, etc.]**
H 1200
Complete the subdivision by repeating the generic term for the type of engagement contained in the heading.
Use as a topical subdivision under individual wars.

—**Radio broadcasting of proceedings**
H 1155
Use as a topical subdivision under names of individual legislative bodies.

—Radio control of models
USE —Models—Radio control

—**Radio equipment**
H 1195
Use as a topical subdivision under individual land vehicles and types of land vehicles.
BT —Equipment and supplies

———**Security measures**   *(May Subd Geog)*
H 1195
Use as a topical subdivision under individual land vehicles and types of land vehicles.
BT —Security measures

—**Radio installations**
H 1159
Use as a topical subdivision under military services.

—**Radio tracking**   *(May Subd Geog)*
H 1147
Use as a topical subdivision under individual animals and groups of animals.
UF —Tracking, Radio

—**Radioactive contamination**
(May Subd Geog)
H 1180
Use as a topical subdivision under individual plants and groups of plants and individual animals and groups of animals.
UF —Contamination, Radioactive

—**Radiography**   *(May Subd Geog)*
H 1158; H 1164; H 1180
Use as a topical subdivision under individual materials and types of materials, individual organs and regions of the body, and individual plants and groups of plants.
NT —Tomography

———**Law and legislation**   *(May Subd Geog)*
H 1164
Further subdivide by subdivisions used under legal topics.
Use as a topical subdivision under individual organs and regions of the body.
BT —Law and legislation

———**Positioning**   *(May Subd Geog)*
H 1164
Use as a topical subdivision under individual organs and regions of the body.
UF —Positioning for radiography

—**Radioimmunoimaging**   *(May Subd Geog)*
H 1150
Use as a topical subdivision under individual diseases and types of diseases.
BT —Immunodiagnosis
—Radionuclide imaging

—**Radioimmunotherapy**   *(May Subd Geog)*
H 1150
Use as a topical subdivision under individual diseases and types of diseases.
BT —Immunotherapy
—Radiotherapy

—**Radioiodination**   *(May Subd Geog)*
H 1149
Use as a topical subdivision under individual chemicals and groups of chemicals.

—Radioisotopes
USE —Isotopes

—Radiology, Interventional
USE —Interventional radiology

—**Radiomen**
H 1159
Further subdivide by subdivisions used under classes of persons.
Use as a topical subdivision under military services.

—**Radionuclide imaging**   *(May Subd Geog)*
H 1150; H 1164
Use as a topical subdivision under individual diseases and types of diseases and individual organs and regions of the body.
UF —Diseases—Radionuclide imaging
BT —Imaging
NT —Radioimmunoimaging

—**Radiotherapy**   *(May Subd Geog)*
H 1150
Use as a topical subdivision under individual diseases and types of diseases.
BT —Treatment
NT —Intraoperative radiotherapy
—Radioimmunotherapy

———**Complications**   *(May Subd Geog)*
H 1150
Further subdivide by subdivisions used under diseases.
Use as a topical subdivision under individual diseases and types of diseases.
UF —Radiotherapy—Complications and sequelae
   [Former subdivision]
BT —Complications

———Complications and sequelae
USE —Radiotherapy—Complications

—Rankings
USE —Ratings and rankings

—**Rapid solidification processing**
(May Subd Geog)
H 1158
Use as a topical subdivision under individual materials and types of materials.

—Rate of diffusion
USE —Diffusion rate

—**Rates**   *(May Subd Geog)*
H 1095
Use as a topical subdivision under types of services, utilities, transportation systems, etc., for works on prices charged for services provided or items sold according to a specific ratio, scale, or standard.

—**Rating of**   *(May Subd Geog)*
H 1100
Use as a topical subdivision under classes of persons.
BT —Evaluation

—**Ratings and rankings**   *(May Subd Geog)*
H 1151.5
Use as a topical subdivision under types of educational institutions.
UF —Rankings

—Ratings, Credit
USE —Credit ratings

—Ration, Rum
USE —Rum ration

—**Reactivity**   *(May Subd Geog)*
H 1149
Use as a topical subdivision under individual chemicals and groups of chemicals.
BT —Properties

—**Reader-response criticism**
H 1188
Use as a topical subdivision under uniform titles of sacred works.
BT —Criticism, interpretation, etc.

—**Readers**
H 1154
Use as a form subdivision under languages other than English.
UF —Chrestomathies and readers
   [Former subdivision]

———**[form]**
H 1154
Use as a form subdivision under languages other than English for readers in those languages in those literary forms.

———**[topic]**
H 1154
Use as a form subdivision under languages other than English for readers in those languages on those topics.

—**Readers for new literates**
> H 1154
> Use as a form subdivision under languages other than English.

—**Readiness, Operational**
> USE —Operational readiness

—**Reading** *(May Subd Geog)*
> H 1188
> Use as a topical subdivision under uniform titles of sacred works.

—**Reading habits**
> USE —Books and reading

—**Reading interests**
> USE —Books and reading

—**Readings, Marginal**
> USE —Marginal readings

—**Readings with music**
> H 1095
> Use as a form subdivision under topical headings.

—**Receptors**
> H 1149
> Use as a topical subdivision under individual chemicals and groups of chemicals.

——**Effect of drugs on** *(May Subd Geog)*
> H 1149
> Use as a topical subdivision under chemicals and groups of chemicals.
> BT —Effect of drugs on

—**Recolonization** *(May Subd Geog)*
> H 1147
> Use as a topical subdivision under individual animals and groups of animals.
> BT —Colonization

—**Reconnaissance operations**
> H 1200
> Use as a topical subdivision under individual wars.

—**Reconnaissance operations, American,** ₍German, etc.₎
> H 1200
> Use as a topical subdivision under individual wars.

—**Records and correspondence**
> H 1095; H 1105; H 1153; H 1159
> Use as a topical subdivision under names of individual corporate bodies and under types of industries, organizations, etc., and military services for works about records of those organizations.
> UF —Office records
> BT —Correspondence
> NT —Personnel records
> —Public records

—**Records and correspondence**
> H 1095; H 1105; H 1153; H 1159
> Use as a form subdivision under names of individual corporate bodies and under types of industries, organizations, etc. and military services for collections of records of those organizations.
> UF —Office records
> BT —Correspondence

—**Records, Performance**
> USE —Performance records

—**Recreation** *(May Subd Geog)*
> H 1100; H 1103
> Use as a topical subdivision under classes of persons and ethnic groups.
> UF —Amusements

—**Recreational use** *(May Subd Geog)*
> H 1095
> Use as a topical subdivision under types of land, types of bodies of water, types of geographic features, and types of buildings with other functions.

—**Recruiting** *(May Subd Geog)*
> H 1100
> Use as a topical subdivision under occupational groups and types of employees.

—**Recruiting, enlistment, etc.**
> H 1159
> Use as a topical subdivision under military services.
> UF —Enlistment

——**Revolution, 1775-1783,** ₍Spanish-American War, 1898, etc.₎
> H 1159
> Use as a topical subdivision under military services.

——**Law and legislation**
> H 1159
> Further subdivide by subdivisions used under legal topics.
> Use as a topical subdivision under military services.
> BT —Law and legislation

—**Recurrence**
> USE —Relapse

—**Recycling** *(May Subd Geog)*
> H 1149; H 1158
> Use as a topical subdivision under individual chemicals and groups of chemicals and individual materials and types of materials.

—**Redaction criticism**
> USE —Criticism, Redaction

—**Reduplication**
> H 1154
> Use as a topical subdivision under individual languages and groups of languages.

—**Reference**
> H 1154
> Use as a topical subdivision under individual languages and groups of languages.
> NT —Switch-reference

—**Reference books**
> H 1095
> Use as a topical subdivision under subjects for works about reference works on those subjects.

—**Reference editions**
> H 1188
> Use as a form subdivision under uniform titles of sacred works.

—**Refining** *(May Subd Geog)*
> H 1158
> Use as a topical subdivision under individual materials and types of materials.

—**Reflexives**
> H 1154
> Use as a topical subdivision under individual languages and groups of languages.

—**Reform**
> H 1154; H 1155
> Use as a topical subdivision under names of individual legislative bodies and individual languages and groups of languages.

—**Refugees** *(May Subd Geog)*
> H 1200
> Further subdivide by subdivisions used under classes of persons.
> Use as a topical subdivision under individual wars.
> UF —Displaced persons
> ₍Former subdivision₎

—**Regeneration** *(May Subd Geog)*
> H 1164; H 1180
> Use as a topical subdivision under individual organs and regions of the body and individual plants and groups of plants.

—**Regeneration, Population**
> USE —Population regeneration

—**Regimental histories** *(May Subd Geog)*
> H 1200
> Use as a topical subdivision under individual wars.

—**Regional disparities**
> H 1095
> Use as a topical subdivision under topical headings.
> UF —Disparities, Regional
> NT —Economic conditions—₍period subdivision₎—Regional disparities
> —Economic conditions—Regional disparities
> —Officials and employees—Salaries, etc.—Regional disparities

—**Regions**
> H 1095
> Use only under countries whose legally designated first order political divisions are called regions.
> Use as a topical subdivision under headings of the type ₍topic₎—₍country₎ for works discussing collectively the regions of a country in relation to the topic.
> BT —Administrative and political divisions

—**Registers**
> H 1095; H 1100; H 1103; H 1105; H 1120; H 1140; H 1159; H 1200
> Use as a form subdivision under names of countries, cities, etc., families, and individual corporate bodies, and under classes of persons, ethnic groups, individual wars, and topical headings for lists of names of persons, organizations, or objects, etc., without addresses or other identifying data.
> UF —Registers, lists, etc.
> ₍Former subdivision₎
> NT —Registers of dead

—**Registers, lists, etc.**
> USE —Registers

—**Registers of dead** *(May Subd Geog)*
> H 1159; H 1200
> Do not subdivide geographically under military services.
> Use as a form subdivision under military services and individual wars.
> UF —Dead, Registers of
> BT —Registers

—**Registration and transfer** *(May Subd Geog)*
> H 1195
> Use as a topical subdivision under individual land vehicles and types of land vehicles.
> UF —Transfer and registration

——**Fees** *(May Subd Geog)*
> H 1195
> Use as a topical subdivision under individual land vehicles and types of land vehicles.
> UF —Fees for registration and transfer

—**Regulation**
> H 1145.5
> Use as a topical subdivision under names of individual bodies of water.

—**Regulation of growth**
> USE —Growth—Regulation

—**Regulation of metabolism**
> USE —Metabolism—Regulation

—**Regulation of reproduction**
> USE —Reproduction—Regulation

—**Regulation of secretion**
> USE —Secretion—Regulation

—**Regulation of synthesis**
> USE —Synthesis—Regulation

—**Regulation of vocalization**
> USE —Vocalization—Regulation

—**Regulations**
> H 1151; H 1159
> Use as a topical subdivision under names of individual educational institutions and military services for works about regulations of those institutions or services.

—**Regulations**
> H 1151; H 1159
> Use as a form subdivision under individual educational institutions and military services for collections of regulations of those institutions and services.

—**Rehabilitation** *(May Subd Geog)*
> H 1100; H 1103
> Use as a topical subdivision under classes of persons and ethnic groups.

—**Reimplantation** *(May Subd Geog)*
> H 1164
> Use as a topical subdivision under individual organs and regions of the body.

—**Reinstatement** *(May Subd Geog)*
> H 1100
> Use as a topical subdivision under occupational groups and types of employees.

—**Reintroduction** *(May Subd Geog)*
> H 1147; H 1180
> Use as a topical subdivision under individual animals and groups of animals and individual plants and groups of plants.

—**Relapse** *(May Subd Geog)*
> H 1150
> Further subdivide by other subdivisions used under diseases.
> Use as a topical subdivision under individual diseases and types of diseases.
> UF —Recurrence

—**Relation to Matthew,** ₁Jeremiah, etc.₁
    H 1188
      Use as a topical subdivision under uniform titles for individual books or groups of books of the Bible.

—**Relation to the Old Testament**
    H 1188
      Use as a topical subdivision under uniform titles for individual books or groups of books of the New Testament.

—**Relational grammar**
    H 1154
      Use as a topical subdivision under individual languages and groups of languages.
    BT —Grammar

—**Relations** *(May Subd Geog)*
    H 1140; H 1185; H 1187
      Further subdivide geographically only under names of places.
      Use as a topical subdivision under names of countries, cities, etc., and under individual religions and Christian denominations.
    UF —Relations (Canon law)
          ₁Former subdivision₁
    NT —Foreign relations
          —Military relations
          —Military relations—Foreign countries

——**Anglican Communion,** ₁**Lutheran Church, etc.**₁
    H 1187
      Use as a topical subdivision under individual Christian denominations.

——**Buddhism,** ₁**Judaism, etc.**₁
    H 1187
      Use as a topical subdivision under individual Christian denominations.

——**Christianity,** ₁**Islam, etc.**₁
    H 1185
      Use as a topical subdivision under individual religions.

——**Evangelicalism**
    H 1187
      Use as a topical subdivision under individual Christian denominations.

——**Protestant churches**
    H 1187
      Use as a topical subdivision under individual Christian denominations.

——**Foreign countries**
    H 1140
      Use as a topical subdivision under names of countries, cities, etc.

—Relations (Canon law)
    USE —Relations

—Relations (diplomatic)
    USE —Foreign relations

—Relations, Ethnic
    USE —Ethnic relations

—Relations, Race
    USE —Race relations

—Relations with employees
    USE —Employees

—Relations with family
    USE —Family

—Relations with friends and associates
    USE —Friends and associates

—**Relations with men**
    H 1110; H 1155.2
      Use as a topical subdivision under names of individual authors and groups of literary authors for works on intimate associations.

—**Relations with** ₁**specific class of persons or ethnic group**₁
    H 1110
      Use as a topical subdivision under names of individual persons.

—**Relations with women**
    H 1110; H 1155.2
      Use as a topical subdivision under names of individual persons and groups of literary authors for works on intimate associations.

—**Relative clauses**
    H 1154
      Use as a topical subdivision under individual languages and groups of languages.
    BT —Clauses

—**Reliability**
    H 1095
      Use as a topical subdivision under types of equipment, machinery, technical systems, industrial plants, etc.

—**Relics** *(May Subd Geog)*
    H 1110; H 1120
      Use as a topical subdivision under names of individual persons and families for works on disinterred bones, etc. For works on graves, interred bones, etc., use the subdivisions Tomb under names of individual persons and Tombs under names of individual families.
    NT —Death mask

—**Relief models**
    H 1140
      Use as a form subdivision under names of countries, cities, etc.
    BT —Maps

—**Religion**
    H 1103; H 1105; H 1110; H 1140; H 1149.5; H 1151.5
      Use as a topical subdivision under names of countries, cities, etc., names of individual persons and corporate bodies, and under ethnic groups and types of educational institutions.
    UF —Religion and ethics
          ₁Former subdivision₁
    NT —Colonies—Religion

——**16th century**
    H 1140
      Use as a topical subdivision under names of countries, cities, etc.

——**17th century**
    H 1140
      Use as a topical subdivision under names of countries, cities, etc.

——**18th century**
    H 1140
      Use as a topical subdivision under names of countries, cities, etc.

——**19th century**
    H 1140
      Use as a topical subdivision under names of countries, cities, etc.

——**20th century**
    H 1140
      Use as a topical subdivision under names of countries, cities, etc.

——**21st century**
    H 1140
      Use as a topical subdivision under names of countries, cities, etc.

——**Economic aspects**
    H 1140
      Use as a topical subdivision under names of countries, cities, etc.
    BT —Economic aspects

—Religion and ethics
    USE —Ethics
          —Religion

—**Religious aspects**
    H 1147; H 1149; H 1150; H 1154; H 1158; H 1161; H 1164; H 1180; H 1200
      Use as a topical subdivision under individual animals and groups of animals, individual plants and groups of plants, individual chemicals and groups of chemicals, individual materials and types of materials, individual languages and groups of languages, individual diseases and types of diseases, individual organs and regions of the body, individual musical instruments and families of instruments, and individual wars.

——**Baptists,** ₁**Catholic Church, etc.**₁
    H 1150; H 1154; H 1161; H 1200
      Use as a topical subdivision under individual plants and groups of plants, individual languages and groups of languages, individual diseases and types of diseases, individual musical instruments and families of instruments, and individual wars.

——**Buddhism,** ₁**Christianity, etc.**₁
    H 1147; H 1149; H 1150; H 1154; H 1158; H 1161; H 1164; H 1180; H 1200
      Use as a topical subdivision under individual animals and groups of animals, individual plants and groups of plants, individual chemicals and groups of chemicals, individual materials and types of materials, individual languages and groups of languages, individual diseases and types of diseases, individual organs and regions of the body, individual musical instruments and families of instruments, and individual wars.

——**Protestant churches**
    H 1200
      Use as a topical subdivision under individual wars.

—**Religious life** *(May Subd Geog)*
    H 1100; H 1159
      Further subdivide geographically only under classes of persons.
      Use as a topical subdivision under classes of persons and military services.

—**Religious life and customs**
    H 1140; H 1149.5
      Use as a topical subdivision under names of countries, cities, etc.
    NT —Colonies—Religious life and customs

—**Relocation** *(May Subd Geog)*
    H 1100; H 1103
      Use as a topical subdivision under occupational groups and types of employees and ethnic groups.

—**Remedial teaching** *(May Subd Geog)*
    H 1154
      Use as a topical subdivision under individual languages and groups of languages.

—**Remodeling** *(May Subd Geog)*
    H 1095
      Use as a topical subdivision under types of structures and rooms.

—**Remodeling for other use** *(May Subd Geog)*
    H 1095
      Use as a topical subdivision under types of buildings and structures.

—**Remote sensing**
    H 1095
      Use as a topical subdivision under topical headings.

—**Remote-sensing images**
    H 1140
      Use as a form subdivision under names of countries, cities, etc.
    NT —Aerial photographs

—**Remote-sensing maps**
    H 1095; H 1140
      Use as a form subdivision under names of countries, cities, etc., and under topical headings.
    BT —Maps

—**Remount service**
    H 1159
      Use as a topical subdivision under military services.

—Removal of snow
    USE —Snow protection and removal

—**Reoperation** *(May Subd Geog)*
    H 1150; H 1164
      Use as a topical subdivision under individual diseases and types of diseases and individual organs and regions of the body.
    UF —Diseases—Reoperation
    BT —Surgery

—**Reorganization**
    H 1105; H 1159
      Use as a topical subdivision under individual corporate bodies and military services.

—Repair and maintenance
    USE —Maintenance and repair

—**Repairing** *(May Subd Geog)*
    H 1095
      Use as a topical subdivision under types of objects not requiring maintenance.
    BT —Maintenance and repair
    NT —Tires—Repairing

—**Reparations** *(May Subd Geog)*
    H 1103; H 1200
      Do not subdivide geographically under individual wars.
      Use as a topical subdivision under ethnic groups and individual wars.

—Repatriation, Forced
  USE —Forced repatriation
—**Repatriation of war dead** (May Subd Geog)
    H 1200
    Use as a topical subdivision under individual
    wars.
    UF —Dead, Repatriation of
      —War dead, Repatriation of
—**Reporters and reporting**
    H 1155
    Use as a topical subdivision under names of in-
    dividual legislative bodies.
—**Reporting** (May Subd Geog)
    H 1150
    Use as a topical subdivision under individual dis-
    eases and types of diseases.
    NT —Defects—Reporting
      —Toxicology—Reporting
—**Reporting to** (May Subd Geog)
    H 1100
    Use as a topical subdivision under occupational
    groups and types of employees.
—Representation, Symbolic
  USE —Symbolic representation
—**Reproduction**
    H 1147; H 1148; H 1180
    Use as a topical subdivision under individual art
    forms and headings for national or ethnic art for the
    processes of producing images of the art.
    Also use under individual animals and groups of
    animals and individual plants and groups of plants
    for works on the physiological processes, sexual or
    asexual, by which organisms generate offspring of
    the same kind. For works on the controlled mating
    and selection of the organisms by humans, usually
    for the purpose of improving the species or breed,
    use the subdivision Breeding.
    BT —Physiology
    NT —Parturition
      —Pollination
      —Pregnancy
      —Propagation
      —Spawning
——**Climatic factors** (May Subd Geog)
    H 1147
    Use as a topical subdivision under individual
    animals and groups of animals.
    BT —Climatic factors
——**Effect of altitude on** (May Subd Geog)
    H 1147
    Use as a topical subdivision under individual
    animals and groups of animals.
    BT —Effect of altitude on
——**Effect of light on** (May Subd Geog)
    H 1147
    Use as a topical subdivision under individual
    animals and groups of animals.
    BT —Effect of light on
——**Effect of temperature on**
    (May Subd Geog)
    H 1147
    Use as a topical subdivision under individual
    animals and groups of animals.
    BT —Effect of temperature on
——**Endocrine aspects**
    H 1147
    Use as a topical subdivision under individual
    animals and groups of animals.
    BT —Endocrinology
——**Regulation**
    H 1147
    Use as a topical subdivision under individual
    animals and groups of animals.
    UF —Regulation of reproduction
—**Republics**
    H 1095
    Use as a topical subdivision under headings of
    the type [topic]—country for works discussing col-
    lectively the republics of a country in relation to the
    topic.
    BT —Administrative and political
      divisions
—Requirements for entrance
  USE —Entrance requirements
—Requirements for graduation
  USE —Graduation requirements
—Requirements for residence
  USE —Residence requirements

—Requirements, Insurance
  USE —Insurance requirements
—Requirements, Nutritional
  USE —Nutrition—Requirements
—Requirements, Water
  USE —Water requirements
—Rescue operations
  USE —Search and rescue operations
—**Research** (May Subd Geog)
    H 1095; H 1100; H 1103; H 1105; H 1140;
    H 1149; H 1154.5; H 1180
    Use as a topical subdivision under names of
    countries, cities, etc., individual corporate bodies,
    classes of persons, ethnic groups, and topical head-
    ings.
    NT —Dialects—Research
——**Law and legislation** (May Subd Geog)
    H 1149; H 1180
    Further subdivide by subdivisions used under
    legal topics.
    Use as a topical subdivision under individual
    chemicals and groups of chemicals and individ-
    ual plants and groups of plants.
    BT —Law and legislation
—**Research grants** (May Subd Geog)
    H 1095; H 1105
    Further subdivide geographically only under
    topical headings.
    Use as a topical subdivision under names of indi-
    vidual corporate bodies and under topical headings.
    UF —Grants, Research
—**Reserve fleets**
    H 1159
    Use as a topical subdivision under military ser-
    vices.
—**Reserves**
    H 1159
    Use as a topical subdivision under military ser-
    vices.
    NT —Women's reserves
——**Pay, allowances, etc.**
    H 1159
    Use as a topical subdivision under military
    services.
    BT —Pay, allowances, etc.
——**Personnel records**
    H 1159
    Use as a topical subdivision under military
    services.
    BT —Personnel records
——**Promotions**
    H 1159
    Use as a topical subdivision under military
    services.
    BT —Promotions
—**Residence requirements** (May Subd Geog)
    H 1100; H 1151.5
    Use as a topical subdivision under occupational
    groups, types of employees, and types of educa-
    tional institutions.
    UF —Requirements for residence
      —Residency requirements
—Residences
  USE —Dwellings
      —Homes and haunts
—Residency requirements
  USE —Residence requirements
—**Residues** (May Subd Geog)
    H 1180
    Use as a topical subdivision under individual
    plants and groups of plants.
—**Resignation** (May Subd Geog)
    H 1100
    Use as a topical subdivision under occupational
    groups and types of employees.
—**Resignation from office**
    H 1110
    Use as a topical subdivision under names of in-
    dividual persons.
—Resistance, Chemical
  USE —Chemical resistance
—Resistance, Skid
  USE —Skid resistance
—Resistance to diseases and pests
  USE —Disease and pest resistance
—Resistance to droughts
  USE —Drought tolerance

—Resistance to frost
  USE —Frost resistance
—Resistance to insects
  USE —Insect resistance
—Resistance to penetration
  USE —Penetration resistance
—Resistance to pests
  USE —Disease and pest resistance
—Resistance to venom
  USE —Venom resistance
—**Resolutions**
    H 1155
    Use as a topical subdivision under names of in-
    dividual legislative bodies for works about resolu-
    tions of those bodies.
—**Resolutions**
    H 1155
    Use as a form subdivision under names of indi-
    vidual legislative bodies for collections of resolu-
    tions of those bodies.
—**Respiration** (May Subd Geog)
    H 1147
    Use as a topical subdivision under individual an-
    imals and groups of animals.
    BT —Physiology
—**Respiratory organs**
    H 1147
    Use as a topical subdivision under individual an-
    imals and groups of animals.
    BT —Anatomy
—**Respite care** (May Subd Geog)
    H 1100; H 1103
    Use as a topical subdivision under classes of per-
    sons and ethnic groups.
    BT —Care
—Restoration and conservation
  USE —Conservation and restoration
—Restraint systems, Occupant
  USE —Occupant restraint systems
—**Resultative constructions**
    H 1154
    Use as a topical subdivision under individual
    languages and groups of languages.
—**Retarders** (May Subd Geog)
    H 1195
    Use as a topical subdivision under individual
    land vehicles and types of land vehicles.
—Retired officials and employees
  USE —Officials and employees, Retired
—**Retirement** (May Subd Geog)
    H 1100; H 1103
    Use as a topical subdivision under classes of per-
    sons and ethnic groups.
    NT —Appointments and retirements
—**Reverse indexes**
    H 1154
    Use as a form subdivision under individual lan-
    guages and groups of languages.
    BT —Indexes
—**Reviews**
    H 1095
    Use as a form subdivision under types of books
    and nonbook materials for collections of descrip-
    tive and evaluative accounts of those materials.
    Also use under headings for mass media and the
    performing arts for collections of critical writings
    about programs, performances, etc.
    NT —Book reviews
—**Revival**
    H 1154
    Use as a topical subdivision under individual
    languages and groups of languages.
—**Rhetoric**
    H 1154
    Use as a topical subdivision under individual
    languages and groups of languages.
—**Rhyme**
    H 1154
    Use as a topical subdivision under individual
    languages and groups of languages.
    UF —Rime
      [Former subdivision]
—**Rhythm**
    H 1154
    Use as a topical subdivision under individual
    modern languages and groups of modern lan-
    guages. Under individual ancient languages use
    the subdivision Metrics and rhythmics.

—**Riding qualities** *(May Subd Geog)*
    H 1195
      Use as a topical subdivision under individual
land vehicles and types of land vehicles.
—Right hand studies
    USE —Studies and exercises (Right hand)
—Rights, Civil
    USE —Civil rights
—Rime
    USE —Rhyme
—**Riot, [date]**
    H 1151
      Use as a topical subdivision under names of in-
dividual educational institutions.
—**Riots**
    H 1151
      Use as a topical subdivision under names of in-
dividual educational institutions.
—**Ripening** *(May Subd Geog)*
    H 1180
      Use as a topical subdivision under individual
plants and groups of plants.
—**Risk assessment** *(May Subd Geog)*
    H 1095
      Use as a topical subdivision under topical head-
ings with which physical risk is associated.
—**Risk factors** *(May Subd Geog)*
    H 1150
      Use as a topical subdivision under individual dis-
eases and types of diseases.
    NT —Health risk assessment
           —Surgery—Risk factors
—**Risk management** *(May Subd Geog)*
    H 1153
      Use as a topical subdivision under types of in-
dustries.
    BT —Management
—**Rites and ceremonies**
    H 1103
      Use as a topical subdivision under ethnic groups.
    UF —Ceremonies
    NT —Funeral customs and rites
           —Marriage customs and rites
—**Rituals**
    H 1105; H 1185
      Use as a topical subdivision under names of in-
dividual secret societies and under individual religions other than Judaism and its sects.
——**Texts**
    H 1185
      Use this subdivision combination as a form
subdivision under individual religions other than
Judaism and its sects for individual texts or collections of texts of rituals.
      Use as a topical subdivision under individ-
ual religions other than Judaism and its sects for
works about those texts.
    BT —Texts
———**Concordances**
    H 1185
      Use this subdivision combination as a form
subdivision under individual religions other
than Judaism and its sects for word indexes
to texts of rituals.
    BT —Concordances
———**History and criticism**
    H 1185
      Use as a topical subdivision under individ-
ual religions other than Judaism and its sects.
    BT —History and criticism
—**Riverine operations** *(May Subd Geog)*
    H 1200
      Use as a topical subdivision under individual
wars.
—**Riverine operations, American [British, etc.]**
    (May Subd Geog)
    H 1200
      Use as a topical subdivision under individual
wars.
—**Robots**
    H 1159
      Use as a topical subdivision under military ser-
vices.
—**Rollover protective structures**
    (May Subd Geog)
    H 1195
      Use as a topical subdivision under individual
land vehicles and types of land vehicles.
    BT —Safety appliances

—Roman antiquities
    USE —Antiquities, Roman
—**Roman influences**
    H 1156
      Use as a topical subdivision under individual lit-
eratures.
    BT —Foreign influences
—**Romances**
    H 1095; H 1110
      Use as a form subdivision under names of indi-
vidual persons and legendary characters for texts of
medieval (that is, pre-1501) European tales based
chiefly on legends of chivalric love and adventure
in which those persons or characters are the domi-
nant character.
    UF —Romances, legends, etc.
        [Former subdivision]
    BT —Legends
—Romances, legends, etc.
    USE —Legends
          —Romances
—**Romanian influences**
    H 1156
      Use as a topical subdivision under individual lit-
eratures.
    BT —Foreign influences
—**Roots**
    H 1154; H 1180
      Use as a topical subdivision under individual
languages and groups of languages and individual
plants and groups of plants.
    NT —Seedlings—Roots
——**Anatomy**
    H 1180
      Use as a topical subdivision under individual
plants and groups of plants.
    BT —Anatomy
——**Diseases and pests** *(May Subd Geog)*
    H 1180
      Use as a topical subdivision under individual
plants and groups of plants.
    BT —Diseases and pests
——**Physiology** *(May Subd Geog)*
    H 1180
      Use as a topical subdivision under individual
plants and groups of plants.
    BT —Physiology
—**Rootstocks** *(May Subd Geog)*
    H 1180
      Use as a topical subdivision under individual
plants and groups of plants.
—Rotation, Molecular
    USE —Molecular rotation
—**Rowing**
    H 1151
      Use as a topical subdivision under names of in-
dividual educational institutions.
    BT —Sports
—Rubrics in liturgical texts
    USE —Liturgy—Texts—Rubrics
—**Rugby football**
    H 1151
      Use as a topical subdivision under names of in-
dividual educational institutions.
    BT —Sports
—Rulers
    USE —Kings and rulers
—**Rules**
    H 1095; H 1186
      Use as a topical subdivision under names of in-
dividual religious and monastic orders, individual
contests and sports events and under types of games
and activities for works about rules of those organizations or pertaining to those topics.
    BT —Standards
—**Rules**
    H 1095; H 1186
      Use as a form subdivision under names of in-
dividual religious and monastic orders, individual
contests and sports events and under types of games
and activities for works containing rules of those
organizations or pertaining to those topics.

—**Rules and practice**
    H 1095; H 1105
      Use as a topical subdivision under types of, and
names of individual, courts, legislative bodies, con-
stitutional conventions, and administrative or reg-
ulatory agencies, for works about the rules and
practice of those bodies.
    UF —Practice and rules
    NT —Committees—Rules and practice
—**Rules and practice**
    H 1095; H 1105
      Use as a form subdivision under types of, and
names of individual, courts, legislative bodies, con-
stitutional conventions, and administrative or regu-
latory agencies, for works containing the rules and
practice of those bodies.
    UF —Practice and rules
    NT —Committees—Rules and practice
—**Rum ration**
    H 1159
      Use as a topical subdivision under military ser-
vices.
    UF —Ration, Rum
—**Rupture** *(May Subd Geog)*
    H 1164
      Further subdivide by subdivisions used under
diseases.
      Use as a topical subdivision under individual or-
gans and regions of the body.
    BT —Wounds and injuries
—**Rural conditions**
    H 1140; H 1149.5
      Use as a topical subdivision under names of
countries, etc.
    NT —Colonies—Rural conditions
—**Russian influences**
    H 1156
      Use as a topical subdivision under individual lit-
eratures.
    BT —Foreign influences
—**Sacred books**
    H 1185
      Use as a topical subdivision under individual re-
ligions for works about the sacred books of those
religions.
—**Sacred books**
    H 1185
      Use as a form subdivision under individual reli-
gions for collections of the sacred books of those
religions.
——**Hermeneutics**
    H 1185
      Use as a topical subdivision under individual
religions.
    BT —Hermeneutics
——**Introductions**
    H 1185
      Use this subdivision combination as a form
subdivision under individual religions.
    BT —Introductions
——**Language, style**
    H 1185
      Use as a topical subdivision under individual
religions.
    BT —Language, style
——**Preservation** *(May Subd Geog)*
    H 1185
      Use as a topical subdivision under individual
religions.
    BT —Preservation
——**Quotations**
    H 1185
      Use this subdivision combination as a form
subdivision under individual religions.
    BT —Quotations
—**Safety appliances** *(May Subd Geog)*
    H 1095; H 1195
      Use as a topical subdivision under types of ma-
chines, vehicles, industrial plants, occupations, etc.
    BT —Equipment and supplies
          —Safety measures
    NT —Occupant restraint systems
          —Rollover protective structures
—**Safety measures**
    H 1095; H 1151.5; H 1153; H 1159
      Use as a topical subdivision under individual
military services and under topical headings.
    NT —Housing—Safety measures
          —Safety appliances

—Safety regulations *(May Subd Geog)*
> H 1095; H 1153
>> Further subdivide by subdivisions used under legal topics.
>> Use as a topical subdivision under topical headings.
>> BT —Law and legislation

—Sailors' handbooks
> H 1159
>> Use as a form subdivision under military services.
>> UF —Seamen's handbooks
>>> *[Former subdivision]*
>> BT —Handbooks, manuals, etc.

—Salaries, allowances, etc.
> USE —Salaries, etc.

—Salaries, commissions, etc.
> USE —Salaries, etc.

—Salaries, etc. *(May Subd Geog)*
> H 1100; H 1155
>> Use as a topical subdivision under names of individual legislative bodies and under classes of professional or public employees.
>> UF —Salaries, allowances, etc.
>>> *[Former subdivision]*
>>> —Salaries, commissions, etc.
>>> —Salaries, pensions, etc.
>>> *[Former subdivision]*
>> NT —Officials and employees—Salaries, etc.

— —Cost-of-living adjustments
> *(May Subd Geog)*
> H 1100
>> Use as a topical subdivision under classes of persons.
>> UF —Cost-of-living adjustments to salaries

— —Law and legislation *(May Subd Geog)*
> H 1100
>> Use as a topical subdivision under classes of persons.

—Salaries, pensions, etc.
> USE —Employees—Pensions
>> —Officials and employees—Pensions
>> —Pensions
>> —Salaries, etc.

—Sampling *(May Subd Geog)*
> H 1149; H 1158; H 1180
>> Use as a topical subdivision under individual chemicals and groups of chemicals, individual materials and types of materials, and individual plants and groups of plants.
>> BT —Inspection

—Sanitary affairs
> H 1151; H 1151.5; H 1159
>> Use as a topical subdivision under names of individual educational institutions, types of educational institutions, and military services.

—Sanitation *(May Subd Geog)*
> H 1095; H 1105; H 1153
>> Do not further subdivide geographically under corporate bodies.
>> Use as a topical subdivision under names of individual corporate bodies, types of industries, and topical headings.
>> NT —Housing—Sanitation

—Sanskrit influences
> H 1156
>> Use as a topical subdivision under individual literatures.
>> BT —Foreign influences

—Satire
> USE —Humor

—Satisfaction, Job
> USE —Job satisfaction

—Sayings
> USE —Quotations

—Scandinavian influences
> H 1156
>> Use as a topical subdivision under individual literatures.
>> BT —Foreign influences

—Scenarios
> H 1160
>> Use as a form subdivision under forms and types of musical compositions.

—Scheduled tribes
> H 1140
>> Use as a topical subdivision under names of states, regions, cities, etc., of India.
>> UF —Tribes, Scheduled

—Scholarship
> USE —Knowledge and learning

—Scholarships and funds
> USE —Funds and scholarships

—Scholarships, fellowships, etc.
> *(May Subd Geog)*
> H 1095; H 1100; H 1103
>> Use as a topical subdivision under classes of persons, ethnic groups, and fields of study.
>> UF —Fellowships

—Scholia
> H 1110
>> Use as a form subdivision under names of individual persons for marginal annotations, explanatory comments or remarks, especially on the text of a classical work by an early grammarian.
>> UF —Marginalia

—School yearbooks
> USE —Students—Yearbooks

—Schooling *(May Subd Geog)*
> H 1147
>> Use as a topical subdivision under individual animals and groups of animals.

—Science *(May Subd Geog)*
> H 1103; H 1200
>> Use as a topical subdivision under ethnic groups and individual wars.

—Scientific apparatus collections
> H 1105; H 1110; H 1120
>> Use as a topical subdivision under names of individual persons, families, and corporate bodies for works about their collections of scientific apparatus.

—Scientific applications *(May Subd Geog)*
> H 1095
>> Use as a topical subdivision under types of technical devices or processes used to further scientific advancement.

—Scientific atlases
> USE —Atlases

—Scientific names
> USE —Nomenclature

—Scores
> H 1160
>> Use as a form subdivision under forms and types of musical compositions.

—Scores and parts
> H 1160
>> Use as a form subdivision under forms and types of musical compositions.
>> UF —Parts and scores

—Scores and parts (solo)
> H 1160
>> Use as a form subdivision under forms and types of musical compositions.

—Scottish authors
> H 1156
>> Use as a topical subdivision under individual literatures.

—Scottish influences
> H 1156
>> Use as a topical subdivision under individual literatures.
>> BT —Foreign influences

—Scouts and scouting
> H 1200
>> Use as a topical subdivision under individual wars.

—Scrapping *(May Subd Geog)*
> H 1195
>> Use as a topical subdivision under individual land vehicles and types of land vehicles.

—Screenplays
> USE —Motion picture plays

—Sea life
> H 1159
>> Use as a topical subdivision under military services.

—Seal
> H 1105; H 1110; H 1140
>> Use as a topical subdivision under names of individual persons, corporate bodies, and countries, cities, etc.

—Seamen's handbooks
> USE —Sailors' handbooks

—Search and rescue operations
> *(May Subd Geog)*
> H 1159; H 1200
>> Use as a topical subdivision under military services and individual wars.
>> UF —Rescue operations

—Seasonal distribution *(May Subd Geog)*
> H 1147
>> Use as a topical subdivision under individual animals and groups of animals.
>> UF —Distribution, Seasonal

—Seasonal variations *(May Subd Geog)*
> H 1147; H 1150; H 1153; H 1180
>> Use as a topical subdivision under types of industries, individual diseases and types of diseases, individual animals and groups of animals, and individual plants and groups of plants.

—Seat belts
> H 1195
>> Use as a topical subdivision under individual land vehicles and types of land vehicles.
>> UF —Belts, Seat
>> BT —Occupant restraint systems

— —Law and legislation *(May Subd Geog)*
> H 1195
>> Further subdivide by subdivisions used under legal topics.
>> Use as a topical subdivision under individual land vehicles and types of land vehicles.
>> BT —Law and legislation

—Seats *(May Subd Geog)*
> H 1195
>> Use as a topical subdivision under individual land vehicles and types of land vehicles.

—Secondary education
> USE —Education (Secondary)

—Secret service *(May Subd Geog)*
> H 1200
>> Use as a topical subdivision under individual wars.

—Secretion
> H 1149
>> Use as a topical subdivision under individual chemicals and groups of chemicals.

— —Regulation
> H 1149
>> Use as a topical subdivision under individual chemicals and groups of chemicals.
>> UF —Regulation of secretion

—Secretions
> H 1164
>> Use as a topical subdivision under individual organs and regions of the body.

—Secular employment of clergy
> USE —Clergy—Secular employment

—Security measures *(May Subd Geog)*
> H 1095; H 1105; H 1151.5; H 1153; H 1159
>> Do not subdivide geographically under names of individual corporate bodies and military services.
>> Use as a topical subdivision under names of individual corporate bodies and under individual computers, networks, and systems, and under types of buildings, installations, industries, and institutions.
>> NT —Computer networks—Security measures
>>> —Radio equipment—Security measures

—Seed
> USE —Seeds

—Seedlings
> H 1180
>> Use as a topical subdivision under individual plants and groups of plants.
>> NT —Seedlings, Bareroot
>>> —Seedlings, Container

— —Diseases and pests *(May Subd Geog)*
> H 1180
>> Use as a topical subdivision under individual plants and groups of plants.
>> BT —Diseases and pests

— —Ecophysiology *(May Subd Geog)*
> H 1180
>> Use as a topical subdivision under individual plants and groups of plants.
>> BT —Ecophysiology

— —Effect of browsing on *(May Subd Geog)*
> H 1180
>> Use as a topical subdivision under individual plants and groups of plants.
>> BT —Effect of browsing on

——**Evaluation**
 H 1180
  Use as a topical subdivision under individual plants and groups of plants.
 BT —Evaluation
——**Protection** (*May Subd Geog*)
 H 1180
  Use as a topical subdivision under individual plants and groups of plants.
 BT —Protection
——**Quality** (*May Subd Geog*)
 H 1180
  Use as a topical subdivision under individual plants and groups of plants.
 BT —Quality
——**Roots**
 H 1180
  Use as a topical subdivision under individual plants and groups of plants.
 BT —Roots
—**Seedlings, Bareroot**
 H 1180
  Use as a topical subdivision under individual plants and groups of plants.
 UF —Bareroot seedlings
 BT —Seedlings
—**Seedlings, Container**
 H 1180
  Use as a topical subdivision under individual plants and groups of plants.
 UF —Container seedlings
 BT —Seedlings
—**Seeds** (*May Subd Geog*)
 H 1180
  Use as a topical subdivision under individual plants and groups of plants.
 UF —Seed
   [Former subdivision]
——**Anatomy**
 H 1180
  Use as a topical subdivision under individual plants and groups of plants.
 BT —Anatomy
——**Certification** (*May Subd Geog*)
 H 1180
  Use as a topical subdivision under individual plants and groups of plants.
 BT —Certification
——**Climatic factors** (*May Subd Geog*)
 H 1180
  Use as a topical subdivision under individual plants and groups of plants
 BT —Climatic factors
——**Dispersal** (*May Subd Geog*)
 H 1180
  Use as a topical subdivision under individual plants and groups of plants.
 BT —Dispersal
——**Dormancy** (*May Subd Geog*)
 H 1180
  Use as a topical subdivision under individual plants and groups of plants.
 BT —Dormancy
——**Drying** (*May Subd Geog*)
 H 1180
  Use as a topical subdivision under individual plants and groups of plants.
 BT —Drying
——**Handling** (*May Subd Geog*)
 H 1180
  Use as a topical subdivision under individual plants and groups of plants.
 BT —Handling
——**Harvesting** (*May Subd Geog*)
 H 1180
  Use as a topical subdivision under individual plants and groups of plants.
 BT —Harvesting
——**Identification**
 H 1180
  Use this subdivision combination as a form subdivision under individual plants and groups of plants.
 BT —Identification
——**Marketing**
 H 1180
  Use as a topical subdivision under individual plants and groups of plants.
 BT —Marketing

——**Morphology**
 H 1180
  Use as a topical subdivision under individual plants and groups of plants.
 BT —Morphology
——**Packaging** (*May Subd Geog*)
 H 1180
  Use as a topical subdivision under individual plants and groups of plants.
 BT —Packaging
——**Physiology** (*May Subd Geog*)
 H 1180
  Use as a topical subdivision under individual plants and groups of plants.
 BT —Physiology
——**Postharvest technology**
 (*May Subd Geog*)
 H 1180
  Use as a topical subdivision under individual plants and groups of plants.
 BT —Postharvest technology
——**Predators of** (*May Subd Geog*)
 H 1180
  Use as a topical subdivision under individual plants and groups of plants.
 UF —Predators of seeds
——**Processing** (*May Subd Geog*)
 H 1180
  Use as a topical subdivision under individual plants and groups of plants.
 BT —Processing
——**Quality** (*May Subd Geog*)
 H 1180
  Use as a topical subdivision under individual plants and groups of plants.
 BT —Quality
——**Storage** (*May Subd Geog*)
 H 1180
  Use as a topical subdivision under individual plants and groups of plants.
 BT —Storage
——**Testing**
 H 1180
  Use as a topical subdivision under individual plants and groups of plants.
 BT —Testing
——**Viability** (*May Subd Geog*)
 H 1180
  Use as a topical subdivision under individual plants and groups of plants.
 UF —Viability of seeds
—**Selection** (*May Subd Geog*)
 H 1147; H 1180
  Use as a topical subdivision under individual animals and groups of animals and individual plants and groups of plants.
 NT —Clones—Selection
—**Selection and appointment**
 (*May Subd Geog*)
 H 1100
  Use as a topical subdivision under occupational groups and types of employees.
 UF —Appointment, qualifications, tenure, etc.
   [Former subdivision]
 NT —Appointments and retirements
   —Bishops—Appointment, call, and election
   —Clergy—Appointment, call, and election
—**Selection indexes for breeding**
 USE —Breeding—Selection indexes
—**Self-instruction**
 H 1154
  Use as a topical subdivision under individual languages and groups of languages for works about self-instruction in a language.
—**Self-instruction**
 H 1154
  Use as a form subdivision under individual languages and groups of languages for self-instructional materials.
 NT —Methods—Self-instruction
—**Self-portraits** (*Not Subd Geog*)
 H 1110
  Use as a topical subdivision under names of individual persons for works about self-portraits by those persons.
 BT —Portraits

—**Self-portraits** (*Not Subd Geog*)
 H 1110
  Use as a form subdivision under names of individual persons for reproductions of self-portraits by those persons.
 BT —Portraits
—**Self-regulation** (*May Subd Geog*)
 H 1153
  Use as a topical subdivision under types of industries.
—**Semantics**
 H 1154
  Use as a topical subdivision under individual languages and groups of languages.
—**Semantics, Historical**
 H 1154
  Use as a topical subdivision under individual languages and groups of languages.
 UF —Historical semantics
—**Seniority system of legislative committees**
 USE —Committees—Seniority system
—**Sense organs**
 H 1147
  Use as a topical subdivision under individual animals and groups of animals.
 BT —Nervous system
—**Sensory evaluation** (*May Subd Geog*)
 H 1180
  Use as a topical subdivision under individual plants and groups of plants.
—**Sentences**
 H 1154
 . Use as a topical subdivision under individual languages and groups of languages.
—**Separation** (*May Subd Geog*)
 H 1149
  Use as a topical subdivision under individual chemicals and groups of chemicals.
—**Sepulchral monument**
 USE —Tomb
—**Serial numbers**
 H 1195
  Use as a topical subdivision under land vehicles and types of land vehicles.
 UF —Numbers, Serial
—**Sermons**
 H 1095; H 1110; H 1151.1; H 1185; H 1187; H 1188; H 1200
  Use as a topical subdivision under names of individual persons and under sects of individual religions, Christian denominations, types of educational institutions, uniform titles of sacred works, individual wars, and topical headings for works about sermons on those subjects.
 UF —Addresses, sermons, etc.
   [Former subdivision]
—**Sermons**
 H 1095; H 1110; H 1151.1; H 1185; H 1187; H 1188; H 1200
  Use as a form subdivision under names of individual persons and under sects of individual religions, Christian denominations, types of educational institutions, uniform titles of sacred works, individual wars, and topical headings for individual or collections of sermons on those subjects.
 UF —Addresses, sermons, etc.
   [Former subdivision]
 NT —Biography—Sermons
   —Children's sermons
——**History and criticism** (*Not Subd Geog*)
 H 1095; H 1110; H 1151.5; H 1185; H 1187; H 1188; H 1200
  Use as a topical subdivision under names of individual persons and under sects of individual religions, Christian denominations, types of educational institutions, uniform titles of sacred works, individual wars, and topical headings for works that critically evaluate the style and/or contents of individual or collections of sermons on those subjects.
 BT —History and criticism
——**Outlines, syllabi, etc.**
 H 1188
  Use this subdivision combination as a form subdivision under uniform titles of sacred works.
 BT —Outlines, syllabi, etc.

—Serodiagnosis *(May Subd Geog)*
> H 1150
>> Use as a topical subdivision under individual diseases and types of diseases.
>> BT —Diagnosis

—Servants
> USE —Employees

—Service clubs
> H 1159
>> Use as a topical subdivision under military services.
>> UF —Clubs, Service

—Service craft
> H 1159
>> Use as a topical subdivision under military services.

—Service life *(May Subd Geog)*
> H 1195
>> Use as a topical subdivision under individual land vehicles and types of land vehicles.

—Services for *(May Subd Geog)*
> H 1100; H 1103; H 1147; H 1151.5
>> Use as a topical subdivision under classes of persons, ethnic groups, individual animals and groups of animals, and types of educational institutions.
>> NT —Medical care
>> —Mental health services

——Contracting out *(May Subd Geog)*
> H 1151.5
>> Use as a topical subdivision under types of educational institutions.
>> UF —Contracting out of services for

—Settings
> H 1110
>> Use as a topical subdivision under names of individual literary authors.

—Settings, Instrumental
> USE —Instrumental settings

—Settings, Musical
> USE —Musical settings

—Sex differences *(May Subd Geog)*
> H 1095; H 1154; H 1164
>> Use as a topical subdivision under individual languages, individual organs and regions of the body, and topical headings.
>> UF —Differences, Sex
>> —Gender differences

—Sex factors *(May Subd Geog)*
> H 1150
>> Use as a topical subdivision under individual diseases and types of diseases.

—Sexing *(May Subd Geog)*
> H 1147
>> Use as a topical subdivision under individual animals and groups of animals.

—Sexual behavior *(May Subd Geog)*
> H 1100; H 1103; H 1110; H 1147
>> Do not subdivide geographically under names of individual persons.
>> Use as a topical subdivision under names of individual persons, classes of persons, ethnic groups, and individual animals and groups of animals.

—Shamanistic influences
> H 1156
>> Use as a topical subdivision under individual literatures.

—Shelling *(May Subd Geog)*
> H 1180
>> Use as a topical subdivision under individual plants and groups of plants.

——Machinery *(May Subd Geog)*
> H 1180
>> Use as a topical subdivision under individual plants and groups of plants.
>> BT —Machinery

—Shock absorbers
> H 1195
>> Use as a topical subdivision under individual land vehicles and types of land vehicles.

—Shore patrol
> H 1159
>> Use as a topical subdivision under navies. Under air forces use the subdivision Air police. Under other military services, use the subdivision Military police.

—Showing *(May Subd Geog)*
> H 1147; H 1180
>> Use as a topical subdivision under individual animals and groups of animals and individual plants and groups of plants.

—Shrines *(May Subd Geog)*
> H 1110
>> Use as a topical subdivision under names of individual persons for works discussing structures or places consecrated or devoted to the person and serving as places of religious veneration or pilgrimage.

—Side effects *(May Subd Geog)*
> H 1149
>> Use as a topical subdivision under individual drugs and groups of drugs.
>> NT —Therapeutic use—Side effects

—Signatures (Writing)
> USE —Autographs

—Signers
> H 1095
>> Further subdivide by subdivisions used under classes of persons.
>> Use as a topical subdivision under uniform titles of historic documents.

—Silage *(May Subd Geog)*
> H 1180
>> Use as a topical subdivision under individual plants and groups of plants.

—Silica content *(May Subd Geog)*
> H 1180
>> Use as a topical subdivision under individual plants and groups of plants.
>> BT —Composition

—Simplified editions *(Not Subd Geog)*
> H 1160
>> Use as a form subdivision under forms and types of musical compositions.

—Simulation games
> H 1095
>> Use as a topical subdivision under topical headings.

—Simulation methods
> H 1095
>> Use as a topical subdivision under topical headings.
>> NT —Computer simulation
>> —Electromechanical analogies
>> —Mathematical models
>> —Study and teaching—Simulation methods
>> —Study and teaching (Elementary)—Simulation methods
>> —Study and teaching (Higher)—Simulation methods
>> —Study and teaching (Secondary)—Simulation methods

—Sindhi authors
> H 1156
>> Use as a topical subdivision under individual languages.

—Sisters of kings and rulers
> USE —Kings and rulers—Sisters

—Size *(May Subd Geog)*
> H 1147; H 1164; H 1180
>> Use as a topical subdivision under individual animals and groups of animals, individual plants and groups of plants, and individual organs and regions of the body.
>> NT —Dilatation
>> —Hypertrophy

—Sizes *(May Subd Geog)*
> H 1195
>> Use as a topical subdivision under individual land vehicles and types of land vehicles.

—Sketchbooks
> USE —Notebooks, sketchbooks, etc.

—Ski troops
> H 1159
>> Use as a topical subdivision under military services.

—Skid resistance *(May Subd Geog)*
> H 1158
>> Use as a topical subdivision under individual materials and types of materials.
>> UF —Resistance, Skid

—Skidding *(May Subd Geog)*
> H 1195
>> Use as a topical subdivision under individual land vehicles and types of land vehicles.

—Slang
> H 1095; H 1154
>> Use as a topical subdivision under individual languages and groups of languages and under topical headings.

—Slavic antiquities
> USE —Antiquities, Slavic

—Slavic influences
> H 1156
>> Use as a topical subdivision under individual literatures.
>> BT —Foreign influences

—Slide collections
> H 1105; H 1110; H 1120
>> Use as a topical subdivision under names of individual persons, families, and corporate bodies.

—Slides
> H 1095; H 1110; H 1140
>> Use as a form subdivision under names of countries, cities, etc., and individual persons and under topical headings.

—Slovak influences
> H1156
>> Use as a topical subdivision under individual litertures.
>> BT —Foreign influences

—Small-boat service
> H 1159
>> Use as a topical subdivision under military services.

—Snow protection and removal
> *(May Subd Geog)*
> H 1195
>> Use as a topical subdivision under individual land vehicles and types of land vehicles.
>> UF —Removal of snow
>> —Snow removal
>> BT —Protection

—Snow removal
> USE —Snow protection and removal

—Soccer
> H 1151
>> Use as a topical subdivision under individual educational institutions.

—Social aspects *(May Subd Geog)*
> H 1095; H 1153; H 1154; H 1200
>> Use as a topical subdivision under topical headings for works on the effect of the item, activity, discipline, etc., and society on each other.
>> NT —Emigration and immigration—Social aspects

——Humor
> H 1095
>> Use as a form subdivision under topical headings for works of social satire on those topics.

—Social conditions
> H 1100; H 1103; H 1140; H 1149.5
>> Use as a topical subdivision under names of countries, cities, etc., and under classes of persons and ethnic groups.
>> UF —Social history
>> —Socioeconomic status
>> *[Former subdivision]*
>> NT —Colonies—Social conditions

———16th century
> H 1100; H 1103; H 1140
>> Use as a topical subdivision under names of countries, cities, etc., and under classes of persons and ethnic groups.

———17th century
> H 1100; H 1103; H 1140
>> Use as a topical subdivision under names of countries, cities, etc., and under classes of persons and ethnic groups.

———18th century
> H 1100; H 1103; H 1140
>> Use as a topical subdivision under names of countries, cities, etc., and under classes of persons and ethnic groups.

———19th century
> H 1100; H 1103; H 1140
>> Use as a topical subdivision under names of countries, cities, etc., and under classes of persons and ethnic groups.

———20th century
> H 1100; H 1103; H 1140
>> Use as a topical subdivision under names of countries, cities, etc., and under classes of persons and ethnic groups.

———21st century
> H 1100; H 1103; H 1140
>> Use as a topical subdivision under names of countries, cities, etc., and under classes of persons and ethnic groups.

——**Humor**

H 1100; H 1103; H 1140

Use as a form subdivision under names of countries, cities, etc., classes of persons, and ethnic groups for works of social satire on those places, people, or groups.

— Social history

USE ——Social conditions

—**Social life and customs**

H 1100; H 1103; H 1140; H 1149.5

Use as a topical subdivision under names of countries, cities, etc., and under classes of persons and ethnic groups.

UF ——Customs

NT ——Colonies—Social life and customs

——**16th century**

H 1100; H 1103; H 1140

Use as a topical subdivision under names of countries, cities, etc., and under classes of persons and ethnic groups.

——**17th century**

H 1100; H 1103; H 1140

Use as a topical subdivision under names of countries, cities, etc., and under classes of persons and ethnic groups.

——**18th century**

H 1100; H 1103; H 1140

Use as a topical subdivision under names of countries, cities, etc., and under classes of persons and ethnic groups.

——**19th century**

H 1100; H 1103; H 1140

Use as a topical subdivision under names of countries, cities, etc., and under classes of persons and ethnic groups.

——**20th century**

H 1100; H 1103; H 1140

Use as a topical subdivision under names of countries, cities, etc., and under classes of persons and ethnic groups.

——**21st century**

H 1100; H 1103; H 1140

Use as a topical subdivision under names of countries, cities, etc., and under classes of persons and ethnic groups.

——**Humor**

H 1100; H 1103; H 1140

Use as a form subdivision under names of countries, cities, etc., classes of persons, and ethnic groups for works of social satire on those places, people, or groups.

—**Social networks**   (*May Subd Geog*)

H 1100; H 1103

Use as a topical subdivision under classes of persons and ethnic groups.

UF ——Networks, Social

—**Social policy**

H 1140; H 1149.5

Use as a topical subdivision under names of countries, cities, etc.

BT ——Government policy

NT ——Colonies—Social policy

—**Social scientific criticism**   (*May Subd Geog*)

H 1188

Use as a topical subdivision under uniform titles of sacred works.

BT ——Criticism, interpretation, etc.

—**Social services**

H 1159

Do not use under headings of the type [Place]—Armed Forces. Use Military social work—[Place] instead.

Use as a topical subdivision under military services.

—Social views

USE ——Political and social views

—**Socialization**   (*May Subd Geog*)

H 1103

Use as a topical subdivision under ethnic groups.

—**Societies and clubs**

H 1100

Use as a topical subdivision under age and sex groups.

UF ——Clubs

BT ——Societies, etc.

—**Societies, etc.**

H 1095; H 1100; H 1103; H 1105; H 1110; H 1120; H 1188

Do not use under classes of persons if the corresponding heading for the discipline can be assigned.

Use as a topical subdivision under names of individual persons, families, and corporate bodies, and under classes of persons, ethnic groups, uniform titles of sacred works, and topical headings for works discussing two or more societies or institutions related to those subjects.

NT ——Societies and clubs

—Societies, periodicals, etc.

USE ——Periodicals

—**Socio-rhetorical criticism**

(*May Subd Geog*)

H 1188

Use as a topical subdivision under uniform titles of sacred works.

BT ——Criticism, interpretation, etc.

—Socioeconomic status

USE ——Economic conditions

——Social conditions

—**Sociological aspects**

H 1095; H 1151.5

Use as a topical subdivision under types of institutions for works on the impact of the inherent nature of the institution in question on group interaction within the institution and vice versa.

—**Software**

H 1095

Use as a form subdivision under topical headings for computer programs that are tools to perform tasks, for example, systems software, utilities, or applications programs.

NT ——Computer games

——Juvenile software

—**Soils**   (*May Subd Geog*)

H 1180

Use as a topical subdivision under individual plants and groups of plants.

—**Solo with harpsichord**

H 1160

Use as a form subdivision under forms and types of musical compositions.

—**Solo with harpsichord and piano**

H 1160

Use as a form subdivision under forms and types of musical compositions.

—**Solo with keyboard instrument**

H 1160

Use as a form subdivision under forms and types of musical compositions.

—**Solo with organ**

H 1160

Use as a form subdivision under forms and types of musical compositions.

—**Solo with piano**

H 1160

Use as a form subdivision under forms and types of musical compositions.

—**Solo with piano (4 hands)**

H 1160

Use as a form subdivision under forms and types of musical compositions.

—**Solo with pianos (2)**

H 1160

Use as a form subdivision under forms and types of musical compositions.

—**Solos with organ**

H 1160

Use as a form subdivision under forms and types of musical compositions.

—**Solos with piano**

H 1160

Use as a form subdivision under forms and types of musical compositions.

—**Solos with pianos (2)**

H 1160

Use as a form subdivision under forms and types of musical compositions.

—**Solubility**   (*May Subd Geog*)

H 1149; H 1158

Use as a topical subdivision under individual chemicals and groups of chemicals and individual materials and types of materials.

BT ——Properties

—**Somatic embryogenesis**   (*May Subd Geog*)

H 1180

Use as a topical subdivision under individual plants and groups of plants.

UF ——Embryogenesis, Somatic

—**Songs and music**

H 1095; H 1100; H 1103; H 1105; H 1110; H 1140; H 1159

Use as a topical subdivision under names of countries, cities, etc., and under classes of persons, ethnic groups, military services, and topical headings for works about vocal or instrumental music about those subjects.

UF ——Music and songs

—**Songs and music**

H 1095; H 1100; H 1103; H 1105; H 1110; H 1140; H 1159

Use as a form subdivision under names of countries, cities, etc., names of individual persons and corporate bodies and under classes of persons, ethnic groups, military services, and topical headings for collections or single works of vocal or instrumental music about the subject.

UF ——Music and songs

——**Discography**

H 1095

Use this subdivison combination as a form subdivision under names of countries, cities, etc., names of individual persons and corporate bodies, and under classes of persons, ethnic groups, military services, and topical headings.

BT ——Discography

——**History and criticism**

H 1095

Use as a topical subdivision under names of countries, cities, etc., names of individual persons and corporate bodies, and under classes of persons, ethnic groups, military services, and topical headings.

BT ——History and criticism

NT ——In opera

——**Texts**

H 1095

Use as a form subdivision under names of countries, cities, etc., names of individual persons and corporate bodies, and under classes of persons, ethnic groups, military services, and topical headings for texts of songs about those subjects.

BT ——Texts

—**Sonorants**

H 1154

Use as a topical subdivision under individual languages and groups of languages.

—Sound recordings for children

USE ——Juvenile sound recordings

—**Sound recordings for foreign speakers**

H 1154

Use as a form subdivision under individual languages and groups of languages.

UF ——Phonorecords for foreign speakers

[Former subdivision]

—**Sound recordings for French, [Spanish, etc.] speakers**

H 1154

Use as a form subdivision under individual languages and groups of languages.

UF ——Phonorecords for French, [Spanish, etc.] speakers

[Former subdivision]

—**Soundproofing**   (*May Subd Geog*)

H 1095

Use as a topical subdivision under types of buildings, structures, facilities and equipment.

NT ——Motors—Soundproofing

—**Sounds**   (*Not Subd Geog*)

H 1164; H 1200

Use as a topical subdivision under individual organs and regions of the body and wars.

—**Sources** (*Not Subd Geog*)
H 1095; H 1110; H 1156
Use as a topical subdivision under historical topics and headings for systems of law for works about source materials on those topics or systems. Use under uniform titles for works about sources used by authors in writing the works. Use under types of literature for works about sources of ideas or inspiration for these literary works. Also use under names of individual persons for works about the individual's sources of ideas or inspiration for his works.
UF —Forerunners
—Primary sources
NT —Biography—Sources
—History—[period subdivision]—Biography—Sources
—History—[period subdivision]—Sources
—History—Sources

—**Sources**
H 1095; H 1110; H 1200
Use as a form subdivision under historical topics, and headings for systems of law for collections of source materials of all types on those topics or systems. Also use under names of individual persons for collections of materials that served as sources of their ideas or inspiration.
UF —Primary sources
NT —Biography—Sources
—History—[period subdivision]—Biography—Sources
—History—[period subdivision]—Sources
—History—Sources

—**South Asian authors**
H 1156
Use as a topical subdivision under individual literatures.

—**Soviet influences**
H 1159
Use as a topical subdivision under individual literatures.
BT —Foreign influences

—**Sowing** (*May Subd Geog*)
H 1180
Use as a topical subdivision under individual plants and groups of plants.

—Space photographs
USE —Photographs from space

—**Spacing** (*May Subd Geog*)
H 1180
Use as a topical subdivision under individual plants and groups of plants.

—**Spanish influences**
H 1156
Use as a topical subdivision under individual literatures.
BT —Foreign influences

—**Spawning** (*May Subd Geog*)
H 1147
Use as a topical subdivision under individual aquatic animals and groups of aquatic animals.
BT —Reproduction

—Spawning, Artificial
USE —Artificial spawning

—Spawning, Induced
USE —Induced spawning

—Speaker
USE —Speakers

—**Speakers**
H 1155
Further subdivide by subdivisions used under classes of persons.
Use as a topical subdivision under names of individual legislative bodies.
UF —Speaker
[Former subdivision]
BT —Leadership

—**Speciation** (*May Subd Geog*)
H 1147; H 1149; H 1180
Use as a topical subdivision under individual animals and groups of animals, individual plants and groups of plants, and individual chemicals and groups of chemicals.

—**Specifications** (*May Subd Geog*)
H 1095; H 1153; H 1158
Use under types of industries only when the works are about specifications not limited to a single product of an industry.
Use as a topical subdivision under types of engineering, construction, industries, products, and merchandise for works about detailed written descriptions of an item to be manufactured or supplied.
UF —Contracts and specifications
[Former subdivision]

—**Specifications** (*May Subd Geog*)
H 1095; H 1153; H 1158
Use under types of industries only when the specifications are not limited to a single product of the industry.
Use as a form subdivision under types of engineering, construction, industries, products, and merchandise for works containing detailed written descriptions of an item to be manufactured or supplied.
UF —Contracts and specifications
[Former subdivision]
NT —Housing—Specifications

—**Specimens**
H 1095
Use as a form subdivision under types of publications, printed matter, etc., for actual specimens of the material.
UF —Examples
—Exemplars

—**Spectra**
H 1095; H 1149; H 1158
Use as a topical subdivision under individual chemicals and groups of chemicals, individual materials and types of materials, elementary particles, and celestial bodies.

—**Spectral analysis**
H 1154
Use as a topical subdivision under individual languages and groups of languages.

—**Spectroscopic imaging** (*May Subd Geog*)
H 1150; H 1164
Use as a topical subdivision under individual diseases and types of diseases and individual organs and regions of the body.
UF —Diseases—Spectroscopic imaging
BT —Imaging

—**Speeches in Congress**
H 1095
Use as a form subdivision under topical headings for single speeches or collections of speeches delivered in Congress on those topics.

—**Speed**
H 1147; H 1195
Use as a topical subdivision under individual animals and groups of animals and individual land vehicles and types of land vehicles.
UF —Velocity

—Spelling
USE —Orthography and spelling

—**Spermatozoa**
H 1147
Use as a topical subdivision under individual animals and groups of animals.

——**Abnormalities** (*May Subd Geog*)
H 1147
Use as a topical subdivision under individual animals and groups of animals.
BT —Abnormalities

——**Morphology**
H 1147
Use as a topical subdivision under individual animals and groups of animals.
BT —Morphology

——**Motility**
H 1147
Use as a topical subdivision under individual animals and groups of animals.

—**Spiritual life**
H 1186
Use as a topical subdivision under names of individual religious and monastic orders.

—**Spiritualistic interpretations**
H 1110
Use as a topical subdivision under names of individual persons.

—**Spoken French, [Japanese, etc.]** (*May Subd Geog*)
H 1154
Use as a topical subdivision under languages other than English.

—Spoofs (Parodies)
USE —Parodies, imitations, etc.

—**Spores** (*May Subd Geog*)
H 1180
Use as a topical subdivision under individual plants and groups of plants.

——**Morphology**
H 1180
Use as a topical subdivision under individual plants and groups of plants.
BT —Morphology

—**Sports** (*May Subd Geog*)
H 1103; H 1151; H 1159
Divide geographically only under ethnic groups.
Use as a topical subdivision under names of individual educational institutions, ethnic groups, and military services.
UF —Athletics
[Former subdivision]
NT —Baseball
—Basketball
—Football
—Golf
—Gymnastics
—Hockey
—Rowing
—Rugby football
—Swimming
—Tennis
—Track and field
—Volleyball
—Wrestling

—**Spray control** (*May Subd Geog*)
H 1195
Use as a topical subdivision under individual land vehicles and types of land vehicles.
UF —Control of spray

—**Springs and suspension** (*May Subd Geog*)
H 1195
Use as a topical subdivision under individual land vehicles and types of land vehicles.
UF —Suspension of vehicles
NT —Air suspension

—Sprouting, Preharvest
USE —Preharvest sprouting

—**Spurious and doubtful works**
H 1110
Use as a topical subdivision under names of individual persons for works that discuss works attributed to a person at a previous time.
UF —Doubtful works
BT —Authorship

—**Spurious and doubtful works**
H 1110
Use as a form subdivision under names of individual persons for collections of works attributed to a person at a previous time.
UF —Doubtful works

—**Stability**
H 1095; H 1149; H 1195
Use as a topical subdivision under types of equipment, individual chemicals and groups of chemicals, and individual land vehicles and types of land vehicles.
BT —Properties
NT —Lateral stability

—**Stability operations**
H 1159
Use as a topical subdivision under military services.
BT —Operations other than war

—**Staff corps**
H 1159
Use as a topical subdivision under military services.

—**Staffs**
H 1159
Further subdivide by subdivisions used under classes of persons.
Use as a topical subdivision under military services.

—**Stage guides**
H 1160
Use as a form subdivision under forms and types of musical compositions.
UF —Guides, Stage

—**Stage history** *(May Subd Geog)*
H 1110
Use as a topical subdivision under names of individual literary authors for works on historical aspects of dramatic production. For works on various aspects of stage presentation, e.g. acting, costume, stage setting and scenery, etc., use the subdivision Dramatic production.

—Stage presentation
USE —Dramatic production

—Stage setting and scenery
USE —Dramatic production

—**Stamp collections**
H 1105; H 1110; H 1120
Use as a topical subdivision under names of individual persons, families, and corporate bodies.

—**Standardization**
H 1154
Use as a topical subdivision under individual languages and groups of languages.

—**Standards** *(May Subd Geog)*
H 1095; H 1149; H 1151.5; H 1153
Use as a topical subdivision under individual chemicals and groups of chemicals, types of industries and educational institutions, and topical headings for descriptions of the example or model set up and established by authority as the measure of quantity, quality, value, extent, weight, etc., to be followed.
NT —Production standards
—Rules

—**Starting devices** *(May Subd Geog)*
H 1195
Use as a topical subdivision under individual land vehicles and types of land vehicles.

—**State supervision** *(May Subd Geog)*
H 1095; H 1153
Use as a topical subdivision under topical headings and types of industries.
UF —Supervision, State

—**States**
H 1095
Use as a topical subdivision under headings of the type [topic]—[country] for works discussing collectively the states of a country in relation to the topic.
BT —Administrative and political divisions

—Statistical data
USE —Statistics

—**Statistical methods**
H 1095; H 1153
Use as a topical subdivision under topical headings for discussions of the methods of solving problems in those topics through the use of statistics.
BT —Methodology

—**Statistical services**
H 1095; H 1100; H 1103; H 1140; H 1153
Use as a topical subdivision under names of countries, cities, etc., classes of persons, ethnic groups, types of industries, and topical headings for works on services that collect numerical data located in those places or about those topics.
BT —Information services

——**Law and legislation**
H 1140
Further subdivide by subdivisions used under legal topics.
Use as a topical subdivision under names of countries, cities, etc.
BT —Law and legislation

—**Statistics**
H 1095; H 1100; H 1103; H 1105; H 1140
Use as a topical subdivision under names of countries, cities, etc., and under individual corporate bodies, classes of persons, ethnic groups, and topical headings for works about statistics on those subjects.
NT —Census
—Statistics, Medical
—Statistics, Vital

—**Statistics**
H 1095; H 1100; H 1103; H 1105; H 1140
Use as a form subdivision under names of countries, cities, etc., and individual corporate bodies, classes of persons, ethnic groups, and topical headings for works consisting of statistics about those subjects.
UF —Cases, clinical reports, statistics
[Former subdivision]
—Statistical data
NT —Casualties—Statistics
—Census
—Statistics, Medical
—Statistics, Vital

—**Statistics, Medical**
H 1140
Use as a topical subdivision under names of countries, cities, etc., for works about medical statistics in those places.
UF —Medical statistics
BT —Statistics

—**Statistics, Medical**
H 1140
Use as a form subdivision under names of countries, cities, etc., for works consisting of medical statistics about those places.
UF —Medical statistics
BT —Statistics

—**Statistics, Vital**
H 1103; H 1140
Use as a topical subdivision under names of countries, cities, etc., and ethnic groups for works about vital statistics in those places or about those groups.
UF —Vital statistics
BT —Statistics

—**Statistics, Vital**
H 1103; H 1140
Use as a form subdivision under names of countries, cities, etc., and ethnic groups for works consisting of vital statistics about those places or groups.
UF —Vital statistics
BT —Statistics

—**Statues** *(May Subd Geog)*
H 1110
Use as a topical subdivision under names of individual persons for works about statues representing the person.

—**Steering-gear**
H 1195
Use as a topical subdivision under individual land vehicles and types of land vehicles.

—Sterilization of surgical instruments
USE —Surgery—Instruments—Sterilization

—**Stewards**
H 1159
Further subdivide by subdivisions used under classes of persons.
Use as a topical subdivision under military services.

—**Storage** *(May Subd Geog)*
H 1095; H 1180
Use as a topical subdivision under types of commodities, foods, materials, industrial products, etc., for their safekeeping in a warehouse or other depository.
NT —Seeds—Storage

——**Climatic factors** *(May Subd Geog)*
H 1180
Use as a topical subdivision under individual plants and groups of plants.
BT —Climatic factors

——**Diseases and injuries** *(May Subd Geog)*
H 1180
Use as a topical subdivision under individual plants and groups of plants.
BT —Postharvest diseases and injuries

—**Storekeepers**
H 1159
Further subdivide by subdivisions used under classes of persons.
Use as a topical subdivision under military services.

—Stories
USE —Fiction

—Stories of operas
USE —Stories, plots, etc.

—**Stories, plots, etc.**
H 1110; H 1156; H 1160
Use as a topical subdivision under names of individual composers, choreographers, and literary authors and under individual literatures and forms and types of musical compositions for works about the stories or plots of those composers, authors, literatures, and compositions.
UF —Plots
[Former subdivision]
—Stories of operas
[Former subdivision]

—**Stories, plots, etc.** *(Not Subd Geog)*
H 1110; H 1156; H 1160
Use as a form subdivision under names of individual composers, choreographers, and literary authors and under individual literatures and forms and types of musical compositions for works consisting of summaries of the stories or plots of those composers, authors, literatures, and compositions.
UF —Plots
[Former subdivision]
—Stories of operas
[Former subdivision]
—Summaries, arguments, etc.
[Former subdivision]

—**Stranding** *(May Subd Geog)*
H 1147
Use as a topical subdivision under individual animals and groups of animals.
UF —Beaching

—**Strategic aspects**
H 1140
Use as a topical subdivision under names of countries, cities, etc.

—**Stress corrosion** *(May Subd Geog)*
H 1158
Use as a topical subdivision under individual materials and types of materials.
BT —Corrosion

—Stress, Job
USE —Job stress

—Strike, [date]
USE —Student strike, [date]

—**Structuralist criticism** *(May Subd Geog)*
H 1188
Use as a topical subdivision under uniform titles of sacred works.
BT —Criticism, interpretation, etc.

—**Structure**
H 1149
Use as a topical subdivision under individual chemicals and groups of chemicals.

—**Structure-activity relationships**
H 1149
Use as a topical subdivision under individual chemicals and groups of chemicals.

—Structures, etc.
USE —Buildings, structures, etc.

—Stud-books
USE —Pedigrees

—Studbooks
USE —Pedigrees

—**Student housing**
H 1151
Use as a topical subdivision under names of individual educational institutions.
UF —Students—Housing
BT —Housing

—**Student strike, [date]**
H 1151
Use as a topical subdivision under names of individual educational institutions.
UF —Strike, [date]
[Former subdivision]

—Student yearbooks
USE —Students—Yearbooks

—**Students**
H 1151
Further subdivide by subdivisions used under classes of persons.
Use as a topical subdivision under individual educational institutions.
NT —Graduate students
—Undergraduates

——Housing
USE —Student housing

—**Students** *(Continued)*

——**Yearbooks**
H 1151
Use this subdivision combination as a form subdivision under individual educational institutions.
UF —School yearbooks
—Student yearbooks
BT —Periodicals

—**Studies and exercises**
H 1161
Use as a form subdivision under individual musical instruments and families of instruments.
UF —Exercises and studies
BT —Problems, exercises, etc.

——Fingering
USE —Fingering

——**Juvenile**
H 1161
Use as a form subdivision under individual musical instruments and families of instruments.

——Pedaling
USE —Pedaling

—**Studies and exercises (Alternative rock)**
H 1161
Use as a form subdivision under individual musical instruments and families of instruments.

—**Studies and exercises (Big band)**
H 1161
Use as a form subdivision under individual musical instruments and families of instruments.

—**Studies and exercises (Bluegrass)**
H 1161
Use as a form subdivision under individual musical instruments and families of instruments.

—**Studies and exercises (Blues)**
H 1161
Use as a form subdivision under individual musical instruments and families of instruments.

—**Studies and exercises (Blues-rock)**
H 1161
Use as a form subdivision under individual musical instruments and families of instruments.

—**Studies and exercises (Boogie woogie)**
H 1161
Use as a form subdivision under individual musical instruments and families of instruments.

—**Studies and exercises (Bop)**
H 1161
Use as a form subdivision under individual musical instruments and families of instruments.

—**Studies and exercises (Celtic)**
H 1161
Use as a form subdivision under individual musical instruments and families of instruments.

—**Studies and exercises (Country)**
H 1161
Use as a form subdivision under individual musical instruments and families of instruments.

—**Studies and exercises (Dixieland)**
H 1161
Use as a form subdivision under individual musical instruments and families of instruments.

—**Studies and exercises (Folk)**
H 1161
Use as a form subdivision under individual musical instruments and families of instruments.

—**Studies and exercises (Funk)**
H 1161
Use as a form subdivision under individual musical instruments and families of instruments.

—**Studies and exercises (Gospel)**
H 1161
Use as a form subdivision under individual musical instruments and families of instruments.

—**Studies and exercises (Heavy metal)**
H 1161
Use as a form subdivision under individual musical instruments and families of instruments.

—**Studies and exercises (Honky-tonk)**
H 1161
Use as a form subdivision under individual musical instruments and families of instruments.

—**Studies and exercises (Jazz)**
H 1161
Use as a form subdivision under individual musical instruments and families of instruments.

—**Studies and exercises (Jazz-rock)**
H1161
Use as a form subdivision under individual musical instruments and families of instruments.

—**Studies and exercises (Latin jazz)**
H 1161
Use as a form subdivision under individual musical instruments and families of instruments.

—**Studies and exercises (Left hand)**
H 1161
Use as a form subdivision under individual musical instruments and families of instruments.
UF —Left hand studies

—**Studies and exercises (Popular music)**
H 1161
Use as a form subdivision under individual musical instruments and families of instruments.

—**Studies and exercises (Progressive rock)**
H 1161
Use as a form subdivision under individual musical instruments and families of instruments.

—**Studies and exercises (Ragtime)**
H 1161
Use as a form subdivision under individual musical instruments and families of instruments.

—**Studies and exercises (Reggae)**
H 1161
Use as a form subdivision under individual musical instruments and families of instruments.

—**Studies and exercises (Rhythm and blues)**
H 1161
Use as a form subdivision under individual musical instruments and families of instruments.

—**Studies and exercises (Right hand)**
H 1161
Use as a form subdivision under individual musical instruments and families of instruments.
UF —Right hand studies

—**Studies and exercises (Rock)**
H 1161
Use as a form subdivision under individual musical instruments and families of instruments.

—**Studies and exercises (Salsa)**
H 1161
Use as a form subdivision under individual musical instruments and families of instruments.

—**Studies and exercises (Swing)**
H 1161
Use as a form subdivision under individual musical instruments and families of instruments.

—**Studies and exercises (Western swing)**
H 1161
Use as a form subdivision under individual musical instruments and families of instruments.

—**Study and teaching** *(May Subd Geog)*
H 1095; H 1100; H 1103; H 1140; H 1154; H 1188
Use as a topical subdivision under subjects for works on methods of study and teaching of those subjects.
NT —Web-based instruction

——**Activity programs** *(May Subd Geog)*
H 1095
Use as a topical subdivision under subjects.

——**African American students**
H 1154
Use as a topical subdivision under individual languages and groups of languages.
UF —Study and teaching—Afro-American students
[Former subdivision]

——Afro-American students
USE —Study and teaching—African American students

——**Audio-visual aids**
H 1095
Use as a topical subdivision under subjects for works on the use of audio-visual aids in the learning and teaching of those subjects.
BT —Audio-visual aids

——**Baptists, [Catholic Church, etc.]**
H 1188
Use as a topical subdivision under uniform titles of sacred works.

——**Bilingual method**
H 1154
Use as a topical subdivision under individual languages and groups of languages.
UF —Bilingual method of language teaching

——**Foreign speakers**
H 1154
Use as a topical subdivision under individual languages and groups of languages.
UF —Study and teaching—Foreign students
[Former subdivision]

————**Audio-visual aids**
H 1154
Use as a topical subdivision under individual languages and groups of languages.

———Foreign students
USE —Study and teaching—Foreign speakers

———**French, [Spanish, etc.] speakers**
H 1154
Use as a topical subdivision under individual languages and groups of languages.

———**Immersion method**
H 1154
Use as a topical subdivision under individual languages and groups of languages.
UF —Immersion method of language teaching

——**Law and legislation** *(May Subd Geog)*
H 1140
Further subdivide by subdivisions used under legal topics.
Use as a topical subdivision under names of countries, cities, etc.
BT —Law and legislation

——Outlines, syllabi, etc.
USE —Outlines, syllabi, etc.

——**Simulation methods**
H 1095
Use as a topical subdivision under topical headings.
BT —Simulation methods

——**Supervision** *(May Subd Geog)*
H 1095
Use as a topical subdivision under topical headings.
UF —Supervision of teaching

—**Study and teaching (Continuing education)** *(May Subd Geog)*
H 1095; H 1154
Use as a topical subdivision under subjects.

——**Audio-visual aids**
H 1095
Use as a topical subdivision under subjects.

——**Foreign speakers**
H 1154
Use as a topical subdivision under individual languages and groups of languages.

——**French, [Spanish, etc.] speakers**
H 1154
Use as a topical subdivision under individual languages and groups of languages.

—**Study and teaching (Early childhood)** *(May Subd Geog)*
H 1095; H 1154
Use as a topical subdivision under subjects.

——**Activity programs** *(May Subd Geog)*
H 1095
Use as a topical heading under subjects.

——**Audio-visual aids**
H 1095
Use as a topical subdivision under subjects.

——**Foreign speakers**
H 1154
Use as a topical subdivision under individual languages and groups of languages.

——**French, [Spanish, etc.] speakers**
H 1154
Use as a topical subdivision under individual languages and groups of languages.

—**Study and teaching (Elementary)** *(May Subd Geog)*
H 1095; H 1154
Use as a topical subdivision under subjects.

——**Activity programs** *(May Subd Geog)*
H 1095
Use as a topical subdivision under subjects.

——**Audio-visual aids**
H 1095
Use as a topical subdivision under subjects.

— —Foreign speakers
H 1154
Use as a topical subdivision under individual
languages and groups of languages.
— —French, [Spanish, etc.] speakers
H 1154
Use as a topical subdivision under individual
languages and groups of languages.
— —Simulation methods
H 1095
Use as a topical subdivision under subjects.
BT —Simulation methods
—Study and teaching (Graduate)
(May Subd Geog)
H 1095
Use as a topical subdivision under subjects.
BT —Graduate work
—Study and teaching (Higher)
(May Subd Geog)
H 1095; H 1154
Use as a topical subdivision under subjects.
— —Activity programs (May Subd Geog)
H 1095
Use as a topical subdivision under subjects.
— —Audio-visual aids
H 1095
Use as a topical subdivision under subjects.
— —Foreign speakers
H 1154
Use as a topical subdivision under individual
languages and groups of languages.
— —French, [Spanish, etc.] speakers
H 1154
Use as a topical subdivision under individual
languages and groups of languages.
— —Simulation methods
H 1095
Use as a topical subdivision under topical
headings.
BT —Simulation methods
—Study and teaching (Internship)
(May Subd Geog)
H 1095
Use as a topical subdivision under subjects.
—Study and teaching (Middle school)
(May Subd Geog)
H 1095
Use as a topical subdivision under subjects.
— —Activity programs (May Subd Geog)
H 1095
Use as a topical subdivision under subjects.
— —Audio-visual aids
H 1095
Use as a topical subdivision under subjects.
—Study and teaching (Preschool)
(May Subd Geog)
H 1095; H 1154
Use as a topical subdivision under subjects.
— —Activity programs (May Subd Geog)
H 1095
Use as a topical subdivision under subjects.
— —Audio-visual aids
H 1095
Use as a topical subdivision under subjects.
— —Foreign speakers
H 1154
Use as a topical subdivision under individual
languages and groups of languages.
— —French, [Spanish, etc.] speakers
H 1154
Use as a topical subdivision under individual
languages and groups of languages
—Study and teaching (Primary)
(May Subd Geog)
H 1095; H 1154
Use as a topical subdivision under subjects.
— —Activity programs (May Subd Geog)
H 1095
Use as a topical subdivision under subjects.
— —Audio-visual aids
H 1095
Use as a topical subdivision under subjects.
— —Foreign speakers
H 1154
Use as a topical subdivision under individual
languages and groups of languages.

— —French, [Spanish, etc.] speakers
H 1154
Use as a topical subdivision under individual
languages and groups of languages.
—Study and teaching (Residency)
(May Subd Geog)
H 1095
Use as a topical subdivision under topical head-
ings.
—Study and teaching (Secondary)
(May Subd Geog)
H 1095; H 1154
Use as a topical subdivision under subjects.
— —Activity programs (May Subd Geog)
H 1095
Use as a topical subdivision under subjects.
— —Audio-visual aids
H 1095
Use as a topical subdivision under subjects.
— —Foreign speakers
H 1154
Use as a topical subdivision under individual
languages and groups of languages.
— —French, [Spanish, etc.] speakers
H 1154
Use as a topical subdivision under individual
languages and groups of languages.
— —Simulation methods
H 1095
Use as a topical subdivision under topical
headings.
BT —Simulation methods
—Study guides
H 1095
Use as a form subdivision under individual ex-
aminations and types of examinations and tests for
guides in preparation for those examinations.
NT —Entrance examinations—Study
guides
—Examinations—Study guides
—Style
H 1154; H 1155.8
Use as a topical subdivision under individual
languages and groups of languages and individual
literary works entered under the title.
NT —Literary style
—Style manuals for authorship
USE —Authorship—Style manuals
—Style manuals for dissertations
USE —Dissertations—Style manuals
—Subcontracting (May Subd Geog)
H 1153
Use as a topical subdivision under types of in-
dustries.
—Subjectless constructions
H 1154
Use as a topical subdivision under individual
languages and groups of languages.
BT —Syntax
—Subjunctive
H 1154
Use as a topical subdivision under individual
languages and groups of languages.
BT —Mood
—Submarine forces
H 1159
Use as a topical subdivision under military ser-
vices.
—Submarine operations
USE —Naval operations—Submarine
—Subordinate constructions
H 1154
Use as a topical subdivision under individual
languages and groups of languages.
BT —Syntax
—Subsidies (May Subd Geog)
H 1153
Use as a topical subdivision under types of in-
dustries.
UF —Federal aid
—Government aid
BT —Finance
—Substance abuse
USE —Substance use

—Substance use (May Subd Geog)
H 1100; H 1103
Use as a topical subdivision under classes of per-
sons and ethnic groups.
UF —Abuse of substances
—Substance abuse
NT —Alcohol use
—Drug use
—Tobacco use
—Substitution
H 1154
Use as a topical subdivision under individual
languages and groups of languages.
—Succession of kings and rulers
USE —Kings and rulers—Succession
—Suffixes and prefixes
H 1154
Use as a topical subdivision under individual
languages and groups of languages.
UF —Prefixes
—Suffrage (May Subd Geog)
H 1100; H 1103
Use as a topical subdivision under classes of per-
sons and ethnic groups.
UF —Politics and suffrage
[Former subdivision]
—Suicidal behavior (May Subd Geog)
H 1100; H 1103
Use as a topical subdivision under classes of per-
sons and ethnic groups.
UF —Attempted suicide
—Suicide
—Suicide
USE —Suicidal behavior
—Summaries, arguments, etc.
USE —Stories, plots, etc.
—Summaries of publications
USE —Abstracts
—Summering (May Subd Geog)
H 1147
Use as a topical subdivision under individual an-
imals and groups of animals.
—Superchargers of motors
USE —Motors—Superchargers
—Supervision of (May Subd Geog)
H 1100
Use as a topical subdivision under occupational
groups and types of employees.
—Supervision of teaching
USE —Study and teaching—Supervision
—Supervision, State
USE —State supervision
—Supplementary employment
(May Subd Geog)
H 1100; H 1103
Use as a topical subdivision under classes of per-
sons and ethnic groups.
UF —Outside employment
BT —Employment
—Suppletion
H 1154
Use as a topical subdivision under individual
languages and groups of languages.
—Supplies
USE —Equipment and supplies
—Supplies and stores
H 1159
Use as a topical subdivision under military ser-
vices.
NT —Medical supplies
—Ordnance and ordnance stores
— —Law and legislation
H 1159
Further subdivide by subdivisions used under
legal topics.
Use as a topical subdivision under military
services.
BT —Law and legislation
— —Quality control
H 1159
Use as a topical subdivision under Military
services.
BT —Quality control

—**Supply and demand** *(May Subd Geog)*
H 1100
Use as a topical subdivision under occupational groups and types of employees.
UF —Demand and supply
NT —Employees—Supply and demand
—**Surfaces**
H 1149; H 1158
Use as a topical subdivision under individual chemicals and groups of chemicals and individual materials and types of materials.
——**Defects** *(May Subd Geog)*
H 1158
Use as a topical subdivision under individual materials and types of materials.
BT —Defects
——**Optical properties**
H 1158
Use as a topical subdivision under individual materials and types of materials.
BT —Optical properties
—**Surgeons**
H 1159
Further subdivide by subdivisions used under classes of persons.
Use as a topical subdivision under military services.
BT —Medical personnel
NT —Flight surgeons
——**Malpractice**
H 1159
Use as a topical subdivision under military services.
UF —Malpractice of surgeons
—**Surgery** *(May Subd Geog)*
H 1100; H 1103; H 1147; H 1150; H 1164
Use as a topical subdivision under classes of persons, ethnic groups, individual animals and groups of animals, individual diseases and types of diseases, and individual organs and regions of the body.
UF —Diseases—Surgery
BT —Treatment
NT —Biopsy
—Cryosurgery
—Endoscopic surgery
—Laser surgery
—Reoperation
—Transplantation
——**Complications** *(May Subd Geog)*
H 1100; H 1147; H 1164
Further subdivide by subdivisions used under diseases.
Use as a topical subdivision under classes of persons, individual animals and groups of animals, individual diseases and types of diseases, and individual organs and regions of the body.
UF —Surgery—Complications and sequelae
[Former subdivision]
BT —Complications
——Complications and sequelae
USE —Surgery—Complications
——**Instruments**
H 1164
Use as a topical subdivision under individual organs and regions of the body.
BT —Instruments
———**Sterilization** *(May Subd Geog)*
H 1164
Use as a topical subdivision under individual organs and regions of the body.
UF —Sterilization of surgical instruments
——**Nursing** *(May Subd Geog)*
H 1147; H 1150; H 1164
Use as a topical subdivision under individual animals and groups of animals, individual diseases and types of diseases, and individual organs and regions of the body.
BT —Nursing
——**Nutritional aspects** *(May Subd Geog)*
H 1164
Use as a topical subdivision under individual organs and regions of the body.
BT —Nutritional aspects

——**Patients** *(May Subd Geog)*
H 1164
Further subdivide by subdivisions used under classes of persons.
Use as a topical subdivision under individual organs and regions of the body.
BT —Patients
——**Risk factors** *(May Subd Geog)*
H 1100; H 1164
Use as a topical subdivision under classes of persons and individual organs and regions of the body.
BT —Risk factors
—**Surveys**
H 1140
Use as a form subdivision under names of countries, cities, etc., for works presenting the results of land surveys.
UF —Land surveys
—**Susceptibility** *(May Subd Geog)*
H 1150
Use as a topical subdivision under individual diseases and types of diseases.
—**Suspension** *(May Subd Geog)*
H 1100
Use as a topical subdivision under occupational groups and types of employees.
—Suspension of vehicles
USE —Springs and suspension
—Sustainability of combat
USE —Combat sustainability
—**Swami-Narayani authors**
H 1156
Use as a topical subdivision under individual literatures.
—**Swimming**
H 1151
Use as a topical subdivision under names of individual educational institutions.
BT —Sports
—**Swiss Americans**
H 1159
Further subdivide by subdivisions used under classes of persons.
Use as a topical subdivision under military services.
—**Switch-reference**
H 1154
Use as a topical subdivision under individual languages and groups of languages.
BT —Reference
—Syllabi
USE —Outlines, syllabi, etc.
—**Syllabication**
H 1154
Use as a topical subdivision under individual languages and groups of languages.
—**Symbolic aspects** *(May Subd Geog)*
H 1147; H 1164
Use as a topical subdivision under individual animals and groups of animals and individual organs and regions of the body.
—**Symbolic representation**
H 1140
Use as a topical subdivision under names of countries, cities, etc.
UF —Representation, Symbolic
—**Symbolism**
H 1110
Use as a topical subdivision under names of individual persons for works about the symbols employed by the person in his creative works.
UF —Allegory
—Allegory and symbolism
[Former subdivision]
—Symbols on maps
USE —Maps—Symbols
—Symposia
USE —Congresses
—Symposiums
USE —Congresses
—**Synonyms and antonyms**
H 1154
Use as a topical subdivision under individual languages and groups of languages.
UF —Antonyms

—**Syntax**
H 1154
Use as a topical subdivision under individual languages and groups of languages.
NT —Dialects—Syntax
—Ergative constructions
—Infinitival constructions
—Locative constructions
—Subjectless constructions
—Subordinate constructions
—Temporal constructions
—**Synthesis**
H 1149
Use as a topical subdivision under individual chemicals and groups of chemicals.
——**Inhibitors**
H 1149
Further subdivide by subdivisions used under chemicals.
Use as a topical subdivision under individual chemicals and groups of chemicals.
BT —Inhibitors
——**Regulation**
H 1149
Use as a topical subdivision under individual chemicals and groups of chemicals.
UF —Regulation of synthesis
—**Syphilis** *(May Subd Geog)*
H 1164
Further subdivide by subdivisions used under diseases.
Use as a topical subdivision under individual organs and regions of the body.
BT —Infections
—Table-talk
USE —Quotations
—**Tables**
H 1095
Use as a form subdivision under topical headings for works in tabular form.
UF —Charts, tables, etc.
[Former subdivision]
—Formulae, tables, etc.
[Former subdivision]
—Tables and ready reckoners
[Former subdivision]
—Tables, calculations, etc.
[Former subdivision]
—Tables, etc.
[Former subdivision]
NT —Conversion tables
—Tables and ready reckoners
USE —Tables
—Tables, calculations, etc.
USE —Tables
—Tables, etc.
USE —Tables
—**Tables of contents**
H 1095
Use as a form subdivision under uniform titles of individual works and under types of publications for works that consist of tables of contents of those works.
UF —Contents, Tables of
—**Tactical aviation** *(May Subd Geog)*
H 1159
Use as a topical subdivision under individual military services.
BT —Aviation
—Tagging
USE —Marking
—Tales, Legendary
USE —Legends
—**Tank warfare**
H 1200
Use as a topical subdivision under individual wars.
—**Taoist influences**
H 1156
Use as a topical subdivision under individual literatures.
—**Target practice**
H 1159
Use as a topical subdivision under military services.

—Taxation *(May Subd Geog)*
H 1095; H 1100; H 1103
Use as a topical subdivision under topical headings for works on the taxes levied on income-producing activities or articles of value; also use under classes of persons and ethnic groups for taxes levied on those groups.

———Law and legislation *(May Subd Geog)*
H 1095; H 1100; H 1103
Further subdivide by subdivisions used under legal topics.
Use as a topical subdivision under classes of persons, ethnic groups, and topical headings.
BT —Law and legislation

—Teaching of the Bible
USE —Biblical teaching

—Teaching office
H 1187
Use as a topical subdivision under individual Christian denominations.

—Teaching pieces
H 1160
Use as a form subdivision under forms and types of musical compositions.

—Teachings
H 1110
Use as a topical subdivision under names of individual persons for works discussing in general the body of knowledge, precepts, or doctrines the person taught to others.

—Technique
H 1095; H 1110; H 1148
Use as a topical subdivision under disciplines, especially those involving laboratory routines, for nontheoretical works describing steps to be followed in performing required tasks. Use under names of individual literary authors and under literary form headings for works on writing technique. Also use under individual art forms and headings for national or ethnic art for works on artistic technique.

—Technological innovations
(May Subd Geog)
H 1095; H 1147; H 1153; H 1180
Use as a topical subdivision under topical headings for works on fundamental technological improvements or changes in materials, production methods, processes, organization, or management which increase efficiency or production.
UF —Innovations, Technological

—Technology
H 1200
Use as a topical subdivision under individual wars.

—Teenagers' use *(May Subd Geog)*
H 1188
Use as a topical subdivision under uniform titles of sacred works.
UF —Use by teenagers

—Telephone calls
H 1100; H 1103; H 1110; H 1120; H 1149
Use as a form subdivision under names of individual persons and families, classes of persons, and ethnic groups for recordings or transcripts of telephone calls by or to those persons or groups.

—Telephone directories
H 1095; H 1100; H 1103; H 1105; H 1140; H 1153
Use as a form subdivision under names of countries, cities, etc., individual corporate bodies, classes of persons, ethnic groups, and types of organizations and industries.
UF —Directories—Telephone
[Former subdivision]
BT —Directories

———Yellow pages
H 1140
Use as a form subdivision under names of countries, cities, etc.
UF —Yellow pages

—Television and the war, [revolution, etc.]
H 1200
Complete the subdivision by repeating the generic term for the type of engagement contained in the heading.
Use as a topical subdivision under individual wars.

—Television broadcasting of proceedings
H 1155
Use as a topical subdivision under names of individual legislative bodies.

—Television plays
USE —Radio and television plays

—Temperature *(May Subd Geog)*
H 1180
Use as a topical subdivision under individual plants and groups of plants.

—Tempo
H 1154
Use as a topical subdivision under individual languages and groups of languages.
BT —Phonetics

—Temporal clauses
H 1154
Use as a topical subdivision under individual languages and groups of languages.
BT —Clauses

—Temporal constructions
H 1154
Use as a topical subdivision under individual languages and groups of languages.
BT —Syntax

—Tennis
H 1151
Use as a topical subdivision under names of individual educational institutions.
BT —Sports

—Tense
H 1154
Use as a topical subdivision under individual languages and groups of languages.

—Tenure of land
USE —Land tenure

—Term of office
H 1155
Use as a topical subdivision under names of individual legislative bodies.

—Terminology
H 1095; H 1100; H 1105; H 1188
Use as a topical subdivision under uniform titles of sacred works, and under classes of persons, individual Christian denominations, and topical headings for works about words and expressions found in those works or used in those fields.

—Terminology
H 1095; H 1100; H 1105; H 1188
Use as a form subdivision under uniform titles of sacred works, and under classes of persons, individual Christian denominations, and topical headings for works that list words and expressions found in those works or used in those fields.
NT —Grammar—Terminology

———Pronunciation
H 1095; H 1188
Use as a topical subdivision under uniform titles of sacred works and topical headings.
UF —Pronunciation of terminology

—Terms and phrases
H 1154
Use as a topical subdivision under individual languages and groups of languages for works about expressions, phrases, idioms, etc., found in those languages.
UF —Phrases and terms

—Terms and phrases
H 1154
Use as a form subdivision under individual languages and groups of languages for works that list expressions, phrases, idioms, etc., found in those languages.
UF —Phrases and terms

—Territorial boundaries
USE —Boundaries

—Territorial expansion
H 1140
Use as a topical subdivision under names of countries, etc.
UF —Expansion, Territorial

—Territorial possessions
USE —Territories and possessions

—Territorial questions *(May Subd Geog)*
H 1200
Use as a topical subdivision under individual wars.

—Territoriality *(May Subd Geog)*
H 1147
Use as a topical subdivision under individual animals and groups of animals.

—Territories and possessions
H 1095; H 1140
Use as a topical subdivision under headings of the type [topic]—[country] for works discussing collectively the territories and territorial possessions of a country in relation to the topic, for example, Postmarks—United States—Territories and possessions. Also use under names of regions and countries for works discussing collectively the territorial possessions of the region or country.
UF —Possessions and territories
—Territorial possessions
NT —Colonies

———Politics and government
H 1140
Use as a topical subdivision under names of regions and countries.
BT —Politics and government

—Test shooting
H 1159
Use as a topical subdivision under military services.

—Testing
H 1095; H 1147; H 1149; H 1158
Use as a topical subdivision under topical headings for works on the construction, application, and results of testing pertaining to those topics. Also use under individual drugs and groups of drugs for works on testing their effectiveness and/or safety, and under individual animals and groups of animals, individual chemicals and groups of chemicals, individual materials and types of materials, and types of instruments, equipment, products, etc., for works on testing of those items and/or the results of testing.
NT —Ability testing
—Compression testing
—Crash tests
—Environmental testing
—Fire testing
—Impact testing
—Materials—Dynamic testing
—Nondestructive testing
—Seeds—Testing
—Therapeutic use—Testing

—Testing, Educational
USE —Examinations

—Testing for drug use or abuse
USE —Drug testing

—Testing for toxicity
USE —Toxicity testing

—Text-books
USE —Textbooks

—Text-books for foreign speakers
USE —Textbooks for foreign speakers

—Textbooks
H 1095; H 1154; H 1188
Use as a topical subdivision under names of individual persons and corporate bodies, uniform titles of sacred works, and topical headings, for works about textbooks on those subjects.
UF —Text-books
[Former subdivision]

—Textbooks
H 1095; H 1154; H 1188
Use as a form subdivision under names of individual persons and corporate bodies, uniform titles of sacred works, and topical headings, for textbooks on those subjects.
UF —Text-books

—Textbooks for English, [French, etc.]
speakers
H 1154
Use as a form subdivision under artificial languages.

—Textbooks for foreign speakers
H 1154
Use as a form subdivision under individual languages and groups of languages.
UF —Foreign language textbooks
—Text-books for foreign speakers
[Former subdivision]

———English
H 1154
Use as a form subdivision under languages other than English.

SD-83

—Textbooks for foreign speakers
(Continued)
———German, [Italian, etc.]
H 1154
Use as a form subdivision under individual languages and groups of languages.
——Texts
H 1095; H 1154; H 1160
Use as a topical subdivision under individual lesser-known languages, dialects, early periods of languages, headings of the type [ethnic groups]—Languages and [place]—Languages, liturgy headings, and headings for vocal music for works about texts.
NT —Liturgy—Texts
—Rituals—Texts
—Texts
H 1095; H 1154; H 1160
Use as a form subdivision under individual lesser-known languages, dialects, early periods of languages, headings of the type [ethnic group]—Languages and [place]—Languages, liturgy headings, and headings for vocal music for individual texts or collections of texts.
NT —Dialects—Texts
—Hymns—Texts
—Languages—Texts
—Liturgy—Texts
—Rituals—Texts
—Songs and music—Texts
———Dating
H 1154
Use as a topical subdivision under lesser-known languages, under headings of the type [ethnic group]—Languages, or [place]—Languages, and under early periods of languages (ca. pre-1500).
BT —Dating
—Textual criticism
USE —Criticism, Textual
—Texture *(May Subd Geog)*
H 1158
Use as a topical subdivision under individual materials and types of materials.
—Thai influences
H 1156
Use as a topical subdivision under individual literatures.
—Theater and the war, [revolution, etc.]
H 1200
Complete the subdivision by repeating the generic term for the type of engagement contained in the heading.
Use as a topical subdivision under individual wars.
—Thematic catalogs
H 1110; H 1160
Use as a form subdivision under names of individual composers and forms and types of musical compositions for lists of musical compositions that include musical notation for the opening measures of individual works or section of works.
BT —Catalogs
—Themes, motives
H 1095; H 1110; H 1148; H 1156
Use as a topical subdivision under names of individual persons and individual literary and art forms.
UF —Motives, themes
—Themes, motives, Literary
USE —Literary themes, motives
—Theology
H 1186; H 1188
Use as a topical subdivision under names of individual religions and monastic orders and under uniform titles of sacred works.
NT —Liturgy—Theology
—Therapeutic use *(May Subd Geog)*
H 1095; H 1147; H 1149; H 1180
Do not use under individual drugs and groups of drugs.
Use as a topical subdivision under topical headings for works on their use in treating disease.
UF —Medicinal use
—Use in therapeutics
———Administration
H 1149
Use as a topical subdivision under individual and groups of non-drug chemicals.
BT —Administration

———Controlled release *(May Subd Geog)*
H 1149
Use as a topical subdivision under individual and groups of non-drug chemicals. Under individual drugs and groups of drugs use the subdivision Controlled release.
BT —Controlled release
———Effectiveness *(May Subd Geog)*
H 1149
Use as a topical subdivision under individual and groups of non-drug chemicals.
BT —Effectiveness
———Side effects *(May Subd Geog)*
H 1149; H 1180
Use as a topical subdivision under individual plants and groups of plants and under individual and groups of non-drug chemicals.
BT —Side effects
———Testing
H 1149
Use as a topical subdivision under individual and groups of non-drug chemicals.
BT —Testing
—Therapy
USE —Treatment
—Thermal conductivity *(May Subd Geog)*
H 1149; H 1159
Use as a topical subdivision under individual chemicals and groups of chemicals and individual materials and types of materials.
UF —Conductivity, Thermal
BT —Thermal properties
—Transport properties
—Thermal fatigue *(May Subd Geog)*
H 1158
Use as a topical subdivision under individual materials and types of materials.
BT —Fatigue
—Thermal properties *(May Subd Geog)*
H 1149; H 1158; H 1180
Use as a topical subdivision under individual plants and groups of plants, individual chemicals and groups of chemicals, and individual materials and types of materials.
BT —Properties
NT —Thermal conductivity
—Thermography *(May Subd Geog)*
H 1164
Use as a topical subdivision under individual organs and regions of the body.
—Thermomechanical properties
H 1158
Use as a topical subdivision under individual materials and types of materials.
—Thermomechanical treatment
(May Subd Geog)
H 1158
Use as a topical subdivision under individual materials and types of materials.
BT —Heat treatment
—Thermotherapy *(May Subd Geog)*
H 1150
Use as a topical subdivision under individual diseases and types of diseases.
BT —Treatment
—Thinning *(May Subd Geog)*
H 1180
Use as a topical subdivision under individual plants and groups of plants.
—Threshing *(May Subd Geog)*
H 1180
Use as a topical subdivision under individual plants and groups of plants.
———Machinery *(May Subd Geog)*
H 1180
Use as a topical subdivision under individual plants and groups of plants.
BT —Machinery
—Threshold limit values *(May Subd Geog)*
H 1149
Use as a topical subdivision under individual chemicals and groups of chemicals.
UF —Exposure limits, Occupational
—Maximum allowable concentrations
—Occupational exposure limits
—Time management *(May Subd Geog)*
H 1100; H 1103
Use as a topical subdivision under classes of persons and ethnic groups.

—Time of flowering
USE —Flowering time
—Time of harvesting
USE —Harvesting time
—Time of planting
USE —Planting time
—Timing belts of motors
USE —Motors—Timing belts
—Tires
H 1195
Use as a topical subdivision under individual land vehicles and types of land vehicles.
———Inflation pressure
H 1195
Use as a topical subdivision under individual land vehicles and types of land vehicles.
UF —Inflation pressure of tires
———Repairing *(May Subd Geog)*
H 1195
Use as a topical subdivision under individual land vehicles and types of land vehicles.
BT —Repairing
—Title abbreviations
USE —Abbreviations of titles
—Titles
H 1100; H 1110
Use as a topical subdivision under names of individual persons and classes of persons.
UF —Address, Titles of
—Nobility, Titles of
—Titles of books
H 1188
Use as a topical subdivision under uniform titles of sacred works.
—Tobacco use *(May Subd Geog)*
H 1100; H 1103
Use as a topical subdivision under classes of persons and ethnic groups.
BT —Substance use
—Tolerance, Drought
USE —Drought tolerance
—Tomb
H 1110
Use as a topical subdivision under names of individual persons for works about the person's grave, interred bones, etc. For works on disinterred bones use the subdivision Relics.
UF —Grave
[Former subdivision]
—Sepulchral monument
BT —Tombs
—Tombs *(May Subd Geog)*
1120; H 1095; H 1100
Use as a topical subdivision under names of individual families, royal houses, dynasties, etc., and under classes of persons.
NT —Kings and rulers—Tombs
—Tomb
—Tomography *(May Subd Geog)*
H 1150; H 1164
Use as a topical subdivision under individual diseases and types of diseases and individual organs and regions of the body.
UF —Diseases—Tomography
BT —Cross-sectional imaging
—Radiography
—Tonguing
H 1161
Use as a topical subdivision under individual musical instruments and families of instruments.
—Tools
USE —Implements
—Topic and comment
H 1154
Use as a topical subdivision under individual languages and groups of languages.
—Topographic maps
USE —Maps, Topographic
—Tourist maps
USE —Maps, Tourist

—Tours
H 1105; H 1140
Use as a form subdivision under names of countries, cities, etc., and individual corporate bodies for guidebooks providing planned itineraries to those places or bodies, usually including descriptions and historical information about items to be seen.
UF —Description and travel—Tours
[Former subdivision]
—Itineraries
BT —Guidebooks

—Towing *(May Subd Geog)*
H 1195
Use as a topical subdivision under individual land vehicles and types of land vehicles.

—Toxicity
USE —Toxicology

—Toxicity testing *(May Subd Geog)*
H 1149
Use as a topical subdivision under individual chemicals and groups of chemicals.
UF —Testing for toxicity

—Toxicology *(May Subd Geog)*
H 1095; H 1147; H 1149; H 1158; H 1180
Use as a topical subdivision under individual chemicals and groups of chemicals, individual materials and types of materials, individual animals and groups of animals, and individual plants and groups of plants for works on their poisonous effects on human beings or animals.
UF —Poisoning
—Toxicity

——Age factors *(May Subd Geog)*
H 1149
Use as a topical subdivision under individual chemicals and groups of chemicals.
BT —Age factors

——Biography
H 1149
Use this subdivision combination as a form subdivision under individual chemicals and groups of chemicals.
BT —Biography

——Reporting *(May Subd Geog)*
H 1149
Use as a topical subdivision under individual chemicals and groups of chemicals.
BT —Reporting

—Track and field
H 1151
Use as a topical subdivision under names of individual educational institutions.
UF —Track-athletics
[Former subdivision]
BT —Sports

—Track-athletics
USE —Track and field

—Tracking, Radio
USE —Radio tracking

—Traction *(May Subd Geog)*
H 1164; H 1195
Use as a topical subdivision under individual organs and regions of the body and individual land vehicles and types of land vehicles.

—Trade
USE —Commerce

—Trade-marks
USE —Trademarks

—Trade policy
USE —Commercial policy

—Trademarks
H 1095; H 1153
Use as a topical subdivision under individual industries and under products and articles that may be trademarked for works about trademarks.
UF —Trade-marks
[Former subdivision]

—Trademarks
H 1095; H 1153
Use as a form subdivision under individual industries and under products and articles that may be trademarked for works listing trademarks.
UF —Trade-marks
[Former subdivision]

—Tragedies
H 1110
Do not use under dramatists who write principally tragedies.
Use as a topical subdivision under names of individual literary authors for criticism of tragedies by the author.
BT —Dramatic works

—Tragicomedies
H 1110
Do not use under dramatists who write principally tragicomedies.
Use as a topical subdivision under names of individual literary authors for criticism of tragicomedies by the author.
BT —Dramatic works

—Training *(May Subd Geog)*
H 1147; H 1180
Use as a topical subdivision under individual animals and groups of animals and individual plants and groups of plants.

—Training administrators
H 1159
Further subdivide by subdivisions used under classes of persons.
Use as a topical subdivision under military services.

—Training of *(May Subd Geog)*
H 1100
Use as a topical subdivision under occupational groups and types of employees.
NT —Employees—Training of
—Guided missile personnel—Training of
—In-service training

—Transaxles
H 1195
Use as a topical subdivision under individual land vehicles and types of land vehicles.

—Transcribing
USE —Transcription

—Transcription *(May Subd Geog)*
H 1154
Use as a topical subdivision under individual languages and groups of languages.
UF —Transcribing

—Transcriptions, Phonetic
USE —Phonetic transcriptions

—Transfer
H 1100
Use as a topical subdivision under classes of persons.

—Transfer and registration
USE —Registration and transfer

—Transition periods
H 1155
Use as a topical subdivision under names of individual legislative bodies.
UF —Periods, Transition

—Transitivity
H 1154
Use as a topical subdivision under individual languages and groups of languages.

—Translating *(May Subd Geog)*
H 1095; H 1154; H 1188
Use as a topical subdivision under uniform titles of sacred works, individual languages and groups of languages, and topical headings.
UF —Translating services
[Former subdivision]
NT —Machine translating

—Translating into French, [German, etc.]
H 1154
Use as a topical subdivision under individual languages and groups of languages.

—Translating services
USE —Translating

—Translations
H 1095; H 1110; H 1155.8; H 1156
Use as a topical subdivision under names of individual literary authors, individual literary works entered under title, individual literatures, types of publications, and topical headings for works about translations.

—Translations
H 1095; H 1110; H 1155.8; H 1156
Do not use for single translations.
Use as a form subdivision under names of individual literary authors, individual literary works entered under title, individual literatures, types of publications, and topical headings, for collections of translated works.
NT —Interlinear translations

———History and criticism
H 1110; H 1155.8; H 1156
Use as a topical subdivision under names of individual literary authors, literary works entered under title, and individual literatures.
BT —History and criticism

—Translations into French, [German, etc.]
H 1095; H 1110; H 1155.8; H 1156
Use as a topical subdivision under names of individual literary authors, individual literary works entered under title, individual literatures, types of publications and topical headings for works about translations in those languages.

—Translations into French, [German, etc.]
H 1095; H 1110; H 1155.8; H 1156
Use as a form subdivision under names of individual literary authors, individual literary works entered under title, individual literatures, types of publications and topical headings for collections of translated works in those languages.

———History and criticism
H 1110; H 1155.8; H 1156
Use as a topical subdivision under names of individual literary authors, literary works entered under title and individual literatures.
BT —History and criticism

—Transliterating
USE —Transliteration

—Transliteration
H 1154
Use as a topical subdivision under individual languages and groups of languages.
UF —Transliterating

—Transliteration into Korean, [Russian, etc.]
H 1154
Use as a topical subdivision under individual languages and groups of languages.

—Transmission *(May Subd Geog)*
H 1150
Use as a topical subdivision under individual diseases and types of diseases.

—Transmission devices
H 1195
Use as a topical subdivision under individual land vehicles and types of land vehicles.

—Transmission devices, Automatic
H 1195
Use as a topical subdivision under individual land vehicles and types of land vehicles.
UF —Automatic transmission devices

——Parts *(May Subd Geog)*
H 1195
Use as a topical subdivision under individual land vehicles and types of land vehicles.
BT —Parts

—Transmutation
H 1154
Use as a topical subdivision under individual languages and groups of languages.

—Transplantation *(May Subd Geog)*
H 1164
Use as a topical subdivision under individual organs and regions of the body.
BT —Surgery
NT —Embryos—Transplantation

——Complications *(May Subd Geog)*
H 1164
Further subdivide by subdivisions used under diseases.
Use as a topical subdivision under individual organs and regions of the body.

——Immunological aspects
H 1164
Use as a topical subdivision under individual organs and regions of the body.
BT —Immunology

—**Transplantation** *(Continued)*
——**Law and legislation** *(May Subd Geog)*
    H 1164
    Further subdivide by subdivisions used under
    legal topics.
      Use as a topical subdivision under individual
    organs and regions of the body.
    BT —Law and legislation
——**Nursing** *(May Subd Geog)*
    H 1164
      Use as a topical subdivision under individual
    organs and regions of the body.
    BT —Nursing
——**Patients** *(May Subd Geog)*
    H 1164
    Further subdivide by subdivisions used under
    classes of persons.
      Use as a topical subdivision under individual
    organs and regions of the body.
    BT —Patients
—**Transplanting** *(May Subd Geog)*
    H 1180
    Use as a topical subdivision under individual
    plants and groups of plants.
——**Machinery** *(May Subd Geog)*
    H 1180
      Use as a topical subdivision under individual
    plants and groups of plants.
    BT —Machinery
—**Transport of sick and wounded**
    H 1159
    Use as a topical subdivision under military ser-
    vices.
    BT —Transportation
—**Transport properties** *(May Subd Geog)*
    H 1149; H 1158
      Use as a topical subdivision under individual
    chemicals and groups of chemicals and individual
    materials and types of materials.
    BT —Properties
    NT —Thermal conductivity
—**Transport service**
    H 1159
    Use as a topical subdivision under military ser-
    vices.
    BT —Transportation
—**Transportation** *(May Subd Geog)*
    H 1095; H 1100; H 1103; H 1147; H 1158;
    H 1159; H 1180; H 1195; H 1200
    Do not subdivide geographically under military
    services.
      Use as a topical subdivision under military ser-
    vices, and under classes of persons, ethnic groups,
    types of objects, merchandise, individual animals
    and groups of animals, individual plants and groups
    of plants, and individual wars for works on trans-
    portation of or applied to those topics.
    NT —Transport of sick and wounded
        —Transport service
——**Diseases and injuries** *(May Subd Geog)*
    H 1180
    Use as a topical subdivision under individual
    plants and groups of plants.
    BT —Postharvest diseases and injuries
——**Law and legislation** *(May Subd Geog)*
    H 1158; H 1195
    Further subdivide by subdivisions used under
    legal topics.
      Use as a topical subdivision under individual
    materials and types of materials and individual
    land vehicles and types of land vehicles.
    BT —Law and legislation
—**Trapping** *(May Subd Geog)*
    H 1103
    Use as a topical subdivision under ethnic groups.
—**Travel** *(May Subd Geog)*
    H 1100; H 1103; H 1105; H 1110
    Use as a topical subdivision under names of in-
    dividual persons and corporate bodies, classes of
    persons and ethnic groups.
    UF —Itineraries
        —Journeys
          [Former subdivision]
        —Travel restrictions
          [Former subdivision]
        —Travels
        —Voyages
    NT —Kings and rulers—Travel

—Travel restrictions
    USE —Travel
—Travels
    USE —Travel
—Travesties (Parodies)
    USE —Parodies, imitations, etc.
—**Treaties**
    H 1103; H 1200
      Use as a topical subdivision under ethnic groups
    and individual wars for works about treaties related
    to those groups or wars.
    NT —Commercial treaties
        —Foreign relations—Treaties
—**Treaties**
    H 1103; H 1200
      Use as a form subdivision under ethnic groups
    and individual wars for individual or collections of
    treaties related to those groups or wars.
    NT —Commercial treaties
        —Foreign relations—Treaties
—**Treatment** *(May Subd Geog)*
    H 1150
      Use as a topical subdivision under individual dis-
    eases and types of diseases.
    UF —Therapy
    NT —Adjuvant treatment
        —Alternative treatment
        —Ayurvedic treatment
        —Chemotherapy
        —Chiropractic treatment
        —Cryotherapy
        —Diet therapy
        —Differentiation therapy
        —Diseases—Treatment
        —Dosimetric treatment
        —Eclectic treatment
        —Gene therapy
        —Homeopathic treatment
        —Hormone therapy
        —Immunotherapy
        —Palliative treatment
        —Phototherapy
        —Physical therapy
        —Radiotherapy
        —Surgery
        —Thermotherapy
——**Complications** *(May Subd Geog)*
    H 1150
    Further subdivide by subdivisions used under
    diseases.
      Use as a topical subdivision under individual
    diseases and types of diseases.
    UF —Treatment—Complications and
        sequelae
        [Former subdivision]
    BT —Complications
——Complications and sequelae
    USE —Treatment—Complications
—**Trench warfare**
    H 1200
      Use as a topical subdivision under individual
    wars.
—**Trial practice**
    H 1154.5
    Use as a topical subdivision under individual le-
    gal topics.
—Trial proceedings
    USE —Trials, litigation, etc.
—**Trials, litigation, etc.**
    H 1105; H 1110; H 1120; H 1140
      Use as a topical subdivision under names of
    countries, cities, etc., individual persons, families,
    and corporate bodies for works about civil or crim-
    inal actions to which they are parties.
    UF —Litigation
—**Trials, litigation, etc.**
    H 1105; H 1110; H 1120; H 1140
      Use as a form subdivision under names of coun-
    tries, cities, etc., individual persons, families, and
    corporate bodies for the proceedings of civil or
    criminal actions to which they are parties.
    UF —Proceedings of trials
        —Trial proceedings

—**Trials of vessels**
    H 1159
    Use as a topical subdivision under military ser-
    vices.
—**Tribal citizenship** *(May Subd Geog)*
    H 1103
    Use as a topical subdivision under ethnic groups.
    UF —Citizenship, Tribal
—Tribes, Scheduled
    USE —Scheduled tribes
—**Tritium content** *(May Subd Geog)*
    H 1158
    Use as a topical subdivision under individual
    materials and types of materials.
—**Trophies**
    H 1200
    Use as a topical subdivision under individual
    wars.
—**Tropical conditions**
    H 1095
    Use as a topical subdivision under topical head-
    ings for works on methods or procedures employed
    when working in a tropical climate.
—**Trypanotolerance** *(May Subd Geog)*
    H 1147
    Use as a topical subdivision under individual an-
    imals and groups of animals.
    BT —Immunology
—**Tuberculosis** *(May Subd Geog)*
    H 1164
    Use as a topical subdivision under individual or-
    gans and regions of the body.
    BT —Infections
—**Tuition**
    H 1151
    Use as a topical subdivision under names of in-
    dividual educational institutions.
—**Tumors** *(May Subd Geog)*
    H 1164
    Further subdivide by subdivisions used under
    diseases.
      Use as a topical subdivision under individual or-
    gans and regions of the body.
    BT —Diseases
—**Tuning** *(May Subd Geog)*
    H 1161
    Use as a topical subdivision under individual
    musical instruments and families of instruments.
—**Tunnel warfare** *(May Subd Geog)*
    H 1200
    Use as a topical subdivision under individual
    wars.
—Turbochargers of motors
    USE —Motors—Turbochargers
—**Turkic authors**
    H 1156
    Use as a topical subdivision under individual lit-
    eratures.
—**Turkic influences**
    H 1156
    Use as a topical subdivision under individual lit-
    eratures.
    BT —Foreign influences
—Turkish antiquities
    USE —Antiquities, Turkish
—**Turkish authors**
    H 1156
    Use as a topical subdivision under individual lit-
    eratures.
—Turnover of officials and employees
    USE —Officials and employees—Turnover
—Two-stroke cycle motors
    USE —Motors (Two-stroke cycle)
—**Type specimens** *(May Subd Geog)*
    H 1147; H 1180
    Use as a topical subdivision under individual an-
    imals and groups of animals and individual plants
    and groups of plants.
—**Ukrainian authors**
    H 1156
    Use as a topical subdivision under individual lit-
    eratures.
—**Ukrainian influences**
    H 1156
    Use as a topical subdivision under individual lit-
    eratures.
    BT —Foreign influences

—**Ulcers** *(May Subd Geog)*
     H 1164
        Further subdivide by subdivisions used under diseases.
        Use as a topical subdivision under individual organs and regions of the body.
     BT —Diseases
—**Ultrasonic imaging** *(May Subd Geog)*
     H 1150; H 1164
        Use as a topical subdivision under individual diseases and types of diseases and individual organs and regions of the body other than brain and heart.
     UF —Diseases—Ultrasonic imaging
     BT —Cross-sectional imaging
—**Ultrastructure**
     H 1164; H 1180
        Use as a topical subdivision under individual organs and regions of the body and individual plants and groups of plants.
     BT —Cytology
—Unclaimed pension benefits
     USE —Pensions—Unclaimed benefits
—Undergraduate students
     USE —Undergraduates
—**Undergraduates**
     H 1151
        Further subdivide by subdivisions used under classes of persons.
        Use as a topical subdivision under individual educational institutions.
     UF —Undergraduate students
     BT —Students
     NT —Freshmen
—**Underground literature** *(May Subd Geog)*
     H 1200
        Use as a topical subdivision under individual wars.
     BT —Literature and the war, [revolution, etc.]
—**Underground movements**
     (May Subd Geog)
     H 1200
        Use as a topical subdivision under individual wars.
     UF —Guerrillas
        [Former subdivision]
—**Underground printing plants**
     (May Subd Geog)
     H 1200
        Use as a topical subdivision under individual wars.
     UF —Printing plants, Underground
—**Uniforms**
     H 1100; H 1105; H 1159
        Use as a topical subdivision under names of individual corporate bodies and under classes of persons and military services.
     BT —Clothing
—Union catalogs
     USE —Union lists
—**Union lists**
     H 1095
        Use as a form subdivision under types of printed or nonbook materials for catalogs of those materials held by two or more libraries.
     UF —Lists, Union
        —Union catalogs
     BT —Catalogs
     NT —Bibliography—Union lists
—**Union territories**
     H 1095
        Use as a topical subdivision under headings of the type [topic]—[country] for works discussing collectively the union territories of a country in relation to the topic.
     BT —Administrative and political divisions
—**Unit cohesion**
     H 1159
        Use as a topical subdivision under military services.
     UF —Cohesion, Unit
—**Unknown military personnel**
     H 1200
        Further subdivide by subdivisions used under classes of persons.
        Use as a topical subdivision under individual wars.

—**Unknown military personnel, American, [British, etc.]**
     H 1200
        Further subdivide by subdivisions used under classes of persons.
        Use as a topical subdivision under individual wars.
—Untouchable authors
     USE —Dalit authors
—**Upholstery** *(May Subd Geog)*
     H 1195
        Use as a topical subdivision under individual land vehicles and types of land vehicles.
—**Urdu influences**
     H 1156
        Use as a topical subdivision under individual literatures.
     BT —Foreign influences
—**Usage**
     H 1154
        Use as a topical subdivision under individual languages and groups of languages.
     UF —Idioms, corrections, errors
        [Former subdivision]
—Usage errors
     USE —Errors of usage
—**Use**
     H 1188
        Use as a topical subdivision under uniform titles of sacred works.
—Use by children
     USE —Children's use
—Use by teenagers
     USE —Teenagers' use
—Use in devotion
     USE —Devotional use
—Use in diagnosis
     USE —Diagnostic use
—**Use in hymns**
     H 1188
        Use as a topical subdivision under uniform titles of sacred works.
—Use in liturgy
     USE —Liturgical use
—Use in therapeutics
     USE —Therapeutic use
—Use in wars
     USE —War use
—Use of
     USE —Utilization
—Use of fire
     USE —Fire use
—**Use studies**
     H 1095
        Use as a topical subdivision under types of information resources, information services, libraries, library resources, and publications for works about use studies of those resources or services.
—**Use studies**
     H 1095
        Use as a form subdivision under types of information resources, information services, libraries, library resources, and publications for use studies of those resources or services.
—**Utilization** *(May Subd Geog)*
     H 1180
        Use as a topical subdivision under individual plants and groups of plants.
        Use as a topical subdivision under individual animals and groups of animals and individual plants and groups of plants.
     UF —Use of
—Vacancies, Job
     USE —Job vacancies
—**Vaccination** *(May Subd Geog)*
     H 1147; H 1150
        Use as a topical subdivision under individual diseases and types of diseases and individual animals and groups of animals.
     UF —Diseases—Vaccination
        [Former subdivision]
        —Preventive inoculation
        [Former subdivision]
     BT —Prevention

——**Complications** *(May Subd Geog)*
     H 1150
        Further subdivide by subdivisions used under diseases.
        Use as a topical subdivision under individual diseases and types of diseases.
     BT —Complications
—Vade-mecums
     USE —Handbooks, manuals, etc.
—**Validity** *(May Subd Geog)*
     H 1095
        Use as a topical subdivision under individual tests and types of tests.
—**Valuation** *(May Subd Geog)*
     H 1095
        Use as a topical subdivision under types of property, businesses, structures, etc., for works on the values set upon those topics or their estimated or determined market value.
—Valves of motors
     USE —Motors—Valves
—Vapor lock of fuel systems
     USE —Fuel systems—Vapor lock
—**Vapor pressure** *(May Subd Geog)*
     H 1149
        Use as a topical subdivision under individual chemicals and groups of chemicals.
     UF —Pressure, Vapor
—**Variation** *(May Subd Geog)*
     H 1147; H 1154; H 1164; H 1180
        Use as a topical subdivision under individual animals and groups of animals, individual organs and regions of the body, individual plants and groups of plants, and individual languages and groups of languages.
     NT —Clones—Variation
—**Varieties** *(May Subd Geog)*
     H 1180
        Use as a topical subdivision under individual plants and groups of plants.
     NT —Heirloom varieties
—**Vegetative propagation** *(May Subd Geog)*
     H 1180
        Use as a topical subdivision under individual plants and groups of plants.
     BT —Propagation
—Vehicle bodies
     USE —Bodies
—Velocity
     USE —Speed
—**Venom** *(May Subd Geog)*
     H 1147
        Use as a topical subdivision under individual animals and groups of animals.
—**Venom resistance** *(May Subd Geog)*
     H 1147
        Use as a topical subdivision under individual animals and groups of animals.
     UF —Resistance to venom
     BT —Physiology
—Ventilation
     USE —Heating and ventilation
—**Verb**
     H 1154
        Use as a topical subdivision under individual languages and groups of languages.
—**Verb phrase**
     H 1154
        Use as a topical subdivision under individual languages and groups of languages.
—**Verbals**
     H 1154
        Use as a topical subdivision under individual languages and groups of languages.
—**Versification**
     H 1110; H 1154; H 1155.8
        Use as a topical subdivision under names of individual literary authors for works on the author's technique of writing verse, and under literary works entered under title. Also use as a topical subdivision under individual modern languages and groups of modern languages. Under individual ancient languages use the subdivision Metrics and rhythmics.
—**Versions**
     H 1188
        Use as a topical subdivision under uniform titles of sacred works.

—Versions *(Continued)*
——Authorized, [Living Bible, Revised Standard, etc.]
H 1188
Use as a topical subdivision under uniform titles of sacred works.
—Versions, African, [Indic, Slavic, etc.]
H 1188
Use adjectival qualifers only for groups of languages. For translations of sacred works into individual languages, assign headings of the type [uniform title of sacred work]. [language]—Versions.
Use as a topical subdivision under uniform titles of sacred works.
—Versions, Baptist
H 1188
Use as a topical subdivision under uniform titles of sacred works.
UF —Baptist versions
—Versions, Catholic
H 1188
Use as a topical subdivision under uniform titles of sacred works.
UF —Catholic versions
—Versions, Catholic vs. Protestant
H 1188
Use as a topical subdivision under uniform titles of sacred works.
UF —Catholic vs. Protestant versions
—Versions, Hussite
H 1188
Use as a topical subdivision under uniform titles of sacred works.
UF —Hussite versions
—Versions, Jehovah's Witnesses
H 1188
Use as a topical subdivision under uniform titles of sacred works.
UF —Jehovah's Witnesses versions
—Vertical distribution *(May Subd Geog)*
H 1147; H 1180
Use as a topical subdivision under individual animals and groups of animals, and individual plants and groups of plants.
UF —Distribution, Vertical
—Vertical integration *(May Subd Geog)*
H 1153
Use as a topical subdivision under individual industries.
UF —Integration, Vertical
—Veterans *(May Subd Geog)*
H 1200
Further subdivide by subdivisions used under classes of persons.
Use as a topical subdivision under individual wars.
—Veterinary service *(May Subd Geog)*
H 1200
Use as a topical subdivision under individual wars.
—Viability of seeds
USE —Seeds—Viability
—Vibration *(May Subd Geog)*
H 1095; H 1195
Use as a topical subdivision under types of equipment, structures, and vehicles.
NT —Motors—Vibration
—Video adaptations
USE —Film and video adaptations
—Video catalogs
H 1095
Use as a form subdivision under subjects for lists of video recordings about those subjects.
UF —Video tape catalogs
[Former subdivision]
BT —Catalogs
—Video recordings for foreign speakers
H 1154
Use as a form subdivision under individual languages and groups of languages.
—Video recordings for French, [Spanish, etc.] speakers
H 1154
Use as a form subdivision under individual languages and groups of languages.
—Video tape catalogs
USE —Video catalogs
—Views, Aerial
USE —Aerial views

—Violence against *(May Subd Geog)*
H 1100; H 1103
Use as a topical subdivision under classes of persons and ethnic groups.
UF —Assaults against
[Former subdivision]
—Virus diseases *(May Subd Geog)*
H 1147; H 1164
Further subdivide by subdivisions used under diseases.
Use as a topical subdivision under individual animals and groups of animals and individual plants and groups of plants.
BT —Infections
—Viruses *(May Subd Geog)*
H 1147; H 1164
Use as a topical subdivision under individual animals and groups of animals and individual plants and groups of plants.
—Viscosity *(May Subd Geog)*
H 1149; H 1158
Use as a topical subdivision under individual chemicals and groups of chemicals and individual materials and types of materials.
BT —Properties
—Vital statistics
USE —Statistics, Vital
—Vitality *(May Subd Geog)*
H 1180
Use as a topical subdivision under individual plants and groups of plants.
—Vocabularies, glossaries, etc.
USE —Glossaries, vocabularies, etc.
—Vocabulary
H 1154
Use as a topical subdivision under individual languages other than English and groups of languages.
NT —Cognate words
—New words
—Obscene words
—Obsolete words
—Onomatopoeic words
—Vocal scores with accordion
H 1160
Use as a form subdivision under forms and types of musical compositions.
—Vocal scores with continuo
H 1160
Use as a form subdivision under forms and types of musical compositions.
—Vocal scores with guitar
H 1160
Use as a form subdivision under forms and types of musical compositions.
—Vocal scores with harp
H 1160
Use as a form subdivision under forms and types of musical compositions.
—Vocal scores with harpsichord
H 1160
Use as a form subdivision under forms and types of musical compositions.
—Vocal scores with keyboard instrument
H 1160
Use as a form subdivision under forms and types of musical compositions.
—Vocal scores with organ
H 1160
Use as a form subdivision under forms and types of musical compositions.
—Vocal scores with organ and piano
H 1160
Use as a form subdivision under forms and types of musical compositions.
UF —Vocal scores with piano and organ
[Former subdivision]
—Vocal scores with piano
H 1160
Use as a form subdivision under forms and types of musical compositions.
—Vocal scores with piano (4 hands)
H 1160
Use as a form subdivision under forms and types of musical compositions.
—Vocal scores with piano and organ
USE —Vocal scores with organ and piano

—Vocal scores with pianos (2)
H 1160
Use as a form subdivision under forms and types of musical compositions.
—Vocal scores without accompaniment
H 1160
Use as a form subdivision under forms and types of musical compositions.
—Vocalization *(May Subd Geog)*
H 1147; H 1154
Use as a topical subdivision under individual animals and groups of animals. Also use under individual Semitic languages. Under other languages use the subdivision Vowels.
——Regulation
H 1147
Use as a topical subdivision under individual animals and groups of animals.
UF —Regulation of vocalization
—Vocational guidance *(May Subd Geog)*
H 1095; H 1100; H 1105; H 1153; H 1154; H 1159
Use as a topical subdivision under names of individual corporate bodies and military services and under occupations, fields of endeavor, and types of industries. Use under classes of persons only if a heading for the corresponding field or activity does not exist or cannot be established.
UF —Guidance, Vocational
—Voice
H 1154
Use as a topical subdivision under individual languages and groups of languages.
NT —Passive voice
—Voivodeships
H 1095
Use as a topical subdivision under headings of the type [topic]—Poland for works discussing collectively the voivodeships of Poland in relation to the topic.
UF —Voivodships
BT —Administrative and political divisions
—Voivodships
USE —Voivodeships
—Volleyball
H 1151
Use as a topical subdivision under names of individual educational institutions.
BT —Sports
—Voting
H 1155
Use as a topical subdivision under names of individual legislative bodies.
—Vowel gradation
H 1154
Use as a topical subdivision under names of individual languages and groups of languages.
—Vowel reduction
H 1154
Use as a topical subdivision under individual languages and groups of languages.
—Vowels
H 1154
Use as a topical subdivision under individual languages and groups of languages other then Semitic languages. Under Semitic languages, use Vocalization.
—Voyages
USE —Travel
—Wage fixing
H 1159
Use as a topical subdivision under individual military services.
—War dead, Repatriation of
USE —Repatriation of war dead
—War use *(May Subd Geog)*
H 1158
Use as a topical subdivision under individual materials and types of materials.
UF —Use in wars
—War work *(May Subd Geog)*
H 1200
Use as a topical subdivision under individual wars.
UF —Hospitals, charities, etc.
[Former subdivision]

——**American Legion**
H 1200
Use as a topical subdivision under individual wars.

——**Boy Scouts**
H 1200
Use as a topical subdivision under individual wars.

——**Catholic Church,** [**Methodist Church, etc.**]
H 1200
Use as a topical subdivision under individual wars.
BT —War work—Churches

——**Churches**
H 1200
Use as a topical subdivision under individual wars.
NT —War work—Catholic Church, [Methodist Church, etc.]

——**Elks**
H 1200
Use as a topical subdivision under individual wars.

——**Girl Scouts**
H 1200
Use as a topical subdivision under individual wars.

——**Red Cross**
H 1200
Use as a topical subdivision under individual wars.

——**Salvation Army**
H 1200
Use as a topical subdivision under individual wars.

——**Schools**
H 1200
Use as a topical subdivision under individual wars.

——**Young Men's Christian associations**
H 1200
Use as a topical subdivision under individual wars.

——**Young Women's Christian associations**
H 1200
Use as a topical subdivision under individual wars.

—**Warfare** *(May Subd Geog)*
H 1103
Use as a topical subdivision under ethnic groups for works on the group's methods and technology of waging war.

—**Warrant officers**
H 1159
Further subdivide by subdivisions used under classes of persons.
Use as a topical subdivision under military services.

—**Wars** *(May Subd Geog)*
H 1103
Use as a topical subdivision under ethnic groups for works discussing collectively the wars in which the group has participated.

—**Waste disposal** *(May Subd Geog)*
H 1095; H 1151.5; H 1153
Use as a topical subdivision under types of industries, industrial processes, facilities, and institutions.
UF —Disposal of wastes
NT —Finishing—Waste disposal
—Housing—Waste disposal
—Pickling—Waste disposal

—**Waste minimization** *(May Subd Geog)*
H 1095; H 1151.5; H 1153
Use as a topical subdivision under types of industries, industrial processes, facilities, and institutions.
UF —Minimization of wastes
NT —Finishing—Waste minimization

—**Watch duty**
H 1159
Use as a topical subdivision under individual navies.

—**Water requirements** *(May Subd Geog)*
H 1147; H 1180
Use as a topical subdivision under individual animals and groups of animals, and individual plants and groups of plants.
UF —Requirements, Water

—**Water rights**
H 1145.5
Use as a topical subdivision under names of individual bodies of water.

—**Water-supply**
H 1095; H 1153
Use as a topical subdivision under types of industries and other topical headings.

—**Weapons systems**
H 1159
Use as a topical subdivision under military services.

—**Web-based instruction** *(May Subd Geog)*
H 1095
Use as a topical subdivision under topical headings.
BT —Study and teaching

—Weblogs
USE —Blogs

—**Weed control** *(May Subd Geog)*
H 1180
Use as a topical subdivision under individual crops and groups of crops.

—**Weight**
H 1095; H 1147; H 1164
Use as a topical subdivision under types of objects, substances, individual animals and groups of animals, and organs and regions of the body for works on the techniques of making weight measurements of those items, or for the results of such measurements.
UF —Weight and measurement
[Former subdivision]

—Weight and measurement
USE —Weight
—Weights and measures

—**Weights and measures**
H 1095
Use as a topical subdivision under types of commodities and merchandise for systems of weights and measures of those groups or established for those items.
UF —Weight and measurement
[Former subdivision]

—**Weldability** *(May Subd Geog)*
H 1158
Use as a topical subdivision under individual materials and types of materials.

—**Welding** *(May Subd Geog)*
H 1149; H 1195
Use as a topical subdivision under individual chemicals and groups of chemicals and individual land vehicles and types of land vehicles.

—**Welsh authors**
H 1156
Use as a topical subdivision under individual literatures.

—**West Indian influences**
H 1156
Use as a topical subdivision under individual literatures.
BT —Foreign influences

—**Western influences**
H 1156
Use as a topical subdivision under individual literatures.
UF —Occidental influences
[Former subdivision]
BT —Foreign influences

—**Wheels**
H 1195
Use as a topical subdivision under individual land vehicles and types of land vehicles.

——**Alignment** *(May Subd Geog)*
H 1195
Use as a topical subdivision under individual land vehicles and types of land vehicles.
UF —Alignment of wheels

——**Balancing** *(May Subd Geog)*
H 1195
Use as a topical subdivision under individual land vehicles and types of land vehicles.
UF —Balancing of wheels

—**White authors**
H 1156
Use as a topical subdivision under individual literatures.

—**Will**
H 1110
Use as a topical subdivision under names of individual persons for discussions of the person's legal declaration regarding the disposition of the person's property or estate, including discussions or cases of contested wills.

—**Windows and windshields** *(May Subd Geog)*
H 1195
Use as a topical subdivision under individual land vehicles and types of land vehicles.
UF —Windshields

——**Law and legislation** *(May Subd Geog)*
H 1195
Further subdivide by subdivisions used under legal topics.
Use as a topical subdivision under individual land vehicles and types of land vehicles.
BT —Law and legislation

—Windshields
USE —Windows and windshields

—**Wintering** *(May Subd Geog)*
H 1147
Use as a topical subdivision under individual animals and groups of animals.

—Wiring, Electric
USE —Electric wiring

—**Women** *(May Subd Geog)*
H 1159; H 1200
Further subdivide by subdivisions used under classes of persons.
Do not subdivide geographically under military services.
Use as a topical subdivision under military services. Also use under individual wars for works on aspects of the war in relation to women, including its effect on them. For works on the participation of women in the military actions of the war, use the subdivision Participation, Female.
UF —Women's work
[Former subdivision]

—**Women authors**
H 1156
Use as a topical subdivision under individual literatures.
UF —Female authors

—**Women's reserves**
H 1159
Use as a topical subdivision under individual military services.
BT —Reserves

—Women's work
USE —Women

—**Word formation**
H 1154
Use as a topical subdivision under individual languages and groups of languages.
UF —Formation of words

—**Word frequency**
H 1154
Use as a topical subdivision under individual languages and groups of languages.
UF —Frequency of words

—Word indexes
USE —Concordances

—**Word order**
H 1154
Use as a topical subdivision under individual languages and groups of languages.
UF —Order of words

—Words, Code
USE —Code words

—Workbooks
USE —Problems, exercises, etc.

—Working conditions
USE —Employment

—**Workload** *(May Subd Geog)*
H 1100
Use as a topical subdivision under occupational groups and types of employees.

—**Wounds and injuries**   *(May Subd Geog)*
> H 1100; H 1103; H 1147; H 1164; H 1180
> Further subdivide by subdivisions used under diseases.
> Use as a topical subdivision under classes of persons, ethnic groups, individual animals and groups of animals, individual organs and regions of the body, and individual plants and groups of plants.
>> UF   —Accidents and injuries
>>> *[Former subdivision]*
>> —Injuries
>> NT   —Blunt trauma
>> —Fractures
>> —Frost damage
>> —Hemorrhage
>> —Herbicide injuries
>> —Radiation injuries
>> —Rupture

——**Diagnosis**   *(May Subd Geog)*
> H 1180
> Use as a topical subdivision under individual plants and groups of plants.
>> BT   —Diagnosis

—**Wrestling**
> H 1151
> Use as a topical subdivision under individual educational institutions.
>> BT   —Sports

—**Writing**
> H 1154
> Use as a topical subdivision under individual languages and groups of languages.

—Writing skill
> USE   —Literary art

—**Written works**
> H 1110
> Do not use under persons also known as literary authors.
> Use as a topical subdivision under names of persons active in the fine arts, music, and performing arts for discussions, listings, etc., of their non-literary textual works.

—Yearbooks
> USE   —Periodicals

—Yellow pages
> USE   —Telephone directories—Yellow pages

—**Yeomen**
> H 1159
> Further subdivde by subdivisions used under classes of persons.
> Use as a topical subdivision under military services.

—**Yiddish influences**
> H 1156
> Use as a topical subdivision under individual literatures.
>> BT   —Foreign influences

—Yield
> USE   —Yields

—**Yields**   *(May Subd Geog)*
> H 1180
> Use as a topical subdivision under individual plants and groups of plants.
>> UF   —Yield
>>> *[Former subdivision]*

—**Yoruba authors**
> H 1156
> Use as a topical subdivision under individual literatures.

—Youth
> H 1156
> Use as a topical subdivision under individual literatures.

Introduction to Library of Congress Genre/Form Terms for Library and Archival Materials

In 2007 the Library of Congress began a project to develop genre/form terms, which describe what a work *is*, rather than what it is *about*, as subject headings do. This introduction provides a brief history of the development of genre/form terms at LC and outlines the ways that genre/form terms differ from *LC Subject Headings* in application.

HISTORY

Library of Congress Subject Headings (*LCSH*) has for many decades included headings that denote what a work *is* rather than what it is *about* (e.g., **Horror films**, **Detective and mystery stories**, **Constitutions**). While these headings refer to genres and forms of works, that information is often not made explicit to library users, through notes, computer displays, or otherwise.

Since the 1980s the Library of Congress has supplemented *LCSH* by developing discipline-specific guides and thesauri of genre/form terms, including for example the *Thesaurus for Graphic Materials*, compiled by the Prints and Photographs Division; the *Radio Form-Genre Guide* and *Moving Image Genre-Form Guide*, both compiled by the Motion Picture, Broadcasting, and Recorded Sound Division (MBRS); and Martha M. Yee's *Moving Image Materials: Genre Terms*, which was coordinated by MBRS and published by LC's Cataloging Distribution Service. Additionally, other discipline-specific thesauri developed at the Library of Congress, such as the *Ethnographic Thesaurus* developed by the American Folklife Center and the *Children's Subject Headings*, include genre/form terms.

The Library of Congress has also used genre/form thesauri compiled by third parties, such as *Guidelines on Subject Access to Individual Works of Fiction, Drama, Etc.*, which is published by the American Library Association, and the *Art & Architecture Thesaurus*, developed by the Getty Art History Information Program and published by Oxford University Press. The LC online catalog also includes genre/form terms from *Medical Subject Headings (MeSH)*, a system that is developed and maintained by the U.S. National Library of Medicine.

The development of LC-authorized genre/form terms was undertaken in 2007 at the behest of the library community, which for many years has recognized the utility and value of such terms and has long petitioned the Library of Congress to create a genre/form list, along with policies for its use. LC genre/form terms mimic the structure of LC subject headings while incorporating terminology from other genre/form lists and thesauri. The intent is to develop a dynamic, multi-disciplinary body of genre/form terms that is cohesive, unified, intuitive, and user-friendly.

In 2007 a pilot project was conducted to establish genre/form terms in the area of moving images (films, television programs, and video recordings). The *Moving Image Genre-Form Guide* (*MIGFG*) and existing LC subject headings were used as the basis for development. Since the existing subject headings constitute a relatively small, defined subgroup of *LCSH*, the project would serve as an experiment to determine and resolve issues that would arise in the creation of genre/form terms. The resolutions would in turn serve as the model for future projects.

A second project, for radio program genre/form terms, was begun in late 2007. Based on the *Radio Form/Genre Guide* (*RADFG*) and LC subject headings, this project was smaller than the first, but it helped identify issues that will arise as terms for new disciplines are added to the genre/form term list.

In September 2007 the first moving image genre/form terms were approved and distributed through the Cataloging Distribution Service. Terms continue to be approved.

CONSISTENCY BETWEEN GENRE/FORM TERMS AND SUBJECT HEADINGS

In most cases, the wording of genre/form terms and subject headings is identical, although the headings serve different purposes (e.g., the genre/form term **Animated films** is identical to the subject heading **Animated films**). This assists searchers by allowing them to use the same terminology to discover works *about* a genre or form that they do to discover *examples of* the genre or form.

There are a few cases in which the same general concept is represented by both genre/form terms and subject headings, but the headings are phrased differently because of their different purposes. For example, a cinéma vérité film is entered under the genre/form term **Cinéma vérité films**, but a work about the cinéma vérité movement and style is entered under the subject heading **Cinéma vérité**.

There are also some genre/form terms that do not currently have an equivalent subject heading, and instead introduce new terminology (e.g., **Disc jockey radio programs**). Since *LCSH* is a dynamic system, it is anticipated that subject headings mimicking the genre/form terms will be proposed as they are needed for works *about* individual genres and forms.

Although the the wording of genre/form term and subject heading pairs is usually identical (as in the **Animated films** example above), computer systems and applications are able to distinguish between them based on MARC 21 tagging conventions. Genre/form terms employ MARC 21 tag 155 in authority records and tag 655 in bibliographic records, while topical subject headings use tags 150 and 650, respectively. This ability to differentiate on the basis of the MARC tag allows the two types of headings to be manipulated and searched separately if desired.

APPLICATION OF GENRE/FORM TERMS

The chief difference between genre/form terms and subject headings in the *LCSH* system lies in their application. Unlike most subject headings, genre/form terms are intended to be used as facets without further subdivision.

Full descriptions of the rules for the application of genre/form terms are provided in the *Subject Headings Manual* (*SHM*). Instruction sheets specific to the type of works being cataloged should be consulted (e.g., H 1969.5 provides

information about the application of genre/form terms for radio programs).

REFERENCES AND SCOPE NOTES

References within the genre/form terms follow the same rules that references for LC subject headings do. A note may also be included to define the scope of the genre/form term. The rules for references and scope notes are described in full in the *SHM*.

PRODUCTS

Four services provide information about new and revised genre/form terms.

1. Genre/form terms are distributed as part of the MARC Distribution Service Subject-Authorities product that provides records in MARC 21 and MARCMXL formats via FTP. This fee-based subscription service provides new and updated records on a weekly basis to supplement the master database of subject authority records.
2. New and changed genre/form terms appear on *LC Subject Headings Weekly Lists*, which are posted on the World Wide Web at http://www.loc.gov/aba/cataloging/subject/weeklylists/; free subscriptions to the *Weekly Lists*, via e-mail or RSS feed, can be arranged at <http://www.loc.gov/rss>.
3. Genre/form terms are included in *Classification Web*, a fee-based World Wide Web service that also provides access to *Library of Congress Subject Headings* and *Library of Congress Classification*.
4. Genre/form records are included in LC Authorities <http://authorities.loc.gov>, a free web-based database that allows for browsing, display, and download (in MARC 21 format) of the authority records.

COVERAGE

The genre/form list contains 582 terms established through December, 2009.

CONTACT

Questions and comments may be sent to:

> Policy and Standards Division
> Library of Congress
> 101 Independence Avenue, S.E.
> Washington, DC 20540-4262
> Phone: 202-707-4467
> Email: policy@loc.gov

3-D films *(Not Subd Geog)*
UF Stereoscopic films
Three-dimensional films
BT Motion pictures
3D game-based animated films
USE Machinima films
3D game-based films
USE Machinima films
Abstract animation films
USE Abstract films
Abstract films *(Not Subd Geog)*
This heading is used as a genre/form heading for nonrepresentational films that avoid narrative and instead convey impressions and emotions by way of color, rhythm and movement.
UF Abstract animation films
Abstract live action films
Concrete films
Nonobjective films
Nonrepresentational films
BT Experimental films
RT Animated films
Abstract live action films
USE Abstract films
Action-adventure films
USE Action and adventure films
Action and adventure films *(Not Subd Geog)*
UF Action-adventure films
Action films
Action movies
Adventure and action films
Adventure films
Adventure movies
BT Motion pictures
RT Swashbuckler films
NT Flash Gordon films
Indiana Jones films
James Bond films
Jungle films
Martial arts films
Action and adventure television programs
(Not Subd Geog)
UF Action television programs
Adventure and action television programs
Adventure television programs
BT Television programs
NT Indiana Jones television programs
Jungle television programs
Action films
USE Action and adventure films
Action films, Black
USE Blaxploitation films
Action movies
USE Action and adventure films

Action television programs
USE Action and adventure television programs
Actualités (Motion pictures)
USE Actualities (Motion pictures)
Actualities (Motion pictures)
(Not Subd Geog)
This heading is used as a genre/form heading for short, unedited, silent films, primarily from the period of early cinema, that portray daily life or specific events or occurrences as filmed by a camera in a fixed location without commentary.
UF Actualités (Motion pictures)
Actuality films
BT Nonfiction films
Short films
Silent films
RT Documentary films
Newsreels
Actuality films
USE Actualities (Motion pictures)
Adaptations, Film
USE Film adaptations
Adaptations, Radio
USE Radio adaptations
Adaptations, Television
USE Television adaptations
Addresses (Motion pictures)
USE Filmed speeches
Addresses, Radio
USE Radio speeches
Addresses, Television
USE Televised speeches
Ads, Radio
USE Radio commercials (Advertisements)
Ads, Television
USE Television commercials
Adult films (Pornographic films)
USE Pornographic films
Adventure and action films
USE Action and adventure films
Adventure and action television programs
USE Action and adventure television programs
Adventure films
USE Action and adventure films
Adventure movies
USE Action and adventure films
Adventure radio programs
UF Radio adventure programs
BT Radio programs
Adventure television programs
USE Action and adventure television programs

Advertisements, Radio
USE Radio commercials (Advertisements)
Advertisements, Television
USE Television commercials
Advertising films
USE Promotional films
Air checks, Radio
USE Radio airchecks
Air movies
USE Aviation films
Airchecks, Radio
USE Radio airchecks
Airplane films
USE Aviation films
Alien films *(Not Subd Geog)*
This heading is used as a genre/form heading for films that feature the character Ellen Ripley, Aliens, Alien 3, and Alien resurrection.
BT Science fiction films
Amateur films *(Not Subd Geog)*
UF Home movies
Home videos
Personal films
BT Motion pictures
NT Fan films
Amateur talent shows (Radio programs)
USE Talent shows (Radio programs)
Amusement ride films *(Not Subd Geog)*
UF Ride films
Ride movies
Thrill ride films
BT Motion pictures
Andy Hardy films *(Not Subd Geog)*
BT Motion pictures
Angel films *(Not Subd Geog)*
BT Fantasy films
Angélique films *(Not Subd Geog)*
BT Motion pictures
Animal films *(Not Subd Geog)*
BT Motion pictures
Animal television programs *(Not Subd Geog)*
BT Television programs
Animated cartoons (Motion pictures)
USE Animated films
Animated films *(Not Subd Geog)*
This heading is used as a genre/form heading for films that create the illusion of movement in drawings, clay, inanimate objects, or the like, through an animation technique.
UF Animated cartoons (Motion pictures)
Cartoons, Animated (Motion pictures)
Motion picture cartoons
BT Motion pictures
RT Abstract films
NT Cameraless animation films
Clay animation films

Animated films   *(Continued)*
    Computer animation films
    Cutout animation films
    Live-action/animation films
    Machinima films
    Pixilated animation films
    Private Snafu films
    Silhouette animation films
    Tom and Jerry films
Animated/live-action films, Hybrid
  USE   Live-action/animation films
Animated television programs
(Not Subd Geog)
    This heading is used as a genre/form heading for television programs that create the illusion of movement in drawings, clay, inanimate objects, or the like, through an animation technique.
  UF   Cartoons (Television programs)
     Television cartoon shows
  BT   Television programs
  NT   Clay animation television programs
     Computer animation television
      programs
     Pink Panther television programs
     Scooby-Doo television programs
Animation and live-action films, Combination
  USE   Live-action/animation films
Animation/live-action films, Hybrid
  USE   Live-action/animation films
Announcements, Theater (Motion pictures)
  USE   Theater announcements (Motion
     pictures)
Anthologies (Motion pictures)
  USE   Anthology films
Anthologies, Radio
  USE   Radio anthologies
Anthologies (Television programs)
  USE   Anthology television programs
Anthology films   *(Not Subd Geog)*
    This heading is used as a genre/form heading for feature-length films made up of different episodes or stories which are usually connected by a theme, event, location or original author, often having a wraparound tale.   Films that are composed of pre-existing published or unpublished films, or portions thereof, are entered under Compilation films.
  UF   Anthologies (Motion pictures)
     Composite films
     Episode films
     Episodic films
     Omnibus films
     Portmanteau films
     Sketch films
  BT   Motion pictures
Anthology radio programs
  USE   Radio anthologies
Anthology television programs
(Not Subd Geog)
    This heading is used as a genre/form heading for television programs made up of different episodes or stories which are usually connected by a theme, event, location or original author, often having a wraparound tale. Television programs that are composed of pre-existing broadcast or unbroadcast television programs, or portions thereof, are entered under Compilation television programs.
  UF   Anthologies (Television programs)
     Omnibus television programs
  BT   Television programs
Anthropological films
  USE   Ethnographic films
Anthropological television programs
  USE   Ethnographic television programs
Anti-militarism films
  USE   Anti-war films
Anti-militarism television programs
  USE   Anti-war television programs

Anti-war films   *(Not Subd Geog)*
  UF   Anti-militarism films
     Antimilitarism films
     Antiwar films
     Pacifist films
  BT   Motion pictures
  RT   War films
Anti-war television programs
(Not Subd Geog)
  UF   Anti-militarism television programs
     Antimilitarism television programs
     Antiwar television programs
     Pacifist television programs
  BT   Television programs
  RT   War television programs
Antimilitarism films
  USE   Anti-war films
Antimilitarism television programs
  USE   Anti-war television programs
Antiwar films
  USE   Anti-war films
Antiwar television programs
  USE   Anti-war television programs
Arts television programs
  USE   Cultural television programs
Audience participation radio programs
  UF   Radio audience participation shows
  BT   Radio talk shows
  RT   Radio call-in shows
Audience participation television programs
(Not Subd Geog)
  BT   Nonfiction television programs
  RT   Television talk shows
Audio books
  USE   Audiobooks
Audio interviews
  USE   Interviews (Sound recordings)
Audiobooks
  UF   Audio books
     Books, Audio
     Books, Cassette
     Books on tape
     Books, Recorded
     Cassette books
     Recorded books
  BT   Sound recordings
  NT   Talking books
Auditions, Film
  USE   Screen tests
Auditions, Motion picture
  USE   Screen tests
Auditions, Radio
  USE   Radio auditions
Auditions, Television
  USE   Screen tests
Autobiographical films   *(Not Subd Geog)*
  BT   Biographical films
Autobiographical television programs
(Not Subd Geog)
  BT   Nonfiction television programs
Avant-garde films
  USE   Experimental films
Aviation films   *(Not Subd Geog)*
  UF   Air movies
     Airplane films
     Flying films
  BT   Motion pictures
Aviation television programs
(Not Subd Geog)
  BT   Television programs
Award presentation films
  USE   Award presentations (Motion pictures)
Award presentation television programs
  USE   Award presentations (Television
     programs)

Award presentations (Motion pictures)
(Not Subd Geog)
    This heading is used as a genre/form heading for films that record the presentation of awards or prizes.
  UF   Award presentation films
     Awards ceremonies (Motion pictures)
     Awards presentations (Motion pictures)
     Filmed award presentations
     Presentations, Award (Motion pictures)
  BT   Nonfiction films
Award presentations (Television programs)
(Not Subd Geog)
    This heading is used as a genre/form heading for television programs that record the presentation of awards or prizes.
  UF   Award presentation television programs
     Awards ceremonies (Television
      programs)
     Awards presentations (Television
      programs)
     Television award presentations
  BT   Nonfiction television programs
Awards ceremonies (Motion pictures)
  USE   Award presentations (Motion pictures)
Awards ceremonies (Television programs)
  USE   Award presentations (Television
     programs)
Awards presentations (Motion pictures)
  USE   Award presentations (Motion pictures)
Awards presentations (Television programs)
  USE   Award presentations (Television
     programs)
B films   *(Not Subd Geog)*
    This heading is used as a genre/form heading for low budget feature films that were usually shown in a double feature program along with the major production, the A film.
  UF   B movies
     B pictures
  BT   Low budget films
B movies
  USE   B films
B pictures
  USE   B films
Ballet films
  BT   Dance films
  NT   Filmed ballets
Ballet television programs   *(Not Subd Geog)*
  BT   Dance television programs
  NT   Televised ballets
Bandit gangster films
  USE   Gangster films
Baseball films   *(Not Subd Geog)*
  BT   Sports films
Baseball television programs
(Not Subd Geog)
  BT   Sports television programs
  NT   Televised baseball games
Basketball films   *(Not Subd Geog)*
  UF   Cage films (Basketball films)
  BT   Sports films
Basketball television programs
(Not Subd Geog)
  BT   Sports television programs
  NT   Televised basketball games
Batman and Robin films
  USE   Batman films
Batman films   *(Not Subd Geog)*
  UF   Batman and Robin films
  BT   Superhero films
Beach-blanket films
  USE   Beach party films
Beach-bunny films
  USE   Beach party films
Beach party films   *(Not Subd Geog)*
    This heading is used as a genre/form heading for films that feature groups of teens who gather on the beach to party, surf, etc.
  UF   Beach-blanket films
     Beach-bunny films
     Sand-and-surf films
     Sun-and-sand films
  BT   Teen films

Beauty contest films (*Not Subd Geog*)
     This heading is used as a genre/form heading for films of competitions in which the entrants are judged as to physical beauty and sometimes personality and talent, with the winners awarded prizes or titles.
     UF Beauty contests (Motion pictures)
          Beauty pageant films
          Beauty pageants (Motion pictures)
     BT Nonfiction films
Beauty contest television programs
     (*Not Subd Geog*)
     This heading is used as a genre/form heading for television programs of competitions in which the entrants are judged as to physical beauty and sometimes personality and talent, with the winners awarded prizes or titles.
     UF Beauty contests (Television programs)
          Beauty pageant television programs
          Beauty pageants (Television programs)
     BT Nonfiction television programs
Beauty contests (Motion pictures)
     USE Beauty contest films
Beauty contests (Television programs)
     USE Beauty contest television programs
Beauty pageant films
     USE Beauty contest films
Beauty pageant television programs
     USE Beauty contest television programs
Beauty pageants (Motion pictures)
     USE Beauty contest films
Beauty pageants (Television programs)
     USE Beauty contest television programs
Bergfilme
     USE Mountain films
Bible films (*Not Subd Geog*)
     This heading is used as a genre/form heading for film versions of Biblical stories.
     UF Biblical films
     BT Religious films
Bible television programs (*Not Subd Geog*)
     This heading is used as a genre/form heading for television versions of Biblical stories.
     UF Biblical television programs
     BT Religious television programs
Biblical films
     USE Bible films
Biblical television programs
     USE Bible television programs
Big Brother television programs
     (*Not Subd Geog*)
     BT Reality television programs
Big-caper films
     USE Caper films
Big-caper television programs
     USE Caper television programs
Biker films
     USE Motorcycle films
Bildungsfilms
     USE Coming-of-age films
Bio-pics
     USE Biographical films
Biographical films (*Not Subd Geog*)
     This heading is used as a genre/form heading for films that depict lives of real people.
     UF Bio-pics
          Biopics
          Film biographies
          Screen biographies
     BT Motion pictures
     NT Autobiographical films
Biographical radio programs
     UF Radio biographies
     BT Nonfiction radio programs

Biographical television programs
     (*Not Subd Geog*)
     This heading is used as a genre/form heading for television programs that depict the lives of real people.
     UF Portraits (Biographical television
               programs)
          Profiles (Biographical television
               programs)
          Television biographies
     BT Television programs
Biopics
     USE Biographical films
Black action films
     USE Blaxploitation films
Black comedy films
     USE Dark comedy films
Black comedy television programs
     USE Dark comedy television programs
Black exploitation films
     USE Blaxploitation films
Blacksploitation films
     USE Blaxploitation films
Blaxploitation films (*Not Subd Geog*)
     UF Action films, Black
          Black action films
          Black exploitation films
          Blacksploitation films
          Exploitation films, Black
     BT Motion pictures
Blue movies
     USE Pornographic films
Bond films
     USE James Bond films
Book review programs, Radio
     USE Book review radio programs
Book review programs, Television
     USE Book review television programs
Book review radio programs
     UF Book review programs, Radio
          Radio book review programs
     BT Nonfiction radio programs
Book review television programs
     (*Not Subd Geog*)
     UF Book review programs, Television
          Television book review programs
     BT Nonfiction television programs
Books, Audio
     USE Audiobooks
Books, Cassette
     USE Audiobooks
Books, Filmed
     USE Film adaptations
Books on tape
     USE Audiobooks
Books, Recorded
     USE Audiobooks
Bowery Boys films (*Not Subd Geog*)
     UF Dead End Kids films
          Eastside Kids films
     BT Motion pictures
Boxing films (*Not Subd Geog*)
     UF Fight films
          Prize-fight films
          Prize-fighting films
          Prizefight films
          Prizefighting films
     BT Sports films
     NT Filmed boxing matches
Broadcasts, Shortwave radio
     USE Shortwave radio broadcasts
Buddy films (*Not Subd Geog*)
     BT Motion pictures
Buddy television programs (*Not Subd Geog*)
     BT Television programs
Business films
     USE Industrial films
Cage films (Basketball films)
     USE Basketball films
Call-in radio programs
     USE Radio call-in shows

Call-in radio shows
     USE Radio call-in shows
Cameraless animated films
     USE Cameraless animation films
Cameraless animation films (*Not Subd Geog*)
     This heading is used as a genre/form heading for films created by drawing, painting, or scratching the images directly on film stock.
     UF Cameraless animated films
          Direct animation films
          Direct-on film animation films
          Drawn-on films
          Graphic animation films
          Hand-drawn films
          Noncamera films
          Out-of-camera films
     BT Animated films
Campaign commercials
     USE Political television commercials
Campaign debates (Radio programs)
     USE Radio debates
Campaign spots (Television commercials)
     USE Political television commercials
Campus films
     USE College life films
Caper films (*Not Subd Geog*)
     This heading is used as a genre/form heading for films that feature the execution of a particularly difficult undertaking, often questionable or illegal, the success of which depends on skill and careful planning.
     UF Big-caper films
          Heist films
     BT Motion pictures
     RT Crime films
Caper television programs (*Not Subd Geog*)
     This heading is used as a genre/form heading for television programs that feature the execution of a particularly difficult undertaking, often questionable or illegal, the success of which depends on skill and careful planning.
     UF Big-caper television programs
          Heist television programs
     BT Television programs
     RT Television crime shows
Captioned films
     USE Films for the hearing impaired
Captioned television programs
     USE Television programs for the hearing
               impaired
Captioned video recordings
     USE Video recordings for the hearing
               impaired
Car-chase films (*Not Subd Geog*)
     UF Car-crash films
          Crash-and-wreck films
     BT Motion pictures
Car-crash films
     USE Car-chase films
Carmen films (*Not Subd Geog*)
     BT Motion pictures
Carry On films (*Not Subd Geog*)
     BT Comedy films
Cartoons, Animated (Motion pictures)
     USE Animated films
Cartoons (Television programs)
     USE Animated television programs
Cassette books
     USE Audiobooks
Catastrophe films
     USE Disaster films
CG films (Computer animation)
     USE Computer animation films
CG television programs (Computer animation)
     USE Computer animation television
               programs
CGI films (Computer animation)
     USE Computer animation films
CGI television programs (Computer animation)
     USE Computer animation television
               programs

Chambara films
  USE Samurai films
Chapterplay films
  USE Film serials
Charlie Chan films *(Not Subd Geog)*
  BT Detective and mystery films
Chase films *(Not Subd Geog)*
  This heading is used as a genre/form heading for short films, primarily from the early period of cinema, in which an incident results in someone being chased, usually by a steadily-growing group of people.
  UF Chaser films
    Runaway films
  BT Short films
Chaser films
  USE Chase films
Chick flicks
  USE Romance films
Children's films *(Not Subd Geog)*
  This heading is used as a genre/form heading for films produced especially for children.
  UF Juvenile films
  BT Motion pictures
Children's radio programs
  This heading is used as a genre/form heading for radio programs produced especially for children.
  BT Radio programs
Children's television programs
(Not Subd Geog)
  This heading is used as a genre/form heading for television programs produced especially for children.
  UF Juvenile television programs
  BT Television programs
Christian films *(Not Subd Geog)*
  BT Religious films
Christian radio programs
  BT Religious radio programs
Christian television programs
(Not Subd Geog)
  BT Religious television programs
Christmas films *(Not Subd Geog)*
  UF Christmas movies
  BT Motion pictures
Christmas movies
  USE Christmas films
Christmas radio programs
  BT Radio programs
Christmas television programs
(Not Subd Geog)
  UF Christmas television specials
    Christmas TV specials
  BT Television programs
Christmas television specials
  USE Christmas television programs
Christmas TV specials
  USE Christmas television programs
Cinéma noir
  USE Film noir
Cinéma vérité films *(Not Subd Geog)*
  UF Direct cinema films
    Truth cinema films
  BT Documentary films
Cisco Kid films *(Not Subd Geog)*
  BT Western films
City symphonies (Motion pictures)
(Not Subd Geog)
  This heading is used as a genre/form heading for films that use a montage of images of a city and city life to capture the essence of a particular city.
  UF City symphony films
  BT Nonfiction films
City symphony films
  USE City symphonies (Motion pictures)
Classical music radio programs
  UF Western art music radio programs
  BT Radio programs
Clay animation films *(Not Subd Geog)*
  UF Claymation films
    Sculptmation films
  BT Animated films

Clay animation television programs
(Not Subd Geog)
  UF Claymation television programs
    Sculptmation television programs
  BT Animated television programs
Claymation films
  USE Clay animation films
Claymation television programs
  USE Clay animation television programs
Cliffhanger films
  USE Film serials
Clips, Film
  USE Film clips
Clips, Radio program
  USE Radio program excerpts
Clips, Television program
  USE Television program clips
Cloak and dagger films
  USE Spy films
Closed caption video recordings
  USE Video recordings for the hearing
    impaired
Closed captioned films
  USE Films for the hearing impaired
Closed captioned television programs
  USE Television programs for the hearing
    impaired
Collage animation films
  USE Cutout animation films
College football films
  USE Football films
College life films *(Not Subd Geog)*
  UF Campus films
    Collegiate films
  BT Motion pictures
College life television programs
(Not Subd Geog)
  BT Television programs
Collegiate films
  USE College life films
Combat films
  USE War films
Combination animation and live-action films
  USE Live-action/animation films
Combination live-action and animation films
  USE Live-action/animation films
Comedies, Radio
  USE Radio comedies
Comedies, Television
  USE Television comedies
Comedy-drama films
  USE Comedy films
Comedy-drama television programs
  USE Television comedies
Comedy fantasy films
  USE Fantasy comedies (Motion pictures)
Comedy fantasy television programs
  USE Fantasy comedies (Television programs)
Comedy films *(Not Subd Geog)*
  UF Comedy-drama films
    Farces (Motion pictures)
    Farcical films
  BT Motion pictures
  NT Carry On films
    Dark comedy films
    Domestic comedy films
    Fantasy comedies (Motion pictures)
    Filmed stand-up comedy routines
    Parody films
    Romantic comedy films
    Rural comedy films
    Screwball comedy films
    Slapstick comedy films
    Sophisticated comedy films
    Three Stooges films
    Trapalhões films
Comedy programs, Radio
  USE Radio comedies
Comedy programs, Television
  USE Television comedies

Comedy radio programs
  USE Radio comedies
Comedy television programs
  USE Television comedies
Comic strip superhero films
  USE Superhero films
Comic strip superheroes films
  USE Superhero films
Coming-of-age films *(Not Subd Geog)*
  UF Bildungsfilms
    Rite of passage films
  BT Teen films
Coming-of-age television programs
(Not Subd Geog)
  UF Rite of passage television programs
  BT Teen television programs
Commentaries, Radio
  USE Radio commentaries
Commercials, Radio (Advertisements)
  USE Radio commercials (Advertisements)
Commercials, Television
  USE Television commercials
Commissario Montalbano television programs
(Not Subd Geog)
  UF Montalbano television programs,
    Commissario
  BT Television programs
Community access television programs
  USE Public access television programs
Community affairs radio programs
  This heading is used as a genre/form heading for radio programs that provide information about issues or events concerning a community or locale.
  BT Nonfiction radio programs
Community service announcements (Motion
pictures)
  USE Public service announcements (Motion
    pictures)
Community service announcements, Radio
  USE Radio public service announcements
Community television programs
  USE Public access television programs
Company promotion films
  USE Promotional films
Compilation films *(Not Subd Geog)*
  This heading is used as a genre/form heading for films that are composed of pre-existing published or unpublished films, or portions thereof. Feature-length films made up of different episodes or stories which are usually connected by a theme, event, location or original author, often having a wrap-around tale are entered under Anthology films.
  UF Compilation reels (Motion pictures)
    Compilations (Motion pictures)
  BT Motion pictures
Compilation radio programs
  This heading is used as a genre/form heading for radio programs that are composed of pre-existing broadcast or unbroadcast radio programs, or portions thereof. Radio programs made up of different episodes or stories which are usually connected by a theme, event, location or original author, often having a wrap-around tale, are entered under Radio anthologies.
  UF Compilations, Radio
    Radio compilations
  BT Radio programs
Compilation reels (Motion pictures)
  USE Compilation films
Compilation reels (Television programs)
  USE Compilation television programs
Compilation television programs
(Not Subd Geog)
  This heading is used as a genre/form heading for television programs that are composed of pre-existing broadcast or unbroadcast television programs, or portions thereof. Television programs made up of different episodes or stories which are usually connected by a theme, event, location or original author, often having a wrap-around tale are entered under Anthology television programs.
  UF Compilation reels (Television programs)
    Compilations (Television programs)
  BT Television programs

Compilations (Motion pictures)
  USE Compilation films
Compilations, Radio
  USE Compilation radio programs
Compilations (Television programs)
  USE Compilation television programs
Composite films
  USE Anthology films
Computer animated films
  USE Computer animation films
Computer animated television programs
  USE Computer animation television
        programs
Computer animation films   *(Not Subd Geog)*
  UF CG films (Computer animation)
      CGI films (Computer animation)
      Computer animated films
  BT Animated films
Computer animation television programs
  (Not Subd Geog)
  UF CG television programs (Computer
        animation)
      CGI television programs (Computer
        animation)
      Computer animated television programs
  BT Animated television programs
Concert films   *(Not Subd Geog)*
    This heading is used as a genre/form heading for
  films of musical concert performances recorded in
  front of a live audience.
  UF In-concert films
      Live concert films
      Live-in-concert films
  BT Nonfiction films
  RT Musical films
  NT Rock concert films
Concert television programs   *(Not Subd Geog)*
    This heading is used as a genre/form heading for
  television programs of musical concert performances
  recorded in front of a live audience.
  UF Television concerts
  BT Nonfiction television programs
  RT Television musicals
Concrete films
  USE Abstract films
Contests, Radio
  USE Radio game shows
      Radio quiz shows
Continuing education radio programs
  USE Educational radio programs
Continuous films
  USE Loop films
Continuous motion pictures
  USE Loop films
Cooking shows, Television
  USE Television cooking shows
Cooking television programs
  USE Television cooking shows
Cop films
  USE Police films
Cop television programs
  USE Television cop shows
Costume spectacles (Motion pictures)
  USE Epic films
Costume spectacles (Television programs)
  USE Epic television programs
Country and western music radio programs
  USE Country music radio programs
Country music radio programs
  UF Country and western music radio
        programs
      Hillbilly music radio programs
      Music radio programs, Country and
        western
      Music radio programs, Hillbilly
      Music radio programs, Western and
        country
      Western and country music radio
        programs
  BT Radio programs
Courtroom films
  USE Legal films

Courtroom television programs
  USE Legal television programs
Cowboy and Indian films
  USE Western films
Cowboy films
  USE Western films
Crash-and-wreck films
  USE Car-chase films
Crazy comedy films
  USE Screwball comedy films
Creature features (Motion pictures)
  USE Monster films
Crime films   *(Not Subd Geog)*
    This heading is used as a genre/form heading for
  fictional films that feature the commission and inves-
  tigation of crimes.
  UF Criminal films
  BT Fiction films
  RT Caper films
      Thrillers (Motion pictures)
  NT Detective and mystery films
      Film noir
      Gangster films
      Juvenile delinquency films
      Police films
      Prison films
Crime programs, Radio
  USE Radio crime shows
Crime reenactment television programs
  USE True crime television programs
Crime shows, Radio
  USE Radio crime shows
Crime television programs
  USE Television crime shows
Criminal films
  USE Crime films
Criminal radio programs
  USE Radio crime shows
Criminal shows
  USE Television crime shows
Criminal television programs
  USE Television crime shows
CSAs (Motion pictures)
  USE Public service announcements (Motion
        pictures)
CSAs, Radio
  USE Radio public service announcements
CSAs, Television
  USE Television public service
        announcements
Cult films, Subculture
  USE Subculture films
Cultural television programs
  (Not Subd Geog)
  UF Arts television programs
  BT Television programs
  NT Dance television programs
Cut-out animation films
  USE Cutout animation films
Cutout animation films   *(Not Subd Geog)*
  UF Collage animation films
      Cut-out animation films
      Paper cut-out animation films
  BT Animated films
Dailies (Motion pictures)
  USE Rushes (Motion pictures)
Dailies (Television programs)
  USE Rushes (Television programs)
Dance films
  BT Motion pictures
  NT Ballet films
      Filmed dance
Dance parties, Television
  USE Television dance parties
Dance television programs
  BT Cultural television programs
  NT Ballet television programs
      Televised dance

Dark comedy films   *(Not Subd Geog)*
    This heading is used as a genre/form heading for
  films that treat serious and often tragic subjects in a
  comic fashion.
  UF Black comedy films
  BT Comedy films
Dark comedy television programs
  (Not Subd Geog)
    This heading is used as a genre/form heading for
  television programs that treat serious and often tragic
  subjects in a comic fashion.
  UF Black comedy television programs
  BT Television comedies
Dark crime films
  USE Film noir
De Grassi television programs
  USE DeGrassi television programs
Dead End Kids films
  USE Bowery Boys films
Deaf, Video recordings for the
  USE Video recordings for the hearing
        impaired
Debates, Radio
  USE Radio debates
Debates, Television
  USE Television debates
Deejay radio programs
  USE Disc jockey radio programs
DeGrassi television programs
  (Not Subd Geog)
  UF De Grassi television programs
  BT Television programs
Detective and mystery films   *(Not Subd Geog)*
  UF Murder mystery films
      Mystery films
      Private eye films
      Who-done-it films
      Whodunit films
      Whodunnit films
  BT Crime films
  RT Police films
  NT Charlie Chan films
      Fantômas films
      Sherlock Holmes films
Detective and mystery radio programs
  UF Detective radio programs
      Mystery radio programs
      Private eye radio programs
  BT Radio crime shows
Detective and mystery television programs
  (Not Subd Geog)
  UF Murder mystery television programs
      Mystery television programs
      Private eye television programs
      Who-done-it television programs
  BT Television crime shows
  RT Television cop shows
  NT Sherlock Holmes television programs
Detective radio programs
  USE Detective and mystery radio programs
Direct animation films
  USE Cameraless animation films
Direct cinema films
  USE Cinéma vérité films
Direct-on film animation films
  USE Cameraless animation films
Disaster films   *(Not Subd Geog)*
    This heading is used as a genre/form heading for
  films that feature a man-made or natural calamity that
  places people in imminent danger. Films that feature
  individuals or groups struggling for their lives in a
  harsh setting are entered under Survival films.
  UF Catastrophe films
      Disaster movies
  BT Motion pictures
  RT Survival films
Disaster movies
  USE Disaster films

Disaster television programs   *(Not Subd Geog)*
This heading is used as a genre/form heading for television programs that feature a man-made or natural calamity that places people in imminent danger. Television programs that feature individuals or groups struggling for their lives in a harsh setting are entered under Survival television programs.
BT   Television programs
RT   Survival television programs

Disc jockey radio programs
This heading is used as a genre/form heading for radio programs in which a host introduces and plays recorded music.
UF   Deejay radio programs
Disk jockey radio programs
DJ radio programs
BT   Radio programs

Discussion shows, Radio
USE   Radio panel discussions

Discussion shows (Television programs)
USE   Television panel discussions

Discussion television programs
USE   Television panel discussions

Disk jockey radio programs
USE   Disc jockey radio programs

DJ radio programs
USE   Disc jockey radio programs

Doctor films (Motion pictures)
USE   Medical films (Motion pictures)

Doctor Mabuse films   *(Not Subd Geog)*
UF   Doktor Mabuse films
Dr. Mabuse films
BT   Motion pictures

Doctor radio programs
USE   Medical radio programs

Doctor television programs
USE   Medical television programs

Docudramas (Motion pictures)
USE   Historical films

Docudramas, Radio
USE   Radio docudramas

Docudramas (Television programs)
USE   Historical television programs

Documentaries, Fake (Motion pictures)
USE   Documentary-style films

Documentaries, Fake (Television programs)
USE   Documentary-style television programs

Documentaries, Motion picture
USE   Documentary films

Documentaries, Radio
USE   Documentary radio programs

Documentaries, Television
USE   Documentary television programs

Documentary films   *(Not Subd Geog)*
UF   Documentaries, Motion picture
Factual films
Motion picture documentaries
BT   Nonfiction films
RT   Actualities (Motion pictures)
NT   Cinéma vérité films
Educational films
Ethnographic films
Historical reenactments (Motion pictures)
Travelogues (Motion pictures)

Documentary films, Fake
USE   Documentary-style films

Documentary films, Fictionalized
USE   Documentary-style films

Documentary films, Mock
USE   Documentary-style films

Documentary programs, Television
USE   Documentary television programs

Documentary radio programs
UF   Documentaries, Radio
Radio documentaries
BT   Nonfiction radio programs
NT   Travelogues (Radio programs)

Documentary-style films   *(Not Subd Geog)*
This heading is used as a genre/form heading for fictional films made to resemble documentary films.
UF   Documentaries, Fake (Motion pictures)
Documentary films, Fake
Documentary films, Fictionalized
Documentary films, Mock
Fake documentaries (Motion pictures)
Fake documentary films
Fictionalized documentary films
Mock documentary films
Mockumentaries
Mockumentary films
Pseudo-documentary films
Quasi-documentary films
Semidocumentary films
BT   Fiction films

Documentary-style television programs
(Not Subd Geog)
This heading is used as a genre/form heading for fictional television programs made to resemble documentary television programs.
UF   Documentaries, Fake (Television programs)
Documentary television programs, Fake
Documentary television programs, Fictionalized
Documentary television programs, Mock
Fake documentaries (Television programs)
Fake documentary television programs
Fictionalized documentary television programs
Mock documentary television programs
Mockumentaries (Television programs)
Mockumentary television programs
Pseudo-documentary television programs
Quasi-documentary television programs
Semidocumentary television programs
BT   Fiction television programs

Documentary television programs
(Not Subd Geog)
UF   Documentaries, Television
Documentary programs, Television
Telementaries
Television documentaries
Television documentary programs
BT   Nonfiction television programs
NT   Educational television programs
Ethnographic television programs
Historical reenactments (Television programs)
Travelogues (Television programs)

Documentary television programs, Fake
USE   Documentary-style television programs

Documentary television programs, Fictionalized
USE   Documentary-style television programs

Documentary television programs, Mock
USE   Documentary-style television programs

Doktor Mabuse films
USE   Doctor Mabuse films

Domestic comedy films   *(Not Subd Geog)*
This heading is used as a genre/form heading for films that find humor in domestic situations and are normally set in the home.
UF   Family comedy films
BT   Comedy films

Domestic comedy television programs
(Not Subd Geog)
This heading is used as a genre/form heading for television programs that find humor in domestic situations and are usually set in the home.
UF   Family comedy television programs
BT   Television comedies
RT   Situation comedies (Television programs)

Don Camillo films   *(Not Subd Geog)*
BT   Motion pictures

Don Juan films   *(Not Subd Geog)*
BT   Motion pictures

Don Juan television programs
(Not Subd Geog)
BT   Television programs

Dr. Mabuse films
USE   Doctor Mabuse films

Dracula films   *(Not Subd Geog)*
BT   Vampire films

Dracula television programs   *(Not Subd Geog)*
BT   Vampire television programs

Dramatic-narrative films
USE   Fiction films

Dramatic readings (Radio programs)
USE   Literary readings (Radio programs)

Drawn-on films
USE   Cameraless animation films

Dystopia films
USE   Dystopian films

Dystopian films   *(Not Subd Geog)*
UF   Dystopia films
BT   Science fiction films
NT   Planet of the Apes films

Eastside Kids films
USE   Bowery Boys films

Editorials, Radio
USE   Radio commentaries

Educational films   *(Not Subd Geog)*
This heading is used as a genre/form heading for films that are intended to impart knowledge and information, including those for classroom viewing. Films that use a structured format to teach or train the audience are entered under Instructional films.
UF   Informational films
BT   Documentary films
NT   Science films
Social guidance films

Educational radio programs
This heading is used as a genre/form heading for radio programs intended to impart knowledge and information. Radio programs that use a structured format to teach or train the audience are entered under Instructional radio programs.
UF   Continuing education radio programs
Informational radio programs
BT   Radio programs
RT   Instructional radio programs
NT   Science radio programs

Educational television programs
(Not Subd Geog)
This heading is used as a genre/form heading for television programs intended to impart knowledge and information. Television programs that use a structured format to teach or train the audience are entered under Instructional television programs.
UF   Informational television programs
BT   Documentary television programs
NT   Science television programs

Entertainment films
USE   Fiction films

Entertainment news programs
(Not Subd Geog)
UF   Entertainment news shows (Television programs)
BT   Television news programs

Entertainment news shows (Television programs)
USE   Entertainment news programs

Environmental films   *(Not Subd Geog)*
BT   Motion pictures

Epic films   *(Not Subd Geog)*
This heading is used as a genre/form heading for films that employ large casts and lavish sets to depict action on a grand scale.
UF   Costume spectacles (Motion pictures)
Film epics
Heroic films
Monumental films
Spectacles (Motion pictures)
Spectaculars (Motion pictures)
BT   Motion pictures

Epic television programs *(Not Subd Geog)*
This heading is used as a genre/form heading for television programs that employ large casts and lavish sets to depict action on a grand scale.
UF Costume spectacles (Television programs)
Heroic television programs
Monumental television programs
Spectacles (Television programs)
Spectaculars (Television programs)
Television epics
BT Television programs
Episode films
USE Anthology films
Film serials
Episodes, Web
USE Webisodes
Episodic films
USE Anthology films
Erotic films *(Not Subd Geog)*
BT Motion pictures
RT Pornographic films
NT Gay erotic films
Schulmädchen-Report films
Erotic television programs *(Not Subd Geog)*
BT Television programs
RT Pornographic television programs
Espionage films
USE Spy films
Espionage radio programs
USE Spy radio programs
Espionage television programs
USE Spy television programs
Ethnic broadcasts (Radio programs)
USE Ethnic radio programs
Ethnic films *(Not Subd Geog)*
This heading is used as a genre/form heading for films made by or intended for a specific ethnic audience and that often feature ethnic experiences.
BT Motion pictures
RT Race films
Yiddish films
Ethnic radio programs
This heading is used as a genre/form heading for radio programs made by or intended for a specific ethnic audience and that often feature ethnic experiences.
UF Ethnic broadcasts (Radio programs)
Minority radio programs
BT Radio programs
Ethnic television programs *(Not Subd Geog)*
This heading is used as a genre/form heading for television programs that are made by or intended for a specific ethnic audience and that often feature ethnic experiences.
BT Television programs
Ethnographic films *(Not Subd Geog)*
UF Anthropological films
Ethnological films
BT Documentary films
Ethnographic television programs *(Not Subd Geog)*
UF Anthropological television programs
Ethnological television programs
BT Documentary television programs
Ethnological films
USE Ethnographic films
Ethnological television programs
USE Ethnographic television programs
Eurowesterns
USE Spaghetti Westerns
Excerpts, Film
USE Film excerpts
Excerpts, Radio program
USE Radio program excerpts
Excerpts, Television program
USE Television program excerpts

Experimental films *(Not Subd Geog)*
UF Avant-garde films
Personal films
Underground films
BT Motion pictures
NT Abstract films
Lyrical films
Structural films
Surrealist films
Exploitation films *(Not Subd Geog)*
This heading is used as a genre/form heading for films of a sensational nature, usually offering subject matter taboo in mainstream cinema, usually produced on a low budget and often presented in the guise of preachy exposés or pseudo-documentaries.
BT Motion pictures
NT Snuff films
Exploitation films, Black
USE Blaxploitation films
Factual films
USE Documentary films
Fairy tales (Radio programs)
USE Fantasy radio programs
Fake documentaries (Motion pictures)
USE Documentary-style films
Fake documentaries (Television programs)
USE Documentary-style television programs
Fake documentary films
USE Documentary-style films
Fake documentary television programs
USE Documentary-style television programs
Family comedy films
USE Domestic comedy films
Family comedy television programs
USE Domestic comedy television programs
Fan films *(Not Subd Geog)*
This heading is used as a genre/form heading for amateur films created by fans of a film, television program, comic book, etc.
BT Amateur films
Fantastic comedies (Motion pictures)
USE Fantasy comedies (Motion pictures)
Fantastic comedies (Television programs)
USE Fantasy comedies (Television programs)
Fantastic television programs
USE Fantasy television programs
Fantasy comedies (Motion pictures) *(Not Subd Geog)*
This heading is used as a genre/form heading for films that feature benevolent intervention by mythological or supernatural beings with comic results, or that feature incredible inventions or machines having a mind of their own.
UF Comedy fantasy films
Fantastic comedies (Motion pictures)
Fantasy comedy films
Ghost comedies (Motion pictures)
Heavenly comedies (Motion pictures)
BT Comedy films
Fantasy films
Fantasy comedies (Television programs) *(Not Subd Geog)*
This heading is used as a genre/form heading for television programs that feature benevolent intervention by mythological or supernatural beings with comic results, or that feature incredible inventions or machines having a mind of their own.
UF Comedy fantasy television programs
Fantastic comedies (Television programs)
Fantasy comedy television programs
Ghost comedies (Television programs)
Heavenly comedies (Television programs)
BT Fantasy television programs
Television comedies
Fantasy comedy films
USE Fantasy comedies (Motion pictures)
Fantasy comedy television programs
USE Fantasy comedies (Television programs)

Fantasy films *(Not Subd Geog)*
This heading is used as a genre/form heading for films that feature elements of the fantastic, often including magic, supernatural forces, or exotic fantasy worlds.
BT Fiction films
NT Angel films
Fantasy comedies (Motion pictures)
Harry Potter films
Lord of the Rings films
Superhero films
Wizard of Oz films
Fantasy radio programs
This heading is used as a genre/form heading for fictional radio programs that feature elements of the fantastic, often including magic, supernatural forces, or exotic fantasy worlds.
UF Fairy tales (Radio programs)
BT Radio programs
Fantasy television programs *(Not Subd Geog)*
This heading is used as a genre/form heading for television programs that feature elements of the fantastic, often including magic, supernatural forces, or exotic fantasy worlds.
UF Fantastic television programs
Telefantasy
BT Fiction television programs
NT Fantasy comedies (Television programs)
Superhero television programs
Fantômas films *(Not Subd Geog)*
BT Detective and mystery films
Fantozzi films *(Not Subd Geog)*
BT Motion pictures
Farces (Motion pictures)
USE Comedy films
Farces (Television programs)
USE Television comedies
Farcical films
USE Comedy films
Farcical television programs
USE Television comedies
Farm comedy films
USE Rural comedy films
Farm comedy television programs
USE Rural comedy television programs
Farmer comedy films
USE Rural comedy films
Feature films *(Not Subd Geog)*
This heading is used as a genre/form heading for individual full-length films with a running time of 40 minutes or more.
UF Features (Motion pictures)
BT Motion pictures
Feature films, Made-for-TV
USE Made-for-TV movies
Features (Motion pictures)
USE Feature films
Features, Television
USE Made-for-TV movies
Feminist cinema
USE Feminist films
Feminist films *(Not Subd Geog)*
UF Feminist cinema
Women's liberation films
BT Motion pictures
Fiction films *(Not Subd Geog)*
UF Dramatic-narrative films
Entertainment films
Fictional films
Fictive films
BT Motion pictures
NT Crime films
Documentary-style films
Fantasy films
Haunted house films
Journalism films
Melodramas (Motion pictures)
Mood films
Political films
Science fiction films

Fiction radio programs
  BT Radio programs
  NT Historical radio dramas
      Science fiction radio programs
      War radio dramas
Fiction television programs *(Not Subd Geog)*
    This heading is used as a genre/form heading for television programs portraying imaginary characters and events.
  UF Fictional television programs
  BT Television programs
  NT Documentary-style television programs
      Fantasy television programs
      Haunted house television programs
      Journalism television programs
      Political television programs
      Science fiction television programs
      Television crime shows
      Television melodramas
Fictional films
  USE Fiction films
Fictional television programs
  USE Fiction television programs
Fictionalized documentary films
  USE Documentary-style films
Fictionalized documentary television programs
  USE Documentary-style television programs
Fictive films
  USE Fiction films
Field reports, Radio
  USE Radio field reports
Fight films
  USE Boxing films
Film adaptations *(Not Subd Geog)*
  UF Adaptations, Film
      Books, Filmed
      Filmed books
      Films from books
      Motion picture adaptations
  BT Motion pictures
Film addresses (Motion pictures)
  USE Filmed speeches
Film auditions
  USE Screen tests
Film biographies
  USE Biographical films
Film clips *(Not Subd Geog)*
    This heading is used as a genre/form heading for short segments, usually incomplete scenes, of films. Parts, usually complete scenes or sequences, extracted from a complete film are entered under Film excerpts.
  UF Clips, Film
  BT Motion pictures
Film criticism television programs
  USE Movie review television programs
Film epics
  USE Epic films
Film excerpts *(Not Subd Geog)*
    This heading is used as a genre/form heading for parts, usually complete scenes or sequences, extracted from a complete film. Short segments, usually incomplete scenes, of films are entered under Film clips.
  UF Excerpts, Film
  BT Motion pictures
Film genre parodies
  USE Parody films
Film interviews
  USE Filmed interviews
Film loops
  USE Loop films
Film musicals
  USE Musical films
Film noir *(Not Subd Geog)*
  UF Cinéma noir
      Dark crime films
      Film noirs
      Films noirs
      Noir films
  BT Crime films
Film noirs
  USE Film noir

Film parodies
  USE Parody films
Film previews
  USE Film trailers
Film remakes *(Not Subd Geog)*
  UF Motion picture remakes
      Remakes, Film
  BT Motion pictures
Film sequels *(Not Subd Geog)*
  UF Follow-up films
      Motion picture sequels
      Sequels, Film
  BT Film series
Film serials *(Not Subd Geog)*
    This heading is used as a genre/form heading for films that were shown in weekly installments and usually featured cliffhanger endings. Successive films that feature the same characters and remain true to a common premise are entered under Film series.
  UF Chapterplay films
      Cliffhanger films
      Episode films
      Serial films
      Serials, Film
  BT Motion pictures
Film series *(Not Subd Geog)*
    This heading is used as a genre/form heading for successive films that feature the same characters and remain true to a common premise. Individual film series are entered under the heading appropriate to the series, e.g. Star Wars films; James Bond films. Films that were shown in weekly installments and usually featured cliffhanger endings are entered under Film serials.
  BT Motion pictures
  NT Film sequels
Film speeches
  USE Filmed speeches
Film thrillers
  USE Thrillers (Motion pictures)
Film trailers *(Not Subd Geog)*
  UF Film previews
      Motion picture previews
      Motion picture trailers
      Movie previews
      Movie trailers
      Previews, Motion picture
      Theatrical trailers
      Trailers, Motion picture
  BT Motion pictures
Film travelogues
  USE Travelogues (Motion pictures)
Filmed addresses
  USE Filmed speeches
Filmed award presentations
  USE Award presentations (Motion pictures)
Filmed ballets *(Not Subd Geog)*
  BT Ballet films
      Filmed dance
Filmed books
  USE Film adaptations
Filmed boxing matches *(Not Subd Geog)*
  BT Boxing films
      Filmed sports events
Filmed dance
  BT Dance films
      Filmed performances
  NT Filmed ballets
Filmed football games *(Not Subd Geog)*
  BT Filmed sports events
      Football films
Filmed interviews *(Not Subd Geog)*
  UF Film interviews
      Interview films
      Interviews, Filmed
      Motion picture interviews
  BT Nonfiction films
  NT Oral histories
Filmed lectures *(Not Subd Geog)*
  UF Lecture films
      Lectures, Filmed
  BT Nonfiction films

Filmed musicals *(Not Subd Geog)*
  BT Filmed performances
      Musical films
Filmed operas *(Not Subd Geog)*
  BT Filmed performances
      Opera films
Filmed operettas *(Not Subd Geog)*
  BT Filmed performances
      Operetta films
Filmed panel discussions *(Not Subd Geog)*
    This heading is used as a genre/form heading for films that feature discussions of topics by panels of speakers or experts.
  UF Filmed roundtables
      Panel discussions, Filmed
      Roundtables, Filmed
  BT Nonfiction films
Filmed performances *(Not Subd Geog)*
  UF Performance films
      Performances, Filmed
  BT Nonfiction films
  NT Filmed dance
      Filmed musicals
      Filmed operas
      Filmed operettas
      Filmed plays
      Filmed shadow shows
      Filmed stand-up comedy routines
Filmed plays *(Not Subd Geog)*
    This heading is used as a genre/form heading for films that record the performances of plays.
  UF Filmed stage productions
      Plays, Filmed
      Stage productions, Filmed
  BT Filmed performances
Filmed roundtables
  USE Filmed panel discussions
Filmed shadow plays
  USE Filmed shadow shows
Filmed shadow shows *(Not Subd Geog)*
  UF Filmed shadow plays
      Shadow plays, Filmed
      Shadow shows, Filmed
  BT Filmed performances
Filmed speeches *(Not Subd Geog)*
  UF Addresses (Motion pictures)
      Film addresses (Motion pictures)
      Film speeches
      Filmed addresses
      Speeches (Motion pictures)
  BT Nonfiction films
Filmed sports events *(Not Subd Geog)*
  BT Nonfiction films
      Sports films
  NT Filmed boxing matches
      Filmed football games
Filmed stage productions
  USE Filmed plays
Filmed stand-up comedy routines
(Not Subd Geog)
  BT Comedy films
      Filmed performances
Films
  USE Motion pictures
Films for people with visual disabilities
(Not Subd Geog)
  BT Motion pictures
Films for the deaf
  USE Films for the hearing impaired
Films for the hearing impaired
(Not Subd Geog)
  UF Captioned films
      Closed captioned films
      Films for the deaf
      Motion pictures for the deaf
      Motion pictures for the hearing impaired
  BT Motion pictures
Films from books
  USE Film adaptations
Films noirs
  USE Film noir

Filmstrips, Newsreel
  USE Newsreels
Flash Gordon films *(Not Subd Geog)*
  BT Action and adventure films
      Superhero films
Flat-figure animation films
  USE Silhouette animation films
Flying films
  USE Aviation films
Follow-up films
  USE Film sequels
Food shows (Television programs)
  USE Television cooking shows
Football films *(Not Subd Geog)*
  UF College football films
      Grid films
      Gridiron films
  BT Sports films
  NT Filmed football games
Football television programs *(Not Subd Geog)*
  BT Sports television programs
  NT Televised football games
Forums, Radio
  USE Radio panel discussions
Found footage (Motion pictures, television, etc.)
  USE Stock footage
Frankenstein films *(Not Subd Geog)*
  BT Monster films
Friday the 13th films *(Not Subd Geog)*
  UF Friday the Thirteenth films
  BT Slasher films
Friday the Thirteenth films
  USE Friday the 13th films
Game shows (Radio programs)
  USE Radio game shows
Game shows (Television programs)
  USE Television game shows
Gang films
  USE Gangster films
      Juvenile delinquency films
Gangland films
  USE Gangster films
Gangster films *(Not Subd Geog)*
  UF Bandit gangster films
      Gang films
      Gangland films
      Hoodlum drama (Motion pictures)
      Mafia films
      Organized crime films
      Outlaw-couple films
      Outlaw gangster films
      Rural bandit films
      Syndicate films
      Syndicate-oriented films
  BT Crime films
Gangster shows, Radio
  USE Radio crime shows
Gangster television programs
(Not Subd Geog)
  UF Hoodlum television programs
      Mafia television programs
      Organized crime television programs
      Rural bandit television programs
  BT Television crime shows
Gay erotic films *(Not Subd Geog)*
  BT Erotic films
  NT Lesbian erotic films
Genre parodies (Motion pictures)
  USE Parody films
Genre parodies (Television programs)
  USE Parody television programs
Genre parody films
  USE Parody films
Genre parody television programs
  USE Parody television programs
Ghost comedies (Motion pictures)
  USE Fantasy comedies (Motion pictures)
Ghost comedies (Television programs)
  USE Fantasy comedies (Television programs)

Ghost films *(Not Subd Geog)*
  UF Ghost movies
  BT Monster films
  RT Haunted house films
Ghost movies
  USE Ghost films
Ghost shows (Television programs)
  USE Ghost television programs
Ghost stories (Television programs)
  USE Ghost television programs
Ghost television programs *(Not Subd Geog)*
  UF Ghost shows (Television programs)
      Ghost stories (Television programs)
  BT Monster television programs
  RT Haunted house television programs
Gladiator films
  USE Peplum films
Godfather films *(Not Subd Geog)*
  BT Motion pictures
Godzilla films *(Not Subd Geog)*
  BT Monster films
Golf matches, Radio
  USE Radio golf matches
Golf television programs *(Not Subd Geog)*
  BT Sports television programs
  NT Televised golf matches
Gossip radio programs
  UF Radio gossip columns
  BT Nonfiction radio programs
Graphic animation films
  USE Cameraless animation films
Grid films
  USE Football films
Gridiron films
  USE Football films
Guidance films, Social
  USE Social guidance films
Hand-drawn films
  USE Cameraless animation films
Harry Potter films
  BT Fantasy films
Haunted house films *(Not Subd Geog)*
    This heading is used as a genre/form heading for
fictional films set in houses that appear to be inhabited
by spirits.
  UF Old dark house mysteries (Motion
      pictures)
      Old house thrillers (Motion pictures)
  BT Fiction films
  RT Ghost films
      Horror films
Haunted house television programs
(Not Subd Geog)
    This heading is used as a genre/form heading for
fictional television programs set in houses that appear
to be inhabited by spirits.
  UF Old dark house mysteries (Television
      programs)
      Old house thrillers (Television
      programs)
  BT Fiction television programs
  RT Ghost television programs
      Horror television programs
Heavenly comedies (Motion pictures)
  USE Fantasy comedies (Motion pictures)
Heavenly comedies (Television programs)
  USE Fantasy comedies (Television programs)
Heimat Films
  USE Heimatfilme
Heimatfilme *(Not Subd Geog)*
    This heading is used as a genre/form heading for
films produced in Germany that present an idealized
view of country life in southern Germany.
  UF Heimat Films
      Homeland films
  BT Motion pictures
Heist films
  USE Caper films
Heist television programs
  USE Caper television programs
Hellraiser films *(Not Subd Geog)*
  BT Motion pictures

Heroic films
  USE Epic films
Heroic television programs
  USE Epic television programs
High comedy films
  USE Sophisticated comedy films
Hillbilly comedy films
  USE Rural comedy films
Hillbilly comedy television programs
  USE Rural comedy television programs
Hillbilly music radio programs
  USE Country music radio programs
Historical dramas (Radio programs)
  USE Historical radio dramas
Historical films *(Not Subd Geog)*
    This heading is used as a genre/form heading for
films that portray historical events or famous people.
  UF Docudramas (Motion pictures)
  BT Motion pictures
  NT Historical reenactments (Motion
      pictures)
Historical radio dramas
    This heading is used as a genre/form heading for
fictional radio programs that feature historic events
or famous people. Nonfiction radio programs that
present accounts of historic events or famous people
are entered under Historical radio programs.
  UF Historical dramas (Radio programs)
      Historical recreations, Radio
      Historical reenactments, Radio
      Radio dramas, Historical
      Radio historical dramas
      Radio historical recreations
      Radio historical reenactments
  BT Fiction radio programs
Historical radio programs
    This heading is used as a genre/form heading for
nonfiction radio programs that present accounts of
historic events and famous people. Fictional radio
programs that feature historic events or famous peo-
ple are entered under Historical radio dramas.
  UF Histories (Radio programs)
      History radio programs
      Radio histories
  BT Nonfiction radio programs
Historical recreations, Radio
  USE Historical radio dramas
Historical reenactments (Motion pictures)
  UF Reenactments, Historical (Motion
      picture)
  BT Documentary films
      Historical films
Historical reenactments, Radio
  USE Historical radio dramas
Historical reenactments (Television programs)
  UF Reenactments, Historical (Television
      programs)
      Television historical reenactments
  BT Documentary television programs
      Historical television programs
Historical television programs
(Not Subd Geog)
    This heading is used as a genre/form heading for
television programs that portray historical events or
famous people.
  UF Docudramas (Television programs)
  BT Television programs
  NT Historical reenactments (Television
      programs)
Histories (Radio programs)
  USE Historical radio programs
History radio programs
  USE Historical radio programs
Hockey films *(Not Subd Geog)*
  UF Ice hockey films
  BT Sports films
Hockey television programs *(Not Subd Geog)*
  BT Sports television programs
  NT Televised hockey games
Hollywood romance films
  USE Romance films
Home movies
  USE Amateur films

Home shopping television programs
(Not Subd Geog)
    This heading is used as a genre/form heading for live television programs that purvey a wide variety of goods that can be purchased by the viewers. Program length television commercials that are devoted to one product, and that usually include a discussion or demonstration, are entered under Infomercials.
    BT Television programs
    RT Infomercials
Home videos
    USE Amateur films
Homeland films
    USE Heimatfilme
Hoodlum drama (Motion pictures)
    USE Gangster films
         Juvenile delinquency films
Hoodlum television programs
    USE Gangster television programs
Hopalong Cassidy films *(Not Subd Geog)*
    BT Western films
Horror films *(Not Subd Geog)*
    UF Spookfests (Motion pictures)
    BT Motion pictures
    RT Haunted house films
         Monster films
    NT Nightmare on Elm Street films
         Slasher films
Horror radio programs
    UF Monster radio programs
    BT Radio programs
Horror television programs *(Not Subd Geog)*
    BT Television programs
    RT Haunted house television programs
         Monster television programs
Hospital films (Motion pictures)
    USE Medical films (Motion pictures)
Hospital radio programs
    USE Medical radio programs
Hospital television programs
    USE Medical television programs
Hybrid animated/live-action films
    USE Live-action/animation films
Hybrid animation/live-action films
    USE Live-action/animation films
Hybrid live-action/animation films
    USE Live-action/animation films
Ice hockey films
    USE Hockey films
Ichi films
    USE Zatoichi films
In-concert films
    USE Concert films
Independent films *(Not Subd Geog)*
    UF Indie films
    BT Motion pictures
Indiana Jones films *(Not Subd Geog)*
    BT Action and adventure films
Indiana Jones television programs
(Not Subd Geog)
    BT Action and adventure television
         programs
Indie films
    USE Independent films
Industrial films *(Not Subd Geog)*
    UF Business films
         Industry-sponsored films
    BT Instructional films
Industrial television programs
(Not Subd Geog)
    This heading is used as a genre/form heading for nonfiction television programs that teach or train the audience about industrial and manufacturing processes or issues.
    BT Instructional television programs
Industry-sponsored films
    USE Industrial films

Infomercials *(Not Subd Geog)*
    This heading is used as a genre/form heading for program-length television commercials that are devoted to one product, and that usually include a discussion or demonstration.   Live television programs that purvey a wide variety of goods that can be purchased by viewers are entered under Home shopping television programs.
    UF Infomercials
    BT Television programs
    RT Home shopping television programs
Informational films
    USE Educational films
Informational radio programs
    USE Educational radio programs
         Instructional radio programs
Informational television programs
    USE Educational television programs
Informercials
    USE Infomercials
Inspirational radio programs
    This heading is used as a genre/form heading for radio programs that are designed to uplift, inspire, or motivate listeners and are often of a religious nature.
    UF Motivational radio programs
    BT Radio programs
    RT Religious radio programs
Instructional films *(Not Subd Geog)*
    This heading is used as a genre/form heading for films that use a structured format to teach or train the audience. Films that are intended to impart knowledge and information, including those for classroom viewing, are entered under Educational films.
    BT Nonfiction films
    NT Industrial films
Instructional radio programs
    This heading is used as a genre/form heading for radio programs that use a structured format to teach or train the audience. Radio programs intended to impart knowledge and information are entered under Educational radio programs.
    UF Informational radio programs
         Lessons, Radio
         Radio instructional programs
         Radio lessons
         Radio training programs
         Training radio programs
    BT Nonfiction radio programs
    RT Educational radio programs
    NT Science radio programs
Instructional television programs
(Not Subd Geog)
    This heading is used as a genre/form heading for television programs that use a structured format to teach or train the audience. Films that are intended to impart knowledge and information are entered under Educational television programs.
    UF Training television programs
    BT Nonfiction television programs
    NT Industrial television programs
Internet films
    USE Internet videos
Internet videos *(Not Subd Geog)*
    UF Internet films
         Net films
         Net videos
         Online films
         Online videos
         Web films
         Web videos
    BT Motion pictures
    RT Webisodes
Interview films
    USE Filmed interviews
Interview radio programs
    USE Radio interviews
Interview television programs
    USE Television interviews
Interviews, Filmed
    USE Filmed interviews
Interviews (Radio programs)
    USE Radio interviews

Interviews (Sound recordings)
    UF Audio interviews
         Recorded sound interviews
         Tape recorded interviews
    BT Sound recordings
    NT Oral histories
         Radio interviews
Interviews (Television programs)
    USE Television interviews
J.D. films
    USE Juvenile delinquency films
James Bond films *(Not Subd Geog)*
    UF Bond films
    BT Action and adventure films
         Spy films
Jazz music radio programs
    USE Jazz radio programs
Jazz radio programs
    UF Jazz music radio programs
         Music radio programs, Jazz
    BT Radio programs
Journalism films *(Not Subd Geog)*
    This heading is used as a genre/form heading for fictional films that feature reporters and news-gathering.
    UF Newspaper films
         Reporter films
    BT Fiction films
Journalism television programs
(Not Subd Geog)
    This heading is used as a genre/form heading for fictional television programs that feature reporters and news-gathering.
    UF Newspaper television programs
         Reporter television programs
    BT Fiction television programs
Jungle films *(Not Subd Geog)*
    This heading is used as a genre/form heading for adventure films that feature a jungle background.
    BT Action and adventure films
Jungle television programs *(Not Subd Geog)*
    This heading is used as a genre/form heading for adventure television programs that feature a jungle background.
    BT Action and adventure television
         programs
Juvenile delinquency films *(Not Subd Geog)*
    UF Gang films
         Hoodlum drama (Motion pictures)
         J.D. films
         Juvenile delinquent films
         Youth gang films
         Youth street films
    BT Crime films
         Teen films
Juvenile delinquency television programs
(Not Subd Geog)
    BT Teen television programs
         Television crime shows
Juvenile delinquent films
    USE Juvenile delinquency films
Juvenile films
    USE Children's films
Juvenile television programs
    USE Children's television programs
King Kong films *(Not Subd Geog)*
    BT Monster films
Kung fu films
    USE Martial arts films
Kung fu television programs
    USE Martial arts television programs
Law films
    USE Legal films
Law television programs
    USE Legal television programs
Lawyer films
    USE Legal films
Lawyer television programs
    USE Legal television programs
Lecture films
    USE Filmed lectures

Lectures, Filmed
  USE Filmed lectures
Lectures, Radio
  USE Radio speeches
Lectures, Television
  USE Television lectures
Legal films *(Not Subd Geog)*
    This heading is used as a genre/form heading for fiction or nonfiction films that feature the interaction of lawyers, prosecutors, clients, witnesses, and judges.
  UF Courtroom films
      Law films
      Lawyer films
      Trial films
  BT Motion pictures
Legal television programs *(Not Subd Geog)*
    This heading is used as a genre/form heading for fiction or nonfiction television programs that feature the interaction of lawyers, prosecutors, clients, witnesses, and judges.
  UF Courtroom television programs
      Law television programs
      Lawyer television programs
      Trial television programs
  BT Television programs
Lesbian erotic films *(Not Subd Geog)*
  BT Gay erotic films
Lessons, Radio
  USE Instructional radio programs
Library film
  USE Stock footage
Library shots (Motion pictures, television, etc.)
  USE Stock footage
Limited serials (Television programs)
  USE Television mini-series
Literary readings (Radio programs)
  UF Dramatic readings (Radio programs)
      Literature readings (Radio programs)
      Poetry readings (Radio programs)
  BT Radio programs
Literature readings (Radio programs)
  USE Literary readings (Radio programs)
Little Rascals films
  USE Our Gang films
Live-action and animation films, Combination
  USE Live-action/animation films
Live-action/animated films
  USE Live-action/animation films
Live-action/animation films *(Not Subd Geog)*
    This heading is used as a genre/form heading for films that feature interaction between live-action and animated elements.
  UF Animated/live-action films, Hybrid
      Animation and live-action films,
        Combination
      Animation/live-action films, Hybrid
      Combination animation and live-action
        films
      Combination live-action and animation
        films
      Hybrid animated/live-action films
      Hybrid animation/live-action films
      Hybrid live-action/animation films
      Live-action and animation films,
        Combination
      Live-action/animated films
  BT Animated films
Live concert films
  USE Concert films
Live-in-concert films
  USE Concert films
Live shows (Television programs)
  USE Live television programs
Live sound recordings
    This heading is used as a genre/form heading for sound recordings containing concerts, theatrical performances, or other cultural events typically performed in front of an audience and transmitted, broadcast, or recorded as they occur.
  BT Sound recordings

Live television programs *(Not Subd Geog)*
  UF Live shows (Television programs)
  BT Television programs
Lone Ranger films *(Not Subd Geog)*
  BT Western films
Loop films *(Not Subd Geog)*
  UF Continuous films
      Continuous motion pictures
      Film loops
      Motion picture loops
  BT Motion pictures
Lord of the Rings films *(Not Subd Geog)*
  BT Fantasy films
Love films
  USE Romance films
Love television programs
  USE Romance television programs
Low budget films *(Not Subd Geog)*
  UF Low budget motion pictures
      Low budget movies
      Low budget pictures
  BT Motion pictures
  NT B films
Low budget motion pictures
  USE Low budget films
Low budget movies
  USE Low budget films
Low budget pictures
  USE Low budget films
Lyrical films *(Not Subd Geog)*
    This heading is used as a genre/form heading for films in which the images and other content are presented as subjective experiences as seen through the eyes of the filmmaker.
  BT Experimental films
Machinima films *(Not Subd Geog)*
  UF 3D game-based animated films
      3D game-based films
      Machinimas
  BT Animated films
Machinimas
  USE Machinima films
Mad scientist films *(Not Subd Geog)*
  BT Monster films
Madcap comedy films
  USE Screwball comedy films
Madcap romantic comedies
  USE Screwball comedy films
Made-for-television films
  USE Made-for-TV movies
Made-for-television motion pictures
  USE Made-for-TV movies
Made-for-television movies
  USE Made-for-TV movies
Made-for-TV feature films
  USE Made-for-TV movies
Made-for-TV films
  USE Made-for-TV movies
Made-for-TV motion pictures
  USE Made-for-TV movies
Made-for-TV movies *(Not Subd Geog)*
  UF Feature films, Made-for-TV
      Features, Television
      Made-for-television films
      Made-for-television motion pictures
      Made-for-television movies
      Made-for-TV feature films
      Made-for-TV films
      Made-for-TV motion pictures
      Tele-features
      Telefeatures
      Telefilms
      Telemovies
      Telepics
      Television features
      Television films
      Television movies
      Vidpics
  BT Television programs
Mafia films
  USE Gangster films

Mafia television programs
  USE Gangster television programs
Magazine format radio programs
  UF Magazine radio programs
      News magazines (Radio programs)
      Newsmagazines (Radio programs)
  BT Nonfiction radio programs
Magazine format television programs
  (Not Subd Geog)
  UF Magazine television programs
      Magazines (Television programs)
      News magazines (Television programs)
      Newsmagazines (Television programs)
  BT Nonfiction television programs
Magazine radio programs
  USE Magazine format radio programs
Magazine television programs
  USE Magazine format television programs
Magazines (Television programs)
  USE Magazine format television programs
Makeover reality television programs
  USE Makeover television programs
Makeover shows (Television programs)
  USE Makeover television programs
Makeover television programs
  (Not Subd Geog)
  UF Makeover reality television programs
      Makeover shows (Television programs)
      Makeover television shows
  BT Reality television programs
Makeover television shows
  USE Makeover television programs
Man-on-the-street interviews (Radio programs)
  USE Vox pop radio programs
Marionette films
  USE Puppet films
Marionette television programs
  USE Puppet television programs
Martial arts films *(Not Subd Geog)*
  UF Kung fu films
      Spaghetti Easterns
  BT Action and adventure films
Martial arts television programs
  (Not Subd Geog)
  UF Kung fu television programs
  BT Sports television programs
  NT Televised martial arts events
Medical films (Motion pictures)
  (Not Subd Geog)
    This heading is used as a genre/form heading for fiction or nonfiction films that feature medical personnel and the practice of medicine.
  UF Doctor films (Motion pictures)
      Hospital films (Motion pictures)
  BT Motion pictures
Medical radio programs
    This heading is used as a genre/form heading for fiction or nonfiction radio programs that feature medical personnel and the practice of medicine.
  UF Doctor radio programs
      Hospital radio programs
      Nurse radio programs
  BT Radio programs
Medical television programs *(Not Subd Geog)*
    This heading is used as a genre/form heading for fiction or nonfiction television programs that feature medical personnel and the practice of medicine.
  UF Doctor television programs
      Hospital television programs
  BT Television programs
Melodrama films
  USE Melodramas (Motion pictures)
Melodramas (Motion pictures)
  (Not Subd Geog)
  UF Melodrama films
      Melodramatic films
  BT Fiction films
Melodramas, Television
  USE Television melodramas
Melodramatic films
  USE Melodramas (Motion pictures)

Melodramatic television programs
USE Television melodramas
Mental hygiene films
USE Social guidance films
Military films *(Not Subd Geog)*
This heading is used as a genre/form heading for films that feature the military lifestyle and loyalty to the armed forces and its codes and are generally set during peacetime. Films that feature military conflicts are entered under War films.
BT Motion pictures
RT War films
Military television programs *(Not Subd Geog)*
This heading is used as a genre/form heading for television programs that feature the military lifestyle and loyalty to the armed forces and its codes and are generally set during peacetime. Television programs that feature military conflicts are entered under War television programs.
BT Television programs
RT War television programs
Mini-series, Television
USE Television mini-series
Miniseries, Television
USE Television mini-series
Minority radio programs
USE Ethnic radio programs
Mock documentary films
USE Documentary-style films
Mock documentary television programs
USE Documentary-style television programs
Mockumentaries
USE Documentary-style films
Mockumentaries (Television programs)
USE Documentary-style television programs
Mockumentary films
USE Documentary-style films
Mockumentary television programs
USE Documentary-style television programs
Monster films *(Not Subd Geog)*
UF Creature features (Motion pictures)
BT Motion pictures
RT Horror films
NT Frankenstein films
Ghost films
Godzilla films
King Kong films
Mad scientist films
Mothra films
Mummy films
Vampire films
Werewolf films
Zombie films
Monster radio programs
USE Horror radio programs
Monster television programs
(Not Subd Geog)
BT Television programs
RT Horror television programs
NT Ghost television programs
Mummy television programs
Vampire television programs
Werewolf television programs
Montalbano television programs, Commissario
USE Commissario Montalbano television programs
Monumental films
USE Epic films
Monumental television programs
USE Epic television programs
Mood films *(Not Subd Geog)*
This heading is used as a genre/form heading for films that emphasize a mood or atmosphere rather than a plot.
BT Fiction films
Mothra films *(Not Subd Geog)*
BT Monster films
Motion picture adaptations
USE Film adaptations
Motion picture auditions
USE Screen tests

Motion picture cartoons
USE Animated films
Motion picture documentaries
USE Documentary films
Motion picture interviews
USE Filmed interviews
Motion picture loops
USE Loop films
Motion picture musicals
USE Musical films
Motion picture parodies
USE Parody films
Motion picture previews
USE Film trailers
Motion picture remakes
USE Film remakes
Motion picture screen tests
USE Screen tests
Motion picture sequels
USE Film sequels
Motion picture stock materials
USE Stock footage
Motion picture trailers
USE Film trailers
Motion pictures *(Not Subd Geog)*
This heading is used as a genre/form heading for collections of films that are composed of multiple genres and/or forms to which more specific headings such as Nonfiction films or Comedy films cannot be applied.
UF Films
Movies
NT 3-D films
Action and adventure films
Amateur films
Amusement ride films
Andy Hardy films
Angélique films
Animal films
Animated films
Anthology films
Anti-war films
Aviation films
Biographical films
Blaxploitation films
Bowery Boys films
Buddy films
Caper films
Car-chase films
Carmen films
Children's films
Christmas films
College life films
Comedy films
Compilation films
Dance films
Disaster films
Doctor Mabuse films
Don Camillo films
Don Juan films
Environmental films
Epic films
Erotic films
Ethnic films
Experimental films
Exploitation films
Fantozzi films
Feature films
Feminist films
Fiction films
Film adaptations
Film clips
Film excerpts
Film remakes
Film serials
Film series
Film trailers
Films for people with visual disabilities
Films for the hearing impaired
Godfather films
Heimatfilme

Hellraiser films
Historical films
Horror films
Independent films
Internet videos
Legal films
Loop films
Low budget films
Medical films (Motion pictures)
Military films
Monster films
Motorcycle films
Musical films
New wave films
Niskavuori films
Nonfiction films
Opera films
Operetta films
Our Gang films
Outtakes
Peplum films
Pink Panther films
Podcasts
Populist films
Pornographic films
Propaganda films
Public service announcements (Motion pictures)
Puppet films
Race films
Religious films
Road films
Rocky films
Romance films
Rubble films
Rushes (Motion pictures)
Samurai films
Scooby-Doo films
Screen tests
Short films
Show business films
Silent films
Social problem films
Sports films
Spy films
Stock footage
Street films
Subculture films
Survival films
Swashbuckler films
Tarzan films
Teen films
Theater announcements (Motion pictures)
Theater commercials (Motion pictures)
Thrillers (Motion pictures)
Time-lapse films
Torchy Blane films
Trick films
Unedited footage
Unfinished films
War films
Western films
Yiddish films
Motion pictures for the deaf
USE Films for the hearing impaired
Motion pictures for the hearing impaired
USE Films for the hearing impaired
Motivational radio programs
USE Inspirational radio programs
Motorcycle films *(Not Subd Geog)*
UF Biker films
BT Motion pictures
Mountain films *(Not Subd Geog)*
UF Bergfilme
Mountaineering films
BT Sports films
Mountaineering films
USE Mountain films
Movie parodies
USE Parody films

Movie previews
  USE Film trailers
Movie review television programs
  (Not Subd Geog)
  UF Film criticism television programs
  BT Nonfiction television programs
Movie theater ads (Motion pictures)
  USE Theater commercials (Motion pictures)
Movie trailers
  USE Film trailers
Movies
  USE Motion pictures
Mummy films *(Not Subd Geog)*
  BT Monster films
Mummy television programs
  (Not Subd Geog)
  BT Monster television programs
Murder mystery films
  USE Detective and mystery films
Murder mystery television programs
  USE Detective and mystery television
      programs
Music radio programs, Country and western
  USE Country music radio programs
Music radio programs, Hillbilly
  USE Country music radio programs
Music radio programs, Jazz
  USE Jazz radio programs
Music radio programs, Rock
  USE Rock music radio programs
Music radio programs, Western and country
  USE Country music radio programs
Music videos *(Not Subd Geog)*
  BT Television programs
      Video recordings
  NT Rock videos
Musical films *(Not Subd Geog)*
  UF Film musicals
      Motion picture musicals
      Musicals (Motion pictures)
  BT Motion pictures
  RT Concert films
  NT Filmed musicals
      Rock films
Musical television programs
  USE Television musicals
Musicals (Motion pictures)
  USE Musical films
Musicals (Television programs)
  USE Television musicals
Mystery films
  USE Detective and mystery films
Mystery radio programs
  USE Detective and mystery radio programs
Mystery television programs
  USE Detective and mystery television
      programs
Nanny television programs *(Not Subd Geog)*
  BT Television programs
Nature films *(Not Subd Geog)*
     This heading is used as a genre/form heading for
  nonfiction films that depict or explain the natural
  world and its phenomena.
  BT Science films
  NT Wildlife films
Nature television programs *(Not Subd Geog)*
     This heading is used as a genre/form heading for
  nonfiction television programs that depict or explain
  the natural world and its phenomena.
  BT Science television programs
  NT Wildlife television programs
Net films
  USE Internet videos
Net videos
  USE Internet videos
New wave cinema
  USE New wave films

New wave films *(Not Subd Geog)*
  UF New wave cinema
      New wave (Motion pictures)
      Nouvelle vague (Motion pictures)
      Nouvelles vagues (Motion pictures)
  BT Motion pictures
New wave (Motion pictures)
  USE New wave films
News bulletins, Radio
  USE Radio news bulletins
News conferences, Radio
  USE Radio press conferences
News conferences, Television
  USE Television press conferences
News films
  USE Newsreels
News flashes, Radio
  USE Radio news bulletins
News magazines (Radio programs)
  USE Magazine format radio programs
News magazines (Television programs)
  USE Magazine format television programs
News programs, Radio
  USE Radio news programs
News programs, Television
  USE Television news programs
News television programs
  USE Television news programs
Newscasts, Radio
  USE Radio news programs
Newsmagazines (Radio programs)
  USE Magazine format radio programs
Newsmagazines (Television programs)
  USE Magazine format television programs
Newspaper films
  USE Journalism films
Newspaper television programs
  USE Journalism television programs
Newsreels *(Not Subd Geog)*
  UF Filmstrips, Newsreel
      News films
  BT Nonfiction films
  RT Actualities (Motion pictures)
Nightmare on Elm Street films
  (Not Subd Geog)
  BT Horror films
Niskavuori films *(Not Subd Geog)*
  BT Motion pictures
Noir films
  USE Film noir
Noncamera films
  USE Cameraless animation films
Nonfiction films *(Not Subd Geog)*
  UF Nonstory films
  BT Motion pictures
  NT Actualities (Motion pictures)
      Award presentations (Motion pictures)
      Beauty contest films
      City symphonies (Motion pictures)
      Concert films
      Documentary films
      Filmed interviews
      Filmed lectures
      Filmed panel discussions
      Filmed performances
      Filmed speeches
      Filmed sports events
      Instructional films
      Newsreels
      Promotional films
      Variety shows (Motion pictures)

Nonfiction radio programs
  BT Radio programs
  NT Biographical radio programs
      Book review radio programs
      Community affairs radio programs
      Documentary radio programs
      Gossip radio programs
      Historical radio programs
      Instructional radio programs
      Magazine format radio programs
      Public affairs radio programs
      Public service radio programs
      Radio commentaries
      Radio debates
      Radio field reports
      Radio interviews
      Radio news programs
      Radio panel discussions
      Radio speeches
      Radio sports events
      Radio talk shows
      Reality radio programs
      Special events radio coverage
      Talent shows (Radio programs)
      Variety shows (Radio programs)
      War radio programs
Nonfiction television programs
  (Not Subd Geog)
  BT Television programs
  NT Audience participation television
        programs
      Autobiographical television programs
      Award presentations (Television
        programs)
      Beauty contest television programs
      Book review television programs
      Concert television programs
      Documentary television programs
      Instructional television programs
      Magazine format television programs
      Movie review television programs
      Public access television programs
      Public affairs television programs
      Public service television programs
      Reality television programs
      Special events television coverage
      Televised performances
      Televised speeches
      Televised sports events
      Television cooking shows
      Television debates
      Television interviews
      Television lectures
      Television news programs
      Television panel discussions
      Television talk shows
      True crime television programs
      Variety shows (Television programs)
Nonobjective films
  USE Abstract films
Nonrepresentational films
  USE Abstract films
Nonstory films
  USE Nonfiction films
Nouvelle vague (Motion pictures)
  USE New wave films
Nouvelles vagues (Motion pictures)
  USE New wave films
Novelties (Motion pictures)
  USE Novelty films
Novelty films *(Not Subd Geog)*
     This heading is used as a genre/form heading for
  whimsical or humorous short films designed to catch
  one's attention momentarily with something with a
  novel twist.
  UF Novelties (Motion pictures)
  BT Short films
Nurse radio programs
  USE Medical radio programs
Oddball comedy films
  USE Screwball comedy films

Old dark house mysteries (Motion pictures)
  USE Haunted house films
Old dark house mysteries (Television programs)
  USE Haunted house television programs
Old house thrillers (Motion pictures)
  USE Haunted house films
Old house thrillers (Television programs)
  USE Haunted house television programs
Omnibus films
  USE Anthology films
Omnibus television programs
  USE Anthology television programs
Online films
  USE Internet videos
Online videos
  USE Internet videos
Opera films *(Not Subd Geog)*
  BT Motion pictures
  NT Filmed operas
Opera television programs *(Not Subd Geog)*
  BT Television programs
  NT Televised operas
Operetta films *(Not Subd Geog)*
  BT Motion pictures
  NT Filmed operettas
Oral histories
  BT Filmed interviews
      Interviews (Sound recordings)
Organized crime films
  USE Gangster films
Organized crime television programs
  USE Gangster television programs
Our Gang films *(Not Subd Geog)*
  UF Little Rascals films
  BT Motion pictures
Out-of-camera films
  USE Cameraless animation films
Out-takes, Radio
  USE Radio outtakes
Outlaw-couple films
  USE Gangster films
Outlaw gangster films
  USE Gangster films
Outtakes *(Not Subd Geog)*
    This heading is used as a genre/form heading for excerpts from films and television programs usually excluded from the final versions of completed films or programs.
  BT Motion pictures
      Television programs
  RT Unedited footage
Outtakes, Radio
  USE Radio outtakes
Oz films
  USE Wizard of Oz films
Pacifist films
  USE Anti-war films
Pacifist television programs
  USE Anti-war television programs
Panel discussions, Filmed
  USE Filmed panel discussions
Panel discussions, Radio
  USE Radio panel discussions
Panel discussions, Television
  USE Television panel discussions
Paper cut-out animation films
  USE Cutout animation films
Parody films *(Not Subd Geog)*
    This heading is used as a genre/form heading for films that comically imitate another work or group of works of a more serious nature.
  UF Film genre parodies
      Film parodies
      Genre parodies (Motion pictures)
      Genre parody films
      Motion picture parodies
      Movie parodies
      Send-up films
      Spoof films
      Spoofs (Motion pictures)
      Takeoff films
  BT Comedy films

Parody television programs *(Not Subd Geog)*
    This heading is used as a genre/form heading for television programs that comically imitate another work or group of works of a more serious nature.
  UF Genre parodies (Television programs)
      Genre parody television programs
      Spoof television programs
      Spoofs (Television programs)
      Television parodies
  BT Television comedies
Peplum films *(Not Subd Geog)*
    This heading is used as a genre/form heading for films that feature mythological, biblical, or invented strongmen as heroes.
  UF Gladiator films
      Sandal-and-spear epics (Motion pictures)
      Sex-and-sand films
      Sword-and-sandal epics (Motion pictures)
  BT Motion pictures
Performance films
  USE Filmed performances
Performances, Filmed
  USE Filmed performances
Performances, Televised
  USE Televised performances
Personal films
  USE Amateur films
      Experimental films
Pilot programs, Television
  USE Television pilot programs
Pilots (Television programs)
  USE Television pilot programs
Pink Panther films *(Not Subd Geog)*
  BT Motion pictures
Pink Panther television programs
(Not Subd Geog)
  BT Animated television programs
Pixilated animation films *(Not Subd Geog)*
  UF Pixilation animation films
      Pixillated animation films
      Pixillation animation films
  BT Animated films
Pixilation animation films
  USE Pixilated animation films
Pixillated animation films
  USE Pixilated animation films
Pixillation animation films
  USE Pixilated animation films
Planet of the Apes films *(Not Subd Geog)*
  BT Dystopian films
Plays, Filmed
  USE Filmed plays
Plays, Televised
  USE Televised plays
Podcasts
  BT Motion pictures
      Sound recordings
      Television programs
Poetry readings (Radio programs)
  USE Literary readings (Radio programs)
Police films *(Not Subd Geog)*
  UF Cop films
  BT Crime films
  RT Detective and mystery films
Police radio shows
  USE Radio crime shows
Police shows (Television programs)
  USE Television cop shows
Police television programs
  USE Television cop shows
Political commercials
  USE Political television commercials
Political debates (Radio programs)
  USE Radio debates
Political films *(Not Subd Geog)*
    This heading is used as a genre/form heading for fictional films that feature the political milieu.
  BT Fiction films

Political radio commercials
  UF Political radio spots
      Political spots (Radio commercials)
  BT Radio commercials (Advertisements)
Political radio spots
  USE Political radio commercials
Political spots (Radio commercials)
  USE Political radio commercials
Political spots (Television commercials)
  USE Political television commercials
Political television commercials
(Not Subd Geog)
  UF Campaign commercials
      Campaign spots (Television commercials)
      Political commercials
      Political spots (Television commercials)
      Political television spots
  BT Television commercials
Political television programs *(Not Subd Geog)*
    This heading is used as a genre/form heading for fictional television programs that feature the political milieu.
  BT Fiction television programs
Political television spots
  USE Political television commercials
Populist films *(Not Subd Geog)*
  BT Motion pictures
Porno films
  USE Pornographic films
Pornographic films *(Not Subd Geog)*
  UF Adult films (Pornographic films)
      Blue movies
      Porno films
      Stag films
      XXX films
  BT Motion pictures
  RT Erotic films
  NT Snuff films
Pornographic television programs
(Not Subd Geog)
  BT Television programs
  RT Erotic television programs
Portmanteau films
  USE Anthology films
Portraits (Biographical television programs)
  USE Biographical television programs
Pre-feature advertisements
  USE Theater commercials (Motion pictures)
Presentations, Award (Motion pictures)
  USE Award presentations (Motion pictures)
Press conferences, Radio
  USE Radio press conferences
Press conferences, Television
  USE Television press conferences
Pressings, Test (Sound recordings)
  USE Test pressings (Sound recordings)
Previews, Motion picture
  USE Film trailers
Prison films *(Not Subd Geog)*
  BT Crime films
Prison television programs *(Not Subd Geog)*
  BT Television crime shows
Private eye films
  USE Detective and mystery films
Private eye radio programs
  USE Detective and mystery radio programs
Private eye television programs
  USE Detective and mystery television programs
Private Snafu films *(Not Subd Geog)*
  UF Snafu films
  BT Animated films
      Short films
Prize-fight films
  USE Boxing films
Prize-fighting films
  USE Boxing films
Prizefight films
  USE Boxing films

Prizefighting films
USE Boxing films
Production footage
USE Unedited footage
Profiles (Biographical television programs)
USE Biographical television programs
Programs, Radio
USE Radio programs
Programs, Television
USE Television programs
Promo films
USE Promotional films

Promos (Television commercials)
(Not Subd Geog)
This heading is used as a genre/form heading for television announcements promoting a particular network or station, or upcoming programs from a network or station.
UF Promotional announcements, Television
   Television promos
   Television promotional announcements
BT Television commercials
Promotional announcements, Television
USE Promos (Television commercials)
Promotional films *(Not Subd Geog)*
This heading is used as a genre/form heading for films that promote or advertise a product, industry, service, organization, etc. Films produced, subsidized, financed, or otherwise significantly supported by a business, government body, organization, etc. are entered under Sponsored films.
UF Advertising films
   Company promotion films
   Promo films
   Public relations films
BT Nonfiction films
RT Sponsored films
Promotional radio spots
USE Radio commercials (Advertisements)
Propaganda films *(Not Subd Geog)*
This heading is used as a genre/form heading for films designed primarily to instill or reinforce a specific ideological belief or set of beliefs in the viewer.
BT Motion pictures
Propaganda, Radio
USE Radio propaganda
Propaganda television programs
(Not Subd Geog)
This heading is used as a genre/form heading for television programs designed primarily to instill or reinforce a specific ideological belief or set of beliefs in the viewer.
BT Television programs
PSAs (Motion pictures)
USE Public service announcements (Motion pictures)
PSAs, Radio
USE Radio public service announcements
PSAs, Television
USE Television public service announcements
Pseudo-documentary films
USE Documentary-style films
Pseudo-documentary television programs
USE Documentary-style television programs
Psycho thrillers (Motion pictures)
USE Thrillers (Motion pictures)
Psycho thrillers (Television programs)
USE Thrillers (Television programs)
Psychological thrillers (Motion pictures)
USE Thrillers (Motion pictures)
Psychological thrillers (Radio programs)
USE Thrillers (Radio programs)
Psychological thrillers (Television programs)
USE Thrillers (Television programs)
Public access television programs
(Not Subd Geog)
UF Community access television programs
   Community television programs
BT Nonfiction television programs

Public affairs radio programs
This heading is used as a genre/form heading for radio programs about public policy or politics. Radio programs aired by or on behalf of nonprofit or governmental organizations to promote the common well-being or general welfare of society are entered under Public service radio programs.
BT Nonfiction radio programs
Public affairs television programs
(Not Subd Geog)
This heading is used as a genre/form heading for television programs about public policy or politics. Television programs aired by or on behalf of nonprofit or governmental organizations to promote the common well-being or general welfare of society are entered under Public service television programs.
BT Nonfiction television programs
Public interest radio programs
USE Public service radio programs
Public relations films
USE Promotional films
Public service advertisments, Radio
USE Radio public service announcements
Public service announcements (Motion pictures) *(Not Subd Geog)*
UF Community service announcements (Motion pictures)
   CSAs (Motion pictures)
   PSAs (Motion pictures)
BT Motion pictures
Public service announcements, Radio
USE Radio public service announcements
Public service announcements, Television
USE Television public service announcements
Public service radio announcements
USE Radio public service announcements
Public service radio programs
This heading is used as a genre/form heading for radio programs aired by or on behalf of nonprofit or governmental organizations to promote the common well-being or general welfare of society. Radio programs about public policy or politics are entered under Public affairs radio programs. Radio announcements aired by or on behalf of nonprofit or governmental organizations to persuade the audience to take some specific action or adopt a favorable view toward a service, institution, or cause are entered under Radio public service announcements.
UF Public interest radio programs
BT Nonfiction radio programs
Public service television programs
(Not Subd Geog)
This heading is used as a genre/form heading for television programs aired by or on behalf of nonprofit or governmental organizations to promote the common well-being or general welfare of society. Television programs about public policy or politics are entered under Public affairs television programs. Television announcements aired by or on behalf of nonprofit or governmental organizations to persuade the audience to take some specific action or adopt a favorable view toward a service, institution, or cause are entered under Television public service announcements.
BT Nonfiction television programs
Puppet films *(Not Subd Geog)*
UF Marionette films
BT Motion pictures
Puppet shows (Television programs)
USE Puppet television programs
Puppet television programs *(Not Subd Geog)*
UF Marionette television programs
   Puppet shows (Television programs)
   Television puppet shows
BT Television programs
Quasi-documentary films
USE Documentary-style films
Quasi-documentary television programs
USE Documentary-style television programs
Quiz shows (Radio programs)
USE Radio quiz shows
Quiz shows (Television programs)
USE Television quiz shows

Race films *(Not Subd Geog)*
This heading is used as a genre/form heading for films produced with African American casts specifically for African American audiences beginning in the late silent-film days and continuing until the end of the 1940s.
UF Race movies
BT Motion pictures
RT Ethnic films
Race movies
USE Race films
Radio adaptations
UF Adaptations, Radio
BT Radio programs
Radio addresses
USE Radio speeches
Radio ads
USE Radio commercials (Advertisements)
Radio adventure programs
USE Adventure radio programs
Radio advertisements
USE Radio commercials (Advertisements)
Radio air checks
USE Radio airchecks
Radio airchecks
UF Air checks, Radio
   Airchecks, Radio
   Radio air checks
BT Radio programs
RT Radio auditions
NT Telescoped radio airchecks
   Untelescoped radio airchecks
Radio anthologies
This heading is used as a genre/form heading for radio programs made up of different episodes or stories which are usually connected by a theme, event, location or original author, often having a wrap-around tale. Radio programs that are composed of pre-existing broadcast or unbroadcast radio programs, or portions thereof, are entered under Compilation radio programs.
UF Anthologies, Radio
   Anthology radio programs
BT Radio programs
Radio audience participation shows
USE Audience participation radio programs
Radio auditions
UF Auditions, Radio
BT Radio programs
RT Radio airchecks
Radio biographies
USE Biographical radio programs
Radio book review programs
USE Book review radio programs
Radio broadcasts, Shortwave
USE Shortwave radio broadcasts
Radio call-in programs
USE Radio call-in shows
Radio call-in shows
UF Call-in radio programs
   Call-in radio shows
   Radio call-in programs
BT Radio talk shows
RT Audience participation radio programs
Radio comedies
UF Comedies, Radio
   Comedy programs, Radio
   Comedy radio programs
   Radio comedy programs
   Radio situation comedies
   Situation comedies, Radio
BT Radio programs
Radio comedy programs
USE Radio comedies
Radio commentaries
This heading is used as a genre/form heading for radio programs, or segments of programs, that consist of an informed speaker's analysis of events or trends.
UF Commentaries, Radio
   Editorials, Radio
   Radio editorials
BT Nonfiction radio programs

Radio commercials (Advertisements)
    UF Ads, Radio
        Advertisements, Radio
        Commercials, Radio (Advertisements)
        Promotional radio spots
        Radio ads
        Radio advertisements
        Radio promotional spots
        Radio spots (Advertisements)
        Spots, Radio (Advertisements)
    BT Radio programs
    NT Political radio commercials
Radio community service announcements
    USE Radio public service announcements
Radio compilations
    USE Compilation radio programs
Radio contests
    USE Radio game shows
         Radio quiz shows
Radio coverage, Special events
    USE Special events radio coverage
Radio crime programs
    USE Radio crime shows
Radio crime shows
    UF Crime programs, Radio
        Crime shows, Radio
        Criminal radio programs
        Gangster shows, Radio
        Police radio shows
        Radio crime programs
        Radio gangster shows
        Radio police shows
    BT Radio programs
    RT Spy radio programs
        Thrillers (Radio programs)
    NT Detective and mystery radio programs
Radio CSAs
    USE Radio public service announcements
Radio debates
    UF Campaign debates (Radio programs)
        Debates, Radio
        Political debates (Radio programs)
    BT Nonfiction radio programs
Radio discussion shows
    USE Radio panel discussions
Radio docudramas
    This heading is used as a genre/form heading for radio programs that use drama to portray factual events or conditions.
    UF Docudramas, Radio
    BT Radio programs
Radio documentaries
    USE Documentary radio programs
Radio dramas, Historical
    USE Historical radio dramas
Radio editorials
    USE Radio commentaries
Radio espionage programs
    USE Spy radio programs
Radio field reports
    This heading is used as a genre/form heading for radio reportorial pieces recorded on location. Radio programs that feature commentators in the studio reporting on current events and noteworthy issues are entered under Radio news programs. Radio reports of noteworthy events, often featuring several commentators and combining studio reports with on-the-scene coverage, are entered under Special events radio coverage.
    UF Field reports, Radio
    BT Nonfiction radio programs
Radio forums
    USE Radio panel discussions
Radio game shows
    This heading is used as a genre/form heading for radio programs that feature contestants participating in various types of competitive activities for prizes. Radio programs that feature a question-and-answer format are entered under Radio quiz shows.
    UF Contests, Radio
        Game shows (Radio programs)
        Radio contests
    BT Radio programs

Radio gangster shows
    USE Radio crime shows
Radio golf matches
    UF Golf matches, Radio
    BT Radio sports events
Radio gossip columns
    USE Gossip radio programs
Radio historical dramas
    USE Historical radio dramas
Radio historical recreations
    USE Historical radio dramas
Radio historical reenactments
    USE Historical radio dramas
Radio histories
    USE Historical radio programs
Radio instructional programs
    USE Instructional radio programs
Radio interviews
    UF Interview radio programs
        Interviews (Radio programs)
    BT Interviews (Sound recordings)
        Nonfiction radio programs
    RT Radio talk shows
    NT Vox pop radio programs
Radio lectures
    USE Radio speeches
Radio lessons
    USE Instructional radio programs
Radio news bulletins
    This heading is used as a genre/form heading for news announcements that interrupt regularly scheduled programming.
    UF News bulletins, Radio
        News flashes, Radio
        Radio news flashes
    BT Radio programs
    RT Radio news programs
Radio news conferences
    USE Radio press conferences
Radio news flashes
    USE Radio news bulletins
Radio news programs
    This heading is used as a genre/form heading for radio programs that feature commentators in the studio reporting on current events and noteworthy issues. Radio reportorial pieces recorded on location are entered under Radio field reports. Radio reports of noteworthy events, often featuring several commentators and combining studio reports with on-the-scene coverage, are entered under Special events radio coverage.
    UF News programs, Radio
        Newscasts, Radio
        Radio newscasts
    BT Nonfiction radio programs
    RT Radio news bulletins
        Radio press conferences
    NT Radio press conferences
        Sports radio news programs
Radio newscasts
    USE Radio news programs
Radio out-takes
    USE Radio outtakes
Radio outtakes
    This heading is used as a genre/form heading for excerpts from radio programs usually excluded from the final versions of completed radio programs.
    UF Out-takes, Radio
        Outtakes, Radio
        Radio out-takes
    BT Radio programs
Radio panel discussions
    This heading is used as a genre/form heading for radio programs that feature discussions of topics by panels of speakers or experts.
    UF Discussion shows, Radio
        Forums, Radio
        Panel discussions, Radio
        Radio discussion shows
        Radio forums
        Radio roundtables
        Roundtables, Radio
    BT Nonfiction radio programs

Radio police shows
    USE Radio crime shows
Radio press conferences
    UF News conferences, Radio
        Press conferences, Radio
        Radio news conferences
    BT Radio news programs
Radio program clips
    USE Radio program excerpts
Radio program excerpts
    This heading is used as a genre/form heading for portions of complete radio programs.
    UF Clips, Radio program
        Excerpts, Radio program
        Radio program clips
    BT Radio programs
Radio programs *(Not Subd Geog)*
    This heading is used as a genre/form heading for collections of radio programs that are composed of multiple genres and/or forms to which more specific headings such as Nonfiction radio programs or Radio comedies cannot be applied.
    UF Programs, Radio
        Radio shows
        Shows, Radio
    BT Sound recordings
    NT Adventure radio programs
        Children's radio programs
        Christmas radio programs
        Classical music radio programs
        Compilation radio programs
        Country music radio programs
        Disc jockey radio programs
        Educational radio programs
        Ethnic radio programs
        Fantasy radio programs
        Fiction radio programs
        Horror radio programs
        Inspirational radio programs
        Jazz radio programs
        Literary readings (Radio programs)
        Medical radio programs
        Nonfiction radio programs
        Radio adaptations
        Radio airchecks
        Radio anthologies
        Radio auditions
        Radio comedies
        Radio commercials (Advertisements)
        Radio crime shows
        Radio docudramas
        Radio game shows
        Radio news bulletins
        Radio outtakes
        Radio program excerpts
        Radio propaganda
        Radio public service announcements
        Radio quiz shows
        Radio rehearsals
        Radio serials
        Radio specials
        Religious radio programs
        Rock music radio programs
        Shortwave radio broadcasts
        Spy radio programs
        Thrillers (Radio programs)
        Western radio programs
Radio promotional spots
    USE Radio commercials (Advertisements)
Radio propaganda
    UF Propaganda, Radio
    BT Radio programs
Radio PSAs
    USE Radio public service announcements
Radio public service advertisments
    USE Radio public service announcements

Radio public service announcements

This heading is used as a genre/form heading for radio announcements aired by or on behalf of nonprofit or governmental organizations to persuade the audience to take some specific action or adopt a favorable view toward a service, institution, or cause. Radio programs aired by or on behalf of nonprofit or governmental organizations to promote the common well-being or general welfare of society are entered under Public service radio programs.

UF Community service announcements, Radio
      CSAs, Radio
      PSAs, Radio
      Public service advertisments, Radio
      Public service announcements, Radio
      Public service radio announcements
      Radio community service announcements
      Radio CSAs
      Radio PSAs
      Radio public service advertisments
BT Radio programs

Radio quiz shows

This heading is used as a genre/form heading for radio programs that feature a question-and-answer format. Radio programs that feature contestants participating in various types of competitive activities for prizes are entered under Radio game shows.

UF Contests, Radio
      Quiz shows (Radio programs)
      Radio contests
BT Radio programs

Radio rehearsals

UF Rehearsals, Radio
BT Radio programs

Radio roundtables
USE Radio panel discussions

Radio serials

UF Serials, Radio
BT Radio programs
NT Radio soap operas

Radio sermons

UF Sermons, Radio
BT Religious radio programs

Radio shows
USE Radio programs

Radio situation comedies
USE Radio comedies

Radio soap operas

UF Soap operas, Radio
BT Radio serials

Radio specials

UF Specials, Radio
BT Radio programs

Radio speeches

This heading is used as a genre/form heading for speeches presented specifically to radio audiences or speeches that are presented to other audiences and broadcast on the radio.

UF Addresses, Radio
      Lectures, Radio
      Radio addresses
      Radio lectures
      Radio talks
      Speeches, Radio
      Talks, Radio
BT Nonfiction radio programs

Radio sporting events
USE Radio sports events

Radio sports events

UF Radio sporting events
      Sporting events, Radio
      Sports events, Radio
BT Nonfiction radio programs
NT Radio golf matches

Radio spots (Advertisements)
USE Radio commercials (Advertisements)

Radio spy programs
USE Spy radio programs

Radio talent shows
USE Talent shows (Radio programs)

Radio talk shows

UF Talk radio programs
      Talk radio shows
      Talk shows, Radio
BT Nonfiction radio programs
RT Radio interviews
NT Audience participation radio programs
      Radio call-in shows

Radio talks
USE Radio speeches

Radio thrillers
USE Thrillers (Radio programs)

Radio training programs
USE Instructional radio programs

Radio variety shows
USE Variety shows (Radio programs)

Radio war dramas
USE War radio dramas

Reality-based radio programs
USE Reality radio programs

Reality-based television programs
USE Reality television programs

Reality radio programs

UF Reality-based radio programs
BT Nonfiction radio programs

Reality shows (Television programs)
USE Reality television programs

Reality television programs *(Not Subd Geog)*

UF Reality-based television programs
      Reality shows (Television programs)
BT Nonfiction television programs
NT Big Brother television programs
      Makeover television programs

Recorded books
USE Audiobooks

Recorded sound interviews
USE Interviews (Sound recordings)

Recordings, Sound
USE Sound recordings

Reenactments, Historical (Motion picture)
USE Historical reenactments (Motion pictures)

Reenactments, Historical (Television programs)
USE Historical reenactments (Television programs)

Rehearsals, Radio
USE Radio rehearsals

Reimagined television programs
USE Television remakes

Religion films
USE Religious films

Religion television programs
USE Religious television programs

Religious films *(Not Subd Geog)*

UF Religion films
BT Motion pictures
NT Bible films
      Christian films

Religious radio programs

BT Radio programs
RT Inspirational radio programs
NT Christian radio programs
      Radio sermons

Religious television programs
(Not Subd Geog)

UF Religion television programs
BT Television programs
NT Bible television programs
      Christian television programs

Remade television programs
USE Television remakes

Remakes, Film
USE Film remakes

Remakes, Television
USE Television remakes

Reporter films
USE Journalism films

Reporter television programs
USE Journalism television programs

Ride films
USE Amusement ride films

Ride movies
USE Amusement ride films

Rite of passage films
USE Coming-of-age films

Rite of passage television programs
USE Coming-of-age television programs

Road films *(Not Subd Geog)*

This heading is used as a genre/form heading for films that are set on the open road.

UF Road movies
BT Motion pictures

Road movies
USE Road films

Road television programs *(Not Subd Geog)*

This heading is used as a genre/form heading for television programs that are set on the open road.

BT Television programs

Rock and roll music radio programs
USE Rock music radio programs

Rock concert documentaries
USE Rock concert films

Rock concert documentary films
USE Rock concert films

Rock concert films *(Not Subd Geog)*

UF Rock concert documentaries
      Rock concert documentary films
      Rock docs (Motion pictures)
      Rock documentaries
      Rock documentary films
BT Concert films

Rock docs (Motion pictures)
USE Rock concert films

Rock documentaries
USE Rock concert films

Rock documentary films
USE Rock concert films

Rock films

BT Musical films

Rock music radio programs

UF Music radio programs, Rock
      Rock and roll music radio programs
      Rock-n-roll music radio programs
BT Radio programs

Rock music videos
USE Rock videos

Rock-n-roll music radio programs
USE Rock music radio programs

Rock videos *(Not Subd Geog)*

UF Rock music videos
      Videos, Rock
BT Music videos

Rocky Balboa films
USE Rocky films

Rocky films *(Not Subd Geog)*

UF Rocky Balboa films
BT Motion pictures

Romance films *(Not Subd Geog)*

This heading is used as a genre/form heading for films that feature the development of love between the main characters.

UF Chick flicks
      Hollywood romance films
      Love films
      Romance (Motion pictures)
      Romance movies
      Romance pictures (Motion pictures)
      Romantic films
      Romantic movies
BT Motion pictures
NT Romantic comedy films

Romance (Motion pictures)
USE Romance films

Romance movies
USE Romance films

Romance pictures (Motion pictures)
USE Romance films

Romance television programs
(Not Subd Geog)
   This heading is used as a genre/form heading for television programs that feature the development of love between the main characters.
   UF Love television programs
   BT Television programs
   NT Romantic comedy television programs
Romantic comedies (Motion pictures)
   USE Romantic comedy films
Romantic comedies (Television programs)
   USE Romantic comedy television programs
Romantic comedy films *(Not Subd Geog)*
   UF Romantic comedies (Motion pictures)
   BT Comedy films
        Romance films
   RT Screwball comedy films
        Sophisticated comedy films
Romantic comedy television programs
(Not Subd Geog)
   UF Romantic comedies (Television programs)
   BT Romance television programs
        Television comedies
   RT Sophisticated comedy television programs
Romantic films
   USE Romance films
Romantic movies
   USE Romance films
Romantic screwball comedy films
   USE Screwball comedy films
Roundtables, Filmed
   USE Filmed panel discussions
Roundtables, Radio
   USE Radio panel discussions
Rubble films *(Not Subd Geog)*
   This heading is used as a genre/form heading for films produced in the years after World War II, often featuring exteriors in bombed-out cities.
   BT Motion pictures
Runaway films
   USE Chase films
Rural bandit films
   USE Gangster films
Rural bandit television programs
   USE Gangster television programs
Rural comedies (Motion pictures)
   USE Rural comedy films
Rural comedies (Television programs)
   USE Rural comedy television programs
Rural comedy films *(Not Subd Geog)*
   This heading is used as a genre/form heading for films that feature rural locations or characters with rural origins and often depict the clash between rural and urban lifestyles and behavior.
   UF Farm comedy films
        Farmer comedy films
        Hillbilly comedy films
        Rural comedies (Motion pictures)
        Rustic comedy films
   BT Comedy films
Rural comedy television programs
(Not Subd Geog)
   This heading is used as a genre/form heading for television programs that feature rural locations or characters with rural origins and often depict the clash between rural and urban lifestyles and behavior.
   UF Farm comedy television programs
        Hillbilly comedy television programs
        Rural comedies (Television programs)
        Rustic comedy television programs
   BT Television comedies
Rushes (Motion pictures) *(Not Subd Geog)*
   This heading is used as a genre/form heading for workprints of a day's shooting of a film, usually meant to be shown and studied before the next day's shooting begins.
   UF Dailies (Motion pictures)
   BT Motion pictures
   RT Unedited footage

Rushes (Television programs)
(Not Subd Geog)
   This heading is used as a genre/form heading for workprints of a day's shooting of a television program, usually meant to be shown and studied before the next day's shooting begins.
   UF Dailies (Television programs)
   BT Television programs
   RT Unedited footage
Rustic comedy films
   USE Rural comedy films
Rustic comedy television programs
   USE Rural comedy television programs
Samurai films *(Not Subd Geog)*
   This heading is used as a genre/form heading for films that feature samurai, usually set in the Tokugawa period of Japanese history.
   UF Chambara films
   BT Motion pictures
   NT Zatoichi films
Sand-and-surf films
   USE Beach party films
Sand animation films
   USE Silhouette animation films
Sandal-and-spear epics (Motion pictures)
   USE Peplum films
Schulmädchen-Report films *(Not Subd Geog)*
   BT Erotic films
Science fiction films *(Not Subd Geog)*
   BT Fiction films
   NT Alien films
        Dystopian films
        Star Trek films
        Star Wars films
        Superhero films
Science fiction radio programs
   BT Fiction radio programs
Science fiction television programs
(Not Subd Geog)
   BT Fiction television programs
   NT Star Trek television programs
        Superhero television programs
Science films *(Not Subd Geog)*
   This heading is used as a genre/form heading for films that are intended to educate or inform about science or scientific topics.
   BT Educational films
   NT Nature films
Science radio programs
   BT Educational radio programs
        Instructional radio programs
Science television programs *(Not Subd Geog)*
   This heading is used as a genre/form heading for television programs that are intended to educate or inform about science or scientific topics.
   BT Educational television programs
   NT Nature television programs
Scooby-Doo films
   BT Motion pictures
Scooby-Doo television programs
(Not Subd Geog)
   BT Animated television programs
Scoped radio airchecks
   USE Telescoped radio airchecks
Screen biographies
   USE Biographical films
Screen-reliant installations (Art)
   USE Video installations (Art)
Screen tests *(Not Subd Geog)*
   This heading is used as a genre/form heading for recordings of screen tests.
   UF Auditions, Film
        Auditions, Motion picture
        Auditions, Television
        Film auditions
        Motion picture auditions
        Motion picture screen tests
        Television auditions
        Television screen tests
   BT Motion pictures
        Television programs
Screwball comedies
   USE Screwball comedy films

Screwball comedy films *(Not Subd Geog)*
   UF Crazy comedy films
        Madcap comedy films
        Madcap romantic comedies
        Oddball comedy films
        Romantic screwball comedy films
        Screwball comedies
        Wacky comedy films
        White telephone comedy films
   BT Comedy films
   RT Romantic comedy films
Sculptmation films
   USE Clay animation films
Sculptmation television programs
   USE Clay animation television programs
Secret agent films
   USE Spy films
Secret service films
   USE Spy films
Semi-object animation films
   USE Silhouette animation films
Semidocumentary films
   USE Documentary-style films
Semidocumentary television programs
   USE Documentary-style television programs
Send-up films
   USE Parody films
Sequels, Film
   USE Film sequels
Sequels, Television
   USE Television sequels
Serial films
   USE Film serials
Serials, Film
   USE Film serials
Serials, Limited (Television programs)
   USE Television mini-series
Serials, Radio
   USE Radio serials
Serials, Television
   USE Television series
Series, Television
   USE Television series
Sermons, Radio
   USE Radio sermons
Sex-and-sand films
   USE Peplum films
Shadow plays, Filmed
   USE Filmed shadow shows
Shadow shows, Filmed
   USE Filmed shadow shows
Sherlock Holmes films *(Not Subd Geog)*
   BT Detective and mystery films
Sherlock Holmes television programs
(Not Subd Geog)
   BT Detective and mystery television
        programs
Short feature films
   USE Short films
Short films *(Not Subd Geog)*
   This heading is used as a genre/form heading for films usually limited to a running time of less than 40 minutes.
   UF Short feature films
        Shorts (Motion pictures)
   BT Motion pictures
   NT Actualities (Motion pictures)
        Chase films
        Novelty films
        Private Snafu films
        Trigger films
Shorts (Motion pictures)
   USE Short films
Shortwave radio broadcasts
   UF Broadcasts, Shortwave radio
        Radio broadcasts, Shortwave
   BT Radio programs
Show business films *(Not Subd Geog)*
   This heading is used as a genre/form heading for films that feature a behind-the-scenes look at the show business industry.
   BT Motion pictures

Show business television programs
(Not Subd Geog)
This heading is used as a genre/form heading for television programs that feature a behind-the-scenes look at the show business industry.
BT   Television programs
Shows, Radio
USE   Radio programs
Shows, Television
USE   Television programs
Silent films   *(Not Subd Geog)*
This heading is used as a genre/form heading for films produced in the early days of the motion picture industry before the advent of talking films.
UF   Silent motion pictures
BT   Motion pictures
NT   Actualities (Motion pictures)
Silent motion pictures
USE   Silent films
Silhouette animation films   *(Not Subd Geog)*
UF   Flat-figure animation films
Sand animation films
Semi-object animation films
BT   Animated films
Singing cowboy films   *(Not Subd Geog)*
This heading is used as a genre/form heading for films that feature a non-violent, singing cowboy hero.
BT   Western films
Singing cowboy television programs
(Not Subd Geog)
This heading is used as a genre/form heading for television programs that feature a non-violent, singing cowboy hero.
BT   Western television programs
Sitcoms (Television programs)
USE   Situation comedies (Television programs)
Situation comedies, Radio
USE   Radio comedies
Situation comedies (Television programs)
(Not Subd Geog)
UF   Sitcoms (Television programs)
Television sitcoms
Television situation comedies
BT   Television comedies
RT   Domestic comedy television programs
Skating films   *(Not Subd Geog)*
BT   Sports films
Sketch comedy television programs
(Not Subd Geog)
UF   Sketch shows (Television programs)
Skit shows (Television programs)
Television sketch comedy programs
BT   Television comedies
Sketch films
USE   Anthology films
Sketch shows (Television programs)
USE   Sketch comedy television programs
Skit shows (Television programs)
USE   Sketch comedy television programs
Slapstick comedy films   *(Not Subd Geog)*
This heading is used as a genre/form heading for films that derive humor from physical comedy.
BT   Comedy films
Slapstick comedy television programs
(Not Subd Geog)
This heading is used as a genre/form heading for television programs that derive humor from physical comedy.
BT   Television comedies
Slasher films   *(Not Subd Geog)*
UF   Slashers (Motion pictures)
Splatter flicks
BT   Horror films
NT   Friday the 13th films
Slashers (Motion pictures)
USE   Slasher films
Snafu films
USE   Private Snafu films

Snuff films   *(Not Subd Geog)*
This heading is used as a genre/form heading for films that feature a murder as the climax of sexual activity.
BT   Exploitation films
Pornographic films
Soap operas, Radio
USE   Radio soap operas
Soap operas, Television
USE   Television soap operas
Soccer films   *(Not Subd Geog)*
BT   Sports films
Soccer television programs   *(Not Subd Geog)*
BT   Sports television programs
NT   Televised soccer games
Social comedy films
USE   Sophisticated comedy films
Social consciousness films
USE   Social problem films
Social consciousness television programs
USE   Social problem television programs
Social guidance films   *(Not Subd Geog)*
This heading is used as a genre/form heading for films that guide people, especially teenagers, in proper behavior, dating, personal safety, etc.
UF   Guidance films, Social
Mental hygiene films
BT   Educational films
Social problem films   *(Not Subd Geog)*
This heading is used as a genre/form heading for films that dramatize a specific social ill, or a contemporary political issue, to draw attention to it.
UF   Social consciousness films
BT   Motion pictures
Social problem television programs
(Not Subd Geog)
This heading is used as a genre/form heading for television programs that dramatize a specific social ill, or a contemporary political issue, to draw attention to it.
UF   Social consciousness television programs
BT   Television programs
Sophisticated comedy films   *(Not Subd Geog)*
This heading is used as a genre/form heading for films that feature the lives of the rich and urbane, particularly their marital and romantic relationships.
UF   High comedy films
Social comedy films
BT   Comedy films
RT   Romantic comedy films
Sophisticated comedy television programs
(Not Subd Geog)
This heading is used as a genre/form heading for television comedies that feature the lives of the rich and urbane, particularly their marital and romantic relationships.
BT   Television comedies
RT   Romantic comedy television programs
Sound recordings
This heading is used as a genre/form heading for collections of sound recordings that are composed of multiple genres and/or forms to which more specific headings such as Oral histories or Audiobooks cannot be applied.
UF   Recordings, Sound
NT   Audiobooks
Interviews (Sound recordings)
Live sound recordings
Podcasts
Radio programs
Test pressings (Sound recordings)
Spaghetti Easterns
USE   Martial arts films
Spaghetti Western films
USE   Spaghetti Westerns
Spaghetti Westerns   *(Not Subd Geog)*
This heading is used as a genre/form heading for Western films usually produced or co-produced by Italian companies and filmed in Europe.
UF   Eurowesterns
Spaghetti Western films
BT   Western films

Special events radio coverage
This heading is used as a genre/form heading for radio reports of noteworthy events, often featuring several commentators and combining studio reports with on-the-scene coverage. Radio programs that feature commentators in the studio reporting on current events and noteworthy issues are entered under Radio news programs. Radio reportorial pieces recorded on location are entered under Radio field reports.
UF   Radio coverage, Special events
BT   Nonfiction radio programs
Special events television coverage
(Not Subd Geog)
This heading is used as a genre/form heading for television programs that record live, on-the-scene coverage of special events. Television programs that report and comment on recent events are entered under Television news programs.
UF   Special events (Television programs)
BT   Nonfiction television programs
RT   Television news programs
Special events (Television programs)
USE   Special events television coverage
Special television programs
USE   Television specials
Specials, Radio
USE   Radio specials
Spectacles (Motion pictures)
USE   Epic films
Spectacles (Television programs)
USE   Epic television programs
Spectaculars (Motion pictures)
USE   Epic films
Spectaculars (Television programs)
USE   Epic television programs
Speeches (Motion pictures)
USE   Filmed speeches
Speeches, Radio
USE   Radio speeches
Speeches, Television
USE   Televised speeches
Splatter flicks
USE   Slasher films
Spoof films
USE   Parody films
Spoof television programs
USE   Parody television programs
Spoofs (Motion pictures)
USE   Parody films
Spoofs (Television programs)
USE   Parody television programs
Spookfests (Motion pictures)
USE   Horror films
Sporting events, Radio
USE   Radio sports events
Sporting films
USE   Sports films
Sports events, Radio
USE   Radio sports events
Sports events, Televised
USE   Televised sports events
Sports films   *(Not Subd Geog)*
UF   Sporting films
BT   Motion pictures
NT   Baseball films
Basketball films
Boxing films
Filmed sports events
Football films
Hockey films
Mountain films
Skating films
Soccer films
Surfing films
Sports news radio programs
USE   Sports radio news programs
Sports radio news programs
UF   Sports news radio programs
BT   Radio news programs

Sports television programs *(Not Subd Geog)*
  BT Television programs
  NT Baseball television programs
     Basketball television programs
     Football television programs
     Golf television programs
     Hockey television programs
     Martial arts television programs
     Soccer television programs
     Televised sports events
     Tennis television programs
Spots, Radio (Advertisements)
  USE Radio commercials (Advertisements)
Spy films *(Not Subd Geog)*
  UF Cloak and dagger films
     Espionage films
     Secret agent films
     Secret service films
  BT Motion pictures
  NT James Bond films
Spy radio programs
  UF Espionage radio programs
     Radio espionage programs
     Radio spy programs
  BT Radio programs
  RT Radio crime shows
Spy television programs *(Not Subd Geog)*
  UF Espionage television programs
  BT Television programs
Stag films
  USE Pornographic films
Stage productions, Filmed
  USE Filmed plays
Stage productions, Televised
  USE Televised plays
Stand-up comedy routines, Televised
  USE Televised stand-up comedy routines
Star Trek films *(Not Subd Geog)*
  BT Science fiction films
Star Trek television programs
  (Not Subd Geog)
  BT Science fiction television programs
Star Wars films *(Not Subd Geog)*
  BT Science fiction films
Stereoscopic films
  USE 3-D films
Stock footage *(Not Subd Geog)*
    This heading is used as a genre/form heading for pre-recorded footage used or collected and organized to be used in the production of films, television programs, and video recordings.
  UF Found footage (Motion pictures, television, etc.)
     Library film
     Library shots (Motion pictures, television, etc.)
     Motion picture stock materials
     Stock materials (Motion pictures, television, etc.)
     Stock shots (Motion pictures, television, etc.)
     Stockshot (Motion pictures, television, etc.)
  BT Motion pictures
     Television programs
     Video recordings
  RT Unedited footage
Stock materials (Motion pictures, television, etc.)
  USE Stock footage
Stock shots (Motion pictures, television, etc.)
  USE Stock footage
Stockshot (Motion pictures, television, etc.)
  USE Stock footage
Street films *(Not Subd Geog)*
    This heading is used as a genre/form heading for films that represent the downtown street as a dangerous lure.
  BT Motion pictures

Structural films *(Not Subd Geog)*
    This heading is used as a genre/form heading for films that use photographic techniques to investigate the nature of film as an aesthetic experience.
  UF Structuralist films
  BT Experimental films
Structuralist films
  USE Structural films
Subcultural films
  USE Subculture films
Subculture cult films
  USE Subculture films
Subculture films *(Not Subd Geog)*
  UF Cult films, Subculture
     Subcultural films
     Subculture cult films
     Subculture movies
  BT Motion pictures
Subculture movies
  USE Subculture films
Submarine films *(Not Subd Geog)*
  UF Submarine movies
     Submarine war films
  BT War films
Submarine movies
  USE Submarine films
Submarine war films
  USE Submarine films
Sun-and-sand films
  USE Beach party films
Superhero films *(Not Subd Geog)*
  UF Comic strip superhero films
     Comic strip superheroes films
     Superheroes films
  BT Fantasy films
     Science fiction films
  NT Batman films
     Flash Gordon films
     Superman films
Superhero television programs
  (Not Subd Geog)
  BT Fantasy television programs
     Science fiction television programs
Superheroes films
  USE Superhero films
Superman films *(Not Subd Geog)*
  BT Superhero films
Surfer films
  USE Surfing films
Surfing films *(Not Subd Geog)*
  UF Surfer films
  BT Sports films
Surrealist films *(Not Subd Geog)*
    This heading is used as a genre/form heading for films that employ symbolism, juxtaposition of unlike objects, dream-like sequences, etc., to allow the viewer's subconscious to make free associations.
  BT Experimental films
Survival films *(Not Subd Geog)*
    This heading is used as a genre/form heading for films that feature individuals or groups struggling for their lives in a harsh setting. Films that feature a man-made or natural calamity that places people in imminent danger are entered under Disaster films.
  UF Survival pictures (Motion pictures)
  BT Motion pictures
  RT Disaster films
Survival pictures (Motion pictures)
  USE Survival films
Survival television programs
  (Not Subd Geog)
    This heading is used as a genre/form heading for television programs that feature individuals or groups struggling for their lives in a harsh setting. Television programs that feature a man-made or natural calamity that places people in imminent danger are entered under Disaster television programs.
  BT Television programs
  RT Disaster television programs
Suspense films
  USE Thrillers (Motion pictures)
Suspense radio programs
  USE Thrillers (Radio programs)

Suspense television programs
  USE Thrillers (Television programs)
Suspense thrillers (Motion pictures)
  USE Thrillers (Motion pictures)
Suspense thrillers (Radio programs)
  USE Thrillers (Radio programs)
Suspense thrillers (Television programs)
  USE Thrillers (Television programs)
Swashbuckler films *(Not Subd Geog)*
    This heading is used as a genre/form heading for films that feature heroic characters in period costume and have swordplay as a central element.
  UF Swashbucklers (Motion pictures)
     Swashbuckling films
     Sword-fight films
     Swordplay films
  BT Motion pictures
  RT Action and adventure films
Swashbucklers (Motion pictures)
  USE Swashbuckler films
Swashbuckling films
  USE Swashbuckler films
Sword-and-sandal epics (Motion pictures)
  USE Peplum films
Sword-fight films
  USE Swashbuckler films
Swordplay films
  USE Swashbuckler films
Syndicate films
  USE Gangster films
Syndicate-oriented films
  USE Gangster films
Takeoff films
  USE Parody films
Talent shows (Radio programs)
  UF Amateur talent shows (Radio programs)
     Radio talent shows
  BT Nonfiction radio programs
Talk radio programs
  USE Radio talk shows
Talk radio shows
  USE Radio talk shows
Talk shows, Radio
  USE Radio talk shows
Talk shows (Television programs)
  USE Television talk shows
Talk television programs
  USE Television talk shows
Talk television shows
  USE Television talk shows
Talking books
    This heading is used as a genre/form heading for spoken texts recorded specifically for use by the blind or people with visual disabilities.
  BT Audiobooks
Talks, Radio
  USE Radio speeches
Talks, Television
  USE Televised speeches
Tape recorded interviews
  USE Interviews (Sound recordings)
Tarzan films *(Not Subd Geog)*
  BT Motion pictures
Teen cinema
  USE Teen films
Teen drama (Motion pictures)
  USE Teen films
Teen drama (Television programs)
  USE Teen television programs

Teen films   (Not Subd Geog)
    This heading is used as a genre/form heading for films produced especially for a teenage audience (i.e., the general age range of thirteen through eighteen years) and films with teenagers and teen issues as the primary subject.
    UF Teen cinema
          Teen drama (Motion pictures)
          Teen movies
          Teen-targeted films
          Teenage films
          Teenage movies
          Teenpics
          Youth films
    BT Motion pictures
    NT Beach party films
          Coming-of-age films
          Juvenile delinquency films
Teen movies
    USE Teen films
Teen-targeted films
    USE Teen films
Teen television programs   (Not Subd Geog)
    UF Teen drama (Television programs)
          Teenage television programs
          Youth television programs
    BT Television programs
    NT Coming-of-age television programs
          Juvenile delinquency television
             programs
Teenage films
    USE Teen films
Teenage movies
    USE Teen films
Teenage television programs
    USE Teen television programs
Teenpics
    USE Teen films
Tele-features
    USE Made-for-TV movies
Telefantasy
    USE Fantasy television programs
Telefeatures
    USE Made-for-TV movies
Telefilms
    USE Made-for-TV movies
Telementaries
    USE Documentary television programs
Telemovies
    USE Made-for-TV movies
Telenovelas
    USE Television soap operas
Telepics
    USE Made-for-TV movies
Telescoped airchecks (Radio programs)
    USE Telescoped radio airchecks
Telescoped radio airchecks
    UF Scoped radio airchecks
          Telescoped airchecks (Radio programs)
    BT Radio airchecks
Televised ballets   (Not Subd Geog)
    BT Ballet television programs
          Televised dance
Televised baseball games   (Not Subd Geog)
    BT Baseball television programs
          Televised sports events
Televised basketball games   (Not Subd Geog)
    BT Basketball television programs
          Televised sports events
Televised dance
    BT Dance television programs
          Televised performances
    NT Televised ballets
Televised debates
    USE Television debates
Televised football games   (Not Subd Geog)
    BT Football television programs
          Televised sports events
Televised golf matches   (Not Subd Geog)
    BT Golf television programs
          Televised sports events

Televised hockey games   (Not Subd Geog)
    BT Hockey television programs
          Televised sports events
Televised martial arts events   (Not Subd Geog)
    BT Martial arts television programs
          Televised sports events
Televised musicals   (Not Subd Geog)
    BT Televised performances
          Television musicals
Televised operas   (Not Subd Geog)
    BT Opera television programs
          Televised performances
Televised performances   (Not Subd Geog)
    UF Performances, Televised
    BT Nonfiction television programs
    NT Televised dance
          Televised musicals
          Televised operas
          Televised plays
          Televised stand-up comedy routines
Televised plays   (Not Subd Geog)
    This heading is used as a genre/form heading for television broadcasts of performances of plays.
    UF Plays, Televised
          Stage productions, Televised
          Televised stage productions
    BT Televised performances
Televised soccer games   (Not Subd Geog)
    BT Soccer television programs
          Televised sports events
Televised speeches   (Not Subd Geog)
    This heading is used as a genre/form heading for speeches presented specifically to television audiences or speeches that are presented to other audiences and broadcast on television.
    UF Addresses, Television
          Speeches, Television
          Talks, Television
          Television addresses
          Television speeches
            [Former heading]
          Television talks
    BT Nonfiction television programs
Televised sports events   (Not Subd Geog)
    UF Sports events, Televised
    BT Nonfiction television programs
          Sports television programs
    NT Televised baseball games
          Televised basketball games
          Televised football games
          Televised golf matches
          Televised hockey games
          Televised martial arts events
          Televised soccer games
          Televised tennis matches
Televised stage productions
    USE Televised plays
Televised stand-up comedy routines
    (Not Subd Geog)
    UF Stand-up comedy routines, Televised
    BT Televised performances
          Television comedies
Televised tennis matches   (Not Subd Geog)
    BT Televised sports events
          Tennis television programs
Television adaptations   (Not Subd Geog)
    UF Adaptations, Television
    BT Television programs
Television addresses
    USE Televised speeches
Television ads
    USE Television commercials
Television advertisements
    USE Television commercials
Television auditions
    USE Screen tests
Television award presentations
    USE Award presentations (Television
            programs)
Television biographies
    USE Biographical television programs

Television book review programs
    USE Book review television programs
Television cartoon shows
    USE Animated television programs
Television clips
    USE Television program clips
Television comedies   (Not Subd Geog)
    UF Comedies, Television
          Comedy-drama television programs
          Comedy programs, Television
          Comedy television programs
          Farces (Television programs)
          Farcical television programs
          Television comedy programs
    BT Television programs
    NT Dark comedy television programs
          Domestic comedy television programs
          Fantasy comedies (Television programs)
          Parody television programs
          Romantic comedy television programs
          Rural comedy television programs
          Situation comedies (Television
            programs)
          Sketch comedy television programs
          Slapstick comedy television programs
          Sophisticated comedy television
            programs
          Televised stand-up comedy routines
Television comedy programs
    USE Television comedies
Television commercials   (Not Subd Geog)
    UF Ads, Television
          Advertisements, Television
          Commercials, Television
          Television ads
          Television advertisements
          Television commercials
           (Advertisements)
           [Former heading]
    BT Television programs
    NT Political television commercials
          Promos (Television commercials)
Television commercials (Advertisements)
    USE Television commercials
Television community service announcements
    USE Television public service
           announcements
Television concerts
    USE Concert television programs
Television cooking shows   (Not Subd Geog)
    UF Cooking shows, Television
          Cooking television programs
          Food shows (Television programs)
    BT Nonfiction television programs
Television cop shows   (Not Subd Geog)
    UF Cop television programs
          Police shows (Television programs)
          Police television programs
    BT Television crime shows
    RT Detective and mystery television
           programs
Television crime shows   (Not Subd Geog)
    This heading is used as a genre/form heading for fictional television programs that feature the commission and investigation of crimes.   Nonfiction television programs that feature actual footage and reenactments of criminal and police activities are entered under True crime television programs.
    UF Crime television programs
          Criminal shows
          Criminal television programs
    BT Fiction television programs
    RT Caper television programs
          Thrillers (Television programs)
    NT Detective and mystery television
           programs
          Gangster television programs
          Juvenile delinquency television
           programs
          Prison television programs
          Television cop shows

Television CSAs
  USE Television public service
      announcements
Television dance parties *(Not Subd Geog)*
  UF Dance parties, Television
  BT Television programs
Television debates *(Not Subd Geog)*
  UF Debates, Television
      Televised debates
  BT Nonfiction television programs
Television discussions
  USE Television panel discussions
Television documentaries
  USE Documentary television programs
Television documentary programs
  USE Documentary television programs
Television epics
  USE Epic television programs
Television excerpts
  USE Television program excerpts
Television features
  USE Made-for-TV movies
Television films
  USE Made-for-TV movies
Television forums
  USE Television panel discussions
Television game shows *(Not Subd Geog)*
    This heading is used as a genre/form heading for
  television programs that feature contestants partici-
  pating in various types of competitive activities for
  prizes. Television programs that feature a question-
  and-answer format are entered under Television quiz
  shows.
  UF Game shows (Television programs)
  BT Television programs
Television historical reenactments
  USE Historical reenactments (Television
      programs)
Television interviews *(Not Subd Geog)*
  UF Interview television programs
      Interviews (Television programs)
      TV interviews
  BT Nonfiction television programs
  RT Television talk shows
Television lectures *(Not Subd Geog)*
  UF Lectures, Television
  BT Nonfiction television programs
Television melodramas *(Not Subd Geog)*
    This heading is used as a genre/form heading
  for fictional television programs that feature suffer-
  ing protagonists victimized by situations or events, in
  which emotion is emphasized.
  UF Melodramas, Television
      Melodramatic television programs
  BT Fiction television programs
  RT Television soap operas
Television mini-series *(Not Subd Geog)*
  UF Limited serials (Television programs)
      Mini-series, Television
      Miniseries, Television
      Serials, Limited (Television programs)
      Television miniseries
  BT Television series
Television miniseries
  USE Television mini-series
Television movies
  USE Made-for-TV movies
Television musicals *(Not Subd Geog)*
  UF Musical television programs
      Musicals (Television programs)
  BT Television programs
  NT Televised musicals
Television news conferences
  USE Television press conferences

Television news programs *(Not Subd Geog)*
    This heading is used as a genre/form heading for
  television programs that report and comment on re-
  cent events. Television programs that record live, on-
  the-scene coverage of special events are entered under
  Special events television coverage.
  UF News programs, Television
      News television programs
      Television newscasts
  BT Nonfiction television programs
  RT Special events television coverage
  NT Entertainment news programs
      Television press conferences
Television newscasts
  USE Television news programs
Television panel discussions *(Not Subd Geog)*
    This heading is used as a genre/form heading for
  television programs that feature discussions of topics
  by panels of speakers or experts.
  UF Discussion shows (Television programs)
      Discussion television programs
      Panel discussions, Television
      Television discussions
      Television forums
      Television roundtables
  BT Nonfiction television programs
Television parodies
  USE Parody television programs
Television pilot programs *(Not Subd Geog)*
  UF Pilot programs, Television
      Pilots (Television programs)
      Television pilots
  BT Television series
Television pilots
  USE Television pilot programs
Television press conferences *(Not Subd Geog)*
  UF News conferences, Television
      Press conferences, Television
      Television news conferences
  BT Television news programs
Television program clips *(Not Subd Geog)*
    This heading is used as a genre/form heading for
  short segments, usually incomplete scenes, of tele-
  vision programs. Parts, usually complete scenes or
  sequences, extracted from a complete television pro-
  gram are entered under Television program excerpts.
  UF Clips, Television program
      Television clips
  BT Television programs
Television program excerpts *(Not Subd Geog)*
    This heading is used as a genre/form heading for
  parts, usually complete scenes or sequences, extracted
  from a complete television program. Short segments,
  usually incomplete scenes, of television programs are
  entered under Television program clips.
  UF Excerpts, Television program
      Television excerpts
  BT Television programs
Television programs *(Not Subd Geog)*
    This heading is used as a genre/form heading for
  collections of television programs that are composed
  of multiple genres and/or forms to which more specific headings such as Nonfiction television programs
  or Television comedies cannot be applied.
  UF Programs, Television
      Shows, Television
      Television shows
      TV shows
  NT Action and adventure television
        programs
      Animal television programs
      Animated television programs
      Anthology television programs
      Anti-war television programs
      Aviation television programs
      Biographical television programs
      Buddy television programs
      Caper television programs
      Children's television programs
      Christmas television programs
      College life television programs
      Commissario Montalbano television
        programs

      Compilation television programs
      Cultural television programs
      DeGrassi television programs
      Disaster television programs
      Don Juan television programs
      Epic television programs
      Erotic television programs
      Ethnic television programs
      Fiction television programs
      Historical television programs
      Home shopping television programs
      Horror television programs
      Infomercials
      Legal television programs
      Live television programs
      Made-for-TV movies
      Medical television programs
      Military television programs
      Monster television programs
      Music videos
      Nanny television programs
      Nonfiction television programs
      Opera television programs
      Outtakes
      Podcasts
      Pornographic television programs
      Propaganda television programs
      Puppet television programs
      Religious television programs
      Road television programs
      Romance television programs
      Rushes (Television programs)
      Screen tests
      Show business television programs
      Social problem television programs
      Sports television programs
      Spy television programs
      Stock footage
      Survival television programs
      Teen television programs
      Television adaptations
      Television comedies
      Television commercials
      Television dance parties
      Television game shows
      Television musicals
      Television program clips
      Television program excerpts
      Television programs for people with
        visual disabilities
      Television programs for the hearing
        impaired
      Television public service
        announcements
      Television quiz shows
      Television remakes
      Television sequels
      Television series
      Television specials
      Thrillers (Television programs)
      Unedited footage
      War television programs
      Webisodes
      Western television programs
**Television programs for people with visual
  disabilities** *(Not Subd Geog)*
  BT Television programs
Television programs for the deaf
  USE Television programs for the hearing
      impaired
Television programs for the hearing impaired
  (Not Subd Geog)
  UF Captioned television programs
      Closed captioned television programs
      Television programs for the deaf
  BT Television programs
Television promos
  USE Promos (Television commercials)
Television promotional announcements
  USE Promos (Television commercials)

Television PSAs
  USE Television public service
       announcements
Television public service announcements
  (Not Subd Geog)
       This heading is used as a genre/form heading for
  television announcements aired by or on behalf of
  nonprofit or governmental organizations to persuade
  the audience to take some specific action or adopt a
  favorable view toward a service, institution, or cause.
  Television programs aired by or on behalf of nonprofit
  or governmental organizations to promote the common well-being or general welfare of society are entered under Public service television programs.
  UF CSAs, Television
      PSAs, Television
      Public service announcements,
        Television
      Television community service
        announcements
      Television CSAs
      Television PSAs
  BT Television programs
Television puppet shows
  USE Puppet television programs
Television quiz shows *(Not Subd Geog)*
       This heading is used as a genre/form heading
  for television programs that feature a question-and-
  answer format. Television programs that feature con-
  testants participating in various types of competitive
  activities for prizes are entered under Television game
  shows.
  UF Quiz shows (Television programs)
  BT Television programs
Television reimaginings
  USE Television remakes
Television remakes
  UF Reimagined television programs
      Remade television programs
      Remakes, Television
      Television reimaginings
  BT Television programs
Television roundtables
  USE Television panel discussions
Television screen tests
  USE Screen tests
Television sequels
  UF Sequels, Television
  BT Television programs
Television serials
  USE Television series
Television series *(Not Subd Geog)*
  UF Serials, Television
      Series, Television
      Television serials
  BT Television programs
  NT Television mini-series
      Television pilot programs
      Television soap operas
Television shows
  USE Television programs
Television sitcoms
  USE Situation comedies (Television
       programs)
Television situation comedies
  USE Situation comedies (Television
       programs)
Television sketch comedy programs
  USE Sketch comedy television programs
Television soap operas *(Not Subd Geog)*
  UF Soap operas, Television
      Telenovelas
  BT Television series
  RT Television melodramas
Television specials *(Not Subd Geog)*
  UF Special television programs
  BT Television programs
Television speeches
  USE Televised speeches
Television talk programs
  USE Television talk shows

Television talk shows *(Not Subd Geog)*
  UF Talk shows (Television programs)
      Talk television programs
      Talk television shows
      Television talk programs
      TV talk shows
  BT Nonfiction television programs
  RT Audience participation television
       programs
      Television interviews
Television talks
  USE Televised speeches
Television thrillers
  USE Thrillers (Television programs)
Television travelogues
  USE Travelogues (Television programs)
Television variety shows
  USE Variety shows (Television programs)
Tennis television programs *(Not Subd Geog)*
  BT Sports television programs
  NT Televised tennis matches
Test pressings (Sound recordings)
       This heading is used as a genre/form heading for
  pressed or molded disc sound recordings, usually with
  plain, typed or handwritten labels, that are frequently
  either rough, first off the press recordings made to as-
  sist in judging whether a recording or take is suitable
  for issue, or recordings pressed by special order.
  UF Pressings, Test (Sound recordings)
  BT Sound recordings
Theater ads (Motion pictures)
  USE Theater commercials (Motion pictures)
Theater announcements (Motion pictures)
  (Not Subd Geog)
       This heading is used as a genre/form heading for
  short, non-commercial films shown to theater audi-
  ences for various purposes, including requesting the
  audience not to smoke, talk, etc.
  UF Announcements, Theater (Motion
        pictures)
  BT Motion pictures
Theater commercials (Motion pictures)
  (Not Subd Geog)
  UF Movie theater ads (Motion pictures)
      Pre-feature advertisements
      Theater ads (Motion pictures)
  BT Motion pictures
Theatrical trailers
  USE Film trailers
Three-dimensional films
  USE 3-D films
Three Stooges films *(Not Subd Geog)*
  BT Comedy films
Thrill ride films
  USE Amusement ride films
Thriller films
  USE Thrillers (Motion pictures)
Thriller radio programs
  USE Thrillers (Radio programs)
Thriller television programs
  USE Thrillers (Television programs)
Thrillers (Motion pictures) *(Not Subd Geog)*
       This heading is used as a genre/form heading for
  films that feature a build up of suspense, tension, un-
  certainty, menace, and anxiety as primary elements
  and in which the audience is kept on tenterhooks.
  UF Film thrillers
      Psycho thrillers (Motion pictures)
      Psychological thrillers (Motion pictures)
      Suspense films
      Suspense thrillers (Motion pictures)
      Thriller films
  BT Motion pictures
  RT Crime films

Thrillers (Radio programs)
       This heading is used as a genre/form heading for
  radio programs that feature a build up of suspense,
  tension, uncertainty, menace, and anxiety as primary
  elements and in which the audience is kept on tenterhooks.
  UF Psychological thrillers (Radio programs)
      Radio thrillers
      Suspense radio programs
      Suspense thrillers (Radio programs)
      Thriller radio programs
  BT Radio programs
  RT Radio crime shows
Thrillers (Television programs)
  (Not Subd Geog)
       This heading is used as a genre/form heading for
  television programs that feature a build up of sus-
  pense, tension, uncertainty, menace, and anxiety as
  primary elements and in which the audience is kept
  on tenterhooks.
  UF Psycho thrillers (Television programs)
      Psychological thrillers (Television
        programs)
      Suspense television programs
      Suspense thrillers (Television programs)
      Television thrillers
      Thriller television programs
  BT Television programs
  RT Television crime shows
Time-lapse films *(Not Subd Geog)*
  UF Timelapse films
  BT Motion pictures
Timelapse films
  USE Time-lapse films
Tom and Jerry films *(Not Subd Geog)*
  BT Animated films
Torchy Blane films *(Not Subd Geog)*
  BT Motion pictures
Trailers, Motion picture
  USE Film trailers
Training radio programs
  USE Instructional radio programs
Training television programs
  USE Instructional television programs
Trapalhões films *(Not Subd Geog)*
  BT Comedy films
Travel radio programs
  USE Travelogues (Radio programs)
Travel shows
  USE Travelogues (Television programs)
Travelogs (Motion pictures)
  USE Travelogues (Motion pictures)
Travelogs (Radio programs)
  USE Travelogues (Radio programs)
Travelogs (Television programs)
  USE Travelogues (Television programs)
Travelogue films
  USE Travelogues (Motion pictures)
Travelogue radio programs
  USE Travelogues (Radio programs)
Travelogue television programs
  USE Travelogues (Television programs)
Travelogues (Motion pictures)
  (Not Subd Geog)
       This heading is used as a genre/form heading for
  nonfiction films that depict travel, peoples, and places.
  UF Film travelogues
      Travelogs (Motion pictures)
      Travelogue films
  BT Documentary films
Travelogues (Radio programs)
       This heading is used as a genre/form heading for
  nonfiction radio programs that depict travel, peoples,
  and places.
  UF Travel radio programs
      Travelogs (Radio programs)
      Travelogue radio programs
  BT Documentary radio programs

Travelogues (Television programs)
(Not Subd Geog)
    This heading is used as a genre/form heading for nonfiction television programs that depict travel, peoples, and places.
    UF Television travelogues
          Travel shows
          Travelogs (Television programs)
          Travelogue television programs
    BT Documentary television programs
Trial films
    USE Legal films
Trial television programs
    USE Legal television programs
Trick films *(Not Subd Geog)*
    This heading is used as a genre/form heading for short films from the early years of cinema that emphasize apparent transformations through the use of trick photography or special optical effects.
    BT Motion pictures
Trigger films *(Not Subd Geog)*
    This heading is used as a genre/form heading for open-ended films that are designed to spark a discussion on a controversial or difficult problem or issue.
    BT Short films
True crime television programs
(Not Subd Geog)
    This heading is used as a genre/form heading for nonfiction television programs that feature actual footage and reenactments of criminal and police activities. Fictional television programs that feature the commission and investigation of crimes are entered under Television crime shows.
    UF Crime reenactment television programs
    BT Nonfiction television programs
Truth cinema films
    USE Cinéma vérité films
TV interviews
    USE Television interviews
TV shows
    USE Television programs
TV talk shows
    USE Television talk shows
Underground films
    USE Experimental films
Unedited footage *(Not Subd Geog)*
    UF Production footage
    BT Motion pictures
          Television programs
          Video recordings
    RT Outtakes
          Rushes (Motion pictures)
          Rushes (Television programs)
          Stock footage
Unfinished films *(Not Subd Geog)*
    UF Unfinished motion pictures
    BT Motion pictures
Unfinished motion pictures
    USE Unfinished films
Unscoped radio airchecks
    USE Untelescoped radio airchecks
Untelescoped airchecks (Radio programs)
    USE Untelescoped radio airchecks
Untelescoped radio airchecks
    UF Unscoped radio airchecks
          Untelescoped airchecks (Radio programs)
    BT Radio airchecks
Vampire films *(Not Subd Geog)*
    BT Monster films
    NT Dracula films
Vampire television programs
(Not Subd Geog)
    BT Monster television programs
    NT Dracula television programs
Variety films
    USE Variety shows (Motion pictures)
Variety programs (Radio programs)
    USE Variety shows (Radio programs)
Variety programs (Television programs)
    USE Variety shows (Television programs)
Variety radio programs
    USE Variety shows (Radio programs)

Variety shows (Motion pictures)
(Not Subd Geog)
    UF Variety films
    BT Nonfiction films
Variety shows (Radio programs)
    UF Radio variety shows
          Variety programs (Radio programs)
          Variety radio programs
    BT Nonfiction radio programs
Variety shows (Television programs)
(Not Subd Geog)
    UF Television variety shows
          Variety programs (Television programs)
          Variety television programs
    BT Nonfiction television programs
Variety television programs
    USE Variety shows (Television programs)
Video installations (Art)
    UF Screen-reliant installations (Art)
    BT Video recordings
Video recordings *(Not Subd Geog)*
    This heading is used as a genre/form heading for collections of video recordings that are composed of multiple genres and/or forms to which more specific headings such as Video recordings for the hearing impaired cannot be applied.
    UF Videorecordings
          Videos
    NT Music videos
          Stock footage
          Unedited footage
          Video installations (Art)
          Video recordings for people with visual disabilities
          Video recordings for the hearing impaired
Video recordings for people with visual disabilities *(Not Subd Geog)*
    BT Video recordings
Video recordings for the deaf
    USE Video recordings for the hearing impaired
Video recordings for the hearing impaired
(Not Subd Geog)
    UF Captioned video recordings
          Closed caption video recordings
          Deaf, Video recordings for the
          Video recordings for the deaf
    BT Video recordings
Videorecordings
    USE Video recordings
Videos
    USE Video recordings
Videos, Rock
    USE Rock videos
Vidpics
    USE Made-for-TV movies
Vox pop radio programs
    UF Man-on-the-street interviews (Radio programs)
          Vox populi radio programs
    BT Radio interviews
Vox populi radio programs
    USE Vox pop radio programs
Wacky comedy films
    USE Screwball comedy films
War dramas (Radio programs)
    USE War radio dramas
War films *(Not Subd Geog)*
    This heading is used as a genre/form heading for films that feature military conflicts. Films that feature the military lifestyle and loyalty to the armed forces and its codes and are generally set during peacetime are entered under Military films.
    UF Combat films
    BT Motion pictures
    RT Anti-war films
    NT Submarine films

War radio dramas
    This heading is used as a genre/form heading for fictional radio programs that feature military conflicts. Nonfiction radio programs that feature military conflicts are entered under War radio programs.
    UF Radio war dramas
          War dramas (Radio programs)
    BT Fiction radio programs
War radio programs
    This heading is used as a genre/form heading for nonfiction radio programs that feature military conflicts. Fictional radio programs that feature military conflicts are entered under War radio dramas.
    BT Nonfiction radio programs
War television programs *(Not Subd Geog)*
    This heading is used as a genre/form heading for television programs that feature military conflicts. Television programs that feature the military lifestyle and loyalty to the armed forces and its codes and are generally set during peacetime are entered under Military television programs.
    BT Television programs
    RT Anti-war television programs
Web episodes
    USE Webisodes
Web films
    USE Internet videos
Web videos
    USE Internet videos
Webisodes *(Not Subd Geog)*
    UF Episodes, Web
          Web episodes
    BT Television programs
    RT Internet videos
Werewolf films *(Not Subd Geog)*
    BT Monster films
Werewolf television programs
(Not Subd Geog)
    BT Monster television programs
Western and country music radio programs
    USE Country music radio programs
Western art music radio programs
    USE Classical music radio programs
Western films *(Not Subd Geog)*
    This heading is used as a genre/form heading for films that feature the American West during the period of westward expansion.
    UF Cowboy and Indian films
          Cowboy films
          Westerns (Motion pictures)
    BT Motion pictures
    NT Cisco Kid films
          Hopalong Cassidy films
          Lone Ranger films
          Singing cowboy films
          Spaghetti Westerns
          Zorro films
Western radio programs
    This heading is used as a genre/form heading for radio programs that feature the American West during the period of westward expansion.
    UF Westerns (Radio programs)
    BT Radio programs
Western television programs *(Not Subd Geog)*
    This heading is used as a genre/form heading for television programs that feature the American West during the period of westward expansion.
    UF Westerns (Television programs)
    BT Television programs
    NT Singing cowboy television programs
          Zorro television programs
Westerns (Motion pictures)
    USE Western films
Westerns (Radio programs)
    USE Western radio programs
Westerns (Television programs)
    USE Western television programs
White telephone comedy films
    USE Screwball comedy films
Who-done-it films
    USE Detective and mystery films
Who-done-it television programs
    USE Detective and mystery television programs

Whodunit films
    USE Detective and mystery films
Whodunnit films
    USE Detective and mystery films
Wildlife films *(Not Subd Geog)*
        This heading is used as a genre/form heading for
    nonfiction films about animals, insects, and plants.
    BT Nature films
Wildlife television programs *(Not Subd Geog)*
        This heading is used as a genre/form heading for
    nonfiction television programs about animals, insects,
    and plants.
    BT Nature television programs
Wizard of Oz films
    UF Oz films
    BT Fantasy films
Women's liberation films
    USE Feminist films
XXX films
    USE Pornographic films
Yiddish films *(Not Subd Geog)*
        This heading is used as a genre/form heading for
    films in Yiddish produced from the 1920s to the 1940s
    in Europe and the United States.
    BT Motion pictures
    RT Ethnic films
Youth films
    USE Teen films
Youth gang films
    USE Juvenile delinquency films
Youth street films
    USE Juvenile delinquency films
Youth television programs
    USE Teen television programs
Zato-ichi films
    USE Zatoichi films
Zatō-no-ichi films
    USE Zatoichi films
Zatoichi films
    UF Ichi films
        Zato-ichi films
        Zatō-no-ichi films
    BT Samurai films
Zombie films *(Not Subd Geog)*
        This heading is used as a genre/form heading for
    fictional films that feature the reanimation of corpses
    that prey on human beings.
    BT Monster films
Zorro films *(Not Subd Geog)*
    BT Western films
Zorro television programs *(Not Subd Geog)*
    BT Western films

Introduction to Children's Subject Headings

Children's subject heading cataloging (formerly called the Annotated Card Program, or AC Program) provides data tailored to the needs of children and young adults who use school and public libraries. The cataloging is available from many sources because of its distribution in the Library of Congress MARC files and inclusion in the Library of Congress Cataloging-In-Publication Program. Records are prepared using the MARC 21 format for authorities, AACR2 rules, valid Library of Congress subject headings, valid children's subject headings, current Library of Congress subject cataloging policies and practices, and current children's subject cataloging policies and practices.

The Children's Literature Section in the U.S. and Publisher Liaison Division of the Library of Congress is responsible for *Children's Subject Headings*. The Section not only catalogs items in scope for the children's subject cataloging program by creating a bibliographic citation complete with children's subject headings and a brief noncritical summary but it also develops new children's subject headings and proposes changes to existing headings as necessary and monitors the policies and practices of children's subject cataloging.

This introduction provides a brief history and outlines ways in which children's subject headings differ from standard LC headings in form and application. Terms not used, sources consulted in establishing headings, and subdivisions that are an exception to LC standard policies or patterns are described. The *Children's Subject Headings* list includes headings which vary in application or form from the standard LC subject headings and those especially created for the children's subject cataloging program. The *Children's Subject Headings* list must be used in conjunction with *Library of Congress Subject Headings (LCSH)*, and its cross-reference structure is to be observed except as noted. When headings which appeared in earlier editions of *Subject Headings for Children's Literature* are incorporated into *LCSH*, they are removed from the following list if the children's subject cataloging interpretation and LC interpretation are identical.

In MARC bibliographic records children's subject headings are identified by the second indicator of 1 in 6XX fields. Records created prior to January 1, 1999, have the notation AC in the b subfield of the 001 field. Records created or updated after January 1, 1999, have the notation lcac in the a subfield of the 042 field.

HISTORY

In the fall of 1965 the Library of Congress initiated the Annotated Card Program. The purpose of this program was to provide a more appropriate and in-depth subject treatment of juvenile titles and to offer easier subject access to those materials. This was accomplished chiefly through a more liberal application of the subject headings in *LCSH*. In some cases the rules for application were changed and headings were simplified; in a few instances headings were created where none had previously existed.

In 1969 the first edition of *Subject Headings for Children's Literature* was published. The Annotated Card Program list was a list of exceptions to the Library of Congress subject headings list and therefore was to be consulted and used in conjunction with it. It explained guiding principles of the AC program and listed those headings that varied from *LCSH* in application or form.

While the AC list contained certain departures from *LCSH*, it was intended primarily to provide a liberal extension of *LCSH*. Any departure from *LCSH* was to be guided by the headings in the *Sears List of Subject Headings (Sears)*, the advice of the ALA RTSD CCS Cataloging of Children's Materials Committee, and the needs of children's libraries as articulated by authorities in the field.

Since then the list has continued to evolve. New policies have been initiated and old ones changed or terminated as the Children's Literature Section catalogs the wide range of material published for children and young adults and receives feedback from the American Library Association ALCTS CCS

Committee on Cataloging of Children's Materials, librarians, and other users.

In 1996 the AC list which had been maintained in a word processing file was converted to individual authority records in the MARC 21 format for authorities. New and changed children's subject headings are now distributed as part of the weekly MARC distribution service for subject authorities.

CATEGORIES OF CHILDREN'S SUBJECT HEADINGS

The headings used in children's subject heading cataloging represent three categories: standard LC, modified LC, and headings established for exclusive use in children's subject heading cataloging .

By far the most numerous are the standard LC headings. Included are topical headings, most proper names, geographic names, and subdivisions. The following headings are typical of standard LC headings applied to children's materials: **Biology—Laboratory manuals; Conductors (Music); Nuclear power plants; People with disabilities; Utah—History; Vietnamese War, 1961–1975; Marshall, Thurgood, 1908–1993.**

The modified LC headings contain the following types of adjustments:

(1) Hyphens are removed from headings like **Water supply; Fortune telling; Art metalwork.**

(2) Foreign names are frequently used in forms more commonly known in the United States. Therefore, names of persons, organizations, or titles may be changed from the AACR 2 form used in regular LC cataloging to conform with popular English usage, as with **Magellan, Ferdinand, d. 1521** rather than **Magalhães, Fernão de, d. 1521; Solidarity (Polish labor organization)** rather than **NSZZ "Solidarnosc" (Labor organization);** and **Dostoyevsky, Fyodor, 1821–1881. Crime and punishment** rather than **Dostoyevsky, Fyodor, 1821–1881. Prestuplenie i nakazanie.**

(3) Subdivisions are sometimes used instead of inversion or qualification, as with **Cookery—Meat** instead of **Cookery (Meat).**

(4) Words and phrases that would be superfluous in a juvenile catalog are deleted in headings like **Separation anxiety [in children]** and **First aid [in illness and injury].** The adjective **Children's** is usually deleted, so that a heading such as **Children's parties** becomes **Parties,** and **Children's songs** becomes **Songs.**

(5) Some headings and subdivisions used instead of the *LCSH* equivalents are: **Sports—Fiction** instead of **Sports stories, Trees—Planting** instead of **Tree planting,** and **Christmas—Drama** instead of **Christmas plays.**

(6) The common names of plants and animals are often used instead of the scientific ones. For those names not appearing in the following *Children's Subject Headings* pages, consult the *LCSH* headings.

Headings are established for use in children's subject heading cataloging when *LCSH* does not provide suitable terminology, form, or scope. Into this group fall such headings as **Clay modeling; Moon rocks; Safety; Seaweed;** and **Bedwetting.**

In establishing a heading that varies from LC, catalogers consult numerous sources in order to arrive at the term thought to be the most effective for children's subject cataloging purposes. Literature in the subject area is consulted; spelling is accepted from *Webster's Third New International Dictionary* and *Random House Dictionary of the English Language,* except for some hyphenated terms; index terms are checked in indexing sources widely used by the public, such as the *Reader's Guide to Periodical Literature* and the *New York Times Index. Sears,* children's encyclopedias, and reference sources usually found in public and school libraries are also consulted.

APPLICATION OF CHILDREN'S SUBJECT HEADINGS

Some of the chief differences between the children's subject headings and LC headings are in application rather than in form. For example:

(1) Omission of subdivisions containing the word "juvenile," such as **—Juvenile fiction** and **—Juvenile literature** which would be superfluous in a children's literature catalog.

(2) Restriction of the use of the subdivision **—United States** and the qualifying term **American** to topics that are predominantly international in scope, such as **Art, Music,** and **Folklore.** In these cases where the presentation is limited to the United States, qualification or subdivision is used, as with **Art, American, Folklore—United States, Music—United States.** Otherwise, **—United States** and **American** are seldom used since most of the material purchased by children's libraries in the United States reflects an American orientation rather than an international one. Thus LC's **Cities and towns—United States** becomes the children's subject heading **Cities and towns,** denoting both works about United States cities and towns and works about cities and towns in several different countries. However, other geographical subdivisions are retained and are used for books limited to a particular country or state, as in the headings **Cities and towns—Great Britain** and **Cities and towns—Virginia.**

(3) Omission of any geographic subdivision for subject headings denoting classes of persons, such as **Athletes, Composers,** and **Explorers.**

(4) Assignment of subject headings to fiction to provide a helpful approach to the literature. For example, if a story adds to the reader's information about a country, a social problem, or a disease, headings are used such as: **Switzerland—Fiction; Drug abuse—Fiction; AIDS (Disease)—Fiction.** Abstract concepts are also recognized, such as **Friendship— Fiction** and **Self-reliance—Fiction.**

(5) Use of specific together with general subject headings. In a catalog for a children's collection a young reader can locate works through both a specific and a general approach, whereas the regular assignment of subject headings may provide only the specific subject heading. Examples of this expanded analysis are: 1. **Incas.** 2. **Indians of South America.,**

1. **Yosemite National Park (Calif.)** 2. **National parks and reserves.,** and 1. **Veterinary medicine—Vocational guidance.** 2. **Vocational guidance.** Only the first subject would be assigned in regular cataloging.

(6) Use of both popular and scientific terms, sometimes assigned to the same work. For material intended for very young children, the popular term is used, as in the headings **Weather** and **Fossils.** When the book is intended for older children, both the popular and scientific terms are frequently assigned. Thus a single record may carry such headings as 1. **Weather.** 2. **Meteorology.** or 1. **Fossils.** 2. **Paleontology.** When books are intended for young adults, ordinarily only the scientific term is provided: **Meteorology** or **Paleontology.**

(7) Use of headings denoting form or kind. Such headings, created to make certain types of material more accessible to the reader, include **Jokes, Stories in rhyme, Spanish language materials.**

SUBDIVISIONS

While many of the most commonly used LC subdivisions can be used in a catalog devoted exclusively to children's literature, some subdivisions require modifications in form or application. The following subdivisions are exceptions to *LCSH* form and practice. Other subdivisions are used as they are in standard LC practice.

Biography

Used for both collected and individual biographies but only under names of ethnic groups, as in **Indians of North America—Biography,** and under subject fields where no specific term designates the profession or contributions of the biographee, as in **Aeronautics—Biography.** However, where a term designates the profession, such as **Engineers,** the subdivision is not used.

Cartoons and comics

Used on topical materials presented through cartoons and comics.

Collections

Used for belles lettres publications containing works by more than one author with the exception of works which take specific form headings such as Nonsense verses, Short stories, Humorous stories, Horror stories, Humorous poetry, Humorous plays, Nursery rhymes, Science fiction, Mystery and detective stories, Fairy tales, etc.

Fiction

Used under all subjects for individual or collected works of fiction on identifiable topics.

Guides

Used instead of the LC subdivision Guidebooks.

Habits and behavior

Used under any kind of animal, bird, reptile, or fish.

Humor

Used on topical wit and humor, including jokes and riddles.

Illustrations

Not used. See Pictorial works.

Pictorial works

Used under all subjects presented exclusively or predominantly through pictorial matter.

REFERENCES

While complete hierarchies are usually not provided for terms in the *Children's Subject Headings* list, most headings have at least one reference. The most common reference occurs when one term is used to designate a particular topic or concept, and UF (Used for) references are made from synonyms or alternative expressions to that heading. For example, for children's subject cataloging purposes the term **Tumbleweeds** is preferred to the LC heading **Russian thistle** and a UF reference reflects this fact. If a complete hierarchy is needed, consult the LC list under **Russian thistle.**

In some cases, a valid term from *LCSH* may be printed in the *Children's Subject Headings* list in order to provide references that show how the term is related to others for children's subject cataloging purposes.

When a heading appears with no references, it usually means that the spelling or form differs from that used in *LCSH*. **Wood carving** has no references; it appears in *Children's Subject Headings* list as two words but is hyphenated in *LCSH*. **Cookery—Bananas** has no references; it appears on the *Children's Subject Headings* list as a heading with a subdivision but appears in *LCSH* as **Cookery (Bananas),** a heading with a parenthetical qualifier.

SCOPE NOTES

A note may be included to define the scope of a heading, especially if it is being used in a way that differs from *LCSH*.

PRODUCTS

Three services provide information about new and changed children's subject headings.

(1) Children's subject headings are distributed as part of the Internet FTP distribution service that provides headings in the MARC 21 authorities format on a weekly basis to supplement the master database of children's subject heading authority records.

(2) Children's subject headings appear at the end of *L.C. Subject Headings Weekly Lists* which are posted weekly to the World Wide Web at <URL http://www.loc.gov/aba/ cataloging/ subject/weeklylists>.

(3) Children's subject headings are included in Classification Web, a World Wide Web service providing access to *Library of Congress Subject Headings* and *Library of Congress Classification.*

COVERAGE

The *Children's Subject Headings* list contains 949 headings established for use through December 2009.

CONTACT

Questions about children's subject cataloging and the construction and use of *Children's Subject Headings* should be sent to:

U.S. and Publisher Liaison Division
Children's Literature Section
Library of Congress
101 Independence Avenue, S.E.
Washington, D.C. 20540–4354
Telephone: (202) 707–5815
Internet: jegi@loc.gov

Aboriginal Australians
—Folklore
UF Folklore, Aboriginal Australian
Abraham Lincoln Brigade
UF Lincoln Brigade
Spain. Ejército Popular de la
República. 15th International
Brigade
Spain. Ejército Popular de la
República. Abraham Lincoln
Brigade
Spain. Ejército Popular de la
República. Brigada Internacional,
XV
Academic rites and ceremonies
USE Graduation (School)
Accidents
—Prevention
USE Safety
Accipitridae
USE Hawk family (Birds)
Actors
USE Actors and actresses
Actors and actresses
UF Actors
Actresses
Male actors
Motion picture actors and actresses
Movie stars
Television actors and actresses
BT Motion pictures—Biography
Actresses
USE Actors and actresses
Adventure and adventurers
—Fiction
UF Adventure stories
Adventure stories
USE Adventure and adventurers—Fiction
African Americans
—Folklore
UF Folklore, African American
Folklore, Negro
Agelenidae
USE Funnel-web spiders
Agkistrodon piscivorus
USE Water moccasin
Ailurus fulgens
USE Lesser panda
Akashi Kaikyō Bridge (Kōbe-shi, Japan)
UF Akashi Kaikyō Ōhashi (Kōbe-shi,
Japan)
Akashi Kaikyō Ōhashi (Kōbe-shi, Japan)
USE Akashi Kaikyō Bridge (Kōbe-shi, Japan)

Alabama
—Social life and customs
——1865-1918
Alaska
—Discovery and exploration
Alcohol
UF Alcohol and youth
Alcohol and youth
USE Alcohol
Alcoholism
Alcoholism
UF Alcohol and youth
Alien beings
USE Extraterrestrial beings
Alopiidae
USE Thresher sharks
Alphabet
UF Alphabet books
Alphabet books
USE Alphabet
Altai (Turkic people)
—Folklore
UF Folklore, Altai
Amaryllis (Hippeastrum)
UF Hippeastrum
American chameleon
USE Anoles
American ₍Danish, English, etc.₎ poetry
Here are entered single poems or collections of po-
etry by individual American ₍Danish, English, etc.₎ au-
thors. Collections of poetry by several authors of the
same nationality are entered under American ₍Danish,
English, etc.₎ poetry—Collections.
—Collections
American drama (Comedy)
USE Humorous plays
American wit and humor
USE Wit and humor
Amusements
**Anastasia, Grand Duchess, daughter of
Nicholas II, Emperor of Russia, 1901-1918**
UF Anastasiîa Nikolaevna, Grand Duchess,
daughter of Nicholas II, Emperor of
Russia, 1901-1918
Anastasiîa Nikolaevna, Grand Duchess, daughter
of Nicholas II, Emperor of Russia, 1901-1918
USE Anastasia, Grand Duchess, daughter
of Nicholas II, Emperor of Russia,
1901-1918
Androids
USE Robots
Angel fish
USE Angelfish

Angelfish
UF Angel fish
Freshwater angelfishes
Scalare
Animal behavior
USE Animals—Habits and behavior
Animal distribution
UF Biogeography
Geographical distribution of animals
and plants
Zoogeography
Animal sounds
UF Sound production by animals
Animal welfare
USE Animals—Treatment
Animals
—Air transportation
—Courtship
UF Courtship in animals
—Grooming behavior
UF Grooming behavior in animals
—Habits and behavior
UF Animal behavior
—Migration
—Play behavior
UF Play behavior in animals
—Sleep behavior
UF Sleep behavior in animals
—Training
—Treatment
UF Animal welfare
Animals, Imaginary
USE Imaginary creatures
Animals, Mythical
Here are entered works on creatures found in
myths and legends, such as the unicorn, griffin, and
phoenix. Works on imaginary animals and other fan-
ciful creatures that do not exist are entered under
Imaginary creatures.
UF Mythical animals
RT Imaginary creatures
Animals, Prehistoric
USE Prehistoric animals
Animated films
RT Animation (Cinematography)
Animation (Cinematography)
RT Animated films
Annelida
USE Annelids
Annelids
UF Annelida
Anoles
UF American chameleon
Anolis carolinensis
Chameleon, American
RT Chameleons

Anolis carolinensis
USE Anoles
Anteaters
Antoninus, Marcus, 83?-30 B.C.
USE Antony, Mark, 83?-30 B.C.
Antony, Mark, 83?-30 B.C.
UF Antoninus, Marcus, 83?-30 B.C.
Arabic language
—**Readers**
Here are entered reading texts in Arabic containing material for instruction and practice in reading that language. Works written in Arabic intended primarily for general information or recreational reading are entered under Arabic language materials.
Arabic language materials
Here are entered works written in Arabic intended primarily for general information or recreational reading. Such works with text also given in English are further subdivided by the subdivision Bilingual, i.e., Arabic language materials—Bilingual. Reading texts in Arabic containing material for instruction and practice in reading that language are entered under Arabic language—Readers.
—**Bilingual**
Arabs
—**Folklore**
UF Folklore, Arab
Arachnida
USE Arachnids
Arachnids
UF Arachnida
Aramaic language
—**Readers**
Here are entered reading texts in Aramaic containing material for instruction and practice in reading that language. Works written in Aramaic intended primarily for general information or recreational reading are entered under Aramaic language materials.
Aramaic language materials
Here are entered works written in Aramaic intended primarily for general information or recreational reading. Such works with text also given in English are further subdivided by the subdivision Bilingual, i.e., Aramaic language materials—Bilingual. Reading texts in Aramaic containing material for instruction and practice in reading that language are entered under Aramaic language—Readers.
—**Bilingual**
Argüello, Concha, d. 1857 (*Not Subd Geog*)
UF Argüello y Morago, María de la Concepción Marcela, d. 1857
Argüello y Morago, María de la Concepción Marcela, d. 1857
USE Argüello, Concha, d. 1857
Art metalwork
Arthropoda
USE Arthropods
Arthropoda, Poisonous
USE Arthropods, Poisonous
Arthropods
UF Arthropoda
Arthropods, Poisonous
UF Arthropoda, Poisonous
Arthur, King
—**Legends**
UF Arthurian romances—Adaptations
Arthurian romances
—**Adaptations**
USE Arthur, King—Legends
Artists
UF Painters
Portrait painters
Ashanti (African people)
—**Folklore**
UF Folklore, Ashanti
Atlantic ridley turtle
UF Kemp's loggerhead turtle
Kemp's turtle
Lepidochelys kempii
Automata
Here are entered works on robots which do not take human form.
RT Robots

Avarice
USE Greed
Ave Maria
USE Hail Mary
Babies
UF Infants
Infants (Newborn)
RT Brothers and sisters
Baikal-Amur Railroad
UF Baĭkalo-Amurskaia magistral´
Baĭkalo-Amurskaia magistral´
USE Baikal-Amur Railroad
Bakeries
USE Bakers and bakeries
Bakers
USE Bakers and bakeries
Bakers and bakeries
UF Bakeries
Bakers
Banded penguins
UF Spheniscus
Bandicoots
UF Peramelidae
Bantu speaking peoples
—**Folklore**
UF Folklore, Bantu
Baseball
—**Fiction**
UF Baseball stories
BT Sports—Fiction
Baseball stories
USE Baseball—Fiction
Basketball
—**Fiction**
UF Basketball stories
BT Sports—Fiction
Basketball stories
USE Basketball—Fiction
Basque language
—**Readers**
Here are entered reading texts in Basque containing material for instruction and practice in reading that language. Works written in Basque intended primarily for general information or recreational reading are entered under Basque language materials.
Basque language materials
Here are entered works written in Basque intended primarily for general information or recreational reading. Such works with text also given in English are further subdivided by the subdivision Bilingual, i.e., Basque language materials—Bilingual. Reading texts in Basque containing material for instruction and practice in reading that language are entered under Basque language—Readers.
—**Bilingual**
Baths
BT Cleanliness
Beckett, Samuel, 1906-1989. Innommable
USE Beckett, Samuel, 1906-1989. Unnamable
Beckett, Samuel, 1906-1989. Malone dies
UF Beckett, Samuel, 1906-1989. Malone meurt
Beckett, Samuel, 1906-1989. Malone meurt
USE Beckett, Samuel, 1906-1989. Malone dies
Beckett, Samuel, 1906-1989. Unnamable
UF Beckett, Samuel, 1906-1989. Innommable
Bedwetting
UF Enuresis
BT Urinary incontinence
Behavior
RT Conduct of life
Etiquette
Bellamy, Francis. Pledge of allegiance to the flag
USE Pledge of Allegiance
Belly button
UF Navel
Umbilicus

Belongings, Personal
UF Personal belongings
Personal paraphernalia
Stuff
Bengali (South Asian people)
—**Folklore**
UF Folklore, Bengali
Bengali language
—**Readers**
Here are entered reading texts in Bengali containing material for instruction and practice in reading that language. Works written in Bengali intended primarily for general information or recreational reading are entered under Bengali language materials.
Bengali language materials
Here are entered works written in Bengali intended primarily for general information or recreational reading. Such works with text also given in English are further subdivided by the subdivision Bilingual, i.e., Bengali language materials—Bilingual. Reading texts in Bengali containing material for instruction and practice in reading that language are entered under Bengali language—Readers.
—**Bilingual**
Best friends
UF Friends, Best
BT Friendship
Bible
—**Selections**
Bicycles
USE Bicycles and bicycling
Bicycles and bicycling
UF Bicycles
Cycling
Tricycles
Bicyclists
UF Cyclists
Bildungsroman
USE Coming of age—Fiction
Biogeography
USE Animal distribution
Plant distribution
Bird-eating spiders
USE Bird spiders
Bird spiders
UF Bird-eating spiders
RT Tarantulas
Birds
—**Attracting**
—**Protection**
UF Birds, Protection of
Birds, Protection of
USE Birds—Protection
Birds as pets
BT Pets
Birth
Here are entered works on birth in general or on animal birth in particular. Works on human birth are entered under Childbirth.
UF Parturition
BT Reproduction
RT Childbirth
Birth control
UF Contraception
Blackbeard, d. 1718
UF Teach, Edward, d. 1718
Blacks
—**Folklore**
UF Folklore, Black
Blanche, de Navarre, comtesse de Champagne, d. 1229
USE Blanche, of Champagne, Lady, d. 1229
Blanche, of Champagne, Lady, d. 1229
UF Blanche, de Navarre, comtesse de Champagne, d. 1229
Blaue Reiter (Group of artists)
USE Blue Rider (Group of artists)
Blue Rider (Group of artists)
UF Blaue Reiter (Group of artists)
Blue-streaked cleaner wrasse
USE Cleaner fish

Borrowing
   USE Borrowing and lending
Borrowing and lending
   UF Borrowing
       Lending
Bosque Eterno de los Niños (Costa Rica)
   USE International Children's Rain Forest
       (Costa Rica)
Bovine spongiform encephalopathy
   USE Mad cow disease
Boxing
  —Fiction
      UF Boxing stories
      BT Sports—Fiction
Boxing stories
   USE Boxing—Fiction
Brazilian free-tailed bat
   USE Mexican free-tailed bat
Bridge (Game)
   UF Bridge whist
       Contract bridge
Bridge whist
   USE Bridge (Game)
Brigands and robbers
   USE Robbers and outlaws
Bromeliaceae
   USE Bromeliads
Bromeliads
   UF Bromeliaceae
Brothers and sisters
   RT Babies
Brush-tailed penguins
   UF Pygoscelis
Bstan-'dzin-rgya-mtsho, Dalai Lama XIV, 1935-
   USE Tenzin Gyatso, Dalai Lama XIV, 1935-
Buddha
   UF Gautama Buddha
Buddhist saints
   USE Saints
Budgerigar
   USE Parakeets
Buffets (Cookery)
   USE Cookery—Buffets
Bufo marinus
   USE Giant toad
Bulldog bats
   USE Fisherman bats
Bullies
   UF Bully
Bully
   USE Bullies
Buried treasure
   UF Sunken treasure
       Treasure troves
Businessmen
   USE Businesspeople
Businesspeople
   UF Businessmen
       Businesswomen
Businesswomen
   USE Businesspeople
Cabeza de Vaca, Alvar Núñez, 16th cent.
   UF Núñez Cabeza de Vaca, Alvar, 16th cent.
Cacomistle
   USE Ringtail
Calculating machines
   USE Calculators
Calculators
   UF Calculating machines
       Pocket calculators
   RT Computers
Caliphs
   USE Kings, queens, rulers, etc.
Camouflage (Biology)
   UF Mimicry (Biology)
Camus, Albert, 1913-1960. Etranger
   USE Camus, Albert, 1913-1960. Stranger
Camus, Albert, 1913-1960. Stranger
   UF Camus, Albert, 1913-1960. Etranger
Cane toad
   USE Giant toad

Canidae
   USE Dog family (Mammals)
Canis simensis
   USE Ethiopian wolf
Canoes and canoeing
   RT Kayaks and kayaking
Cappella Sistina (Vatican Palace, Vatican City)
   USE Sistine Chapel (Vatican Palace, Vatican
       City)
Card tricks
   RT Magic tricks
Cardiovascular system
   USE Circulatory system
Caricatures and cartoons
   USE Cartoons and comics
Carnivora
   USE Carnivores
Carnivores
   UF Carnivora
Cartilaginous fishes
   UF Chondrichthyes
   BT Fishes
Cartoons and comics
     For fictional cartoons and comics, an additional
entry is made under the heading [topic]—Fiction. For
nonfiction cartoons and comics, an additional en-
try is made under the heading [topic]—Cartoons and
comics.
   UF Caricatures and cartoons
       Comic books, strips, etc.
       Comics and cartoons
   NT Goofy (Fictitious character)
Cat family (Mammals)
   UF Felidae
Cats
   UF Kittens
Cattails
   UF Typha
Cavallo di Leonardo (Milan, Italy)
   USE Leonardo's horse (Milan, Italy)
Cave dwellings
Celts
  —Folklore
      UF Folklore, Celtic
Cephalopoda
   USE Cephalopods
Cephalopods
   UF Cephalopoda
Ceratopsians
   UF Ceratopsidae
Ceratopsidae
   USE Ceratopsians
Cercopithecus aethiops
   USE Vervet monkey
Cetacea
   USE Cetaceans
Cetaceans
   UF Cetacea
Chameleon, American
   USE Anoles
Chameleons
   RT Anoles
Chan, Jackie, 1954-
   UF Cheng, Long, 1954-
Characters and characteristics in literature
   USE Characters in literature
Characters in literature
   UF Characters and characteristics in
       literature
       Literary characters
Cheating
   UF Cheating (Education)
   BT Honesty
Cheating (Education)
   USE Cheating
Chekhov, Anton Pavlovich, 1860-1904.
  Cherry orchard
      UF Chekhov, Anton Pavlovich, 1860-1904.
         Vishnevyi sad

Chekhov, Anton Pavlovich, 1860-1904.
  Vishnevyi sad
   USE Chekhov, Anton Pavlovich, 1860-1904.
       Cherry orchard
Chelm (Chelm, Poland)
   USE Chelm (Lublin, Poland)
Chelm (Lublin, Poland)
   UF Chelm (Chelm, Poland)
       [Former heading]
Cheng, Long, 1954-
   USE Chan, Jackie, 1954-
Chicken pox
   UF Chickenpox
Chickenpox
   USE Chicken pox
Chickens
   UF Chicks
Chicks
   USE Chickens
Chiefs, Indian
   USE Kings, queens, rulers, etc.
Child sexual abuse
   USE Sexual abuse
Childbirth
     Here are entered works on human birth. Works on
birth in general or on animal birth in particular are en-
tered under Birth.
   BT Reproduction
   RT Birth
Children and strangers
   USE Strangers
Children's Day (Japan)
   UF Kodomo no hi
Children's plays
   USE Plays
Chinese Americans
  —Folklore
      UF Folklore, Chinese American
Chinese language
  —Readers
       Here are entered reading texts in Chinese con-
     taining material for instruction and practice in
     reading that language. Works written in Chi-
     nese intended primarily for general information
     or recreational reading are entered under Chi-
     nese language materials.
Chinese language materials
     Here are entered works written in Chinese in-
tended primarily for general information or recre-
ational reading. Such works with text also given
in English are further subdivided by the subdivision
Bilingual, i.e., Chinese language materials—Bilingual. Reading texts in Chinese containing material
for instruction and practice in reading that language
are entered under Chinese language—Readers.
  —Bilingual
Chipewyan language
  —Readers
       Here are entered reading texts in Chipewyan
     containing material for instruction and practice
     in that language. Works written in Chipewyan
     intended primarily for general information or
     recreational reading are entered under
     Chipewyan language materials.
Chipewyan language materials
     Here are entered works written in Chipewyan in-
tended primarily for general information or recre-
ational reading. Such works with text also given
in English are further subdivided by the subdivision
Bilingual, i.e., Chipewyan language materials—Bilingual. Reading texts in Chipewyan containing material
for instruction and practice in reading that language
are entered under Chipewyan language—Readers.
  —Bilingual
Chippewa language
  —Readers
       Here are entered reading texts in Chippewa
     containing material for instruction and practice
     in reading that language. Works written in
     Chippewa intended primarily for general infor-
     mation or recreational reading are entered under
     Chippewa language materials.

Chippewa language materials

Here are entered works written in Chippewa intended primarily for general information or recreational reading. Such works with text also given in English are further subdivided by the subdivision Bilingual, i.e., Chippewa language materials—Bilingual. Reading texts in Chippewa containing material for instruction and practice in reading that language are entered under Chippewa language—Readers.

—**Bilingual**

Chivalry

Here are entered nonfiction works only. Works of fiction are entered under Knights and Knighthood—Fiction.

—**Fiction**

USE Knights and knighthood—Fiction

Choctaw language

—**Readers**

Here are entered reading texts in Choctaw containing material for instruction and practice in reading that language. Works written in Choctaw intended primarily for general information or recreational reading are entered under Choctaw language materials.

Choctaw language materials

Here are entered works written in Choctaw intended primarily for general information or recreational reading. Such works with text also given in English are further subdivided by the subdivision Bilingual, i.e. Choctaw language materials—Bilingual. Reading texts in Choctaw containing material for instruction and practice in reading that language are entered under Choctaw language—Readers.

—**Bilingual**

Choice

Chondrichthyes

USE Cartilaginous fishes

Chordata

USE Chordates

Chordates

UF Chordata

Christian fiction

USE Christian life—Fiction

Christian life

Here are entered works on the effect of Christian religions on everyday life.

RT Religious life

—**Fiction**

UF Christian fiction

Christian saints

USE Saints

Christian sects

USE Sects

Christianity

—**History**

UF Church history

Christmas

—**Drama**

UF Christmas plays

—**Fiction**

UF Christmas stories

—**Poetry**

UF Christmas poetry

—**Prayer books and devotions**

Christmas plays

USE Christmas—Drama

Christmas poetry

USE Christmas—Poetry

Christmas stories

USE Christmas—Fiction

Chronology

Chumash language

—**Readers**

Here are entered reading texts in Chumash containing material for instruction and practice in reading that language. Works written in Chumash intended primarily for general information or recreational reading are entered under Chumash language materials.

Chumash language materials

Here are entered works written in Chumash intended primarily for general information or recreational reading. Such works with text also given in English are further subdivided by the subdivision Bilingual, i.e., Chumash language materials—Bilingual. Reading texts in Chumash containing material for instruction and practice in reading that language are entered under Chumash language—Readers.

—**Bilingual**

Church history

USE Christianity—History

Ciconiiformes

USE Wading birds

Ciliata

USE Ciliates

Ciliates

UF Ciliata

Cipher stories

USE Ciphers—Fiction

Ciphers

—**Fiction**

UF Cipher stories

Code stories

Cryptogram stories

BT Mystery and detective stories

Circulatory system

UF Cardiovascular system

Circus

—**Fiction**

UF Circus stories

Circus stories

USE Circus—Fiction

Clay modeling

BT Modeling

Cleaner fish

UF Blue-streaked cleaner wrasse

Labroides dimidiatus

Cleanliness

UF Dirtiness

Hygiene

Messiness

Neatness

Tidiness

Untidiness

BT Health

Sanitation

RT Grooming

Orderliness

NT Baths

Cliff dwellers

Cliff dwellings

Code stories

USE Ciphers—Fiction

Coelenterata

USE Coelenterates

Coelenterates

UF Coelenterata

Coins

UF Numismatics

—**Collectors and collecting**

Collared peccary

USE Javelina

Collective settlements

—**China**

UF Communes (China)

College stories

USE Universities and colleges—Fiction

Colón, Diego, d. 1526

USE Columbus, Diego, d. 1526

Colón, Fernando, 1488-1539

USE Columbus, Ferdinand, 1488-1539

Color

UF Colors

Colorado

—**Social life and customs**

——**19th century**

Colors

USE Color

Columbus, Diego, d. 1526

UF Colón, Diego, d. 1526

Columbus, Ferdinand, 1488-1539

UF Colón, Fernando, 1488-1539

Comedies

USE Humorous plays

Comic books, strips, etc.

USE Cartoons and comics

Comics and cartoons

USE Cartoons and comics

Coming of age

Here are entered works about coming to a new awareness of life and the world during the passage from youth to adulthood.

—**Fiction**

UF Bildungsroman

Coming-of-age stories

Coming-of-age stories

USE Coming of age—Fiction

Commencement ceremonies

USE Graduation (School)

Commencements

USE Graduation (School)

Communes (China)

USE Collective settlements—China

Computers

UF Electronic digital computers

RT Calculators

Data processing

—**Programming**

USE Programming (Computers)

Conduct of life

Here are entered works on moral and ethical values in everyday life.

RT Behavior

NT Selfishness

Conservation of natural resources

UF Nature conservation

Contraception

USE Birth control

Contract bridge

USE Bridge (Game)

Cookery

—**Apples**

—**Bananas**

—Bean curd

USE Cookery—Tofu

—**Beans**

—**Beef**

—**Bread**

—**Buffets**

UF Buffets (Cookery)

—**Butter**

—**Cereals**

—**Chicken**

—**Coconut**

—**Crabs**

—**Dairy products**

—**Ducks**

—**Eggs**

—**Fish**

—**Frankfurters**

—**Fruit**

—**Garlic**

—**Garnishes**

—Health foods

USE Cookery—Natural foods

—**Herbs**

—**Honey**

—**Lamb and mutton**

—Macaroni

USE Cookery—Pasta

—**Meat**

—**Milk**

—**Molasses**

—**Natural foods**

UF Cookery—Health foods

Cookery—Organic foods

—Noodles

USE Cookery—Pasta

—**Nuts**

—Organic foods

USE Cookery—Natural foods

—Pasta
UF Cookery—Macaroni
Cookery—Noodles
Cookery—Spaghetti
Cookery—Vermicelli
RT Pasta products
—Peanut butter
—Peanuts
—Pork
—Poultry
—Pumpkin
—Rice
—Seafood
—Spaghetti
USE Cookery—Pasta
—Sprouts
—Tea
—Tofu
UF Cookery—Bean curd
—Veal
—Vegetables
—Venison
—Vermicelli
USE Cookery—Pasta
—Wild foods
—Wine
Cortés, Hernán, 1485-1547
USE Cortés, Hernando, 1485-1547
Cortés, Hernando, 1485-1547
UF Cortés, Hernán, 1485-1547
Cortez, Hernando, 1485-1547
Cortez, Hernando, 1485-1547
USE Cortés, Hernando, 1485-1547
Cosmogony
USE Cosmology
Universe
Cosmography
USE Cosmology
Universe
Cosmology
Here are entered works on the general science or philosophy of the universe. Works limited to the physical description of the universe are entered under the heading Universe.
UF Cosmogony
Cosmography
BT Universe
Cottonmouth
USE Water moccasin
Counting
RT Counting-out rhymes
Counting games
BT Mathematical recreations
Number games
Counting-out rhymes
Here are entered rhymes traditionally used to count out or eliminate a player in a child's game. Counting books in rhyme are entered under Counting.
RT Counting
Courtesy
USE Etiquette
Courtship in animals
USE Animals—Courtship
Covetousness
USE Greed
Coypu
USE Nutria
Creative activities and seat work
USE Handicraft
Indoor games
Mathematical recreations
Puzzles
Creatures, Imaginary
USE Imaginary creatures
Cree language
—**Readers**
Here are entered reading texts in Cree containing material for instruction and practice in reading that language. Works written in Cree intended primarily for general information or recreational reading are entered under Cree language materials.

Cree language materials
Here are entered works written in Cree intended primarily for general information or recreational reading. Such works with text also given in English are further subdivided by the subdivision Bilingual, i.e., Cree language materials—Bilingual. Reading texts in Cree containing material for instruction and practice in reading that language are entered under Cree language—Readers.
—**Bilingual**
Crested penguins
UF Eudyptes
Cricket
—**Fiction**
UF Cricket stories
BT Sports—Fiction
Cricket stories
USE Cricket—Fiction
Crustacea
USE Crustaceans
Crustaceans
UF Crustacea
Cryptogram stories
USE Ciphers—Fiction
Cycling
USE Bicycles and bicycling
Cyclists
USE Bicyclists
Czechs
—**Folklore**
UF Folklore, Czech
Daddy longleg spiders
UF Pholcidae
Daddy longlegs
UF Opiliones
Danish language
—**Readers**
Here are entered reading texts in Danish containing material for instruction and practice in reading that language. Works written in Danish intended primarily for general information or recreational reading are entered under Danish language materials.
Danish language materials
Here are entered works written in Danish intended primarily for general information or recreational reading. Such works with text also given in English are further subdivided by the subdivision Bilingual, i.e., Danish language materials—Bilingual. Reading texts in Danish containing material for instruction and practice in reading that language are entered under Danish language—Readers.
—**Bilingual**
Dante Alighieri, 1265-1321. Divina commedia
USE Dante Alighieri, 1265-1321. Divine comedy
Dante Alighieri, 1265-1321. Divine comedy
UF Dante Alighieri, 1265-1321. Divina commedia
Data processing
UF Electronic data processing
RT Computers
Programming (Computers)
Programming languages (Computers)
Day
De Ruyter, Michael, 1607-1676
(Not Subd Geog)
UF Ruyter, Michiel Adriaanszoon de, 1607-1676
De Soto, Hernando, ca. 1500-1542
UF Soto, Hernando de, ca. 1500-1542
Delphinidae
USE Dolphin family (Mammals)
Dendrobatidae
USE Poison frogs
Detective and mystery plays
USE Mystery and detective plays
Detective and mystery stories
USE Mystery and detective stories
Detective and mystery television programs
USE Mystery and detective television programs
Devotional exercises
USE Prayer books and devotions

Diaries
UF Diaries (Blank-books)
Diaries (Blank-books)
USE Diaries
Dictators
RT Kings, queens, rulers, etc.
Diet
RT Weight control
Dietrich, von Freiberg, ca. 1250-ca. 1310
USE Theodoric of Freiberg, ca. 1250-ca. 1310
Digestive system
Dinosaurs
RT Fossils
Dirt, Household
USE Household dirt
Dirtiness
USE Cleanliness
Disappointment
BT Hope
Doctors without Borders (Association)
UF Médecins sans frontières (Association)
Dog family (Mammals)
UF Canidae
Dogs
UF Puppies
Dolphin family (Mammals)
UF Delphinidae
Domestics
USE Household employees
Dostoyevsky, Fyodor, 1821-1881. Crime and punishment
UF Dostoyevsky, Fyodor, 1821-1881. Prestuplenie i nakazanie
Dostoyevsky, Fyodor, 1821-1881. Prestuplenie i nakazanie
USE Dostoyevsky, Fyodor, 1821-1881. Crime and punishment
Drama
—Collections
USE Plays—Collections
Driftwood
BT Wood
Drug abuse
UF Drugs and youth
Drugs
UF Drugs and youth
Drugs and youth
USE Drug abuse
Drugs
Duck-billed dinosaurs
USE Hadrosaurs
Duckbill dinosaurs
USE Hadrosaurs
Dust
NT Household dirt
Dysfunctional families
USE Family problems
E. coli infections
UF Escherichia coli infections
Easter
—**Fiction**
UF Easter stories
Easter stories
USE Easter—Fiction
Eating customs
RT Table etiquette
Echidnas
UF Spiny anteaters
Tachyglossidae
Echinodermata
USE Echinoderms
Echinoderms
UF Echinodermata
Egyptian Islamic Jihad
UF Tanẓīm al-Jihād al-Islāmī (Organization)
Eiffel Tower (Paris, France)
UF Tour Eiffel (Paris, France)
Eighteen wheelers
USE Tractor trailers

Elaphe
USE   Rat snakes
Electric power plants
Electric power plants, Underground
Electronic data processing
USE   Data processing
Electronic digital computers
USE   Computers
Electronic mail messages
USE   Email
Email
UF   Electronic mail messages
Emancipation Proclamation
UF   United States.   President (1861-1865
: Lincoln).   Emancipation
Proclamation
Emotional problems
UF   Emotional problems of children
Emotional problems of teenagers
Emotional problems of children
USE   Emotional problems
Emotional problems of teenagers
USE   Emotional problems
Emperors
USE   Kings, queens, rulers, etc.
Empresses
USE   Kings, queens, rulers, etc.
Encopresis in children
USE   Soiling
End of the world
UF   End of the world (Astronomy)
End of the world (Islam)
End of the world (Astronomy)
USE   End of the world
End of the world (Islam)
USE   End of the world
English language
—Orthography and spelling
USE   English language—Spelling
—**Spelling**
UF   English language—Orthography
and spelling
—**Textbooks for foreign speakers**
English wit and humor
USE   Wit and humor
Entertaining
RT   Parties
Enuresis
USE   Bedwetting
Equidae
USE   Horse family (Mammals)
Ericson, Leif, d. ca. 1020
UF   Leif Ericson, d. ca. 1020
Leiv Eiriksson, d. ca. 1020
Escherichia coli infections
USE   E. coli infections
Eskimo language
—**Readers**
Here are entered reading texts in the Eskimo
languages containing material for instruction
and practice in reading that language. Works
written in the Eskimo languages intended pri-
marily for general information or recreational
reading are entered under Eskimo language ma-
terials.
Eskimo language materials
Here are entered works written in the Eskimo lan-
guages intended primarily for general information or
recreational reading. Such works with text also given
in English are further subdivided by the subdivision
Bilingual, i.e., Eskimo language materials—Bilingual. Reading texts in the Eskimo languages containing material for instruction and practice in reading that
language are entered under Eskimo language—Read-
ers.
—**Bilingual**
Eskimos
—**Folklore**
Espionage
Here are entered works on the art and techniques
of espionage.
RT   Intelligence service
Spies

—Fiction
USE   Spies—Fiction
Essayists, American, ⟨French, German, etc.⟩
Estádio do Maracanã (Rio de Janeiro, Brazil)
USE   Maracanã Stadium (Rio de Janeiro,
Brazil)
Ethiopian wolf
UF   Canis simensis
Etiquette
Here are entered works on prescribed patterns and
conventions of social behavior.
UF   Courtesy
RT   Behavior
Eudyptes
USE   Crested penguins
Evolution
UF   Human evolution
—**Study and teaching**
——**Law and legislation**
Excretion
USE   Excretory system
Excretory organs
RT   Excretory system
Excretory system
UF   Excretion
RT   Excretory organs
Experiments
SA   *subdivision* Experiments *under subjects,
e.g.,* Chemistry—Experiments
Exposition universelle de 1889 (Paris, France)
USE   Paris World's Fair (1889)
Extinct amphibians
USE   Extinct animals
Extinct animals
UF   Extinct amphibians
Extinct birds
Extinct insects
Extinct mammals
Extinct birds
USE   Extinct animals
Extinct insects
USE   Extinct animals
Extinct mammals
USE   Extinct animals
Extraterrestrial beings
UF   Alien beings
Interplanetary visitors
Extraterrestrial beings in art
Fabrics
USE   Textiles
Fairies
NT   Menehune
—**Poetry**
UF   Fairy poetry
Fairy poetry
USE   Fairies—Poetry
Falcons
NT   Kestrels
Families
Here are entered works stressing the sociological
concept and structure of families. Works stressing the
everyday life, interaction, and relationships of family
members are entered under Family life.
UF   Family
⟨Former heading⟩
RT   Family life
Family
USE   Families
Family life
Here are entered works stressing the everyday
life, interaction, and relationships of family members.
Works stressing the sociological concept and structure
of families are entered under Families.
RT   Families
Family problems
UF   Dysfunctional families
Problem families

Fantasy
Here are entered works of fiction, generally char-
acterized as "High Fantasy," primarily set in imagi-
nary worlds, often peopled by extraordinary creatures,
and featuring heroic deeds, epic quests, and elements
of magic.
UF   Fantasy fiction
Fantasy fiction
USE   Fantasy
Fecal incontinence
RT   Soiling
Felidae
USE   Cat family (Mammals)
Fertilization in vitro, Human
USE   Test tube babies
Fibers
UF   Textile fibers
RT   Textiles
Figure skating
USE   Ice skating
Fin M'Coul
USE   Finn MacCool
Finding things
USE   Lost and found possessions
Fingal, 3rd cent.
USE   Finn MacCool
Finn Mac Cool
USE   Finn MacCool
Finn mac Cumal
USE   Finn MacCool
Finn MacCool
UF   Fin M'Coul
Fingal, 3rd cent.
Finn Mac Cool
Finn mac Cumal
Finn MacCumal
Finn MacCumhaill, 3rd cent.
Finn McCool
Fionn Mac Cumhail
MacCool, Finn
Finn MacCumal
USE   Finn MacCool
Finn MacCumhaill, 3rd cent.
USE   Finn MacCool
Finn McCool
USE   Finn MacCool
Fionn Mac Cumhail
USE   Finn MacCool
Fire departments
UF   Fire stations
Fire stations
USE   Fire departments
First aid
First ladies
UF   Presidents—Wives
Presidents' wives
Fisher spiders
UF   Fishing spiders
Fisherman bats
UF   Bulldog bats
Noctilio
Fishes
NT   Cartilaginous fishes
Fishing
—**Fiction**
UF   Fishing stories
BT   Sports—Fiction
Fishing spiders
USE   Fisher spiders
Fishing stories
USE   Fishing—Fiction
Flags
—**United States**
RT   Pledge of Allegiance
Flatworms
UF   Plathelminthes
Platyhelminthes
Flemings
—**Folklore**
UF   Folklore, Flemish
Flying machines

Folklore
    UF Legends
        Tales
    SA *subdivision* Folklore *under specific*
        ethnic groups (e.g. Eskimos, Indians
        of North America, Australian
        aborigines, etc.)
—Asia
    UF Folklore, Oriental
—Iran
    UF Folklore, Persian
—[State, country, region, continent, etc.]
        Here are entered single folktales or collec-
    tions of folklore originating in a particular ge-
    ographic area. Single folktales or collections of
    folklore of ethnic groups are entered under the
    heading for the group with the subdivision Folk-
    lore and are given a second heading for the folk-
    lore of the appropriate geographic area, e.g. 1.
    Ashanti (African people)—Folklore. 2. Folk-
    lore—Ghana; 1. Navajo Indians—Folklore. 2.
    Folklore—Southwest, New.
Folklore, Aboriginal Australian
    USE Aboriginal Australians—Folklore
Folklore, African American
    USE African Americans—Folklore
Folklore, Altai
    USE Altai (Turkic people)—Folklore
Folklore, Arab
    USE Arabs—Folklore
Folklore, Ashanti
    USE Ashanti (African people)—Folklore
Folklore, Bantu
    USE Bantu speaking peoples—Folklore
Folklore, Bengali
    USE Bengali (South Asian people)—Folklore
Folklore, Black
    USE Blacks—Folklore
Folklore, Celtic
    USE Celts—Folklore
Folklore, Chinese American
    USE Chinese Americans—Folklore
Folklore, Czech
    USE Czechs—Folklore
Folklore, Flemish
    USE Flemings—Folklore
Folklore, French Canadian
    USE French Canadians—Folklore
Folklore, Frisian
    USE Frisians—Folklore
Folklore, Germanic
    USE Germanic peoples—Folklore
Folklore, Hmong
    USE Hmong (Asian people)—Folklore
Folklore, Igbo
    USE Igbo (African people)—Folklore
Folklore, Jewish
    USE Jews—Folklore
Folklore, Kamba
    USE Kamba (African people)—Folklore
Folklore, Kazakh
    USE Kazakhs—Folklore
Folklore, Khoikhoi
    USE Khoikhoi (African people)—Folklore
Folklore, Maasai
    USE Maasai (African people)—Folklore
Folklore, Malay
    USE Malays (Asian people)—Folklore
Folklore, Maori
    USE Maori (New Zealand people)—Folklore
Folklore, Mpongwe
    USE Mpongwe (African people)—Folklore
Folklore, Negro
    USE African Americans—Folklore
Folklore, Oriental
    USE Folklore—Asia
Folklore, Persian
    USE Folklore—Iran
Folklore, San
    USE San (African people)—Folklore
Folklore, Slavic
    USE Slavs—Folklore

Folklore, Tonga (Zambezi)
    USE Tonga (Zambezi people)—Folklore
Folklore, Yoruba
    USE Yoruba (African people)—Folklore
Folklore, Zulu
    USE Zulu (African people)—Folklore
Football
—Fiction
        UF Football stories
        BT Sports—Fiction
Football stories
    USE Football—Fiction
Foreign Legion, French
    USE France. Army. Foreign Legion
Fortune
    USE Luck
Fortune telling
Fossils
    RT Dinosaurs
        Prehistoric animals
—Collectors and collecting
Fourth of July
    UF Fourth of July celebrations
Fourth of July celebrations
    USE Fourth of July
France. Armée. Légion étrangere
    USE France. Army. Foreign Legion
France. Army. Foreign Legion
    UF Foreign Legion, French
        France. Armée. Légion étrangere
        French Foreign Legion
Freedom
    UF Liberty
French Canadians
—Folklore
        UF Folklore, French Canadian
French Foreign Legion
    USE France. Army. Foreign Legion
French language
—Readers
        Here are entered reading texts in French con-
    taining material for instruction and practice in
    reading that language. Works written in French
    intended primarily for general information or
    recreational reading are entered under French
    language materials.
French language materials
        Here are entered works written in French intended
    primarily for general information or recreational read-
    ing. Such works with text also given in English are
    further subdivided by the subdivision Bilingual, i.e.,
    French language materials—Bilingual. Reading texts
    in French containing material for instruction and prac-
    tice in reading that language are entered under French
    language—Readers.
—Bilingual
French Quarter (New Orleans, La.)
        UF New Orleans (La.). Vieux Carré
            Old French Quarter (New Orleans, La.)
            Vieux Carré (New Orleans, La.)
Fresh air charity
Freshwater angelfishes
    USE Angelfish
Friars
        Here are entered works on members of a men-
    dicant order, whose members are not attached to a
    monastery and own no property. Works on members
    of a monastery who are bound by a vow of stability
    and are co-owners of the community property of the
    monastery are entered under the heading Monks.
    RT Monks
Friends, Best
    USE Best friends
Friends, Imaginary
    USE Imaginary playmates
Friendship
    NT Best friends
        Imaginary playmates
Friesians
    USE Frisians
Frisians
    UF Friesians
—Folklore
        UF Folklore, Frisian

Frog hopper
    USE Spittle insects
Frost Jack
    USE Jack Frost
Fruit culture
Fulgoridae
    USE Fulgorids
Fulgorids
    UF Fulgoridae
Funnel-web spiders
    UF Agelenidae
Galapagos Islands Biosphere Reserve
    (Galapagos Islands)
    UF Reserva Biosferica en los Galápagos
        (Galapagos Islands)
Galilei, Galileo, 1564-1642
    USE Galileo, 1564-1642
Galileo, 1564-1642
    UF Galilei, Galileo, 1564-1642
Game and game birds
Games
Ganeśa (Hindu deity)
    USE Ganesha (Hindu deity)
Ganesha (Hindu deity)
    UF Ganeśa (Hindu deity)
García Márquez, Gabriel, 1928- Cien años de
    soledad
    USE García Márquez, Gabriel, 1928- One
        hundred years of solitude
García Márquez, Gabriel, 1928- One hundred
    years of solitude
    UF García Márquez, Gabriel, 1928- Cien
        años de soledad
Gas
    UF Natural gas
Gautama Buddha
    USE Buddha
Generative organs, Female
    USE Reproductive system, Female
Generative organs, Male
    USE Reproductive system, Male
Genetic engineering
    NT Test tube babies
Genies
    UF Jinn
Geographical distribution of animals and plants
    USE Animal distribution
        Plant distribution
German Alîaskinskiĭ, Saint, 1756-1837
    USE Herman, of Alaska, Saint, 1756-1837
German language
—Readers
        Here are entered reading texts in German con-
    taining material for instruction and practice in
    reading that language. Works written in Ger-
    man intended primarily for general information
    or recreational reading are entered under Ger-
    man language materials.
German language materials
        Here are entered works written in German in-
    tended primarily for general information or recre-
    ational reading. Such works with text also given
    in English are further subdivided by the subdivision
    Bilingual, i.e., German language materials—Bilin-
    gual. Reading texts in German containing material
    for instruction and practice in reading that language
    are entered under German language—Readers.
—Bilingual
Germanic peoples
—Folklore
        UF Folklore, Germanic
Ghost stories
    USE Ghosts—Fiction
Ghosts
—Fiction
        UF Ghost stories
Giant toad
    UF Bufo marinus
        Cane toad
        Marine toad
Ginglymostoma
    USE Nurse sharks

Glees, catches, rounds, etc.
    USE Rounds (Music)
Gliding
Goofy (Cartoon character)
    USE Goofy (Fictitious character)
Goofy (Fictitious character)
    UF Goofy (Cartoon character)
    BT Cartoons and comics
Gophers
    UF Pocket gophers
Graduation (School)
    UF Academic rites and ceremonies
        Commencement ceremonies
        Commencements
        School graduation
Gravitation
    USE Gravity
Gravity
    UF Gravitation
Greed
    UF Avarice
        Covetousness
Greek language
    —Readers
        Here are entered reading texts in Greek containing material for instruction and practice in reading that language. Works written in Greek intended primarily for general information or recreational reading are entered under Greek language materials.
Greek language materials
    Here are entered works written in Greek intended for general information or recreational reading. Such works with text also given in English are further subdivided by the subdivision Bilingual, i.e., Greek language materials—Bilingual. Reading texts in Greek containing material for instruction and practice in reading that language are entered under Greek language—Readers.
    —Bilingual
Grooming
    UF Grooming for men
    RT Cleanliness
Grooming behavior in animals
    USE Animals—Grooming behavior
Grooming for men
    USE Grooming
Ground Forces of the Soviet Union
    USE Soviet Union. Ground Forces
Gruber, Franz Xaver, 1787-1863. Silent night, holy night
    UF Gruber, Franz Xaver, 1787-1863. Stille Nacht, heilige Nacht
Gruber, Franz Xaver, 1787-1863. Stille Nacht, heilige Nacht
    USE Gruber, Franz Xaver, 1787-1863. Silent night, holy night
Guggenheim Museum Bilbao
    UF Museo Guggenheim Bilbao
Guide-books *(Not Subd Geog)*
    USE *subdivision* Description—Guides *or* Description and travel—Guides *under countries, regions, cities, etc., e.g.* United States—Description and travel—Guides; Pittsburgh—Description—Guides
Hadrosauridae
    USE Hadrosaurs
Hadrosaurs
    UF Duck-billed dinosaurs
        Duckbill dinosaurs
        Hadrosauridae
Hail Mary
    UF Ave Maria
Hall, Susanna Shakespeare, 1583-1649
    USE Shakespeare, Susanna, 1583-1649
Hamas
    UF Ḥarakat al-Muqāwamah al-Islāmīyah
        Islamic Resistance Movement
Handbooks, manuals, etc.
    UF Handbooks, vade-mecums, etc.
Handbooks, vade-mecums, etc.
    USE Handbooks, manuals, etc.

Handicraft
    UF Creative activities and seat work
Hanukkah
    —Fiction
        UF Hanukkah stories
Hanukkah stories
    USE Hanukkah—Fiction
Ḥarakat al-Muqāwamah al-Islāmīyah
    USE Hamas
Harvest mouse, European
    UF Micromys minutus
Hawaiian language
    —Readers
        Here are entered reading texts in Hawaiian containing material for instruction and practice in reading that language. Works written in Hawaiian intended primarily for general information or recreational reading are entered under Hawaiian language materials.
Hawaiian language materials
    Here are entered works written in Hawaiian intended primarily for general information or recreational reading. Such works with text also given in English are further subdivided by the subdivision Bilingual, i.e., Hawaiian language materials—Bilingual. Reading texts in Hawaiian containing material for instruction and practice in reading that language are entered under Hawaiian language—Readers.
    —Bilingual
Hawk family (Birds)
    UF Accipitridae
Heads of state
    NT Kings, queens, rulers, etc.
Health
    UF Hygiene
    NT Cleanliness
Hebrew language
    —Readers
        Here are entered reading texts in Hebrew containing material for instruction and practice in reading that language. Works written in Hebrew intended primarily for general information or recreational reading are entered under Hebrew language materials.
Hebrew language materials
    Here are entered works written in Hebrew intended primarily for general information or recreational reading. Such works with text also given in English are further subdivided by the subdivision Bilingual, i.e., Hebrew language materials—Bilingual. Reading texts in Hebrew containing material for instruction and practice in reading that language are entered under Hebrew language—Readers.
    —Bilingual
Helpfulness
    UF Helping behavior
Helping behavior
    USE Helpfulness
Henrique, o Navegador, Infante of Portugal, 1394-1460
    USE Henry the Navigator, 1394-1460
Henry, Infante of Portugal, 1394-1460
    USE Henry the Navigator, 1394-1460
Henry the Navigator, 1394-1460
    UF Henrique, o Navegador, Infante of Portugal, 1394-1460
        Henry, Infante of Portugal, 1394-1460
Herman, of Alaska, Saint, 1756-1837
    UF German Aliaskinskiĭ, Saint, 1756-1837
High school students' writings
    USE Youths' writings
Hindi language
    —Readers
        Here are entered reading texts in Hindi containing material for instruction and practice in reading that language. Works written in Hindi intended primarily for general information or recreational reading are entered under Hindi language materials.

Hindi language materials
    Here are entered works written in Hindi intended primarily for general information or recreational reading. Such works with text also given in English are further subdivided by the subdivision Bilingual, i.e. Hindi language materials—Bilingual. Reading texts in Hindi containing material for instruction and practice in reading that language are entered under Hindi language—Readers.
    —Bilingual
Hippeastrum
    USE Amaryllis (Hippeastrum)
Hitler-Jugend
    USE Hitler Youth
Hitler Youth
    UF Hitler-Jugend
        Nazi Youth Movement
    BT National socialism
        Youth movement—Germany
Hmong (Asian people)
    —Folklore
        UF Folklore, Hmong
Hmong language
    —Readers
        Here are entered reading texts in Hmong containing material for instruction and practice in reading that language. Works written in Hmong intended primarily for general information or recreational reading are entered under Hmong language materials
Hmong language materials
    Here are entered works written in Hmong intended primarily for general information or recreational reading. Such works with text also given in English are further subdivided by the subdivision Bilingual, i.e. Hmong language materials—Bilingual. Reading texts in Hmong containing material for instruction and practice in reading that language are entered under Hmong language—Readers.
    —Bilingual
Homeless children
    USE Homeless persons
Homeless persons
    UF Homeless children
Homoptera
    USE Homopterans
Homopterans
    UF Homoptera
Honesty
    UF Truthfulness and falsehood
    NT Cheating
Hope
    NT Disappointment
Hopi language
    —Readers
        Here are entered reading texts in Hopi containing material for instruction and practice in reading that language. Works written in Hopi intended primarily for general information or recreational reading are entered under Hopi language materials.
Hopi language materials
    Here are entered works written in Hopi intended for general information or recreational reading. Such works with text also given in English are further subdivided by the subdivision Bilingual, i.e. Hopi languge materials—Bilingual. Reading texts in Hopi containing material for instruction and practice in reading that language are entered under Hopi language—Readers.
    —Bilingual
Horokōsuto Kyōiku Shiryō Sentā
    USE Tokyo Holocaust Education Resource Center
Horror
    —Fiction
        USE Horror stories
Horror stories
    UF Horror—Fiction
        Horror tales
Horror tales
    USE Horror stories
Horse family (Mammals)
    UF Equidae
Horses

Horseshoe crabs

Hotels
  USE Hotels, motels, etc.

Hotels, motels, etc.
  UF Hotels
      Motels

Household dirt
  UF Dirt, Household
  BT Dust

Household employees
  UF Domestics
      Servants

Human evolution
  USE Evolution

Humorous plays
  UF American drama (Comedy)
      Comedies
  BT Plays

Hunting
  —Fiction
      UF Hunting stories
      BT Sports—Fiction

Hunting stories
  USE Hunting—Fiction

Hygiene
  USE Cleanliness
       Health

Hylidae
  USE Tree frogs

Ibsen, Henrik, 1828-1906. Doll's house
  UF Ibsen, Henrik, 1828-1906. Dukkehjem

Ibsen, Henrik, 1828-1906. Dukkehjem
  USE Ibsen, Henrik, 1828-1906. Doll's
       house

Ice skaters
  UF Skaters

Ice skating
  UF Figure skating
      Skating

Identity
  UF Identity (Philosophical concept)
      Identity (Psychology)
      Personal identity

Identity (Philosophical concept)
  USE Identity

Identity (Psychology)
  USE Identity

Igbo (African people)
  —Folklore
      UF Folklore, Igbo

Imaginary animals
  USE Imaginary creatures

Imaginary companions
  USE Imaginary playmates

Imaginary creatures
    Here are entered works on imaginary animals and
  other fanciful creatures that do not exist. Works on
  creatures found in myths and legends, such as the unicorn, griffin, and phoenix, are entered under Animals,
  Mythical.
  UF Animals, Imaginary
      Creatures, Imaginary
      Imaginary animals
  RT Animals, Mythical

Imaginary friends
  USE Imaginary playmates

Imaginary playmates
  UF Friends, Imaginary
      Imaginary companions
      Imaginary friends
      Invisible playmates
      Make-believe playmates
      Playmates, Imaginary
  BT Friendship
      Imagination
      Play

Imagination
  NT Imaginary playmates

Immortalism
  USE Immortality

Immortality
    Here are entered works on both the concept of the
  survival of the soul after death and the concept of living indefinitely in the flesh.
  UF Immortalism

Improvisation (Acting)
  USE Plays—Improvisation

Indian chiefs
  USE Kings, queens, rulers, etc.

Indian mythology
  —North America, [South America, etc.]
      USE Indians of North America, [South
           America, etc.]—Folklore

Indians
  —Treatment
      UF Indians, Treatment of

Indians, Treatment of
  USE Indians—Treatment

Indians of North America

Indians of North America, [South America, etc.]
  —Folklore
      Single myths or collections of mythology of a
    specific tribe are entered under the name of the
    tribe with the subdivision Folklore.
      UF Indian mythology—North America,
           [South America, etc.]
          Indians of North America, [South
           America, etc.]—Legends
  —Legends
      USE Indians of North America, [South
           America, etc.]—Folklore

Indoor games
  UF Creative activities and seat work

Infants
  USE Babies

Infants (Newborn)
  USE Babies

Infants (Premature)
  USE Premature babies

Insectivora
  USE Insectivores

Insectivores
  UF Insectivora

Intelligence service
    Here are entered works on the organization, func-
  tion, and activities of particular intelligence services.
  RT Espionage
      Spies
  —Fiction
      Here are entered fictional works on the activ-
    ities of agents of an intelligence service.
  RT Spy stories

International Children's Rain Forest (Costa Rica)
  UF Bosque Eterno de los Niños (Costa
       Rica)

Interplanetary visitors
  USE Extraterrestrial beings

Inuit language
  —Readers
      Here are entered reading texts in Inuit con-
    taining material for instruction and practice in
    reading that language. Works written in Inuit
    intended primarily for general information or
    recreational reading are entered under Inuit lan-
    guage materials.

Inuit language materials
    Here are entered works written in Inuit intended
  primarily for general information or recreational reading. Such works with text also given in English are
  further subdivided by the subdivision Bilingual, i.e.,
  Inuit language materials—Bilingual. Reading texts in
  Inuit containing material for instruction and practice
  in reading that language are entered under Inuit language—Readers.
  —Bilingual

Inupiaq dialect
  —Readers
      Here are entered reading texts in Inupiaq con-
    taining material for instruction and practice in
    reading that dialect. Works written in Inupiaq
    intended primarily for general information or
    recreational reading are entered under Inupiaq
    dialect materials.

Inupiaq dialect materials
    Here are entered works written in Inupiaq intended
  primarily for general information or recreational reading. Such works with text also given in English are
  further subdivided by the subdivision Bilingual, i.e.,
  Inupiaq dialect materials—Bilingual. Reading texts in
  Inupiaq containing material for instruction and practice in reading that dialect—Readers.
  —Bilingual

Invisible playmates
  USE Imaginary playmates

Irish language
  —Readers
      Here are entered reading texts in Irish con-
    taining material for instruction and practice in
    reading that language. Works written in Irish
    intended primarily for general information or
    recreational reading are entered under Irish lan-
    guage materials.

Irish language materials
    Here are entered works written in Irish intended
  primarily for general information or recreational reading. Such works with text also given in English are
  further subdivided by the subdivision Bilingual, i.e.
  Irish language materials—Bilingual. Reading texts in
  Irish containing material for instruction and practice
  in reading that language are entered under Irish language—Readers.
  —Bilingual

Ironworks

Iroquois Indians

Islamic Resistance Movement
  USE Hamas

Isopoda
  USE Isopods

Isopods
  UF Isopoda

Isopods as pets

Israel Museum (Jerusalem)
  UF Muze'on Yisra'el (Jerusalem)

Israel Philharmonic Orchestra
  UF Tizmoret ha-filharmonit ha-Yisre'elit

Italian language
  —Readers
      Here are entered reading texts in Italian con-
    taining material for instruction and practice in
    reading that language. Works written in Ital-
    ian intended primarily for general information
    or recreational reading are entered under Italian
    language materials.

Italian language materials
    Here are entered works written in Italian intended
  primarily for general information or recreational reading. Such works with text also given in English are
  further subdivided by the subdivision Bilingual, i.e.,
  Italian language materials—Bilingual. Reading texts
  in Italian containing material for instruction and practice in reading that language are entered under Italian
  language—Readers.
  —Bilingual

Jack Frost
  UF Frost Jack
  BT Winter

Japanese language
  —Readers
      Here are entered reading texts in Japanese
    containing material for instruction and practice
    in reading that language. Works written in
    Japanese intended primarily for general infor-
    mation or recreational reading are entered under
    Japanese language materials.

Japanese language materials
    Here are entered works written in Japanese in-
  tended primarily for general information and recreational reading. Such works with text also given
  in English are further subdivided by the subdivision
  Bilingual, i.e., Japanese language materials—Bilingual. Reading texts in Japanese containing material
  for instruction and practice in reading that language
  are entered under Japanese language—Readers.
  —Bilingual

Japanese Red Army
  UF Nihon Sekigun
      Red Army Faction (Japan)

Javelina
  UF Collared peccary

Jews

—**Folklore**

UF Folklore, Jewish

Legends, Jewish

Jinn

USE Genies

Jogging

USE Running

Joke books

USE Jokes

Jokes

UF Joke books

BT Wit and humor

Journalism

UF Journalism, School

Journalism, School

USE Journalism

Jumping bean

UF Mexican jumping bean

Jungle stories

USE Jungles—Fiction

Jungles

—**Fiction**

UF Jungle stories

Junk

Here are entered works on secondhand, worn, or discarded articles of any kind, such as one might find stored in attics, at yard sales, garage sales, thrift shops, etc.

RT Recycling (Waste)

Refuse and refuse disposal

K.G.B.

USE KGB

Kafka, Franz, 1883-1924. Metamorphosis

UF Kafka, Franz, 1883-1924. Verwandlung

Kafka, Franz, 1883-1924. Prozess

USE Kafka, Franz, 1883-1924. Trial

Kafka, Franz, 1883-1924. Trial

UF Kafka, Franz, 1883-1924. Prozess

Kafka, Franz, 1883-1924. Verwandlung

USE Kafka, Franz, 1883-1924. Metamorphosis

Kamba (African people)

—**Folklore**

UF Folklore, Kamba

Kayaking

USE Kayaks and kayaking

Kayaks and kayaking

UF Kayaking

RT Canoes and canoeing

Kazakhs

—**Folklore**

UF Folklore, Kazakh

Kazunomiya Princess of Japan, 1846-1877

UF Seikan'in no Miya, 1846-1877

Kelps

RT Seaweed

Kemp's loggerhead turtle

USE Atlantic ridley turtle

Kemp's turtle

USE Atlantic ridley turtle

Kestrels

BT Falcons

KGB

UF K.G.B.

Soviet Union. Komitet gosudarstvennoi bezopasnosti

Khmer language

—**Readers**

Here are entered reading texts in Khmer containing material for instruction and practice in reading that language. Works written in Khmer intended primarily for general information or recreational reading are entered under Khmer language materials.

Khmer language materials

Here are entered works written in Khmer intended primarily for general information or recreational reading. Such works with text also given in English are further subdivided by the subdivision Bilingual, i.e., Khmer language material—Bilingual. Reading texts in Khmer containing material for instruction and practice in reading that language are entered under Khmer language—Readers.

—**Bilingual**

Khoikhoi (African people)

—**Folklore**

UF Folklore, Khoikhoi

King snakes

UF Lampropeltis

Kings, queens, rulers, etc.

UF Caliphs

Chiefs, Indian

Emperors

Empresses

Indian chiefs

Monarchs

Pharaohs

Queens

Roman emperors

Royalty

Rulers

Russian empresses

Shahs

Sovereigns

Sultans

BT Heads of state

RT Dictators

Presidents

Prime ministers

Statesmen

Kirov Ballet Academy

UF Kirov Ballet School

Leningradiskoe akademicheskoe khoreograficheskoe uchilishche im. ÎA. Vaganovoĭ

Vaganova Choreographic Institute

Kirov Ballet Company

UF Leningradskiĭ gosudarstvennyĭ akademicheskiĭ teatr opery i baleta imeni S.M. Kirova

Kirov Ballet School

USE Kirov Ballet Academy

Kittens

USE Cats

Knights and knighthood

—**Fiction**

UF Chivalry—Fiction

Kodomo no hi

USE Children's Day (Japan)

Korean language

—**Readers**

Here are entered reading texts in Korean containing material for instruction and practice in reading that language. Works written in Korean intended primarily for general information or recreational reading are entered under Korean language materials.

Korean language materials

Here are entered works written in Korean intended primarily for general information or recreational reading. Such works with text also given in English are further subdivided by the subdivision Bilingual, i.e., Korean language materials—Bilingual. Reading texts in Korean containing material for instruction and practice in reading that language are entered under Korean language—Readers.

—**Bilingual**

Kukatja language

—**Readers**

Here are entered reading texts in Kukatja containing material for instruction and practice in reading that language. Works written in Kukatja intended primarily for general information or recreational reading are entered under Kukatja language materials.

Kukatja language materials

Here are entered works written in Kukatja intended primarily for general information or recreational reading. Such works with text also given in English are further subdivided by the subdivision Bilingual, i.e., Kukatja language materials—Bilingual. Reading texts in Kukatja containing material for instruction and practice in reading that language are entered under Kukatja language—Readers.

—**Bilingual**

Labor unions

—**Poland**

NT Solidarity (Polish labor organization)

Labroides dimidiatus

USE Cleaner fish

Lampropeltis

USE King snakes

Latin language

—**Readers**

Here are entered reading texts in Latin containing material for instruction and practice in reading that language. Works written in Latin intended primarily for general information or recreational reading are entered under Latin language materials.

Latin language materials

Here are entered works written in Latin intended primarily for general information or recreational reading. Such works with text also given in English are further subdivided by the subdivision Bilingual, i.e., Latin language materials—Bilingual. Reading texts in Latin containing material for instruction and practice in reading that language are entered under Latin language—Readers.

—**Bilingual**

Learning

This heading is used only with subdivisions.

—**Psychology**

Left and right

Here are entered works on left and right as indications of location or direction. Works on political beliefs are entered under Right and left (Political science). Works on the physical characteristics of favoring one hand or the other are entered under Left- and right-handedness.

UF Right and left

Left- and right-handedness

Here are entered works on the physical characteristics of favoring one hand or the other. Works on left and right as indications of location or direction are entered under Left and right. Works on political beliefs are entered under Right and left (Political science).

Legends

USE Folklore

Legends, Jewish

USE Jews—Folklore

Legends, Maori

USE Maori (New Zealand people)—Folklore

Leif Ericson, d. ca. 1020

USE Ericson, Leif, d. ca. 1020

Leigh-Mallory, George Herbert, 1886-1924

USE Mallory, George, 1886-1924

Leiv Eiriksson, d. ca. 1020

USE Ericson, Leif, d. ca. 1020

Lending

USE Borrowing and lending

Leningradiskoe akademicheskoe khoreograficheskoe uchilishche im. ÎA. Vaganovoĭ

USE Kirov Ballet Academy

Leningradskiĭ gosudarstvennyĭ akademicheskiĭ teatr opery i baleta imeni S.M. Kirova

USE Kirov Ballet Company

Leonardo's horse (Milan, Italy)

UF Cavallo di Leonardo (Milan, Italy)

Lepidochelys kempii

USE Atlantic ridley turtle

Lepidoptera

USE Lepidopterans

Lepidopterans

UF Lepidoptera

Lesser panda
　UF　Ailurus fulgens
　　　Red panda
　　　Wah
Liberty
　USE　Freedom
Light
　UF　Lights
Lights
　USE　Light
Lincoln Brigade
　USE　Abraham Lincoln Brigade
Literary characters
　USE　Characters in literature
Literary recreations
　　　Here are entered collections of literary recreations
　and individual literary works involving reader partici-
　pation, when no more specific form heading (i.e. Re-
　buses, Plot-your-own stories, or Palindromes) is ap-
　propriate.
Livebearers (Fish)
　UF　Poeciliidae
Lodging houses
Log chopping (Sports)
Long-eared bat
　UF　Plecotus auritus
Losing and winning
　USE　Winning and losing
Losing things
　USE　Lost and found possessions
Lost and found possessions
　UF　Finding things
　　　Losing things
　　　Lost animals
　　　Lost articles
　　　Lost pets
　　　Possessions, Lost and found
　RT　Lost children
Lost animals
　USE　Lost and found possessions
Lost articles
　USE　Lost and found possessions
Lost children
　RT　Lost and found possessions
Lost pets
　USE　Lost and found possessions
Love
　—**Fiction**
　　　UF　Love stories
　—**Poetry**
　　　UF　Love poetry
Love poetry
　USE　Love—Poetry
Love stories
　USE　Love—Fiction
Luck
　UF　Fortune
Lumber and lumbering
　—**Terminology**
　　　Here are entered works on technical terms of
　　the industry.
　　　RT　Lumbermen—Language
Lumbermen
　—**Language**
　　　Here are entered works on slang used by men
　　in lumber camps, etc.
　　　RT　Lumber and lumbering—
　　　　　Terminology
Lunar petrology
　USE　Moon rocks
Lymphatic system
　UF　Lymphatics
Lymphatics
　USE　Lymphatic system
Maasai (African people)
　—**Folklore**
　　　UF　Folklore, Maasai
MacCool, Finn
　USE　Finn MacCool
Machine tools
Mad cow disease
　UF　Bovine spongiform encephalopathy

Magalhães, Fernão de, d. 1521
　USE　Magellan, Ferdinand, d. 1521
Magellan, Ferdinand, d. 1521
　UF　Magalhães, Fernão de, d. 1521
Magic
　RT　Magic tricks
Magnetic recorders and recording
　USE　Tape recorders and recording
Make-believe playmates
　USE　Imaginary playmates
Malays (Asian people)
　—**Folklore**
　　　UF　Folklore, Malay
Male actors
　USE　Actors and actresses
Mallory, George, 1886-1924　*(Not Subd Geog)*
　UF　Leigh-Mallory, George Herbert,
　　　　1886-1924
Malraux, Andre, 1901-1976.　Condition
　humaine
　USE　Malraux, Andre, 1901-1976.　Man's
　　　　fate
Malraux, Andre, 1901-1976.　Man's estate
　USE　Malraux, Andre, 1901-1976.　Man's
　　　　fate
Malraux, Andre, 1901-1976.　Man's fate
　UF　Malraux, Andre, 1901-1976.
　　　　Condition humaine
　　　Malraux, Andre, 1901-1976.　Man's
　　　　estate
Mann, Thomas, 1875-1955.　Magic mountain
　UF　Mann, Thomas, 1875-1955.
　　　　Zauberberg
Mann, Thomas, 1875-1955.　Zauberberg
　USE　Mann, Thomas, 1875-1955.　Magic
　　　　mountain
Manta rays
　UF　Mobulidae
Maori (New Zealand people)
　—**Folklore**
　　　UF　Folklore, Maori
　　　　Legends, Maori
Maracanã Stadium (Rio de Janeiro, Brazil)
　UF　Estádio do Maracanã (Rio de Janeiro,
　　　　Brazil)
Mardi Gras
Marine algae
　NT　Seaweed
Marine toad
　USE　Giant toad
Marmots
　　　Here are entered works on several species of mar-
　mots.
Marriage
　UF　Teenage marriage
Mathematical recreations
　UF　Creative activities and seat work
　NT　Counting games
　　　Number games
Measurement
　UF　Measuring
　　　Mensuration
　　　Physical measurements
Measuring
　USE　Measurement
Médecins sans frontières (Association)
　USE　Doctors without Borders (Association)
Menara Berkembar Petronas (Kuala Lumpur,
　Malaysia)
　USE　Petronas Twin Towers (Kuala Lumpur,
　　　　Malaysia)
Menehune
　BT　Fairies
Menstrual cycle
　USE　Menstruation
Menstruation
　UF　Menstrual cycle
Mensuration
　USE　Measurement

Mental illness
　　　Here are entered works on specific kinds of men-
　tal illness and on the special problems encountered by
　those dealing with mentally ill persons.
　RT　Mentally ill
Mentally ill
　　　Here are entered works on mentally ill persons and
　their relationship to their environment.
　RT　Mental illness
Mermaids
　RT　Mermen
Mermen
　RT　Mermaids
Messiness
　USE　Cleanliness
　　　Orderliness
Metalwork
Metazoa
　USE　Metazoans
Metazoans
　UF　Metazoa
Mexican free-tailed bat
　UF　Brazilian free-tailed bat
　　　Tadarida brasiliensis
　　　Tadarida mexicana
Mexican jumping bean
　USE　Jumping bean
Micromys minutus
　USE　Harvest mouse, European
Mime
　USE　Pantomime
Mimicry (Biology)
　USE　Camouflage (Biology)
Mimosas
　UF　Sensitive plants
Missing persons
　NT　Runaways
Mobulidae
　USE　Manta rays
Modeling
　NT　Clay modeling
Mohr, Joseph, 1792-1848.　Silent night, holy
　night
　UF　Mohr, Joseph, 1792-1848.　Stille
　　　　Nacht, heilige Nacht
Mohr, Joseph, 1792-1848.　Stille Nacht, heilige
　Nacht
　USE　Mohr, Joseph, 1792-1848.　Silent
　　　　night, holy night
Monarchs
　USE　Kings, queens, rulers, etc.
Monastic and religious life
　USE　Religious life
Money-making projects for children
　USE　Moneymaking projects
Moneymaking projects
　UF　Money-making projects for children
Monks
　　　Here are entered works on members of a
　monastery who are bound by a vow of stability and
　are co-owners of the community property of the
　monastery. Works on members of a mendicant order,
　whose members are not attached to a monastery and
　own no community property are entered under the
　heading Friars.
　RT　Friars
Monorail railroads
　USE　Monorails
Monorails
　UF　Monorail railroads
Monteverde Cloud Forest Preserve (Costa
　Rica)
　UF　Reserva del Bosque Nuboso de
　　　　Monteverde (Costa Rica)
Moon rocks
　UF　Lunar petrology
Motels
　USE　Hotels, motels, etc.
Motion picture actors and actresses
　USE　Actors and actresses
Motion picture producers and directors
　USE　Producers and directors

Motion pictures
— **Biography**
   NT   Actors and actresses
Mound builders
Movie stars
   USE   Actors and actresses
Movimiento Revolucionario Túpac Amaru
   USE   Túpac Amaru Revolutionary Movement
Mpongwe (African people)
— **Folklore**
   UF   Folklore, Mpongwe
MRTA
   USE   Túpac Amaru Revolutionary Movement
Muḥammad, Prophet, d. 632
— **Ascension**
   UF   Muḥammad, Prophet, d. 632—Isrā'
           and Mi'rāj
       Muḥammad, Prophet, d. 632—
           Night journey to Jerusalem
— Isrā' and Mi'rāj
   USE   Muḥammad, Prophet, d. 632—
           Ascension
— Night journey to Jerusalem
   USE   Muḥammad, Prophet, d. 632—
           Ascension
Muscles
   NT   Muscular system
Muscular system
   UF   Musculoskeletal system
   BT   Muscles
Musculoskeletal system
   USE   Muscular system
Museo Guggenheim Bilbao
   USE   Guggenheim Museum Bilbao
Mussorgsky, Modest Petrovich, 1839-1881.
   Night on Bald Mountain
   UF   Mussorgsky, Modest Petrovich,
           1839-1881. Noch'na Lysoĭ gore
           (1880)
Mussorgsky, Modest Petrovich, 1839-1881.
   Noch'na Lysoĭ gore (1880)
   USE   Mussorgsky, Modest Petrovich,
           1839-1881. Night on Bald Mountain
Muze'on Yisŕa'el (Jerusalem)
   USE   Israel Museum (Jerusalem)
Myriapoda
   USE   Myriapods
Myriapods
   UF   Myriapoda
Mysteries and miracle plays
Mystery and detective plays
   UF   Detective and mystery plays
Mystery and detective stories
   UF   Detective and mystery stories
   NT   Ciphers—Fiction
Mystery and detective television programs
   UF   Detective and mystery television
           programs
Mythical animals
   USE   Animals, Mythical
National socialism
   NT   Hitler Youth
Natural gas
   USE   Gas
Nature conservation
   USE   Conservation of natural resources
Nature printing and nature prints
Navajo language
— **Readers**
       Here are entered reading texts in Navajo con-
   taining material for instruction and practice in
   reading that language. Works written in Navajo
   intended primarily for general information or
   recreational reading are entered under Navajo
   language materials.

Navajo language materials
       Here are entered works written in Navajo intended
   primarily for general information or recreational read-
   ing. Such works with text also given in English are
   further subdivided by the subdivision Bilingual, i.e.,
   Navajo language materials—Bilingual. Reading texts
   in Navajo containing material for instruction and prac-
   tice in reading that language are entered under Navajo
   language—Readers.
— **Bilingual**
Navel
   USE   Belly button
Nazi Youth Movement
   USE   Hitler Youth
Neatness
   USE   Cleanliness
           Orderliness
Neighbors
   BT   Persons
New England
— **Social life and customs**
— — **1783-1865**
New Orleans (La.).   Vieux Carré
   USE   French Quarter (New Orleans, La.)
New York (State)
— **Social life and customs**
— — **1918-1945**
Newspapers
   UF   School newspapers
           Student newspapers and periodicals
Nihon Sekigun
   USE   Japanese Red Army
Noctilio
   USE   Fisherman bats
Novels in verse
       Here are entered juvenile and young adult novels
   written as a series of poems, not necessarily in rhyme.
   Stories that are not novels but are written in rhymed
   text are entered under Stories in rhyme.
   UF   Verse novels
NSZZ "Solidarność" (Labor organization)
   USE   Solidarity (Polish labor organization)
Nudibranchia
   USE   Sea slugs
Number games
   BT   Mathematical recreations
   NT   Counting games
Number systems
   UF   Numeration
Numeration
   USE   Number systems
Numerology
   UF   Symbolism of numbers
Numismatics
   USE   Coins
Núñez Cabeza de Vaca, Alvar, 16th cent.
   USE   Cabeza de Vaca, Alvar Núñez, 16th
           cent.
Nurse sharks
   UF   Ginglymostoma
Nutria
   UF   Coypu
Occult fiction
   USE   Occultism—Fiction
           Witchcraft—Fiction
Occultism
— **Fiction**
       UF   Occult fiction
Old age
   UF   Older people
Old French Quarter (New Orleans, La.)
   USE   French Quarter (New Orleans, La.)
Older people
   USE   Old age
One-act plays
   USE   Plays
Opera producers and directors
   USE   Producers and directors
Opiliones
   USE   Daddy longlegs

Orderliness
   UF   Messiness
           Neatness
           Tidiness
           Untidiness
   RT   Cleanliness
Ornithischia
   USE   Ornithischians
Ornithischians
   UF   Ornithischia
Outlaws
   USE   Robbers and outlaws
Oxyuranus
   USE   Taipans (Reptiles)
Painters
   USE   Artists
Pantomime
   UF   Mime
Papilionidae
   USE   Swallowtail butterflies
Parakeets
   UF   Budgerigar
Paris World's Fair (1889)
   UF   Exposition universelle de 1889 (Paris,
           France)
       World's Fair (1889 : Paris, France)
Parties
   RT   Entertaining
Parturition
   USE   Birth
Passeriformes
   USE   Passerines
Passerines
   UF   Passeriformes
           Perching birds
Pasta products
   RT   Cookery—Pasta
   NT   Spaghetti
Pastry
   NT   Pies
           Turnovers (Pastry)
Paws
Peacocks
   UF   Peafowl
Peafowl
   USE   Peacocks
Pearl diving
       Here are entered works on old methods of diving
   with rocks, baskets, etc.
   RT   Pearl industry and trade
Pearl industry and trade
       Here are entered works on the modern industry and
   modern diving methods.
   RT   Pearl diving
People with disabilities, Teachers of the
   USE   Teachers of people with disabilities
Peramelidae
   USE   Bandicoots
Perching birds
   USE   Passerines
Periodicals
   UF   Student newspapers and periodicals
Peromyscus
   USE   White-footed mouse
Perseverance (Ethics)
   RT   Persistence
Persian language
— **Readers**
       Here are entered reading texts in Persian con-
   taining material for instruction and practice in
   reading that language. Works written in Per-
   sian intended primarily for general information
   or recreational reading are entered under Persian
   language materials.
Persian language materials
       Here are entered works written in Persian intended
   primarily for general information or recreational reading. Such works with text also given in English
   are further subdivided by the subdivision Bilingual,
   i.e., Persian language materials—Bilingual. Reading
   texts in Persian containing material for instruction and
   practice in reading that language are entered under
   Persian language—Readers.

—Bilingual
Persistence
   RT Perseverance (Ethics)
Personal belongings
   USE Belongings, Personal
Personal identity
   USE Identity
Personal paraphernalia
   USE Belongings, Personal
Persons
   NT Neighbors
Petrarca, Francesco, 1304-1374
   USE Petrarch, 1304-1374
Petrarch, 1304-1374
   UF Petrarca, Francesco, 1304-1374
Petronas Twin Towers (Kuala Lumpur, Malaysia)
   UF Menara Berkembar Petronas (Kuala Lumpur, Malaysia)
Pets
   NT Birds as pets
Pharaohs
   USE Kings, queens, rulers, etc.
Pholcidae
   USE Daddy longleg spiders
Photography
  —**Collections**
     Here are entered collections of photographs by one or more photographers intended as examples of the art of photography.
Phyllostomus
   USE Spearnosed bats
Physical measurements
   USE Measurement
Phytogeography
   USE Plant distribution
Pies
   BT Pastry
Piglets
   USE Pigs
Pigs
   UF Piglets
        Swine
Pinnipedia
   USE Pinnipeds
Pinnipeds
   UF Pinnipedia
Pitjandjara language
  —**Readers**
     Here are entered reading texts in Pitjandjara containing material for instruction and practice in reading that language. Works written in Pitjandjara intended primarily for general information or recreational reading are entered under Pitjandjara language materials.
Pitjandjara language materials
     Here are entered works written in Pitjandjara intended primarily for general information or recreational reading. Such works with text also given in English are further subdivided by the subdivision Bilingual, i.e. Pitjandjara language materials—Bilingual. Reading texts in Pitjandjara containing material for instruction and practice in reading that language are entered under Pitjandjara language—Readers.
  —**Bilingual**
Plain-nosed bats
   UF Vespertilionidae
Planetaria
   USE Planetariums
Planetariums
   UF Planetaria
Plant distribution
   UF Biogeography
        Geographical distribution of animals and plants
        Phytogeography
Plathelminthes
   USE Flatworms
Platyhelminthes
   USE Flatworms
Play
   NT Imaginary playmates

Play behavior in animals
   USE Animals—Play behavior
Play houses
   USE Playhouses
Playhouses   *(May Subd Geog)*
   UF Play houses
Playmates, Imaginary
   USE Imaginary playmates
Plays
     Here are entered single or collected plays by one author or joint authors. Collections of plays by several authors are entered under Plays—Collections. Works on plays as acted on the stage are entered under Theater.
   UF Children's plays
        One-act plays
        School plays
   NT Humorous plays
  —**Collections**
     Here are entered collections of plays by several authors. Single or collected plays by one author or joint authors are entered under Plays. Works on plays as acted on the stage are entered under Theater.
   UF Drama—Collections
  —Fiction
   USE Theater—Fiction
  —**Improvisation**
   UF Improvisation (Acting)
  —Presentation, etc.
   USE Plays—Production and direction
  —**Production and direction**
   USE Plays—Presentation, etc.
Plecotus auritus
   USE Long-eared bat
Pledge of Allegiance
   UF Bellamy, Francis.   Pledge of allegiance to the flag
   RT Flags—United States
Pocket calculators
   USE Calculators
Pocket gophers
   USE Gophers
Poeciliidae
   USE Livebearers (Fish)
Poison-arrow frogs
   USE Poison frogs
Poison-dart frogs
   USE Poison frogs
Poison frogs   *(May Subd Geog)*
   UF Dendrobatidae
        Poison-arrow frogs
        Poison-dart frogs
Police, Private
   USE Security guards
Polyglot materials
   UF Polyglot texts, selections, quotations, etc.
Polyglot texts, selections, quotations, etc.
   USE Polyglot materials
Portrait painters
   USE Artists
Possessions, Lost and found
   USE Lost and found possessions
Prayer-books
   USE Prayer books and devotions
Prayer books and devotions
   UF Devotional exercises
        Prayer-books
   SA *subdivision* Prayer books and devotions *under individual religions, names of individual religious denominations, names of individual religious and monastic orders, classes of persons for whose use the prayers are intended, or names of saints, deities, etc. to whom the devotions are directed, and under subjects, e.g.* Catholic Church—Prayer books and devotions; Jesus Christ—Prayer books and devotions; Christmas—Prayer books and devotions

Prehistoric animals
   UF Animals, Prehistoric
   RT Fossils
Premature babies
   UF Infants (Premature)
Presidents
   RT Kings, queens, rulers, etc.
  —Wives
     USE First ladies
Presidents' wives
   USE First ladies
Prime ministers
   RT Kings, queens, rulers, etc.
Primers
     This heading is not subdivided by date or subject.
Prison reformers
   USE Reformers
Private secretaries
   USE Secretaries
Problem families
   USE Family problems
Procyonidae
   USE Procyonids
Procyonids
   UF Procyonidae
Producers and directors
   UF Motion picture producers and directors
        Opera producers and directors
        Radio producers and directors
        Television producers and directors
        Theatrical producers and directors
Programming (Computers)
   UF Computers—Programming
        Programming (Electronic computers)
   RT Data processing
        Programming languages (Computers)
Programming (Electronic computers)
   USE Programming (Computers)
Programming languages (Computers)
   UF Programming languages (Electronic computers)
   RT Data processing
        Programming (Computers)
Programming languages (Electronic computers)
   USE Programming languages (Computers)
Prophecies
   UF Prophecies (Occultism)
Prophecies (Occultism)
   USE Prophecies
Protista
   USE Protists
Protists
   UF Protista
Protozoa
   USE Protozoans
Protozoans
   UF Protozoa
Proust, Marcel, 1871-1922. A la recherche du temps perdu
   USE Proust, Marcel, 1871-1922. Remembrance of things past
Proust, Marcel, 1871-1922. Remembrance of things past
   UF Proust, Marcel, 1871-1922. A la recherche du temps perdu
Pterodactyls
   BT Pterosaurs
Pterosauria
   USE Pterosaurs
Pterosaurs
   UF Pterosauria
   NT Pterodactyls
Pulaski, Casimir, 1747-1779.
   UF Pułaski, Kazimierz, 1747-1779.
Pułaski, Kazimierz, 1747-1779.
   USE Pulaski, Casimir, 1747-1779.
Puppies
   USE Dogs
Puzzles
   UF Creative activities and seat work

Pygoscelis
    USE Brush-tailed penguins
Queens
    USE Kings, queens, rulers, etc.
Rack railroads
Radio producers and directors
    USE Producers and directors
Railroad stories
    USE Railroad trains—Fiction
          Railroads—Fiction
Railroad trains
    —Fiction
        UF Railroad stories
Railroads
    —Fiction
        UF Railroad stories
Railroads, Cable
Rare amphibians
    USE Rare animals
Rare animals
    UF Rare amphibians
        Rare birds
        Rare fishes
        Rare insects
        Rare invertebrates
        Rare mammals
        Rare reptiles
Rare birds
    USE Rare animals
Rare fishes
    USE Rare animals
Rare insects
    USE Rare animals
Rare invertebrates
    USE Rare animals
Rare mammals
    USE Rare animals
Rare reptiles
    USE Rare animals
Rat snakes
    UF Elaphe
Readers
        This heading is not subdivided by date or subject.
Recycling (Waste)
    UF Salvage (Waste, etc.)
    RT Junk
Red Army Faction (Japan)
    USE Japanese Red Army
Red panda
    USE Lesser panda
Red squirrels
    UF Tamiasciurus
Reducing
    USE Weight control
Reformers
    UF Prison reformers
        Social reformers
Refuse and refuse disposal
    RT Junk
Religious biography
    USE Religious leaders
Religious leaders
    UF Religious biography
Religious life
        Here are entered works on the religious and
    monastic life of monks, priests, saints, nuns, etc.
    UF Monastic and religious life
    RT Christian life
Reproduction
    NT Birth
        Childbirth
Reproductive system, Female
    UF Generative organs, Female
Reproductive system, Male
    UF Generative organs, Male
Rescue work
    UF Search and rescue operations
Reserva Biosferica en los Galápagos (Galapagos
    Islands)
    USE Galapagos Islands Biosphere Reserve
        (Galapagos Islands)

Reserva del Bosque Nuboso de Monteverde
    (Costa Rica)
    USE Monteverde Cloud Forest Preserve
        (Costa Rica)
Respiratory system
Right and left
    USE Left and right
Right and left (Political science)
        Here are entered works on political beliefs.
    Works on the physical characteristics of favoring
    one hand or the other are entered under Left- and
    right-handedness. Works on left and right as indica-
    tions of location or direction are entered under Left
    and right.
Ringtail
    UF Cacomistle
Roads, Norman
Robbers and outlaws
    UF Brigands and robbers
        Outlaws
        Thieves
Robots
        Here are entered works on automata which take
    human form and perform human activities.
    UF Androids
    RT Automata
Roller skating
    UF Skating
Roman emperors
    USE Kings, queens, rulers, etc.
Rounds (Music)
    UF Glees, catches, rounds, etc.
Royalty
    USE Kings, queens, rulers, etc.
Rulers
    USE Kings, queens, rulers, etc.
Runaways
    BT Missing persons
Running
    UF Jogging
**Russia (Federation).   External Intelligence
Service**
    UF Sluzhba vneshneĭ razvedki Rossiĭskoĭ
        Federat͡sii
        SVR
Russian empresses
    USE Kings, queens, rulers, etc.
Russian language
    —Readers
        Here are entered reading texts in Russian con-
        taining material for instruction and practice in
        reading that language. Works written in Rus-
        sian intended primarily for general information
        or recreational reading are entered under Rus-
        sian language materials.
Russian language materials
        Here are entered works written in Russian in-
    tended primarily for general information or recre-
    ational reading. Such works with text also given
    in English are further subdivided by the subdivision
    Bilingual, i.e., Russian language materials—Bilin-
    gual. Reading texts in Russian containing material for
    instruction and practice in reading that language are
    entered under Russian language—Readers.
    —Bilingual
Russian thistle
    USE Tumbleweeds
Ruyter, Michiel Adriaanszoon de, 1607-1676
    USE De Ruyter, Michael, 1607-1676
Saber-toothed tigers
    UF Smilodon
Safety
    UF Accidents—Prevention
        Safety education
Safety education
    USE Safety
Saint-Saens, Camille, 1835-1921. Carnaval des
    animaux
    USE Saint-Saens, Camille, 1835-1921.
        Carnival of the animals
**Saint-Saens, Camille, 1835-1921.   Carnival of
the animals**
    UF Saint-Saens, Camille, 1835-1921.
        Carnaval des animaux

Saints
    UF Buddhist saints
        Christian saints
Salvage (Waste, etc.)
    USE Recycling (Waste)
San (African people)
    —Folklore
        UF Folklore, San
Sandman
Sanitation
    NT Cleanliness
Saurischia
    USE Saurischians
Saurischians
    UF Saurischia
Scalare
    USE Angelfish
School graduation
    USE Graduation (School)
School newspapers
    USE Newspapers
School plays
    USE Plays
        Theater
School stories
    USE Schools—Fiction
Schools
    —Fiction
        UF School stories
Sea slugs
    UF Nudibranchia
Search and rescue operations
    USE Rescue work
Seaweed
    BT Marine algae
    RT Kelps
Secretaries
    UF Private secretaries
Secrets
Sects
    UF Christian sects
Security guards
    UF Police, Private
Seikan Tonneru (Japan)
    USE Seikan Tunnel (Japan)
Seikan Tunnel (Japan)
    UF Seikan Tonneru (Japan)
Seikan'in no Miya, 1846-1877
    USE Kazunomiya Princess of Japan,
        1846-1877
Selfishness
    BT Conduct of life
Sendero Luminoso (Guerrilla group)
    USE Shining Path (Guerrilla group)
Sensitive plants
    USE Mimosas
Separation anxiety
    UF Separation anxiety in children
Separation anxiety in children
    USE Separation anxiety
Sergiĭ, Radonezhskiĭ, Saint, ca. 1314-1391 or 2
    USE Sergius, of Radonezh, Saint, ca.
        1314-1391 or 2
**Sergius, of Radonezh, Saint, ca. 1314-1391 or
2** *(Not Subd Geog)*
    UF Sergiĭ, Radonezhskiĭ, Saint, ca.
        1314-1391 or 2
Serpents
    USE Snakes
Servants
    USE Household employees
Sex crimes
    USE Sexual abuse
Sexual abuse *(May Subd Geog)*
    UF Child sexual abuse
        Sex crimes
Shades and shadows
    USE Shadows
Shadow pictures
Shadows
    UF Shades and shadows

Shahs
USE Kings, queens, rulers, etc.

Shakespeare, Susanna, 1583-1649
UF Hall, Susanna Shakespeare, 1583-1649

Shape
UF Size and shape

Sharpshooters
UF Shooters (of arms)
Shooters of firearms

Shells
—Collection and preservation

Shining Path (Guerrilla group)
UF Sendero Luminoso (Guerrilla group)

Shooters (of arms)
USE Sharpshooters

Shooters of firearms
USE Sharpshooters

Short stories
Here are entered collections of two or more short stories regardless of format, age level, or previous publication history. This heading is not used for collections of episodic stories that feature multiple adventures of the same character(s), e.g., Arnold Lobel's Frog and Toad books. Collections of such episodic stories are treated as single works of fiction.

Show-and-tell presentations
Here are entered works on the activity, usually performed in school, in which each participant presents an object of special interest and tells something about it.

Sistine Chapel (Vatican Palace, Vatican City)
UF Cappella Sistina (Vatican Palace, Vatican City)

Size
UF Size and shape
Stature

Size and shape
USE Shape
Size

Skaters
USE Ice skaters

Skating
USE Ice skating
Roller skating

Slavs
—Folklore
UF Folklore, Slavic

Sleep behavior in animals
USE Animals—Sleep behavior

Slide rule

Sluzhba vneshneĭ razvedki Rossiĭskoĭ Federatsii
USE Russia (Federation). External Intelligence Service

Smilodon
USE Saber-toothed tigers

Snakes
UF Serpents

Soccer
—Fiction
UF Soccer stories

Soccer stories
USE Soccer—Fiction

Social reformers
USE Reformers

Soiling
UF Encopresis in children
RT Fecal incontinence

Solidarity (Polish labor organization)
UF NSZZ "Solidarność" (Labor organization)
BT Labor unions—Poland

Somali language
—Readers
Here are entered reading texts in Somali containing material for instruction and practice in reading that language. Works written in Somali intended primarily for general information or recreational reading are entered under Somali language materials.

Somali language materials
Here are entered works written in Somali intended primarily for general information or recreational reading. Such works with text also given in English are further subdivided by the subdivision Bilingual, i.e., Somali language materials—Bilingual. Reading texts in Somali containing material for instruction and practice in reading that language are entered under Somali language—Readers.
—Bilingual

Song-books
USE Songs

Songs
UF Song-books

Sonī Kabushiki Kaisha
USE Sony Corporation

Sony Corporation
UF Sonī Kabushiki Kaisha

Soto, Hernando de, ca. 1500-1542
USE De Soto, Hernando, ca. 1500-1542

Sound
UF Sounds

Sound production by animals
USE Animal sounds

Sounds
USE Sound

Sovereigns
USE Kings, queens, rulers, etc.

Soviet Ground Forces
USE Soviet Union. Ground Forces

Soviet Navy
USE Soviet Union. Navy

Soviet Union. Ground Forces
UF Ground Forces of the Soviet Union
Soviet Ground Forces
Soviet Union. Ground Troops
Soviet Union. Sukhoputnye voiska

Soviet Union. Ground Troops
USE Soviet Union. Ground Forces

Soviet Union. Komitet gosudarstvennoi bezopasnosti
USE KGB

Soviet Union. Navy
UF Soviet Navy
Soviet Union. Soviet Navy
Soviet Union. Voenno-Morskoĭ Flot

Soviet Union. Soviet Navy
USE Soviet Union. Navy

Soviet Union. Sukhoputnye voiska
USE Soviet Union. Ground Forces

Soviet Union. Voenno-Morskoĭ Flot
USE Soviet Union. Navy

Space and time

Spaghetti
BT Pasta products

Spain. Ejército Popular de la República. 15th International Brigade
USE Abraham Lincoln Brigade

Spain. Ejército Popular de la República. Abraham Lincoln Brigade
USE Abraham Lincoln Brigade

Spain. Ejército Popular de la República. Brigada Internacional, XV
USE Abraham Lincoln Brigade

Spanische Reitschule (Vienna, Austria)
USE Spanish Riding School (Vienna, Austria)

Spanish language
—Readers
Here are entered reading texts in Spanish containing material for instruction and practice in reading that language. Works written in Spanish intended primarily for general information or recreational reading are entered under Spanish language materials.

Spanish language materials
Here are entered works written in Spanish intended primarily for general information or recreational reading. Such works with text also given in English are further subdivided by the subdivision Bilingual, i.e., Spanish language materials—Bilingual. Reading texts in Spanish containing material for instruction and practice in reading that language are entered under Spanish language—Readers.

—Bilingual

Spanish Riding School (Vienna, Austria)
UF Spanische Reitschule (Vienna, Austria)

Spearnosed bats
UF Phyllostomus

Spheniscus
USE Banded penguins

Spies
Here are entered nonfiction works on individuals involved in espionage.
RT Espionage
Intelligence service
—Fiction
Here are entered fictional works on individuals working independently to secure information for an organization or government.
UF Espionage—Fiction

Spinner dolphin
UF Stenella longirostris

Spiny anteaters
USE Echidnas

Spit bug
USE Spittle insects

Spittle insects
UF Frog hopper
Spit bug
Spittlebug

Spittlebug
USE Spittle insects

Sports
—Fiction
UF Sports stories
NT Baseball—Fiction
Basketball—Fiction
Boxing—Fiction
Cricket—Fiction
Fishing—Fiction
Football—Fiction
Hunting—Fiction

Sports stories
USE Sports—Fiction

Spotted dolphins
UF Stenella

Spy stories
RT Intelligence service—Fiction

Statesmen
RT Kings, queens, rulers, etc.

Statue of Liberty (New York, N.Y.)
Here are entered works on the Statue of Liberty itself, as well as works on the Statue of Liberty National Monument comprising Liberty Island and the former immigration station on Ellis Island.
UF Statue of Liberty National Monument (N.Y. and N.J.)

Statue of Liberty National Monument (N.Y. and N.J.)
USE Statue of Liberty (New York, N.Y.)

Stature
USE Size

Stealing
UF Theft

Steam engines

Stendhal, 1783-1842. Red and the black
UF Stendhal, 1783-1842. Rouge et le noir

Stendhal, 1783-1842. Rouge et le noir
USE Stendhal, 1783-1842. Red and the black

Stenella
USE Spotted dolphins

Stenella longirostris
USE Spinner dolphin

Stock exchange

Stonecutters

Stores or stock room keeping

Stories in rhyme
Here are entered fictional works that are not novels but are written in rhymed text. Juvenile and young adult novels written as a series of poems, not necessarily in rhyme, are entered under Novels in verse.

Storytelling
—Collections
Here are entered collections of stories compiled primarily for oral presentation.

Strangers
> UF   Children and strangers

Student newspapers and periodicals
> USE   Newspapers
> > Periodicals

Stuff
> USE   Belongings, Personal

Sultans
> USE   Kings, queens, rulers, etc.

Sunday schools

Sunken treasure
> USE   Buried treasure

Survival
> UF   Survival (after airplane accidents,
> > shipwrecks, etc.)

Survival (after airplane accidents, shipwrecks, etc.)
> USE   Survival

SVR
> USE   Russia (Federation).   External
> > Intelligence Service

Swahili language
> **—Readers**
> > Here are entered reading texts in Swahili containing material for instruction and practice in reading that language. Works written in Swahili intended primarily for general information or recreational reading are entered under Swahili language materials.

Swahili language materials
> Here are entered works written in Swahili intended primarily for general information or recreational reading.   Such works with text also given in English are further subdivided by the subdivision Bilingual, i.e., Swahili language materials—Bilingual. Reading texts in Swahili containing material for instruction and practice in reading that language are entered under Swahili language—Readers.
> **—Bilingual**

Swallowtail butterflies
> UF   Papilionidae

Swine
> USE   Pigs

Symbolism of numbers
> USE   Numerology

Table etiquette
> RT   Eating customs

Tachyglossidae
> USE   Echidnas

Tadarida brasiliensis
> USE   Mexican free-tailed bat

Tadarida mexicana
> USE   Mexican free-tailed bat

Tagalog language
> **—Readers**
> > Here are entered reading texts in Tagalog containing material for instruction and practice in reading that language. Works written in Tagalog intended primarily for general information or recreational reading are entered under Tagalog language materials.

Tagalog language materials
> Here are entered works written in Tagalog intended primarily for general information or recreational reading.   Such works with text also given in English are further subdivided by the subdivision Bilingual, i.e., Tagalog language materials—Bilingual. Reading texts in Tagalog containing material for instruction and practice in reading that language are entered under Tagalog language—Readers.
> **—Bilingual**

Taipans (Reptiles)
> UF   Oxyuranus

Tales
> USE   Folklore

Tamberlain, 1336-1405
> USE   Tamerlane, 1336-1405

Tamburlaine, 1336-1405
> USE   Tamerlane, 1336-1405

Tamerlane, 1336-1405
> UF   Tamberlain, 1336-1405
> > Tamburlaine, 1336-1405
> > Timur, 1336-1405

Tamiasciurus
> USE   Red squirrels

Tanẓīm al-Jihād al-Islāmī (Organization)
> USE   Egyptian Islamic Jihad

Tape recorders and recording
> UF   Magnetic recorders and recording

Tarantulas
> RT   Bird spiders

Teach, Edward, d. 1718
> USE   Blackbeard, d. 1718

Teachers of people with disabilities
> UF   People with disabilities, Teachers of the
> > Teachers of the physically handicapped
> > > *[Former heading]*

Teachers of the physically handicapped
> USE   Teachers of people with disabilities

Teenage marriage
> USE   Marriage

Teenagers' writings
> USE   Youths' writings

Television actors and actresses
> USE   Actors and actresses

Television producers and directors
> USE   Producers and directors

Tell, Wilhelm
> USE   Tell, William

Tell, William
> UF   Tell, Wilhelm

Tennis
> **—Fiction**
> > UF   Tennis stories

Tennis stories
> USE   Tennis—Fiction

Tenzin Gyatso, Dalai Lama XIV, 1935-
> UF   Bstan-'dzin-rgya-mtsho, Dalai Lama
> > XIV, 1935-

Test tube babies
> UF   Fertilization in vitro, Human
> BT   Genetic engineering

Textile fabrics
> USE   Textiles

Textile fibers
> USE   Fibers

Textile industry
> RT   Textiles

Textiles
> UF   Fabrics
> > Textile fabrics
> RT   Fibers
> > Textile industry

Textures

Thai language
> **—Readers**
> > Here are entered reading texts in Thai containing material for instruction and practice in reading that language. Works written in Thai intended primarily for general information or recreational reading are entered under Thai language materials.

Thai language materials
> Here are entered works written in Thai intended primarily for general information or recreational reading.   Such works with text also given in English are further subdivided by the subdivision Bilingual, i.e. Thai language materials—Bilingual. Reading texts in Thai containing material for instruction and practice in reading that language are entered under Thai language—Readers.
> **—Bilingual**

Theater
> Here are entered works on plays as acted on the stage. Single or collected plays by one author or joint authors are entered under Plays. Collections of plays by several authors are entered under Plays—Collections.
> UF   School plays
> **—Fiction**
> > UF   Plays—Fiction

Theaters
> **—Stage setting and scenery**

Theatrical producers and directors
> USE   Producers and directors

Theft
> USE   Stealing

Theodoric of Freiberg, ca. 1250-ca. 1310
> UF   Dietrich, von Freiberg, ca. 1250-ca.
> > 1310

Thieves
> USE   Robbers and outlaws

Thresher sharks
> UF   Alopiidae

Tibetan language
> **—Readers**
> > Here are entered reading texts in Tibetan containing material for instruction and practice in reading that language. Works written in Tibetan intended primarily for general information or recreational reading are entered under Tibetan language materials.

Tibetan language materials
> Here are entered works written in Tibetan intended primarily for general information or recreational reading.   Such works with text also given in English are further subdivided by the subdivision Bilingual, i.e. Tibetan language materials—Bilingual. Reading texts in Tibetan containing material for instruction and practice in reading that language are entered under Tibetan language—Readers.
> **—Bilingual**

Tidiness
> USE   Cleanliness
> > Orderliness

Tie dyeing

Time

Timur, 1336-1405
> USE   Tamerlane, 1336-1405

Tizmoret ha-filharmonit ha-Yiśre'elit
> USE   Israel Philharmonic Orchestra

Tokyo Holocaust Education Resource Center
> UF   Horokōsuto Kyōiku Shiryō Sentā

Tolstoy, Leo, graf, 1828-1910.   Voĭna i mir
> USE   Tolstoy, Leo, graf, 1828-1910.   War
> > and peace

Tolstoy, Leo, graf, 1828-1910.   War and peace
> UF   Tolstoy, Leo, graf, 1828-1910.   Voĭna i
> > mir

Tonga (Zambesi people)

Tonga (Zambezi people)
> **—Folklore**   *(May Subd Geog)*
> > UF   Folklore, Tonga (Zambezi)

Tooth Fairy

Torpedo boats

Tour Eiffel (Paris, France)
> USE   Eiffel Tower (Paris, France)

Tractor trailer combinations
> USE   Tractor trailers

Tractor trailers
> UF   Eighteen wheelers
> > Tractor trailer combinations

Trans-Siberian Railway
> UF   Velikaia Sibirskaia magistral

Treasure troves
> USE   Buried treasure

Tree frogs
> UF   Hylidae
> > Tree toads

Tree planting
> USE   Trees—Planting

Tree toads
> USE   Tree frogs

Trees
> **—Planting**
> > UF   Tree planting

Tricycles
> USE   Bicycles and bicycling

Truthfulness and falsehood
> USE   Honesty

Tumbleweeds
> UF   Russian thistle

Túpac Amaru Revolutionary Movement
> UF   Movimiento Revolucionario Túpac
> > Amaru
> > MRTA

Turnovers (Pastry)
> BT   Pastry

Typha
USE Cattails
Ukrainian language
—Readers
Here are entered reading texts in Ukrainian containing material for instruction and practice in reading that language. Works written in Ukrainian intended primarily for general information or recreational reading are entered under Ukrainian language materials.
Ukrainian language materials
Here are entered works written in Ukrainian intended primarily for general information or recreational reading. Such works with text also given in English are further subdivided by the subdivision Bilingual, i.e., Ukrainian language materials—Bilingual. Reading texts in Ukrainian containing material for instruction and practice in reading that language are entered under Ukrainian language—Readers.
—Bilingual
Umbilicus
USE Belly button
United States. President (1861-1865 : Lincoln). Emancipation Proclamation
USE Emancipation Proclamation
Universe
Here are entered works limited to the physical description of the universe. Works dealing with the general science or philosophy of the universe are entered under the heading Cosmology.
UF Cosmogony
Cosmography
NT Cosmology
Universities and colleges
—Fiction
UF College stories
Untidiness
USE Cleanliness
Orderliness
Urinary incontinence
NT Bedwetting
Vacation Bible schools
UF Vacation schools, Christian
Vacation schools, Christian
USE Vacation Bible schools
Vaganova Choreographic Institute
USE Kirov Ballet Academy
Valley animals
UF Valley fauna
Valley fauna
USE Valley animals
Velikaia Sibirskaia magistral
USE Trans-Siberian Railway
Verse novels
USE Novels in verse
Vervet monkey
UF Cercopithecus aethiops
Vespertilionidae
USE Plain-nosed bats
Vietnamese language
—Readers
Here are entered reading texts in Vietnamese containing material for instruction and practice in reading that language. Works written in Vietnamese intended primarily for general information or recreational reading are entered under Vietnamese language materials.
Vietnamese language materials
Here are entered works written in Vietnamese intended primarily for general information or recreational reading. Such works with text also given in English are further subdivided by the subdivision Bilingual, i.e., Vietnamese language materials—Bilingual. Reading texts in Vietnamese containing material for instruction and practice in reading that language are entered under Vietnamese language—Readers.
—Bilingual
Vieux Carré (New Orleans, La.)
USE French Quarter (New Orleans, La.)
Virgil. Aeneid
UF Virgil. Aeneis
Virgil. Aeneis
USE Virgil. Aeneid

Wading birds
UF Ciconiiformes
Wah
USE Lesser panda
Waiters
USE Waiters and waitresses
Waiters and waitresses
UF Waiters
Waitresses
Waitresses
USE Waiters and waitresses
Walesa, Lech, 1943-
War
—Fiction
UF War stories
—Poetry
UF War poetry
War poetry
USE War—Poetry
War stories
USE War—Fiction
Water bugs
Water moccasin
UF Agkistrodon piscivorus
Cottonmouth
Water power
Water supply
Wax modeling
Weight control
UF Reducing
RT Diet
Weisse Rose (Resistance group)
USE White Rose (German resistance group)
West (U.S.)
—Fiction
UF Western stories
Western stories
USE West (U.S.)—Fiction
White-footed mouse
UF Peromyscus
White Rose (German resistance group)
UF Weisse Rose (Resistance group)
Winning and losing
UF Losing and winning
Winter
NT Jack Frost
Wit and humor
UF American wit and humor
English wit and humor
SA subdivision Humor under names of individual persons, corporate bodies, and sacred works, and under topical subjects
NT Jokes
Witchcraft
Here are entered works on those practicing or accused of practicing sorcery or witchery. Works on Halloween witches and other witches of fantasy are entered under Witches.
RT Witches
—Fiction
UF Occult fiction
Witches
Here are entered works on Halloween witches and other witches of fantasy. Works on those practicing or accused of practicing sorcery or witchery are entered under Witchcraft.
RT Witchcraft
Women
Women and religion
USE Women in religion
Women in religion
UF Women and religion
Wood
NT Driftwood
Wood carvers
Wood carving
World War, 1939-1945
—Displaced persons
USE World War, 1939-1945—Refugees

—Refugees
UF World War, 1939-1945—Displaced persons
World's Fair (1889 : Paris, France)
USE Paris World's Fair (1889)
X rays
Yiddish language
—Readers
Here are entered reading texts in Yiddish containing material for instruction and practice in reading that language. Works written in Yiddish intended primarily for general information or recreational reading are entered under Yiddish language materials.
Yiddish language materials
Here are entered works written in Yiddish intended primarily for general information or recreational reading. Such works with text also given in English are further subdivided by the subdivision Bilingual, i.e., Yiddish language materials—Bilingual. Reading texts in Yiddish containing material for instruction and practice in reading that language are entered under Yiddish language—Readers.
—Bilingual
Yoruba (African people)
—Folklore
UF Folklore, Yoruba
Youth movement
—Germany
NT Hitler Youth
Youths' writings
UF High school students' writings
Teenagers' writings
Zoogeography
USE Animal distribution
Zulu (African people)
—Folklore
UF Folklore, Zulu
Zulu language
—Readers
Here are entered reading texts in Zulu containing material for instruction and practice in reading that language. Works written in Zulu intended primarily for general information or recreational reading are entered under Zulu language materials.
Zulu language materials
Here are entered works written in Zulu intended primarily for general information or recreational reading. Such works with text also given in English are further subdivided by the subdivision Bilingual, i.e., Zulu language materials—Bilingual. Reading texts in Zulu containing material for instruction and practice in reading that language are entered under Zulu language—Readers.
—Bilingual
Here are entered works written in Zulu intended primarily for general information or recreational reading. Such works with text also given in English are further subdivided by the subdivision Bilingual, i.e., Zulu language materials—Bilingual. Reading texts in Zulu containing material for instruction and practice in reading that language—Readers.